Webster's Color
ATLAS
of the
WORLD

Webster's Color
ATLAS
of the
WORLD

Consultant Editor
Professor Emrys Jones

Introduction by
Magnus Magnusson

CRESCENT BOOKS
New York

Contents

THE PHYSICAL WORLD

THE LIVING WORLD

HUMAN GEOGRAPHY

Introduction

The world we live in is the most marvellous place imaginable. At one time, no one had any idea how the Earth had come about, or how large it was, or what shape it was, or how it fitted into the visible universe of Sun and Moon and planets and stars. They were all great marvels, the ultimate mystery for man's mind to grapple with.

We know that people have always been fascinated by this subject because, as soon as man developed the ability to express his thoughts in writing, some 5,000 years ago, just about the first thing he did was to try to answer some of the riddles of the Universe. Who created it? And why? And how?

Questions of that kind were answered in terms of mythology: the Universe was created by gods, for the enjoyment of mankind. These gods had different functions — a god of the storms, a god of the sea, a god of the plants, and so on. In this way, early man recognized that there were innumerable natural forces which he could observe, but not control; and he tried to come to terms with these natural

phenomena by attributing them to personified gods with whom he could negotiate, or to whom he could pray.

Today we are still asking the same sort of questions: what *is* the Universe? How was it formed? When did it happen? How and when did our planet Earth come into being? What is it made of? What makes the weather happen? What made the mountains? And what is man's place on this great planet, which is such a tiny speck in the infinite vastness of the Universe?

Many of these questions can now be answered with some assurance — and the answers are to be found in this book. There are still marvels and mysteries that are beyond our understanding, of course (and I hope there always will be!); there are almost unimaginable stretches of time and space that are far beyond the reach of even our most powerful telescopes. But we know a great deal now about the world today — about our world, and our place in it.

Finding out about the world has been one of the great achievements of the human mind. The wonder of the world is by no means lessened by knowing more and more about it; on the contrary, it is greatly increased.

Knowledge about our world is not only useful; it is tremendous fun. When you travel from one part of the country to another, or from one part of the world to another, the journey becomes infinitely more exciting if you know why the landscapes are so different, why the people are so different, why customs and languages and styles of living are so different.

Knowing about the world — which means knowing about yourself and all the other people in it, whether they are black, white or yellow — is the beginning of all knowledge. Enjoy it!

Magnus Magnusson

Maps

Half title page **Tilling with a primitive plough and a donkey near Marrakech in Morocco.**

Title pages **Clouds over Seram, Moluccas.**

Page 6 above left **A modern combine harvester is manoeuvred beside a loading wagon during the harvesting of green crops in Germany.**

Page 6 above right **Peasant farmers ploughing with oxen in the Benares region of Northern India.**

Page 6 below right **A lioness keeps a watchful eye on her cubs at play.**

Acknowledgments

The publishers would like to thank the following individuals and organizations for their kind permission to reproduce the photographs in this book:

Heather Angel 42 below right, 43 below; Aquila Photographics (W S Paton) 6 below right, (P D V Weaving) 40 above right; Ardea Photograhics (Ian Beames) 40 centre right, (M D England) 42 below left, (K W Fink) 40 above left, (Su Gooders) 35 below right, (P Green) 36, (Eric Lindgren) 40 below left, (R F Porter) 44, (Swedberg) 45 above, (R &V Taylor) 43 above left; Barnaby's Picture Library (H Kanus) 55 below; BBC 4-5; Almanna Bokenfeld, Iceland 23; Camera Press Ltd. 24; John Cleare, Mountain Camera 33; Bruce Coleman Ltd. 39, (J Burton) 11 above; Sonia Halliday 49 left; Robert Harding Associates 2-3, 30 above right, 66, (J M Stewart) 51 Above; Angelo Hornak 49 right, 92; Alan Hutchison Library endpapers, 25 above, 68, 71, (S E Porlock) 57, 58; London Features International 86; Photri 87 above; National Coal Board 70; Photo Aquatics (Hermann Gruhl) 43 above right; Pic on Tour/Charlie 40-41 below, 55 above; Picturepoint Ltd. 7, 47 left, 77, 81, 82, 84-85, 85 above, below left and below right, 87 below left and below right, 89 above, 91 below, 94; R K Pilsbury 17, (2) (3) (5) (6) (7) (8) (9) (10); Popperfoto 21, 54, 75, 89 above centre and below centre, 93, (W M Simmons) 91 above; David Prout 12 below; Rex Features Ltd. 14; Spectrum Colour Library 8 below, 16-17, 26, 30-31 below, 31, 35 below left, 41 above, 51 below, 56 right; John Topham Picture Library (Dumas) 42 above, (L Garbison) 35 above, (Mousseau) 45 below left, (M Wilkins) 12 above, (Windridge) 17, (1) (4); A G Waltham 29; Keith Wicks 13 above, 73; ZEFA (R Everts) 27, 82-83, (R Halin) 17 centre below, 32, 62, 63, (H Helbing) 6 above left, 59, (H Hoffmann-Buchardi) 47 right, (Dr Hans Kramarz) 64, (E Landschak) 45 below right, (Photo Leidmann) 1, (Th Luttge) 56 left, (G Marche) 95, (Dr F Sauer) 37, (D H Teuffen) 30 left, (F Walther) 6 above right, 46.

Illustrations by: Diagram Ltd., Eric Jewell Associates, Illustra Design Ltd., Osborne/Marks

First published in Great Britain 1977 by Octopus Books Limited 59 Grosvenor Street London W1

This edition published 1982 by Crescent Books Distributed by Crown Publishers, Inc. One Park Avenue, New York, NY 10016

© MCMLXXVII Hennerwood Publications Limited

Map section and index, illustrations pages 18-19, 22, 34-35, 48-49, 78 below
© MCMLXXVII George Philip & Son Ltd

Library of Congress Catalog Card Number 82-71586

ISBN 0-517-230062

Produced by Mandarin Publishers Limited 22a Westlands Road, Quarry Bay, Hong Kong

Printed in Hong Kong

The Physical World

The Earth in Space

To most of us, the Earth seems to be a very big place. Our hands would have to be enlarged more than 100 million times to be able to grasp the Earth. Yet, in their journeys to the Moon, American astronauts saw the Earth appear to shrink until it seemed small enough to hold in their hands. With their own eyes, these men have been able to see just how tiny our world really is in comparison with the great depths of space.

But we, too, can get an idea of our place in the Universe just by looking up into the sky. Only two bodies in the heavens appear to be of any size — the Moon and the Sun. The Moon is a small world, its diameter being only a quarter of the Earth's diameter, whereas the Sun is huge — 109 times greater in diameter than the Earth. But the Sun and Moon look the same size from the Earth because, although the Sun is about 400 times bigger in diameter than the Moon, it is about 400 times farther from the Earth than the Moon is.

Nine main planets move in oval paths around the Sun. The Earth is one of these planets. All the planets are lit by the Sun and do not produce their own light. Some are smaller and some larger but, whatever their size, they are all so far away from the Earth that they appear merely as dots of light in the night sky. Like our world, most of them have one or more moons moving around them, but these are so small that they can be seen from Earth only with the aid of a telescope. The Sun's group of planets, together with their moons and other bodies, such as comets and asteroids (minor planets), is called the Solar System. The orbit of its outermost member, Pluto, averages nearly 6,000 million kilometres (3,750 million miles) from the Sun; your hand would have to be more than 100 million million times its actual size to hold the Solar System!

Almost all the asteroids orbit the Sun in a broad belt between the orbits of Mars and Jupiter. Thousands of asteroids have been discovered and all are extremely small compared with the main planets of the Solar System. Comets are bodies that come from the depths of space. As they approach the Sun, they become visible and usually display a glowing tail of charged particles. After passing close to the Sun, comets travel back to the outer edges of the Solar System. Some comets reappear at regular intervals.

Although the Solar System may seem enormous, in fact it is only a tiny corner of the Universe. A glance into the night sky reveals thousands of stars, many of them like our Sun, which is a common kind of star. The Sun is in fact a member of a vast group of stars called the Galaxy. With the naked eye, we can see only a small proportion of these — the ones that are relatively close or very bright. All together, the Galaxy contains 100,000 million stars, all so distant that they appear, even through the most powerful telescopes, as dots of light. Distances are so great in astronomy that they have to be measured in light-years. One light-year is the distance that light travels in a year, and it is equal to nearly 10 million million kilometres (6.2 million million miles). On this scale, the Galaxy is 100,000 light-years across, and the Universe does not stop there. Scattered throughout space are millions of other galaxies. No one knows how big the Universe really is because it extends beyond the reach of our telescopes. But these instruments have detected bodies that could be as much as 15,600 million light-years away. For comparison, the farthest distance that man has travelled into space — to the Moon — takes light a mere 1¼ seconds to cross.

The Motion of the Earth

Every day, the Sun crosses the sky, rising at dawn in the east and setting at dusk in the west. Night comes as the Sun moves beyond •

Above: **The planets, to scale, with their moons (top), and the Solar System with distances to scale (bottom). The nine planets, with their average distances from the Sun, are:**

1. Mercury:	57,900,000 km
2. Venus:	108,210,000 km
3. Earth:	149,600,000 km
4. Mars:	227,930,000 km
5. Jupiter:	778,340,000 km
6. Saturn:	1,427,000,000 km
7. Uranus:	2,869,600,000 km
8. Neptune:	4,496,700,000 km
9. Pluto:	5,900,000,000 km

The asteroids, or minor planets, make up the belt between Mars and Jupiter.

Left: **The Earth, as seen from space by American Apollo astronauts.**

Right: **The Earth is in the Solar System, which is a small part of the Galaxy, one of millions of galaxies in the Universe.**

the horizon to the other side of the world and our side is shaded from its light. We say, for convenience, that the Sun crosses or moves in the sky, but it is, in fact, the Earth that is moving, and not the Sun. The Earth rotates once every 24 hours, spinning in a west-to-east direction but, to anyone on the Earth's surface, the Sun *appears* to move from east to west. With one rotation of the Earth, a day and night passes. However, the length of day and night vary throughout the year. In summer, the days are long and nights short, while winter is a time of short days and long nights. These changes happen because the Earth's axis is tilted. The Earth's axis is an imaginary line about which the Earth rotates; it runs through the middle of the Earth from the North Pole to the South Pole. If this line were exactly at right angles to the plane of the Earth's orbit around the Sun, then all days and nights would be exactly the same length — 12 hours each — and there would be no seasons. But the axis is tilted at an angle of 23½°. As the Earth moves around the Sun in its orbit, first one pole tilts towards the Sun and then the other pole does. The Earth's movement around the Sun thus causes seasonal changes in world climate.

When it is summer in the Northern Hemisphere, the North Pole is tilted towards the Sun, making the Sun appear to be high in the sky at midday. Days are long and it is warm, because the Sun's rays come straight down through the atmosphere and can heat the ground for a long time. At the same time, it is winter in the Southern Hemisphere. The South Pole is pointing away from the Sun, making the Sun appear to be low in the sky in the Southern Hemisphere. The days are short and nights long, and it is cold because the Sun's rays enter the atmosphere at a narrow angle and have little time to heat the ground. Six months later, the poles are pointing the other way and it is winter in the Northern

Hemisphere and summer in the Southern Hemisphere. In between, spring and autumn occurs in each hemisphere. Then neither pole is tilted very much towards or away from the Sun. As a result, days and nights are about the same length during both the spring and autumn months.

The day on which the Sun appears to get to its highest point in the sky is the longest day of the year and is called the *summer solstice*. In the Northern Hemisphere, it is about June 21. The shortest day is called the *winter solstice* and is about December 22 in the Northern Hemisphere. In the Southern Hemisphere, these dates are reversed. On days called *equinoxes,* day and night last exactly the same time all over the world. The vernal (spring) equinox occurs on about March 21 and the autumnal equinox on about September 22. However, these days tend to mark the beginnings of the seasons rather than their midpoints. This is because it takes time for the ground to warm up after winter or cool down after summer.

The Motion of the Moon

The Moon moves around the Earth in an orbit, just as the Earth moves around the Sun, and takes nearly 27⅓ days to go once around the Earth. However, the Moon rotates very slowly, spinning only once in the time it takes to go around the Earth. This means that the Moon always keeps the same face towards the Earth and, from Earth, we can never see the other side.

But the Moon does appear to change. Sometimes, it looks like a crescent, then a semi-circle and a full circle. These changes are called *phases*. They happen because we do not always see all of the side of the Moon that is lit up by the Sun. At new moon, the dark

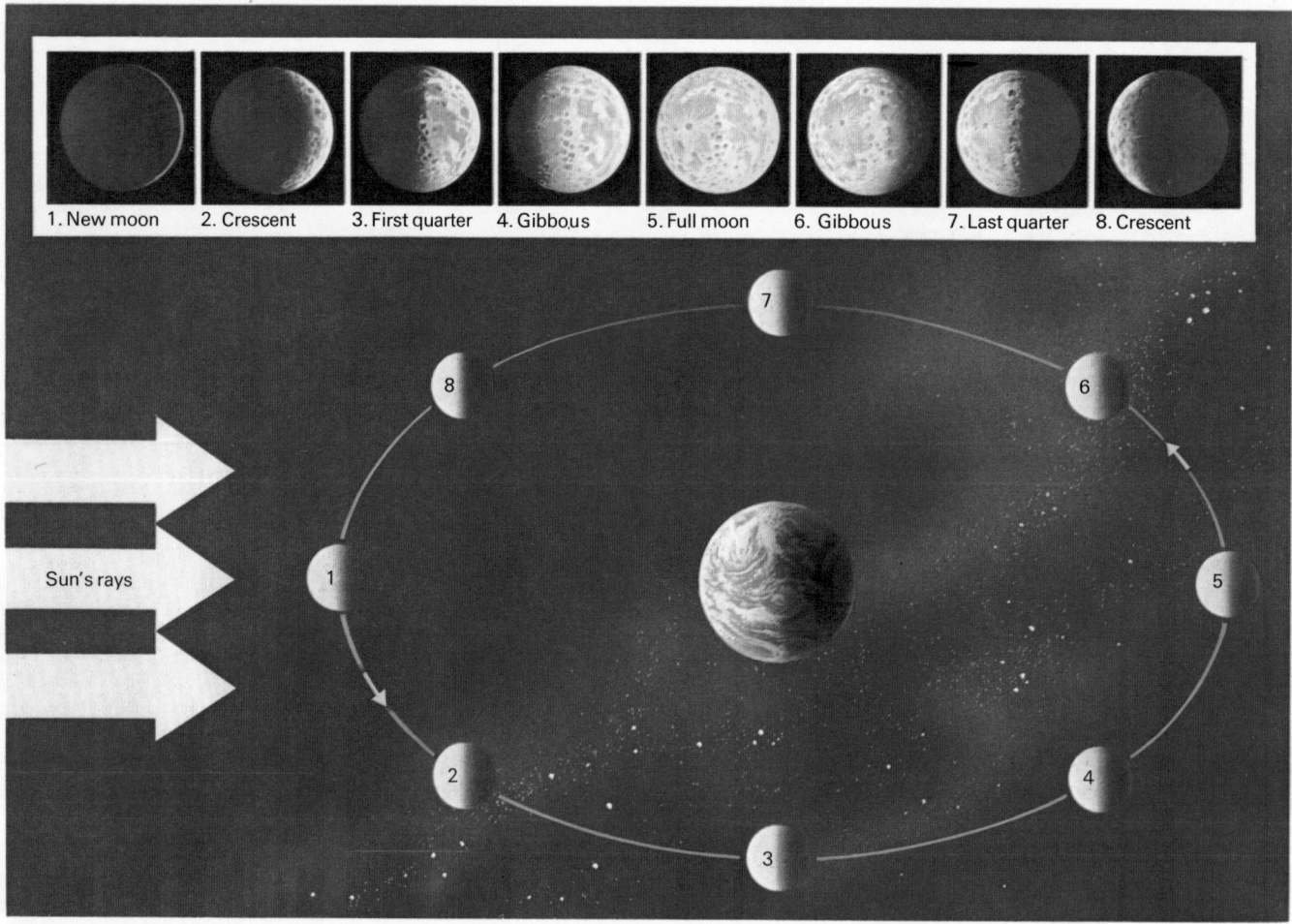

1. New moon　2. Crescent　3. First quarter　4. Gibbous　5. Full moon　6. Gibbous　7. Last quarter　8. Crescent

Sun's rays

side is towards us and we see nothing. Then, as the Moon moves around the Earth, a little of the lit-up side comes into view and we see a crescent. As more of the lit-up side comes round, the crescent grows into a semi-circle and then we have half moon. This grows into a full circle — full moon — when we can see all the lit-up side. Then the full moon shrinks to a half moon and then to a crescent again before we have another new moon. The time it takes for the Moon to go through one complete cycle of phases is just over 29½ days. This is also the length of one complete day and night at any point on the Moon.

The Moon's motion also causes *eclipses* to occur from time to time. When the Moon comes directly between the Earth and the Sun, its shadow sweeps across the Earth's surface. Anyone within the shadow will see the Sun's disc blocked out by the Moon, producing a total eclipse of the Sun, or total *solar eclipse.* Around the Moon's shadow or *umbra,* is a region of partial shadow called the *penumbra.* In places where only the penumbra falls, only part of the Sun's disc is hidden by the Moon. This kind of eclipse is called a partial eclipse. A total eclipse lasts only a few minutes, but a partial eclipse may last for an hour or so. A *lunar eclipse,* or eclipse of the Moon, happens when the Earth comes directly between the Moon and the Sun and the Earth's shadow falls across the Moon, hiding it from view for a short while. Because the orbit of the Moon is tilted, eclipses do not happen every month but usually only once or twice a year.

The Moon also causes tides to occur on the Earth. The gravitational attraction of the Moon slightly raises the level of the ocean beneath the Moon. At the same time, the motion of the Earth causes another rise in level to occur on the opposite side of the world. As the Earth rotates beneath these rises, they appear to move around the world, producing a high tide twice a day. In between, the level falls, giving low tides. The rises in level are also influenced by the Sun. When the Sun is in line with the Moon and the Earth — at new moon and full moon — the rise and fall of the tides is large, giving *spring tides.* Between new moon and full moon, when the Sun, Earth and Moon form a right angle, the rise and fall is small, giving *neap tides.*

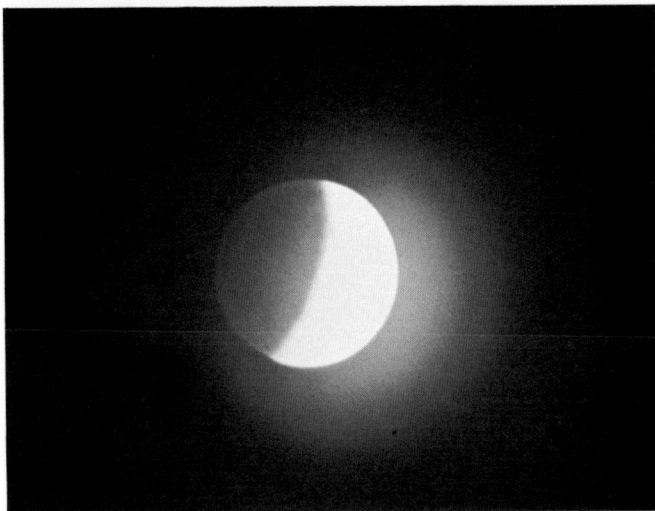

Above: **An eclipse of the Moon occurs when the Earth's shadow passes over the Moon.**

Right: **A total eclipse of the Moon occurs when the Moon is completely within the Earth's shadow. Before and after, when it is partly in the Earth's shadow, a partial eclipse occurs.**

Below right: **An eclipse of the Sun occurs when the Moon's shadow falls on the Earth's surface. A total eclipse, in which the Sun is completely obscured by the Moon, occurs only in a small region. But, on either side of this region, the Moon partly shades the surface and a partial eclipse can be seen.**

Left: **The Moon goes through a cycle of phases as it revolves around the Earth. At new moon (1), the dark side is towards the Earth, and the Moon is almost invisible. Then, as the Moon moves in its orbit, the illuminated side comes into view. First we see a crescent moon (2) and this widens into a half moon (3). Then comes a gibbous moon (4) before a full moon is reached (5), when the Moon is halfway through its orbit and the illuminated side faces the Earth. Then the shape shrinks to become gibbous (6), half moon (7) and crescent (8), before we are back to new moon. The whole cycle takes just over 29½ days.**

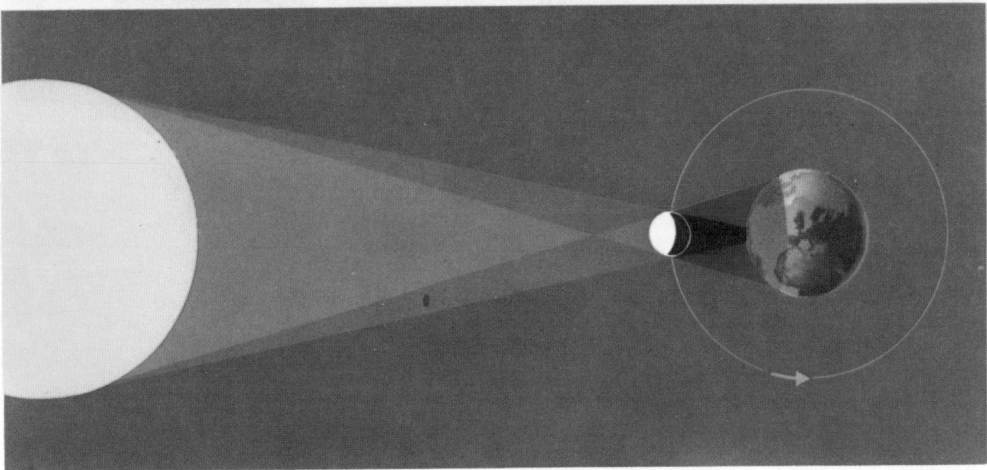

Latitude, Longitude and Time

Latitude and Longitude

Imaginary lines of latitude and longitude divide up the Earth's surface. These lines enable us to locate any place with precision. Latitude shows that a place is on a line running east-west a certain distance north (N) or south (S) of the Equator. The Equator is at 0° latitude, the North Pole at 90°N and the South Pole at 90°S. All other places come somewhere in between. Longitude shows that the place is also on a particular line running north-south. The line of 0° longitude runs from the North Pole to the South Pole through Greenwich Observatory in Britain. All other lines of longitude are related to this line, being up to 180° west (W) or 180° east (E) of it. To find the position of any place on the Earth's surface, it is necessary to give its latitude and longitude. This defines a pair of lines, and the place is at their intersection.

Latitude can be found by observing the positions of certain stars or the Sun in relation to the horizon. Longitude is found by measuring the time at which the Sun or certain stars reach a particular height in the sky.

Time

Although we have many kinds of clocks and watches to tell the time, basically time is measured by the motion of the Earth. A day is the time it takes for the Earth to rotate once on its axis in relation to the Sun. This length of time is then divided into 24 hours, each consisting of 60 minutes, each of 60 seconds. This division into hours, minutes and seconds has no special meaning; it is simply convenient for our everyday lives. We also use months in measuring time, but this is a very approximate method as our months vary in length from 28 to 31 days. A year — the time it takes the Earth to go once around the Sun — is a good unit for measuring long periods of time, not only because it is long, but also because it can be measured very precisely. To the nearest second, a year is 365 days 5 hours 48 minutes and 46 seconds.

These odd hours, minutes and seconds have given people a lot of trouble in producing a calendar in which a particular date always occurs at the same time of the year. This is necessary to keep the months and days in step with the seasons. The ancient Egyptians thought that the year was exactly 365 days long, but every new year arrived one quarter of a day too early with such a calendar. After a time, the seasons began to get obviously later in the year. Julius Caesar realized what was wrong and, in 46 BC, produced a calendar in which most years still had 365 days, but every fourth year — a leap year — had 366 days. This made the average year longer by 6 hours, but this was now 11 minutes too much. By the 1500s, the calendar was several days out and, in 1582, Pope Gregory XIII changed the calendar again. He decreed that every century year (for example 1700, 1800) would not be a leap year unless it could be divided by 400 (for example 1600, 2000). This calendar reduced the error in the length of the year to an average of 26 seconds and it is the calendar that we now use.

However, for all this scientific accuracy, our calendar still has months of different lengths named by the ancient Romans, and the same date falls on a different day of the week from year to year. People have worked out a calendar in which every date always falls on the same day of the week. With this calendar, it would not be necessary to print new diaries and calendars every year, as each year would be exactly the same as the one before.

Another problem that occurs with telling the time is one's location on the Earth's surface. Because everyone expects it to be light at noon and dark at midnight (except in polar regions, where it may be light or dark for months at a time), the world is divided into several different time zones.

Left: **A naval officer uses a sextant to find his position. The sextant measures the angle between the horizon and the Sun or a star. With this information and the exact time, he can work out his position.**

Right: **One kind of sundial, man's first reliable clock. The angle of the shadows changes as the Sun moves from east to west, and thus shows the time of day. The length of the shadows at any particular time varies according to the season.**

Below left: **The line of 0° longitude, which is called the prime meridian, passes through Greenwich Observatory in London. All positions of longitude are measured in degrees east or west of this line.**

Below: **The world is divided into several time zones. As people travel from one zone to another, they change their watches to match the local time.**

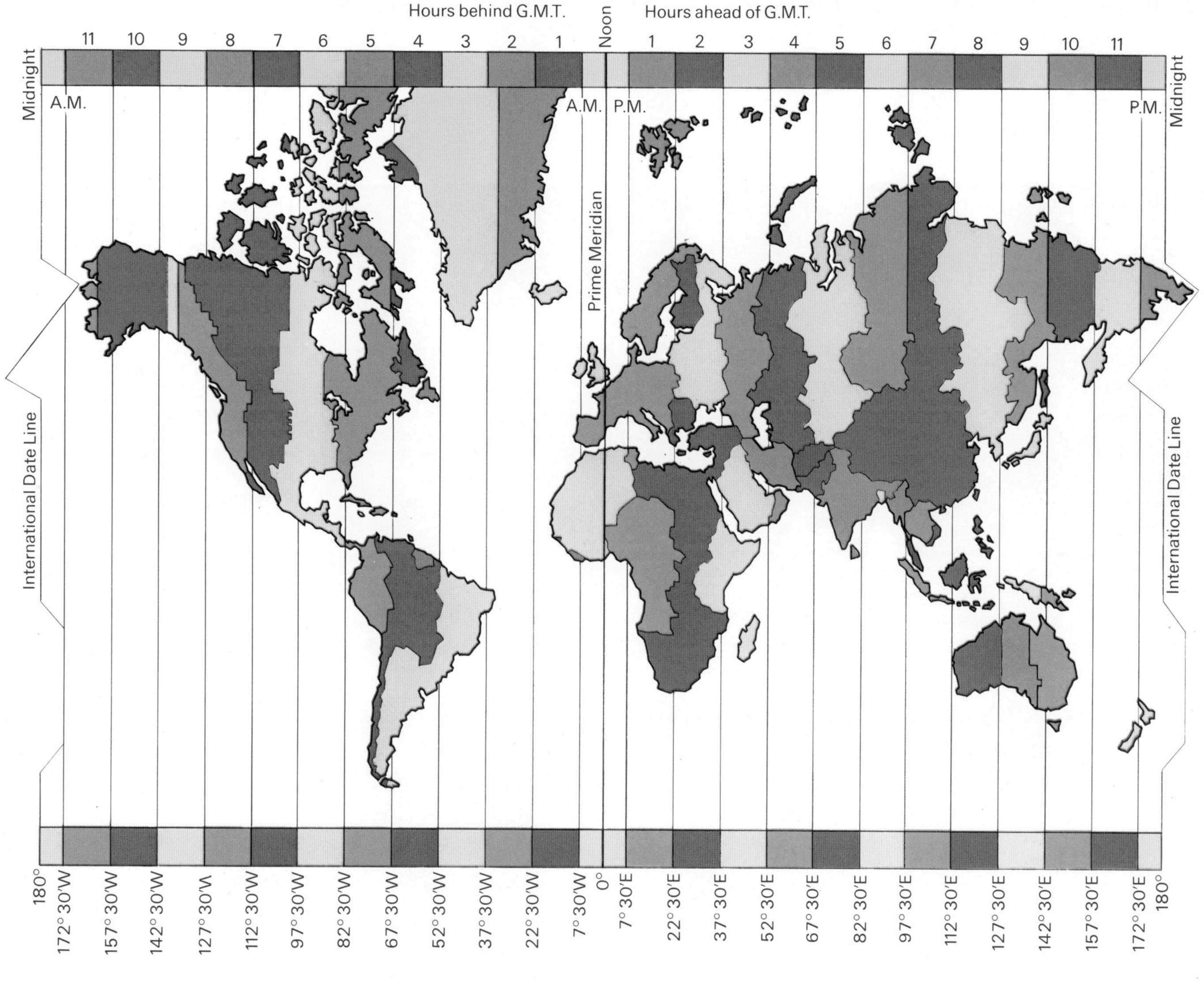

Hours behind G.M.T.   Hours ahead of G.M.T.

The Atmosphere

About 5,000 million million tonnes of gas make up the Earth's atmosphere. A column of air, weighing about one tonne, is pressing down on our shoulders. But we do not feel this pressure, because it is balanced by the same air pressure within our bodies.

The atmosphere is essential for life on Earth. It contains oxygen for animals and carbon dioxide for plants. The ozone layer in the stratosphere protects life on Earth by absorbing most of the Sun's harmful ultraviolet radiation. And the general circulation of the atmosphere redistributes heat around the globe, thus acting like a giant thermostat.

Dry air is composed of nitrogen (78.09% by volume), oxygen (20.95%) and argon (0.93%), together with minute proportions of other gases, including carbon dioxide, neon, helium, methane, krypton, nitrous oxide, hydrogen, ozone and xenon. The amount of carbon dioxide varies considerably from place to place, being greatest over cities and lowest over countryside. Air also contains tiny specks of dust and other substances, such as salt crystals (derived from ocean spray). There are also varying amounts of water vapour evaporated from the Earth's surface, especially from the oceans.

About five-sixths of the total mass of the atmosphere, including nearly all the water vapour, is confined to the lowest zone — the troposphere. Most of the weather we experience originates in this zone. The temperature in the troposphere decreases upwards to the tropopause — the upper limit of the troposphere. There, the temperature becomes stable at about −55°C (−67°F). The height of the tropopause varies between about 8 kilometres (5 miles) over the poles to about 11 kilometres (7 miles) over the middle latitudes and 18 kilometres (11 miles) over the Equator.

Above the tropopause is the lower stratosphere, where conditions are relatively calm and so jet aircraft often fly there. However, strong winds called jet streams blow through the upper troposphere and the lower stratosphere. Reaching speeds of 160 kilometres per hour (100 m.p.h.), these winds can be an obstacle or an aid to high-flying aircraft. Above the tropopause, temperatures remain stable at first but, eventually, they start to rise, reaching about 2°C (36°F) just above the ozone layer.

Beyond the stratosphere, from about 50 to 500 kilometres (30 to 300 miles) above sea level is the ionosphere. Here, temperatures decrease at first, reaching about −70°C (−94°F) at a height of 80 kilometres (50 miles) above sea level. Then temperatures start to rise steadily in the ionosphere, reaching more than 2,000°C (3,600°F) at 400 kilometres (250 miles). The ionosphere is so called because the thinly-distributed gas molecules are ionized (electrically charged) by solar radiation. These charged particles are important in radio communications because they reflect some radio waves. Radio communications are sometimes interrupted by occasional magnetic storms, when the ionosphere is disturbed by streams of charged particles from the Sun. These particles are deflected through the ionosphere by the Earth's magnetic field. Over the magnetic poles, they collide with molecules in the ionosphere and cause spectacular glowing displays of light called *aurorae*. Beyond the ionosphere lies the exosphere, where the thin air gradually merges into space.

Left: **A weather-satellite photograph of a typhoon, or tropical cyclone, over the Pacific Ocean. These large rotating air systems, which are called hurricanes in the Atlantic Ocean, bring fierce winds and may cause serious flooding and great devastation as they move over coastal areas. Information from weather satellites has enabled meteorologists to study the formation of typhoons, chart their movements and issue advance warnings to shipping and threatened coastal areas.**

Right: **A section through the atmosphere, including the troposphere, stratosphere, ionosphere and exosphere. Alongside the diagram are the temperatures and air pressures at different levels.**

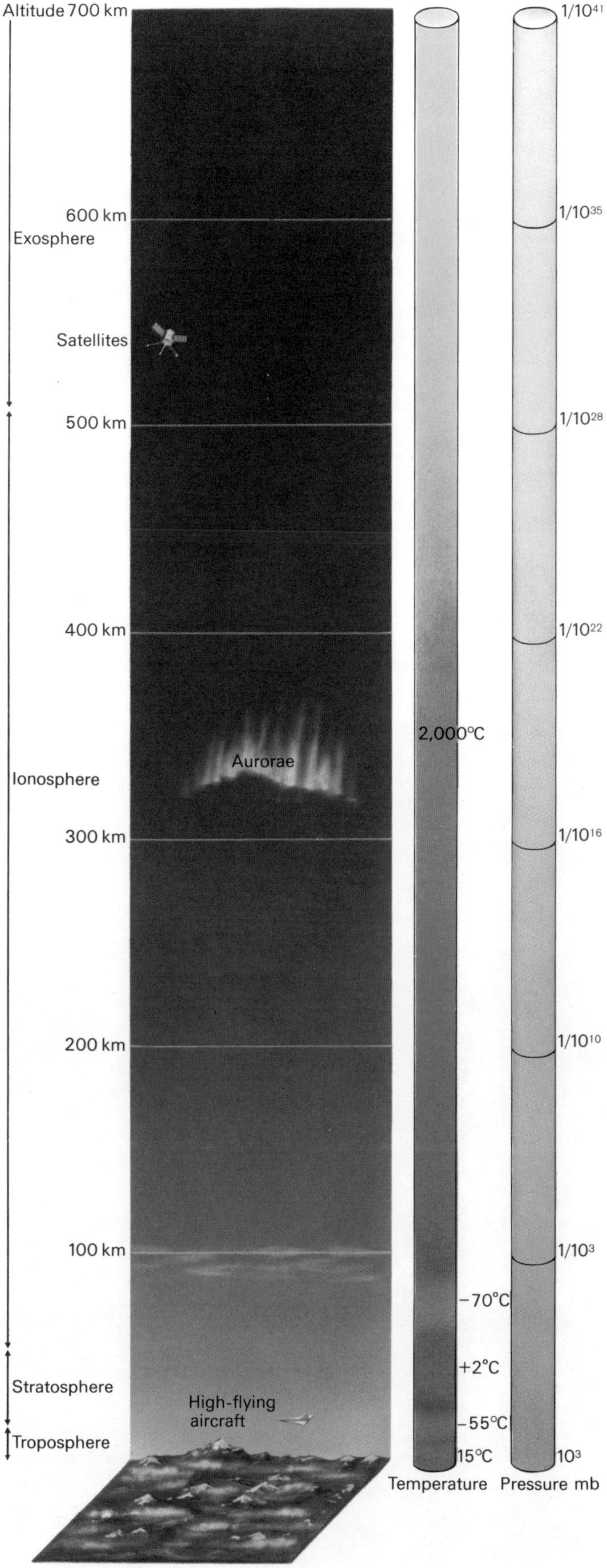

Altitude 700 km

600 km

Exosphere

Satellites

500 km

400 km

Aurorae

Ionosphere

300 km

200 km

100 km

Stratosphere

High-flying
aircraft

Troposphere

2,000°C

−70°C

+2°C

−55°C

15°C

Temperature

1/10⁴¹

1/10³⁵

1/10²⁸

1/10²²

1/10¹⁶

1/10¹⁰

1/10³

10³

Pressure mb

Winds

The air in the atmosphere is constantly circulating. It is like a vast machine powered by the Sun. But heat is unevenly distributed, the effect of the Sun being greatest at the Equator, where it passes directly overhead. As a result, there are great variations in air pressure, causing air currents (winds) to flow from high pressure areas towards low pressure areas.

At the Equator, air near the ground is heated, making it expand and rise. As a result, equatorial regions are characterized by a low-pressure air system, called the *doldrums*. On both sides of the Equator, air flows towards the doldrums in the trade-wind belts. The warm air rising above the equatorial zone cools as it ascends and spreads out north and south. Finally it sinks back to Earth around latitudes 30° North and 30° South, creating two high-pressure belts called the *horse latitudes*. At the surface, some of the descending air flows into the trade winds, and some flows polewards in the westerlies. The westerlies meet cold, dense air flowing from the poles along the polar front. The intermingling of warm, light, sub-tropical air with cold, dense polar air creates rotating low-pressure systems, called *depressions*. These bring changeable, stormy weather to middle latitudes.

This simple pattern of atmospheric circulation is complicated by several factors. First, because the Earth spins on its axis, winds do not flow north-south, but are deflected to the right in the northern hemisphere and to the left in the southern hemisphere. Winds are also deflected by mountain ranges. Another important factor is the seasonal development of large and fairly stable air masses. For example, the interiors of large mid-latitude continents heat up in summer. Large low-pressure air masses form, into which winds are drawn. But, in winter, these continental interiors are cold, and so high-pressure air masses form, from which icy winds blow outwards.

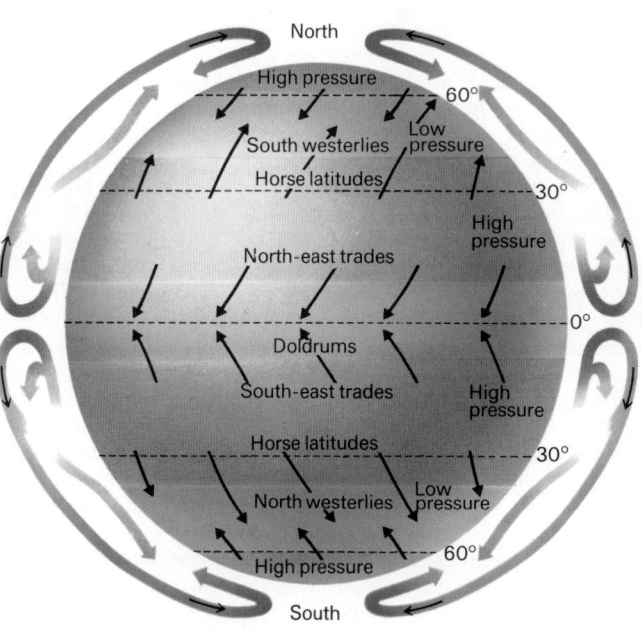

North

High pressure

60°

Low pressure

South westerlies

Horse latitudes

30°

High pressure

North-east trades

0°

Doldrums

South-east trades

High pressure

Horse latitudes

30°

North westerlies

Low pressure

High pressure

60°

South

Above: **The main wind belts on the Earth's surface, and the main air-circulation currents in the atmosphere. Air circulates because uneven heating of the Earth gives rise to air-pressure variations in the** **atmosphere. The air moves as winds, from high-pressure to low-pressure regions. The general pattern of prevailing winds shown here does not take account of local and seasonal variations.**

Weather

Weather is the day-to-day condition of the air. The chief elements of weather are the temperature and pressure of the air, wind speeds and directions, and the amount of moisture in the air — particularly if the moisture is being precipitated as rain, snow, hail, sleet, dew or frost.

All air contains moisture in the form of water vapour, which is water in gaseous form. Warm air can hold more water vapour than cold air. When warm air is cooled, usually by moving upwards in the troposphere, its capacity to hold water vapour decreases. Finally, *dew point* is reached — that is, the air is completely saturated, having a relative humidity of 100 per cent. Further cooling beyond dew point leads to water vapour condensing around nucleii, such as specks of dust or salt, to form water droplets or, in cold air, minute ice crystals. Large quantities of condensed water vapour form clouds.

There are two main kinds of clouds: cumuliform ('heap' clouds) and stratiform ('layer' clouds). Clouds are classified according to their height. Low clouds, within 2.5 kilometres (1.6 miles) of the surface, include: grey stratus; cumulus, a white heap cloud; cumulonimbus, a heap thundercloud; nimbostratus, a layer cloud often blurred by rain or snow; and stratocumulus, a greyish-white layer cloud. Medium-height clouds, from 2.5 to 6 kilometres (1.6 to 3.7 miles) are the greyish-white, rounded altocumulus, and the altostratus, which is a greyish layer cloud. Above 6 kilometres (3.7 miles) are the high clouds, including the feathery cirrus, cirrocumulus and cirrostratus.

Clouds form part of the water cycle, by which water is continually conveyed from the salty oceans to the land, where it is released from the air as precipitation. This provides the land with the fresh water needed by animal and plant life. Finally, the water completes the cycle by returning to the oceans.

Rainfall is of three main kinds. *Convectional rain* occurs, especially in the tropics, when hot air rises and water vapour condenses into towering, often anvil-topped cumulonimbus clouds. Inside the turbulent clouds, the water droplets collide, fuse together and fall as raindrops. *Cyclonic rain* occurs in depressions when warm air rises above wedges of cold air along cold and warm fronts and occlusions. In the middle latitudes, clouds contain super-cooled water droplets, which are still liquid although their temperature may be as low as $-40°C$ ($-40°F$), and ice crystals. The ice crystals collide with supercooled droplets and grow in size. They then start to fall, melting near the surface to become raindrops or, if the air is cold, they join together to form snowflakes. *Orographic rain* is caused when air rises over a mountain range.

Precipitation is a feature of storms. The commonest storms are thunderstorms, about 45,000 of which break out every day somewhere in the world. Thunderstorms occur when strongly rising air currents cause cumulonimbus clouds to form. As temperatures within the clouds fall, the outer shells of super-cooled water droplets freeze and acquire a positive electrical charge. But, when the core subsequently freezes, it has a negative charge. The core expands as it freezes and shatters the outer shell, tiny splinters of which waft upwards, giving the top of the cloud a positive charge. The heavier cores remain lower down, building up a large negative charge. The air between the cloud and ground normally acts as an electrical insulator. But, when the charge on the cloud becomes great enough, the insulation breaks down and lightning — a gigantic spark — occurs. Along the lightning's path, heat causes a violent expansion of the air, and the resultant compression wave is heard as thunder.

Other storms include large, rotating hurricanes, also called tropical cyclones. Hurricanes strike the coasts of Central America and the southeastern United States about 11 times per year. They cause much damage, especially because strong winds hurl high waves onto the shore, causing flooding. Tornadoes are smaller, measuring about 500 metres (1,600 feet) across. Wind speeds in these rotating, funnel-like columns of air may reach 650 kilometres per hour (400 m.p.h.). In tornadoes, buildings may explode because the air pressure outside the buildings is far lower than the air pressure inside them.

Weather satellites orbiting the Earth help forecasters to track hurricanes and give warnings of their advance, besides supplying much other information. At surface weather stations, on land and at sea, meteorologists take regular measurements of air conditions, including temperature, pressure, humidity, precipitation, and wind speeds and directions. Information about conditions in the upper air is provided by radiosondes — hydrogen-filled balloons carrying instruments.

Information from weather stations is sent to forecast centres, where it is often analysed by computers. Synoptic charts are prepared, summarizing weather conditions over a large area. By comparing the latest synoptic chart with preceding charts, developments are noted. Meteorologists deduce how weather conditions will probably change and express them on a forecast chart, from which forecasts are made for the general public.

Grey stratus clouds

Cumulus clouds

Cumulonimbus clouds

Nimbostratus clouds

Stratocumulus clouds

Altocumulus clouds

Altostratus clouds

Cirrus clouds

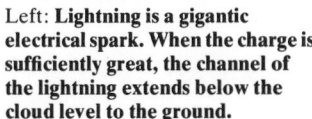

Cirrocumulus clouds

Cirrostratus clouds

Above: **Weather stations use white shelters, called Stevenson screens, to enclose thermometers and, sometimes, other instruments used to measure air conditions. The air can circulate freely through the louvres, so that the instruments, protected from the Sun and the wind, make true readings.**

Left: **Lightning is a gigantic electrical spark. When the charge is sufficiently great, the channel of the lightning extends below the cloud level to the ground.**

Right: **The diagram shows how water continuously circulates from sea to land and back again in the water, or hydrologic cycle. Through this cycle, land areas obtain a regular supply of fresh water, which is essential to the Earth's plant and animal life.**

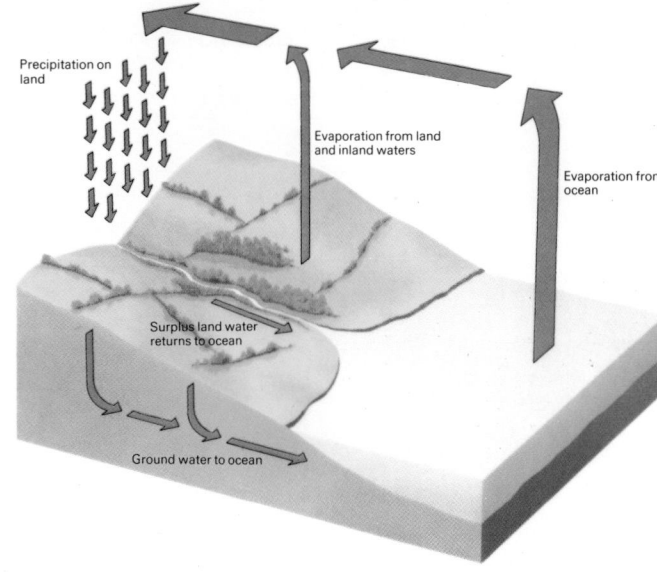

Precipitation on land

Evaporation from land and inland waters

Evaporation from ocean

Surplus land water returns to ocean

Ground water to ocean

Climate

Climate is the typical or average weather of a place based on records covering a period of years. The word climate comes from the Greek word *klima,* which means slope. The Greeks believed that the Earth 'sloped' from the Mediterranean southwards to the hot equatorial zone and northwards to the cold polar region. Hence, a Greek scholar Parmenides suggested in about 500 BC that there were five climatic zones. The central equatorial zone was hot all the year round. The middle latitudes in both hemispheres had summer and winter seasons. And the polar regions were cold all the year round.

But other factors, such as the terrain and the proximity to the sea, complicate this simple pattern. For example, mountains and plateaux have cooler climates than surrounding plains, because temperatures fall, on average, by about 6°C (11°F) for every kilometre (0.6 mile) of altitude. For example, in Kenya, which straddles the Equator, the coastal port of Mombasa has average temperatures of 27°C (81°F) all the year round. But, on the high southwestern plateau in the interior, average temperatures are

10°C to 20°C (50°F to 68°F), and so the plateau has proved more attractive to European settlers than the coast.

The terrain influences the rainfall too. For example, when winds from the oceans are forced to rise over coastal mountain ranges, they lose most of their moisture during their ascent. Beyond the crest of the mountains, the winds are dry and there is often a 'rain shadow' area.

The oceans have a considerable effect on climate. The Sun's rays heat the surfaces of land areas more intensely and faster than they heat the sea. But land areas cool extremely quickly, whereas bodies of water retain heat about two-and-a-half times as readily as land. Generally, in maritime areas, winds from the oceans warm the land in winter and cool it in summer. This moderating influence is particularly pronounced, for example, along the west coasts of land masses in the middle latitudes of the northern hemisphere, where the prevailing winds are southwesterlies. But, beyond the moderating influence of the oceans, the continental interiors have extreme climates. In southwestern Ireland, the

Left: **Climate around the world.**

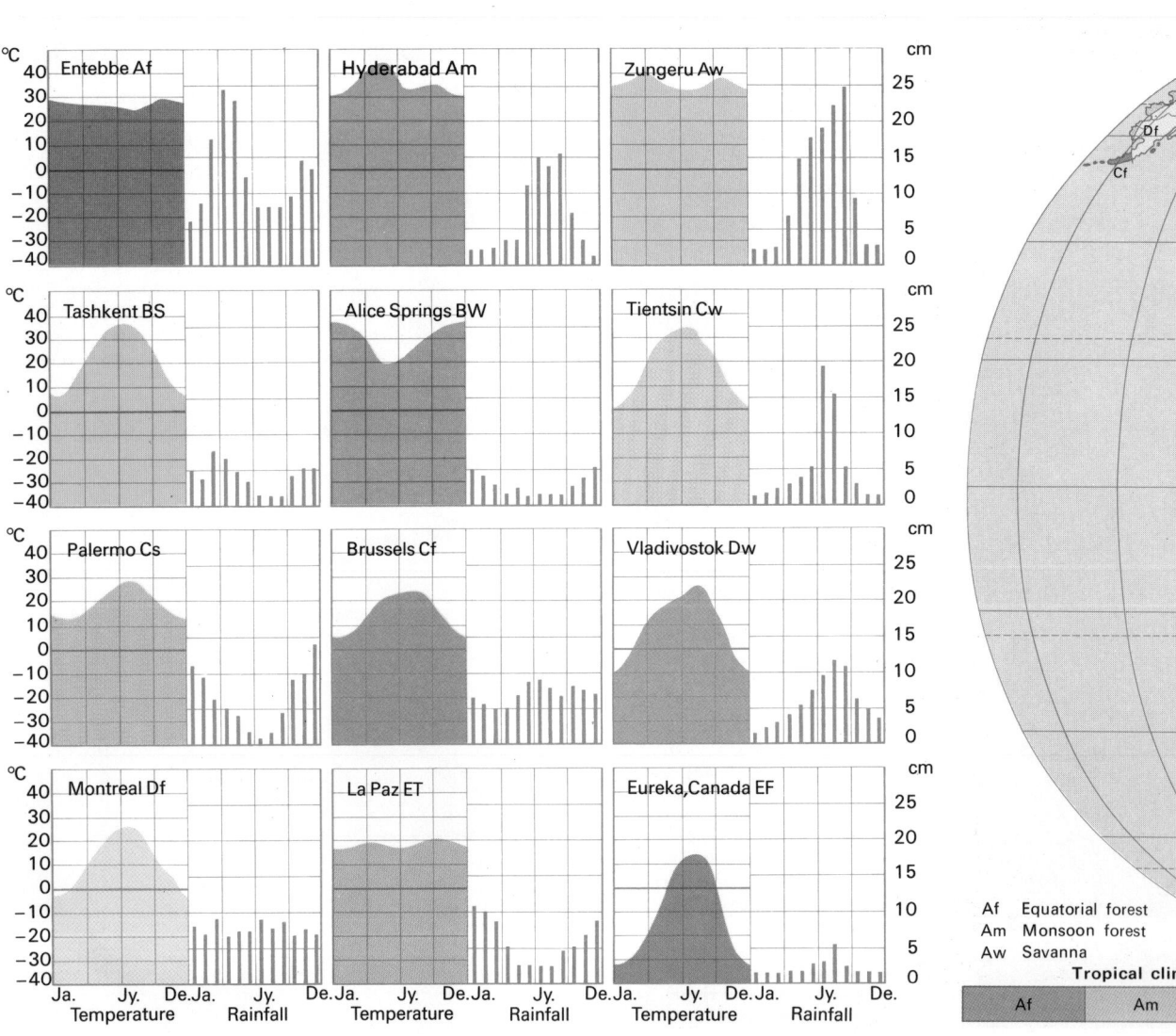

average temperature in the coldest month is 5°C (41°F) and the average in the warmest month is 16°C (61°F) — an average annual temperature range of only 11°C (20°F). But, in the same latitude, south of Moscow, the average temperature in the coldest month is −11°C (12°F) and, in the warmest month, it is 21°C (70°F) — an average annual temperature range of 32°C (58°F).

Ocean currents affect climate too. The icy Labrador current flows southwards down the eastern coast of Canada, and St. John's in Newfoundland, for example, has cold winters, with an average temperature in the coldest month of −5°C (23°F). St. John's lies in the same latitude as Brittany, which has mild winters. The coastlands of northwestern Europe are warmed in winter by onshore winds that pass over an extension of the warm Gulf Stream — an ocean current that originates in the Caribbean.

There are various ways of classifying climates, but most classifications used today are based on the work of Russian meteorologist Vladimir Köppen in the early 1900s. Köppen classified climates according to temperature and rainfall. He distinguished five main climatic types, coding them **A, B, C, D** and **E**. Type **A** is the tropical, rainy climate, with average temperatures of over 18°C (64°F) in every month of the year. Type **B** is a dry climate, with an average of less than 250 millimetres (10 inches) of rain per year and a high evaporation rate. Type **C** is the middle-latitude, warm temperate climate, with average temperatures in the coldest month from −3°C to 18°C (27°F to 64°F). Type **D** is a cold and snowy climate, with an average temperature of less than −3°C (27°F) in the coldest month, but the average temperature in the warmest month is more than 10°C (50°F). And type **E** is the polar climate, with an average temperature of less than 10°C (50°F) in the warmest month. Cold, mountain regions, once included in type **E**, are now usually classified **H**.

To distinguish between rainfall patterns, a second group of symbols has been added: **S** (dry steppelands), **W** (deserts), **f** (places with ample, well-distributed rainfall), **m** (monsoon, or seasonal rainfall), **s** (a dry summer) and **w** (a dry winter). To distinguish between polar climates, the code **T** represents tundra and **F** signifies ice-sheet climates. Hence, type **Af** is equatorial forest, which is hot and wet all the year round, whereas **Aw** is tropical savanna, with summer rains and a winter drought.

Other symbols are: **a** (hot summers), **b** (warm summers), **c** (cool summers), **d** (very cold winters), **h** (dry and hot) and **k** (dry and cold). Hence, the code **Cfb** means a middle-latitude, warm temperate climate, with ample, well-distributed rainfall and warm summers — the characteristic climate of northwestern Europe.

Below: **World climate zones.**

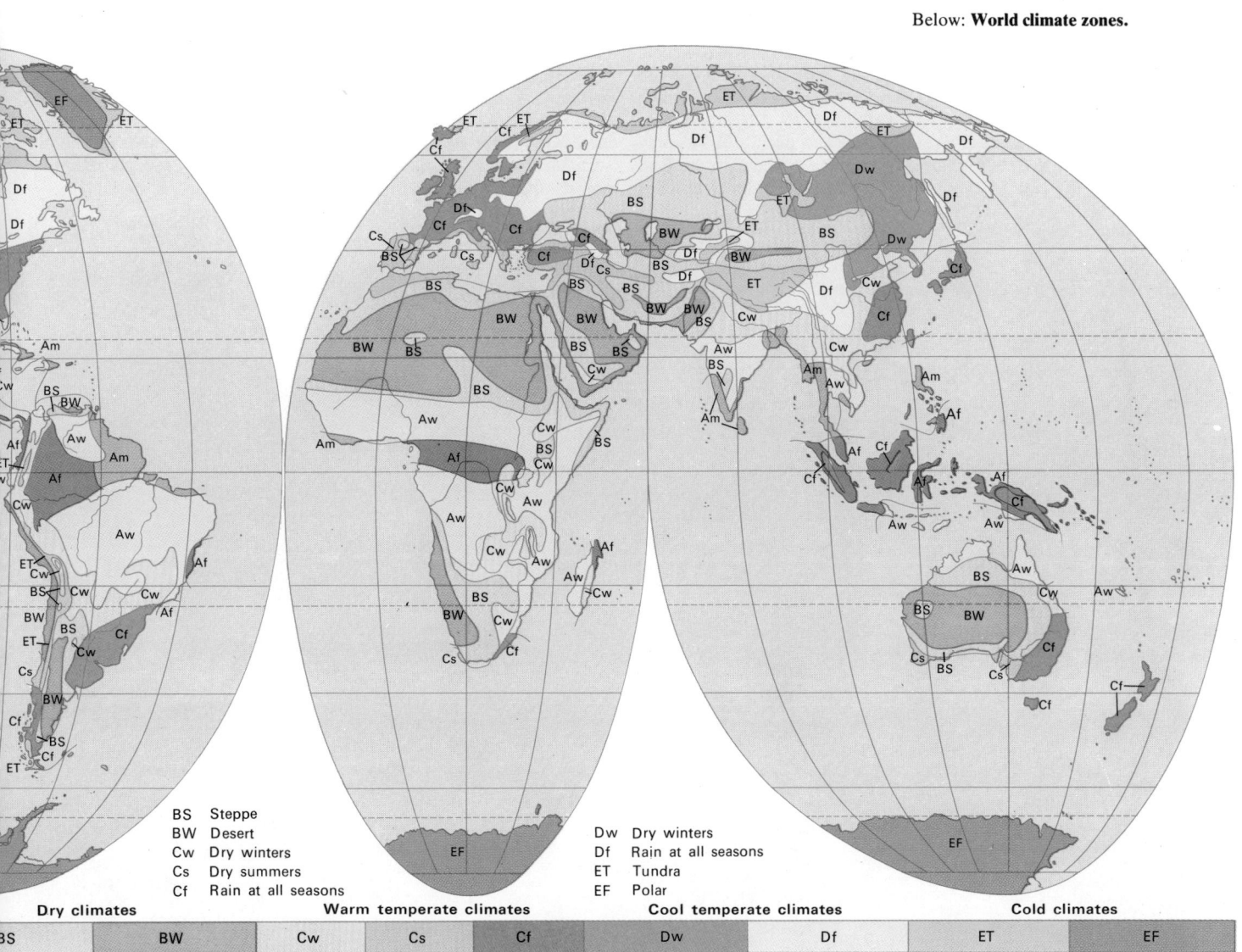

BS	Steppe		Dw	Dry winters
BW	Desert		Df	Rain at all seasons
Cw	Dry winters		ET	Tundra
Cs	Dry summers		EF	Polar
Cf	Rain at all seasons			

Dry climates **Warm temperate climates** **Cool temperate climates** **Cold climates**

BS	BW	Cw	Cs	Cf	Dw	Df	ET	EF

The Oceans

The oceans, which are interconnected, cover 70.8 per cent of the Earth's surface. The largest ocean, the Pacific, sprawls over the vast area of 165,236,000 square kilometres (63,798,000 square miles) — more than the combined area of all the continents. The oceans have an average depth of about 3.5 kilometres (2.2 miles), but the deepest known point is in Challenger Deep, part of the Mariana Trench in the Pacific, which is 11.033 kilometres (6.855 miles) deep.

The water in the oceans totals about 1,300 million cubic kilometres (312 million cubic miles) — more than 97 per cent of the world's total water. On average, seawater contains about 3.5 per cent by weight of dissolved substances. Nearly 3 per cent is composed of chlorine and sodium, which together form sodium chloride (common salt). Other substances, such as sulphur, magnesium, potassium and calcium, are present in abundance in seawater, and there are minute proportions of many other elements. In fact, seawater is a great treasure trove of valuable and useful minerals, but the extraction of most of them is extremely costly and, therefore, uneconomic. The only important substances currently obtained from seawater are common salt, magnesium and bromine. The extraction of other substances will probably not be undertaken until land reserves are nearly exhausted. Also present in seawater are various gases dissolved from the atmosphere. The most important is oxygen, on which marine organisms depend.

The salinity of seawater averages 35 parts per 1,000 (usually expressed as 35‰), but it varies from place to place. In the Red Sea, where the rate of evaporation is high, the salinity reaches 41‰. But, in the Baltic Sea, rivers supply large amounts of fresh water and the salinity is lowered to 7.2‰. Salinity and temperature affect the density of seawater, high salinity and low temperatures both causing the water to have a relatively high density. The temperature of ocean water varies between $-2°C$ (28°F) — its approximate freezing point — and 29°C (84°F).

Density differences contribute to the continuous circulation of ocean waters, because dense water sinks beneath less dense water. However, the chief movements of ocean water are: tides, caused by the gravitational pull of the Moon and, to a lesser extent, the Sun; waves, which move water particles in a circular orbit, but not horizontally, except on shores; and ocean currents.

Surface ocean currents generally follow prevailing winds although, because of the Earth's spin, they swing to the right of the wind direction in the Northern Hemisphere and to the left in the Southern Hemisphere. Generally, currents cause the surface waters of the Northern Hemisphere to circulate in a clockwise direction. In the Southern Hemisphere, the circulation is anti-clockwise. Surface currents are classed as *cold* if they flow from polar regions towards the tropics, and *warm* if they flow polewards from the tropics. The temperature of offshore currents has a great effect on the climates of coastlands.

The effect of surface currents is hardly noticeable at about 350 metres (1,150 feet) below the surface. But the waters in the ocean depths are not still, and several deep, vigorous counter-currents have been found flowing in an opposite direction to those on the surface. Scientists have found that, even in the deepest parts of the oceans, the water is moving. They base this conclusion on the fact

Sea level

Transform fa

Mohorovicic discontinuity

Mantle

that fishes have been found at great depths. If the water were still, the oxygen dissolved from the air would have been used up long ago and no fishes could possibly survive.

The study of the ocean floor has been of tremendous importance in establishing how the oceans were formed and how the continents have drifted around the Earth's surface. The ocean floor consists of three main zones: the continental shelf, the continental slope and the abyss. The gently sloping continental shelves border the continents, extending outwards to a depth of about 180 metres (600 feet). They vary considerably in width. For example, the continental shelf off northwestern Europe extends about 300 kilometres (190 miles) west of Land's End. But, off the west coast of South America, there is practically no continental shelf. The shelves are, in fact, submerged parts of the continents. Islands that rise above water level are called continental islands to distinguish them from oceanic islands, which rise from the abyss.

The continental shelves end at the start of the continental slope, the true edge of the continents. The continental slope descends steeply down to the abyss.

The abyss contains large, sediment-covered plains, interrupted by lofty volcanic mountains, some of which surface as islands, and long, broad ridges, 2 to 4 kilometres (1.2 to 2.5 miles) high and up to 4,000 kilometres (2,500 miles) wide. One ridge runs the whole length of the Atlantic Ocean. These ridges, which surface in places such as Iceland, are centres of volcanic activity and earthquakes. Other important features of the abyss are yawning chasms called oceanic trenches.

Left: **Thor Heyerdahl's papyrus boat _Ra_, like those of ancient Egypt, was driven by winds and currents.**

Below: **A section through the Atlantic Ocean. In order to show the details clearly, the vertical scale has been exaggerated.**

ft

Crust (including sediments)

Asthenosphere

Formation of the Earth

The Restless Earth

The Earth was formed about 4,600 million years ago from a great cloud of gas, rock and dust that was orbiting around a new star, the Sun. Gradually, heavier materials, such as iron and nickel, sank towards the centre, while lighter materials rose to the surface. And parts of the molten surface hardened into a thin, solid crust of igneous rocks, probably consisting mostly of basalt.

But cracking and reheating often broke up the outer shell and, from remelting, even lighter granitic rocks separated out. When they hardened, these rocks formed the first parts of the continental crust. Gases and water vapour were released from the rocks by continuous volcanic eruptions. These gases formed the atmosphere. Great storms must have raged over the Earth and rains eroded the hardened igneous rock. Streams swept eroded fragments into primeval lakes and seas, where they accumulated to form the first sedimentary rocks.

The early atmosphere probably contained only a minute proportion of oxygen, because volcanic gases are deficient in this life-giving gas. But, after the evolution of oxygen-producing plants around 1,900 million years ago, the proportion of oxygen steadily increased.

The Earth today has an equatorial diameter of 12,756 kilometres (7,926 miles). Measured from pole to pole, however, the diameter is 43 kilometres (27 miles) less, because our planet is not a true sphere, being slightly flattened at the poles and bulging at the Equator. Our knowledge of the Earth's interior is based on the behaviour of seismic (earthquake) waves as they travel through the Earth. From a study of how these waves bend, scientists have concluded that the centre of the Earth's core is a solid sphere with a diameter of about 2,740 kilometres (1,700 miles). The rocks in the solid core are about three times as dense as those in the crust. Surrounding the inner core is a liquid outer core, which is about 2,100 kilometres (1,300 miles) thick. Temperatures in the outer core range from 2,000°C to 5,000°C (3,600°F to 9,000°F), and movements in this molten material

probably generate the electricity that gives the Earth its magnetic properties. Between the outer core and the crust is the dense mantle, which is about 2,900 kilometres (1,800 miles) thick. The mantle is mostly solid but, at its top, some rocks are molten or semi-solid. Heating causes these rocks to rise and spread beneath the crust in convection currents.

The Earth's crust beneath the oceanic abyss is only about 6 kilometres (3.7 miles) thick. But the continental crust is mostly 35 to 50 kilometres (22 to 25 miles) in thickness, reaching 60 kilometres (37 miles) under high mountain ranges. There are other contrasts between oceanic and continental crust. First, the basaltic oceanic crust is 3.0 times as dense as water, whereas granitic continental crust is only 2.7 times as dense as water. And all oceanic crust has been formed within the last 200 million years, whereas the continents contain rocks that are more than 3,500 million years old.

The study of the oceanic crust has contributed to the generally accepted theory of *plate tectonics,* or *continental drift.* Scientists now believe that the crust is cracked into a series of 'plates' which are moving around the Earth's surface. The continents are composed of light materials and they rest upon the moving plates.

Plate edges occur along the mid-oceanic ridges. Along these ridges, new crustal rock is being added as molten material wells up from below. For example, in the Atlantic Ocean, studies of rock samples reveal that rocks become progressively older east and west of the mid-Atlantic ridge. These rock samples often contain magnetized particles, which were aligned towards the Earth's magnetic poles when the rock hardened. But these particles have been twisted out of alignment — further evidence of movement.

As a result of this movement, the oceans are widening, or spreading, at 1 to 10 centimetres (0.4 to 4 inches) per year. But the Earth is not expanding, for the crust is being destroyed at other plate edges. These are the oceanic trenches. Here, one plate is pushed beneath another to about 700 kilometres (430 miles) below the surface, before it is finally melted and destroyed. Some

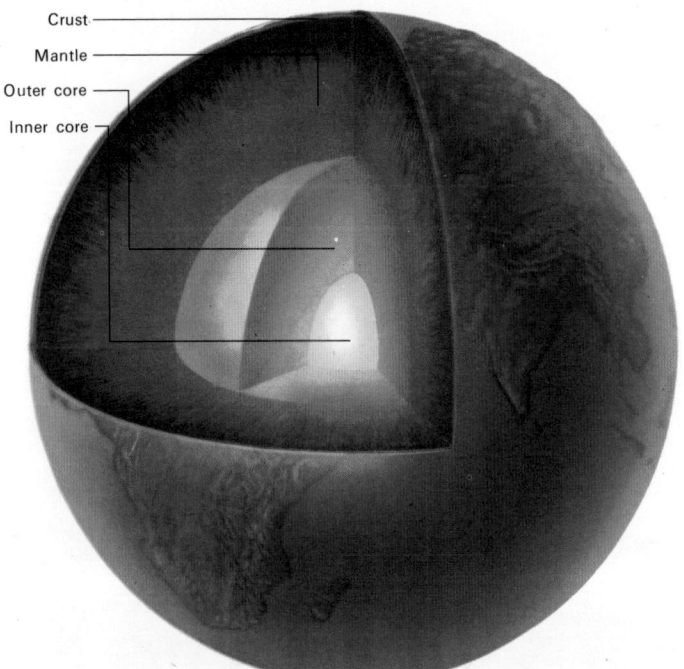

Crust
Mantle
Outer core
Inner core

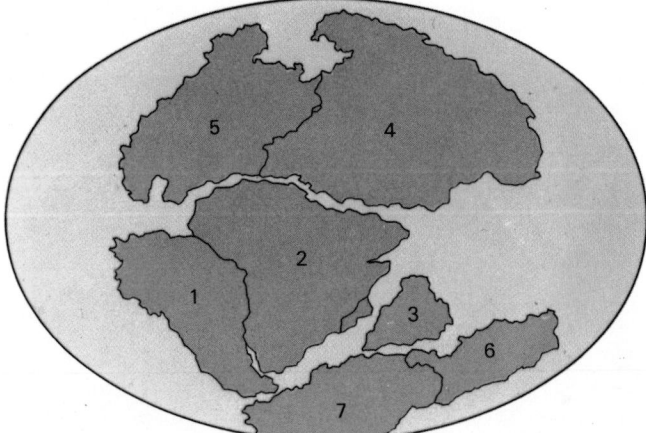

Left: **Zones within the Earth.**

Above: **A super-continent, called Pangaea, existed about 200 million years ago. Since then, the continents have broken away and drifted apart to their present positions.**

Right: **The volcanic island of Surtsey, on the mid-Atlantic ridge. This island appeared off the Icelandic coast in November, 1963 and grew rapidly. After three weeks, its crater had risen to 120 metres (390 feet) above sea level and was almost 1 kilometre (0.6 mile) across.**

of the melted rock may return to the surface through the overriding plate to form a chain of volcanic islands, roughly parallel to the trench. Another type of plate edge, a transform fault, occurs where plates move horizontally alongside each other.

Scientists now believe that, about 200 million years ago, all the continental land masses were grouped together in one super-continent, called Pangaea. The northern part of Pangaea, called Laurasia, consisted of North America and most of Eurasia. The southern part, Gondwanaland, consisted of South America, Africa, the Indian sub-continent, Australia and Antarctica. In the last 180 million years, Pangaea has split apart and the continents have drifted to their present positions. The Indian sub-continent, after separating from Gondwanaland, moved northward and eventually linked up with Asia.

Earthquakes

As plates drift apart, the movement occurs in sudden jerks, which cause earthquakes.

Earthquakes can occur anywhere. They are caused mostly by sudden movements along faults in rocks triggering off destructive vibrations. The most destructive earthquakes occur when the focus (point of origin) is within about 60 kilometres (37 miles) of the Earth's surface. The point on the Earth's surface directly above the focus is called the epicentre. About 10,000 earthquakes are recorded annually, although, on average, only 10 cause major destruction. By plotting the epicentres of all the earthquakes on a world map, it is evident that earthquakes predominate around the edges of the plates. They are much less common in areas away from plate edges.

The intensity of earthquakes is measured on a scale devised by C. F. Richter in 1935. An earthquake rated 2 on the Richter scale is hardly noticeable. But a magnitude of 5 causes some damage, and magnitude 7 is severe. One of the most intensive earthquakes in recent times had a magnitude of 8.9. It occurred in the Prince William Sound off Alaska on March 28, 1964.

This earthquake triggered off a so-called tidal wave — a misnomer because such waves have nothing to do with tides. Hence, scientists use the Japanese term *tsunami*. These fast waves travel through the water at speeds up to 800 kilometres per hour (500 m.p.h.). In the open sea, they may pass unnoticed, because the wave height (the vertical distance between the crest and the trough) is usually less than one metre (three feet). But the energy contained in a tsunami is tremendous, especially because, unlike a normal wave, it extends through the entire depth of the water. As tsunamis approach coasts, the wave height increases rapidly, and they batter the land with terrifying force. The Alaskan earthquake of March 1964 caused a tsunami that reached a height of 67 metres (220 feet).

In recent times, scientists have been trying to find ways of alleviating the tension along faults and producing methods of reliable forecasting. One area of research is California in the United States. A long plate edge in California, called the San Andreas fault, is a transform fault. The jagged plate edges become jammed together until the pressure becomes so intense that the plates suddenly lurch forward. In 1906, the plates along the San Andreas fault, which is 960 kilometres (600 miles) long, moved violently. The ground shook with tremendous force and buildings in San Francisco swayed and collapsed. The shift along the fault near San Francisco was about 4.6 metres (15 feet). Broken gas pipes and overturned stoves caused raging fires.

Since 1906, many minor earthquakes have occurred around the San Andreas fault, and scientists now fear that San Francisco may again be threatened. They have, however, made some interesting discoveries. They have found that waste water pumped down disused wells lubricates faults, causing minor tremors. But, if water is pumped out of a well, the dry rocks become firmly locked together. Scientists have, therefore, suggested that they should

EARTHQUAKES
The most destructive earthquake occurred in September 1923, in Japan. After the earthquake, fires, caused mainly by overturned stoves, raged through Tokyo and Yokohama, and about 143,000 people lost their lives. The highest death toll caused by a single earthquake was 830,000. This disaster occurred in Shensi province, China, in 1556.

Right: **This building in the Philippines collapsed during an earthquake in August 1976.**

Below left: **Earthquake damage in Osoppo, Italy: a fireman inspects a house which is in danger of collapsing.**

Below: **World map showing continental plate boundaries, volcanoes and earthquake zones.**

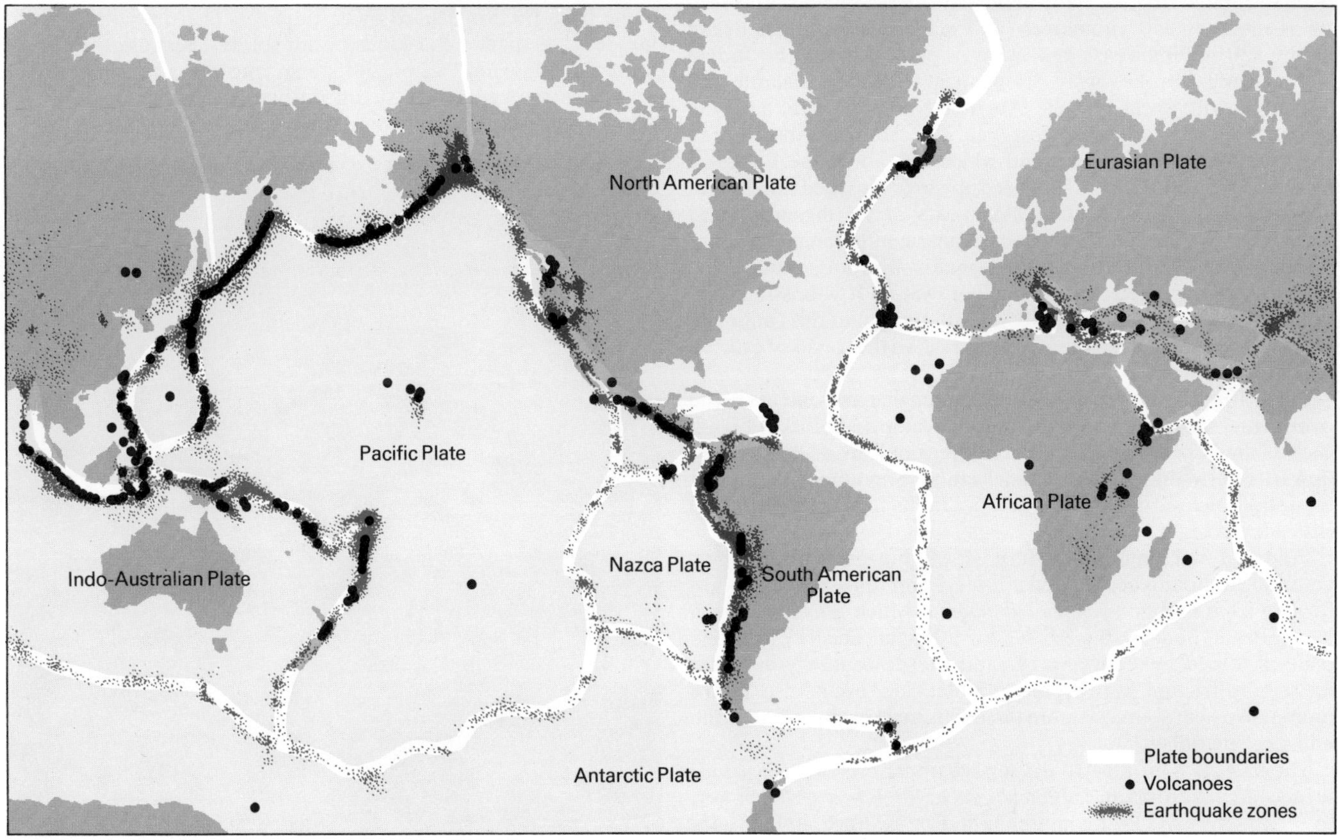

North American Plate

Eurasian Plate

Pacific Plate

Nazca Plate

South American Plate

African Plate

Indo-Australian Plate

Antarctic Plate

Plate boundaries
Volcanoes
Earthquake zones

drill a series of wells along the San Andreas fault. If they pumped all the ground water from two wells, they would lock the fault at those points. Then, if they pumped water into a third well, between the two dry wells, they might set off a minor earthquake, which would relieve the pressure at that point. By leap-frogging along the fault in this way, they might induce many small quakes and avert a major tragedy. This method would be costly, though not as costly as the destruction of San Francisco.

Attempts at earthquake forecasting have been developing recently, especially in China, a country which has had more than its share of earthquake tragedies. Several methods have been proposed. One involves recording any slight tilting of the ground. Such tilting was noticed in the city of Haicheng in early 1975. About 100,000 people were evacuated two hours before a severe earthquake. But, despite this and other claimed successes, a severe earthquake at Tangshan in July, 1976 was not predicted.

Another possible method of forecasting is to record variations in the amount of a radioactive gas, radon, in well water. Radon, which results from the decay of radium, is normally trapped in rocks. But, if the rocks crack and open, the gas escapes and is dissolved in ground water. The onset of earthquakes may also be indicated by changes in the elasticity and electrical resistance of rocks. And, the Chinese claim, odd animal behaviour often precedes earthquakes.

Mountains and Volcanoes

The study of plate tectonics has not only helped us to understand better the causes and nature of earthquakes, it has also provided us with a much deeper understanding of how mountains are formed. There are three main kinds of mountains: fold mountains, block mountains and volcanoes.

Fold mountains are raised up when level layers of rock are squeezed together by tremendous lateral force. The rock layers are buckled upwards into large, complex folds. For example, it has been estimated that the folded Himalayas have been compressed by as much as 650 kilometres (400 miles). This process began about 120 million years ago, when a plate bearing the Indian sub-continent broke away from ancient Gondwanaland and began to drift towards Asia. About 50 million years ago, the Indian plate was pushing against Asia. The sediments that floored the intervening Tethys Sea and which contained the fossils of ancient sea creatures were squeezed upwards into the Himalayas.

Similarly, in the last 30 million years or so, the northward movement of the African plate rammed intervening, smaller plates in the Mediterranean area against Europe, causing the folded Alpine range to rise steadily upwards. It is possible that both the Himalayas and the Alps are still rising, but this cannot be measured because, even as mountains rise, so the forces of erosion plane them down.

The drifting plates create tension and tugging movements in the continental rocks they contain. Faults develop and blocks of land, such as the Vosges and Black Forest areas of Europe, are pushed upwards between roughly parallel faults. Sometimes, blocks of land slip downwards between parallel faults to form steep-sided rift valleys.

Fold and block mountains form slowly but, periodically, new volcanic mountains are created in a very short time. Volcanoes are formed from molten rock, called *magma,* which is erupted from large pockets beneath the Earth's crust. Magma occurs where one plate is forced beneath another and the descending rocks are melted by friction and pressure. Volcanoes occur also above radioactive heat sources within the Earth, such as those under the mid-oceanic ridges.

The magma is erupted to the surface under pressure in various forms, ranging from tiny fragments, such as volcanic dust and ash, to broad rivers of blazing molten lava. For example, in February

1943, a small hole opened up in a cornfield in Mexico, near the village of Parícutin. Hot ash erupted from the hole and piled up in a small cone. One day later, lava began to flow from the vent, and layer upon layer covered the surrounding land, continuously raising the new mountain's level. Two years later, the volcano, which had been christened Parícutin, stood about 500 metres (1,640 feet) above the level of the former cornfield, the greatest height it has yet attained. Parícutin was the first mountain whose birth and growth were witnessed and studied by scientists.

There are about 535 active volcanoes in the world, including 80 under the oceans. They are classified according to the way in which they erupt. Broadly, there are explosive, quiet and intermediate volcanoes. Explosive volcanoes contain magma that is highly charged with explosive gases. These gases expand and explode in the hot magma, shattering it into fragments of dust, ash, cinders and larger lumps called volcanic bombs. Explosive volcanoes are usually cone-shaped with steep sides. The greatest volcanic explosion in recent times destroyed the volcanic island of Krakatoa in 1883. The explosion set off a terrible tsunami, which killed 36,000 people in the nearby islands of Java and Sumatra.

Quiet volcanoes contain magma with little gas. They erupt by discharging streams of bubbling lava, which flows swiftly from the vent, often covering great distances before solidifying. Quiet volcanoes are flattened and shield-like in shape.

Many volcanoes are intermediate and combine both explosive and quiet eruptions. For example, the famous eruption of Vesuvius in AD 79 was explosive. Clouds of hot ash were flung into the air, burying the prosperous town of Pompeii. The nearby town of Herculaneum was engulfed by a mud-flow, consisting of hot ash mixed with rainwater. No lava streams appeared in AD 79, but they have accompanied most later eruptions. Scientific observatories have been set up around many active volcanoes in order to give warning of possible eruptions.

Hot springs and emissions of gas and steam are associated with dormant volcanoes. But the heat required for hot springs may also come from friction caused by earthquakes or from radioactivity. Geysers are spectacular kinds of hot springs, because they erupt tall columns of hot water and steam into the air. Some geyser eruptions are caused by steam pushing the water upwards. In other cases, gases in the heated water force it up.

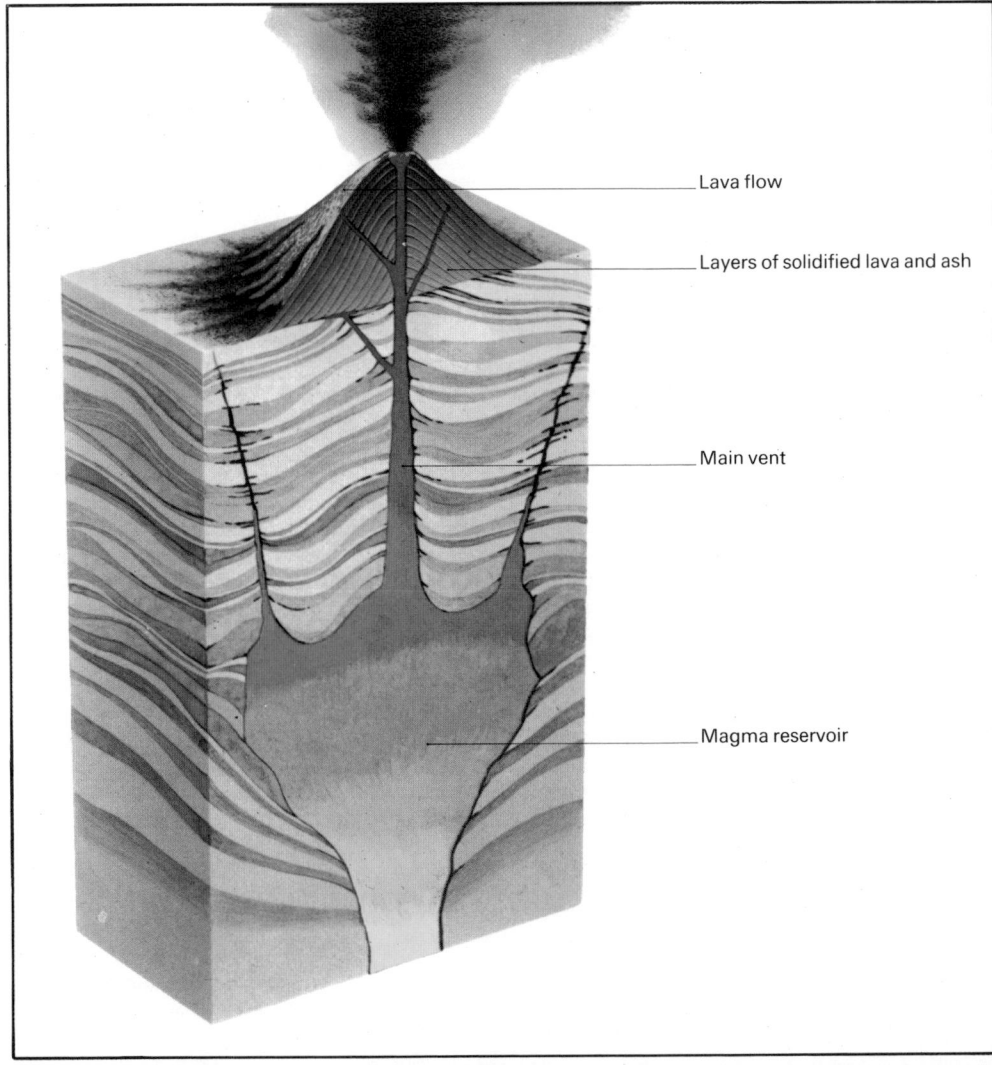

Lava flow

Layers of solidified lava and ash

Main vent

Magma reservoir

Left: **Molten magma is forced upwards through the vent of a volcano, where it forms fine ash, rocky fragments or lava streams.**

Left: **The photograph of exposed rocks in Dyfed (formerly Pembrokeshire) in southwestern Wales shows how rock strata can be folded by Earth movements. In this case, the top part of the fold has been thrust over the bottom part along a fault in the rock.**

Right: **The Alps are a range of recently folded mountains. They were squeezed upwards as the Earth's plate bearing Africa moved towards the European plate. Smaller, intervening plates were rammed against the European mainland and the sedimentary rocks between were folded upwards. But, even as mountains rise, natural forces, such as weathering and valley glaciers, wear them down.**

Shaping of the Land

We tend to think of landscapes as unchanging and, in one person's lifetime, the land does not seem to alter, unless it is subject to human interference. But, in fact, the land is constantly changing, albeit slowly. Geologists estimate that, on average, about 3.4 centimetres (1.3 inches) of land is removed overall from North America every 1,000 years. Over millions of years, therefore, such erosion can remove the highest mountain ranges.

The rate of natural erosion varies considerably. It proceeds at its fastest rate in mountainous regions and is least effective on plains. Eroded material is broken down into smaller and smaller fragments during its transportation until it finally comes to rest, usually on the floors of seas or lakes. There, it accumulates in layers which become compacted together, possibly forming the building material for new mountain ranges which will arise millions of years later, only to be worn down in their turn.

A group of processes instrumental in the break up and decay of rocks are called weathering. Mechanical weathering occurs in hot deserts when rocks are rapidly heated and cooled. The widely alternating temperatures crack the outer shells of rocks, which peel away like layers of an onion — a process called *exfoliation*. And, in moist, temperate regions, water accumulates in rock crevices. But, when it freezes, the ice occupies nine per cent more space than the water. So it exerts such pressure on the rocks that it eventually prises them apart. Also included in mechanical weathering are the actions of plants and animals. For example, the downward-probing roots of trees can break boulders apart, and burrowing animals play a major role in the disintegration of rocks.

Chemical weathering involves the decay or dissolving of rocks. For example, *hydrolysis* is a process of rock decay caused by chemical reactions between water and minerals, such as the conversion of potash feldspar in granite into kaolin, a clay. The removal of rocks in solution results, for example, from a process called *carbonation*. Carbonation occurs in limestone rocks, which consist mostly of calcium carbonate and are insoluble in pure water. But rainwater, which contains carbon dioxide from the air,

is a weak solution of carbonic acid. It reacts chemically with limestone to form soluble calcium bicarbonate.

Limestone plateaux are usually bleak areas. The exposed rocks are riven by vertical joints and horizontal bedding planes. Rainwater dissolves and widens the joints, giving the surface a paving-stone character. The surface is also pitted with deep fissures called swallow-holes, sink-holes or pot-holes. Some of these holes are dry, while others are entrances for streams, which plunge down into the subterranean world of limestone caves. These complex networks of passages and caverns were formed by water percolating through the joints and bedding planes. Many caves contain redeposited calcium carbonate in such features as hanging stalactites, pillar-like stalagmites and thin, wavy deposits resembling rock curtains.

One of the hazards of pot-holing (exploring limestone caves) is that heavy rainstorms can rapidly raise the level of subterranean rivers, trapping and drowning those within. These underground rivers usually return to the surface as a spring at the base of the limestone outcrop. Springs occur when any *aquifer* (water-bearing rock layer), such as limestone or sandstone, appears at the surface. Springs form the sources of streams and rivers.

Rivers are major agents of erosion, transportation and deposition. In their upper reaches, or youthful stage, they tumble down steep gradients, sweeping stones and, occasionally, boulders along their beds. As the loose fragments bump along the river beds they wear away more rock, causing downward erosion. This gives youthful rivers their characteristic steep-sided V-shaped

Below left: **Rivers are agents of erosion and deposition. Oxbow lakes are formed when meandering rivers straighten their courses.** **underground streams. Gorges occur when caves collapse. Stalactites and stalagmites are deposited in caves.**

Below: **This section through limestone shows a typical network of swallow holes, caves and** Right: **Stalactites and stalagmites in a limestone cave at Divica, in Yugoslavia.**

1. Youthful stage
2. Mature stage
3. Ox-bow
4. Old-age stage
5. Delta

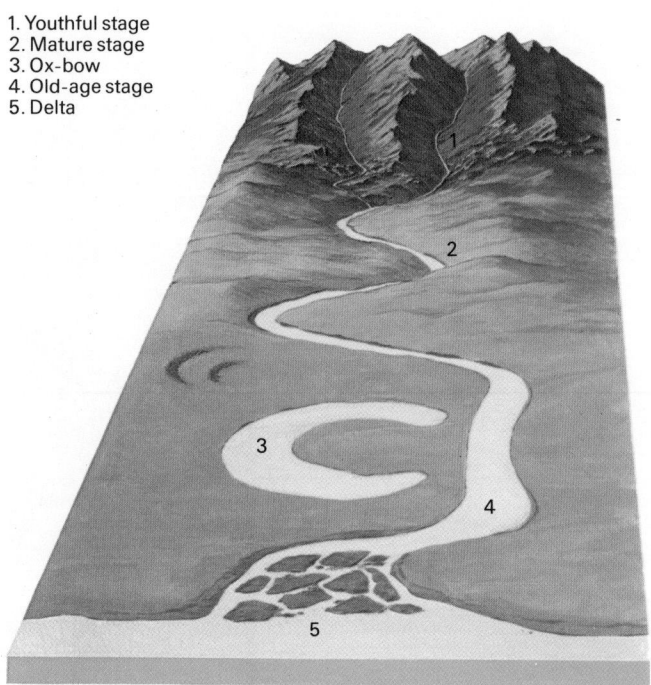

1. Swallow hole	4. Joints	7. Stalactites
2. Chimney	5. Pool	8. Roof fall
3. Chockstone	6. Stalagmites	9. Syphon

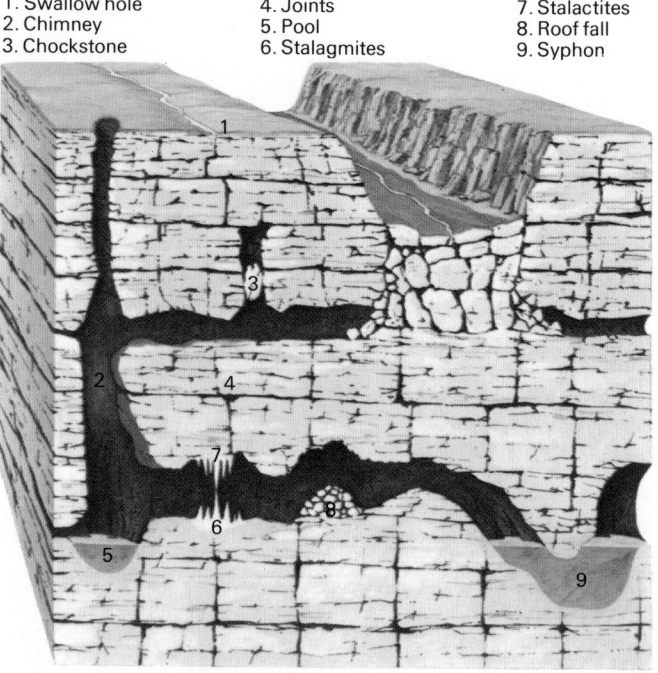

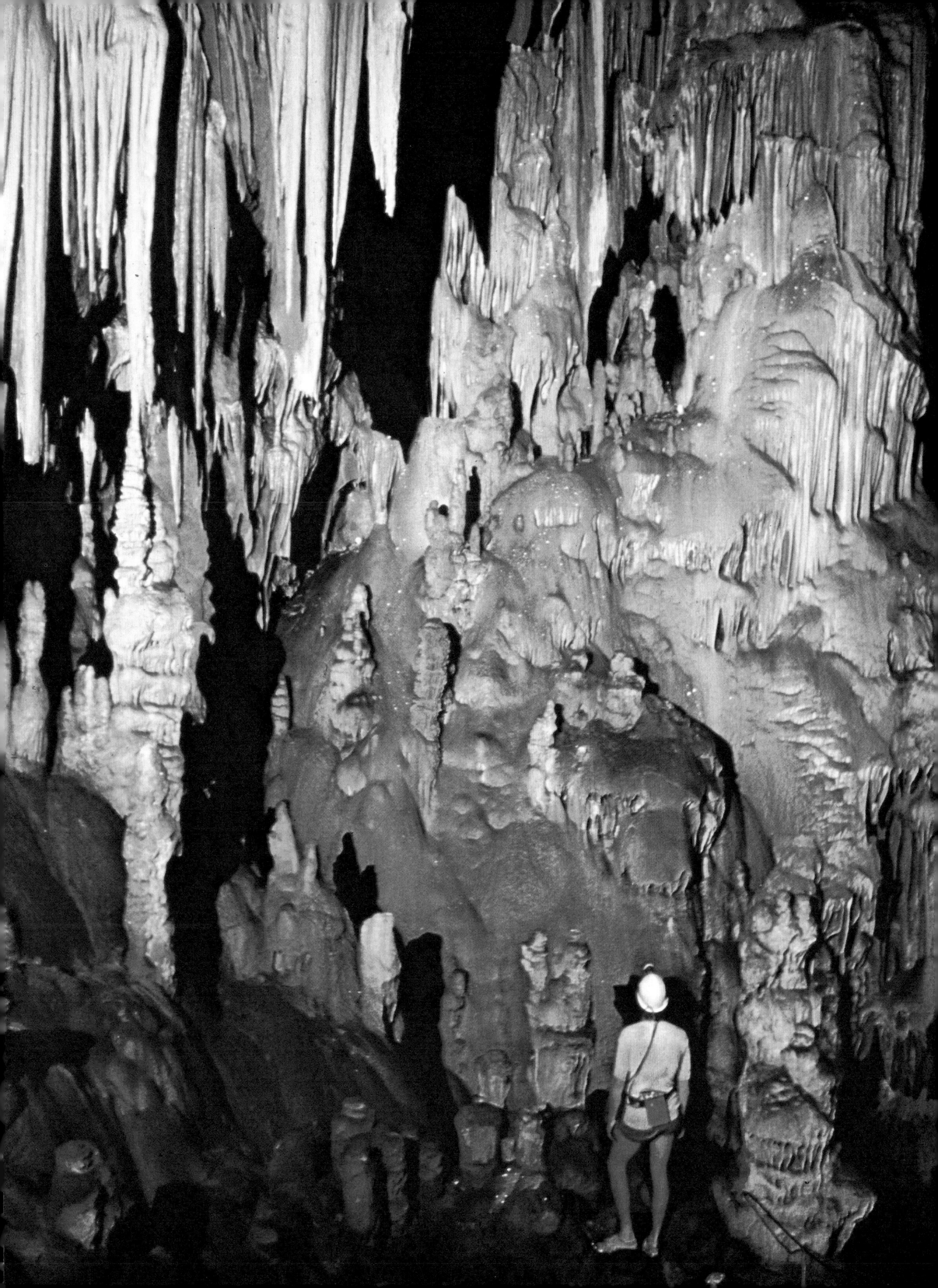

cross-section. But, when youthful rivers cross hard rocks, waterfalls and rapids occur.

In its mature stage, the river valley is broader, but erosion continues, especially as the outer bends are undercut. In old age, there is little river erosion, but sluggish, old-age rivers are major agents of transportation. The eroded material is mostly fine-grained silt or dissolved substances. When an old-age river floods, fertile silt is spread over the land. But most eroded material reaches the sea, at which point it may accumulate in deltas, if tides are weak, or be spread over the sea floor.

Occasionally, spectacular valleys result from the *rejuvenation* of old-age rivers. Rejuvenation occurred, for example, when a flat, coastal plain was uplifted to form the Colorado Plateau in the south-western United States. With a gradually increasing gradient, the Colorado River has etched the magnificent Grand Canyon into the plateau.

Ice sheets and glaciers in polar or mountain regions, the wind in arid and semi-arid areas, and the restless sea around coasts are other agents of erosion, transportation and deposition.

During the Pleistocene Ice Age, which began about 600,000 years ago and ended between 10,000 and 20,000 years ago, thick ice covered much of North America and northern Eurasia. The advance and retreat of the ice had a great effect on scenery.

In the world today, there are only two large ice sheets, one covering nearly all of Antarctica, and the other 85 per cent of Greenland. There are also smaller ice sheets in parts of northern Canada, Iceland, Norway and Spitzbergen. And valley glaciers occur above the permanent snowline in mountain regions in most parts of the world, even on the Equator. The total volume of land ice is the equivalent of 2.15 per cent of the world's total water supply. If all this ice were to melt, the sea level would rise by 60 to 90 metres (200 to 300 feet).

Large bodies of ice mould scenery as they slide downhill. Valley glaciers display the fastest movement, usually about one metre (three feet) per day, whereas the ice sheet of Antactica takes about a year to advance the same distance. Sometimes, the volume of a valley glacier is suddenly increased, for example, by an earthquake that dislodges snow and sends it crashing onto the glacier's source. This happened in 1936–7 on the Black Rapids glacier, Alaska, whose speed, as a result, reached a maximum of 60 metres (200 feet) in one day.

Glaciers transport weathered rock on their surfaces, within the ice or frozen in the base. Jagged rock fragments in the base of glaciers scrape over the land, eroding deep U-shaped valleys. Fiords are formerly glaciated valleys now filled by the sea. Near the source of valley glaciers, the ice freezes around projecting rocks and plucks them away. This action creates armchair-shaped basins called *cirques*. When two cirques are back to back, ice

erosion creates a knife-edge ridge, called an *arête,* between them. When three or more cirques occur back to back, a pyramidal peak, or *horn,* is formed.

Ice-eroded rock fragments, ranging in size from fine clay to boulders, are finally dumped as *moraine.* Around the snouts of glaciers, ridges of terminal moraine often accumulate. And streams issuing from glaciers transport the moraine for some distance. Large boulders composed of different rocks from the bedrock are sometimes dumped by the ice. Such boulders are called *erratics.*

Many land features in hot deserts were carved by water, either in the past, when the climate was different, or during occasional storms that occur every few years. But a major agent of desert erosion is wind-blown sand. Because sand particles are heavy, even the strongest winds cannot lift them much higher than an adult's shoulders. Erosion, therefore, occurs at low levels. But sandstorms can strip the paint off cars and frost their windscreens. Similarly, wind-blown sand can cut deeply into layers of softer rock or lines of weakness. And it can lead to the carving of mushroom rocks, which are supported by a narrow, precarious-looking pedestal. Wind-blown sand also scours rock surfaces, creating extensive depressions.

Sand covers only parts of the world's hot deserts. There are large areas of sandless *hammada* (bare rock) and *reg* (gravelly plains). Areas of sand are called *erg.* The sand accumulates in drifting dunes, some of which are crescent-shaped (*barchans*) and others are long ridges (*seif dunes*). Sand dunes are also features of some coasts.

Around coasts, the sea is constantly wearing away land, breaking up rocks into smaller particles and transporting debris out to sea or along the coast to create new land areas. Storm waves have great power. Hurled at cliffs, the waves trap and compress air in crevices. When the pressure is released, the air expands with explosive force, shattering the cliff rocks. Storm waves also lift up and bombard the shore with loose material, ranging from sand to boulders. The sea's weaponry undermines coastal rocks, cutting bays, caves, and natural arches through headlands. When natural arches collapse, rocky islets, or *stacks,* are left isolated in the sea.

Wave erosion is most effective on softer rocks. The Holderness coast of southeastern Yorkshire, England, is composed of glacial deposits. Since Roman times, the sea has removed a belt of around 4 to 5 kilometres (2.5 to 3 miles) of land from this coast.

Waves usually approach land at an oblique angle but, after the waves break, the water flows back at right angles to the shore. This means that the water and its load of sand and gravel move in a zig-zag path along the shore. When the direction of the coast changes, the loose material is dropped to form low ridges called *spits.* Some spits, called *tombolos,* link the mainland to an island.

Far left: **The Aletsch glacier in Switzerland is Europe's largest.**

Left: **Chesil Beach in Dorset, England has been formed by shingle deposited by the tides.**

Below: **This mushroom rock in Bahrain has been undercut by the abrasive action of wind-blown sand.**

Right: **This stretch of coastline in Northern Ireland is being steadily eroded by the sea. Wave action carves out bays. And caves, worn in headlands, meet to form natural arches. When the arches collapse, isolated stacks remain.**

Physical Statistics

The Earth

Dimensions: The Earth is flattened at the poles and bulges slightly at the Equator. Hence, the equatorial diameter and circumference are larger than the polar diameter and circumference.
Equatorial diameter: 12,756 kilometres (7,926 miles).
Equatorial circumference: 40,075 kilometres (24,901 miles).
Polar diameter: 12,713 kilometres (7,899 miles).
Polar circumference: 40,007 kilometres (24,859 miles).
Area: 510,061,938 square kilometres (196,936,480 square miles).
Land and water: Land covers 148,324,824 square kilometres (57,268,670 square miles) — about 29 per cent of the Earth's surface. Water covers 361,737,114 square kilometres (139,667,810 square miles) — about 71 per cent of the Earth's surface.
Mass: 5,976 million million metric tonnes (5,882 million million tons).

The Oceans

Size: Pacific Ocean 165,236,000 square kilometres (63,798,000 square miles); Atlantic Ocean 81,660,000 square kilometres (31,529,000 square miles); Indian Ocean 73,442,000 square kilometres (28,356,000 square miles); Arctic Ocean 14,351,000 square kilometres (5,541,000 square miles).
Volume of water: 1,300 million cubic kilometres (312 million cubic miles).
Deepest Point: 11.033 kilometres (6.856 miles), Challenger Deep in the Marianas Trench in the Pacific Ocean.
Highest wave in the open sea: 34 metres (112 feet) recorded in the Pacific by the U.S.S. *Ramapo* in 1933.
Largest islands: Greenland, 2,175,485 square kilometres (839,961 square miles); New Guinea 820,617 square kilometres (316,843 square miles); Borneo 743,211 square kilometres (286,956 square miles).
Highest oceanic mountain: Mauna Kea, Hawaii, rises 10,203 metres (33,474 feet) from the sea floor. (Mauna Kea is only 4,205 metres (13,796 feet) above sea level.)

Rivers

The World's Ten Largest Rivers

River	Continent	Length
Nile	Africa	6,670 km (4,145 miles)
Amazon	South America	6,448 km (4,007 miles)
Mississippi-Missouri	North America	6,270 km (3,896 miles)
Yangtze	Asia	4,990 km (3,101 miles)
Zaire	Africa	4,670 km (2,902 miles)
Amur	Asia	4,410 km (2,740 miles)
Hwang Ho	Asia	4,350 km (2,703 miles)
Lena	Asia	4,260 km (2,647 miles)
Mekong	Asia	4,180 km (2,597 miles)
Niger	Africa	4,180 km (2,597 miles)

The Amazon and its tributaries occupy the world's largest river basin, covering 7,045,000 square kilometres (2,720,000 square miles). One tributary, the Madeira, is the world's longest tributary. The Amazon also has the greatest flow of water, with an average discharge into the Atlantic of 120,000 cubic metres per second (4.2 million cubic feet per second).

Lakes

The largest lake, or inland sea, is the salty Caspian Sea, which is enclosed between Iran and the U.S.S.R. It covers 424,198 square kilometres (163,784 square miles). The largest freshwater lake, Lake Superior, lies between Canada and the United States. It has an area of 82,400 square kilometres (31,815 square miles). The highest large lake is Lake Titicaca, which is in the Andes range between Peru and Bolivia. Its surface is 3,812 metres (12,507 feet) above sea level. The lowest lake is the Dead Sea, whose shoreline is 395 metres (1,296 feet) below the mean sea level of the nearby Mediterranean Sea.

Mountains

World's highest mountains: Mount Everest 8,848 metres (29,029 feet) in the Himalayan range; K2 (Mount Godwin-Austen) 8,611 metres (28,251 feet) in the Karakoram range; Kanchenjunga 8,598 metres (28,209 feet) in the Himalayan range.
Highest in Africa: Mount Kilimanjaro 5,895 metres (19,341 feet).
Highest in North America: Mount McKinley 6,194 metres (20,320 feet)
Highest in South America: Mount Aconcagua 6,960 metres (22,835 feet).
Highest in Europe: Mount Elbrus 5,633 metres (18,481 feet).
Highest in Australia: Mount Kosciusko 2,230 metres (7,316 feet).
Highest in New Zealand: Mount Cook 3,764 metres (12,349 feet).

Above: **The River Amazon has a greater flow of water than any other river. It discolours the Atlantic Ocean for about 300 kilometres (190 miles) off the coast of Brazil.**

Right: **Mount Everest, in the Himalayas, is the world's highest peak. The first men to reach the summit were Sir Edmund Hillary and Tensing Norgay on May 29, 1953.**

The Living World

Vegetation

The natural vegetation of a place results from the interaction of soils, landforms and climate. Soils are complex substances, composed mostly of weathered particles, together with some humus (the decayed remains of plants and animals), water, air and countless micro-organisms. The nature of some soils depends on such factors as the bedrock or poor drainage. But the character of most soils is determined by climate. Such *zonal* soils are divided broadly into *pedalfers* in wet regions and *pedocals* in regions with much less rainfall.

For example, in rainy, tropical regions, soils are heavily leached — that is, soluble minerals are dissolved out of the top layer and removed completely or redeposited lower down. Characteristic wet tropical soils are the heavily-leached, reddish latosols, the top layer of which is laterite. This contains mostly insoluble substances, including iron, which colours the soil, bauxite and manganese. Other pedalfers include the greyish podzols of cold, snowy climates. Podzols are also heavily leached.

In regions with comparatively little rainfall, there is much less leaching and the top layers are coloured by humus. For example, the black chernozems of steppelands and the dark brown soils of prairies are pedocals coloured by decayed grass.

Soil and natural vegetation regions, therefore, follow a broadly similar pattern to climatic regions. When geographers talk of natural vegetation, they mean the climax vegetation — that is, the most flourishing vegetation that could occur in an area with particular soils and climate, providing it has not been altered by man. For example, the broadleaf forests of the eastern United States and western and central Europe have been mostly cut down. But, if man ceased to interfere with the natural plant life of these regions, broadleaf forests would probably reassert themselves before long.

Polar ice sheets, ice caps and adjacent areas that are permanently covered by snow are almost devoid of plant life. But the polar tundra has a short warm summer, when the top few centimetres of the soil thaw. Flat areas become marshes, and mosses, lichens and various flowering plants thrive. Beneath the surface layer, however, is permafrost — permanently frozen ground. This factor, together with the cold, prevents the growth of trees, other than dwarf shrubs.

Cold, snowy climates are characterized by vast forests of conifers. Conifers are especially well adapted to cold climates. Their narrow, conical shapes prevent over-loading by snow, their

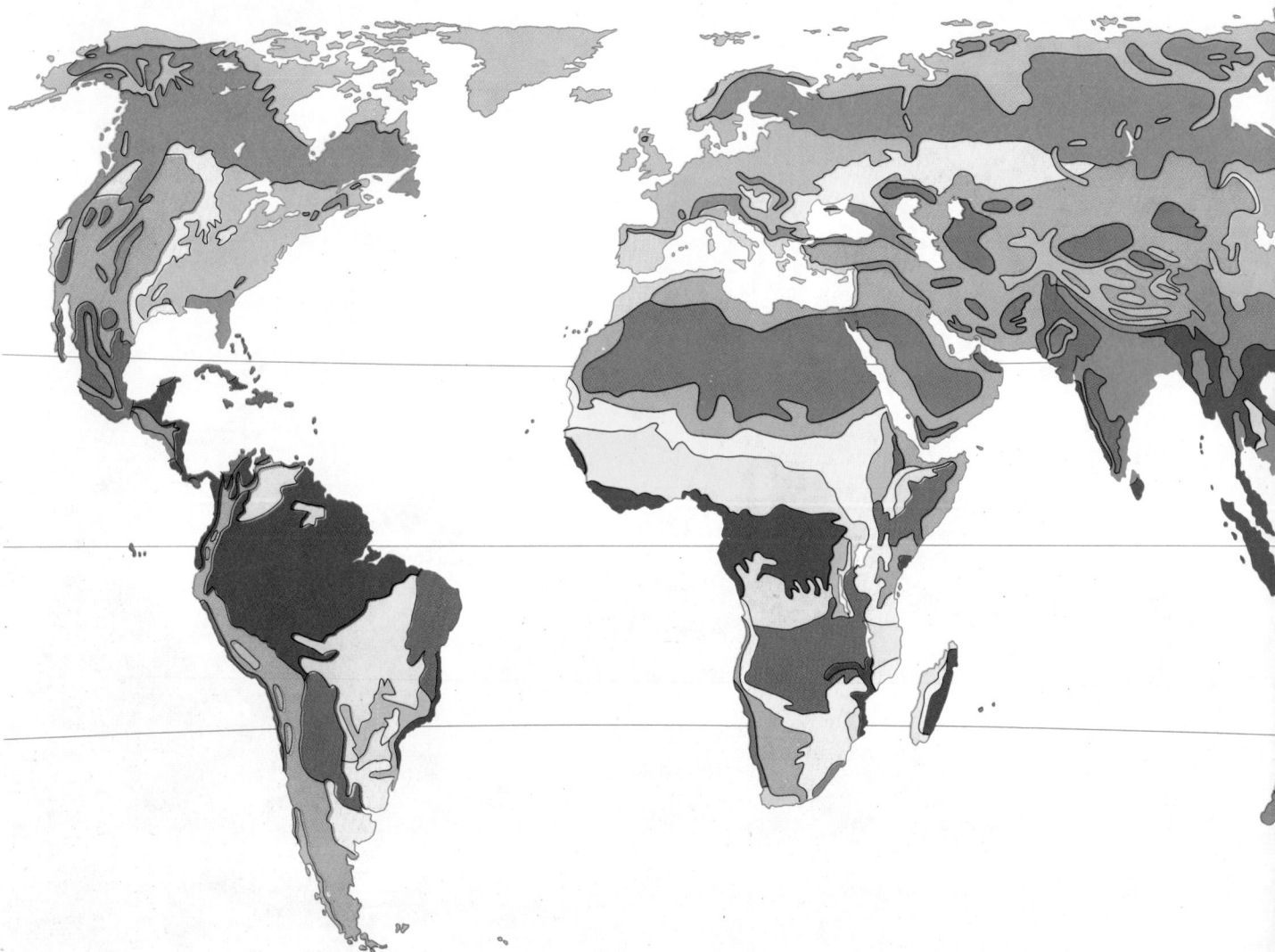

shallow roots absorb moisture, even when the subsoil freezes, and thick barks give protection against the cold. With the exception of larches, conifers are evergreens. Conifers also grow in Mediterranean regions, where their adaptations fit them to withstand the summer drought.

The boreal (northern) coniferous forests merge southwards into the broadleaf, or deciduous, forest belt. Deciduous trees are adapted to moist, temperate climates, with some rainfall throughout the year and temperatures above 6°C (43°F) for six months of the year. In autumn, deciduous trees shed their leaves, which form a thick carpet of humus on the forest floor. When the forests are cut down, their rich brown soils are very productive.

Grasslands are of two main kinds: the mid-latitude grasslands in continental interiors, including steppelands and prairies; and the tropical grasslands. In the mid-latitude grasslands, trees are rare, partly because of the aridity and partly because winters are extremely cold. Savanna is a term for tropical grassland, broken by scattered trees or patches of forest and merging into thorn forest and dry scrub. Tropical grasslands lie broadly between the equatorial forests and the sub-tropical deserts.

The world's hot deserts contain various xerophytes (drought-resistant plants). Adaptations include long, shallow roots, which absorb moisture from a large area; thick stems, which store water; and waxy coverings, which reduce loss of moisture by transpira-tion. Some plants spring to life after the rare, infrequent rainstorms, and they may seed within two weeks of sprouting. The seeds may lie dormant for several years until the next rainstorm starts a new growth cycle.

The tropical forests include rain forests, with rain all the year round, and monsoon forests, where the rainfall is markedly seasonal. With abundant rainfall and high temperatures, tropical forests are luxuriant, and hundreds of species may occur in a small area. Trees grow to 30 to 40 metres (100 to 130 feet), with some protruding to more than 50 metres (160 feet). The thick canopy of leaves in the tree tops blocks out light from the forest floor, so few plants grow on the ground. Most of the other forest plants are climbers, such as vines, or epiphytes (parasitical plants).

Mountain regions have varying vegetation according to the altitude. Ascending some high mountains around the Equator is like taking a short trip to the poles. One can start in tropical forest, then climb through changing belts of vegetation and finally encounter tundra and polar conditions around the peak.

Natural vegetation

Tundra & ice
Coniferous forest
Broadleaf forest
Mediterranean scrub
Grassland
Savanna
Sub tropical forest
Dry tropical scrub & thorn forest
Monsoon forest
Tropical rain forest
Scrub, steppe and semidesert
Desert

Right: **Parts of the world's hot deserts are covered by barren shifting sands. Permanent settlement is possible only at oases.**

Below right: **The Himalayan foothills support luxuriant forests. But the vegetation gradually changes with altitude.**

Below: **The prairies of Alberta, in Canada, are part of the world's vast mid-latitude grasslands.**

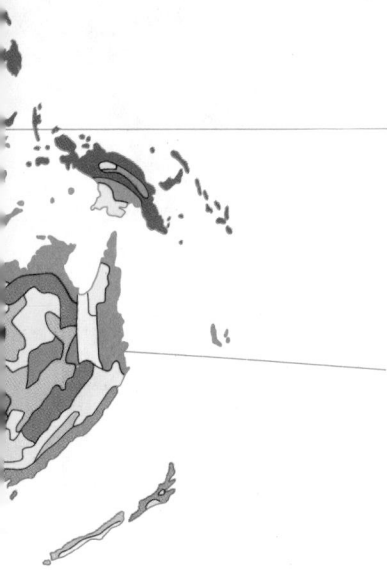

Evolution

Fossils, found in sedimentary rocks, are evidence of ancient life. Fast burial is a prerequisite for fossilization because, otherwise, plants and animals decay quickly. But, once buried, teeth, bones and other hard parts, such as shells and woody tissue, may be preserved. Many remains are petrified (turned to stone) by the replacement of each molecule of the organism by a molecule of a mineral. Some fossils are casts or moulds of organisms, while plant leaves and soft-bodied creatures, such as jellyfish, can be preserved as smears of carbon. Other fossils include animal droppings, footprints and holes bored by worms.

Ancient Greek scholars realized that most fossils were the remains of sea creatures and concluded that the rocks in which they occurred were once under the sea. But, when ancient Greece declined, this understanding was lost. For about 2,000 years, many fanciful ideas were advanced to explain fossils. Some people thought that they were the work of the Devil, who had put them in rocks to confuse us. Fossil belemnites, extinct creatures similar to cuttlefishes, are still sometimes called 'Devil's thunderbolts.'

In the 1700s, the Scottish geologist James Hutton deduced that sedimentary rocks were formed mostly on the floors of seas and

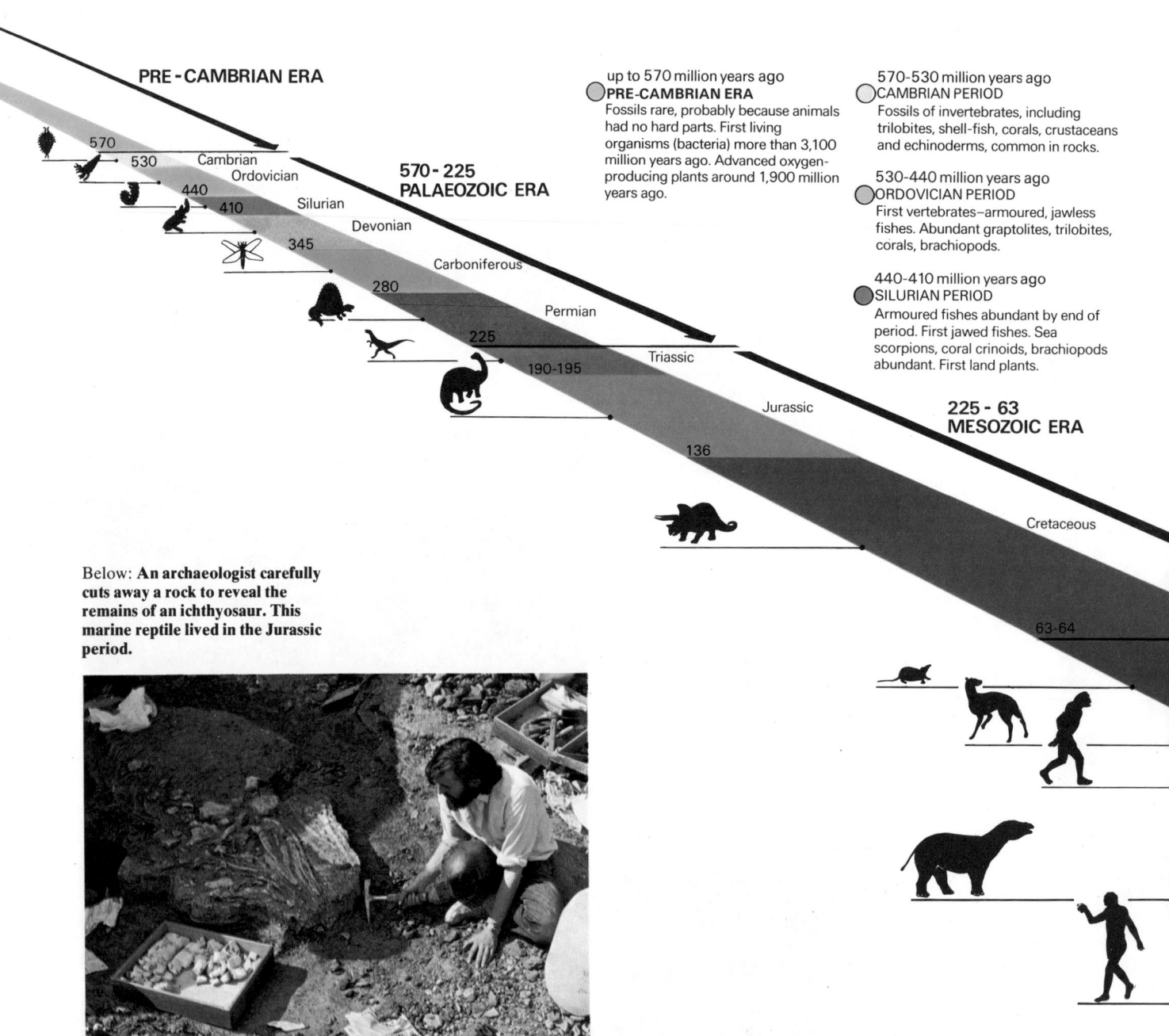

PRE-CAMBRIAN ERA

570

530

Cambrian

440

Ordovician

410

Silurian

345

Devonian

280

Carboniferous

225

Permian

190-195

Triassic

136

Jurassic

63-64

Cretaceous

570 - 225
PALAEOZOIC ERA

225 - 63
MESOZOIC ERA

up to 570 million years ago
PRE-CAMBRIAN ERA
Fossils rare, probably because animals had no hard parts. First living organisms (bacteria) more than 3,100 million years ago. Advanced oxygen-producing plants around 1,900 million years ago.

570-530 million years ago
CAMBRIAN PERIOD
Fossils of invertebrates, including trilobites, shell-fish, corals, crustaceans and echinoderms, common in rocks.

530-440 million years ago
ORDOVICIAN PERIOD
First vertebrates—armoured, jawless fishes. Abundant graptolites, trilobites, corals, brachiopods.

440-410 million years ago
SILURIAN PERIOD
Armoured fishes abundant by end of period. First jawed fishes. Sea scorpions, coral crinoids, brachiopods abundant. First land plants.

Below: **An archaeologist carefully cuts away a rock to reveal the remains of an ichthyosaur. This marine reptile lived in the Jurassic period.**

36

lakes. Their formation was slow, but they accumulated in great thicknesses before, eventually, they were raised up to form new land. The slow rate of sedimentation made Hutton and others appreciate that the Earth must be extremely old.

In the early 1800s, a British canal engineer William Smith collected fossils and began to classify rocks according to the fossils in them. He understood that, if two rock layers, however far apart, contained the same kind of fossils, then they were of the same age. Geologists were then able to work out the sequence, or relative ages, of sedimentary rocks, grouping them into eras, periods and epochs. The meaning of fossils was further clarified by the work of Charles Darwin, who advanced the theory of evolution by natural selection in his *Origin of the Species* (1859). In the early 1900s, the discovery that radioactive elements decay at specific rates made it possible to provide absolute dates for rocks and their associated fossils.

Although many gaps occur in the fossil record, a clear pattern of evolutionary history has emerged. When a plant or animal group evolves from its ancestral form, such as the first reptiles from the amphibians in the Carboniferous period, the group first passes through a *divergence phase,* in which the group diverges from its ancestors by producing new features. *Improvement* follows as the group's new features are adapted by natural selection. Then, by a process called *adaptive radiation,* the group spreads to all available environments. For example, the reptiles evolved large and small species that lived on land, in the sea and in the air. Finally, however, comes *extinction.*

From a study of Earth history, extinction seems to be the fate of all species, even the most successful. Most large reptiles became extinct at the end of the Mesozoic era. Many theories have been advanced to explain what happened, including climatic changes, overpopulation, the bombardment of the Earth by cosmic rays, and the destruction of their eggs by mammals. But the extinction of species, whatever the reason, always seems to involve some change in the environment to which the group is unable to adapt.

410-345 million years ago
DEVONIAN PERIOD
Age of Fishes. Amphibians evolved near end of period. Plants spread on land. First insects. Graptolites died out.

345-280 million years ago
CARBONIFEROUS PERIOD
Amphibians increased. Reptiles evolved. Insects common. Many corals, brachiopods and fishes in seas.

280-225 million years ago
PERMIAN PERIOD
Reptiles spread on land. Ammonites in seas. But trilobites and many other sea creatures died out.

225-190 million years ago
TRIASSIC PERIOD
First dinosaurs and large sea reptiles. Ammonites abundant. First mammals evolved.

190-136 million years ago
JURASSIC PERIOD
Large reptiles, including dinosaurs and flying reptiles (pterosaurs) abundant. First bird (archaeopteryx) appeared. Ammonites and belemnites abundant in seas. Some mammals on land.

136-63 million years ago
CRETACEOUS PERIOD
Reptiles, including dinosaurs, dominated the land, but most died out at end of period, as did ammonites and many other sea creatures. Small mammals lived throughout period.

63-2 million years ago
TERTIARY
Palaeocene 63-44 million years ago
Rapid development of mammals.
Eocene 44-38 million years ago
First horses and elephants.
Oligocene 38-26 million years ago
Early apes; ancestors of many modern mammals.
Miocene 26-7 million years ago
Greatest variety of mammals.
Pliocene 7-2 million years ago
Man-apes in Africa. Many larger mammals died out.

2-0 million years ago
QUATERNARY PERIOD
Pleistocene 2-0.01 million years ago
Rise of man. Woolly mammoths and rhinos in cold northern hemisphere.
Recent 0.01-0 million years ago
Modern man.

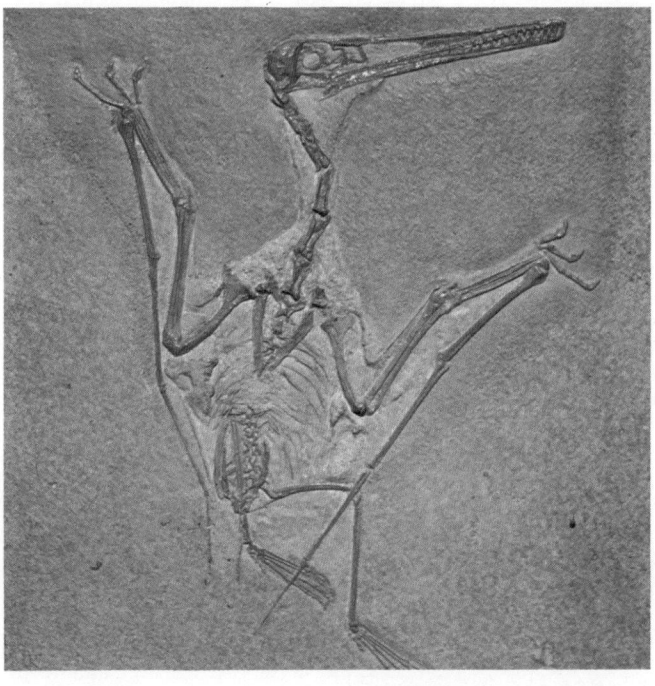

Above: **The petrified remains of a pterosaur (flying reptile), which lived in the Jurassic period.**

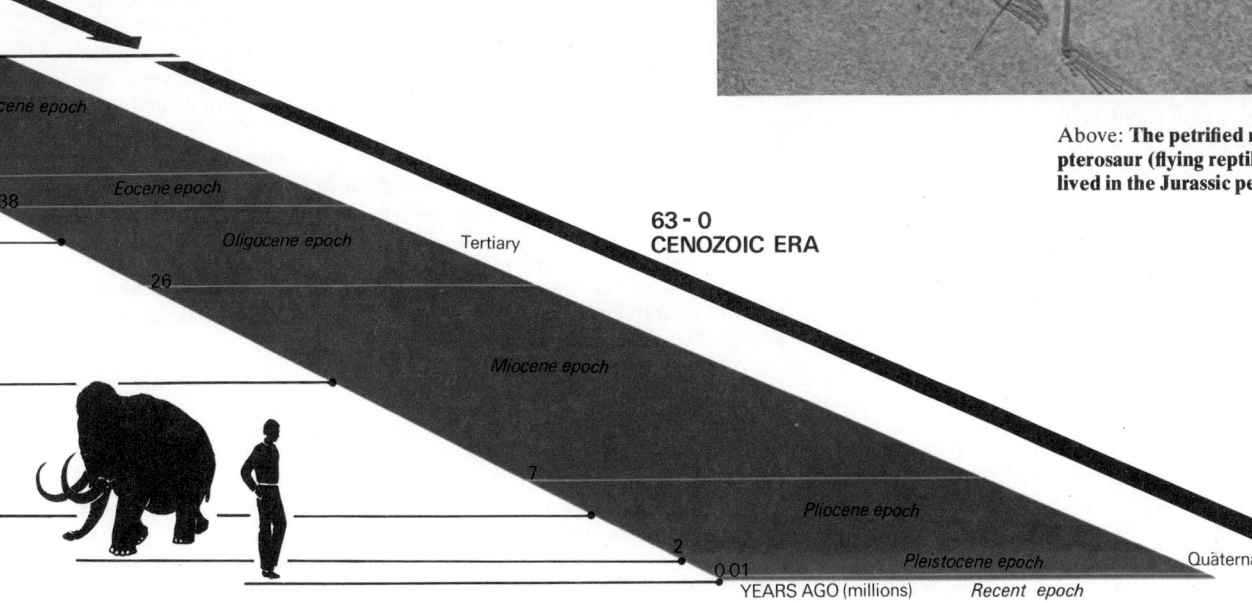

eocene epoch

Eocene epoch
38

Oligocene epoch   Tertiary   63 - 0
26   CENOZOIC ERA

Miocene epoch

7

Pliocene epoch

2
0.01   Pleistocene epoch   Quaternary
YEARS AGO (millions)   *Recent epoch*

Animal Life

Virtually every part of our planet is inhabited by animals. Only the icy wastes at the poles, the chill summits of the highest mountains and the thin air of the upper atmosphere are devoid of life — apart from human visitors. Elsewhere, animals exist in profusion and in great diversity.

There are two main reasons why the Earth possesses a wide range of animals. Physical barriers — mountain chains, oceans and seas, and deserts — separate the land into six zoogeographic regions, each containing its own particular kinds of animals. The barriers prevent the animals from intermixing, and distinct populations have evolved in each one. For example, the Australian region has monotreme animals, such as the duck-billed platypus, and many marsupials, including kangaroos. And the neo-tropical region contains most of the hummingbirds. Because islands in the ocean are isolated from the rest of the world, they often contain special kinds of animals not found elsewhere. In the oceans, different kinds of animals live at different depths.

The second factor that determines the kind of animals that live in a particular region is climate. Each of the climatic zones of the world has its own kind of animal life, because the animals have evolved to suit the conditions there. Similar environments tend to produce similar animals, even though they may be in different parts of the world and of different animal families. Desert animals, for example, are often very alike wherever they are found, having been shaped by the same harsh conditions. In considering the kinds of animals that inhabit the Earth, it is, therefore, better to look at them in the various climatic zones rather than the zoogeographic regions.

Animals of the Polar Regions

The polar regions are basically different from each other: the Arctic consists of a frozen sea surrounded by cold coasts, while the Antarctic is an ice-covered continent surrounded by cold seas. However, both regions are white with snow and ice. In the Arctic, many of the animals are also white so that they cannot easily be seen against their surroundings. In this way, they escape the attentions of other animals that hunt them or, if they are themselves hunters, they cannot easily be spotted by their prey. These white animals include the polar bear, arctic fox, arctic hare and snowy owl. In the Antarctic, few animals live on the ice cap because it is so cold, but many are found on the surrounding islands. Many of them, such as seals and penguins, and Arctic animals such as the polar bear and arctic fox, are large and have rounded bodies with small ears and short tails. All these features help to prevent heat escaping from their bodies, thus keeping them warm. The animals also have thick layers of fat and heavy coats of fur to retain their own heat. Some polar birds even have their feet covered with feathers.

Because the polar seas are so cold, they contain much dissolved oxygen, which supports a huge population of marine life. Feeding on the great shoals of fish and other sea creatures are seals and whales, and penguins and seabirds of several kinds, many of them adept at diving.

Animals of Coniferous Forests

Across Canada and the far north of Europe and Asia stretches a belt of coniferous forest. The needle-leaved evergreen trees stand tightly packed, their leaves cutting out the light all the year round so that little undergrowth surrounds their trunks. Many animals make their homes in this cold, forbidding place. Some feed on the trees. Beavers eat the bark and fell the trees to build their lodges;

grouse consume the leaves and buds, and crossbills can cut open the cones with their special crossing beaks to get at the seeds inside. Squirrels clamber about the trees, opening cones and storing the seeds for winter. Chipmunks also store seeds but hibernate for the winter, waking now and then when they get hungry. Insect-eating birds, such as woodpeckers and tits, work their way over the branches, pecking in crevices in the bark. Small mammals, such as voles and lemmings, wander over the ground eating plants and burrow beneath the snow in winter to find food. Other animals survive by preying on these creatures. Bears, lynxes and weasels hunt among the trees; hawks and falcons swoop from the air by day, and owls do so by night.

Animals of the Deciduous Forests

South of the coniferous forest, and also in the southernmost parts of the southern hemisphere, lies a broad belt of deciduous forest. Here the climate is mild and the trees shed their leaves in winter. Leaf mould builds up on the ground and light comes in, enabling a tangled undergrowth of shrubs and bushes to grow among the trees. Evergreen trees may be found too. Many different kinds of animals live in the forest. The leaves are easier to eat than the tough leaves of conifers, and caterpillars and aphids munch their way through plants, while deer browse among the trees. Birds, such as finches, and squirrels, mice and other small mammals take the seeds and buds. Other birds, including European warblers, and mammals, such as hedgehogs, seek insects in the forest. These insect eaters find food scarce in winter, so the birds migrate to warmer climes or rely on seeds, while the mammals may hibernate for the winter. Predators also hunt among the trees, as they do in coniferous forests. They include foxes, snakes, polecats, badgers, wild cats and birds of prey. However, their prey is not always defenceless — the skunk is famous for the way it squirts an evil-smelling liquid at predators, and many potential victims hide safely among the leaves and undergrowth.

Animals of Mountains

Because it gets colder as you go up a mountain, several different zones of life exist. There may be deciduous forest at the bottom, coniferous forest halfway up, and then a polar scene with scanty plants and snow at the top. Kinds of animals similar to those found in these climatic regions may, therefore, be found on the sides of a mountain, wherever in the world it is situated. However, polar animals will not be found, for they depend ultimately on the ocean for their food.

Some mountain animals have special features that help them to live on rocky slopes, where cold winds howl and few plants grow. Mountain goats have special feet that enable them to leap among the crags, and vicunas and yaks have woolly coats to keep out the cold. These animals can survive on poor plant food, but may have to descend to lower slopes for the winter. Mountain birds are mainly strong fliers, such as eagles, or small birds that nest and find food in rock crevices.

Animals of Grasslands

Between the forests and deserts of the world lie the grasslands, vast grassy plains dotted with a few stunted trees that manage to grow in the dry climate. These regions are known by several names, including steppes, prairies, savannas, pampas and veld. It is warm all the year round.

Great numbers of animals make their homes in grasslands. Many eat the grasses and other plants. They include: large

mammals, such as antelopes, zebras, gazelles, bison, elephants, giraffes, rhinoceroses, wild horses and kangaroos; small mammals, such as hares and rodents; flightless birds, such as emus and ostriches; and flocks of weaver birds that raid crops in the grasslands, as do locusts and other insects. Living on these animals in turn are insect eaters, like anteaters and armadillos, and the much-feared flesh eaters, including rattlesnakes and cobras, vultures, hyenas, wild dogs, lions and cheetahs.

Being in the open, the victims of these hunting animals cannot hide from danger. Many roam the grasslands in herds, finding safety in numbers, and the elephant is just too big to be worth attacking. Smaller animals, which may have to run for their lives, possess powerful legs and feet that enable them to sprint for long periods. The smallest animals retreat into their burrows when danger threatens.

Animals of Deserts

Desert regions occur on each side of the Equator. Little, if any, rain falls throughout the year, and it is usually very hot by day, though often cold by night. The stony or sandy ground supports little plant growth. Some animals do manage to survive in these harsh conditions, but they are faced with two main problems — how to keep cool and how to save water.

Many desert animals are small — a feature that helps them to lose heat — and live in burrows. Some, such as scorpions, avoid the daytime heat by staying in their burrows, seeking food only at night. Others, such as lizards, may prefer to hunt by day, but retire into their burrows or into shade during the hottest hours. The desert fox is one of several desert animals with large ears, which help to radiate excess body heat. And some animals hop or scurry over the hot sand to escape its heat. These adaptations also help the animals to hear and escape their predators. Many desert animals, including camels, are able to withstand high body temperatures and lack of water without harm. Their bodies may even be able to produce water from a diet of seeds or plants, so that they never need to drink. Gerbils survive in this way. And because they do not sweat, they retain as much water as possible inside their bodies. Some water is inevitably lost with body wastes, but desert animals reduce this amount to the minimum possible.

Animals of Tropical Forests

Along the Equator lies a belt of tropical forest. It is always hot and has frequent rain. Trees crowd together and fight for the light, producing a thick tangle of leaves and branches.

Many animals live among the leaves and branches of the forest. They are either able to fly or are good climbers. Toucans, parrots and other birds take fruit, hummingbirds seek nectar in flowers, and butterflies and moths flutter here and there. Many of these animals are brightly coloured, though the colours do not show up so vividly among the leaves. Sloths clamber among the branches, and monkeys swing to and fro, feeding from the trees. Chameleons seek insects in the leaves, changing colour to match their surroundings, and bats hunt insects in the air. Some animals, including several lizards and squirrels, have developed ways of gliding from one tree to another. On the ground, compact animals, such as pigs and rodents, push through the undergrowth, often eating ants and other insects that abound. Pheasants scratch about the forest floor, and lizards and snakes burrow in the litter of dead leaves. Feeding on the plant-eating and insect-eating animals are the hunters, such as tigers, leopards and jaguars, civets and snakes. They seek their victims in the trees and on the ground, often hunting by night.

Below: **A king penguin colony on the island of South Georgia.**

Far top left: **The Rocky Mountain goat lives among the high peaks of the Rocky Mountains in North America, easily scaling the rocky crags.**

Above left: **The red squirrel brings colour and life to the gloom and quiet of the coniferous forest.**

Below left: **The scorpion lives in the desert. It uses its claws to dig a burrow to escape the heat, and stings with its tail.**

Far bottom left: **A tube-nosed bat hangs upside-down from a branch. Bats can fly in the dark, using sound to navigate.**

Right: **A jay feeds its young. Jays are birds of deciduous forests. They collect acorns and bury them to form a winter food reserve.**

Below: **A herd of elephants heads for a water hole. Many elephants live on the grasslands of Africa, mostly in reserves, where they are protected from hunters and ivory poachers.**

Animals of Fresh Water

Rivers, ponds and lakes are home to many different kinds of animals. Fish sweep up food particles from the water, eating water plants, insects and other small water creatures, or even hunting other fish. Birds are a common sight, finding food in the water in several ways. Grebes, for example, dive for their food, while many ducks dabble at the surface. Kingfishers plunge into the water from the air, but herons stand or wade patiently in the shallows, waiting to make a catch. Insects abound, dragonflies hovering in the air, and pond skaters rowing themselves across the water surface. Amphibians breed in water, and many frogs, toads and newts remain in or around water all their lives. Reptiles and mammals are less common, for they feed and breed mostly away from water. However, crocodiles and turtles live in warm inland waters, and some snakes can swim. Otters and water voles can dive for food, and hippos rest in water, but come ashore to feed.

Fish can survive beneath the ice through a freezing winter, though such conditions make life hard for water birds.

Animals of the Seashore

Animals that live permanently on seashores where tides come and go every day face great problems of survival. One moment they are living in cool water and the next they may find themselves in the open air, being scorched by the sun. Only special kinds of animals can live in these conditions. On rocky shores, barnacles, mussels and other shellfish close their shells tightly as the tide goes down. Sea anemones pull in their stinging tentacles and close up, while small mobile animals, such as shrimps and crabs, take refuge in rock pools. On sandy and muddy shores, shellfish and worms burrow into the damp mud or sand to prevent their bodies drying up. Some have tubes that lead to the surface to obtain food and oxygen. These small shore dwellers feed on seaweeds, on minute creatures in the water, sand or mud, or on food particles that they sift from the water or sand. The seashore is also the home of larger animals. Birds wade in the shallows, peck in the sand or mud, or fly out to sea to find food. Seals and turtles come ashore in large numbers to breed.

Above: **Crocodiles live mostly in inland waters, where they often lie with their nostrils just above the surface. They capture other animals in their powerful jaws and drag them beneath the surface, where they tear apart and devour their victims.**

Right: **The common hippopotamus is the largest freshwater mammal. Common hippos live in African rivers, sleeping and resting by day and emerging at night to feed on plants near the water.**

Far right: **A sea anemone lies ready for a small fish or other creature to approach its stinging tentacles. It will then pull in its paralyzed victim and slowly digest it.**

Animals of the Oceans

The world's oceans contain a vast range of animals, from microscopic protozoans to the blue whale, the largest animal that has ever lived. In the oceans' surface layers drift huge numbers of minute plants and animals known as *plankton*. All other sea creatures depend on plankton for food, either by eating it directly or by consuming other plankton-eating animals.

Marine animals are classed into two groups — those that swim in the sea and those that live at the bottom. In waters near the shore, where light penetrates to the sea bed, an interesting array of creatures may be found. Flatfish swim over the sea floor, changing their body patterns to match the background, wherever they settle. This enables them to escape the attention of hunting animals. Lobsters and crabs, armed with a heavy shell and threatening pincers, scuttle about, and octopuses and cuttlefish wander or hide, squirting out a cloud of ink to confuse any enemy that appears. Starfish and sea urchins, and corals and sponges are among the many other strange animals of the seabed.

Fish of all kinds swim out in the open sea. Some live in great shoals, finding safety in numbers, and they are often coloured silvery-white, which makes them almost invisible in the water. Other creatures of the open sea include turtles, squids and sea mammals, such as whales and dolphins, which must continually rise to the surface to breathe air. The depths of the open sea are completely dark as light cannot penetrate very far. There, many animals are luminous and produce their own light to hunt or find a mate. The sea floor is often covered with mud, on which long-legged creatures walk and others lie.

Animal Movements

Not all creatures are content to remain in one place all their lives. Locusts, for example, wander in search of food, settling wherever they find enough to eat, and leaving when they have stripped everything bare. But many animals make regular journeys called migrations to find food and to raise their young.

The best-known migrations are those of birds. In spring, many fly to their breeding grounds, where there will be enough food to feed their young when they are born. This food supply disappears as the winter comes, and so the birds fly back to their winter quarters to find food until the spring arrives again. In the tropics, where there may be no real summer or winter, birds may migrate in the wet and dry seasons instead. Some mammals migrate too. Caribou walk long distances between breeding grounds and winter quarters, and whales may swim from one ocean to another.

Several fishes make extraordinary migrations that take years. Eels are born in mid-ocean and migrate to the rivers of surrounding lands, where they grow up before returning to the ocean to breed. Salmon migrate in the opposite direction, being born inland and then swimming out to sea. After several years, the adult salmon swim back to their birthplace to breed.

Below left: **The shark is one of the most feared animals of the sea, though not all sharks attack man.**

Below right: **A ray, one of the flatfishes, is related to the sharks. Like sharks, rays have cartilage,**

not true bones. Most rays live on the sea bed, their colour matching their surroundings for camouflage.

Bottom: **The lobster lives on the sea bed close to the shore, feeding on plants and animals.**

Threats to Life

Animals are shaped by evolution to fit their environment — unlike man, who can change his environment to suit himself. If an animal cannot change to meet man's demands on nature, then it may find itself in danger. In clearing forests to create fields for farming, or in making space for houses, man destroys the habitats of particular animals and takes away their sources of food. His domestic animals may kill them, or man himself may hunt them for their meat or for valuable products such as ivory and furs.

Animals that live on islands uninhabited by man are highly vulnerable, as they have evolved to suit a special environment. For example, birds may have lost the power to fly because there are no predatory animals with which to contend. The arrival of man changes things so abruptly that these overspecialized animals may not survive for long. The flightless dodo of Mauritius, for example, was extinct less than two centuries after the arrival of Portuguese sailors there in the early 1500s. However, not only rare, defenceless creatures are threatened. In less than a century, man succeeded in wiping out the passenger pigeon, millions of which once lived in North America. The demise of the passenger pigeon is a warning that one should never be complacent about the conservation of wildlife.

Measures are now being organized on a world-wide scale to help save animals in danger of extinction. International conferences limit the number of whales that may be captured, and a vast campaign is under way to raise money to save the tiger. Many governments ban hunting and create national parks and nature reserves to shelter rare animals. But these measures are not always very effective, or may be too late. Whalers are beginning to find that their limits have been too high and that some species of whales have nearly vanished. A hunting ban is difficult to enforce in some countries, and hunters may even enter parks and reserves. Accidents may happen: the use of DDT as a pesticide has done wonders to control insect pests but also nearly succeeded in wiping out several birds of prey. Conservationists are, therefore, also conducting projects to save threatened animals directly by removing them from their endangered habitats to zoos or breeding centres. There, efforts are made to get the animals to breed in captivity. When numbers have increased, the animals are returned to the wild. This has often been successful; the nene, or Hawaiian goose — down to about 30 birds in 1950 — is now up to about 1,000, and many birds have been repatriated.

Wherever man spreads, the waste he creates causes pollution, which threatens life on this planet, including his own existence. Instead of being treated in sewage farms, human wastes are sometimes dumped into rivers and seas. This may be hazardous to health, for example, shellfish caught in a bay near a town may be contaminated with sewage. In addition, particularly in rivers, decomposition of the sewage by bacteria uses up oxygen needed by fish and other animals. Detergents from kitchen sinks make matters worse, and the water may lose virtually all its oxygen, resulting in the loss of its animal life. Industrial wastes are also dumped into rivers and seas, sometimes with harmful effects. At Minamata in Japan, people died in the 1950s from eating fish contaminated with mercury compounds discharged into the sea from a local plastics factory. However, increasing awareness of these dangers has led to anti-pollution measures that are cleaning up many rivers. Less rosy is the outlook for oil pollution, as supertankers carry crude oil about the world in ever-larger quantities, and undersea oil drilling becomes more common. Huge leaks of oil into the sea may now occur with any accident involving a tanker or oil rig, threatening all marine life in the area.

The atmosphere is liable to pollution in several ways too.

Burning fuel causes the release of gases into the air. Sulphur dioxide is among the most dangerous, for it dissolves in rain-water to produce a weak acid that can worsen breathing troubles and eat away the surfaces of buildings and statues. Furthermore, the pollutants may be blown long distances by winds and so affect places far away. In January 1974, all the winds in Europe converged on Norway for 12 days, depositing so much acid that fish were killed in lakes and rivers. Motor-cars emit lead compounds and oxides of nitrogen from their exhausts. Nitrogen oxides may contribute to breathing difficulties. In many places, air pollution has been reduced by banning the burning of coal and by treating fumes before they leave factory chimneys and the exhausts of motor-cars.

In the upper atmosphere, a layer of ozone gas prevents ultraviolet radiation from the Sun reaching the ground in harmful quantities. Scientists are worried that the ozone layer may be affected by pollution. Chemicals called fluorocarbons, released by aerosol sprays, and nitrogen oxides from jet aircraft (especially supersonic airliners, which fly very high) may be slowly destroying the ozone layer. Any resulting increase in ultraviolet rays reaching the ground could produce more skin cancer. So it may become necessary to ban aerosol sprays and there is a slight possibility that supersonic flight could be banned.

A third form of pollution, which may also affect future generations, is radioactivity. All waste from nuclear power stations produces harmful radiation, and some remains dangerous for centuries. At present, it is stored away so that no-one is harmed. But there is cause for alarm. A nuclear accident could release substantial amounts of radioactive material into the air. Nuclear installations have leaked to a small degree, and there are rumours that a nuclear accident killed many people in the U.S.S.R. several years ago. If governments build new 'fast' reactors to produce more energy, then there is a greater likelihood of a nuclear disaster because, unlike today's 'slow' reactors, fast reactors could possibly explode. Furthermore, there will be much greater amounts of long-lived radioactive waste to store, and the reactors will use plutonium, which is extremely poisonous as well as highly radioactive. For these reasons, many people are pressing governments to develop alternative energy supplies, such as wave power and solar energy, which are not polluting.

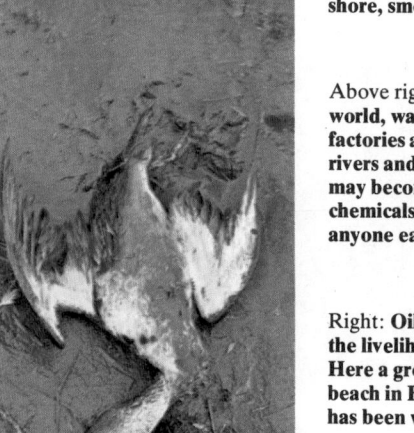

Left: **A seabird lies dead on the shore, smothered in oil.**

Above right: **In many parts of the world, waste products from factories are simply discharged into rivers and seas. As a result, fish may become contaminated with chemicals harmful to the fish or to anyone eating them.**

Right: **Oil pollution may threaten the livelihood of seaside resorts. Here a group of people clean up a beach in Brittany, France, after oil has been washed ashore.**

Far right: **A haze of pollution hangs over a town in Germany.**

Human Geography

The Human Race

Scientists consider that man and the apes are primates with a common, extinct ancestor. From fossil discoveries, we now know that various forms of man-like creatures evolved over the last 12 million years. The chief factors distinguishing man-like creatures from apes are man's larger brain and his ability to walk upright. Around 35,000 years ago, one species of man, *Homo sapiens,* became dominant, and all other forms, such as Neanderthal man, became extinct. *Homo sapiens* had been in existence for at least 70,000 years before that time.

All modern men and women, therefore, belong to the species *Homo sapiens.* And so, scientifically, all people belong to one race — the human race. But people display differing physical features, including skin colour, eye and hair colour, skull shapes, height and build. Anthropologists have devised various methods of classifying mankind, but it is generally accepted that there are three broad sub-groups. They are, in order of population size, the 'white-skinned' Caucasoids, the 'yellow-skinned' Mongoloids and the 'black-skinned' Negroids.

The term Caucasoid was first coined in the 1700s by the scientist J. F. Blumenbach, who used it to describe the people of the Caucasus mountain region between the Black Sea and the Caspian Sea — a region that was probably the original homeland of many of Europe's peoples. The term Caucasoid is now used to include a broad group of people who form the indigenous populations of Europe, southwestern Asia, India and northern and eastern Africa.

Caucasoids vary considerably. For example, skin colour ranges from white to dark brown, and eye colouring from light blue to dark brown. Hair varies from straight to curly, although body and facial hair is more abundant among Caucasoids than among other sub-groups. Caucasoids generally have narrow, prominent noses and thin lips, but all kinds of skull shapes occur, from long-headed to round-headed. The chief Caucasoid groups are the Mediterraneans, Alpines, Nordics, Lapps, East Baltics, Irano-Afghans, southern Indians, and northern and eastern Africans. However, intermixing has blurred the distinguishing features of these types in many areas.

Mediterraneans include the narrow-faced Basques of France and Spain, who are more properly called 'early Mediterraneans', because they are the purest descendants of the prehistoric inhabitants of Europe. The Mediterraneans proper are long-headed and dark-haired, with olive to light brown skins. They are found both north and south of the Mediterranean Sea and include Spaniards, Italians and Arabs. Alpine people are of medium height and they are sturdily built. Their round heads distinguish them from Mediterraneans and Nordics. The Nordics of Scandinavia are typically long-headed, tall people with blue eyes and blond hair.

The short Lapps have round heads, like the East Baltics of northeastern and eastern Europe and many Russians. On the otherhand, the Irano-Afghans of Afghanistan, Baluchistan, northwestern India and Iran are physically similar to Nordics, except for their darker hair and skin colouring. The Dinarics of southeastern Europe and the Armenians are similar to the Irano-Afghans.

The southern Indians are mostly of the Mediterranean type, except for their darker skins. African Caucasoids include the Berbers of northern Africa and some of the peoples of northeastern Africa, including some Ethiopians, Somalis and Sudanese. However, through intermixing, they have acquired some Negroid features. Mixed groups broadly included in the Caucasoid sub-group, include Polynesians, the Vedda of southern India and Australoids, including the Australian Aborigines. The Australoids, also called 'archaic whites', are sometimes considered to be a separate sub-group.

From the early 1500s, Europeans have spread around the world, exploring and colonizing the Americas, Africa and Australia. As a result, Caucasoids are the most widely spread of the three sub-groups.

Mongoloids are distinguished by their yellowish skin, straight black hair, flat faces and noses, high cheek bones and, in many cases, slanted eyes — caused by a skin fold of the upper eyelid. These features are displayed by the short-legged, thick-set Classic Mongoloids, including Eskimoes, Japanese, Koreans and northern Chinese.

The other Mongoloids do not have slanted eyes. They include: the broad-faced, rather thick-lipped Turkics of central Asia; the narrow-faced Tibetans, or Himalayans; the short and graceful Indonesian-Malays, including the Burmese, southern Chinese, Filipinos and Thais; and the American Indians, whose ancestors entered the Americas sometime between 20,000 and 10,000 years ago.

American Indians differ in various ways from typical Mongoloids. Their skin is often reddish or yellowish-brown, and their noses are prominent and seldom flat. But they have black hair, high cheek bones and little body hair.

The Negroids of Africa, south of the Sahara, mostly have very dark skins, thick, outward-turning lips, broad noses and narrow heads, with a protruding upper jaw. This sub-group includes some of the world's tallest people — the Nilotes — and the shortest — the Negrillos, or pygmies. Descendants of African slaves live in large numbers in the Americas, although they have intermixed considerably with Caucasoids. Asian Negroids include the Papuans of New Guinea and the Negritos, or pygmies, of Malaysia and many Pacific islands.

Left: **This woman from northern Thailand belongs to the Indonesian-Malay sub-group of the Mongoloid peoples. The Indonesian-Malays do not have the slanting eyes of the Classic Mongoloids.**

Above right: **Peoples of the world.**

Right: **This European mother and her children belong to the Caucasoid group of mankind. Within the Caucasoid group, there are many variations in the appearance of individuals.**

Far right: **The Hausa of northern Nigeria are essentially Negroid, although they speak a Hamitic tongue and they have intermixed to some extent with peoples from the north. As a result, they tend to be taller and often have narrower noses than the typical Negroes of the West African coastlands.**

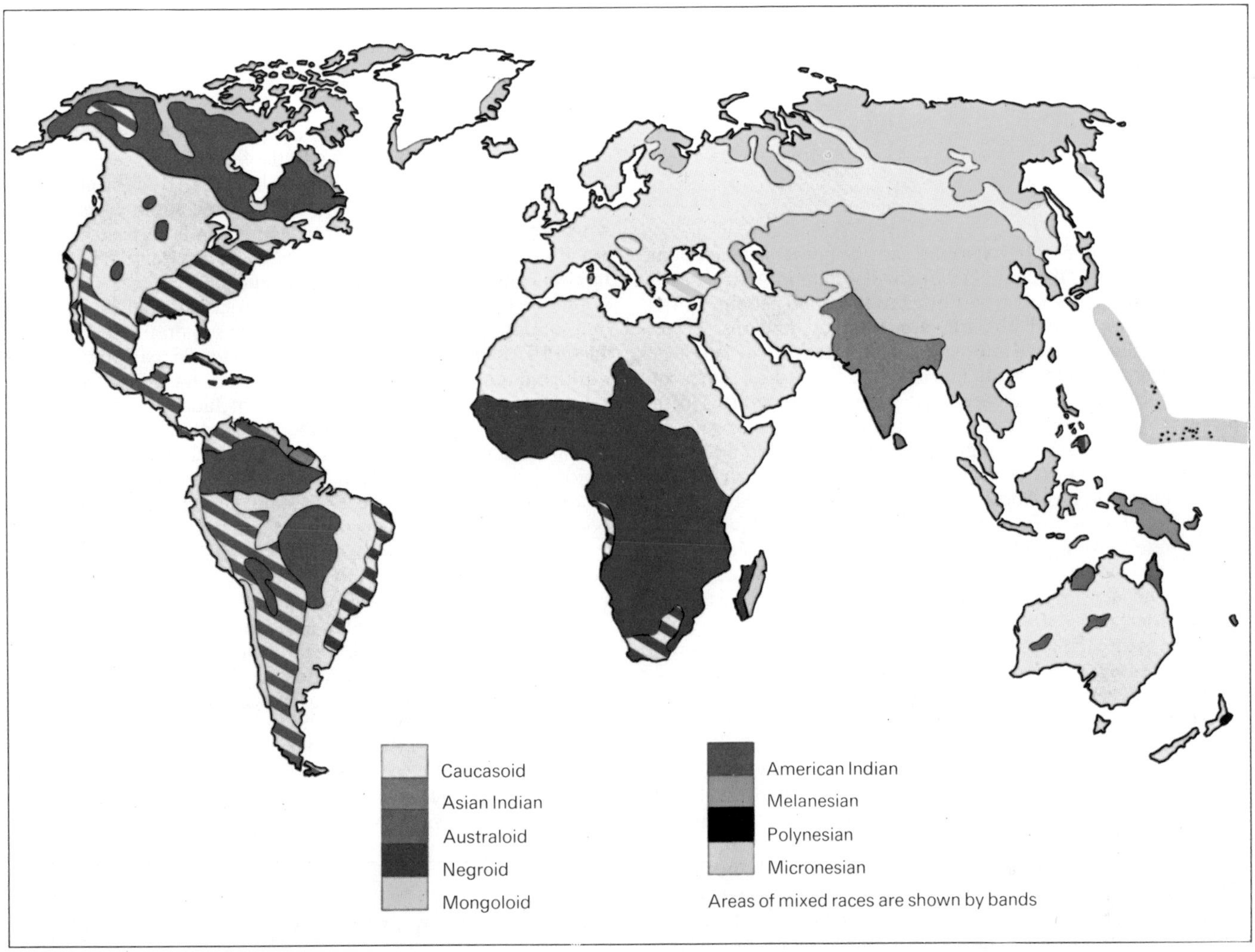

	Caucasoid		American Indian
	Asian Indian		Melanesian
	Australoid		Polynesian
	Negroid		Micronesian
	Mongoloid		Areas of mixed races are shown by bands

Languages and Religions

The world's peoples are divided into many language and religious groups. These divisions have led to conflict between nations and divisions within nations.

Languages

There are nearly 2,800 languages, not including dialects. Some languages, such as those spoken by small groups in Africa and the Amazon basin, are spoken only by a few thousand people. Others, such as Chinese and English, are used by millions. A few languages have achieved international importance. The languages most used in international business are English, French and German, which together are used for about four-fifths of all business transactions. These languages have spread around the world, partly because of migration and colonization and partly because the countries in which these languages are spoken are among the world's foremost trading nations. Other languages that have spread widely from their original area are Spanish and Portuguese (throughout South America), Russian, Italian and Arabic. Chinese is of major importance in terms of the number of people who speak it, but this language is of minor importance in international business.

Of the great languages mentioned above, all except Arabic and Chinese belong to the world's largest single language family — the Indo-European. Languages of this family are used by about one-half of the world's population.

The Indo-European language family has several branches. The Balto-Slavic group includes Bulgarian, Czech, Latvian, Lithuanian, Polish, Russian, Serbo-Croat, Slovak, Slovenian and Ukrainian. The Germanic branch includes English, Dutch, Flemish (a Dutch dialect), German and the Scandinavian languages. Celtic languages include Breton, Gaelic (Irish and Scots) and Welsh. The Romance branch is based on Latin — the language of ancient Rome — and includes French, Italian, Portuguese, Romanian and Spanish. The Greek language forms a branch on its own, as does Albanian. The Iranian group includes Persian and Pushtu, the language of the Afghans. And the Indo-Aryan branch includes Bengali and Hindi.

The second largest language family is the Sino-Tibetan, which accounts for more than one-fifth of the world's population. It includes Burmese, Chinese (Sinitic), Thai and Tibetan. The other main language families are spoken by far fewer people. They include: the Semitic-Hamitic-Kushitic group, which includes Arabic and Hebrew; the Uralic and Altaic families, including Mongol, Finnish, and Turkish; the Japanese and Korean family; the Dravidian family of southern India; the Malayo-Polynesian family; the Mon-Khmer family of southeastern Asia; the languages of black Africa; and the American Indian languages.

Religions

Most religions combine the worship of one or several gods with ethical rules of conduct, although some are chiefly ethical and philosophical. There are 10 major religions: Christianity, Islam, Hinduism, Confucianism, Buddhism, Shinto, Taoism, Judaism, Sikhism and Jainism.

Hinduism is an ancient Indian religion, which is also followed by people in Malaysia, Mauritius, the Pacific islands and parts of eastern and southern Africa. Hinduism dates back to about 2500 BC. Hindus believe in one supreme power, Brahman, but they worship many gods, who are seen as reflections of Brahman. Incorporated in Hinduism are beliefs in reincarnation, the caste system and the sacredness of cattle. Buddhism developed from Hinduism. Its founder was Siddartha Gautama (560–480 BC),

who became the Buddha — the Enlightened One. Buddhists do not worship any god, but seek a state of complete peace and love called Nirvana. Although it began in India, Buddhism is now practised mostly in China, Japan, Tibet and southeastern Asia. Another religion developed from Hinduism is Jainism, which is practised in western India. Founded by Mahavira in the 500s BC, Jainism consists basically of ethical beliefs.

One of the earliest religions to embrace a belief in one God (monotheism) was Judaism, a religion based on the teachings in the Old Testament and the Talmud. Jews live in many parts of the world, but they regard Palestine as their spiritual home. Christianity incorporates most of the teachings of Judaism, together with the teachings of Jesus Christ in the New Testament. Today there are about 3,000 Christian denominations, but there are three major divisions — the Roman Catholic Church, the Eastern Orthodox Church and the Protestant denominations. Islam, a word generally taken to mean peace and submission to God, is a religion taught by Muhammad (AD 570–632). Islam retains much from Judaism and Christianity. Its holy book is the Koran. Islam has spread through northern Africa and southwestern Asia.

Sikhism, which is followed in northwestern India, was founded by Guru Nanak (AD 1469–1538). It combines Hindu and Islamic beliefs. The great religions of China are Buddhism, Confucianism (a philosophical religion founded by Confucius around 500 BC), and Taoism (a mystical religion, founded, according to tradition, by Lao Tzu in the 500s BC). Shinto is Japan's native religion. Dating back 2,500 years, Shinto involves the worship of many gods. In the past, Shintoists regarded the Japanese emperor as a descendant of the Sun God.

Assyrian (carved)

Ancient Hebrew (painted)

Egyptian hieroglyphic (painted)

Some modern non-latin type faces

Greek
ΑΒΓΔΕΖΗΘΙΚΛΜΝΞΟΠΡΣΤΥΦΧΨΩΣ

Cyrillic
АБВГДЕЖЗИЙІКЛМНОПРСТУФХЦЏЧШ

Arabic
فى عام ١٨٩٧ وصل إلى إنجلترا أ نموذج

Bengali
১৮৯৭ খ্রীস্টাব্দে আধুনিক মডেলের একটি

Telugu
విన్న నాయింంటికే వచ్చిన యుత్థ యేమియు

Japanese
国土の位置と地形

Chinese
司 父
在 獨
提 子
印 出
芬 有
刷 之
奧 限
業 地
司 位
上 司，
有 能

Above: **The Sultan Ahmet Mosque in Istanbul, one of the finest of Islamic buildings.**

Right: **A Christian church in Bavaria, in the southern part of West Germany.**

Below left: **Writing styles of ancient and modern times.**

Below: **Distribution of religious groups around the world.**

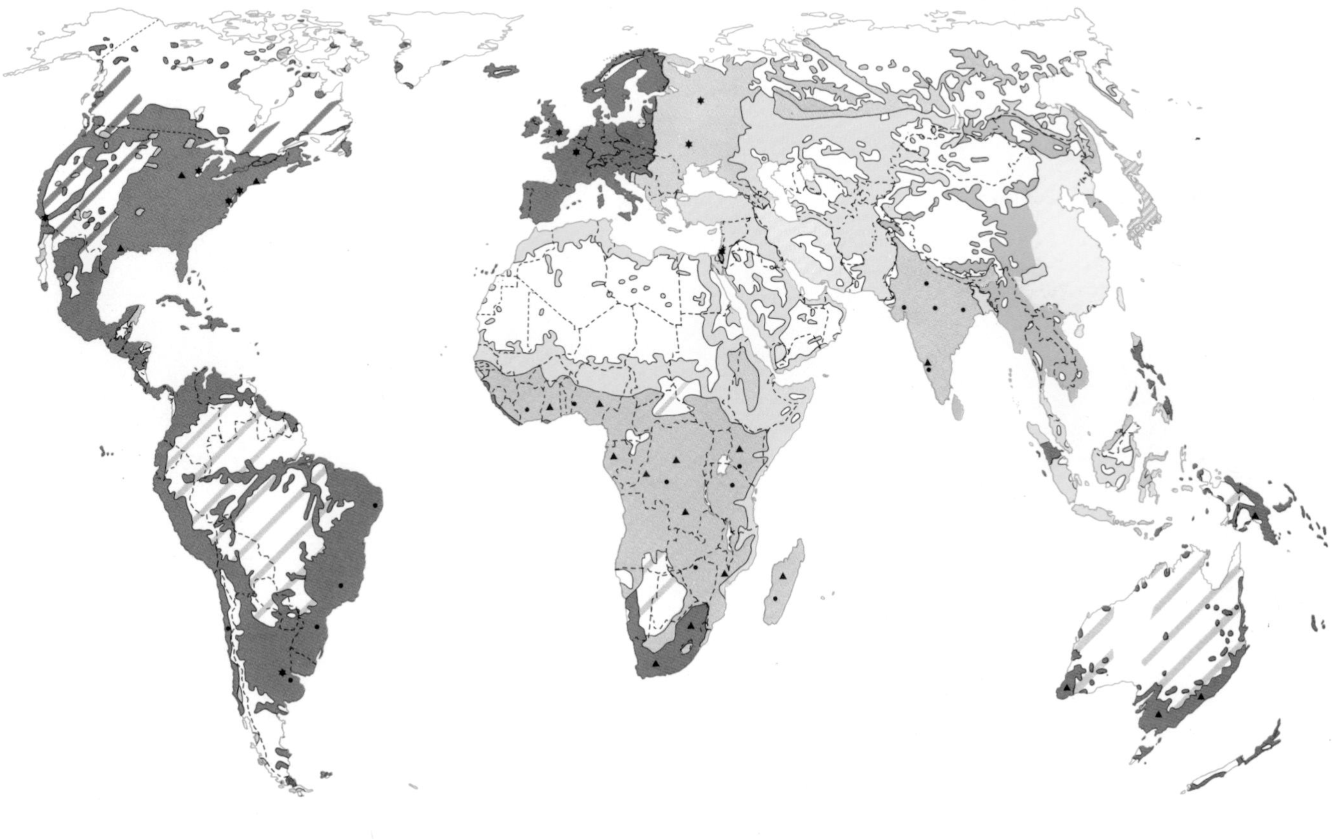

▲ Roman Catholicism	Shiah Islam	★ Judaism
Orthodox and other Eastern Churches	Buddhism	Shintoism
• Protestantism	Hinduism	Primitive religions
Sunni Islam	Confucianism	Uninhabited

Population

The world's population is very unevenly distributed. Vast tracts of land are too cold, too dry or too rugged and mountainous to support more than a few people. On the other hand, in parts of the farming belts, which total no more than 10 per cent of the Earth's land area, and in industrial zones, people are crowded together.

On average, in 1982, there were about 33 people to every square kilometre of land (86 per square mile), excluding the icy continent of Antarctica, which has no permanent population. But

Europe had a population density of 100 per square kilometre (258 per square mile) and Asia was second with 95 per square kilometre (246 per square mile). By contrast, Oceania, which includes Australia — two-thirds of which is virtually empty because it is desert — had only 2.9 people per square kilometre (7.5 per square mile), while the U.S.S.R. and North America had about 12 per square kilometre (31 per square mile).

The world's ten largest countries, by area, are the U.S.S.R..

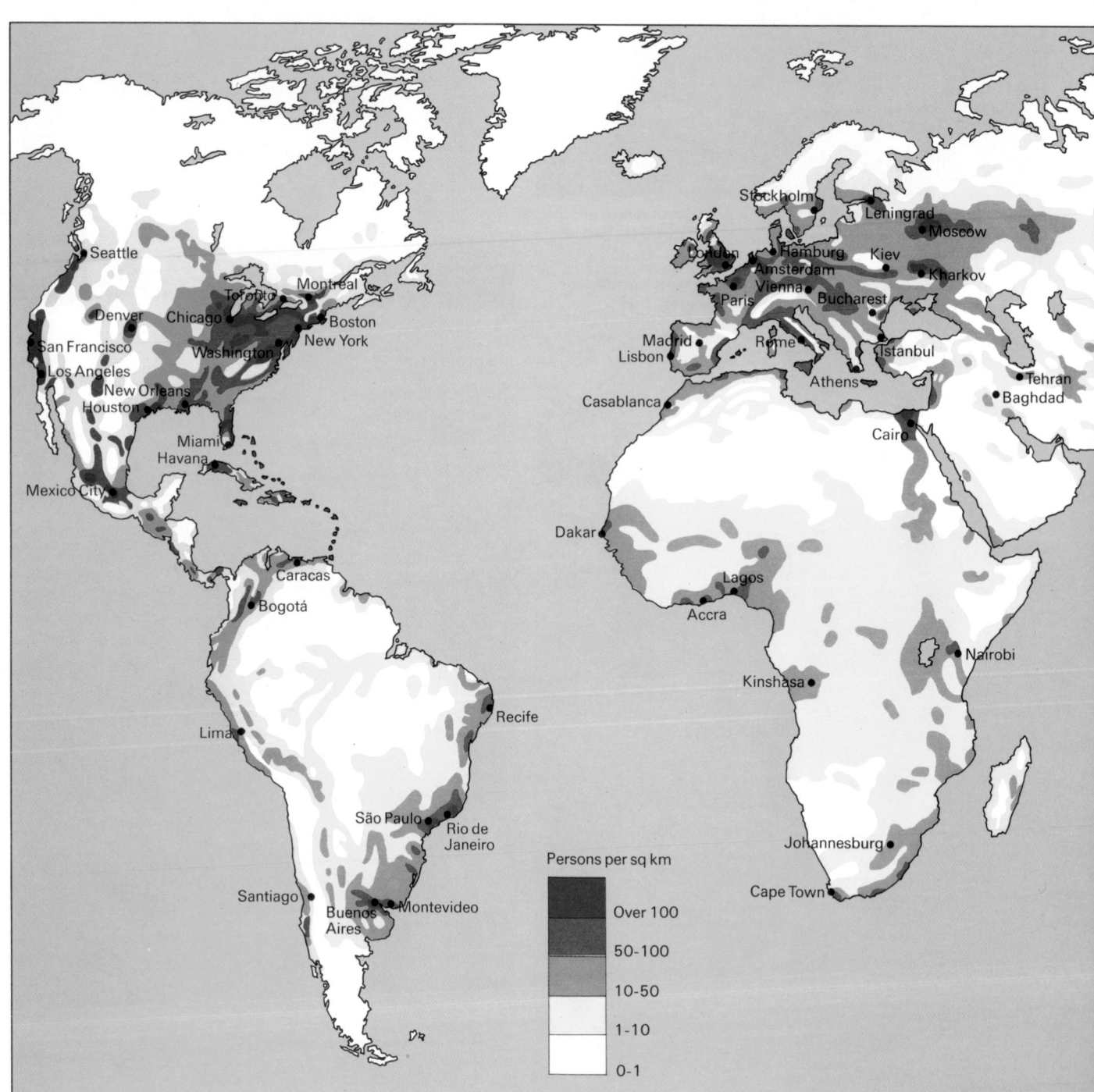

Persons per sq km

Over 100

50-100

10-50

1-10

0-1

Canada, China, the United States, Brazil, Australia, India, Argentina, Sudan and Algeria. But the ten most populated countries in 1980 were China (964 million), India (650 million) the U.S.S.R. (264 million), the United States (226 million), Indonesia (148 million), Japan (118 million), Brazil (118 million), Bangladesh (86 million), Pakistan (79 million) and Nigeria (74 million).

In 1982, the world had an estimated population of 4,506 million, and it was increasing by about 1.6 million per week. This is the fastest and most massive population increase in history. Around 6000 BC, the world had an estimated population of about 200 million. It then increased steadily until, in AD 1000, it had reached just over 300 million. After that, the rate of increase

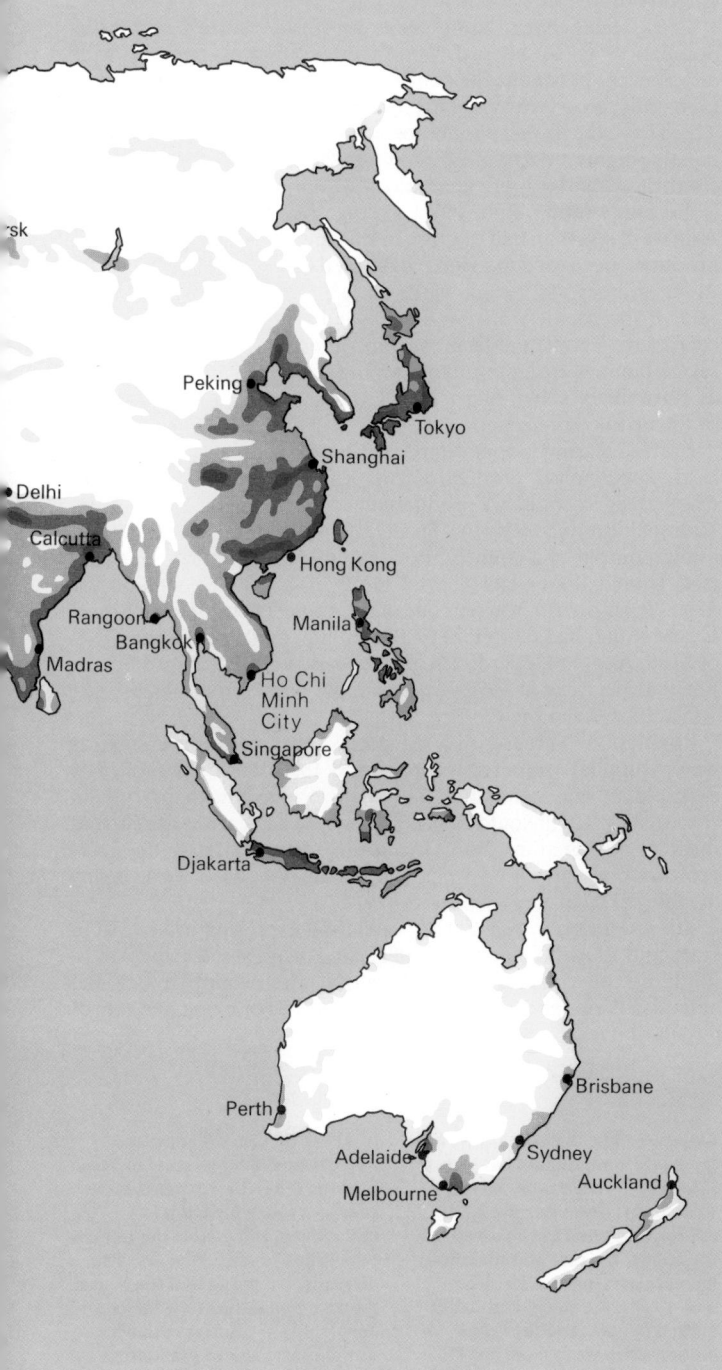

Top: **Mongolia contains large areas of bleak plateaux and mountains. Because of the severe and extreme climate, Mongolia is thinly-populated and most of the people are nomadic pastoralists.**

Above: **A crowded street in Tokyo, Japan's capital. Japan is densely populated but, in recent years, its annual rate of population growth has been reduced to only 1.3 per cent.**

began to accelerate, and the 1,000 million mark was passed in the 1800s. By the mid-1920s, it was nearly 2,000 million, and it doubled again in the following 50 years.

The explosion in world populations results from a net increase of births over deaths, mainly caused by a gradual decrease in infant mortality and longer average life spans. In the world as a whole, the average birth rate for the years 1965–74 was 33 per 1,000 people and the average death rate for the same period was 13 per 1,000. And, in 1970–4, there was a net increase in world population of about 1.9 per cent per year. If this rate continues, the world's population will double in the next 37 years.

There are considerable variations in population increases from country to country and from continent to continent. For example, the population of Pakistan has been estimated to be increasing by 2.9 per cent per year — an extremely fast rate that would double Pakistan's population in only 25 years. But, in France, it would take more than 110 years for the population to double at the slow rate of 0.6 per cent per year.

Among the continents, the populations of Africa and Latin America (including Central America and Caribbean countries) are increasing at the fast rate of 2.7 per cent per year. This rate would double the population in only 26 years. Africa has the highest birth rate of all the continents — 46 per 1,000 people per year — but it also has the highest death rate — 20 per 1,000 people per year. Latin America has a lower birth rate at 37 per 1,000 per year, but its death rate is also much lower at 9 per 1,000 people. Asia's birth rate is almost as high as Latin America's at 34 per 1,000 people per year, but the death rate of 13 per 1,000 is considerably higher. Hence, the net average rate of population increase in Asia is lower at 2.2 per cent per year (1970–7 average) and it would take 33 years for the population to double at this rate.

By contrast, the populations of North America and the U.S.S.R. are increasing by 0.9 per cent per year, which means that it would take 78 years for their populations to double if this rate were maintained. And, in Europe, the average rate of increase is only 0.6 per cent per year. Europe and North America have the lowest birth rates at 17 per 1,000 people per year.

The highest population increases have thus been taking place in the developing world, and the lowest increases have occurred in the developed, industrialized world. In Asia, Japan is the only truly industrialized country and, significantly, its average rate of population increase is well below the average for Asia at 1.2 per cent per year. Part of the reason for this contrast is that, in developing countries, a high proportion of the people live at subsistence level. It is not surprising that many poor farmers may see their only hope for survival in old age as having enough sons to support them.

The average rate of population increase in the developed world is 1.1 per cent per year, whereas the rate in the developing world is more than twice as much, averaging 2.3 per cent. One of the most striking consequences of this difference is reflected in the age structures of the two worlds.

In Africa, Asia and Latin America, the populations are more youthful than in the developed world. On average, about 40 out of every 100 people are under 15 years of age; 56 are between 15 and 64; and only 4 out of every 100 are 65 or over. This contrasts with Europe, North America, Oceania and the U.S.S.R., where 27 out of every 100 people are under 15 years of age; 63 are between 15 and 64; and 10 are 65 or over.

The large and increasing school-age populations in developing countries already have too few educational facilities and teachers. Also, the developing world has a lower proportion of people of working age, and the average life expectation is much lower. The developed countries face different problems, such as the high and increasing proportion of older people, who do not contribute directly to the economy. For example, the average life expectation

for Canadian men and women in 1931 was 60 years and 62.1 years respectively. But by 1978, it had risen to an average of 74 years for both sexes.

The population explosion poses a threat to the Earth's resources. One vital resource is farmland, which is limited in extent by climate and topography. Today the world has about 1,440 million hectares (3,558 million acres) of farmland — that is, land under the plough or under permanent crops. In 1982, when the world's population stood at about 4,506 million, the average amount of farmland per person was just under one-third of a hectre (nearly four-fifths of an acre). By the year 2000, the world's population will have increased to about 6.300 million at current rates of growth. The average amount of farmland per person will then be reduced to just over one-fifth of a hectare (slightly more than half an acre).

Crop yields must, therefore, rise if the world's increasing population is to be fed. But average figures conceal wide differences between the developed and developing worlds. Generally, crop yields per hectare are high in developed countries which have the lowest population growth rates, because farming is mostly highly mechanized and efficient. But, in developing countries, standards are generally low. For example, in Asia, rice is the staple food but, in 1970, average rice yields per hectare in Asia were less than half of those in Europe. Also the United States produces more food than it needs to feed its people, yet only about 2 out of every 100 people work on farms. In Asia, about 64 per cent of the people work on farms. And, in Africa, where 74 per cent of the people are farm workers, mostly at subsistence level, severe famines are all too frequent. In such poor African countries as Burundi, Malawi, Niger and Rwanda, more than 85 per cent of the people are farmers.

Fast-increasing populations, combined with a generally low level of economic production, are causing severe problems in many areas. A country's production is often expressed as its Gross National Product (GNP). The GNP is the total domestic and foreign output of a country. For example, in 1979, the industrialized United States had a total GNP of $2,337,090 million, or $10,820 per person, whereas one of the poorest developing nations, Upper Volta, had a GNP of $1,000 million and a per capita GNP of $180. And, in Upper Volta, the per capita GNP declined by one per cent per year in 1970–8 because the population increased at a faster rate than the GNP.

Population increase also threatens other resources, such as water supplies, mineral reserves and fossil fuel reserves. For example, it was estimated that the world's known petroleum resources in 1973 would be used up in only 27 years at the current rates of production. With increasing demand from an ever-growing population, oil wells will eventually run dry and many metals will be in short supply.

The problems posed by the population explosion are global in scale and must be treated globally, by a sensible distribution of food and other resources. Significantly, when countries develop and raise their per capita GDPs and standards of living, the rate of population increase starts to decline.

Opposite: **The diagram shows how the world's population has grown since 1650. At first, the increase was steady. But, after the 1,000 million mark had been passed in the 1800s, the rate of population increase accelerated. By the mid-1920s, the world had 2,000 million people, and the 4,000 million mark was passed in 1976 — the population having doubled in** just over 50 years. Today, the average rate of population increase is estimated to be 1.9 per cent per year — a rate which, if it is maintained, will double the world's population in only 37 years. The diagram also shows that the fastest growing populations are in the developing, or poorer countries. The slowest rates of population growth occur in developed nations.

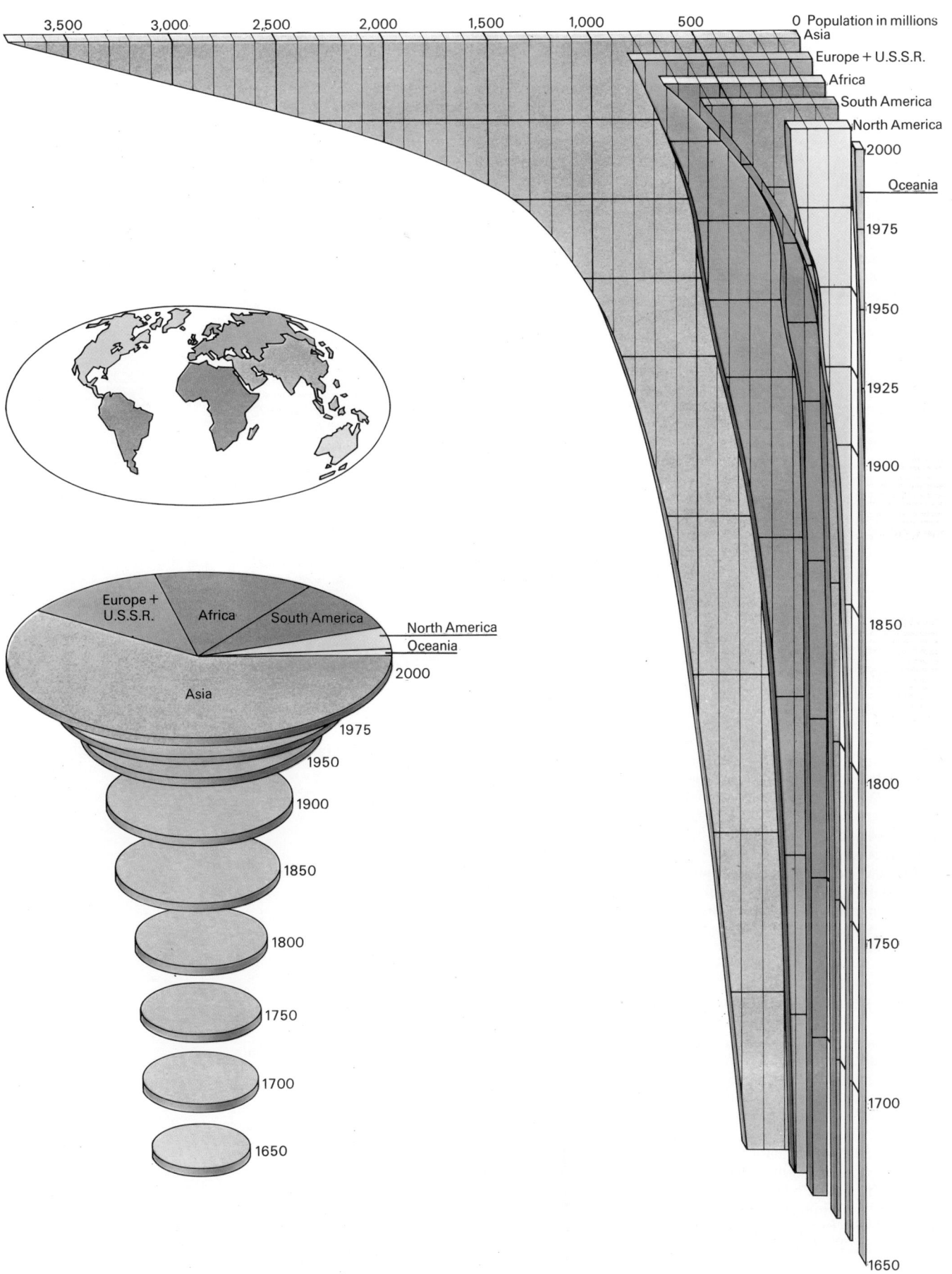

Population

3,500   3,000   2,500   2,000   1,500   1,000   500   0 Population in millions

Asia
Europe + U.S.S.R.
Africa
South America
North America

2000

Oceania

1975

1950

1925

1900

1850

1800

1750

1700

1650

Europe +
U.S.S.R.   Africa   South America

North America
Oceania

2000

Asia

1975
1950
1900
1850
1800
1750
1700
1650

53

The Growth of Towns

One of the main features that distinguishes developed countries from their less fortunate developing neighbours is that developed countries have large manufacturing industries. On the other hand, the economies of most developing countries are based mainly on the production of primary products — food and raw materials, although such developing countries as Brazil and China do have important pockets of manufacturing industries.

Industrialization is the chief factor that has led to the rapid development of cities and towns since the late 1700s, when the Industrial Revolution began, at first in Britain, although rural manufacturing remains important in Norway and Switzerland. In the world as a whole, about one-third of the people live in urban areas. But, in the developed world, between two-thirds and nine-tenths of the people live and work in cities and towns. By contrast, in parts of Africa, only 10 per cent of the people are urbanized. In Asia, an average of only one-third of the people live in urban areas and, in Latin America, about half are town or city dwellers. However, as developing countries try to diversify their economies by establishing manufacturing industries and services, so more and more people are leaving the countryside for the towns and cities.

The earliest towns grew up in Mesopotamia following the start of agriculture and the production of food surpluses 6,000 years ago. By 3500 BC, there were many well-established towns in the area. Towns were later set up in Egypt and the Mediterranean area and, to the east, in India, central Asia and China. These early towns were essentially centres of trade and craft industries, but many of the sites were chosen because they were easily defended. In the towns, people had time to develop the arts and sciences, and so it was the towns that provided the stimulus for the development of the great early civilizations. But most towns remained small, although some ancient Chinese cities may have had about one million inhabitants.

The development of Paris is typical of many cities. It was first established as a settlement on an island in the River Seine. Because of the island, the settlement provided an easy bridging point of the river, and Paris developed as a communications centre. When it was taken by the Romans in 52 BC, it covered about 40 hectares (100 acres). As trade increased, Paris gradually expanded onto the north and south banks of the Seine and, by the Middle Ages, it covered nearly 8 square kilometres (3 square miles) and had a population of about 150,000. France began to industrialize in the early 1800s, and Paris grew quickly as factories sprang up in and around it. By the 1840s, industrial Paris covered 10 times the area of medieval Paris, and its population passed the 900,000 mark. Today, with its large suburbs, it sprawls over an area of 480 square kilometres (185 square miles) and has a population of 8,547,000.

In the early days of the Industrial Revolution, many new towns arose on coalfields, ironfields and other places where natural resources were to hand. But, as communications improved, so cities could be founded far from the resources they required for their people and industries. For example, ports handling imports and exports became industrial centres, and other cities were established on the expanding railway networks, especially at railway junctions.

Modern cities face many problems, including large-scale crime, noise, pollution, communications breakdowns, such as traffic jams, and a lack of community sense that may cause loneliness.

In the developing world, the lack of capital makes it difficult for governments to cope with the rapid expansion of their cities. Country people migrate to urban areas in search of better-paid jobs, higher standards of living and more amenities. The population of Brazil's cities, for example, will increase by an estimated 32 million people during the 1980s. This means that these cities will have to provide at least five million new family houses, otherwise ugly shanty towns with serious health hazards will arise. And, as most of the new arrivals are unskilled, there will be serious urban unemployment, unless the industrial expansion is fast enough to provide sufficient jobs. In one country, communist China, the government has been trying to reverse the world trend towards urbanization by diverting people back to rural communities, which they are trying to make self-sufficient.

The World's Largest 25 Cities*

City	Country	Population
New York City	United States	16,962,000
Mexico City	Mexico	13,993,000
Tokyo	Japan	11,695,000
Los Angeles	United States	10,605,000
Shanghai	China	10,000,000
Buenos Aires	Argentina	9,749,000
Paris	France	8,547,000
Peking	China	8,000,000
Moscow	U.S.S.R.	7,909,000
Chicago	United States	7,662,000
Sao Paulo	Brazil	7,198,000
Calcutta	India	7,031,000
Tientsin	China	6,992,000
London	United Kingdom	6,970,000
Seoul	South Korea	6,879,000
Chongquin	China	6,000,000
Bombay	India	5,970,000
Philadelphia	United States	5,627,000
Cairo	Egypt	5,084,000
Canton	China	5,000,000
Rio de Janeiro	Brazil	4,857,000
San Francisco	United States	4,693,000
Detroit	United States	4,620,000
Hong Kong	Hong Kong	4,610,000
Djakarta	Indonesia	4,576,000

*Including suburban areas

Above left: **Italy, like most developed countries, suffers from traffic congestion in urban areas. The populations of urban areas in most parts of the world are increasing in size, partly as a result of natural population growth and partly because of rural depopulation.**

Above: **Land and housing are so limited in the crowded British colony of Hong Kong that many people have to live in boats.**

Right: **Many towns in Taiwan, like others in developing nations, are surrounded by shanty towns, where crime, disease and poverty are rife. Shanty towns develop when the urban building programmes cannot keep pace with the fast-increasing populations. Yet, in most countries, the exodus of people from the countryside continues, because the best-paid jobs are nearly all to be found in the towns.**

Health, Wealth and Poverty

Developed countries are distinguished from developing countries by their far higher per capita GNPs. For example, in 1979 France had a per capita GNP of US $9,940; West Germany, $11,730; the Netherlands, $10,240; the United Kingdom, $6,340; and the United States, $10,820. People who live in these, or other developed countries, can expect to live much longer, on average, than people in developing countries. For example, average life expectations in 1978 were as follows: France, 73 years (as opposed to 71 in 1960); West Germany, 72 years (69 in 1960); the Netherlands, 74 years (73 in 1960); the United Kingdom, 73 years (70 in 1960); and the United States, 73 years (70 in 1960).

Complete statistics are lacking in many developing countries. But the United Nations estimates for average life expectations in some of them were as follows: Ghana, 48 years; India, 51 years; Indonesia, 47 years; and Senegal, 42 years. The per capita GNPs in 1979 were: Ghana $400; India $190; Indonesia $380; and Senegal $430. Some African countries have even lower average life expectations and per capita GNPs.

Low economic production, poverty and short life expectations are all, therefore, inter-related. Experts estimate that 300 to 400 million people, mostly children in the developing world, are suffering from malnutrition. For good health, people need a balanced diet. They need carbohydrates and fats, which provide energy. They need proteins for the growth of bones, cells and muscles, and smaller amounts of mineral salts and vitamins, which enable the body to make use of foods consumed. But, in the developing world, many people suffer from deficiency diseases, caused by a lack of one or more of these essential elements.

Kwashiokor is a disorder caused by a lack of protein, although sufferers may be eating sufficient carbohydrates in the form of cereals. In fact, it is estimated that about half of the world's population obtain two-thirds or less of the proteins they require for good health. Survivors of deficiency diseases in childhood may be left with impaired mental powers and their bodies may be stunted. Yet these children are the adults of the future, on whose shoulders rests the responsibility for raising their countries' economic production.

In many developing countries, periodic droughts, attacks of pests, and various plant and animal diseases often cause terrible famines. For example, in the dry Sahelian savanna, south of the Sahara Desert, years of drought occurred in the late 1960s and early 1970s. Hundreds of thousands of cattle perished, crops failed and many people suffered great hardship and starvation.

The food that is available in many places is unevenly distributed. Even in developed countries, unequal distribution of wealth causes poverty and malnutrition in some areas. In some cases, in developing nations, the consumption of certain foods has been forbidden by ancient customs. In East Africa, in the early 1960s, many Masai people were starving as a result of drought, but they refused solid foods, such as maize meal, because their traditional diet consisted of milk and blood. Also, in developing countries, many people get poor-quality or inadequate food, which impairs their general health.

People whose general standard of health is low lack resistance to disease. Among such people, the infant mortality rate is also high, standards of hygiene are often low and medical facilities are extremely limited. In northern Nigeria, there was only one doctor for every 100,000 people in the mid-1960s, while the United States had about 150 per 100,000 people. In developing countries, money is lacking for medicines, hospitals and other health facilities. For example, in the mid-1960s, the United States had around 750 times as much money available to spend on health per person as Nigeria.

Much aid for developing countries is channelled through the U.N. For example, the World Health Organization has mounted a campaign in Africa to reduce the incidence of malaria by preventive medicine and the eradication of the mosquitoes' habitats. But new health hazards are sometimes created as developing countries progress. For example, hydro-electric stations at the Kariba Dam in southern Africa and the Aswan High Dam in Egypt provide cheap electricity for manufacturing industries. But, behind the dams, lakes Kariba and Nasser have provided vast breeding grounds for the parasite that communicates the dangerous disease bilharzia.

One interesting development in some countries has been the utilization of the limited cash available to train medical auxiliaries. These are not doctors, but they are given a short and, therefore, cheap training that enables them to diagnose illnesses, treat the simpler cases and educate people in hygiene and birth control. Patients they are unable to help are referred to the few hospitals, which are mostly in the towns. Medical auxiliaries have an especially important role in large developing countries, where the population is widely scattered.

Left: **Many nations have promoted campaigns to educate people in birth control methods in an attempt to slow down fast rates of population increase. Such measures should eventually lead to economic stability and a higher standard of general health. But many people oppose most birth control methods for religious reasons.**

Right: **Victims of the severe drought and famine that occurred in the Sahel region of West Africa in 1972-4.**

The Economic World

Vegetable Food Resources

Vegetable foods — that is, plants of all kinds — are the basis of all animal life, including Man. Even carnivores — flesh-eaters — depend for their food on animals that feed on plants. Man is an omnivore, with teeth adapted to eating either meat or vegetable foods. There are about as many domestic animals as people in the world, and they have to share the vegetable crop. But meat is an extravagant way of using food resources. A given amount of cereal food might provide the nutritional needs of, say, twenty people when eaten as cereal. But it would suffice for only two to eight people when fed to animals and eaten in the form of meat or other animal products.

The world's greatest crop-growing regions are not always those with the highest populations. As a result, many areas of the world are not self-sufficient in food supplies, and have to import a great deal of their needs. For example, Western Europe has to import a large amount of cereals, particularly maize (corn) and hard wheat. Many countries, particularly the poorest of the developing countries, do produce all their own food, but only to a very poor standard of nutrition.

In such countries, farming plays a major part in the lives of the people. For example, over large areas of West Africa, nine workers out of ten are engaged in agriculture. In Bangladesh, eight out of ten are farmers, yet the country still does not produce enough food for its needs. Some difficulties are caused by unreliable climate, poor soil, or a population too large for the available farming land. But generally, the shortage of food is due to old-fashioned and inefficient methods of cultivation.

For these countries, there is hope for the future in what has come to be called the Green Revolution, which has been taking place over the past 20 years. The men behind this revolution are the plant breeders. They are continually raising new varieties of plants that produce heavier crops than those formerly grown. During the late 1960s and early 1970s, yields of rice and wheat in many Asian countries increased by amounts ranging from 20 per cent to 100 per cent. This Green Revolution has also changed trading patterns. For example, Japan and the Philippines, which were big importers of rice in the early 1960s, have now become exporters of this crop.

The most important vegetable crops are the cereals, which provide the bulk of the world's food and the feed for its animals. The two leading cereals are rice, which is the staple food of Asia, and so of about half the world's population, and wheat. Wheat is grown in all parts of the world, including Asia. In the forms of bread, pasta, and breakfast cereals, it forms an important part of the diet in the northern hemisphere. Maize (corn), the third-ranking cereal, is used largely as animal feed.

Root crops are widely cultivated for human and animal consumption. Potatoes are a leading crop in Europe, North America, and the U.S.S.R.; sweet potatoes and yams are grown in China, Japan, and Korea; and cassava is grown in Africa, Asia and parts of South America. Pulses — beans, peas, lentils and chickpeas — form a vital part of the diet in many poor countries. Sugar, from sugar-beet and sugar-cane, is important as a high-energy food. Edible oils, obtained from olives, oilpalms, soybeans and groundnuts, are used in cooking and as an alternative to butter.

Leading Wheat Producers

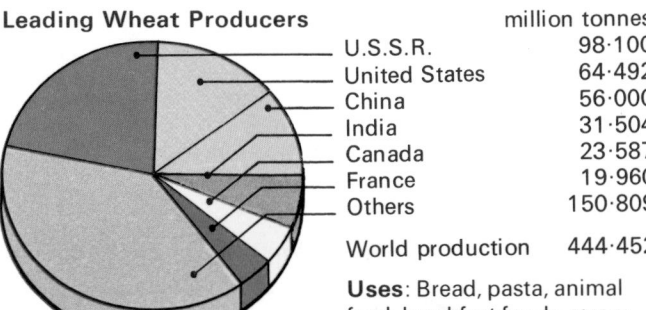

	million tonnes
U.S.S.R.	98·100
United States	64·492
China	56·000
India	31·504
Canada	23·587
France	19·960
Others	150·809
World production	444·452

Uses: Bread, pasta, animal feed, breakfast foods, straw

Leading Rye Producers

	million tonnes
U.S.S.R.	10·200
Poland	6·809
West Germany	2·111
East Germany	1·700
Czechoslovakia	0·741
Turkey	0·705
Others	5·128
World production	27·394

Uses: Bread, animal feed, alcoholic drinks, straw

Leading Millet and Sorghum Producers

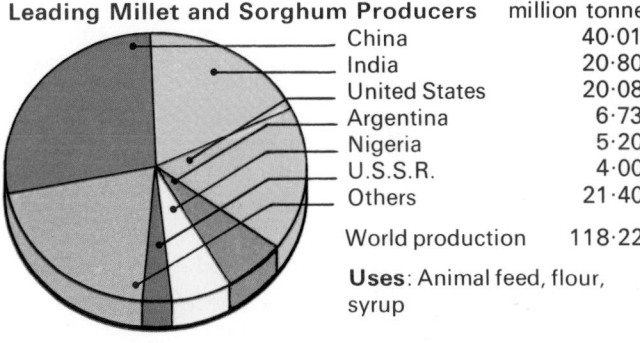

	million tonnes
China	40·014
India	20·800
United States	20·083
Argentina	6·730
Nigeria	5·200
U.S.S.R.	4·000
Others	21·400
World production	118·227

Uses: Animal feed, flour, syrup

Leading Maize (Corn) Producers

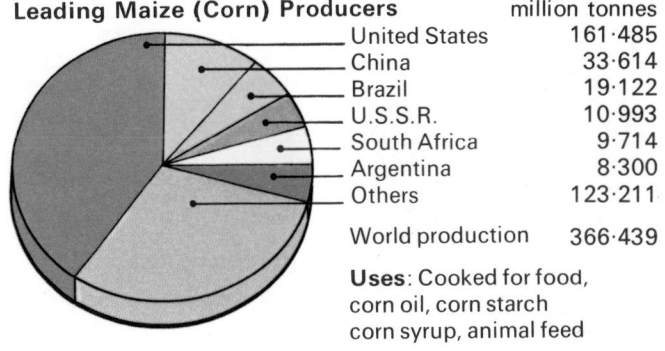

	million tonnes
United States	161·485
China	33·614
Brazil	19·122
U.S.S.R.	10·993
South Africa	9·714
Argentina	8·300
Others	123·211
World production	366·439

Uses: Cooked for food, corn oil, corn starch corn syrup, animal feed

Below left: **Much farm work in developing countries is done by hand, resulting in low production.**

Below: **Machinery like this combine harvester can greatly increase production.**

Vegetable Food Resources

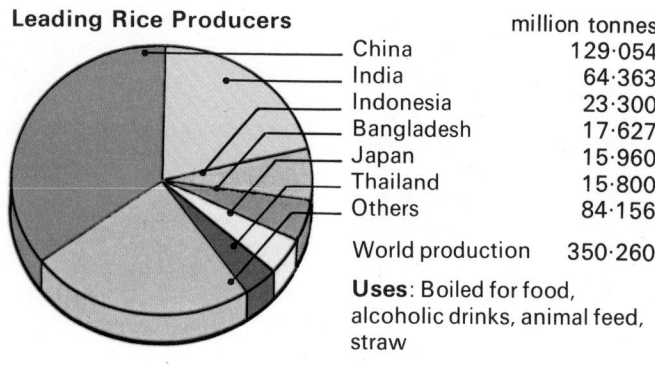

Leading Rice Producers

	million tonnes
China	129·054
India	64·363
Indonesia	23·300
Bangladesh	17·627
Japan	15·960
Thailand	15·800
Others	84·156
World production	350·260

Uses: Boiled for food, alcoholic drinks, animal feed, straw

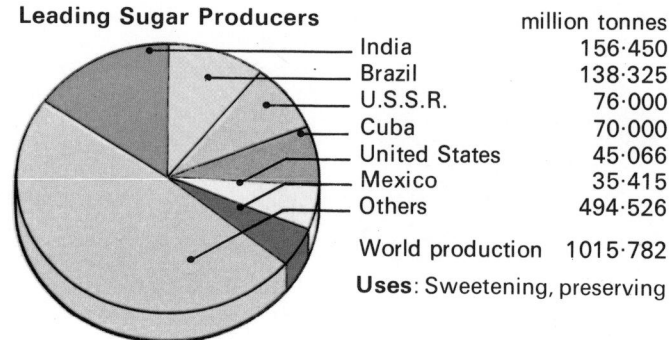

Leading Sugar Producers

	million tonnes
India	156·450
Brazil	138·325
U.S.S.R.	76·000
Cuba	70·000
United States	45·066
Mexico	35·415
Others	494·526
World production	1015·782

Uses: Sweetening, preserving

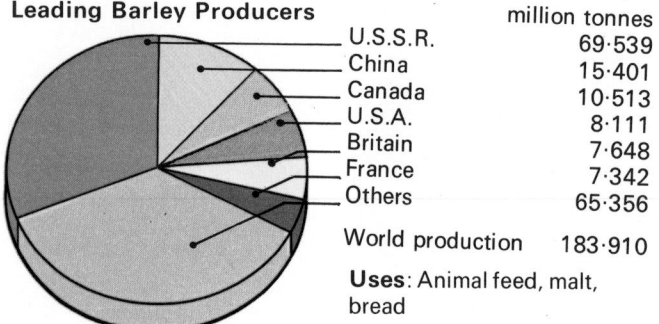

Leading Barley Producers

	million tonnes
U.S.S.R.	69·539
China	15·401
Canada	10·513
U.S.A.	8·111
Britain	7·648
France	7·342
Others	65·356
World production	183·910

Uses: Animal feed, malt, bread

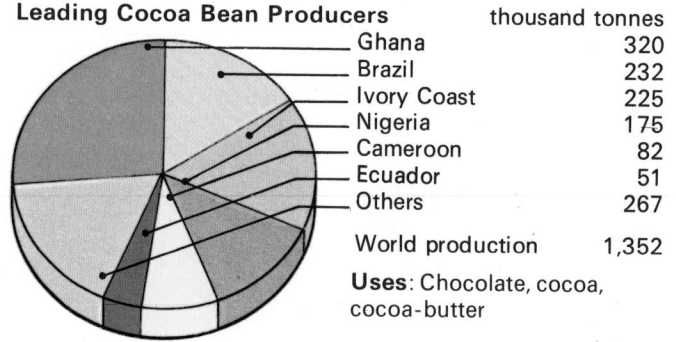

Leading Cocoa Bean Producers

	thousand tonnes
Ghana	320
Brazil	232
Ivory Coast	225
Nigeria	175
Cameroon	82
Ecuador	51
Others	267
World production	1,352

Uses: Chocolate, cocoa, cocoa-butter

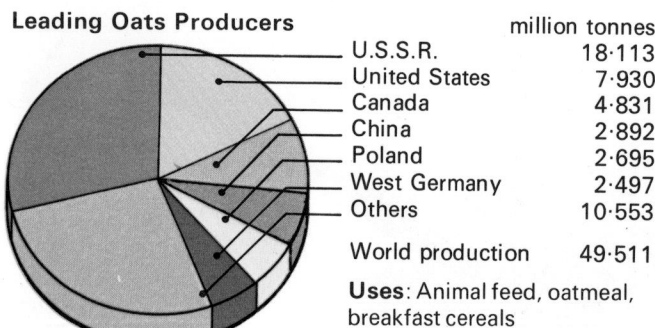

Leading Oats Producers

	million tonnes
U.S.S.R.	18·113
United States	7·930
Canada	4·831
China	2·892
Poland	2·695
West Germany	2·497
Others	10·553
World production	49·511

Uses: Animal feed, oatmeal, breakfast cereals

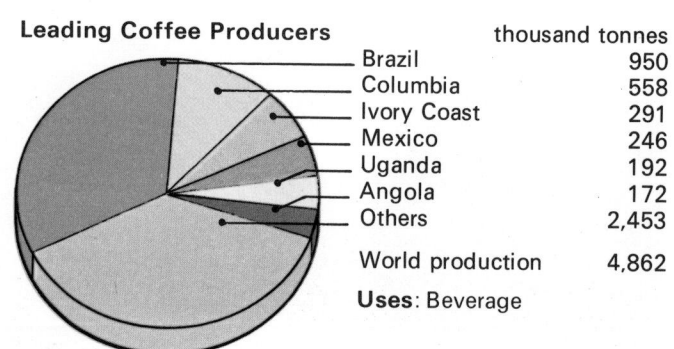

Leading Coffee Producers

	thousand tonnes
Brazil	950
Columbia	558
Ivory Coast	291
Mexico	246
Uganda	192
Angola	172
Others	2,453
World production	4,862

Uses: Beverage

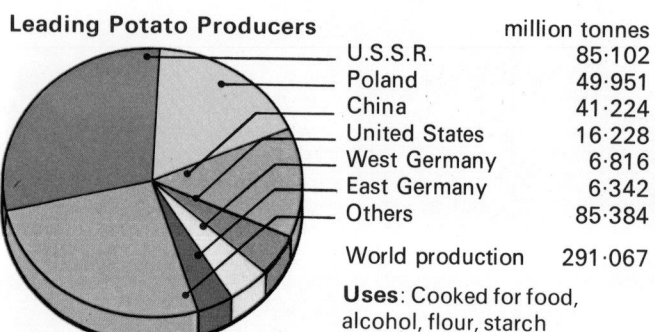

Leading Potato Producers

	million tonnes
U.S.S.R.	85·102
Poland	49·951
China	41·224
United States	16·228
West Germany	6·816
East Germany	6·342
Others	85·384
World production	291·067

Uses: Cooked for food, alcohol, flour, starch

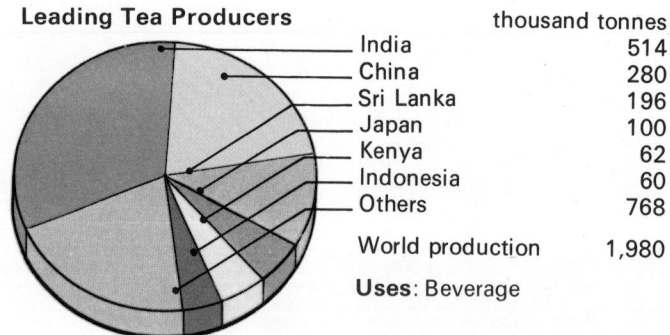

Leading Tea Producers

	thousand tonnes
India	514
China	280
Sri Lanka	196
Japan	100
Kenya	62
Indonesia	60
Others	768
World production	1,980

Uses: Beverage

Animal Food Resources

Although Man is largely a vegetable eater, meat and animal products form a valuable part of his diet. Meat provides a ready source of protein and fat — two essentials for health — and contains many vitamins. It also contains minerals such as iron, copper and phosphorus. The smell of cooked meat has been found to stimulate the digestive juices.

The main meats are beef, mutton and lamb, and pork. In some countries, particularly around the Mediterranean Sea, the flesh of goats is regularly eaten. In all parts of the world, people also eat the flesh of poultry and some other birds, such as ducks and geese.

Another valuable animal product is milk, usually from cows, though goat's milk and ewe's milk are also drunk in small quantities. Milk contains much the same nutrients as meat. A great deal of it is consumed in the form of butter and cheese, which contain a greater concentration of fats than plain milk.

Meat is raised largely in the grassland areas of the world; dairy cattle are kept mostly in the temperate zone countries, particularly in Europe, the United States, New Zealand and Australia. Sheep can be grazed on hilly land with poorer grass than required by cattle.

INDIA'S 'SACRED COWS' Although India leads the world in the number of cattle produced, this can be misleading unless all the factors are known.

The cow is sacred to the Hindus, who form 85 per cent of India's people, and so they eat no beef — and the slaughter of cows, as distinct from bulls, is banned by the country's constitution. Although bullocks are the principal draft animals, India's huge cattle population includes a large number of useless beasts, and the milk yield from cows is among the world's lowest.

Leading Butter Producers

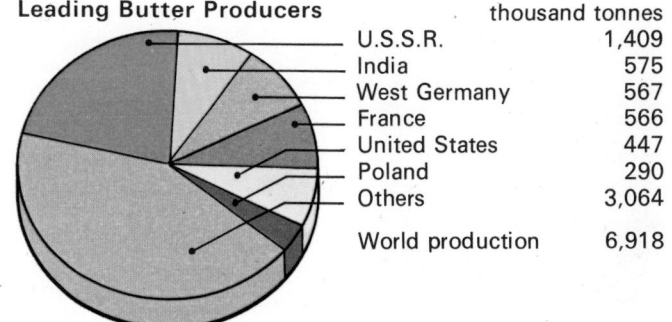

	thousand tonnes
U.S.S.R.	1,409
India	575
West Germany	567
France	566
United States	447
Poland	290
Others	3,064
World production	6,918

Leading Cattle Producers

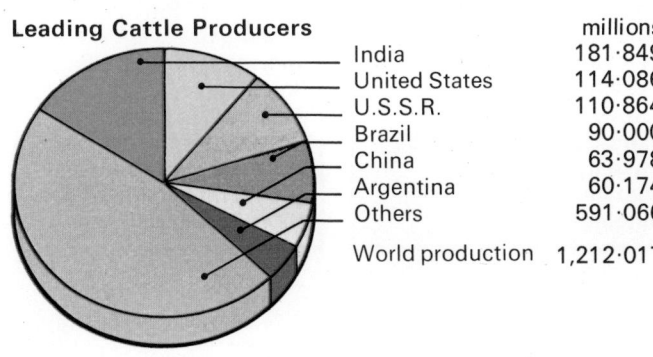

	millions
India	181·849
United States	114·086
U.S.S.R.	110·864
Brazil	90·000
China	63·978
Argentina	60·174
Others	591·066
World production	1,212·017

Leading Hen's Egg Producers

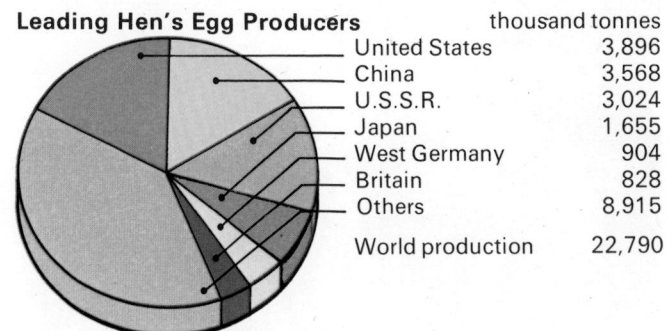

	thousand tonnes
United States	3,896
China	3,568
U.S.S.R.	3,024
Japan	1,655
West Germany	904
Britain	828
Others	8,915
World production	22,790

Leading Pig Producers

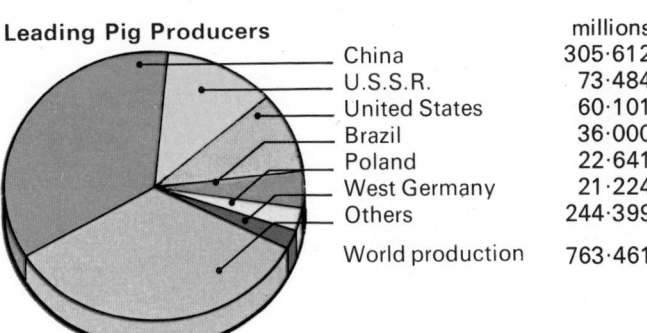

	millions
China	305·612
U.S.S.R.	73·484
United States	60·101
Brazil	36·000
Poland	22·641
West Germany	21·224
Others	244·399
World production	763·461

Leading Sheep Producers

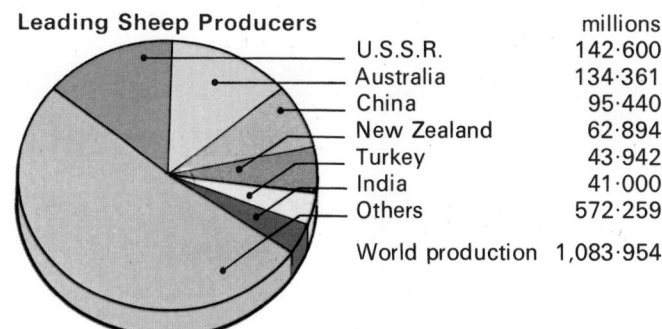

	millions
U.S.S.R.	142·600
Australia	134·361
China	95·440
New Zealand	62·894
Turkey	43·942
India	41·000
Others	572·259
World production	1,083·954

Leading Fish Producers

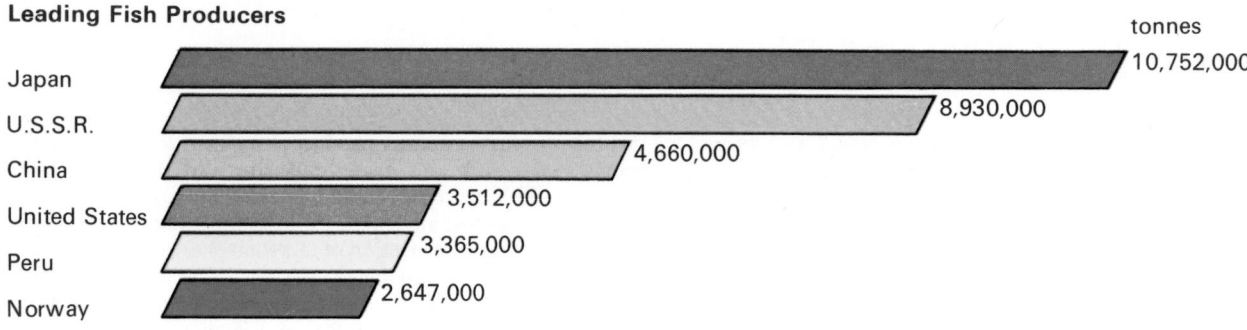

tonnes

Japan	10,752,000
U.S.S.R.	8,930,000
China	4,660,000
United States	3,512,000
Peru	3,365,000
Norway	2,647,000

WORLD FISHERIES
Fishing fleets of the world catch about 72 million tonnes of fish every year, and the total is constantly rising. There is a serious danger of over-fishing, and some traditional fishing grounds, such as those off Iceland, are already yielding significantly lower catches than they used to.

Fish are rich in protein and form an important part of the world diet. But some fish, and the waste of others, are used for other purposes. For example, fish-meal is used for chicken and livestock feed and as fertilizer. Other fish products include glue, isinglass, and oil for use in margarine, soap, candles, paints and linoleum.

WHALING
Whales are hunted largely for their oil, which is mostly made into margarine, but also for their flesh, which is esteemed in some countries, such as Japan. Overhunting has seriously reduced the world's whale population. Strenuous international efforts are now being made to limit whale catches.

The two main whaling countries are the U.S.S.R. and Japan, which take about 74 per cent of the total catch. Smaller whaling fleets are operated by Australia, Brazil, Canada, Chile, Denmark, Iceland, Norway, Peru, Portugal, South Africa and Spain. The world annual catch is about 15,000,000 tonnes.

Left: **Making cheese at Roquefort, France. The cheese, named after its place of origin, is made from the milk of goats and ewes.**

Right: **A worker tapping a rubber tree. Each tree yields about 18 litres (4 gallons) of latex a year, for up to 30 years.**

Leading Cheese Producers

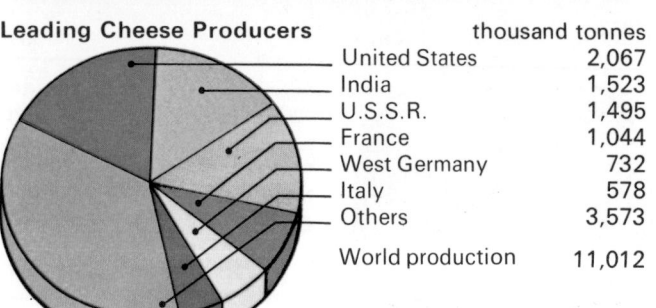

	thousand tonnes
United States	2,067
India	1,523
U.S.S.R.	1,495
France	1,044
West Germany	732
Italy	578
Others	3,573
World production	11,012

Leading Milk Producers

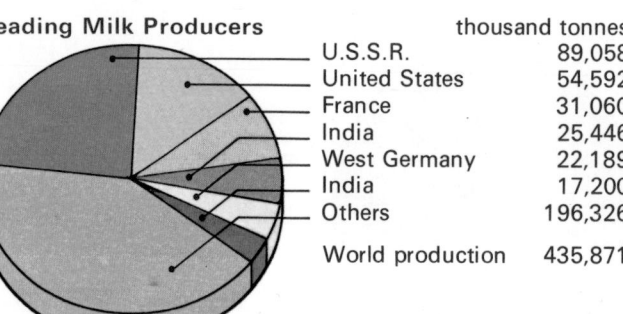

	thousand tonnes
U.S.S.R.	89,058
United States	54,592
France	31,060
India	25,446
West Germany	22,189
India	17,200
Others	196,326
World production	435,871

Natural Products for Manufacturing

Vegetable and animal products are used not only for food, but also as raw materials for manufacturing. Unlike mineral resources, animal and vegetable resources can be continually replenished, though reliance on wild crops has greatly reduced the world's timber stocks.

Before the advent of man-made fibres, people had to rely entirely on natural products for making fabrics and ropes. The most important vegetable fibre is cotton, which is used mostly for cloth. Flax is used for making linen and cord, and the leading producers are the U.S.S.R., Poland, France and Czechoslovakia. Hemp, used for carpeting, ropes, sailcloth and other coarse fabrics, comes mostly from the U.S.S.R., India, Romania and China. Jute, mainly used for sacking and hessian, is produced mostly in India, Bangladesh, China and Burma. Sisal, from which twine is made, comes mostly from East Africa.

The two main animal fibres are wool, produced mostly from sheep — though goats and rabbits also produce limited amounts — and silk, made by the silkworm moth, *Bombyx mori*.

Natural rubber, in great demand for motor-car tyres, is produced largely in southeastern Asia, though synthetic rubber is now made in even larger quantities. Most tobacco is grown for smoking, but it is used for numerous other products, including insecticides and drugs.

The world's forests yield many products. Forest lands have been greatly reduced in the past 2,000 years — for example, in Roman times, a large part of Britain was under forest. But today, careful management is ensuring that new growth is largely keeping up with demand, especially in the quick-growing softwoods.

Timber in its various forms is the most important forest product. Some of it is used as logs for telegraph poles and other items, while a great deal is turned into squared timber of various sections. Some timber is made into veneers, most of which is laminated to form plywood. Wood that is not suitable for such uses can be turned into chips, which are bonded with plastic glues into chipboards, or shredded into fibres for making into hardboards and similar products.

Newsprint is made from woodpulp, which is wood ground up in water. The many substances derived from wood include chemicals, such as acetone, methanol and glycerine, and such products as explosives, plastics and rayon.

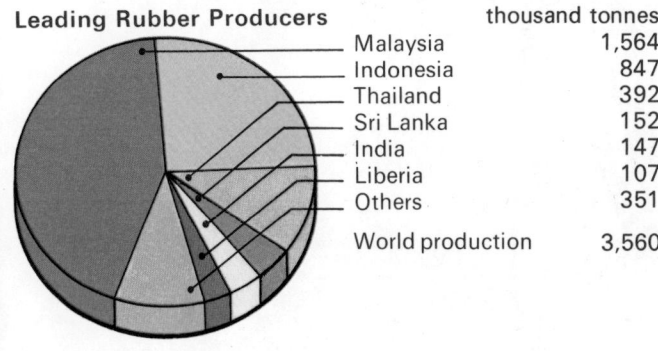

Leading Rubber Producers	thousand tonnes
Malaysia	1,564
Indonesia	847
Thailand	392
Sri Lanka	152
India	147
Liberia	107
Others	351
World production	3,560

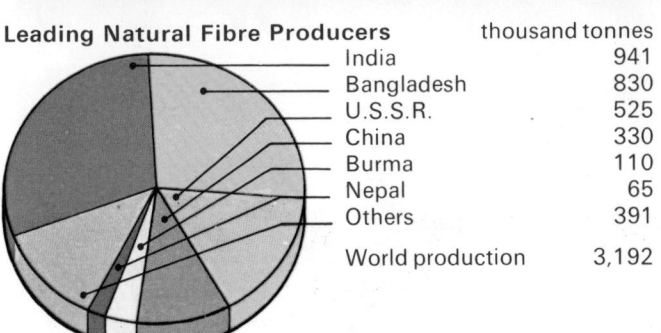

Leading Natural Fibre Producers	thousand tonnes
India	941
Bangladesh	830
U.S.S.R.	525
China	330
Burma	110
Nepal	65
Others	391
World production	3,192

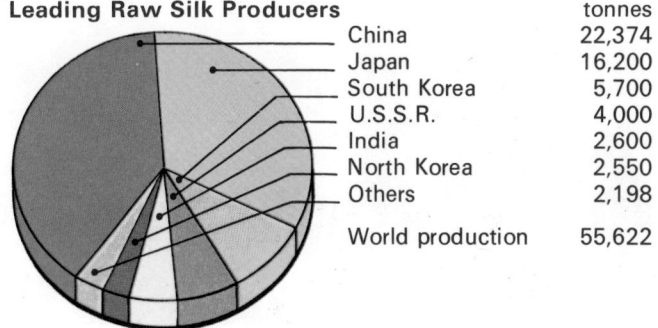

Leading Raw Silk Producers	tonnes
China	22,374
Japan	16,200
South Korea	5,700
U.S.S.R.	4,000
India	2,600
North Korea	2,550
Others	2,198
World production	55,622

Natural Products for Manufacturing

Leading Wool Producers

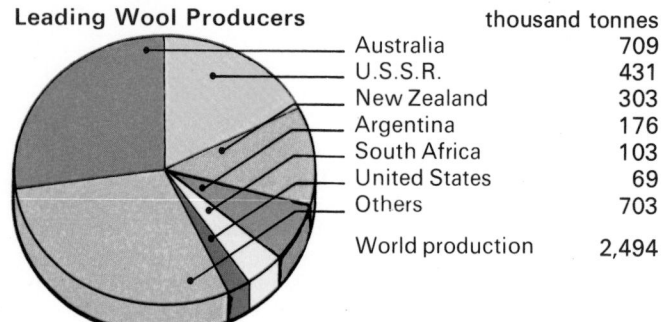

	thousand tonnes
Australia	709
U.S.S.R.	431
New Zealand	303
Argentina	176
South Africa	103
United States	69
Others	703
World production	2,494

Leading Roundwood Timber Producers

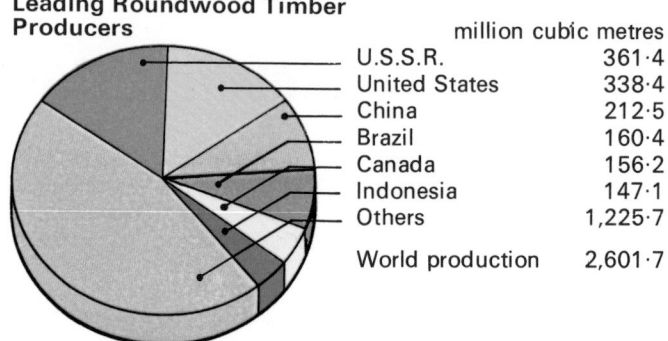

	million cubic metres
U.S.S.R.	361·4
United States	338·4
China	212·5
Brazil	160·4
Canada	156·2
Indonesia	147·1
Others	1,225·7
World production	2,601·7

Leading Cotton Producers

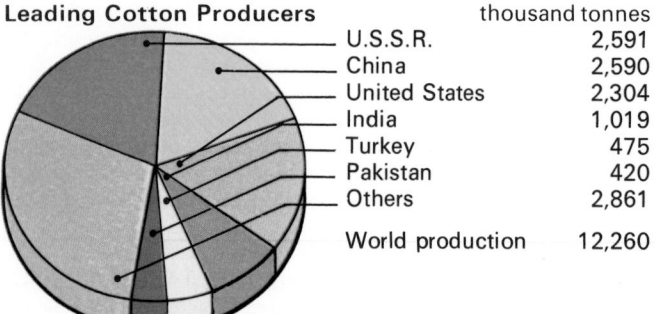

	thousand tonnes
U.S.S.R.	2,591
China	2,590
United States	2,304
India	1,019
Turkey	475
Pakistan	420
Others	2,861
World production	12,260

Leading Tobacco Producers

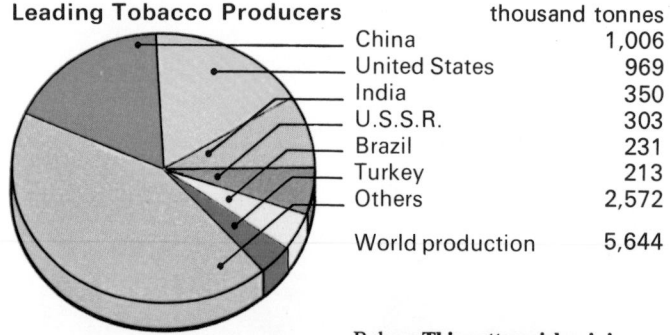

	thousand tonnes
China	1,006
United States	969
India	350
U.S.S.R.	303
Brazil	231
Turkey	213
Others	2,572
World production	5,644

Below: **This cotton picker is in Uzbekistan, in the U.S.S.R.**

Mineral Resources

The wealth of the world's industrialized countries is based on supplies of minerals, particularly the metals. When the Industrial Revolution began in the 1750s, and for many years afterwards, processing plants and factories that used metals were built near their sources. Today the industrialized countries import large quantities of minerals, often from many thousands of miles away, while modern technology demands the use of a great variety of metals and other substances that are found in different locations.

Iron is the most important of all metals, and a United Nations survey in the 1950s showed that the world supply of iron ore would last at least 800 years. The ore is distributed all over the globe, but some deposits, particularly those of Africa and the Americas, are especially rich, and it is cheaper to produce iron from these sources. Of the world's leading iron producers, the

U.S.S.R. has some of the richest deposits and has, therefore, no need to import iron ore.

Most iron is made into steel, an alloy that is harder and more useful than pure iron. All steel contains small quantities of carbon, a chemical element that is readily obtainable, but most steels have some other metal or metals mixed in to give them particular properties. For example, chromium, nickel and cobalt all help to make steel resistant to corrosion; tungsten and vanadium give it hardness; manganese gives it high tensile strength; and molybdenum gives it more elasticity.

These *ferro-alloys,* as they are called, come from much more limited sources than iron, so countries that have them possess a great strategic advantage in world politics. For example, the United States and Canada between them produce more than 75

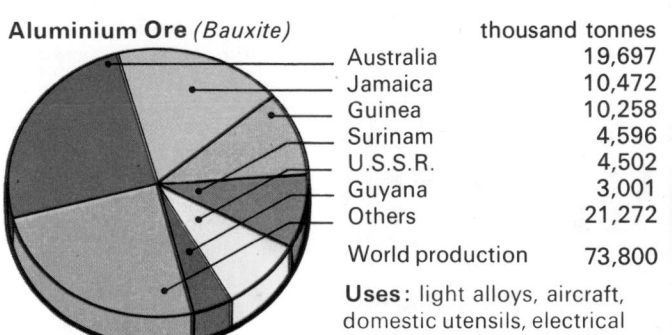

Aluminium Ore *(Bauxite)*

	thousand tonnes
Australia	19,697
Jamaica	10,472
Guinea	10,258
Surinam	4,596
U.S.S.R.	4,502
Guyana	3,001
Others	21,272
World production	73,800

Uses: light alloys, aircraft, domestic utensils, electrical apparatus

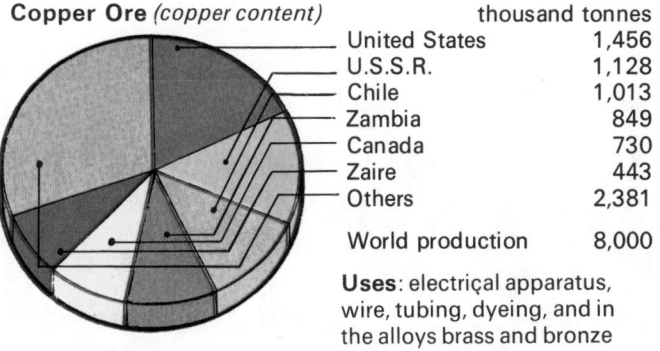

Copper Ore *(copper content)*

	thousand tonnes
United States	1,456
U.S.S.R.	1,128
Chile	1,013
Zambia	849
Canada	730
Zaire	443
Others	2,381
World production	8,000

Uses: electrical apparatus, wire, tubing, dyeing, and in the alloys brass and bronze

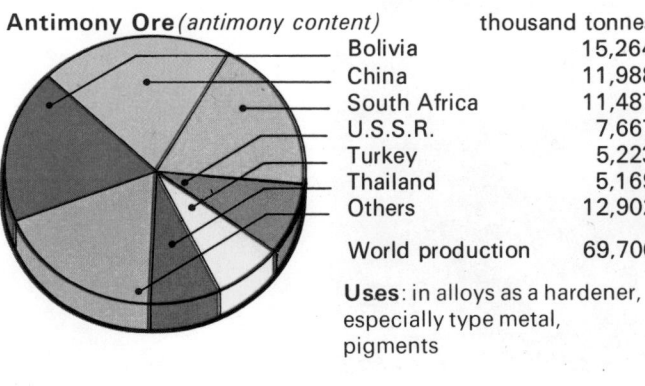

Antimony Ore *(antimony content)*

	thousand tonnes
Bolivia	15,264
China	11,988
South Africa	11,487
U.S.S.R.	7,667
Turkey	5,223
Thailand	5,169
Others	12,902
World production	69,700

Uses: in alloys as a hardener, especially type metal, pigments

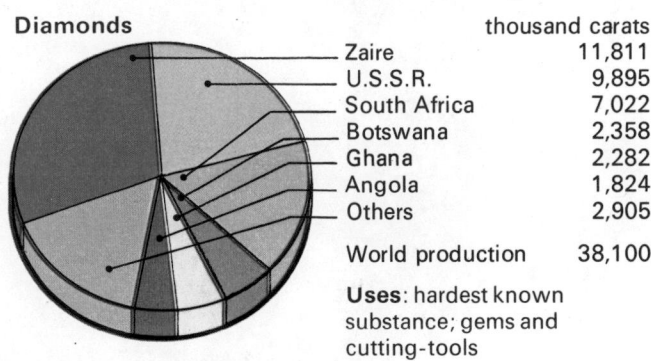

Diamonds

	thousand carats
Zaire	11,811
U.S.S.R.	9,895
South Africa	7,022
Botswana	2,358
Ghana	2,282
Angola	1,824
Others	2,905
World production	38,100

Uses: hardest known substance; gems and cutting-tools

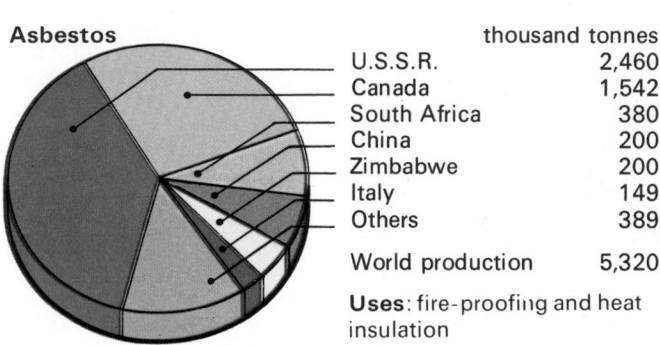

Asbestos

	thousand tonnes
U.S.S.R.	2,460
Canada	1,542
South Africa	380
China	200
Zimbabwe	200
Italy	149
Others	389
World production	5,320

Uses: fire-proofing and heat insulation

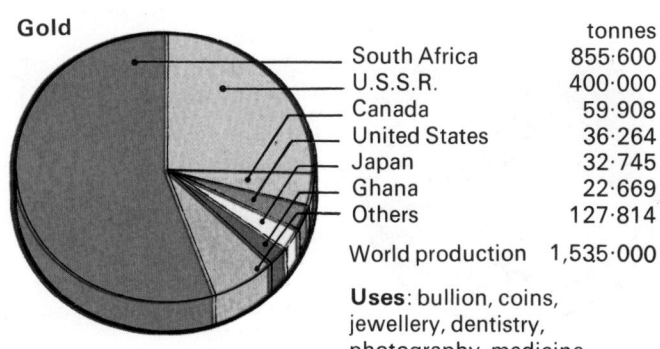

Gold

	tonnes
South Africa	855·600
U.S.S.R.	400·000
Canada	59·908
United States	36·264
Japan	32·745
Ghana	22·669
Others	127·814
World production	1,535·000

Uses: bullion, coins, jewellery, dentistry, photography, medicine

per cent of the world's molybdenum; Canada, New Caledonia and the U.S.S.R. produce 71 per cent of the nickel; and Zaire produces 59 per cent of the cobalt.

Equally vital in modern industry are the non-ferrous metals — that is, those that are not used in alloys with iron. Among the most important of these metals is copper, which is widely used for electrical work and in plumbing. Outside North America and the U.S.S.R., main supplies occur in Zaire and Zambia in Africa, and in Chile and Peru in South America. A fall in the world price of copper caused these four countries to cut production in 1975. But their strategic importance remains, and they will have a considerable influence on world markets when prices are higher again.

Other important non-ferrous metals include aluminium, lead, zinc and tin. Aluminium is one of the most abundant chemical elements in the Earth's crust, and is certainly the most abundant of all metals. But it is difficult to extract, even from its best source, bauxite, which can be either a hard rock or soft mud. Australia and Jamaica head the world's sources of bauxite.

Tin, for which Cornwall in England was once famous as a source, now comes principally from Malaysia and Indonesia in southeastern Asia, and Bolivia. Lead is produced by the United States, the U.S.S.R. and Australia, while zinc has Canada as its principal supplier.

The precious metals — gold, silver and platinum and its related metals, such as palladium — are valued because of their natural beauty as much as for their industrial importance. Gold, of which South Africa has, by far, the largest supply, is used largely as a form of currency. Most of the gold mined goes straight into bank vaults or is used to make jewellery. Silver, less used today for money, has more industrial uses, and the U.S.S.R. and Canada lead in silver production. Platinum metals come from North America, South Africa, the U.S.S.R. and South America.

The world is using minerals, especially metals, at such a rate that scientists are forecasting serious shortages of some of them. Fortunately, pressure for supplies has stimulated research, so that known resources have actually increased. In 1965, for example, copper reserves were estimated at 140 million tonnes but, in 1973, nearly 300 million tonnes were known. But even with scrap copper providing half the world's needs, supplies are being used up at an alarming rate.

A report issued in 1975 by the United States National Academy of Sciences suggested that real shortages of five metals — chromium, gold, mercury, palladium, and tin — could occur during the 1980s. Other metals whose supply also seems to be in danger, though not so imminent, are antimony, silver, tungsten, vanadium and zinc.

Left: **A worker cuts a diamond for use as a gem-stone. This operator is at Martapura, in Indonesian Borneo; major centres of the industry are in the Netherlands and Israel.**

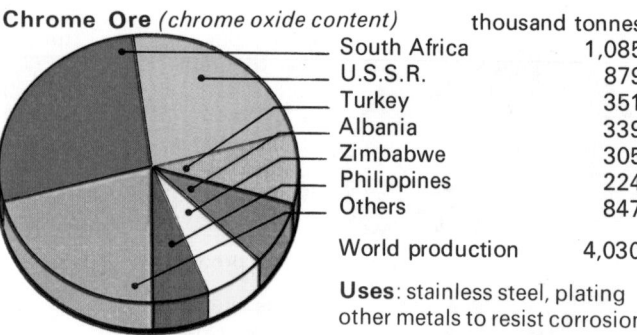

Chrome Ore *(chrome oxide content)* thousand tonnes

South Africa	1,085
U.S.S.R.	879
Turkey	351
Albania	339
Zimbabwe	305
Philippines	224
Others	847
World production	4,030

Uses: stainless steel, plating other metals to resist corrosion

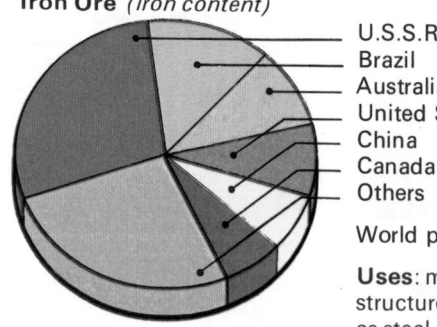

Iron Ore *(iron content)* million tonnes

U.S.S.R.	130·890
Brazil	60·596
Australia	58·263
United States	50·152
China	43·230
Canada	34·992
Others	134·576
World production	512·700

Uses: machinery and structures of all kinds, mostly as steel

Lead Ore *(lead content)*

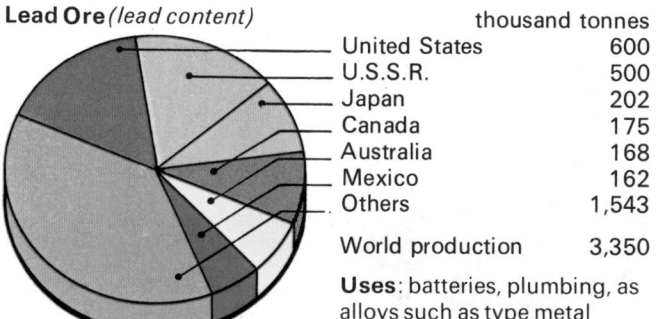

	thousand tonnes
United States	600
U.S.S.R.	500
Japan	202
Canada	175
Australia	168
Mexico	162
Others	1,543
World production	3,350

Uses: batteries, plumbing, as alloys such as type metal

Nickel Ore *(nickel content)*

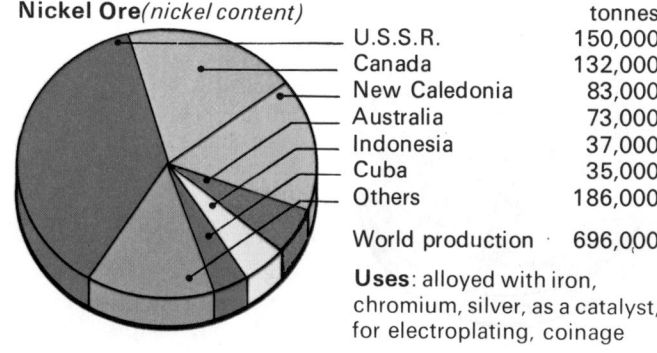

	tonnes
U.S.S.R.	150,000
Canada	132,000
New Caledonia	83,000
Australia	73,000
Indonesia	37,000
Cuba	35,000
Others	186,000
World production	696,000

Uses: alloyed with iron, chromium, silver, as a catalyst, for electroplating, coinage

Magnesium Ore *(crude magnesite)*

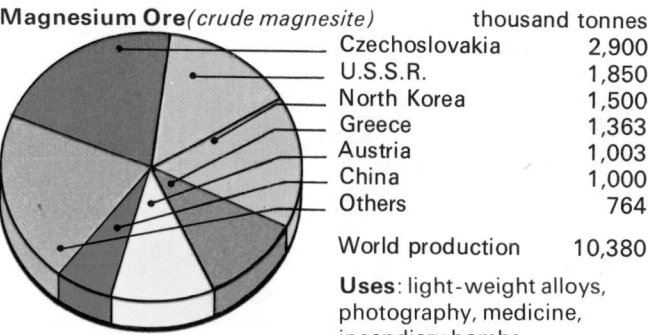

	thousand tonnes
Czechoslovakia	2,900
U.S.S.R.	1,850
North Korea	1,500
Greece	1,363
Austria	1,003
China	1,000
Others	764
World production	10,380

Uses: light-weight alloys, photography, medicine, incendiary bombs

Phosphate Rock *(Phosphorus pentoxide content)*

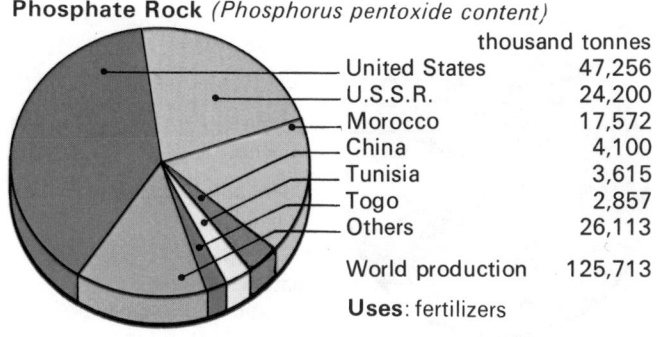

	thousand tonnes
United States	47,256
U.S.S.R.	24,200
Morocco	17,572
China	4,100
Tunisia	3,615
Togo	2,857
Others	26,113
World production	125,713

Uses: fertilizers

Manganese Ore *(manganese content)*

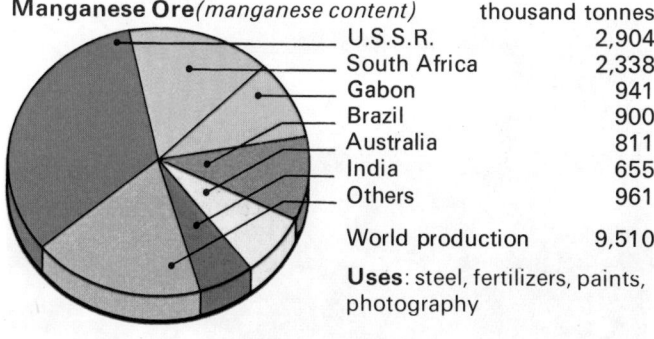

	thousand tonnes
U.S.S.R.	2,904
South Africa	2,338
Gabon	941
Brazil	900
Australia	811
India	655
Others	961
World production	9,510

Uses: steel, fertilizers, paints, photography

Potash *(Potassium monoxide content)*

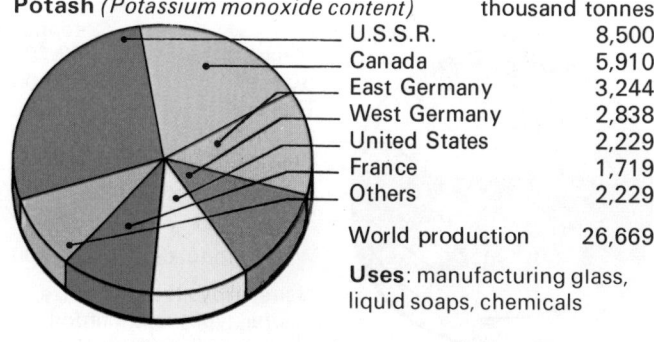

	thousand tonnes
U.S.S.R.	8,500
Canada	5,910
East Germany	3,244
West Germany	2,838
United States	2,229
France	1,719
Others	2,229
World production	26,669

Uses: manufacturing glass, liquid soaps, chemicals

Mercury

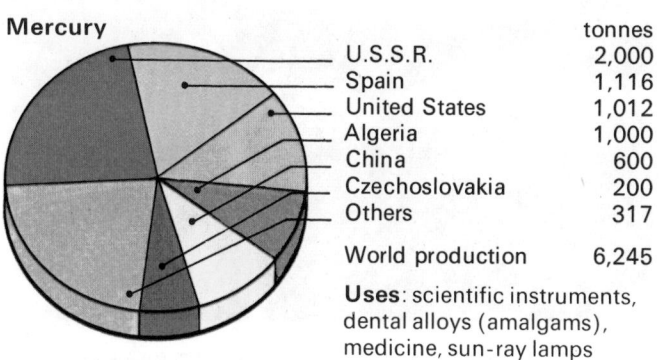

	tonnes
U.S.S.R.	2,000
Spain	1,116
United States	1,012
Algeria	1,000
China	600
Czechoslovakia	200
Others	317
World production	6,245

Uses: scientific instruments, dental alloys (amalgams), medicine, sun-ray lamps

Salt

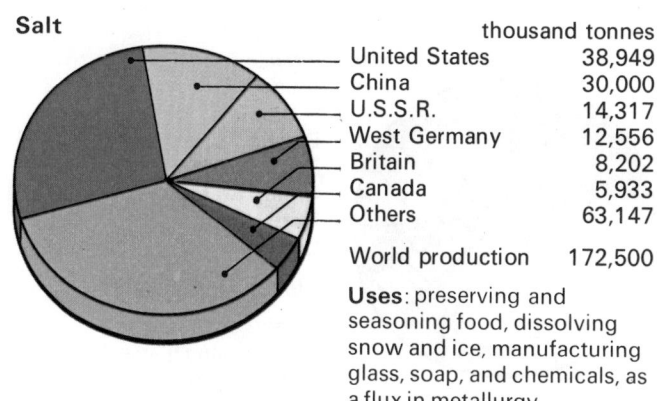

	thousand tonnes
United States	38,949
China	30,000
U.S.S.R.	14,317
West Germany	12,556
Britain	8,202
Canada	5,933
Others	63,147
World production	172,500

Uses: preserving and seasoning food, dissolving snow and ice, manufacturing glass, soap, and chemicals, as a flux in metallurgy

Mineral Resources

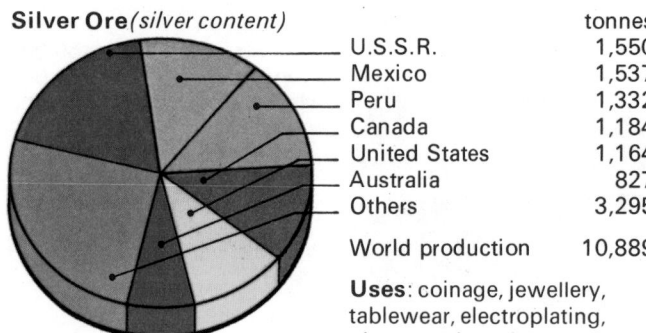

Silver Ore *(silver content)*

	tonnes
U.S.S.R.	1,550
Mexico	1,537
Peru	1,332
Canada	1,184
United States	1,164
Australia	827
Others	3,295
World production	10,889

Uses: coinage, jewellery, tablewear, electroplating, photography, mirrors

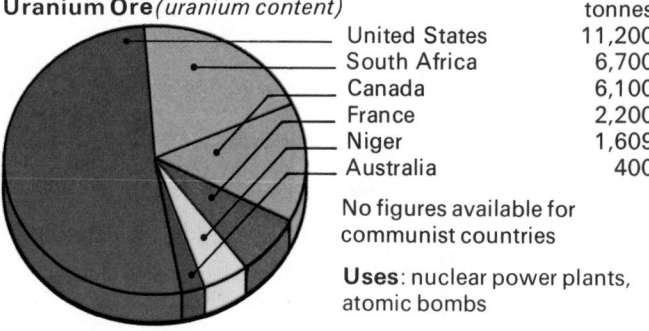

Uranium Ore *(uranium content)*

	tonnes
United States	11,200
South Africa	6,700
Canada	6,100
France	2,200
Niger	1,609
Australia	400

No figures available for communist countries

Uses: nuclear power plants, atomic bombs

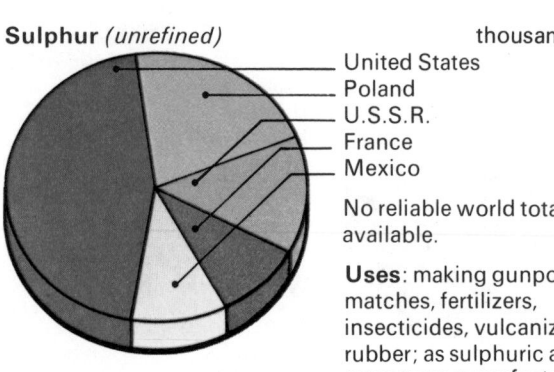

Sulphur *(unrefined)*

	thousand tonnes
United States	5,822
Poland	4,765
U.S.S.R.	2,500
France	1,841
Mexico	1,856

No reliable world total available.

Uses: making gunpowder, matches, fertilizers, insecticides, vulcanizing rubber; as sulphuric acid, in numerous manufacturing processes

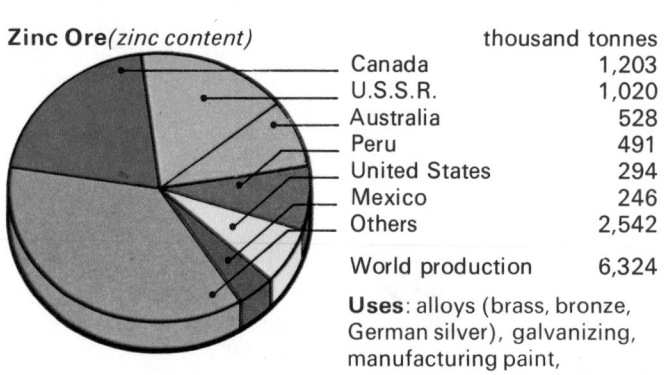

Zinc Ore *(zinc content)*

	thousand tonnes
Canada	1,203
U.S.S.R.	1,020
Australia	528
Peru	491
United States	294
Mexico	246
Others	2,542
World production	6,324

Uses: alloys (brass, bronze, German silver), galvanizing, manufacturing paint, cosmetics, rubber goods, and dental cements; in medicine

Tin Concentrates *(tin content)*

	tonnes
Malaysia	62,700
Bolivia	30,900
Thailand	30,200
Indonesia	27,400
China	18,000
U.S.S.R.	18,000
Others	49,000
World production	236,200

Uses: alloys (brass, bronze, pewter, type metal), tinfoil, tinplate, collapsible tubes, bearings, solder

Tungsten Ore *(tungstic acid content)*

	tonnes
China	11,300
U.S.S.R.	10,350
Bolivia	3,759
South Korea	3,513
United States	3,436
North Korea	2,700
Others	15,542
World production	50,600

Uses: very hard steel, electric-lamp filaments, electronic apparatus, X-ray apparatus

Above: **Mining for gold at Elsburg, in the Witwatersrand of South Africa. Mines here vary in depth from 900 to 3,700 metres (3,000 to 12,000 feet), and are highly mechanized.**

Fuel and Energy

Modern civilization depends largely on plentiful sources of fuel to provide heat and power. The principal sources of heat and power today are provided by the *fossil fuels*, which were formed by decaying plant and animal life millions of years ago. The main fossil fuels are coal, oil and natural gas. In developed countries, all industry has been founded on these three fuels. Most of our electricity is produced in power stations, where coal or oil are used to turn water to steam. The steam drives turbines, which turn huge electricity generators. Coal, the most important fuel of the 1800s, has now taken third place to oil and natural gas.

The principal sources of oil, the most important fossil fuel, are the Middle East, North America, the North Sea, the U.S.S.R., Venezuela, Argentina, Indonesia, Libya and Nigeria. In the mid-1970s, the United States, although itself a big producer, was consuming about 30 per cent more oil than it produced, and relied heavily on imports from Venezuela, Canada and the Middle East. Western Europe produced very little oil and relied almost entirely on imports from the Middle East, Libya and Nigeria. Japan, another major user, also had to import nearly all its oil.

But the discovery and exploitation of new resources means that the pattern of the world's fuel supplies and distribution is changing all the time. The development of North Sea natural gas fields made Britain independent of gas imports in the mid-1970s. And Britain, Norway and the Netherlands were set to be independent in oil from the same source by the early 1980s. The ever-increasing cost of fuel from the Middle East has stimulated research for new sources.

Although the world's stocks of fossil fuels are vast, and more remain to be found and developed, there is already a serious threat of shortages — and, once exhausted, fossil fuels cannot be replaced. World coal stocks may last for about 800 years, but oil and gas are likely to be used up early next century. However, alternative sources of power are being developed.

An extremely important alternative to fossil fuels is hydro-

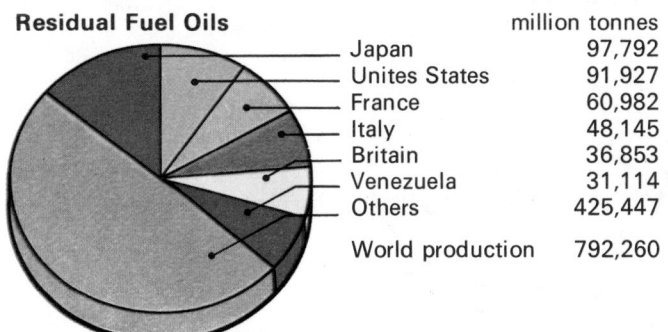

Residual Fuel Oils

	million tonnes
Japan	97,792
Unites States	91,927
France	60,982
Italy	48,145
Britain	36,853
Venezuela	31,114
Others	425,447
World production	792,260

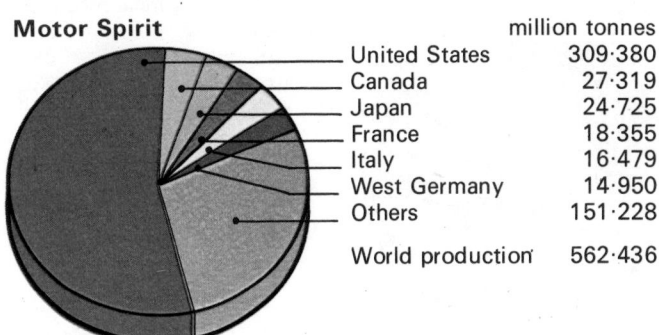

Motor Spirit

	million tonnes
United States	309·380
Canada	27·319
Japan	24·725
France	18·355
Italy	16·479
West Germany	14·950
Others	151·228
World production	562·436

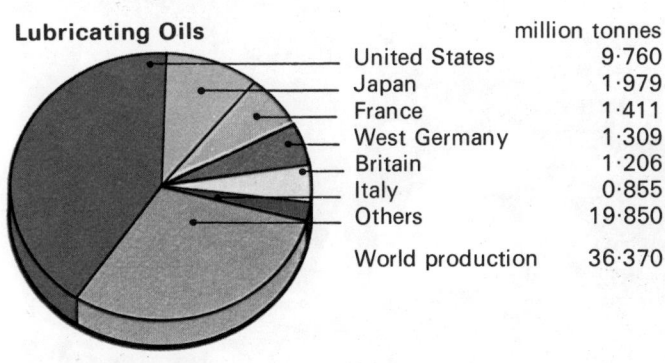

Lubricating Oils

	million tonnes
United States	9·760
Japan	1·979
France	1·411
West Germany	1·309
Britain	1·206
Italy	0·855
Others	19·850
World production	36·370

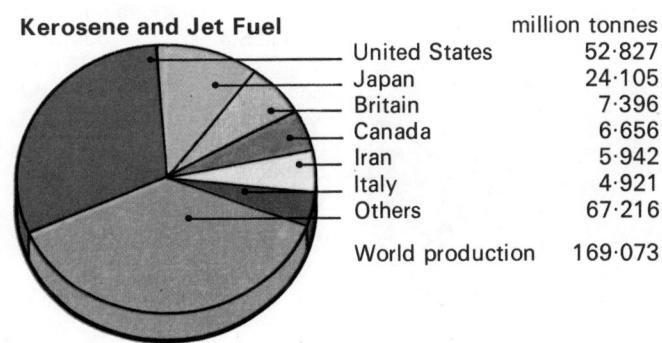

Kerosene and Jet Fuel

	million tonnes
United States	52·827
Japan	24·105
Britain	7·396
Canada	6·656
Iran	5·942
Italy	4·921
Others	67·216
World production	169·073

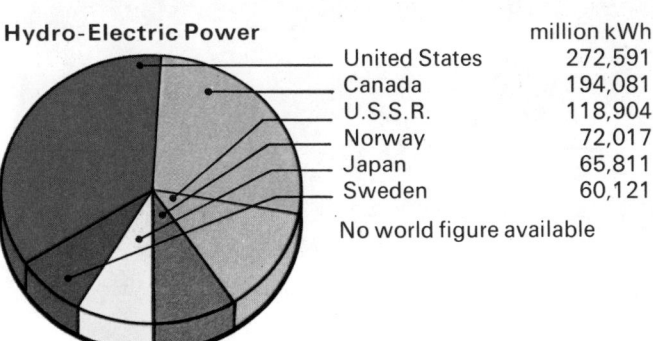

Hydro-Electric Power

	million kWh
United States	272,591
Canada	194,081
U.S.S.R.	118,904
Norway	72,017
Japan	65,811
Sweden	60,121

No world figure available

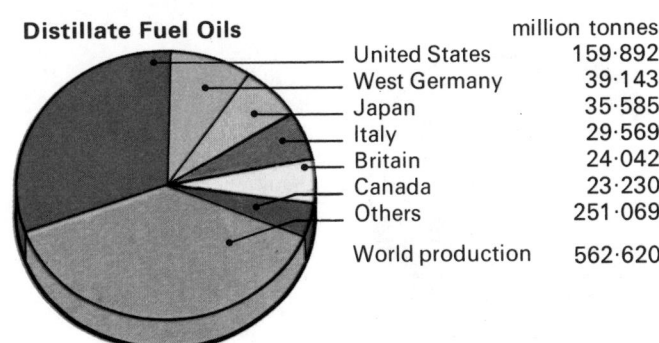

Distillate Fuel Oils

	million tonnes
United States	159·892
West Germany	39·143
Japan	35·585
Italy	29·569
Britain	24·042
Canada	23·230
Others	251·069
World production	562·620

electric power, using the flow of rivers and the movement of the sea to drive generators. Many countries already make great use of hydro-electric power. Norway, for example, generates 99 per cent of its electricity this way.

Nuclear power, using the heat released by the fission (splitting up) of uranium atoms, is extremely important too. Britain is one of the leaders in this field, with about 10 per cent of its electricity coming from nuclear power stations. Uranium is, fortunately, in good supply, though high-grade ores — rocks from which the metal can easily be extracted — are less common. The main known reserves of uranium are in North America, Zaire, South Africa, Australia, France and Czechoslovakia. China and the U.S.S.R. have kept their resources of uranium secret, but it is thought they have substantial reserves. Modern breeder-reactors not only generate heat by nuclear fission, but also 'breed' more fuel at the same time.

A more useful long-term source of power is nuclear fusion. Fusion plants work on the same principle as the sun, fusing together atoms of hydrogen to form helium — a slightly heavier gas. In the process, great heat is released. Research on this process is likely to continue for several years, but success will solve fuel and energy problems for all time, because the hydrogen fuel can be readily extracted from water.

With the increasing use of nuclear power, conservationists are becoming more and more concerned about the possibility of pollution by waste products from nuclear power stations. Most of these products are radioactive and need to be stored extremely carefully in order to reduce the chance of pollution and the consequent endangering of life. Such waste products gradually decrease in radioactivity but, in some cases, it would take thousands of years for the radioactivity to decrease to a safe level.

Two other major sources of power are the heat of the Sun and the internal heat of the Earth. Various forms of solar cells have been devised to absorb the Sun's heat and convert it into electricity. But panels in which running water absorbs the Sun's heat are generally more successful. Even in climates where there is a fair amount of cloud, the use of heat collected by roof-mounted solar panels can considerably reduce fuel bills.

The Earth's heat is easiest to harness in places where there is volcanic activity, or where hot springs exist. Geothermal energy has been most successfully developed in Iceland, New Zealand and the southwestern part of the United States.

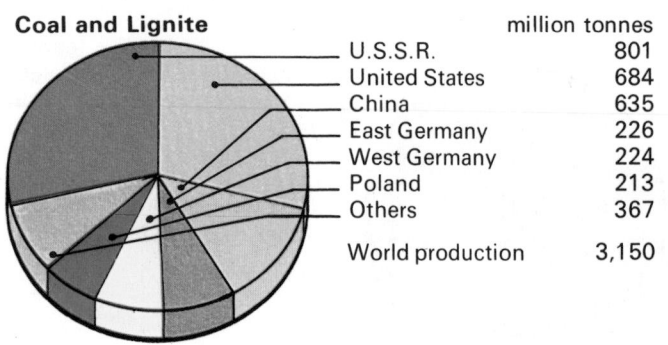

Coal and Lignite

	million tonnes
U.S.S.R.	801
United States	684
China	635
East Germany	226
West Germany	224
Poland	213
Others	367
World production	3,150

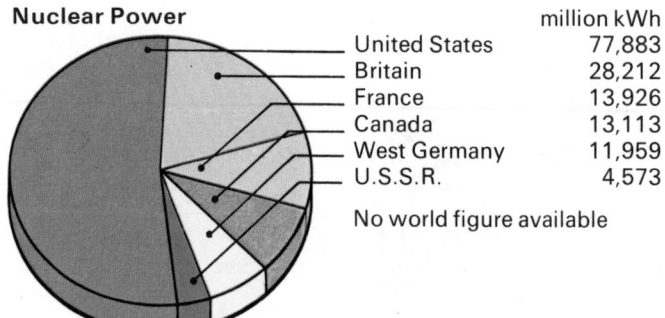

Nuclear Power

	million kWh
United States	77,883
Britain	28,212
France	13,926
Canada	13,113
West Germany	11,959
U.S.S.R.	4,573

No world figure available

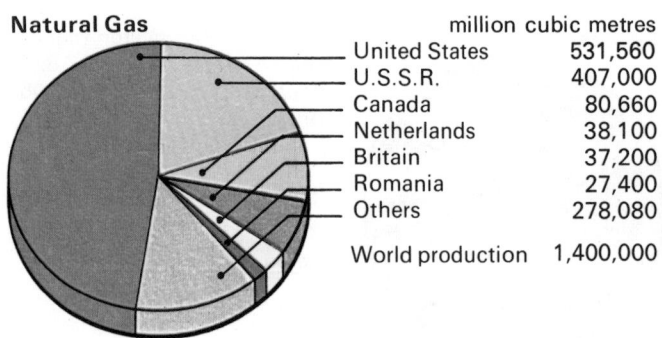

Natural Gas

	million cubic metres
United States	531,560
U.S.S.R.	407,000
Canada	80,660
Netherlands	38,100
Britain	37,200
Romania	27,400
Others	278,080
World production	1,400,000

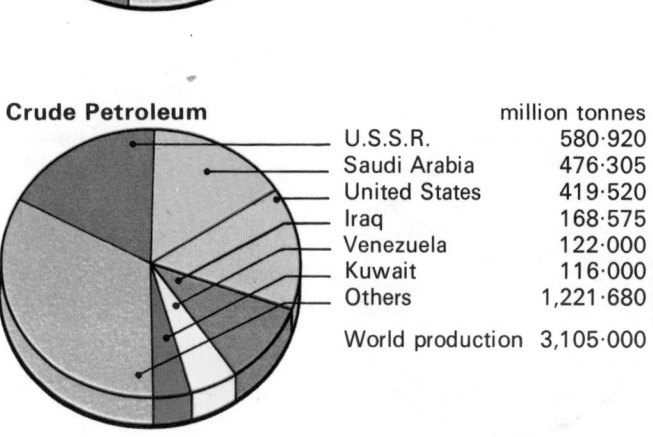

Crude Petroleum

	million tonnes
U.S.S.R.	580·920
Saudi Arabia	476·305
United States	419·520
Iraq	168·575
Venezuela	122·000
Kuwait	116·000
Others	1,221·680
World production	3,105·000

Above: **Drilling for oil in Nigeria, which ranks seventh in world oil production.**

Right: **Modern coal-cutting machinery in a typical, highly mechanized British mine.**

Occupations, Manufacturing and Production

Basic requirements of all peoples are food and shelter, and for this reason the simplest economies are based on the provision of these two things. In parts of Africa and South America, primitive tribes practise subsistence farming, growing just enough food for themselves and their families. The production of a surplus, which can be sold to purchase other goods, is the first step towards development.

Subsistence farming is uneconomic because it requires enormous effort for comparatively little output. Even today, many important countries still have large parts of their working population engaged in agriculture, simply because they are using old-fashioned methods requiring a great deal of labour. For example, 74 per cent of India's workers are in agriculture, but India still has to import some food. In contrast, only 4.2 per cent of the workers are engaged in agriculture in the United States — a major food exporter. Other countries with high proportions of workers in agriculture are Bangladesh (74 per cent) and China (an estimated 62 per cent).

The major manufacturing countries are those of Western and Central Europe, where industrialization began, the United States, Canada and the U.S.S.R. The pattern is changing all the time.

Many of the developing nations, particularly former colonies, are increasing their industries by leaps and bounds, although they still have a long way to go before they catch up with the economies of the European countries.

A measure of a country's industrialization and prosperity is the proportion of its working population engaged in 'services' — non-productive occupations. These include communications, such as transport, press and television, many professional services, such as medicine and law, and the work of civil servants, bankers, shopkeepers, and many more. The United States, for example, has over 60 per cent of workers in services.

Another way of looking at a country's way of working is to consider its Gross Domestic Product — that is, the total value of all the goods and services its people produce in a year. India's 74 per cent engaged in farming contribute 40 per cent of the country's annual wealth, while 48 per cent of West Germany's GDP is produced by the 48 per cent working in industry. It is notable that, in developed countries heavily orientated towards agricultural production — such as Australia, New Zealand and Argentina — the proportion of the GDP produced by it is small: 5 per cent, 10 per cent and 13 per cent respectively.

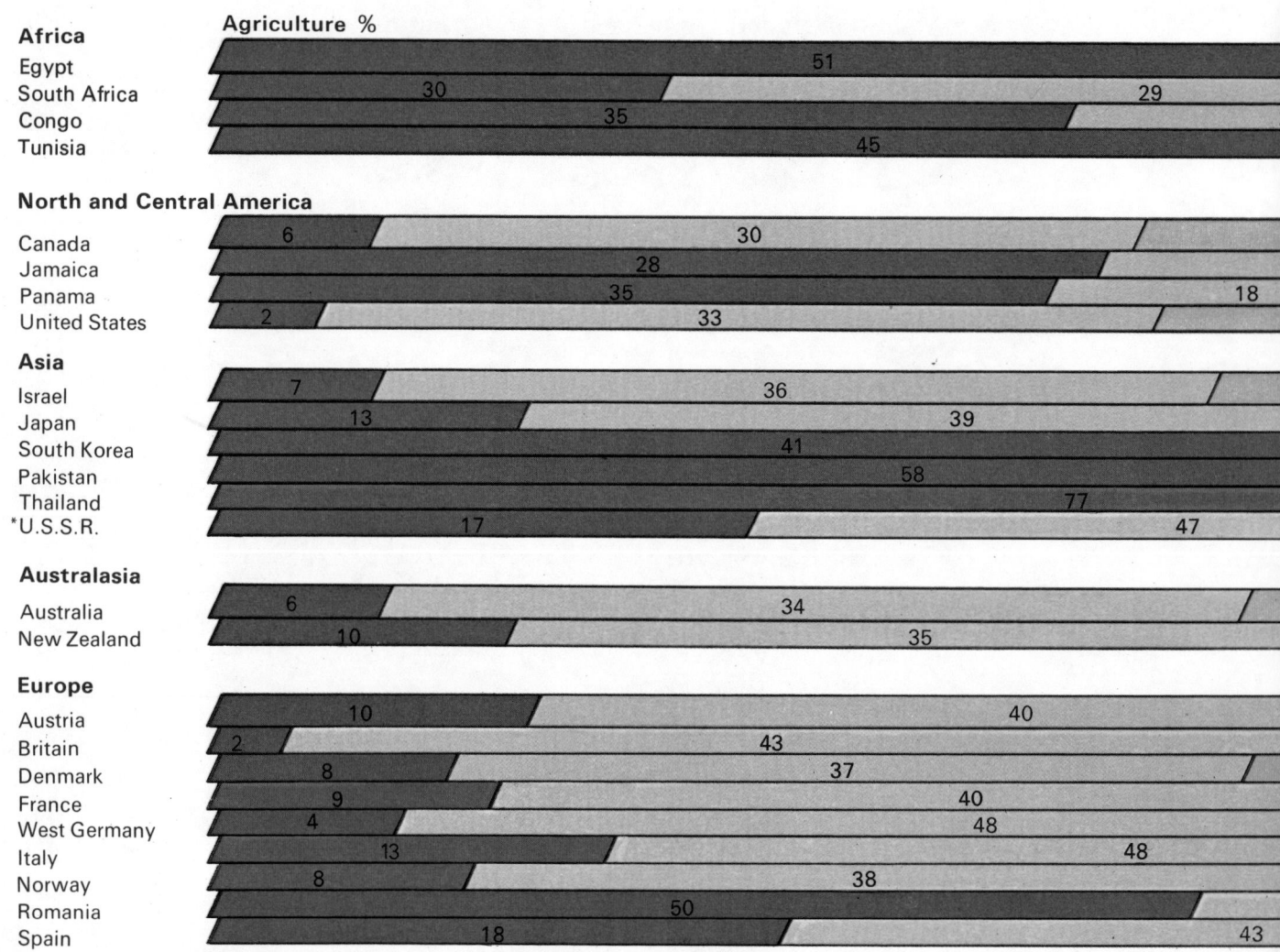

Africa Agriculture %
Egypt · 51
South Africa · 30 · 29
Congo · 35
Tunisia · 45

North and Central America
Canada · 6 · 30
Jamaica · 28
Panama · 35 · 18
United States · 2 · 33

Asia
Israel · 7 · 36
Japan · 13 · 39
South Korea · 41
Pakistan · 58
Thailand · 77
*U.S.S.R. · 17 · 47

Australasia
Australia · 6 · 34
New Zealand · 10 · 35

Europe
Austria · 10 · 40
Britain · 2 · 43
Denmark · 8 · 37
France · 9 · 40
West Germany · 4 · 48
Italy · 13 · 48
Norway · 8 · 38
Romania · 50
Spain · 18 · 43

* Includes European part of the U.S.S.R.

Right: **A television cameraman at work during an outside broadcast. Most workers in radio and television are among those engaged in services – occupations that do not result in the production of goods.**

Below: **The chart shows the proportion of workers engaged in agriculture, industry and services in various countries.**

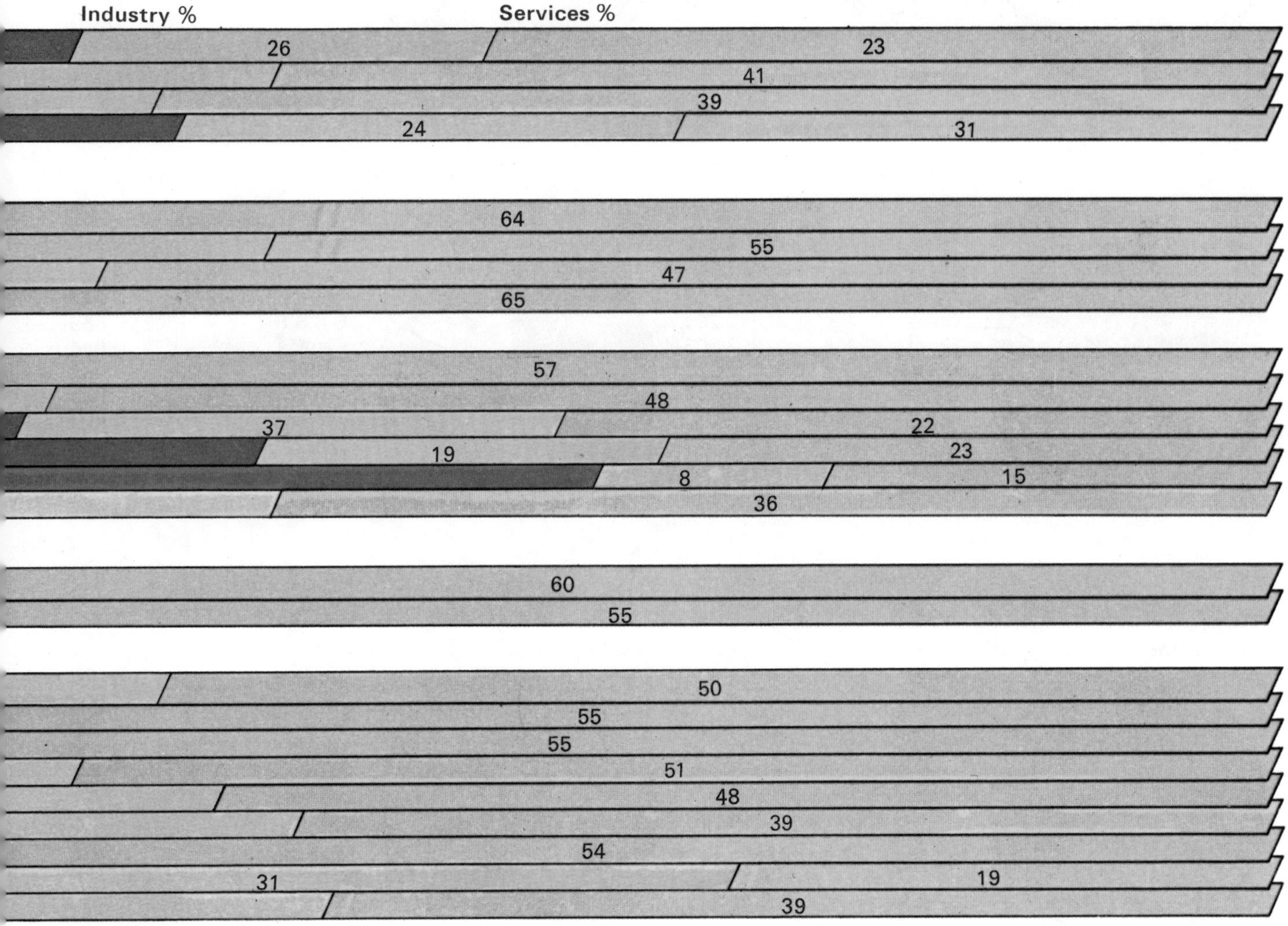

Industry %   Services %

26   23

41

39

24   31

64

55

47

65

57

48

37   22

19   23

8   15

36

60

55

50

55

55

51

48

39

54

31   19

39

Occupations, Manufacturing and Production

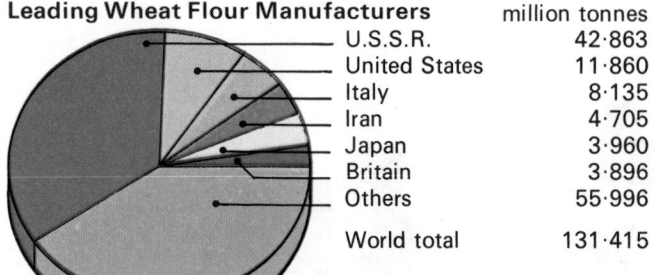

Leading Wheat Flour Manufacturers

million tonnes

U.S.S.R.	42·863
United States	11·860
Italy	8·135
Iran	4·705
Japan	3·960
Britain	3·896
Others	55·996
World total	131·415

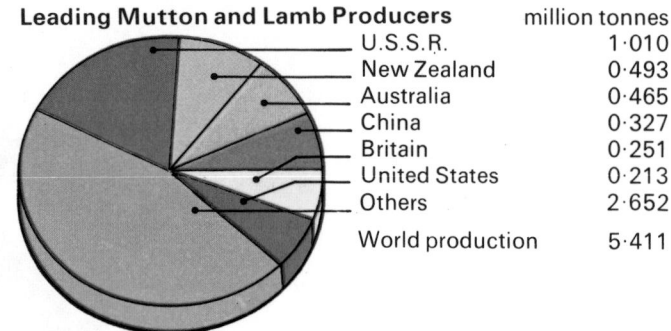

Leading Mutton and Lamb Producers

million tonnes

U.S.S.R.	1·010
New Zealand	0·493
Australia	0·465
China	0·327
Britain	0·251
United States	0·213
Others	2·652
World production	5·411

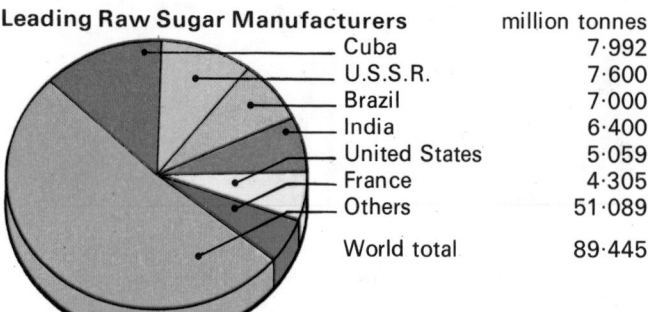

Leading Raw Sugar Manufacturers

million tonnes

Cuba	7·992
U.S.S.R.	7·600
Brazil	7·000
India	6·400
United States	5·059
France	4·305
Others	51·089
World total	89·445

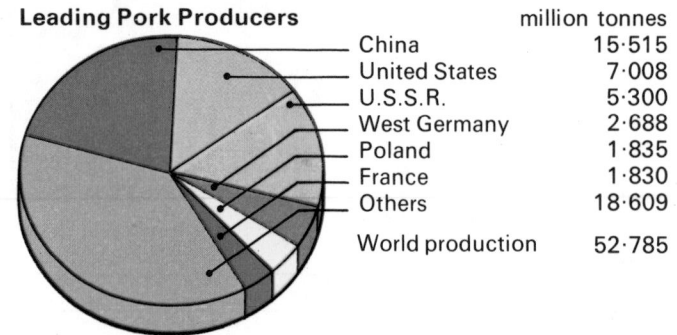

Leading Pork Producers

million tonnes

China	15·515
United States	7·008
U.S.S.R.	5·300
West Germany	2·688
Poland	1·835
France	1·830
Others	18·609
World production	52·785

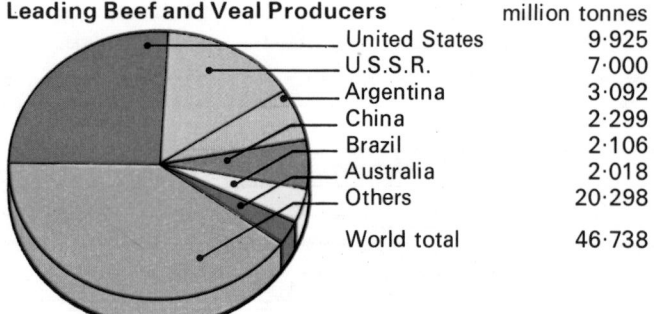

Leading Beef and Veal Producers

million tonnes

United States	9·925
U.S.S.R.	7·000
Argentina	3·092
China	2·299
Brazil	2·106
Australia	2·018
Others	20·298
World total	46·738

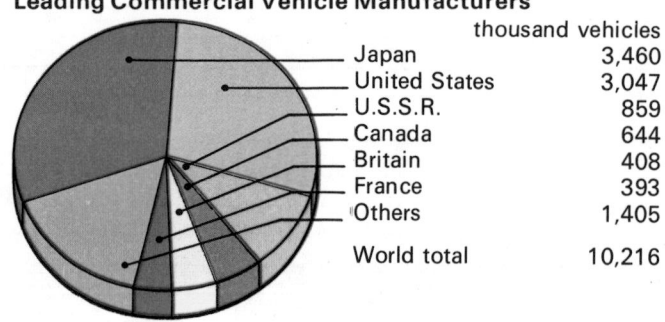

Leading Commercial Vehicle Manufacturers

thousand vehicles

Japan	3,460
United States	3,047
U.S.S.R.	859
Canada	644
Britain	408
France	393
Others	1,405
World total	10,216

Leading Motor-car Manufacturers

thousand cars

United States	8,434
Japan	6,176
West Germany	3,933
France	3,220
Italy	1,481
U.S.S.R.	1,314
Others	6,253
World total	30,811

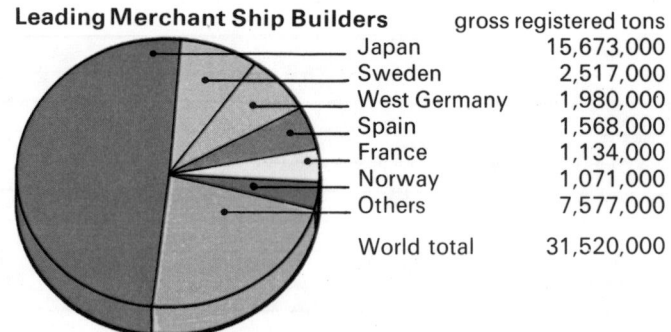

Leading Merchant Ship Builders

gross registered tons

Japan	15,673,000
Sweden	2,517,000
West Germany	1,980,000
Spain	1,568,000
France	1,134,000
Norway	1,071,000
Others	7,577,000
World total	31,520,000

Leading Cotton Yarn Manufacturers

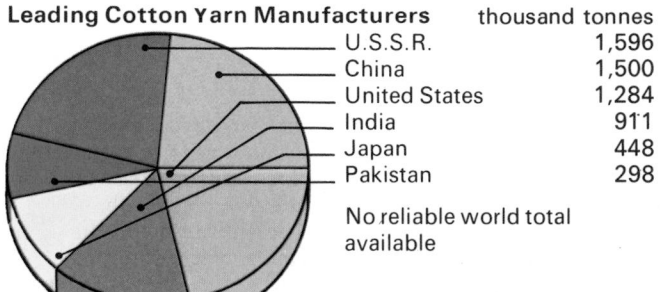

thousand tonnes

U.S.S.R.	1,596
China	1,500
United States	1,284
India	911
Japan	448
Pakistan	298

No reliable world total available

Leading Wood Pulp Manufacturers

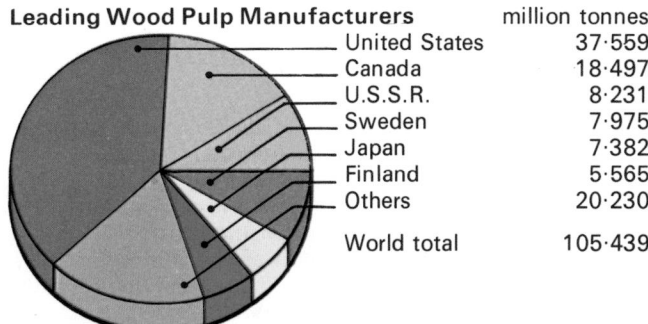

million tonnes

United States	37·559
Canada	18·497
U.S.S.R.	8·231
Sweden	7·975
Japan	7·382
Finland	5·565
Others	20·230
World total	105·439

Leading Wool Yarn Manufacturers

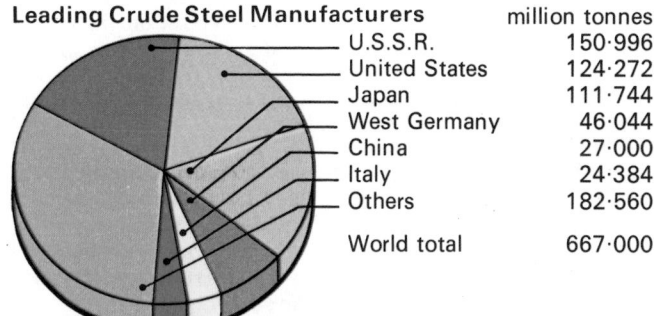

thousand tonnes

U.S.S.R.	393
Britain	235
Italy	199
Japan	198
France	152
United States	89

No reliable world total available

Leading Crude Steel Manufacturers

million tonnes

U.S.S.R.	150·996
United States	124·272
Japan	111·744
West Germany	46·044
China	27·000
Italy	24·384
Others	182·560
World total	667·000

Left: **Car bodies meeting their chassis on an assembly line at the Volkswagen factory in West Germany. Mass production methods were first introduced into the car industry in the United States by Ransom E. Olds in 1901. They have become the pattern for much industrial production of today.**

Transport

Good transport is the key to all industrial development and trade. It is essential to carry raw materials from their sources to where they are processed and turned into manufactured products, and also to carry those products to people who want to buy them. Transport is also needed to carry people from place to place.

The three basic kinds of transport are by land, sea and air. Patterns of transport change with the demands of traffic and the development of technology. Before World War II, most passenger traffic across the Atlantic Ocean was by sea; but, with the development of aviation, most transatlantic travellers now fly. Ships are still the cheapest and most efficient way of moving bulk cargoes from one place to another over long distances and, with the growth of fast highways and powerful trucks, road and sea transport are becoming more and more linked. Containers that can be carried by road and loaded straight onto ships are an increasingly popular way of carrying all but the bulkiest goods.

Liquids such as petroleum and natural gas are carried by a combination of giant, ocean-going tankers and overland pipelines. Major pipeline systems extend across North America, Western Europe and the U.S.S.R. The Russian system links with pipelines from the Arab oil states of the Middle East and also with Western Europe. All these networks are being continually extended as new supplies of oil and gas are developed.

Railways, the backbone of land transport in the late 1800s and for the first half of this century, are giving way in many parts of the world to road traffic, which is more economical to run and delivers goods from door to door. Inland waterways — rivers and canals — have maintained their importance in some parts of the world, particularly Western Europe, where there are many major navigable rivers.

PRINCIPAL MERCHANT FLEETS

It is difficult to say which country in the world actually has the largest merchant shipping fleet, because many shipping companies of other countries register their ships in Liberia and Panama. This is because these two countries charge lower taxes and enforce rules governing wages and safety regulations less severely. The table which follows gives an indication, in gross tonnage rather than numbers of vessels, of ship registrations.

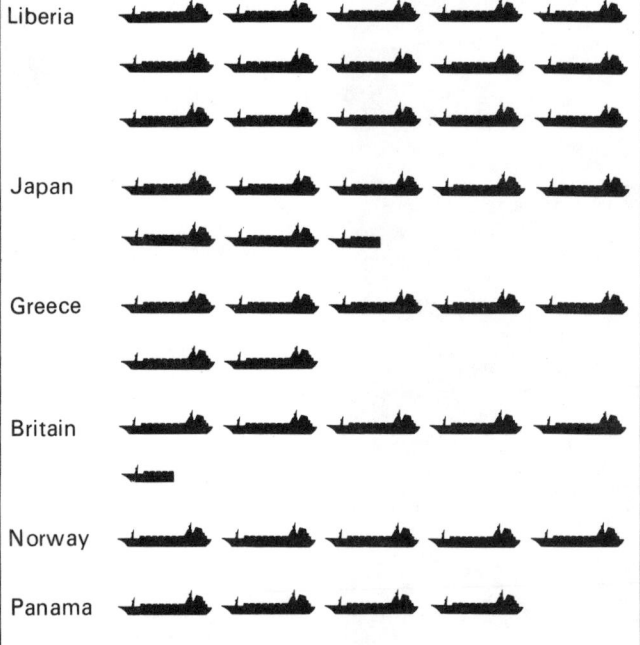

Liberia

Japan

Greece

Britain

Norway

Panama

U.S.S.R.

United States

Each symbol equals 5 million tons. Figures based on Lloyd's Register of Shipping.

Leading Car-owning Countries

United States

New Zealand

Canada

Australia

Sweden

West Germany

Each symbol equals 100 cars per 1000 people.

Leading Commercial-vehicle-owning Countries

United States

Japan

Australia

Canada

New Zealand

Britain

Each symbol equals 20 vehicles per 1000 people.

Below: **Sea transport remains the best and most economical method of carrying bulky cargo over long distances. Here, a bus is being loaded onto a ship at Miami Harbor in Florida.**

The volume of sea and air traffic has meant a great deal of international co-operation to ensure speedy and safe communication. Countries co-operate in providing up-to-date charts for shipping and weather forecasting. Some particularly busy sea routes, such as the English Channel, are 'policed' by the countries bordering them to make sure ships keep to recognized channels and so avoid collisions. Air transport comes under the control of a United Nations agency, the International Civil Aviation Organization, which has its headquarters in Montreal, Canada.

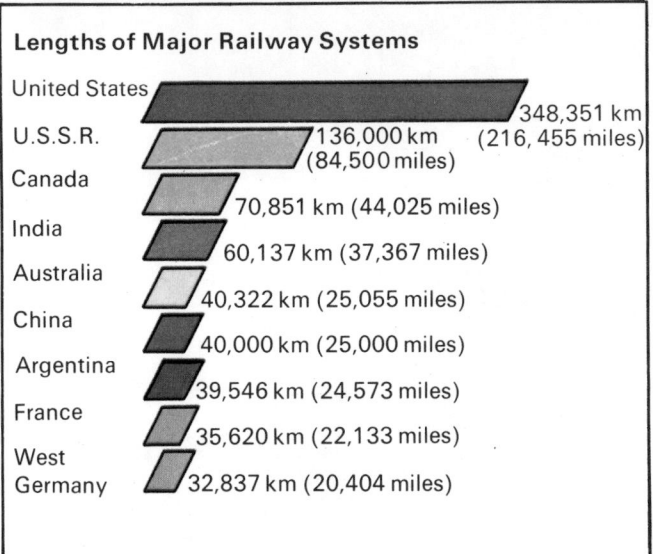

Lengths of Major Railway Systems

Country	Length
United States	348,351 km (216,455 miles)
U.S.S.R.	136,000 km (84,500 miles)
Canada	70,851 km (44,025 miles)
India	60,137 km (37,367 miles)
Australia	40,322 km (25,055 miles)
China	40,000 km (25,000 miles)
Argentina	39,546 km (24,573 miles)
France	35,620 km (22,133 miles)
West Germany	32,837 km (20,404 miles)

AVIATION FLEETS AND CONSTRUCTION

The world's airlines have around 10,000 passenger aircraft in service, but the numbers are constantly fluctuating. This is because new developments, such as faster and larger aircraft, make it possible to operate services efficiently with fewer planes, while developing countries, such as those of Africa, are building up their airlines.

The aircraft industry is concentrated in the United States, which has more than half the market, the U.S.S.R. with one-third, and the countries of Western Europe, particularly Britain, France, West Germany, Italy and the Netherlands. Canada also has a thriving construction industry. The enormous cost of development of new aircraft is tending to concentrate the industry into fewer and larger units, with several countries sharing the development and construction of new kinds of aircraft.

World Trade

World trade has developed over hundreds of years. Even back in medieval times, European countries used to export goods made by their craftsmen to other parts of the globe to pay for raw materials not available at home. With the growth of the Industrial Revolution from the 1750s onwards, this pattern of trade became intensified. Today, the countries of Europe are highly industrialized. Together with the United States, Canada and Japan, which have developed along European lines, they export manufactured goods and import mostly raw materials and food.

The developing countries of the world rely for their trade on minerals they can mine and food they can grow. To an extent, this even applies to the Europeanized countries, such as Australia, New Zealand and South Africa, whose industries still do not play a dominant part in their economies, even though they may absorb the bulk of the workforce.

However, clear-cut trading patterns in the style of the 1800s, when the industrialized countries produced all the world's goods, no longer exist. Most countries now have some industry and are developing more rapidly, while the biggest of all industrialized countries, the United States, is a major exporter of foodstuffs such as cereals. There is a growing tendency for countries to specialize in goods and services. For example, the Netherlands and Israel lead in cutting diamonds; Britain is a centre for banking and insurance; Japan is outstanding for photographic equipment; and Denmark and New Zealand are major producers of butter.

Financing international trade is a complicated business. Banks and other finance organizations, including the International Monetary Fund, operate the international finance market, through which traders can obtain currency to pay for the goods they buy. For example, a merchant in Brazil (currency, cruzeiros) may buy goods from India (rupees), which are carried in an American ship (dollars) and insured in Britain (pounds). Through the international banking network, the merchant can get the money he needs — even though Brazil may not possess any rupees. The necessary currency may well come through New York or London, two of the world's leading financial centres.

The Principal Food Importing and Exporting Countries

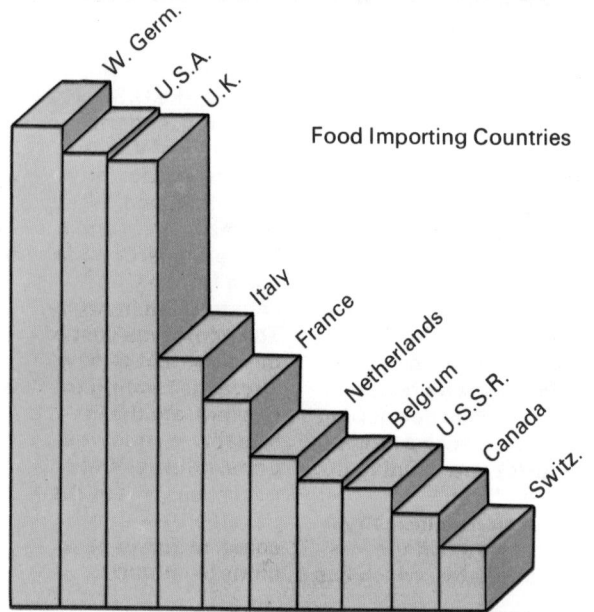

Food Importing Countries

W. Germ. U.S.A. U.K. Italy France Netherlands Belgium U.S.S.R. Canada Switz.

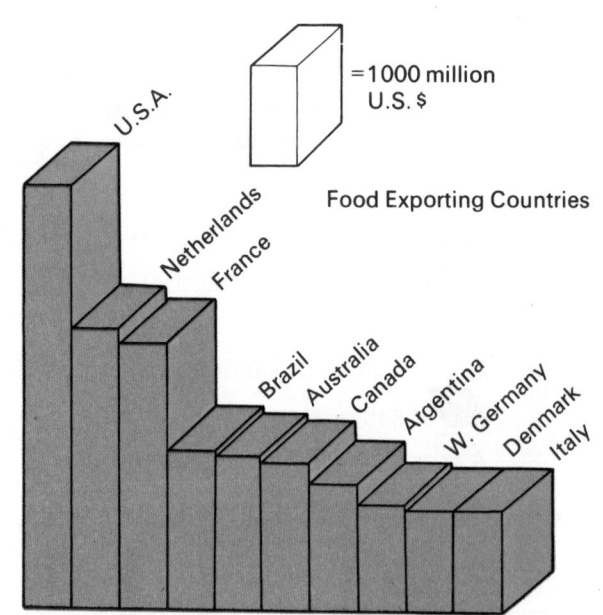

=1000 million U.S. $

Food Exporting Countries

U.S.A. Netherlands France Brazil Australia Canada Argentina W. Germany Denmark Italy

Above left: **A million pounds in gold bullion, notes and coins photographed in the vaults of Hambros Bank in the City of London.**

Overleaf: **A busy dockyard scene at Dar-es-Salaam, Tanzania.**

Annual Imports and Exports of Leading Countries

Figures are in millions of US$.

Country	Imports	Exports	Country	Imports	Exports
Algeria	10,560	12,410	Iraq	12,936	26,352
Argentina	6,400	7,800	Ireland (Republic)	11,153	8,502
Australia	22,331	22,061	Israel	8,593	5,528
Austria	24,456	17,502	Italy	99,475	77,685
			Japan	141,289	130,469
Belgium with Luxembourg	71,612	64,499	Kuwait	7,285	20,332
Brazil	25,002	20,132	Malaysia	7,849	11,077
Britain	120,154	115,117	Mexico	19,460	15,348
Canada	62,566	67,529	Netherlands	78,073	73,826
Chile	5,821	4,818	New Zealand	5,473	5,421
Colombia	4,739	3,925	Nigeria	15,792	26,742
Cuba	5,100	5,300	Norway	16,956	18,299
Czechoslovakia	14,300	13,200	Philippines	8,182	5,704
Denmark	19,322	16,742	Poland	na	na
Finland	15,632	14,168	Portugal	6,534	3,480
France	134,874	116,016	Saudi Arabia	33,060	102,548
Germany (East)	17,600	16,200	Spain	34,078	26,720
Germany (West)	187,933	192,901	Sweden	33,438	30,912
Ghana	937	933	Switzerland	36,360	29,647
Greece	9,614	3,885	Turkey	5,070	2,261
Hungary	10,200	8,800	United States	252,997	220,706
India	12,600	5,906	Venezuela	11,390	23,000
Indonesia	7,202	15,590	Yugoslavia	15,076	8,989
Iran	17,700	21,700	Zaire	835	1,632

The United States of America

The Continental Congress adopted the 'Stars and Stripes' as the U.S. flag in June, 1777. The pattern of stars for the present 50-star flag was fixed by order of President Dwight D. Eisenhower.

Birth and Growth of the Nation

The United States of America came into being on July 4, 1776, as the result of the determination of the citizens of 13 British colonies to control their own destinies. It has become the world's richest country in just three centuries.

The country is the fourth largest in the world — only the U.S.S.R., Canada, and China are larger — and it also has the fourth largest population — only China, India, and the U.S.S.R. have more people. The first census, taken in 1790, showed there were 3,929,214 people in the new young country. Today, the population is 226,000,000, and it is growing at the rate of about 0.75 per cent each year.

The people of the United States are of all races and creeds. During the 1800s, the growing country welcomed immigrants from all over the world and, in particular, from Europe. Today, about 95 per cent of all Americans are native born.

The United States is now one of the most highly mechanized countries in the world. As a result, although it has the highest production of manufactured goods, and is one of the world's major food producers, less than half the working population is engaged in producing goods and food.

The Land and Climate

The Land

The United States, the world's fourth largest nation, is a country of tremendous contrasts. It contains lofty fold mountains and high plateaux, fertile coastal plains and vast inland prairies, enormous forests and barren, burning-hot deserts. The four main physical regions are the coastal lowlands, the Appalachian region, the central lowlands and the western highlands.

The coastal lowlands are in the southeast and east. In the southeast, they extend in a broad belt from Texas to Florida, reaching a maximum width of about 500 kilometres (300 miles). From Florida, the coastal lowlands extend northwards to the New England states, gradually diminishing in width. The Atlantic coast is deeply indented by bays, around which such ports as Baltimore, Boston, New York City and Philadelphia have grown up. The rivers of the eastern coastlands, including the Delaware, Hudson and Potomac, are mostly short. But the central part of the broad southeastern coastlands is dominated by the great Mississippi River.

The Appalachian region extends from Newfoundland, in Canada, to Alabama. It is a complex region of fold mountains, plateaux and valleys. The undulating Piedmont region borders the eastern coastal lowlands. The boundary between the Piedmont and the lowlands is called the 'fall line', because rapids and waterfalls occur along it. West of the Piedmont is the beautiful Great Smokies-Blue Ridge region, where Mount Mitchell, the Appalachians' highest peak, rises to 2,037 metres (6,683 feet) above sea level. To the west is the Ridge and Valley region, which extends from New York to Alabama. Beyond lies the Appalachian Plateau, parts of which are rugged and deeply dissected by rivers.

The central, or interior lowlands extend east-west from the Appalachian Plateau to the western highlands. The area around the Great Lakes on the Canadian border is, strictly, an extension of the Canadian Laurentian (Pre-Cambrian) Shield, the oldest part of North America. The Great Lakes are the world's largest group of freshwater lakes. The magnificent Niagara Falls are on the Niagara River, which links lakes Erie and Ontario.

The central lowlands contain much of the best farmland in the United States and most of the courses of two of the world's mightiest rivers, the Mississippi and Missouri. The region is not all flat. It includes the low plateau of Kentucky and Tennessee, the Ozark Plateau and the Ouachita Mountains. In the west, the central lowlands rise towards the Great Plains, which border the western highlands. The Great Plains are 450 to 1,800 metres (1,476 to 5,906 feet) above sea level, although the Black Hills, a high outlier of the Rockies, rise above the plains.

The western highlands include the folded Rocky Mountains, high plateaux and deep basins, and the Pacific mountains. This upland zone extends from Alaska, through Canada and the United States, into Mexico. The Rockies reach their highest

Above right: **Birches in fall colours in the Berkshire Hills of western Massachusetts.**

Right: **The Red Canyon in Utah, showing the fantastic shapes into which wind and rain have carved the rocks over millions of years.**

UNITED STATES: FACTS AND FIGURES
Total Area: 9,519,853 square kilometres (3,675,633 square miles), including Hawaii
Population: 226 million
Monetary Unit: Dollar ($); 100 cents = $1.00
Political Divisions: 50 States; the Commonwealth of Puerto Rico; Panama Canal Zone; island possessions
Federal Capital: Washington, D.C.
Official Language: English
Flag: Thirteen stripes, red and white, representing the 13 original states, and 50 white stars on a blue ground, representing the present 50 states
Highest Mountain: Mount McKinley, Alaska, 6,194 metres (20,320 feet) above sea level
Longest River: Mississippi, 3,779 kilometres (2,348 miles)
Lowest Elevation: Death Valley, Cal., 86 metres (282 feet) below sea level

extent in Colorado, where many peaks are over 4,250 metres (13,944 feet) above sea level. The plateaux include the lava-covered Columbia Plateau in the northwest and the Colorado Plateau in the south. The gradual uplift of the Colorado Plateau, which was once a flat coastal plain, gave a new cutting edge to the Colorado River, enabling it to carve out one of the world's wonders — the Grand Canyon. Down-faulted basins, such as the Great Basin which contains the Great Salt Lake of Utah, are another striking feature of the western highlands. In the southwest, the Basin and Range region contains uplifted block mountains, often bordered by steep scarp faults.

The Pacific mountains in the far west include two mountain chains, separated by a trough. The eastern chain includes the Alaska range, where Mount McKinley, the highest peak in the United States, towers 6,194 metres (20,231 feet) above sea level. The eastern chain extends through Canada into the United States, where it includes the Cascades and the Sierra Nevadas. Mount Whitney in the Sierra Nevada is 4,418 metres (14,495 feet) above sea level. The western, or coastal chain includes the islands off Alaska and British Columbia (Canada), and the coastal ranges of Washington, Oregon and California. The central trough includes the fertile Great Valley of California. In eastern California, Death Valley contains the lowest point in the United States — 86 metres (282 feet) below sea level.

Hawaii, the 50th state of the United States, lies far away in the central Pacific Ocean. It is a string of volcanic and coral islands.

Climate

The chief factors affecting the climate of the United States are latitude, relief, proximity to the sea and the movements of major air masses.

East of the Rockies, the weather is dominated by the interplay between the polar continental (PC) air mass and the tropical maritime (TM) air mass. The cold, dry PC air brings cold weather to the central lowlands, especially in winter. It is sometimes felt as far south as the Gulf coast. The TM air moves into the interior from the Gulf of Mexico, especially in summer. When it encounters the PC air, it rises and rain falls.

West of the Rockies, the coastal areas of California are affected by TM air from the Pacific. But the northwestern coast gets its abundant rainfall from the moist Polar Maritime (PM) air mass. The PM air flows eastwards, bringing rain to the mountain slopes. Usually, it cannot penetrate beyond the Rockies, because it is forced above the denser PC air. But, if the PC air mass is weak, the PM air descends, becoming gradually warmer and drier. This air movement forms the Chinook wind, which melts the snows of Montana on the leeward side of the Rockies.

East of the Rockies, climatic zones occur in broadly latitudinal strips from subtropical in southern Florida, to humid subtropical in the Southern States, humid continental with a long summer in the midwest and northeast, and humid continental with a short summer around the Canadian border. The west coast has a Mediterranean climate in the southwest (California) and a wet temperate zone in the northwest.

The western highlands have arid or semi-arid climates, which are subtropical in the south and temperate in the north, although the higher parts have true mountain climates. Alaska is a subarctic and tundra region.

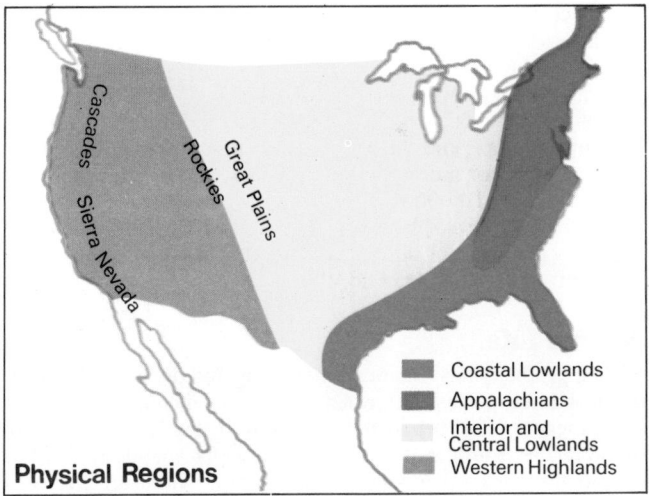

Physical Regions

Coastal Lowlands
Appalachians
Interior and Central Lowlands
Western Highlands

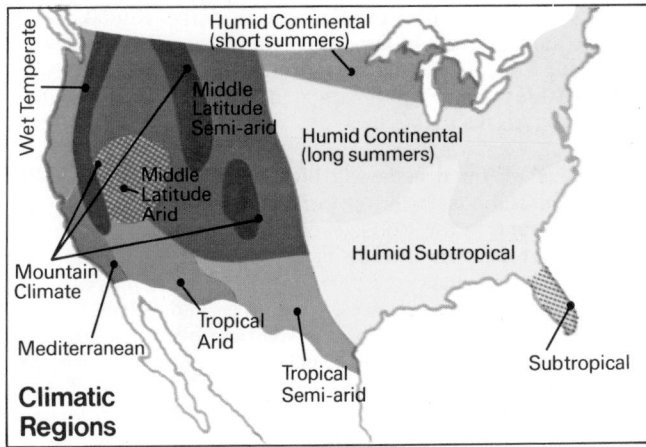

Climatic Regions

Plants and Animals

The huge size of the mainland portion of the United States — over 4,500 kilometres (2,800 miles) east to west, and 2,500 kilometres (1,500 miles) north to south — with all the climatic variations involved, means that there is a great range of plant and animal life. In addition, there is the wild life of Hawaii and Alaska.

Plant Life

The northern part of Alaska is tundra, the polar desert where only lichens, mosses and a few other low-growing plants can withstand the long, cold winters. The short summer months are bright with such flowers as skunk cabbage, red Alpine bearberries and fritillaries. The more southern parts of Alaska have forests of pine, fir and spruce, with a few species of broad-leaved trees. A similar pattern of Arctic and subarctic vegetation occurs farther south in the main part of the country, where the height of the Rocky Mountains cancels out the warmer effects normally associated with lower latitudes.

Forests of mixed deciduous and coniferous trees extend along the Canadian frontier, and southwards in the Appalachian Mountains. Farther south in the Appalachians and in the Blue Ridge area, the forest is a mixture of broadleafed trees, including ash, beech, hickory, maple, oak and walnut. The sandy coastal areas in the east have many pine forests, with mangroves in the swamp region of Florida.

The central part of the United States, between the Appalachians and the Rockies, is basically grassland, much of which has been ploughed for cultivation. The land from Texas, west to California, is essentially desert mixed with grassland. Typical plants of this desert region include yuccas, Joshua trees, mesquites and cacti. Among the trees of the western forests are the giant sequoias and the bristlecone pines. Sequoias have been known to live for more than 3,000 years, and bristlecone pines sometimes exceed 4,000 years.

America's native plants include almost 25,000 species of flowering plants and 1,000 species of trees; but many others have been introduced from the Old World.

Animal Life

Alaska probably has the most interesting and distinctive wildlife in the United States. Large land mammals include the Kodiak bear, biggest of all bears, the grey-coated grizzly, which is also found farther south, and the polar bear, which spends much of its life on the pack ice in the extreme north. There are herds of heavy-shouldered musk-oxen, long-maned caribou, and giant moose, which are often even bigger than the Kodiak bears. Smaller animals include lemmings, white-coated Arctic hares, and Arctic foxes. In the sea are walruses and sea otters. Alaska's rich bird life includes puffins and other seabirds, the willow ptarmigan (Alaska's state bird) and the U.S. emblem – the bald eagle.

In the rest of America, the wild life is closely allied to the type of vegetation. Rabbits, beavers, porcupines, squirrels and other rodents abound in the wooded regions of the mountains in the west. Larger animals include bighorn sheep, mule deer, and Rocky Mountain goats, and these plant-eaters are preyed on by mountain lions (pumas), lynxes, bears, foxes and wolves.

The grasslands are home for the American bison, the so-called 'buffalo' which used to roam the plains in huge herds before the white man came. In 1850 there were nearly 70 million of these huge animals; but, by 1889, only 541 were left. Several thousand bison now live in carefully-protected herds in national parks.

Other animals of the grasslands are jackrabbits, prairie dogs, ground squirrels, and gophers, preyed on by the coyote and the badger. Lizards, turtles and snakes also live in the region. As the grasslands give way to deserts, the animal life becomes less varied, and the larger animals find it difficult to win enough food. But smaller creatures, such as rabbits, survive, and these in turn provide food for foxes.

In the eastern part of the country, including the forests of the Appalachian range and the coastal plains, it is mainly the smaller animals that have survived the presence of man. Woods provide shelter and a living for skunks, raccoons, squirrels, rabbits, muskrats and porcupines.

Down in the swamplands of Florida lives the largest of land reptiles, the alligator, once facing extinction but now preserved and increasing in numbers again. Other reptiles, including many kinds of snakes, lizards, turtles and the Gila monster, are found in various parts of the land.

Many of the animals, though particularly common in certain regions, are also found in nearly every part of the United States. Notable among these animals are squirrels, snapping turtles, rabbits, beavers and deer.

A great many species of birds are native to North America, and settlers have imported many more from the Old World. Songbirds include bluebirds, wrens, warblers, thrushes, robins, orioles, chickadees, finches and sparrows, while birds of prey include eagles, falcons, ospreys, hawks and owls. Distinctive American game birds include wild turkeys, woodcock and prairie chickens. The water birds include the flamingo, the roseate spoonbill and the Louisiana heron.

PIGEON TRAGEDY
Of all the birds in North America, the most numerous was the passenger pigeon, a largish pigeon that nested in the woodlands of the east and central regions. In the early 1800s, there were almost 9,000 million of these birds. One flock seen by the naturalist John James Audubon took three hours to pass overhead. Then the hunters began their deadly work — one killed 24,000 birds in 10 days — and, within a few years, the millions had dwindled to thousands. The last wild passenger pigeon was killed in 1900, and the last survivor in captivity died in a zoo in 1914.

HAWAIIAN WILD LIFE
The tropical volcanic islands of Hawaii have a unique flora and fauna because of their isolation from the rest of the world. There are about 900 species of flowering plants in the islands, and many of them were there long before Europeans arrived. They include the flaming wiliwili, colourful species of hibiscus, the glowing, spiky ohia lehua, the white-petalled pua-kala (poppy) and the bushy silversword, whose long, greyish leaves look like a forest of upward-pointed swordblades under the tall cylinder of small red flowers.

One species of bat, blown there perhaps by some freak wind, was the only native mammal; the Hawaiians themselves introduced dogs, pigs, rats and mice. More than 100 species of birds include the orange-breasted honey creepers.

Below: **Bison – the 'buffalo' of the pioneers – now survive only in national parks. Millions of bison once roamed the plains.**

Above: **A giant sequoia in Yosemite Park, California.**

Below: **A raccoon catching fish.**

Below right: **The saguaro cactus of the Arizona desert may grow as much as 15 metres (50 feet) tall. It is also called the giant cactus.**

The American People

The first men came to what is now the United States possibly some time between 10,000 and 20,000 years ago. They were the ancestors of present-day American Indians and Eskimos, and they came from Asia across the Bering Sea, either over ice or over a land bridge that no longer exists. They were Mongoloid peoples, related to the Chinese and Japanese of today.

The Indians formed hundreds of different tribes, each with its own language and customs. Many of them were nomads, wandering from place to place in search of food. Some gathered seeds, nuts and fruit; others hunted. Some tribes, particularly in the east, led more settled lives and did some farming.

The next arrivals were a group of Norsemen led by the Viking Leif Ericsson in AD 1002. Some Norse colonies were founded soon afterwards, but they did not survive for long. Even the memory of a land across the Atlantic had largely died out in Europe by the time of the epic voyage of Christopher Columbus in 1492. Columbus never realized that he had found a whole New World, but other Spanish and Portuguese explorers quickly did.

Spanish *conquistadores* (conquerors) founded the first settlements in what is now the United States in the 1500s, but the first true colonies were English. The first successful settlement was at Jamestown, Va., in 1607. In 1620 the Pilgrim Fathers, Puritan refugees from England, landed at Plymouth, Mass., and founded the first New England colony. Progress in government was rapid. Virginia had its first legislature by 1619, while the Puritan leaders of Massachusetts established strong government from the first.

Colonies grew quickly all along the Atlantic seaboard. The Dutch set up the colony of New Netherland in 1624, but the English absorbed it and renamed it New York 40 years later. The Quaker colony of Pennsylvania, founded in 1681, attracted Scots, Irish and German settlers, besides the English. The French, with settlements in Canada, claimed the whole of the Mississippi river valley and founded settlements at the river mouth from 1699 onwards. The Spaniards began settling Florida as early as 1689.

When Britain's 13 North American colonies declared their independence in 1776, most of the people were of English or Irish descent. In 1790, when the first U.S. census was taken, three-fourths of the American people were of British origin. But the development of the Industrial Revolution brought a great change. Between 1820 and 1860, more than 5,000,000 immigrants landed in the United States, many of them to work in the growing number of factories. They came from more than 20 countries. Germany contributed 1,486,000; England and Scotland, 1,783,000; Ireland, beset by famine and want, 967,000; and France, 208,000. Other immigrants came from China, Italy, Norway, Poland, Spain and Sweden.

In the 1880s, a new wave of immigration began. Between 1881 and 1890, 4,737,000 immigrants arrived, and many of them were from the poorer regions of southern and eastern Europe, mostly Austria-Hungary, Italy and Russia. Between 1901 and 1910, 8,136,000 immigrants arrived. The flood continued after World War I until, in 1921, Congress finally voted a quota law to slow the rate. The sufferings of Europe in World War II led to a further wave of immigrants — 4,571,000 between 1945 and 1964.

Negro slaves were imported into America from the early 1500s and, by 1776, Negroes formed almost one-third of the population of the new United States. By 1860, there were 4,442,000 Negroes in the country. At the time of the 1970 census, there were 22,580,000 — representing about 11 per cent of the population at that time.

Today, the people of the United States are a mixture of many races. Only about 5 per cent were born in other countries, though 13 per cent are first-generation Americans — children of immigrants. About half the population claim specific ethnic origins — almost 50 million from the British Isles, 25 million from Germany, 9 million from Spain, more than 8.5 million from Italy, 5 million from Poland, and 2 million from Russia.

Each of these many nationalities has brought its own culture to America, but although some traditions persist — such as the Mardi Gras festivities of French-speaking New Orleans, or the Pennsylvania German Folklore Festival in Kutztown, Pa. — the universal educational system and the use of English as the national language has tended to blend together all these varying cultural backgrounds.

HISTORIC AMERICAN UNIVERSITIES

The following 13 U.S. universities and colleges were founded before the outbreak of the Revolutionary War in 1775.

Name	Date	Location
Brown University	1764	Providence, R.I.
Charleston College	1770	Charleston, S.C.
Columbia University	1758	New York, N.Y.
Dartmouth College	1769	Hanover, N.H.
Dickinson College	1773	Carlisle, Pa.
Harvard University	1636	Cambridge, Mass.
Pennsylvania University	1756	Philadelphia, Pa.
Princeton University	1746	Princeton, N.J.
Rutgers University	1766	New Brunswick, N.J.
St. John's College	1696	Annapolis, Md.
Salem College	1772	Winston-Salem, N.C.
William and Mary College	1693	Williamsburg, Va.
Yale University	1701	New Haven, Conn.

The people of Hawaii have their own ethnic and cultural blend. About 15 per cent are Hawaiians — that is, descendants of the Polynesian peoples who first settled the islands. Some 40 per cent are of European stock, and 30 per cent are Japanese. There are also many Chinese and Filipinos.

The people of European stock are principally British (via mainland America), Portuguese, Germans, Italians, Poles, Norwegians, Russians and Spaniards.

EDUCATION IN THE UNITED STATES
Children of school age total about 23 per cent of the population of the United States, while another 4.6 per cent are enrolled in institutions of higher education — universities, colleges and professional schools. Laws vary from state to state but, generally, education is compulsory until age 16 or 17, or until graduation if this is earlier. Despite this, a U.S. Office of Education four-year survey published in 1975 showed that 23 million adult Americans come into the 'functionally illiterate' category, with insufficient knowledge of reading to cope with newspaper advertisements.

Left: **Louis Armstrong ('Satchmo')** helped to popularize the Negro music of jazz all over the world.

Above right: **Navaho women still weave their traditional blankets in their tribal home in Arizona.**

Right: **Most of the people in New York City's Harlem district are Negroes or Latin Americans, living in overcrowded conditions.**

Far right: **A hula dancer from Oahu Island, Hawaii.**

History and Politics

The 13 British colonies that formed the United States of America in 1776 were settled largely by people of independent mind, who had come to America to find political or religious freedom. For many years they had remained generally contented to be under the nominal rule of Britain. But, when the British government attempted to tax the colonies in the late 1760s and early 1770s, the colonists resisted violently. This resistance boiled over into open fighting in 1775, and the historic Declaration of Independence on July 4, 1776.

The Articles of Confederation (ratified 1781), under which the United States' first government was set up, gave that government inadequate powers. This weakness very soon became apparent and, in 1787, a meeting of delegates from 12 of the states devised a new form of administration, embodied in the United States Constitution. The Constitution came into force in 1789, and George Washington, military hero of the Revolutionary War, was elected as the first president.

Two political parties — the Federalists and the Democratic-Republicans — arose almost at once and, for the next 40 years, they controlled the new nation's affairs.

In 1803 came the first big change in the United States, when President Thomas Jefferson bought the Louisiana Territory from the French ruler, Napoleon Bonaparte, who realized he could never defend it. The Lousiana Purchase, for about $15 million, almost doubled the size of the country.

Britain's continuing war with France led it to try to prevent U.S. ships from taking supplies to Napoleon. As a result of these actions, the United States drifted into war with Britain. The war officially ended in 1814, although the last battle was actually fought in 1815 — after the peace treaty had been signed.

American attitudes to Europe were spelt out in 1823 by President James Monroe, who propounded the Monroe Doctrine, stating that the United States would oppose any European interference in the western hemisphere.

Party politics took a new turn in 1828 with the formation of the Democratic Party, largely composed of members of the old Democratic-Republican Party. During the next 30 years, the United States increased its size, partly by annexation (Texas and Oregon country) and partly by war with Mexico. In this period the dominant political issue was slavery, which the possession of new territories served to heighten.

Some states, mostly in the south where slavery was legal, wanted all new territory to be slave-owning; the antislavery northern states wanted it to be free. In 1854 a combination of antislavery groups formed the Republican Party; and, when the party's candidate, Abraham Lincoln, won the presidential election of 1860, six southern states broke away from the Union and formed the Confederate States of America. Civil war followed, and five more states seceded to join the Confederacy. The war brought defeat for the Confederacy and liberty to all slaves, but it tore the country apart and devastated the south.

Civil war ended in 1865; two years later, the United States made another huge purchase of territory, buying Alaska from Russia at the bargain price of $7,200,000, roughly 5 cents per hectare (2 cents per acre). At the time most Americans were more concerned with the problem of reconstruction after the war. This task was bedevilled by bitterness in the defeated southern states, and the desire of many people in the north for revenge against those whose actions had precipitated the war.

The Civil War increased the power of the federal government at the expense of the states, a trend that has continued ever since. The swift development of industrialization led to the rise of big business — which played an ever-increasing role in politics — followed inevitably by the rise of unions for the workers.

In 1898, the United States became involved in another war, this time with Spain over cruelties in Cuba, then a Spanish colony. As a result of its victory, America gained Guam, the Philippines and Puerto Rico. It also became acknowledged as a major world power, and its prestige and influence were underlined when, in 1905, intervention by President Theodore Roosevelt helped to end a war between Japan and Russia.

When World War I broke out in Europe in 1914, the United States under President Woodrow Wilson tried to remain neutral. But Germany's policy of unlimited submarine warfare, which led to the sinking of American ships, forced the United States to declare war in 1917. American forces played an important part in the final victories, which ended the war in 1918.

After the war, Wilson persuaded other countries to form the League of Nations, as an international body designed to prevent future conflicts. But isolationist groups in Congress prevented the United States from joining the League.

The 1920s were a period of prosperity and reaction from the war. It was also the period of Prohibition, which had come into force in 1919. Prohibition did not curb the drinking of alcohol; it merely drove the manufacture and distribution of liquor into the hands of gangsters, and led to an increase in crime.

Prosperity led to wild speculation and, in 1929, a stock market collapse set off the Great Depression of the 1930s, which put 12 million people out of work. President Franklin D. Roosevelt, who took office in 1933, proclaimed a 'New Deal' to help the country out of trouble. Congress passed a series of Acts, one of which established a fund for direct relief and wages for public works, later embodied as the Works Progress Administration (WPA) of 1935. The Tennessee Valley Authority, spending federal funds on dams, hydro-electric plants and agricultural and industrial development, was another part of the New Deal programme. These Acts all increased federal government powers.

The United States again tried to stay neutral in World War II, but was forced into battle when Japan attacked the U.S. naval base at Pearl Harbor in December, 1941. Thereafter, the United States played a major role in the conflict, emerging at the end of the war in 1945 as the world's leading power and richest country.

Since World War II, world politics have been dominated by the Cold War between the communist bloc, led by the U.S.S.R., and the free countries of the Western world, led by the United States. Resistance to communist aggression has flared into shooting wars, first in Korea in the 1950s, where the United States fought at the behest of the United Nations, and in the 1960s and 1970s in Vietnam, where U.S. forces were also heavily involved.

Today, American influence on world affairs is being exerted largely through the means of diplomacy. This is keeping opposing factions talking and preventing the Cold War from developing into a disastrous armed conflict between the eastern and western powers.

Right top: **Ulysses S. Grant was the leading Union general during the Civil War. His fame led to his becoming President in 1869.**

Right upper middle: **Franklin D. Roosevelt became President in 1933. He was re-elected three times.**

Right lower middle: **Dwight D. Eisenhower, supreme commander of the Allied armies in Europe in World War II, became President in 1953.**

Right bottom: **Jimmy Carter, a career sailor turned peanut farmer, became President of the United States in 1977.**

PRESIDENTS OF THE UNITED STATES

Name	Served	Party	Occupation	Vice-President
1 George Washington	1789-1797	Federalist	Planter	John Adams
2 John Adams	1797-1801	Federalist	Lawyer	Thomas Jefferson
3 Thomas Jefferson	1801-1809	Democratic-Republican	Planter	Aaron Burr George Clinton
4 James Madison	1809-1817	Democratic-Republican	Lawyer	George Clinton Elbridge Gerry
5 James Monroe	1817-1825	Democratic-Republican	Lawyer	Daniel D. Tompkins
6 John Quincy Adams	1825-1829	Democratic-Republican	Lawyer	John C. Calhoun
7 Andrew Jackson	1829-1837	Democrat	Lawyer	John C. Calhoun Martin Van Buren
8 Martin Van Buren	1837-1841	Democrat	Lawyer	Richard M. Johnson
9 William H. Harrison*	1841	Whig	Farmer	John Tyler
10 John Tyler	1841-1845	Whig	Lawyer	——————
11 James K. Polk	1845-1849	Democrat	Lawyer	George M. Dallas
12 Zachary Taylor*	1849-1850	Whig	Soldier	Millard Fillmore
13 Millard Fillmore	1850-1853	Whig	Lawyer	——————
14 Franklin Pierce	1853-1857	Democrat	Lawyer	William R. King
15 James Buchanan	1857-1861	Democrat	Lawyer	John C. Breckinridge
16 Abraham Lincoln†	1861-1865	Republican	Lawyer	Hannibal Hamlin Andrew Johnson
17 Andrew Johnson	1865-1869	Democrat	Tailor	——————
18 Ulysses S. Grant	1869-1877	Republican	Soldier	Schuyler Colfax Henry Wilson
19 Rutherford B. Hayes	1877-1881	Republican	Lawyer	William A. Wheeler
20 James A. Garfield†	1881	Republican	Lawyer	Chester A. Arthur
21 Chester A. Arthur	1881-1885	Republican	Lawyer	——————
22 Grover Cleveland	1885-1889	Democrat	Lawyer	Thomas A. Hendricks
23 Benjamin Harrison	1889-1893	Republican	Lawyer	Levi P. Morton
24 Grover Cleveland	1893-1897	Democrat	Lawyer	Adlai E. Stevenson
25 William McKinley†	1897-1901	Republican	Lawyer	Garret A. Hobart Theodore Roosevelt
26 Theodore Roosevelt	1901-1909	Republican	Writer	Charles W. Fairbanks
27 William H. Taft	1909-1913	Republican	Lawyer	James S. Sherman
28 Woodrow Wilson	1913-1921	Democrat	Teacher	Thomas R. Marshall
29 Warren G. Harding*	1921-1923	Republican	Newspaperman	Calvin Coolidge
30 Calvin Coolidge	1923-1929	Republican	Lawyer	Charles G. Dawes
31 Herbert C. Hoover	1929-1933	Republican	Engineer	Charles Curtis
32 Franklin D. Roosevelt*	1933-1945	Democrat	Lawyer	John N. Garner Henry A. Wallace Harry S. Truman
33 Harry S. Truman	1945-1953	Democrat	Businessman	—————— Alben W. Barkley
34 Dwight D. Eisenhower	1953-1961	Republican	Soldier	Richard M. Nixon
35 John F. Kennedy†	1961-1963	Democrat	Writer	Lyndon B. Johnson
36 Lyndon B. Johnson	1963-1969	Democrat	Teacher	—————— Hubert H. Humphrey
37 Richard M. Nixon‡	1969-1974	Republican	Lawyer	Spiro T. Agnew Gerald R. Ford
38 Gerald R. Ford	1974-1977	Republican	Lawyer	Nelson A. Rockefeller
39 Jimmy E. Carter	1977-1981	Democrat	Farmer	Walter F. Mondale
40 Ronald W. Reagan	1981-	Republican	Actor	George Bush

*Died in office   †Assassinated   ‡Resigned

Note: Before the 25th Amendment was ratified in 1967, a Vice-President succeeding to the presidency had no Vice-President serving with him, until and unless he was re-elected.

Farming, Fishing and Mining

Farming

About half the land surface of the United States is devoted to agriculture of various kinds, although fewer than 3,500,000 people — about 4 per cent of the total working population — work on the land. With this relatively small labour force, the United States remains one of the world's foremost agricultural nations, and produces more corn (maize) and cotton each year than any other country in the world.

There are now less than three million farms in the United States, and the number tends to get less every year, while the average size increases. As recently as 1955, there were five million individual farm holdings. This concentration mirrors the country's high degree of mechanization, larger farms being more economical to work with machines.

The leading crop is corn, which is grown in every state. But the principal area of production is the corn belt, in the north-central part of the country. Northwest of the corn belt, the main crop is spring wheat, and winter wheat is grown to the south.

The southern states are the lands of cotton and tobacco, while the east coast states are devoted to mixed farming, truck farming and dairying. Citrus fruits are the specialty of California and Florida, and the United States leads world production of oranges and grapefruit.

Crop production has proved of immense importance to the U.S. economy in recent years, although fluctuations in world markets sometimes cause problems of surpluses. More than one million people are in work connected with agricultural exports.

Over half the farmland of the United States is devoted to raising livestock, particularly cattle. The dairy farms of the northeast, stretching from the Atlantic coast to Minnesota, put America among the world's top producers of milk, butter and cheese. Beef is raised mainly in the midwest and on the traditional ranges of the west. Hogs are raised largely in the corn belt.

About one-fourth of the country is still under forest, which provides large quantities of lumber and woodpulp. A policy of forest farming, which involves the replacement of cut timber, is now helping to conserve the country's supplies, which were formerly decreasing too rapidly.

Mining

The United States is one of the world's largest producers of minerals, and it has rich resources of coal, iron ore, natural gas and petroleum. Even so, these vast supplies are not sufficient for the needs of the nation's ever-growing industries, and a great deal has to be imported.

The main iron-ore sources are in the ancient hematite rocks close to lakes Michigan and Superior. There are also rich deposits near Birmingham, Ala., and in Pennsylvania and the Adirondack Mountains of New York. Many of the best sources have already been worked out, but modern methods of prospecting are finding new reserves. By value, 72 per cent of American mineral production consists of fossil fuels — oil, natural gas and coal. Output continues to rise, but not fast enough to keep pace with the nation's needs, except in coal.

Many other metallic minerals, including chromium, copper, gold, lead, manganese, silver and tungsten, come mainly from the mountain states, particularly Colorado, Utah, Arizona and Idaho. But a number of metals essential in modern industrial production exist either in small quantities or are not found at all. These include cobalt, tin and industrial diamonds, which all have to be imported.

CROP PRODUCTS

The United States holds a high place in the world league of crop producers.

Crop	Annual Production (thousand tonnes)	Rank in World
Barley	8,111	6
Corn	161,485	1
Cotton	2,304	3
Grapefruit	2,491	1
Grapes	4,467	5
Groundnuts	1,804	3
Hops	25	2
Lemons and limes	695	2
Millet and sorghum	20,083	3
Oats	7,930	2
Oranges	8,306	2
Potatoes	16,228	4
Rice	6,040	12
Rye	624	6
Soybeans	61,715	1
Tobacco	969	2
Tomatoes	7,663	1
Wheat	64,492	2

LIVESTOCK PRODUCTION

Product	Annual Production (thousand tonnes)	Rank in World
Cattle	110,864	3
Hogs	60,101	3
Sheep	12,224	22
Beef and veal	9,925	1
Butter	447	5
Cheese	2,067	1
Eggs	4,077	2
Milk	54,592	2
Mutton and lamb	213	6
Pork	7,008	2

MINERAL PRODUCTION

Mineral/Ore	Annual Production	Rank in World
Antimony	655,000 tonnes	15
Asbestos	92,000 tonnes	8
Bauxite (aluminium ore)	1,752,000 tonnes	12
Coal	842,100,000 tonnes	2
Copper ore	1,456,000 tonnes	1
Gold	36 tonnes	4
Iron ore	50,152,000 tonnes	4
Lead ore	600,000 tonnes	1
Magnesite	600,000 tonnes	7
Molybdenum	55,205,000 tonnes	1
Natural gas	531,560 million cu. metres	1
Nickel ore	12,700,000 tonnes	10
Petroleum	419,520 tonnes	3
Silver ore	1,164,000 tonnes	5
Sulfur	5,822,000 tonnes	1
Uranium	11,200,000 tonnes	1
Vanadium	5,900,000 tonnes	3
Wolframite (tungsten ore)	3,436,000 tonnes	5
Zinc	294,000 tonnes	5

Above: **Copper is largely mined in the U.S. by open-cast methods.**

Right: **Pennsylvania has some of the country's richest farm land.**

U.S. FISHING INDUSTRY
The United States ranks fifth in the world league of fishing industries, with a 1978 catch of 3.5 million tonnes. Serious overfishing of the seas around its coasts, and increasing competition from the huge fishing fleets of Japan, the U.S.S.R. and China, are causing problems. But the recent extension of the country's fishing limit from 22 to 370 kilometres (12 to 200 nautical miles) may be the answer. The main fish caught in the two fishing grounds of the Pacific and the Atlantic include anchovy, cod, crab, halibut, herring, lobster, mackerel and tuna. Salmon is caught in the seas off Alaska. Delaware and Chesapeake bays are noted for their oysters.

Manufacturing and Technology

Manufacturing

Just over 34 per cent of the work force in the United States is engaged in industry, in particular in manufacturing. The United States is the world's leading industrial country, although its productivity is increasing at an average rate of less than 4.5 per cent per year — compared with more than 10 per cent for Japan.

One of the secrets of American success in manufacturing is the country's large natural resources, particularly of iron ore, bauxite and copper, and of fuels — coal, petroleum and natural gas. The main manufacturing states are those in the north and northeast — Wisconsin, Illinois, Michigan, Ohio, Pennsylvania, New York, New Jersey, Connecticut, Massachusetts, Rhode Island, Vermont, New Hampshire and Maine — plus a secondary belt of industrialized states to the south, including Alabama, Georgia, Tennessee, South Carolina, North Carolina and Virginia. There is a third, smaller industrial belt along the Pacific seaboard in Washington, Oregon and northern California.

The older industrial belt of the northeast was located close to fuel and mineral sources. Much modern industry has developed in regions where land is cheaper and labour is plentiful.

The main steel-making regions are along the shores of lakes Erie and Michigan, around Pittsburg, Pa., around Birmingham, Ala., and down the northeast coast. The vehicle industry is also concentrated in the north, with Detroit, Mich., as the world's 'car capital'. Textile manufacturing occurs mainly in eastern New England, where woollen goods are made, and in the southern states, where fabrics of cotton and man-made fibres are produced.

The general world recession of the mid-1970s led to a fall-back in total value of manufactured goods produced and a small, but significant drop in the utilization of industrial plant capacity. However, one of the strengths of American manufacturing is the very large home market for goods, which helps to cushion industry against international fluctuations.

Construction

Expenditure on building and construction in the mid-1970s averaged an all-time high of $137 billion per year. This is more than 60 per cent over the figure for the 1960s, but is due more to inflation and the higher cost of labour than to expansion.

The United States building and construction industry has led the world in the pioneering of new construction techniques. Prefabrication of building sections and even of entire new homes has been developed, and the skyscraper, now the characteristic building of all modern cities, was an American invention. The first skyscraper was the Home Insurance Building in Chicago, Ill., built in 1884, while the Sears Tower, also in Chicago, became the world's tallest building in 1974, having a height of 443 metres (1,454 feet), excluding its two TV antennae.

Science and Technology

Since World War II, the United States has been regarded as the world's leading scientific nation, with a more advanced technology than any other country. It owes this partly to the Nazi régime, which dominated Germany from 1933 to 1945. During that time, thousands of scientists, scholars and engineers fled from Germany, and many of them settled in the United States. There they found the laboratory and financial resources they needed in order to continue their work. In 1939, a team of these scientists persuaded President Franklin D. Roosevelt to set up the Office of Scientific Research and Development, with the object of putting the United States ahead of Germany in the race to construct an atomic bomb. The development and eventual use of this bomb against Japan enabled the United States to bring the war to a sudden conclusion in 1945.

Another presidential decision put the United States ahead of the rest of the world in the space race. In 1961, President John F. Kennedy called on the nation to put a man on the Moon by 1970. This feat was accomplished on July 20, 1969, when Neil Armstrong became the first person to set foot on the lunar soil. The Apollo moonflights were important, not so much for the prestige that they brought to American technology as for the huge advances in so many aspects of scientific and technological development.

For economic reasons, the U.S. space programme was scaled down in the mid-1970s, but this stimulated research into less expensive ways of exploring space. One result has been the development of a reusable shuttle for putting spacecraft into orbit in the 1980s. The space shuttle can leave and re-enter the Earth's atmosphere without having to jettison equipment costing billions of dollars. All that is lost is a relatively cheap fuel tank. It has been estimated that the space shuttle system may reduce launching costs to only about 2 per cent of those for the Apollo missions.

The development of nuclear fusion processes for peaceful purposes is now a major field for scientific research in the United States. For fusion, which uses the abundant element hydrogen, could provide man's energy needs for millions of years.

The importance that successive administrations attach to science and technology is shown by the size of the federal budget appropriation for this sector, running at more than $4 billion per year in the mid-1970s. Part of this huge sum is devoted to such projects as earthquake prediction, which is of particular importance in California. There, the San Andreas fault, which produced the earthquake that shattered San Francisco in 1906, is expected to let loose another major quake before the year 2000.

Above: **This view of New York's famous skyscraper skyline was taken from the R.C.A. building at Sixth Avenue and 50th Street.**

Right: **A Saturn rocket blasting the Apollo 16 Moon mission into space in April 1972 from the John F. Kennedy Space Center.**

Trade and Transport

Trade

Because it is one of the world's largest producing countries, the United States naturally has the largest individual share of the market in international trade. The value of both imports and exports has been rising steadily for many years. In the mid-1960s, imports from other countries stood at around $19 billion whereas, in the mid-1970s, they were more than $96 billion. And exports in the mid-1960s were more than $26 billion while, in the 1970s, they had risen to more than $107 billion. Domestic trade runs at about 10 times the volume of external trade.

Part of the recent increase in trading figures is due to a steady increase in the general volume of business, but much of it is to be explained by inflation. This stood at 11 per cent in 1974, at the height of the world energy crisis that followed oil price rises, but has been slowing since.

Although the United States is the world's leading manufacturing country, agricultural products led the export list in the 1970s, followed by transportation equipment. The principal import, by value, is fuel, mainly petroleum, with machinery and foreign-built automobiles ranking next. The trading pattern has fluctuated considerably over the years. In the mid-1960s, manufactured goods led the export field, while a wide range of raw materials formed the principal imports.

Many fluctuations in U.S. trade have been caused by climatic changes, particularly in the field of foodstuffs. The U.S.S.R. has been a large buyer of grain from the United States in recent years, largely because of Russian crop failures caused by bad weather. The erratic nature of these Soviet purchases has been partly ironed out by trading agreements between the U.S.S.R. and the United States.

For the first 70 years of this century, American exports exceeded imports, though capital outflow and other 'invisibles'

produced a negative balance of payments on many occasions. In spite of mounting fuel costs and the world depression in the early 1970s, the U.S. balance of visible trade was showing signs of a healthy recovery by 1975.

LEADING CUSTOMERS OF THE U.S.		LEADING SUPPLIERS TO THE U.S.	
Country	**% of total exports**	**Country**	**% of total imports**
Canada	15·9	Canada	17·3
Japan	9·5	Japan	12·8
United Kingdom	5·7	Saudi Arabia	5·2
Mexico	4·9	West Germany	4·8
West Germany	4·9	Nigeria	4·5
Netherlands	3·9	United Kingdom	4·1
France	3·4	Mexico	3·6
Belgium and Lux.	3·0	Libya	3·0
Others	48·8	Others	44·7

Land Transport

Modern America grew up around its transportation systems. The coming of the railroads in the 1830s soon opened up the west. The railroads formed main routes across the country and, wherever the railroads went, settlers and industry soon followed. More roads were then built to link the ever-increasing number of new, growing communities. Today's modern highways have speeded up overland communications over long distances, and to places that the railroads cannot reach.

Roads and streets in the United States total over 6,100,000 kilometres (3,800,000 miles). Of this, around 16 per cent is in city

and municipal locations; the rest is rural and includes major highways. More than 80 per cent of roads and streets are surfaced, while the rest have been graded and drained.

In 1974, there were 129,893,311 motor vehicles of all types registered in the United States, representing about five vehicles for every eight persons in the country. Trucking is a major industry in the United States, though the recession of the mid-1970s caused a sharp drop in freightage.

Railroads cover 348,270 kilometres (216,405 miles), built almost entirely on the standard gauge of 1,435 millimetres (4 feet 8½ inches). Four transcontinental lines link the Atlantic and Pacific coasts, and the rail network is most dense in the eastern states. In spite of competition from the highways and airlines, the railroads remain the prime means of moving freight, and they have more than 1,350,000 freight cars in regular service. Passenger cars total more than 7,300.

As in many other countries, railroads in the United States are not completely economically viable. So, in the mid-1970s, the government-controlled U.S. Railway Association acted to merge seven bankrupt lines for operation with federal financial backing.

Air Transport

It seems amazing that the first powered flight, made by the Wright brothers, took place as recently as 1903. Since then, a vast, world-wide system of air services has appeared.

U.S. air services are provided by about 60 companies, most of which operate only on domestic flights. After a boom year in 1974, in which almost 207,450,000 passengers were carried over a total distance of 262,190,000,000 kilometres (162,917,000,000 miles) with good profitability, the impact of high fuel costs and, therefore, higher fares resulted in a drop in traffic and considerable losses the following year. Freight and express goods carried annually total about 140 million tonne-kilometres (86 million ton-miles). More than 3,000,000 persons work in aviation. Airlines of many foreign countries provide services to and from the United States.

The bulk of the United States' overseas trade is carried by sea and, at April 1, 1975, the country's mercantile marine had more than 900 vessels capable of carrying over 1,000 tonnes. These included more than 220 tankers, but problems over international fuel supplies hit the tanker market very hard in the mid-1970s, and many giant tankers were idle.

Internal traffic by the country's network of domestic waterways still plays a vital role in the movement of bulk freight. The St. Lawrence Seaway and the Great Lakes allow ocean-going vessels to sail clear through to Chicago, Ill., and that busy port is linked with New Orleans and the Gulf of Mexico by way of the Chicago River, the Chicago Sanitary and Ship Canal, and the Mississippi River. The Atlantic Intracoastal Waterway provides a sheltered route for small vessels from Trenton, N.J., 1,900 kilometres (1,200 miles) south to Miami, with only two short lengths of exposed travel in the open sea. A similar sheltered route is provided along the Gulf of Mexico by the Gulf Intracoastal Waterway, which runs more than 1,600 kilometres (1,000 miles) from Carrabelle, Fla., to Brownsville, Tex., close to the Mexican frontier.

LEADING U.S. PORTS
New York, N.Y.
New Orleans, La.
Houston, Tex
Baton Rouge, La.
Valdez, Alaska
Beaumont, Tex.
Philadelphia, Pa.
Baltimore, Md.
Norfolk, Va.
Tampa, Fla.

Below left: **National Interstate Highway 70 and U.S. Highway 50 crossing the Mississippi River at St. Louis, Mo. – part of the nationwide network of highways.**

Below: **The John F. Kennedy international airport at Idlewild, New York City, was opened in 1948, and given its present name in 1963. It is one of the busiest and most important airports in the world.**

The Fifty States

State	Abbreviation	Area in sq. km	Area in sq. mi	Population	Capital	Date of admission to Union	Popular name
Alabama	Ala.	133,667	51,609	3,890,061	Montgomery	1819	Yellowhammer State
Alaska	Alaska	1,518,770	586,400	400,481	Juneau	1959	Last Frontier
Arizona	Ariz.	295,023	113,909	2,717,866	Phoenix	1912	Grand Canyon State
Arkansas	Ark.	137,539	53,104	2,285,513	Little Rock	1836	Land of Opportunity
California	Calif.	411,013	158,693	23,668,562	Sacramento	1850	Golden State
Colorado	Colo.	269,999	104,247	2,888,834	Denver	1876	Centennial State
Connecticut	Conn.	12,973	5,009	3,107,576	Hartford	1788	Constitution State
Delaware	Del.	5,328	2,057	595,225	Dover	1787	First State
Florida	Fla.	151,670	58,560	9,739,992	Tallahassee	1845	Sunshine State
Georgia	Ga.	152,488	58,876	5,464,265	Atlanta	1788	Empire State of the South
Hawaii	Hawaii	16,638	6,424	965,000	Honolulu	1959	Aloha State
Idaho	Ida.	216,412	83,557	943,935	Boise	1890	Gem State
Illinois	Ill.	146,075	56,400	11,418,461	Springfield	1818	Land of Lincoln
Indiana	Ind.	93,993	36,291	5,490,179	Indianapolis	1816	Hoosier State
Iowa	Ia.	145,791	56,290	2,913,387	Des Moines	1846	Hawkeye State
Kansas	Kans. or Kan.	213,063	82,264	2,363,208	Topeka	1861	Sunflower State
Kentucky	Ky. or Ken.	104,623	40,395	3,661,433	Frankfort	1792	Bluegrass State
Louisiana	La.	125,674	48,523	4,203,972	Baton Rouge	1812	Pelican State
Maine	Me.	86,027	33,215	1,124,660	Augusta	1820	Pine Tree State
Maryland	Md.	27,394	10,577	4,216,446	Annapolis	1788	Old Line State
Massachusetts	Mass.	21,386	8,257	5,737,037	Boston	1788	Bay State
Michigan	Mich.	150,779	58,216	9,258,344	Lansing	1837	Wolverine State
Minnesota	Minn.	217,735	84,068	4,077,148	St. Paul	1858	Gopher State
Mississippi	Miss.	123,584	47,716	2,520,638	Jackson	1817	Magnolia State
Missouri	Mo.	180,486	69,686	4,917,444	Jefferson City	1821	'Show Me' State
Montana	Mont.	381,086	147,138	786,690	Helena	1889	Treasure State
Nebraska	Nebr. or Neb.	200,017	77,227	1,570,006	Lincoln	1867	Cornhusker State
Nevada	Nev.	286,297	110,540	799,184	Carson City	1864	Silver State
New Hampshire	N.H.	24,097	9,304	920,610	Concord	1788	Granite State
New Jersey	N.J.	20,295	7,836	7,364,158	Trenton	1787	Garden State
New Mexico	N.Mex. or N.M.	315,114	121,666	1,299,968	Santa Fe	1912	Land of Enchantment
New York	N.Y.	128,401	49,576	17,557,288	Albany	1788	Empire State
North Carolina	N.C.	136,524	52,712	5,894,429	Raleigh	1789	Tar Heel State
North Dakota	N.Dak. or N.D.	183,022	70,665	652,695	Bismarck	1889	Flickertail State
Ohio	O.	106,765	41,222	10,797,419	Columbus	1803	Buckeye State
Oklahoma	Okla.	181,090	69,919	3,025,266	Oklahoma City	1907	Sooner State
Oregon	Ore. or Oreg.	251,180	96,981	2,632,663	Salem	1859	Beaver State
Pennsylvania	Pa. or Penn.	117,412	45,333	11,866,728	Harrisburg	1787	Keystone State
Rhode Island	R.I.	3,144	1,214	947,154	Providence	1790	Little Rhody
South Carolina	S.C.	80,432	31,055	3,119,208	Columbia	1788	Palmetto State
South Dakota	S. Dak. or S.D.	199,551	77,047	690,178	Pierre	1889	Sunshine State
Tennessee	Tenn.	109,412	42,244	4,590,750	Nashville	1796	Volunteer State
Texas	Tex.	692,405	267,339	14,228,383	Austin	1845	Lone Star State
Utah	Ut.	219,932	84,916	1,461,037	Salt Lake City	1896	Beehive State
Vermont	Vt.	24,887	9,609	511,456	Montpelier	1791	Green Mountain State
Virginia	Va.	105,710	40,815	5,396,279	Richmond	1788	Old Dominion
Washington	Wash.	176,617	68,192	4,130,163	Olympia	1889	Evergreen State
West Virginia	W.Va.	62,629	24,181	1,949,644	Charleston	1863	Mountain State
Wisconsin	Wis.	145,438	56,154	4,705,335	Madison	1848	Badger State
Wyoming	Wyo.	253,596	97,914	470,816	Cheyenne	1890	Equality State

Population figures based on 1980 census

GENERAL REFERENCE

CONVERSION SCALE

Abbreviations of measures used — ft Feet; mm {Millimetres / Millimeters}; cm {Centimetres / Centimeters}; m {Metres / Meters}; Km {Kilometres / Kilometers}; mb Millibars

3386 — Principal Shipping Routes (Distances in Nautical Miles)

City and Town symbols in order of size

Sites of Archæological or Historical Importance

International Boundaries

International Boundaries (Undemarcated or Undefined)

Internal Boundaries

Principal Roads

Tracks, Seasonal and other Roads

Road Tunnels

Principal Railways

Other Railways

Railways under construction

Railway Tunnels

Principal Canals

Principal Oil Pipelines

Principal Air Routes

Principal Airports

Perennial Streams

Seasonal Streams

Seasonal Lakes, Salt Flats

Swamps, Marshes

Wells in Desert

Permanent Ice

Passes

▲ 8848 Height above sea-level
▼ 8050 Depth below sea-level } in metres
1134 Height of lake-level

THE WORLD: Physical

1:150 000 000

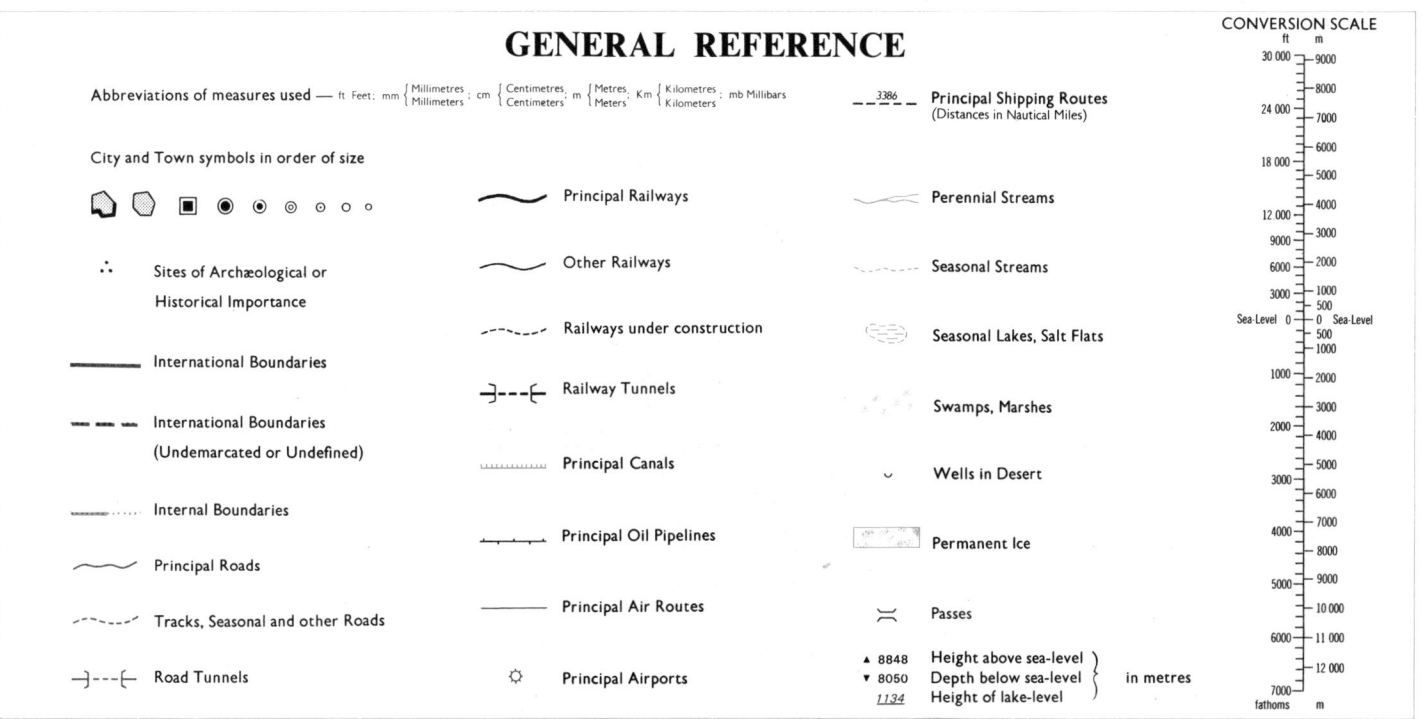

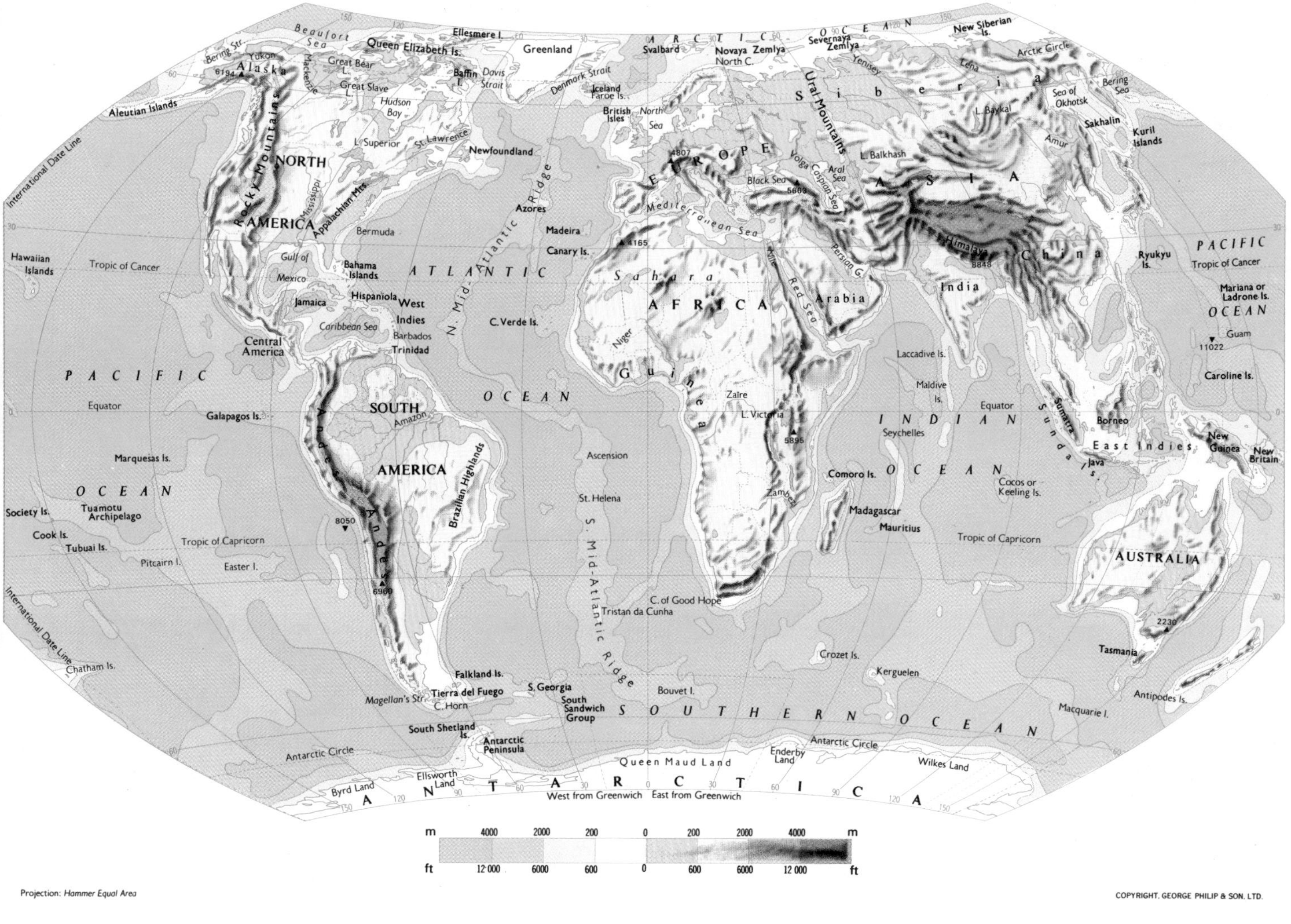

m 4000 2000 200 0 200 2000 4000 m
ft 12 000 6000 600 0 600 6000 12 000 ft

Projection: Hammer Equal Area

Projection: *Hammer Equal Area*

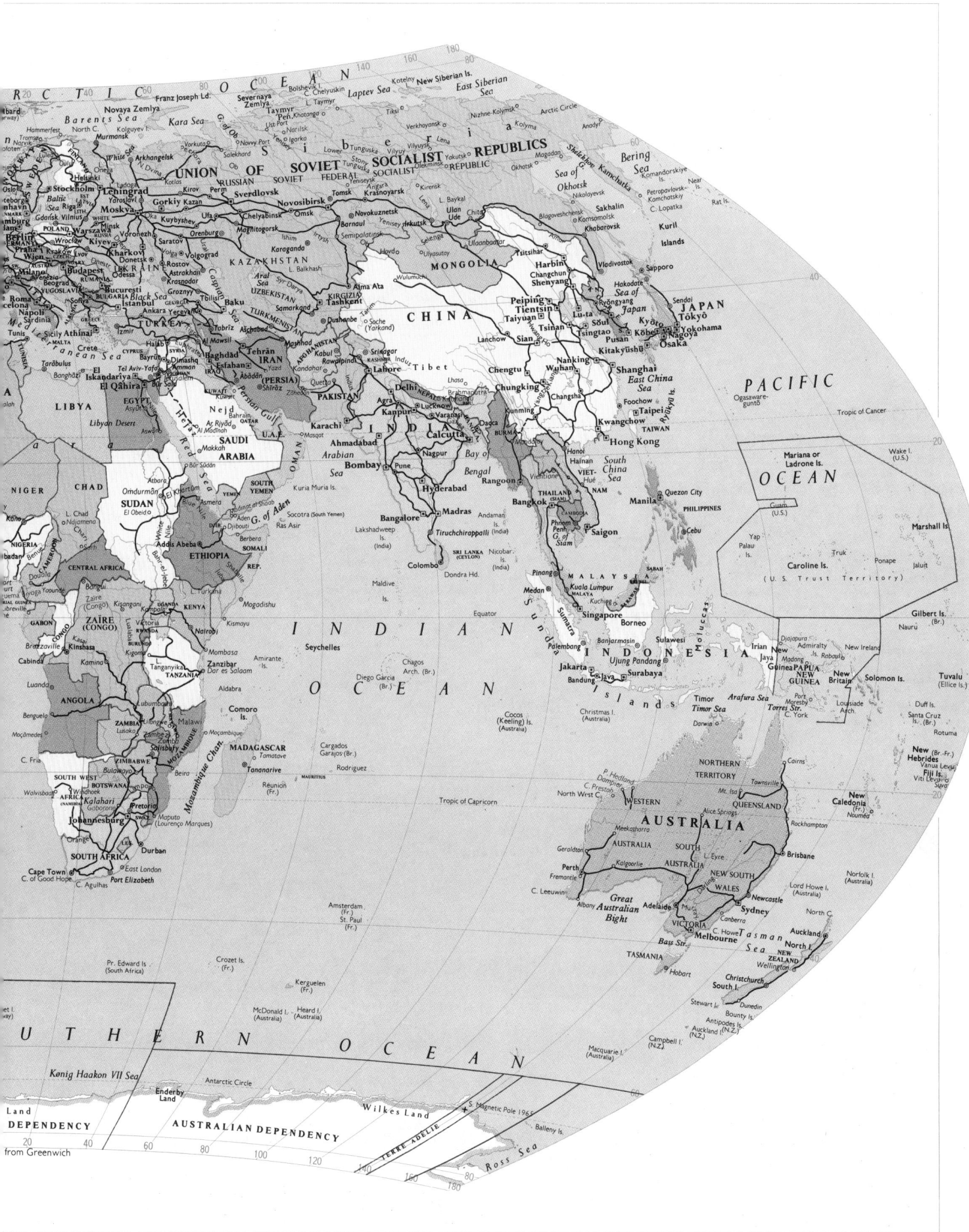

4 POLAR REGIONS

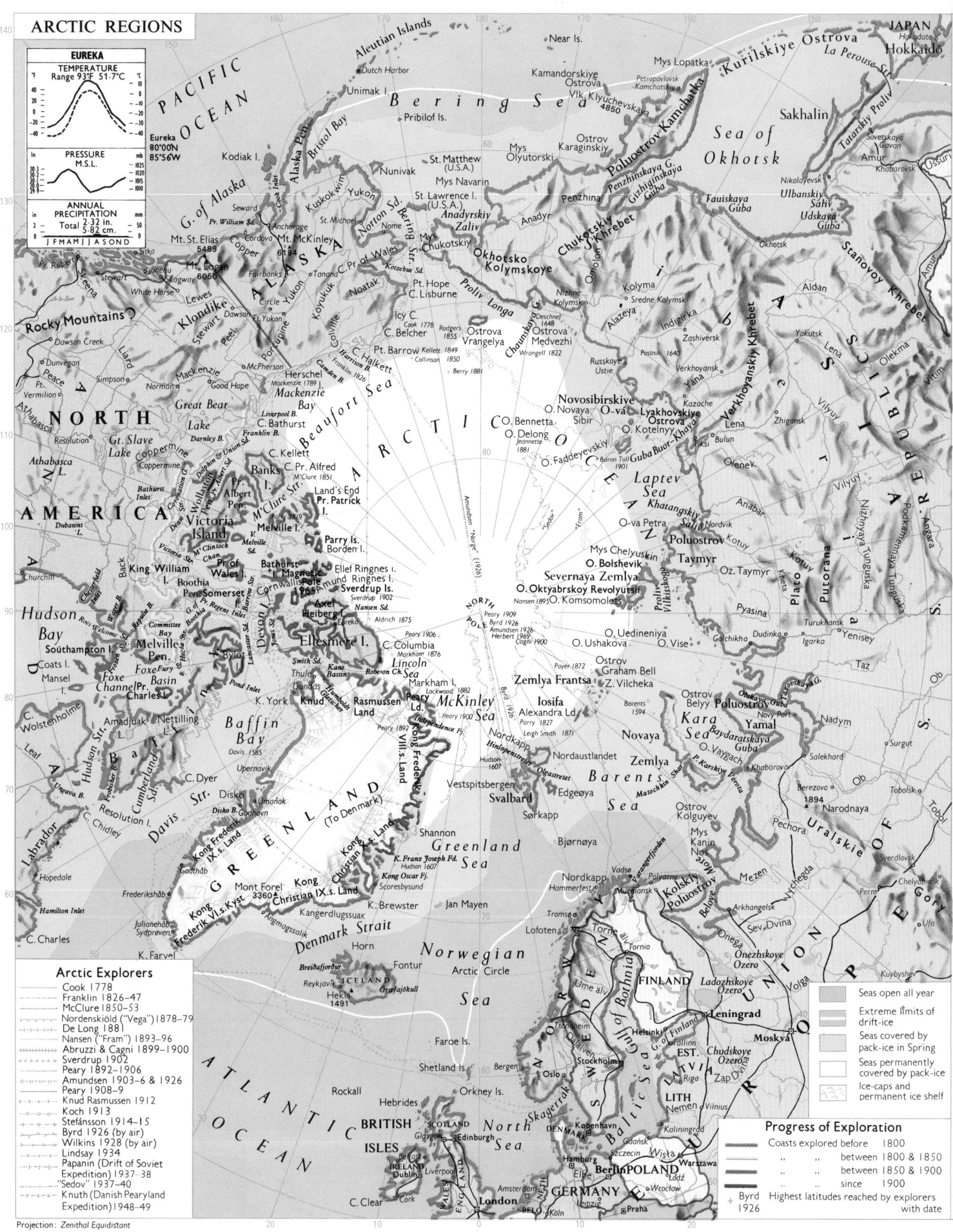

ARCTIC REGIONS

EUREKA

TEMPERATURE
Range 93°F 51.7°C

Eureka
80°00'N
85°56'W

PRESSURE
M.S.L.

ANNUAL
PRECIPITATION
Total 2.32 in.
5.82 cm.

J F M A M J J A S O N D

Arctic Explorers

	Cook 1778
	Franklin 1826–47
	McClure 1850–53
	Nordenskiöld ("Vega") 1878–79
	De Long 1881
	Nansen ("Fram") 1893–96
	Abruzzi & Cagni 1899–1900
	Sverdrup 1902
	Peary 1892–1906
	Amundsen 1903–6 & 1926
	Peary 1908–9
	Knud Rasmussen 1912
	Koch 1913
	Stefánsson 1914–15
	Byrd 1926 (by air)
	Wilkins 1928 (by air)
	Lindsay 1934
	Papanin (Drift of Soviet Expedition) 1937–38
	"Sedov" 1937–40
	Knuth (Danish Pearyland Expedition)1948–49

Projection: Zenithal Equidistant

Progress of Exploration

	Coasts explored before	1800
	" " between	1800 & 1850
	" " between	1850 & 1900
	" " since	1900
+ Byrd 1926	Highest latitudes reached by explorers with date	

Seas open all year

Extreme limits of drift-ice

Seas covered by pack-ice in Spring

Seas permanently covered by pack-ice

Ice-caps and permanent ice shelf

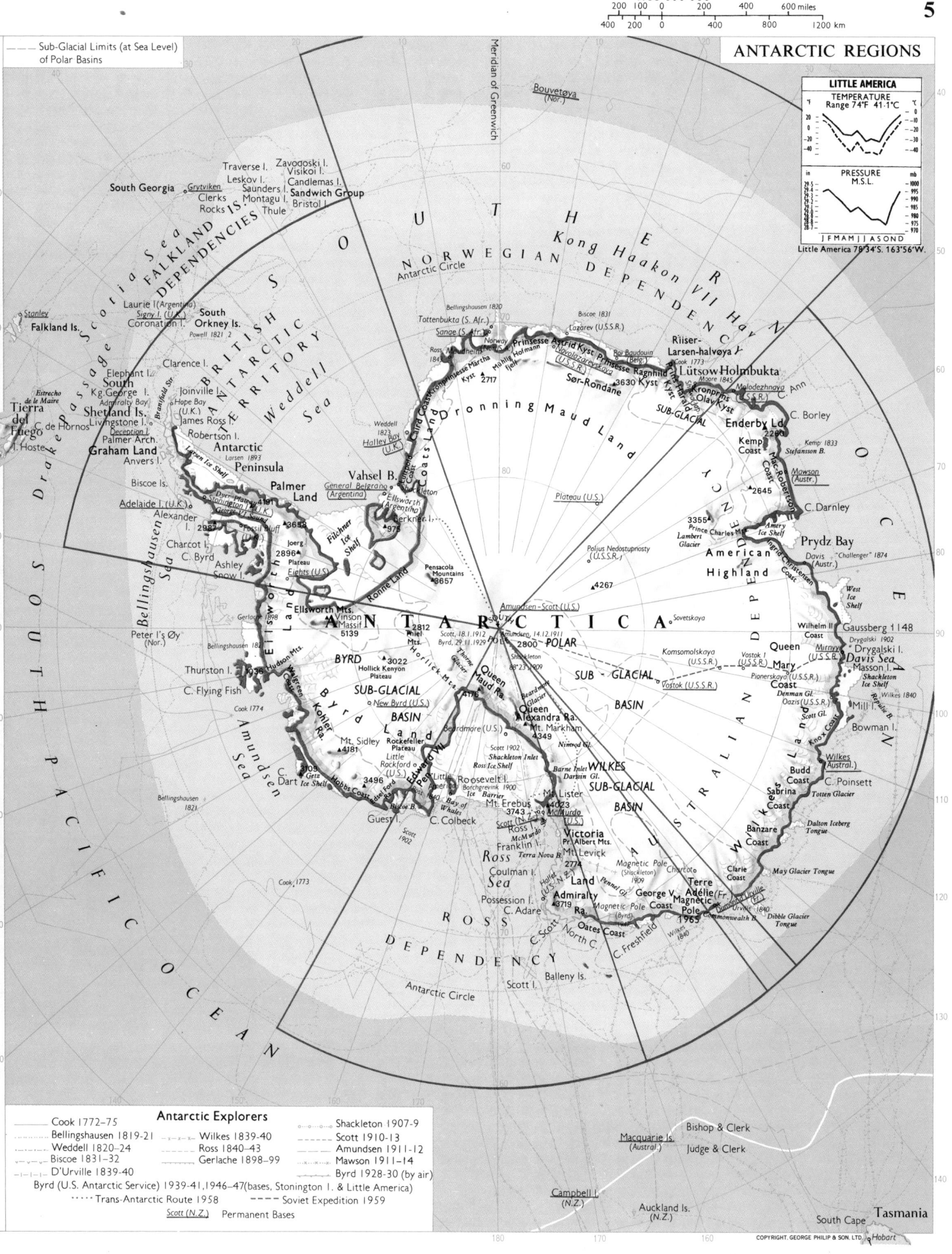

ANTARCTIC REGIONS

1:35 000 000

200 100 0 200 400 600 miles
400 200 0 400 800 1200 km

Sub-Glacial Limits (at Sea Level) of Polar Basins

LITTLE AMERICA

TEMPERATURE
Range 74°F 41.1°C

PRESSURE M.S.L.

J F M A M J J A S O N D

Little America 78°34'S. 163°56'W.

Antarctic Explorers

Cook 1772–75
Bellingshausen 1819–21
Weddell 1820–24
Biscoe 1831–32
D'Urville 1839–40
Wilkes 1839–40
Ross 1840–43
Gerlache 1898–99
Shackleton 1907–9
Scott 1910–13
Amundsen 1911–12
Mawson 1911–14
Byrd 1928–30 (by air)

Byrd (U.S. Antarctic Service) 1939–41, 1946–47 (bases, Stonington I. & Little America)

Trans-Antarctic Route 1958
Soviet Expedition 1959
Scott (N.Z.) Permanent Bases

COPYRIGHT. GEORGE PHILIP & SON. LTD.

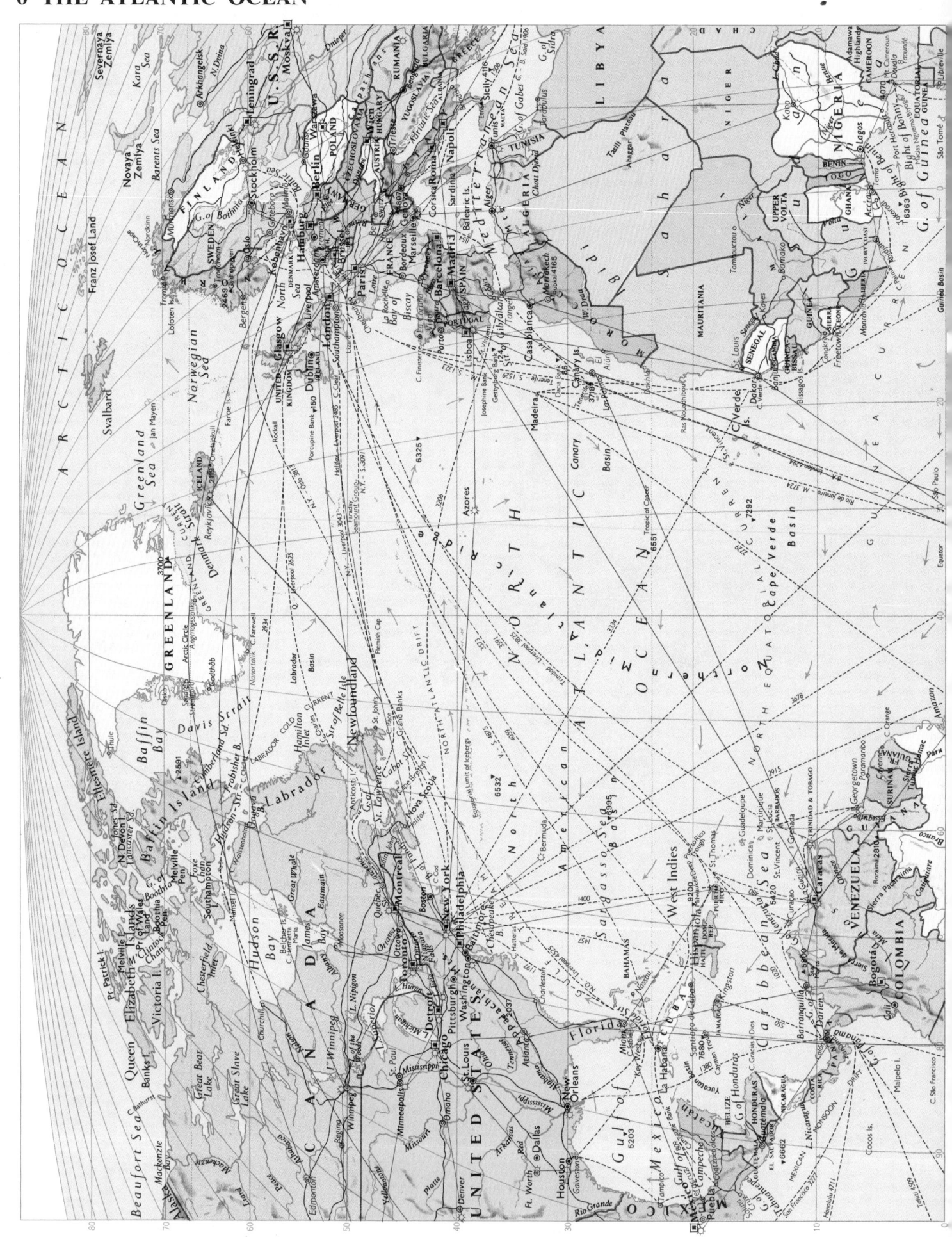

Direction of Currents

Principal Shipping Routes
(Distances in Nautical Miles)

3778

Projection: Mollweide

COPYRIGHT GEORGE PHILIP & SON, LTD.

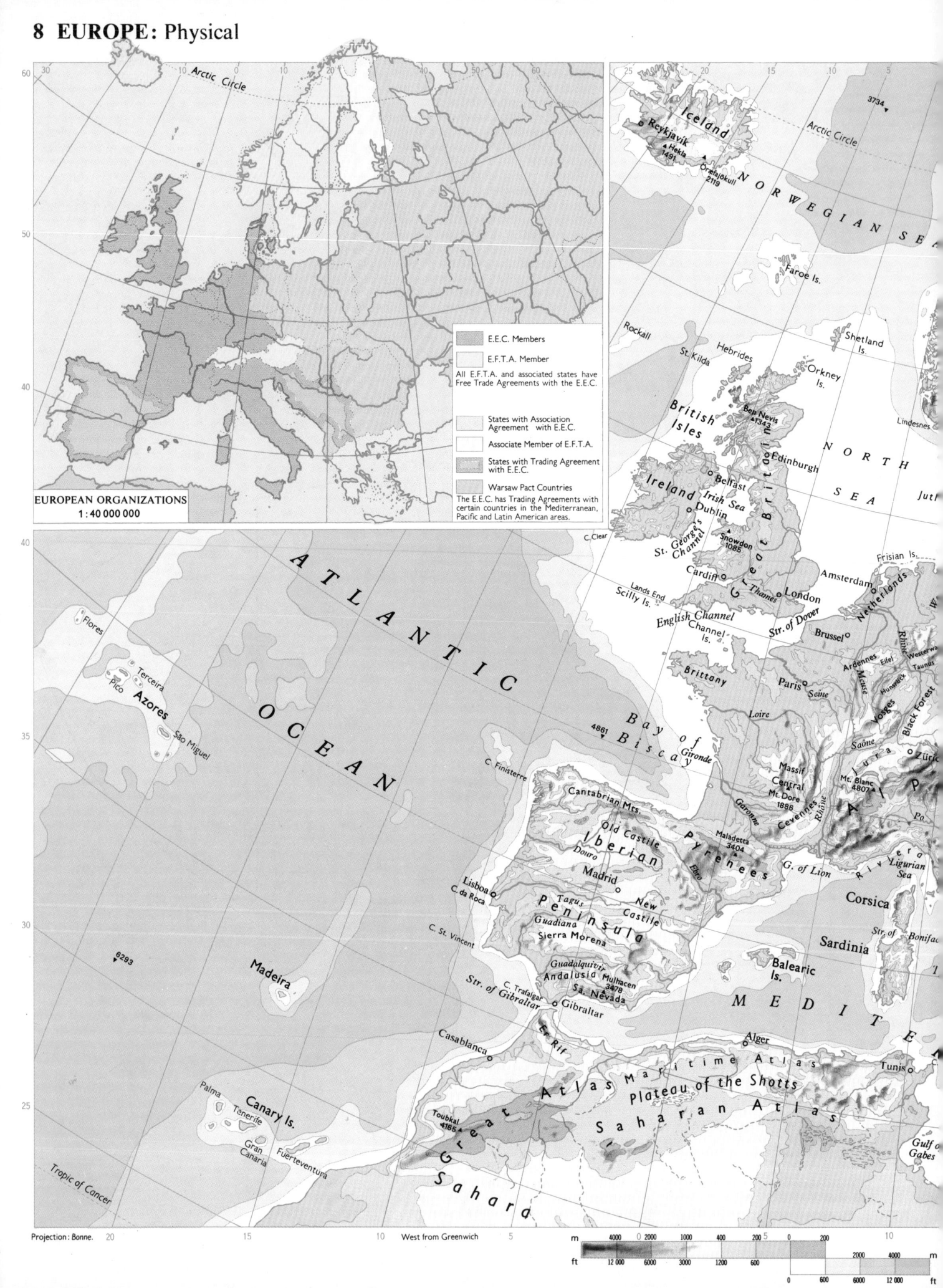

EUROPEAN ORGANIZATIONS
1 : 40 000 000

E.E.C. Members

E.F.T.A. Member

All E.F.T.A. and associated states have Free Trade Agreements with the E.E.C.

States with Association Agreement with E.E.C.

Associate Member of E.F.T.A.

States with Trading Agreement with E.E.C.

Warsaw Pact Countries

The E.E.C. has Trading Agreements with certain countries in the Mediterranean, Pacific and Latin American areas.

Arctic Circle

ICELAND
Reykjavik
Hekla 1491
Öræfajökull 2119

NORWEGIAN SEA

Arctic Circle
3734

Faroe Is.

Shetland Is.

Lindesnes

Rockall
St. Kilda
Hebrides
Orkney Is.

British Isles
Ben Nevis 1343
Edinburgh

NORTH SEA

Jut

Ireland
Belfast
Irish Sea
Dublin

Great Britain
Snowdon 1085

Frisian Is.

Amsterdam
Netherlands

C. Clear
St. George's Channel
Cardiff
Thames
London

Brussel
Rhine
Westerw
Taunus

Lands End
Scilly Is.
English Channel
Channel Is.
Str. of Dover

Paris
Seine

Ardennes
Meuse
Eifel
Hunsrück

ATLANTIC

Brittany

Loire

Vosges
Black Forest
Jura
Zürich

Flores

Bay of Biscay
4861
Gironde

Massif Central
Mt. Dore 1886

Saône

Mt. Blanc 4807

Terceira
Pico
Azores
São Miguel

OCEAN

C. Finisterre

Cantabrian Mts.

Garonne
Cevennes
Rhône

Maladetta 3404

Po

Old Castle
Iberian

Pyrenees

G. of Lion

Ligurian Sea

Douro

Ebro

Riviera

C. St. Vincent

Lisboa
C. da Roca
Tagus
Madrid
New Castle

Corsica

6293

Peninsula
Guadiana
Sierra Morena

Str. of Bonifac

Sardinia

Madeira

Guadalquivir
Andalusia Mulhacen 3478
C. Trafalgar Sa. Nevada
Str. of Gibraltar
Gibraltar

Balearic Is.

MEDITE

Palma
Tenerife
Canary Is.

Casablanca

Er Rif

Alger

Tunis

Gran Canaria
Fuerteventura

Toubkal 4165

Great Atlas Maritime Atlas
Plateau of the Shotts
Saharan Atlas

Gulf of Gabes

Tropic of Cancer

Sahara

Projection: Bonne.   20   15   West from Greenwich   5

m 4000 0 2000 1000 400 200   0 200   2000 4000 m
ft 12 000 6000 3000 1200 600   6000 12 000 ft

1:17 500 000

100   0   100   200   300   400   500 miles

100   0   200   400   600   800 km

Nordkapp   Nordkinn

Lofoten

L. Inari

Kebnekaise 2123

Scandinavia

Lappland

Kanin Peninsula

Tundra

Pechora

Narodnaya 1894

West Siberian Plain

Ob

Irtysh

Kola Peninsula

White Sea

Mezen

Telpos Iz. 1617

Ural Mountains

Tobol

Torne älv

Umeälv

Gulf of Bothnia

Finland

Onega

N. Dvina

Indalsälven

Idhöppiggen 2469

Oslo

Stockholm

Vänern

Måleren

Vättern

Gotland

Åland Is.

Helsinki

Gulf of Finland

L. Chudskoye

Neva

Leningrad

Lake Ladoga

Svir

L. Onega

Rybinsk Res.

Gorkiy

Volga

Kama

Skaw

Kattegat

København

BALTIC SEA

Valdai Hills

Dvina

Volga

Moskva

Oka

Volga

Obshchi Syrt

Ural

Elbe

Berlino

North

Oder

European

Plain

Neman

Central Russian Uplands

Volga Heights

Kirgiz Steppe

Mts. Prahad

Ore

Bohemian Forest

Sudetes

Moravia Hts.

Tatra 2655

Carpathians

Vistula

Warszawa

Pripet

Pripet Marshes

Kiyevo

Dnieper

Ukraine

Tsimlyansk Res.

Volga

Ust Urt Plateau

Karagiye Depression -132

Inn

Wien

Bakony Forest

Budapest

Plain of Hungary

Drava

Danube

Mureş

Tisza

Transylvanian Alps

Dniester

Prut

Bug

Don

Kara Bogaz

Caspian Sea

-28

Dinaric Alps

Sava

Beograd

Wallachia

Bucureşti

Danube

Morava

Odessa

Dnieper

Sea of Azov

Crimea

Kuban

Terek

Caucasus

5633 Elbrus

Transcaucasia

Kura

Araks

Baku

Adriatic Sea

Dalmatia

Mouths of the Danube

Strait of Kerch

Black Sea

2211

Pontine Mts.

Ararat 5165

L. Van

L. Urmia

Elburz Mts.

Tehran

Apennines

Gran Sasso 2914

Roma

Str. of Otranto

Balkan Peninsula

Sofiya

Rhodope

Balkans

Istanbul

Bosporus

Sea of Marmara

Ankara

K Kizil

Anatolia

Taurus Mts.

Kurdistan

Strait of Messina

Etna 3263

Sicily

Calabria

Ionian Sea

Pindus

Ionian Is.

Morea

Dardanelles

Aegean Sea

Athinai

L. Tuz

Erciyas 3770

Euphrates

Tigris

Baghdad

Mesopotamia

Halab

telleria

Malta

5121

C. Matapan

C. Spartivento

Crete

Rhodes

Cyprus

Bayrut

Syrian

Desert

Tel Aviv-Yafo

Dead Sea -395

Nile Delta

Levant

Persian Gulf

Tripoli

MEDITERRANEAN SEA

Gulf of Sidra

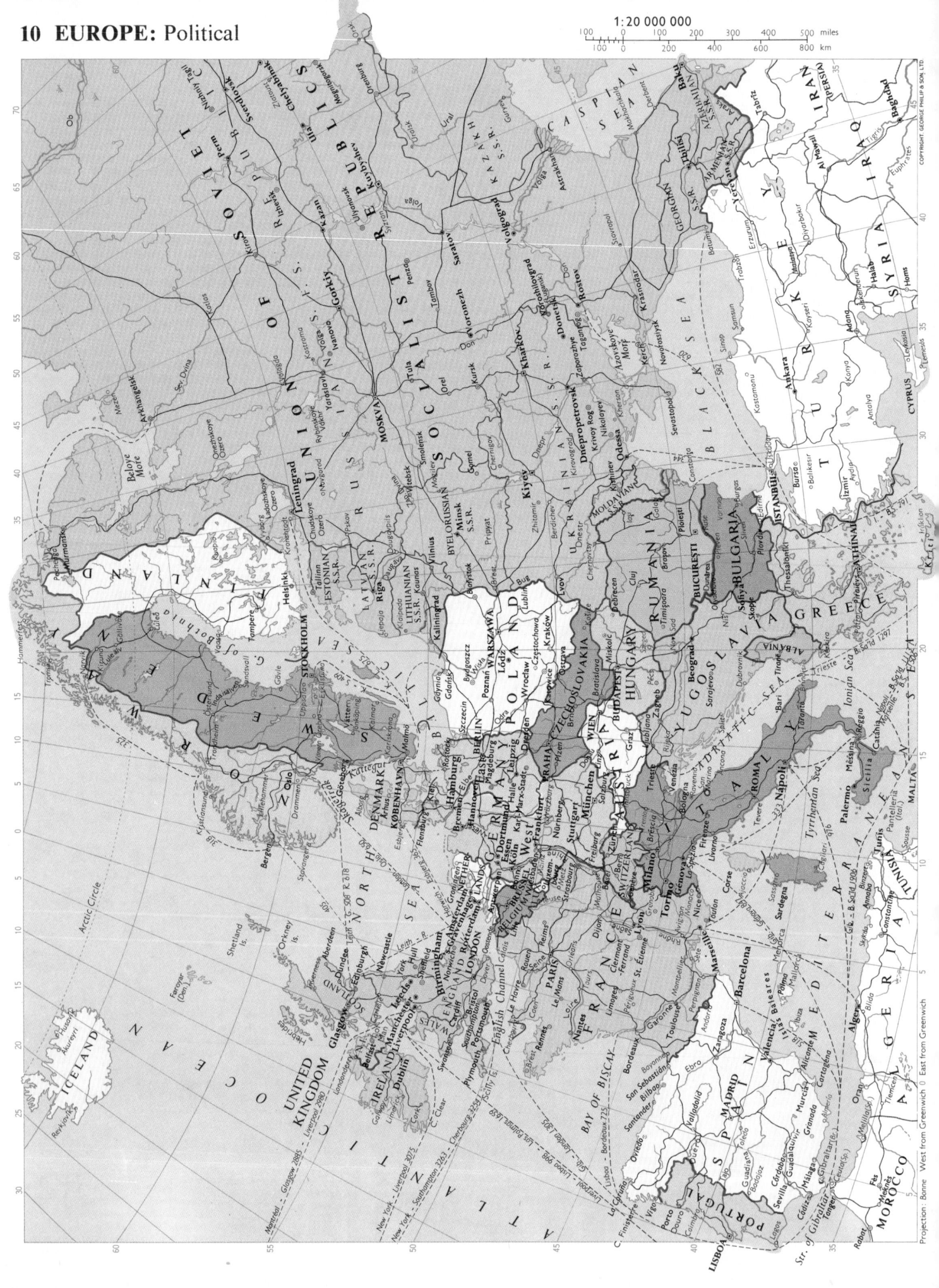

1 : 20 000 000

1 : 4 000 000

The DISTRICTS of Northern Ireland have been numbered and can be identified by reference to this table.

1	Londonderry	14	Craigavon
2	Limavady	15	Armagh
3	Coleraine	16	Newry & Mourne
4	Ballymoney	17	Banbridge
5	Moyle	18	Down
6	Larne	19	Lisburn
7	Ballymena	20	Antrim
8	Magherafelt	21	Newtownabbey
9	Cookstown	22	Carrickfergus
10	Strabane	23	North Down
11	Omagh	24	Ards
12	Fermanagh	25	Castlereagh
13	Dungannon	26	Belfast

1 Merseyside
2 Greater Manchester
3 West Yorkshire
4 South Yorkshire
5 West Glamorgan
6 Mid Glamorgan
7 South Glamorgan

Orkney Is.

Shetland Is.

Projection : Conical with two standard parallels

West from Greenwich   East from Greenwich
COPYRIGHT. GEORGE PHILIP & SON, LTD.

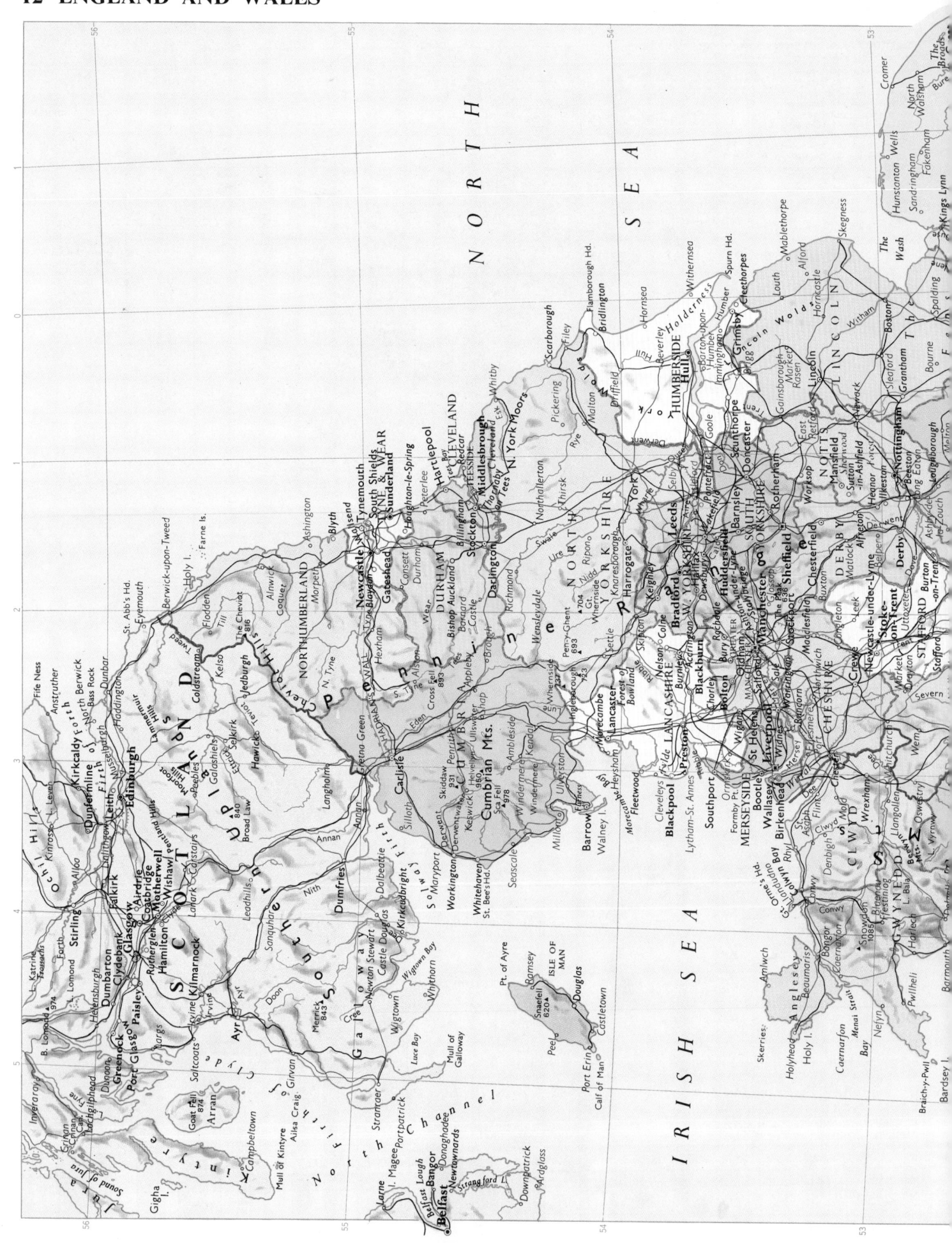

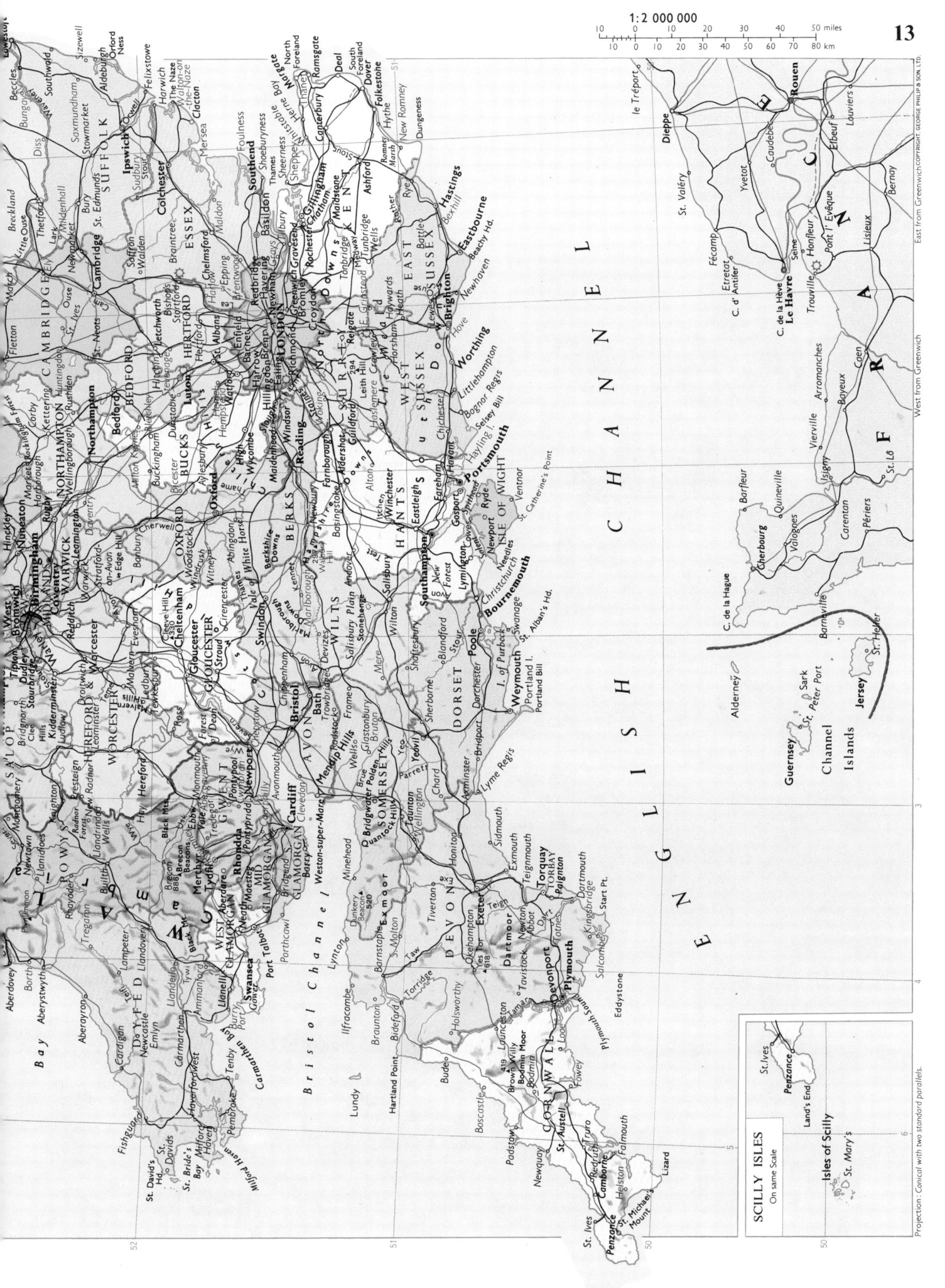

14 SCOTLAND

1:2 000 000

10 0 10 20 30 40 50 miles
10 0 10 20 30 40 50 60 70 80 km

Projection: Conical with two standard parallels.

West from Greenwich

ORKNEY IS.
On same scale

Scapa Flow · Hoy · South Ronaldsay · North Ronaldsay · Westray · Eday · Rousay · Sanday · Stronsay · Stromness · Mainland · Shapinsay · ORKNEY · Kirkwall · Scapa Flow · South Ronaldsay · Hoy · Pentland Firth · Dunnet Hd. · John O'Groats

SHETLAND IS.
On same scale

Unst · Fetlar · Yell · Yell Sound · SHETLAND · Whalsay · Mainland · Bressay · Scalloway · Lerwick · Foula · Sumburgh Hd.

ATLANTIC OCEAN

NORTH SEA

Western Isles / Outer Hebrides / Inner Hebrides

Flannan Is. · Butt of Lewis · Stornoway · Broad Bay · Lewis · Eye Pen. · WESTERN ISLES · Tarbert · Harris · Sound of Harris · North Uist · Lochmaddy · Monach Is. · Benbecula · South Uist · Lochboisdale · Barra · Barra Hd. · Canna · Rhum · Eigg · Muck · Coll · Tiree · Staffa · Iona · Mull · Ben More 966 · Tobermory · Colonsay · Islay · Bowmore · Port Ellen · Gigha · Jura · Rubh a' Mhail · Ardnamurchan Pt.

Highlands

C. Wrath · Durness · Tongue · Strathy Pt. · Dunnet Hd. · Thurso · Dounreay · John O'Groats · Wick · Noss Hd. · Lybster · Ben Hope 927 · Reay Forest · L. Laxford · Lochinver · Enard Bay · L. Assynt · B. More Assynt · Loch Shin · Lairg · Brora · Helmsdale · Ord of Caithness · Ullapool · L. Broom · Oykell · Dornoch · Golspie · Tarbat Ness · Dornoch Firth · Tain · NORTH WEST HIGHLANDS · B. Dearg 1081 · Invergordon · Cromarty · Moray Firth · Lossiemouth · Buckie · Cullen · Portsoy · Banff · Macduff · Kinnaird's Head · Fraserburgh · Rattray Head · Peterhead · Buchan Ness · Elgin · Forres · Rothes · Keith · Deveron · Turriff · BUCHAN · Nairn · Culloden Moor · Inverness · Findhorn · Dufftown · Huntly · Ythan · Ellon · GRAMPIAN · Inverurie · Alford · Don · Aberdeen · Girdle Ness · HIGHLAND · Beauly · Dingwall · Strathpeffer · Fortrose · Conon · Grantown-on-Spey · Tomintoul · L. Fannich · L. Maree · L. Torridon · Trotternish · Strome Ferry · Glen Affric · Glen Moriston · Fort Augustus · Loch Ness · Glen More · Strathspey · Aviemore · Cairn Gorm 1245 · Monadhliath Mts. · Kingussie · Newtonmore · Cairn Toul · Ben Macdhui 1311 · Cairngorm Mts. 1292 · Ballater · Aboyne · Banchory · Stonehaven · Braemar · Lochnagar 1154 · Balmoral · Braes of Angus · Laurencekirk · Inverbervie · Brechin · Montrose

Islands / West coast

Raasay · Sound of Raasay · Rona · Inner Sound · Portree · Skye · L. Bracadale · Scalpay · Cuillin Hills · Cuillin Sound · Kyle of Lochalsh · Dornie · L. Carron · L. Alsh · Sound of Sleat · L. Hourn · Glen Garry · L. Oich · Mallaig · L. Morar · L. Arkaig · Arisaig · L. Eil · Fort William · Ben Nevis 1343 · Ardgour · L. Moidart · L. Shiel · L. Sunart · Morvern · Loch Linnhe · Lismore · Ben Cruachan 1124 · Oban · Firth of Lorn · Ben More 1174 · Inveraray · L. Awe · Crinan · Loch Fyne · Lochgilphead · Sound of Jura · Tarbert · Knapdale · KINTYRE · Campbeltown · Mull of Kintyre · Ailsa Craig

Central / Tayside

Badenoch · Forest of Atholl · Glen Garry · Blair Atholl · Pass of Killiecrankie · Pitlochry · Kirriemuir · N. Esk · S. Esk · Forfar · Strathmore · GRAMPIAN HIGHLANDS · Rannoch Moor · L. Rannoch · L. Tummel · Aberfeldy · Tay · Blairgowrie · Alyth · Sidlaw Hills · Dunkeld · Ballachulish · Glen Coe · L. Etive · Ben Lawers 1214 · L. Tay · Killin · Breadalbane · Ben More 1174 · Earn · Crieff · B. Vorlich 983 · Callander · Scone · TAYSIDE · Dundee · Broughty Ferry · Firth of Tay · Tayport · Arbroath · NORTH SEA · B. Vorlich 942 · L. Katrine · Trossachs · Ben Lomond 974 · CENTRAL · Dunblane · Ochil Hills · Kinross · Cupar · St. Andrews · Fife Ness · FIFE · Leven · Anstruther · L. Lomond · Stirling · Bannockburn · Alloa · Cowdenbeath · Lochgelly · Buckhaven · Kirkcaldy · Dunfermline · Rosyth · Firth of Forth · Bass Rock · North Berwick · Dunbar · St. Abb's Hd. · Eyemouth · Berwick on Tweed · Holy I.

Clyde / Central Belt

Helensburgh · Dunoon · Dumbarton · Clydebank · Greenock · Port Glasgow · Renfrew · Paisley · Glasgow · Rutherglen · Kirkintilloch · Airdrie · Coatbridge · Falkirk · Grangemouth · Bo'ness · Linlithgow · Edinburgh · Leith · Musselburgh · Haddington · Prestonpans · LOTHIAN · Dalkeith · Penicuik · Pentland Hills · Bathgate · Motherwell · Wishaw · Hamilton · Kilbride · STRATHCLYDE · Largs · Bute · Rothesay · Goat Fell 874 · Arran · Brodick · Ardrossan · Saltcoats · Troon · Prestwick · Irvine · Kilmarnock · Ayr · Cumnock · Doon · Leadhills · Sanquhar · Moorfoot Hills · Peebles · Lanark · Carstairs · Biggar · Broad Law 840 · Lammermuir Hills · Duns · Coldstream · Galashiels · Melrose · Selkirk · Hawick · BORDERS · Jedburgh · The Cheviot 816 · Kelso · Flodden · Till · Cheviot Hills · Coquet

South

SOUTHERN UPLANDS · Merrick 843 · Trostan 554 · Newton Stewart · Galloway · DUMFRIES AND GALLOWAY · Dumfries · Lockerbie · Langholm · Gretna Green · Annan · Solway Firth · Carlisle · HADRIAN'S WALL · ENGLAND · Moffat · Nith · Ken · Creel · L. Ryan · Stranraer · Portpatrick · Wigtown · Whithorn · Luce Bay · Wigtown Bay · Castle Douglas · Dalbeattie · Gatehouse of Fleet · Kirkcudbright · Dalmellington · Wear · Cross Fell 893 · Penrith · Alston · N. Tyne · S. Tyne · Hexham · Workington · Skiddaw 931 · Ullswater · Derwent · Cumbrian Mts. · Tees · Barnard Castle

Ireland

NORTHERN IRELAND · Belfast · Belfast Lough · Bangor · Newtownards · Ballymena · Larne · Ballycastle · Rathlin · Fair Hd. · Mull of Galloway · North Channel · Firth of Clyde

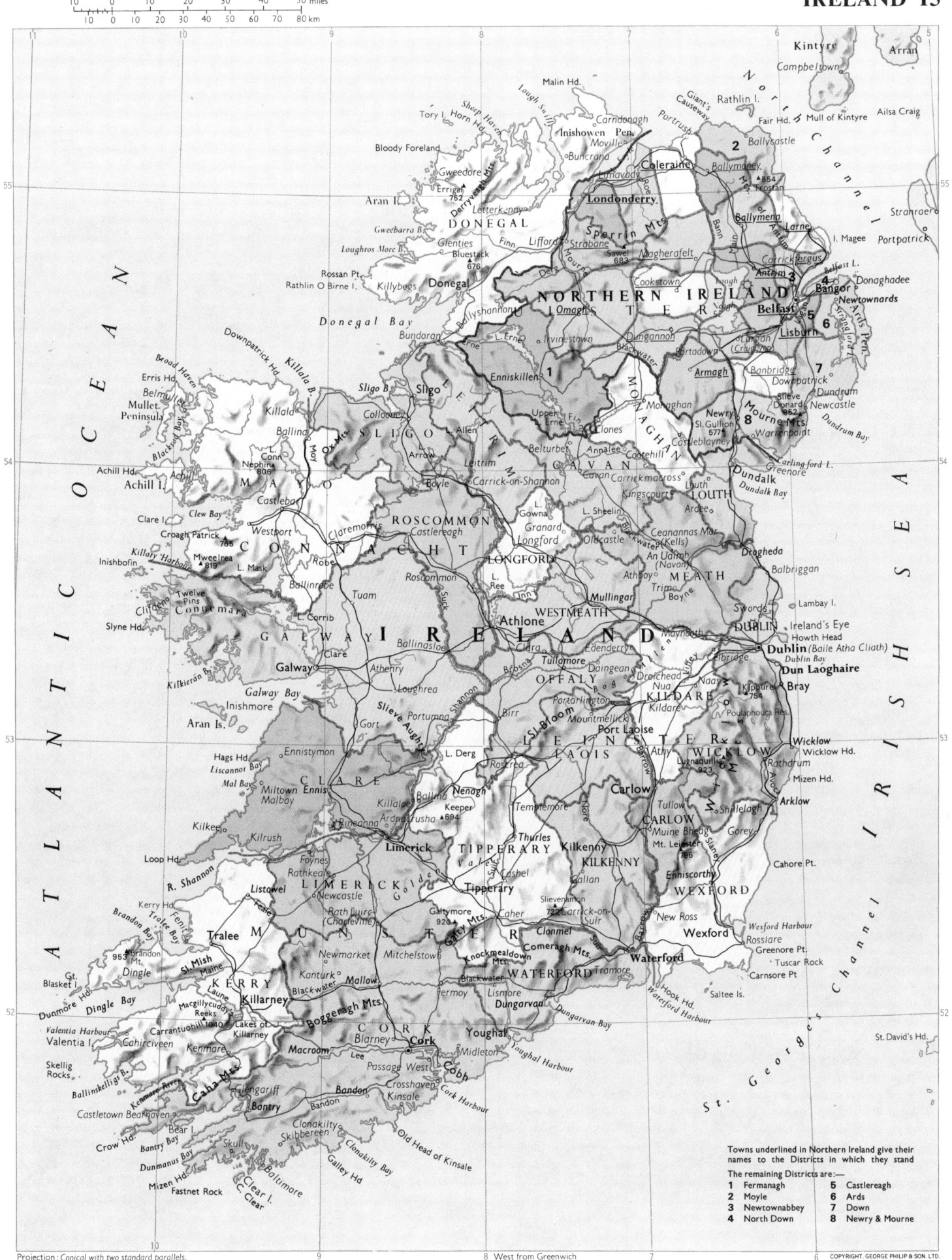

1:2 000 000

Projection: Conical with two standard parallels.

West from Greenwich

Towns underlined in Northern Ireland give their names to the Districts in which they stand

The remaining Districts are:—

1	Fermanagh	5	Castlereagh
2	Moyle	6	Ards
3	Newtownabbey	7	Down
4	North Down	8	Newry & Mourne

1:2 500 000

10 0 10 20 30 40 50 miles
10 0 10 20 30 40 50 60 70 80 km

Countries and seas:

NORTH SEA

ENGLAND

NETHERLANDS

BELGIUM

LUXEMBOURG

FRANCE

Major cities and towns (Netherlands):

AMSTERDAM, 's-GRAVENHAGE (The Hague), ROTTERDAM, Utrecht, Haarlem, Leiden, Delft, Dordrecht, Breda, Tilburg, Eindhoven, 's Hertogenbosch, Nijmegen, Arnhem, Apeldoorn, Deventer, Zwolle, Enschede, Hengelo, Almelo, Groningen, Leeuwarden, Assen, Emmen, Meppel, Hoogeveen, Den Helder, Alkmaar, Zaandam, Hilversum, Amersfoort, Zeist, Gouda, Vlaardingen, Schiedam, Vlissingen, Middelburg, Bergen-op-Zoom, Roosendaal, Oosterhout, Helmond, Venlo, Roermond, Weert, Zutphen, Ede, Veenendaal, Hoek van Holland, Scheveningen, Katwijk-aan-Zee, Noordwijk, Zandvoort, Beverwijk, IJmuiden, Heemstede, Bussum, Soest, Texel, Vlieland, Terschelling, Ameland, Schiermonnikoog

WADDEN ZEE, IJsselmeer, Noordoost-Polder, FRIESLAND, DRENTHE, OVERIJSSEL, GELDERLAND

Belgium:

BRUSSEL (Bruxelles), Antwerpen, Gent (Gand), Brugge (Bruges), Liège, Namur, Charleroi, Mons, Mechelen, Leuven, Aalst, Kortrijk, Roeselare, Oostende (Ostend), Hasselt, Genk, Verviers, Tournai, Mouscron, Roubaix, Tienen, Nivelles, Turnhout, Lier, Dendermonde, Sint Niklaas, Boom, Diest, Aarschot, Waterloo, Ninove, Geeraardsbergen, Ronse, Oudenaarde, Deinze, Wetteren, Herentals, Mol, Maaseik, Tongeren, Eupen, Malmedy, Dinant, Bastogne, Arlon

FLANDRES, HAINAUT, BRABANT, ARDENNES

Luxembourg:

Luxembourg, Esch, Ettelbrück, Diekirch, Wiltz, Clervaux, Echternach

Germany (east):

Bremerhaven, Wilhelmshaven, Oldenburg, Osnabrück, Münster, DORTMUND, ESSEN, DUISBURG, DÜSSELDORF, KÖLN (Cologne), Bonn, Wuppertal, Mönchengladbach, Krefeld, Neuss, Solingen, Remscheid, Leverkusen, Bochum, Gelsenkirchen, Oberhausen, Mülheim, Hagen, Herne, Recklinghausen, Bottrop, Hamm, Lippstadt, Aachen, Siegen, Koblenz, Wiesbaden, Mainz, Trier, Saarbrücken, Kaiserslautern, Neunkirchen, Völklingen, Idar-Oberstein, Emden, Groningen, Papenburg, Meppen, Lingen, Rheine, Nordhorn, Enschede

RHEINLAND-PFALZ, WESTFALEN, NIEDERRHEIN, SAARLAND, HUNSRÜCK, EIFEL

France (south):

PARIS, Versailles, St. Denis, St. Germain, Argenteuil, Lille, Tourcoing, Amiens, Arras, Douai, Valenciennes, Cambrai, St. Quentin, Laon, Soissons, Reims, Châlons-sur-Marne, Épernay, Beauvais, Compiègne, Noyon, Chauny, Calais, Dunkerque, Boulogne-sur-Mer, St. Omer, Béthune, Lens, Abbeville, Montdidier, Charleville-Mézières, Sedan, Verdun, Metz, Thionville, Nancy, Lunéville, Longwy, Montmédy, Strasbourg, Haguenau, Saverne, Sarrebourg, Sarreguemines, Forbach

PICARDIE, CHAMPAGNE, ARDENNES, LORRAINE, ALSACE, ARTOIS, FLANDRE

North Sea coast (England):

Great Yarmouth, Lowestoft, Southwold, Aldeburgh, Orford Ness, Beccles, Bungay, North Walsham, Dover, Caister

Yare, Waveney

Projection: Conical with two standard parallels

East from Greenwich

COPYRIGHT. GEORGE PHILIP & SON. LTD.

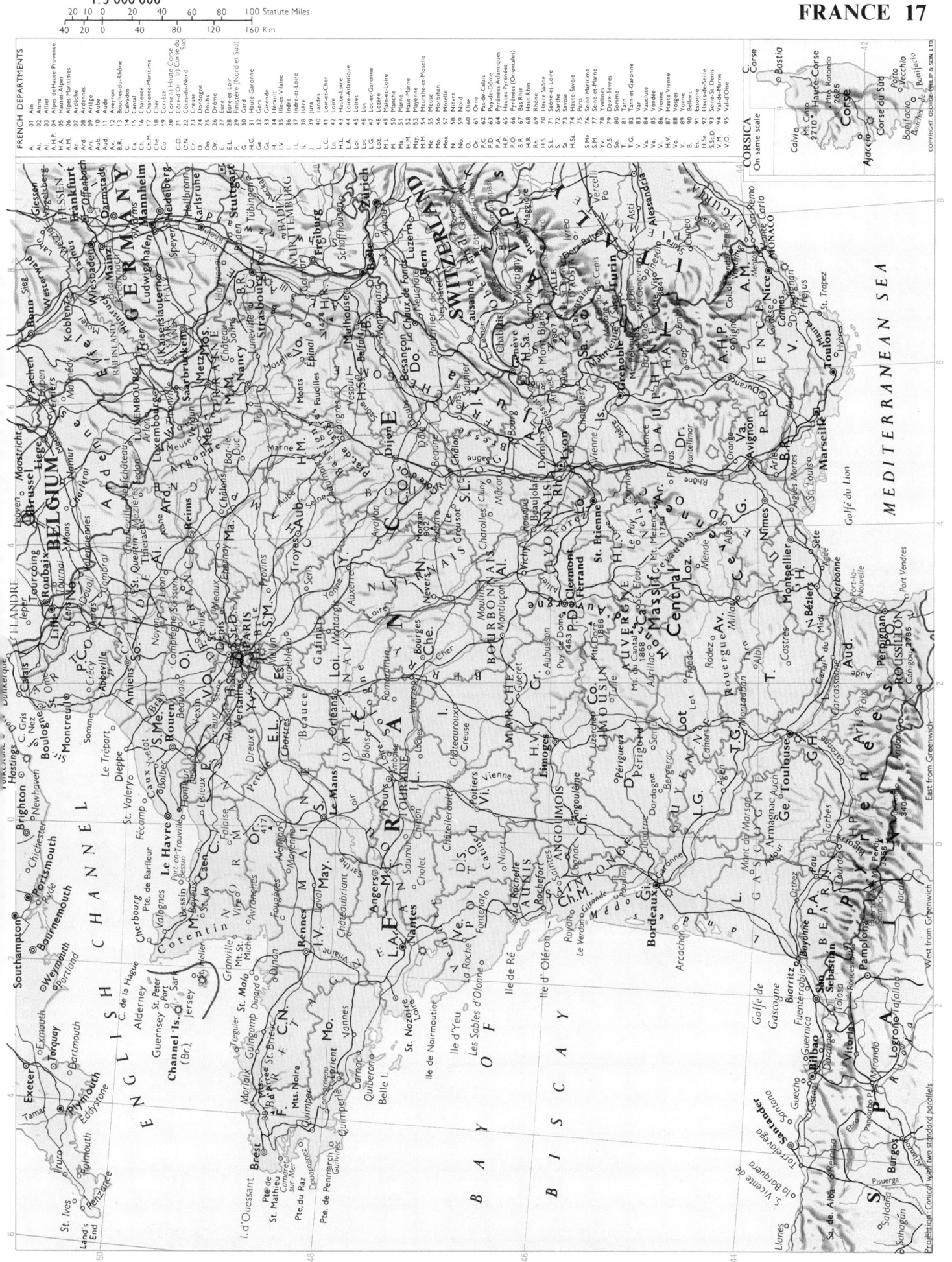

Bideford
South Molton
Bampton
Tiverton
Yeovil
Sherborne
Crewkerne
Romsey
Eastleigh
Midhurst
Haywards Heath
Tenterden
Hythe
Folk

Bude
Holsworthy
Okehampton
621
Chard
Blandford
Southampton
Fareham
Chichester
Lewes
Battle
Rother
Rye
Hastings

Trevose Hd.
Pudstow
Launceston
Princetown
Tavistock
Newton Abbot
Honiton
Dorchester
Lymington
Cowes
I. of Wight
Bognor Regis
Littlehampton
Worthing
Brighton
Bexhill
Eastbourne
Beachy Head
Dungeness

Newquay
Redruth
Camborne
St. Ives
Morazion
Bodmin
Saltash
Plymouth
Fowey
Dartmoor
Torquay
Paignton
Brixham
Dartmouth
Poole
Bournemouth
Swanage
Portland Bill
Wareham
Weymouth
Lyme Bay

Penzance
Helston
Falmouth
Land's End
Lizard Pt.

E n g l i s h   C h a n n e l

CHANNEL
Guernsey
St. Peter Port
ISLANDS
Jersey
St. Helier

B A Y   O F   B I S C A Y

B R E T A G N E

Brest
Quimper
Lorient
Vannes
Rennes
Laval
Le Mans

Nantes
Angers
Tours

La Roche-sur-Yon
Poitiers

La Rochelle
Rochefort
Niort
Châtellerault

Angoulême

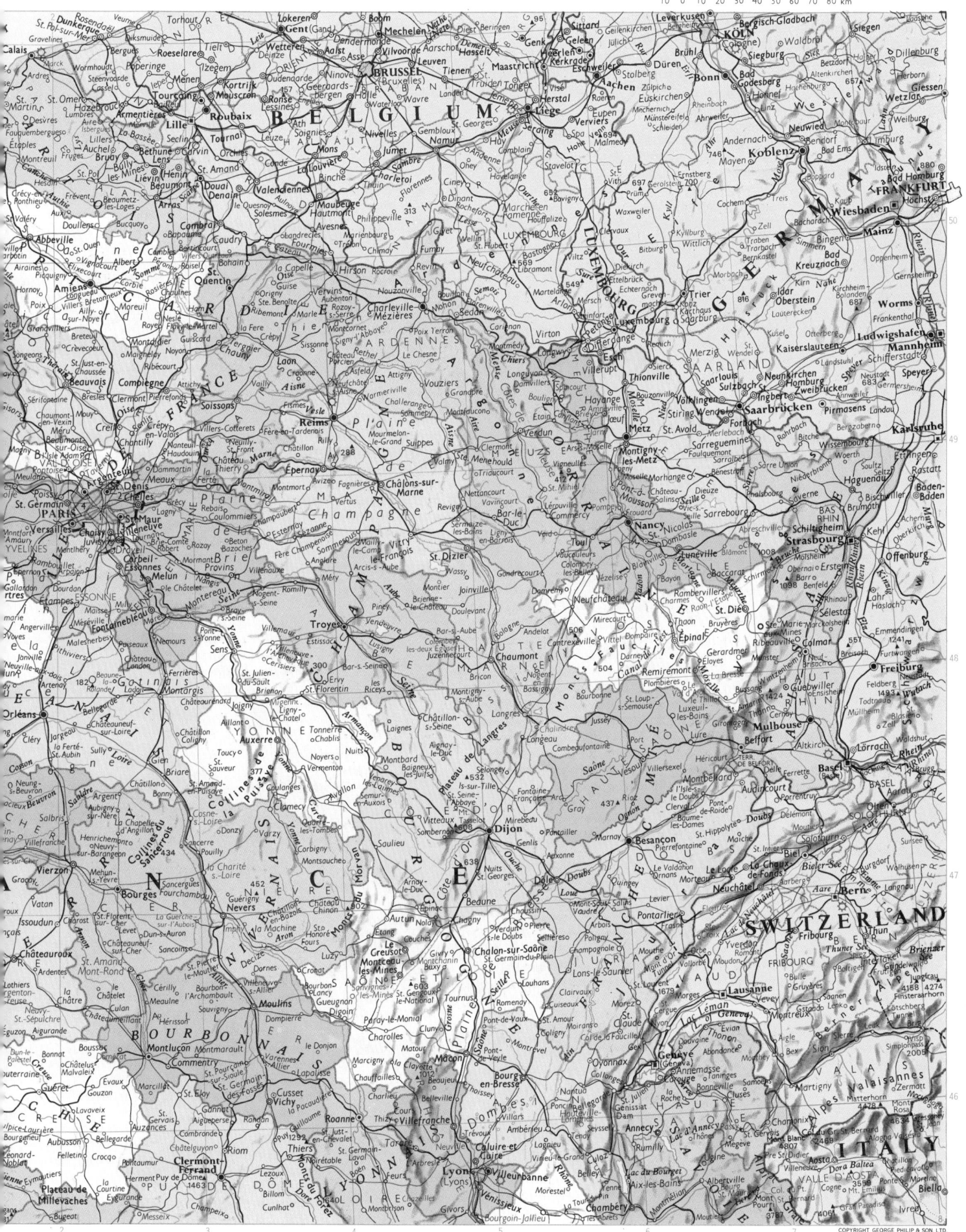

1:2 500 000

1 : 2 500 000

1:5 000 000

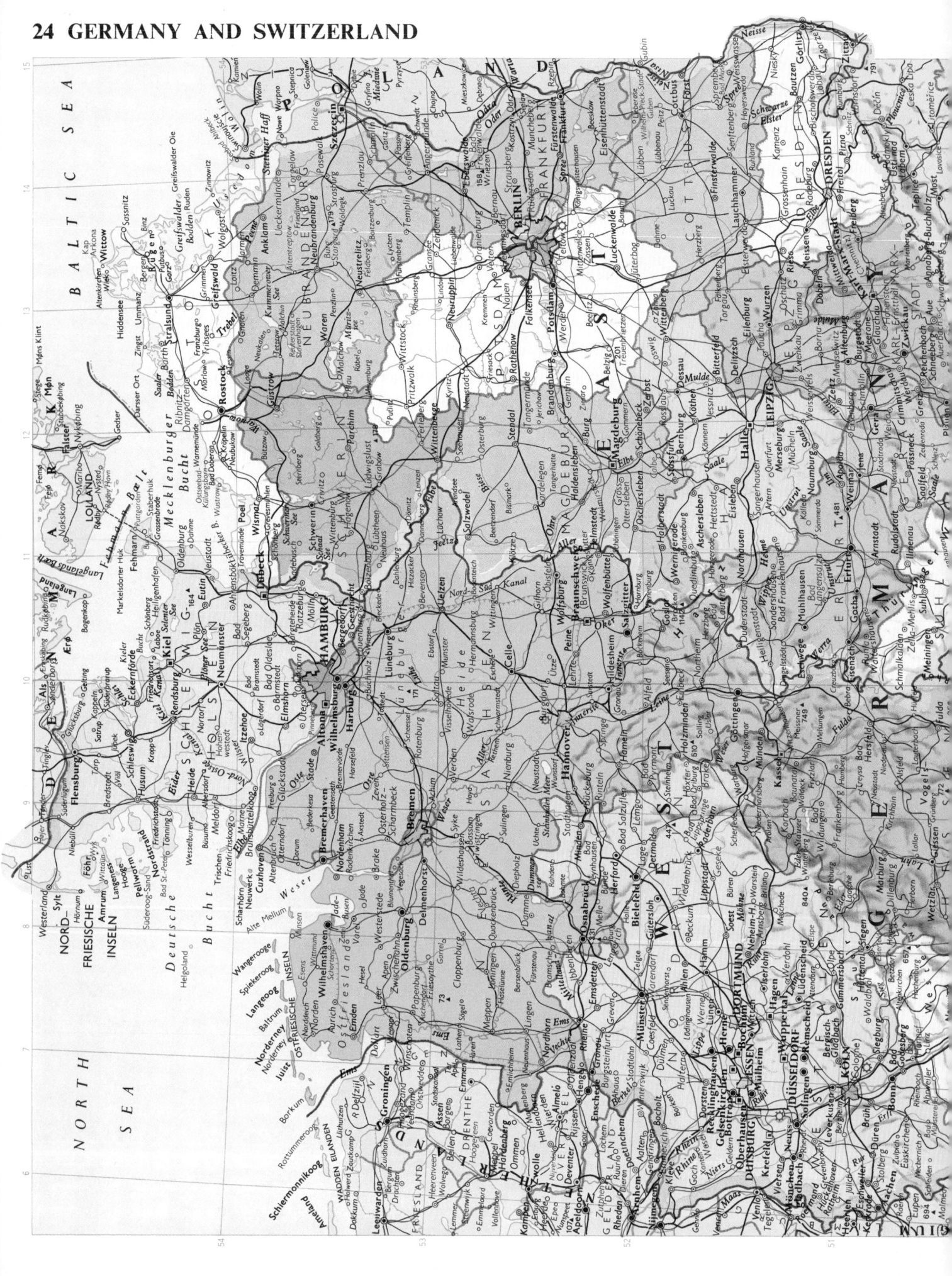

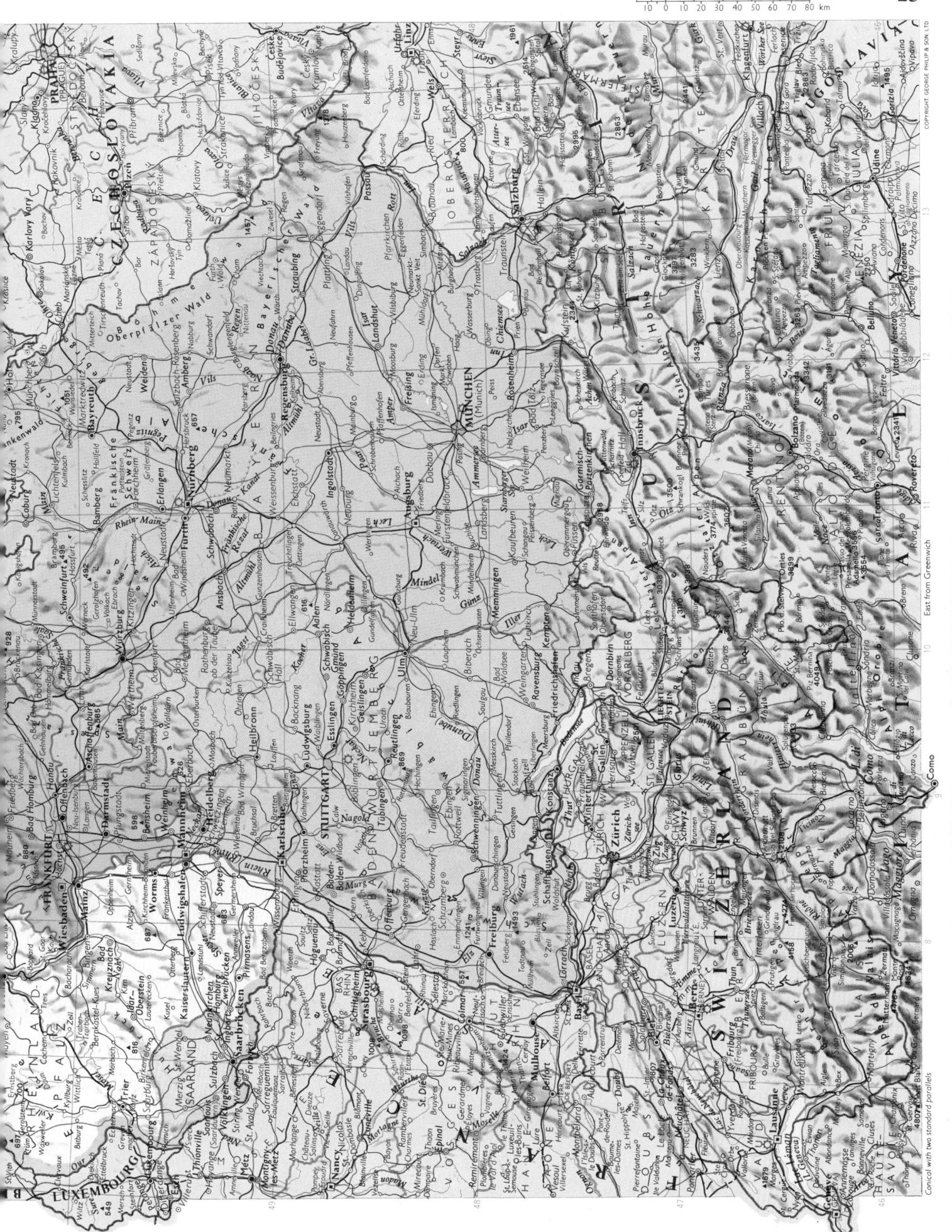

1:2 500 000

50 miles

80 km

East from Greenwich

Conical with two standard parallels

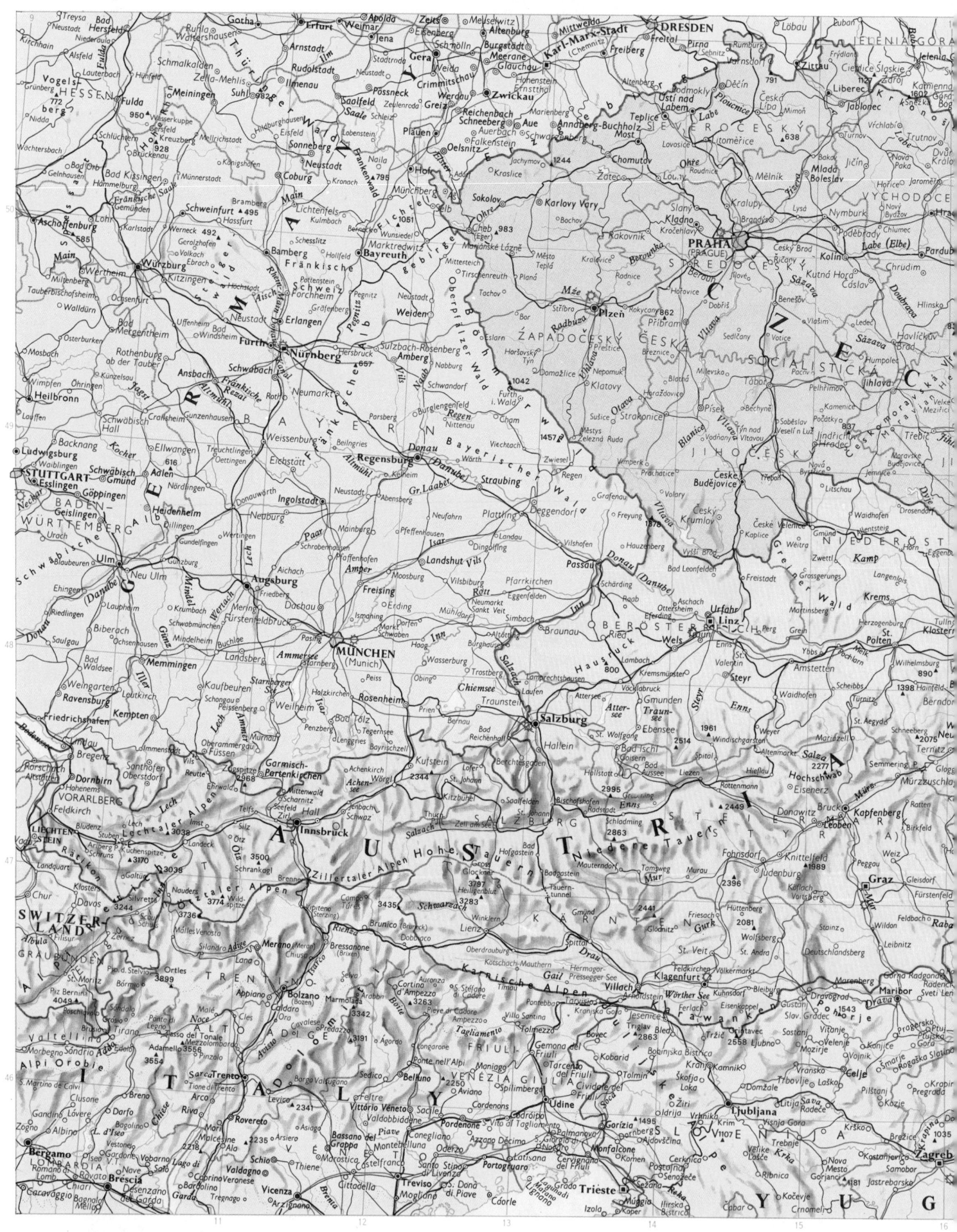

1:2 500 000

10 0 10 20 30 40 50 miles
10 0 10 20 30 40 50 60 70 80 km

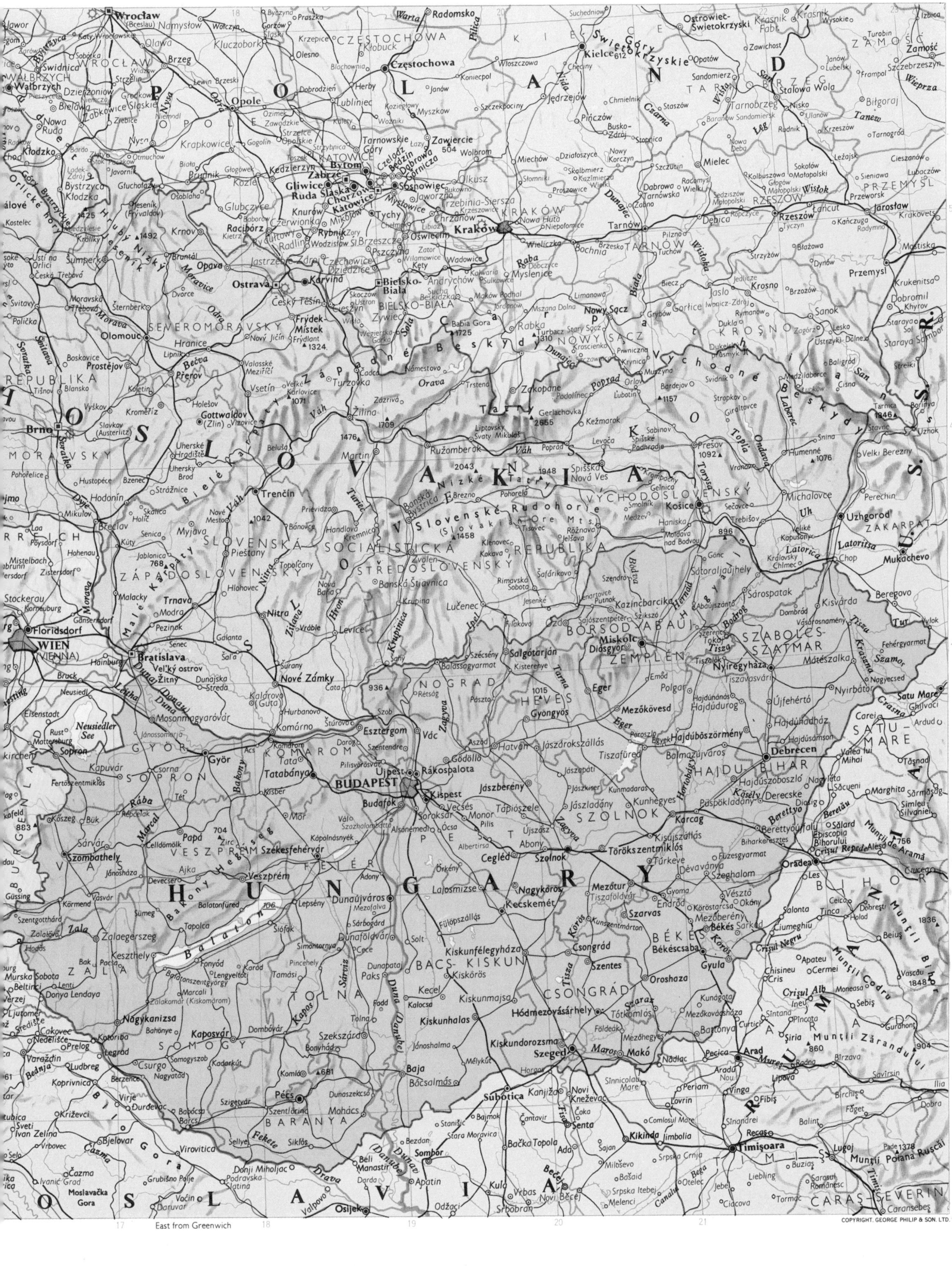

P O L A N D

Wrocław (Breslau)
Częstochowa
Opole
KATOWICE
Kraków
Kielce
Rzeszów
Przemyśl
Tarnów
TARNÓW
KROSNO
NOWY SĄCZ

Ostrava
Olomouc
Brno
Č O S L O V A K I A
SLOVENSKÁ SOCIALISTICKÁ REPUBLIKA
ZÁPADOSLOVENSKÝ
STREDOSLOVENSKÝ
VÝCHODOSLOVENSKÝ
Slovenské Rudohorie (Slovak Ore Mts.)
Nízke Tatry
Vysoké Tatry
Gerlachovka 2655
Žilina
Trenčín
Nitra
Bratislava
Košice
Prešov
Uzhgorod
Mukachevo
ZAKARPAT

WIEN (VIENNA)
Floridsdorf
Neusiedler See
Sopron
GYŐR
Győr
Komárom
Esztergom
Tatabánya
Székesfehérvár
Veszprém
VESZPRÉM

BUDAPEST
Kispest
Budafok
Újpest
Rákospalota
PEST
NÓGRÁD
HEVES
Eger
Gyöngyös
Miskolc
BORSOD-ABAÚJ
ZEMPLÉN
SZABOLCS-SZATMÁR
Nyíregyháza
Debrecen
HAJDÚ-BIHAR
SZOLNOK
Szolnok
Kecskemét
BÁCS-KISKUN
CSONGRÁD
Szeged
BÉKÉS
Békéscsaba
Gyula

H U N G A R Y

Zalaegerszeg
ZALA
SOMOGY
Kaposvár
Pécs
BARANYA
Nagykanizsa
TOLNA
Szekszárd

Y U G O S L A V I A
Subotica
Kikinda
Timişoara
CARAŞ-SEVERIN
R O M A N I A
Arad
Oradea
BIHOR
SATU-MARE
Satu Mare

Balaton

East from Greenwich

COPYRIGHT. GEORGE PHILIP & SON. LTD.

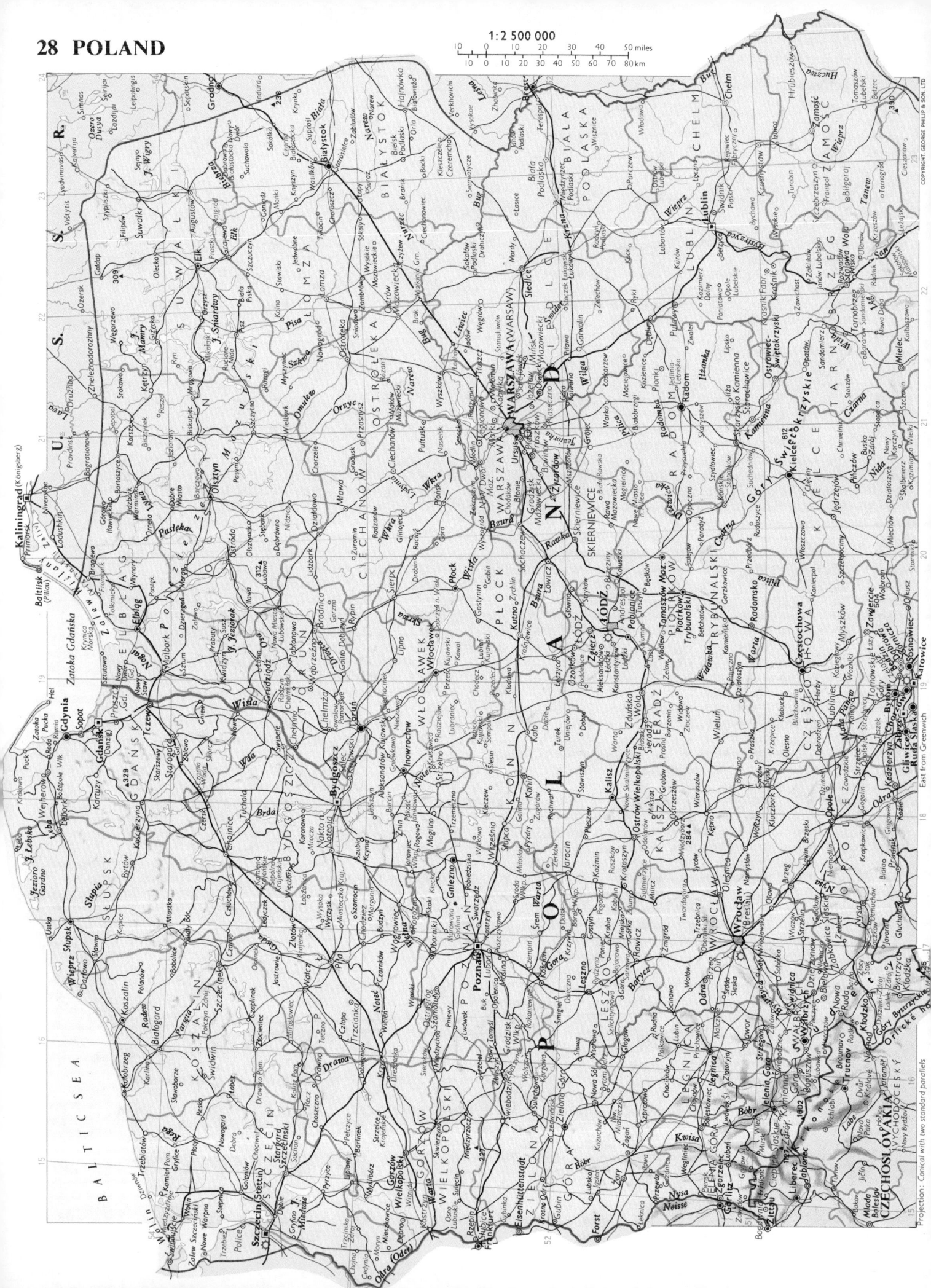

1:5,000,000

50 0 50 100 miles
50 0 50 100 150 km

COPYRIGHT GEORGE PHILIP & SON LTD.

East from Greenwich

West from Greenwich

Projection : Conical with two standard parallels

FRANCE

ANDORRA

SPAIN

PORTUGAL

ALGERIA

MOROCCO

MEDITERRANEAN SEA

ATLANTIC OCEAN

Bay of Biscay

Golfe du Lion

Balearic Islands

Mallorca

Menorca

Ibiza

Formentera

Cabrera

Madrid

Barcelona

Valencia

Sevilla

Zaragoza

Málaga

Bilbao

Murcia

Alicante

Córdoba

Granada

Lisboa (Lisbon)

Porto

Montpellier

Béziers

Narbonne

Perpignan

Toulouse

Pau

Bayonne

Biarritz

San Sebastián

Pamplona

Logroño

Burgos

Valladolid

Palencia

León

Oviedo

Gijón

Avilés

La Coruña

Santiago de Compostela

Pontevedra

Vigo

Orense

Lugo

Ferrol

Salamanca

Zamora

Segovia

Ávila

Toledo

Ciudad Real

Albacete

Cuenca

Guadalajara

Teruel

Castellón de la Plana

Tarragona

Tortosa

Lérida

Huesca

Gerona

Tarrasa

Sabadell

Badalona

Hospitalet

Sitges

Almería

Guadix

Jaén

Linares

Cartagena

Lorca

Elche

Denia

Gibraltar (Br.)

Algeciras

Cádiz

Jerez

Huelva

Badajoz

Cáceres

Mérida

Évora

Coimbra

Braga

Setúbal

Santarém

Ceuta (Sp.)

Tetouán

Tánger

Alger

Oran

Mostaganem

Tenès

Blida

Boufarik

Koléa

Khemis Miliana

El Asnam

GALICIA

ASTURIAS

CANTABRICA

NAVARRA

ARAGÓN

CASTILLA LA VIEJA

CASTILLA LA NUEVA

EXTREMADURA

ANDALUCIA

MURCIA

VALENCIA

CATALUÑA

LEÓN

VASCONGADAS

Sierra de Guadarrama

Sierra de Gredos

Sierra Morena

Sierra Nevada

Sierra de la Demanda

Pyrenees

Picos de Europa

Ebro

Duero

Tajo

Guadiana

Guadalquivir

Miño

Douro

Mondego

Tejo

Golfo de Valencia

Golfo de Cádiz

Golfo de San Jorge

Golfo de Rosas

Strait of Gibraltar

Costa Brava

C. de Gata

C. de Palos

C. Nao

C. de S. Vicente

C. da Roca

C. Finisterre

C. Ortegal

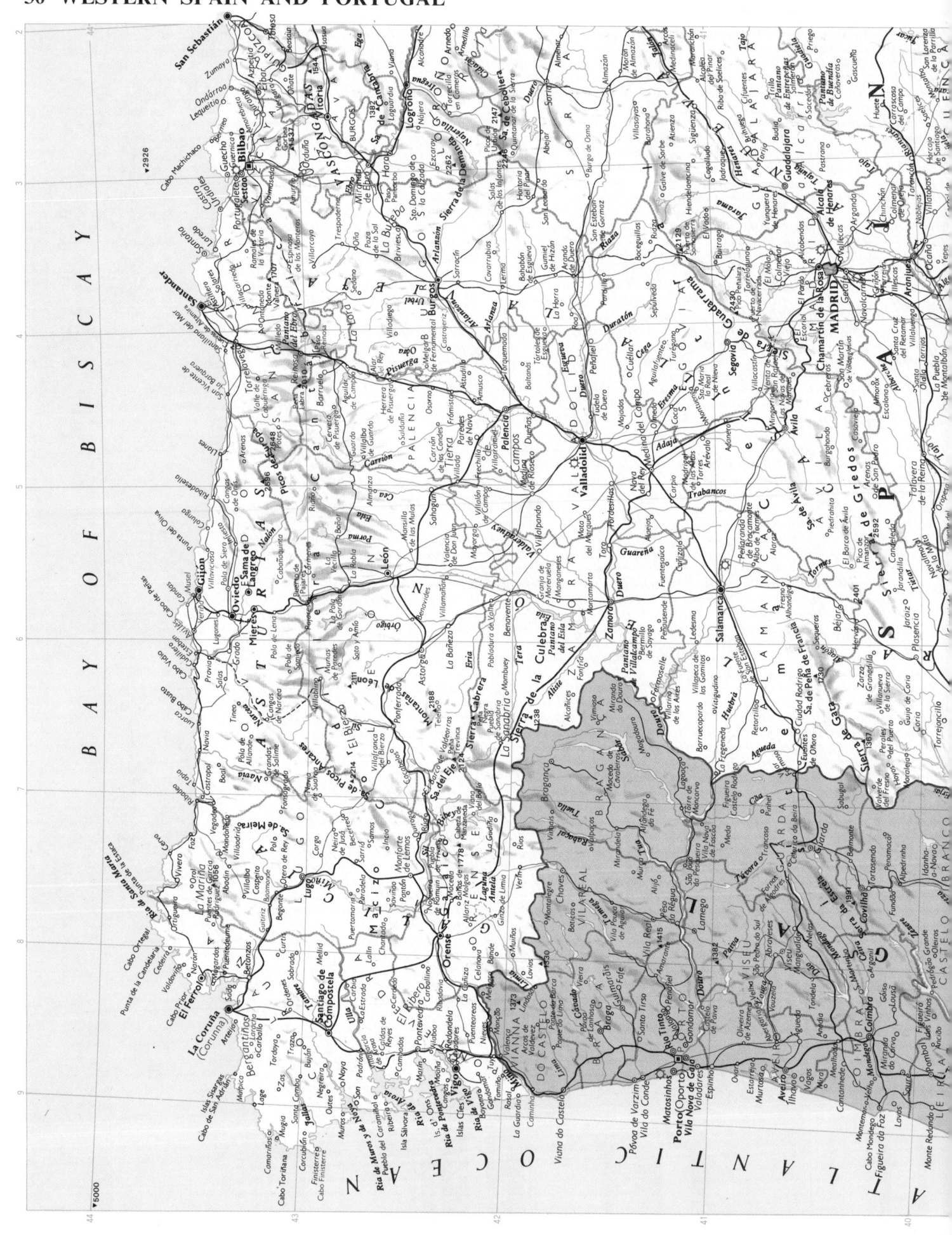

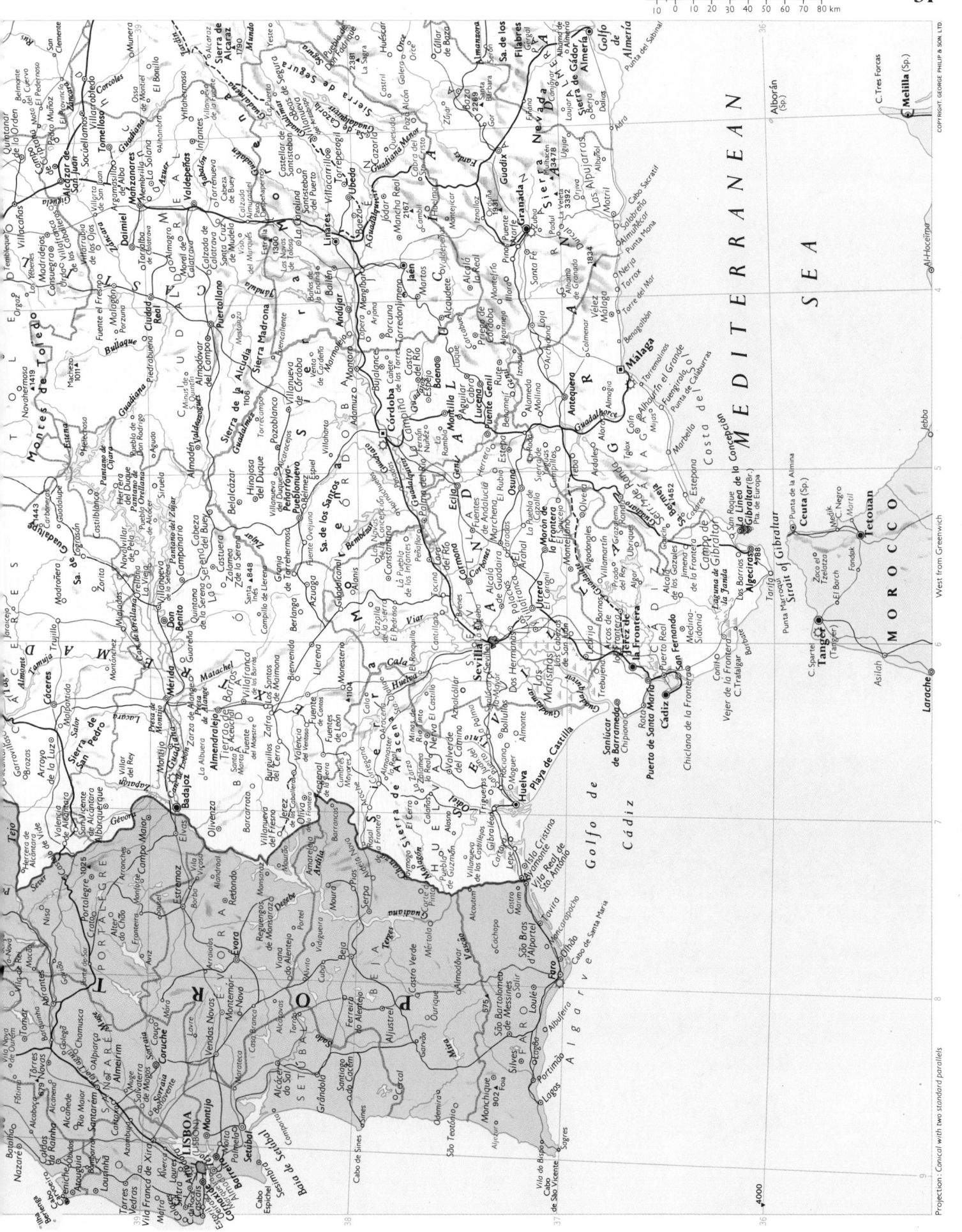

1:2 500 000

10 0 10 20 30 40 50 miles
10 0 10 20 30 40 50 60 70 80 km

COPYRIGHT GEORGE PHILIP & SON LTD.

M E D I T E R R A N E A N

S E A

MOROCCO

Projection: Conical with two standard parallels

West from Greenwich

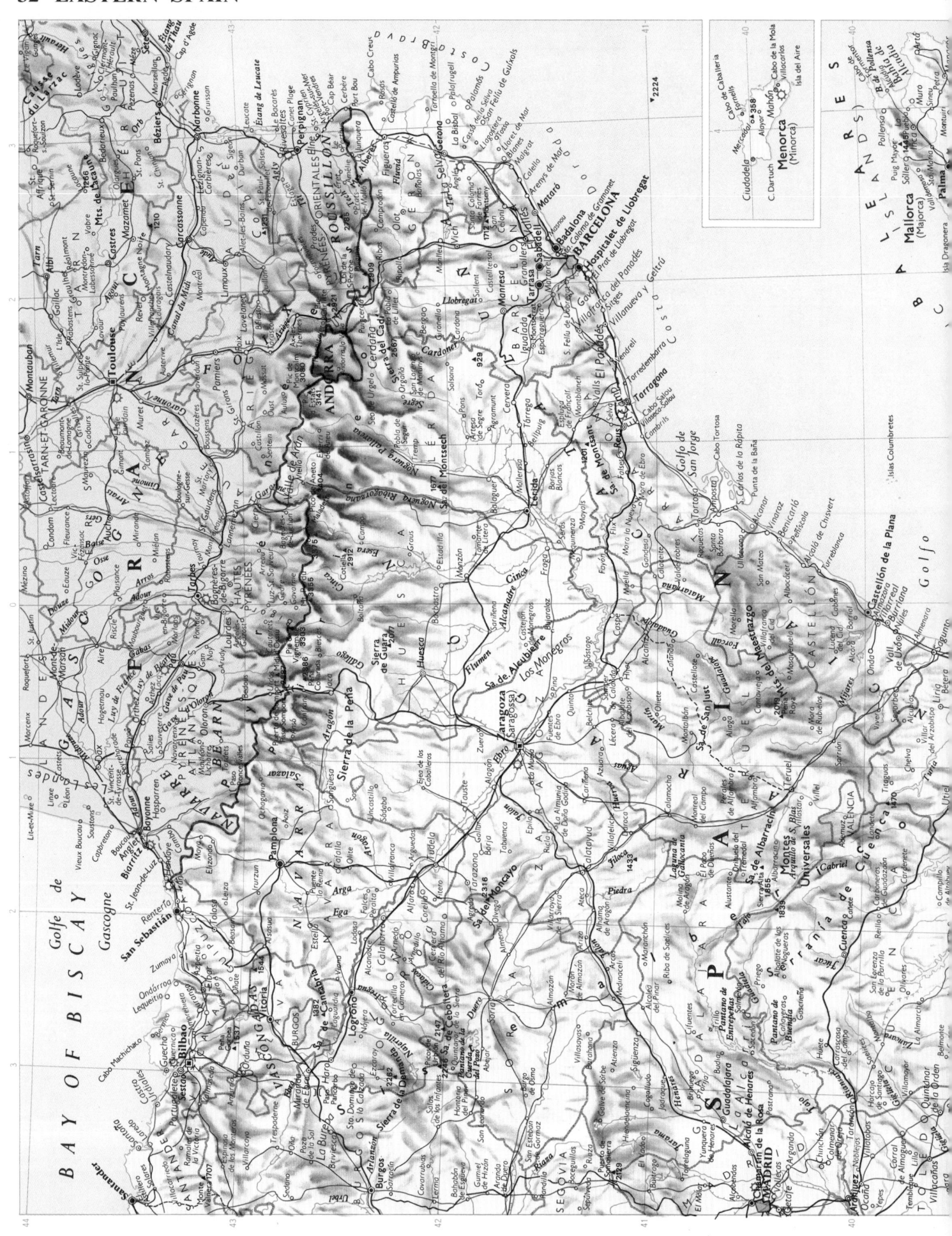

1:2 500 000

10   0   10   20   30   40   50   miles
10 0 10 20 30 40 50 60 70 80   km

COPYRIGHT GEORGE PHILIP & SON, LTD.

Projection : Conical with two standard parallels

West from Greenwich   East from Greenwich

MEDITERRANEAN SEA

BALEARIC SEA

ALGERIA

MOROCCO

ALGER (Algiers)

ORAN

Cartagena

Alicante

Murcia

Granada

Almería

Albacete

Valencia

Ibiza (Iviza)

Formentera

Projection: Conical with two
standard parallels.   West from Greenwich   0   East from Greenwich

LIGURIAN SEA

Golfo di Génova

CORSE
(CORSICA)

Iles Sanguinaires
G. d'Ajaccio
C. di Muro
Tafaroo
Pinarellu
2136 Zonza
Levie
Solenzara
Favone
G. de Valinco
Sartège
Porto-Vecchio
Propriano

CORSE
CORSICA
CORSE-DU-SUD
Iles Cerbicales

Bonifacio
I. de Cavallo

Santa Teresa Gallura
Bouches de Bonifacio
Maddalena
La Maddalena
Caprera
Punta dello Scorno
Asinara

41

Golfo dell'
Asinara
Coghinas
Àggius
Tèmpio Pausania
Calangiànus
G. di Olbia
1362
M. Limbara
Olbia
Golfo Aranci
Tavolara

Porto Tórres
Sorso
Sennori
Uschiri
Osilo
Sássari
L. di Coghinas
Posada
Ittiri
Ozieri
Pattada
Siniscola
C. dell'Argentiera
Fértilia
Alghero
Buddusò
Villanova
Monteleone
1259
Bonòrva
Bitti
C. Comino

Bosa
Macomer
Núoro
Orune
Dorgali

Temo
Ottieri
Golfo di
Orosei

SARDEGNA
Ghilarza
L. del Tirso
Sorgono
Monti del
Gennargentu
1834
Bauner
C. di Monte Santu

40

C. Mannu
Oristano
SARDEGNA
Lacôni
Arbatax

Golfo di
Oristano
M. Arci
812
Lànusei
Àrborea
Terralba
Nurri
Jerzu

SARDINIA

Gúspini
Montevale
S. Gavino
Sànluri
Villaputzu
Muravera

Arbus
1236
Gonnostanadíga
Villacidro
S. Vitao
C. Pécora
M. Linas
Serramanna
Dolianova
Fluminimaggiore
Villacidro
Sestu
Pta. Serpedi
Senorbi
C. Ferrato

Iglésias
Cixerri
Assémini
Sinnai
1069
Portoscuso
Gonnesa
Siliqua
Quartu Sant'Elena
Carloforte
Carbónia
Selárgius
Serpentara
San Pietro
1116
Santadi
Cágliari
C. Carbonara
Sant'Antioco
Porto Botte
Pula
Golfo di
Cágliari

39

Sant'
Antíoco
Teulada

G. di Palmas
C. Spartivento

Projection: Conical with two standard parallels

TYRRHENIAN

SEA

3719

3589

Ustica

Vatican City
ROMA
(Rome)
Tívoli
Sàbiaco
Tràsacco
Conca del Fúcino

Fregene
Palestrina
Volmontone
Anagni
Alatri
Sora
Véroli

Lido di Óstia
(Lido di Roma)
Velletri
Cori
Ferentino
Arpino
Monte S. Giov.

Prática
di Mare
Cisterna
Ceccano
Frosinone
Cassino

Ánzio
Nettuno
Latina
Priverno
Sonnino
Fondi
1533
Ponteco

Pontínia
Sabáudio
541
Terracina
Gaeta
Minturno
Formia

Monte Circeo
Garigliano

Zannone
Golfo di
Cariñ

Palmarola
Ponza
Gaeta
Mondragone

Ísole
Ponziane
283
Voltur

Ventotene
788
Giugl
Pro

Íschia
(Naples)

C. San Vito
del Golfo
Favorotta
C. Gallo

Levanzo
Trápani
Érice
1110
PALERMO
Bagheria
Ísole Égadi
Alcamo
Partinico
Misilmeri

Maréttimo
Paceo
Giuseppe
Jato
Favignana
Calatafimi
Camporeale
1613
Belsito
Stagnone
Carleone
Prizzi
Lercara
Mac

Marsala
Salemi
Gibellina
Marineo
Alia

Partanna
Bisacquino
Sambuca
di Sicília
Lercara
Friddi
Alia

Castelvetrano
Menfi
Burgio
Mussomeli
Cate

Mazara
del Vallo
Belice
Sciacca
Calaboli
Castelterm
San Catalo
Calta

Campobello di Mazara
Ribera
Platani
Racalmuto
Caníco

Sicilian Channel
Cattólica Eraclea
Siculiano
Magna
Naro
Favara

Porto Empédocle
Agrigento
Palma di Montechiaro
Licata
Ryan

Palma di
Campobella

Iles de la
Galite

C. Blanc
Cani

C. Serrat
Bizerte
(Binzert)
Plane

Menzel-Bourguiba
Zembra

Mateur
Golfe de Tunis
C. Bon

El Kala
Tabarka
Halq el Oued
(La Goulette)
Kelibia

TUNIS
Menzel
Temime

Téboursouk
Béja
Soliman

Médjerda
Nabeul

Zaghouan
Hammamet

TUNISIA
Téboursouk

Pantelleria
Pantelleria
836 (It.)

1319

MEDITE

East from Greenwich

Projection: Conical with two standard parallels

East from Greenwich

1:2 500 000

10 0 10 20 30 40 50 miles
10 0 10 20 30 40 50 60 70 80 km

TRANSILVANIA

U.S.S.R.

UKRAINIAN S.S.R.

IZMAIL

ROMÂNIA

WALACHIA / VALAHIA

BUCUREŞTI (Bucharest)

Ploieşti

Braşov (Oraşul Stalin)

Sibiu

Galaţi

Brăila

Constanţa

DOBRUDJA

BULGARIA

Sofiya (Sofia)

Plovdiv (Philippopolis)

Stara Zagora

Varna

Burgas

Burgaski Zaliv

Ruse (Ruschuk)

Pleven

Tolbukhin (Dobrich Bazargic)

Kolarovgrad (Shumen)

BLACK SEA

Istanbul

Üsküdar

TURKEY

Edirne (Adrianople)

KIRKLARELI

TEKIRDAĞ

GREECE / Ἑλλάς

DRÁMA

XÁNTHI

Komotiní

Rodopi

Karadeniz Boğazı (Bosporus)

Dunărea (Danube)

COPYRIGHT GEORGE PHILIP & SON, LTD.

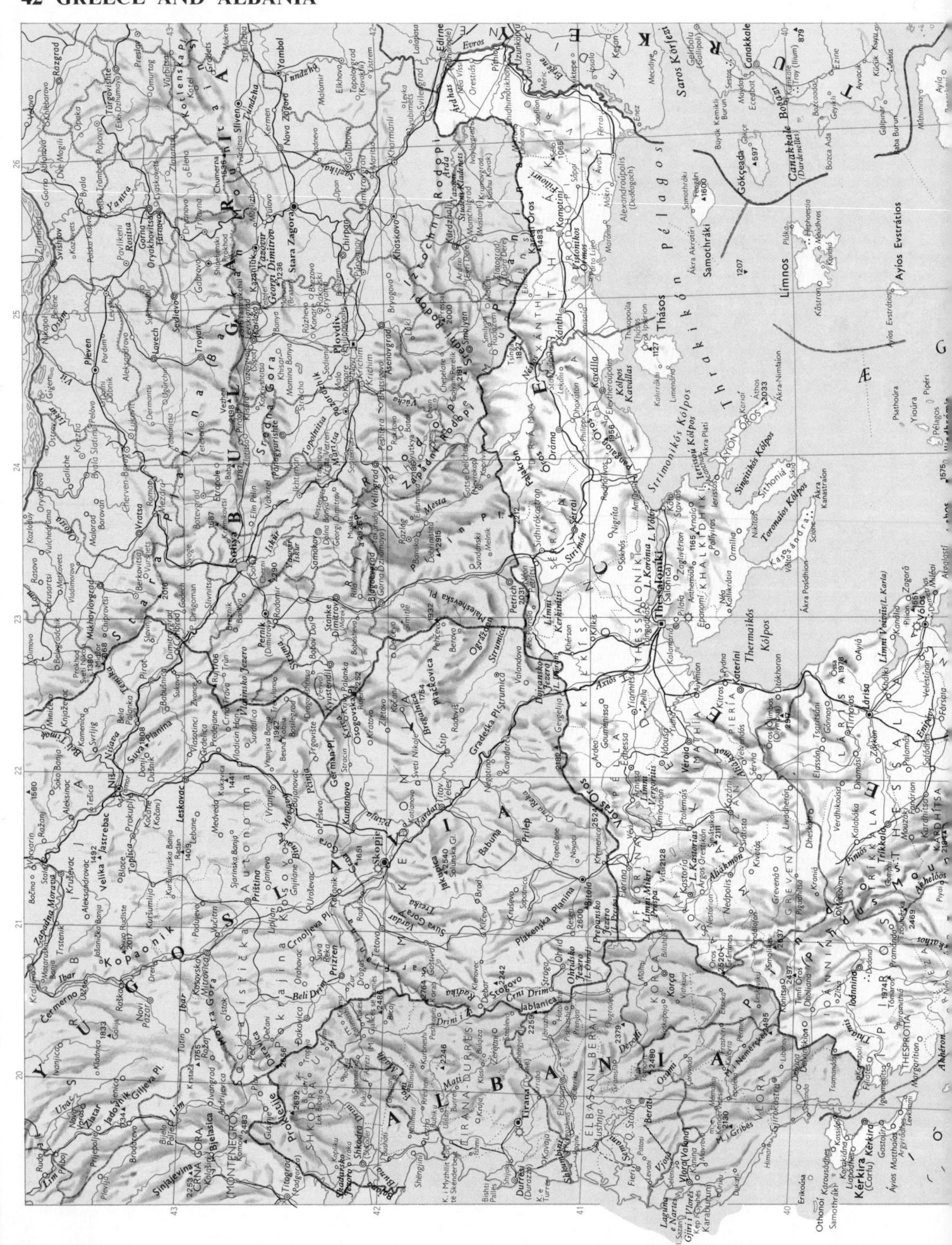

SEA OF CRETE

(Sea of Candia)

KIKLÁDHES

(C Y C L A D E S)

Khíos (Chios)

Psará

Ikaría

Mikonos

Ándros

Tínos

Síros

Náxos

Páros

Íos

Thíra

Sífnos

Mílos

Kíthnos

Kéa

Sérifos

Skíros

Skópelos

(Northern Sporades)

ATTIKÍ

ATHÍNAI

Piraiévs (Piraeus)

Saronikós Kólpos

Korinthiakós Kólpos

Korinthos (Corinth)

Corinth Canal

PELOPÓNNISOS

Taíyetos Óros

Párnon Óros

Árkadía

Lakonikós Kólpos

Messiniakós Kólpos

Kíthira (Cerigo)

Kárpathos

Ródhos (Rhodes)

Stenón Karpáthos

DHODHEKÁNISOS (DODECANESE)

Kos

Sámos

Astipálaia

Amorgós

Astipálaia

Iráklion

KRÍTI (CRETE)

Khersónisos Akrotíri Soúdhas

Khaniá (Canea)

Kólpos Khanion

Kólpos Kisámou

Kólpos Mesará

Kefallinía (Cephalonia)

Zákinthos (Zante)

Levkás (Santa Maura)

Itháki (Ithaca)

Préveza

Nicopolis

Pátrai

Agrínion

Mesolóngion

AITOLÍA

AKARNANÍA

Lamía

Khalkís (Chalcis)

Thívai (Thebes)

Elevsís (Eleusis)

Spárti (Sparta)

Trípolis

Kalámata

Pílos

IONIAN SEA

(Sea of Candia)

Kușada Körfezi

Sámos

Samsun Dağı

Büyük Menderes

Bafa Gölü

Milas

MUĞLA

Kerme Körfezi

Bodrum (Halicarnassus)

Símí

Tílos (Piscopi)

Nísiros

Continuation Eastwards
on same scale

1:2 500 000

miles
10   0   10   20   30   40   50   miles
10   0   10   20   30   40   50   60   70   80   km

BALTIC   SEA

POLAND

Gotland

ÖSTERGÖTLANDS

KALMAR   LÄN

Öland

Oskarshamn

Kalmar

JÖNKÖPINGS   LÄN

KRONOBERGS   LÄN

BLEKINGE   LÄN

Karlskrona

Karlshamn

SKARABORGS   LÄN

ÄLVSBORGS   LÄN

HALLANDS   LÄN

KRISTIANSTADS L.

MALMÖHUS L.

Bornholm

GERMANY

Göteborg

Borås

Halmstad

Helsingborg

Malmö

Trelleborg

Kattegat

Skagerrak

Jammerbugt

Aalborg Bucht

Frederikshavn

NORDJYLLANDS   AMT

VENDSYSSEL

Aarhus

VIBORG   AMT

RINGKJØBING   AMT

VEJLE   AMT

J   Y   L   L   A   N   D

SØNDERJYLLANDS   AMT

RIBE   AMT

Esbjerg

Kolding

Flensburg

Schleswig

Rendsburg

Kiel

FYN

Odense

SJÆLLAND

KØBENHAVN
COPENHAGEN

Roskilde

Næstved

SORØ AMT

STORSTRØMS AMT

LOLLAND

FALSTER

Møn

Kieler Bucht

Fehmarn

East from Greenwich

Projection: Conical with two standard parallels

ICELAND
on the same scale
as general map

NORWEGIAN SEA

1:5 000 000

20 10 0 20 40 60 80 100 miles
40 20 0 40 80 120 160 km

East from Greenwich

Projection: Conical with two standard parallels

S E A

B A L T I C

G U L F   O F   F I N L A N D

GULF OF BOTHNIA

Åland hav

Gulf of Riga (Rigas Jūras Līcis)

Skagerrak

Kattegat

HELSINKI (Helsingfors)
Tampere
Turku (Åbo)
Pori (Björneborg)
Rauma
Hämeenlinna
Lahti
Kotka
Tallinn
Haapsalu
Pärnu
Valga
Viljandi
Rakvere
Saaremaa (Ösel)
Hiiumaa (Dagö)
Riga
Valmiera
Jelgava
Liepāja
Ventspils
Klaipėda
Kaliningrad
Chernyakhovsk
Sovetsk
Kaunas
Vilnius
Grodno
Białystok
Łomża
Ostrołęka
Gdańsk
Gdynia
Elbląg
Grudziądz
Toruń
Bydgoszcz
Szczecin

E S T O N I A N   S.S.R.
L A T V I A N   S.S.R.
L I T H U A N I A N   S.S.R.
R.S.F.S.R.
P O L A N D
G E R M A N Y

STOCKHOLM
Uppsala
Västerås
Eskilstuna
Södertälje
Nyköping
Norrköping
Linköping
Motala
Örebro
Karlstad
Falun
Borlänge
Gävle
Söderhamn
Hudiksvall
Bollnäs
Mariehamn (Maarianhamina)
Åland (Ahvenanmaa)
Gotland
Visby
Fårö
Öland
Kalmar
Karlskrona
Karlshamn
Växjö
Jönköping
Borås
GÖTEBORG
Trollhättan
Vänersborg
Uddevalla
Halmstad
Helsingborg
MALMÖ
Ystad
Kristianstad
Landskrona
Trelleborg
Varberg
Falkenberg
Lidköping
Skövde
Mjölby
Västervik
Oskarshamn
Nässjö
Värnamo
Ljungby
Bornholm
Rønne

SVERIGE
VÄRMLAND
DALARNA
KOPPARBERG
ÖSTERGÖTLAND
SÖDERMANLAND
VÄSTMANLAND
SMÅLAND
HALLAND
SKÅNE
BLEKINGE
KRONOBERG
JÖNKÖPING
ÄLVSBORG
GÖTEBORG OCH BOHUS
GOTLAND
KALMAR
GÄVLEBORG

OSLO
Drammen
Hamar
Lillehammer
Kongsberg
Skien
Larvik
Tønsberg
Arendal
Kristiansand
Grimstad
Lillesand
Mandal
Farsund
Flekkefjord
Egersund (Eigersund)
Stavanger
Sandnes
Haugesund
Bergen

NORGE
OPPLAND
HEDMARK
BUSKERUD
TELEMARK
AUST-AGDER
VEST-AGDER
ROGALAND
HORDALAND
SOGN OG FJORDANE
ØSTFOLD
AKERSHUS
VESTFOLD

D E N M A R K
København
Roskilde
Helsingør
Nykøbing
Odense
Svendborg
Nyborg
Kolding
Fredericia
Vejle
Horsens
Silkeborg
Herning
Viborg
Randers
Århus
Ålborg
Hjørring
Thisted
Esbjerg
Ribe
Sjælland
Fyn
Store Bælt
Lille Bælt
Limfjorden
Falster
Lolland
Møn

Kiel
Lübeck
Hamburg
Rostock
Schwerin
Wismar
Flensburg
Bremerhaven
Wilhelmshaven
Oldenburg
Bremen
Emden
Groningen

G E R M A N Y
N E D E R L A N D

Nordfriesische Inseln
Ostfriesische Inseln
Rügen
Usedom

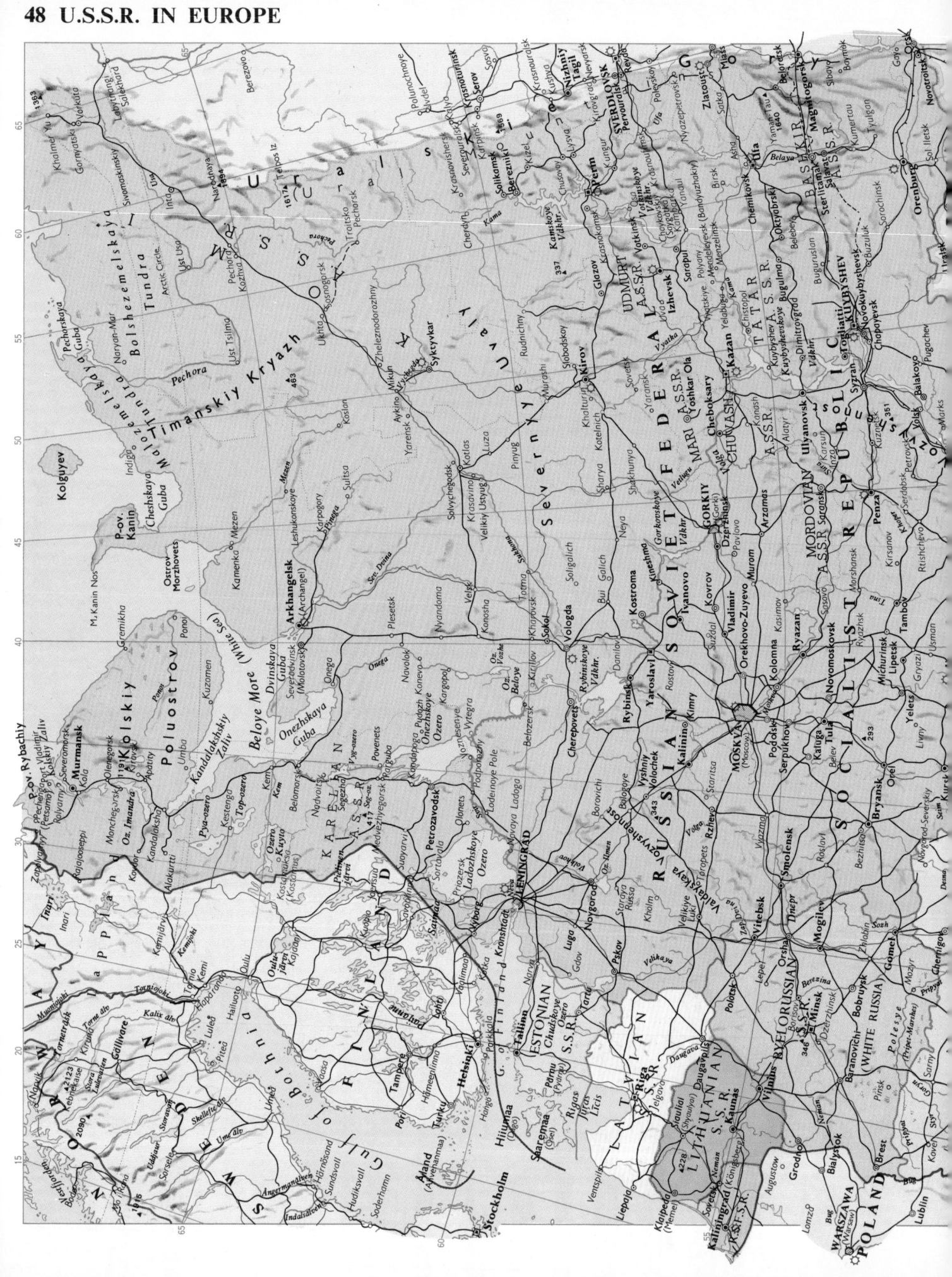

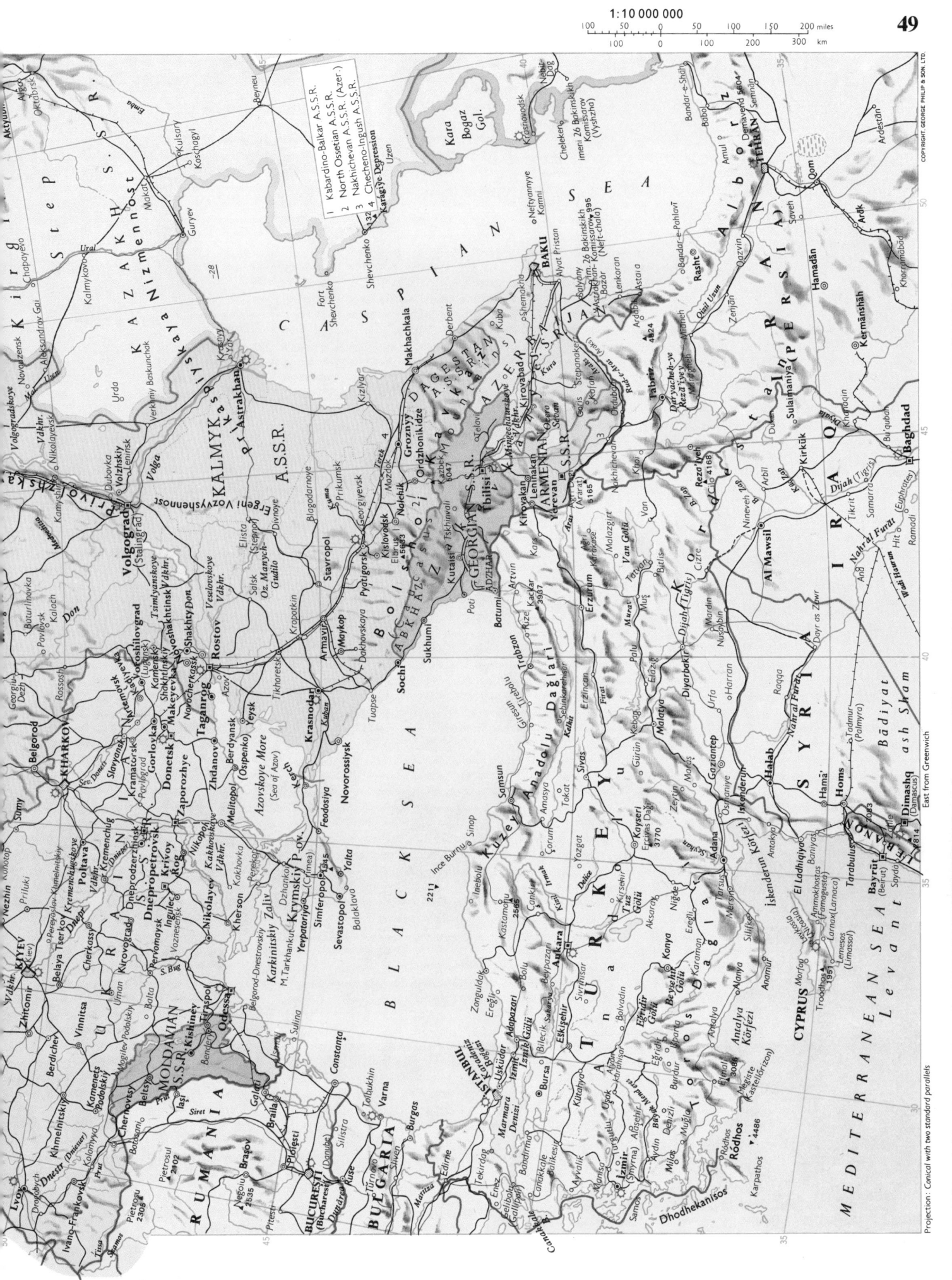

1:10 000 000

100   50   0   50   100   150   200 miles

100   0   100   200   300 km

Kara
Bogaz
Gol.

C A S P I A N   S E A

1 Kabardino-Balkar A.S.S.R.
2 North Ossetian A.S.S.R. (Azer.)
3 Nakhichevan A.S.S.R.
4 Checheno-Ingush A.S.S.R.

TEHRAN

K I r g i z   S t e p

K A Z A K H.   S. S. R.

Kazakhskaya Nizmennost

Ural

Emba

Guryev

Astrakhan

KALMYK
A.S.S.R.

Ergeni Vozvyshennost

Volga

Volgograd
(Stalingrad)

Elista

Privolzhskaya

DAGESTAN
A.S.S.R.

Makhachkala

Derbent

BAKU

A Z E R B A I J A N

Grozny
Ordzhonikidze

Nalchik

K a v k a z

B o l s h o i   K a v k a z

GEORGIAN   S.S.R.

ADZHAR

ARMENIAN
S.S.R.

Yerevan

Ararat
5165

Tabriz

TEHRAN

I r a n   (P E R S I A)

Hamadān

Kermānshāh

Baghdad

A l b o r z

Volgograd

Sevastopol

U K R A I N E

KHARKOV

Rostov

Krasnodar

Novorossiysk

B L A C K   S E A

Sochi

A B K H A Z

Sukhum

Batum

Trabzon

A n a d o l u   D a ğ l a r ı

K u z e y

Samsun

Sinop

Ankara

T U R K E Y

Kayseri
3770

Erzurum

T o r o s   D a ğ l a r ı

Adana

Halab

S Y R I A

Dimashq
(Damascus)

Bādiyat ash Sham

Al Mawsil

I R A Q

Dijah (Tigris)

CYPRUS

MEDITERRANEAN SEA   L e v a n t

Istanbul

Bursa

İzmir

Konya

Antalya

Dhodhekánisos

Ródhos

RUMANIA

BUCUREŞTI
(Bucharest)

B U L G A R I A

Varna

Burgas

MOLDAVIAN
S.S.R.

KIYEV
(Kiev)

Odessa

Kishinev

Constanţa

Poltava

Donetsk

Zaporozhye

Dnepropetrovsk

Simferopol

Krymskiy P-ov.
(Crimea)

Azovskoye More
(Sea of Azov)

Kerch

Yalta

Feodosiya

East from Greenwich

Projection: Conical with two standard parallels

COPYRIGHT GEORGE PHILIP & SON LTD.

51

1:20 000 000

100 0 100 200 300 400 500 miles

100 0 200 400 600 800 km

Boundaries of U.S.S.R.
Boundaries of S.S.R.
Boundaries of A.S.S.R.

1:50 000 000

250 0 250 500 750 1000 miles
250 0 500 1000 1500 km

COPYRIGHT GEORGE PHILIP & SON, LTD.

PACIFIC OCEAN

ARCTIC OCEAN

INDIAN OCEAN

Aleutian Is.
Bering Sea
Kamchatka Peninsula
Sea of Okhotsk
Sakhalin
Kuril Is.
Hokkaido
Sikhote Alin Ra.
Sea of Japan
Honshu
Shikoku
Kyushu
Korea Str.
Korea
Yellow Sea
East China Sea
Ryukyu Is.
Formosa
Tropic of Cancer
Bonin Is.
Guam
Caroline Is.
Pelew Is.
Mindanao
Philippine Is.
Luzon
Palawan
Sulu Sea
Hainan
G. of Tonkin
Celebes Sea
Borneo
Halmahera
Moluccas
Celebes
Ceram
Banda Sea
Arafura Sea
New Guinea
Timor
Flores
Bali
Java Sea
Makasar Strait
Java
Sumatra
Sunda Is.
Str. of Malacca
Malay Peninsula
G. of Siam
Menam
Mekong
Salween
Irrawaddy
Bay of Bengal
Andaman Is.
Nicobar Is.
Ceylon
Polk Strait
Equator
Maldive Is.
Laccadive Is.
Chagos Arch.
Amirantes
Seychelles
Socotra
G. of Aden
Somali Peninsula
Red Sea
Ras Asir (C. Guardafui)
Arabia
Ar Rub' al Khali
Arabian Sea
G. of Oman
Persian Gulf
Tigris
Euphrates
Mesopotamia
Syrian Desert
Dead Sea
Nile
Libyan Desert
Mediterranean Sea
Cyprus
Anatolia
Taurus Mts.
Caucasus
Elbruz 5633
Ararat 5165
Black Sea
Bosporus
Adriatic Sea
Carpathians
Danube
Rhine
Elbe
Oder
Vistula
North Sea
British Isles
Iceland
Greenland
Arctic Circle
Scandinavia
Baltic Sea
Finland
North European Plain
Central Russian Uplands
Don
Dnepr
Volga
Ural
Ural Mountains
1640
Steppes
Caspian Sea
Aral Sea
Syr Darya
Amu Darya
Turan Plain
L. Balkhash
Ili
Chu
Pamirs
Communism Pk. 7495
Hindu Kush
Karakoram Ra.
Koko Nor
Kunlun Shan
Plateau of Tibet
Everest 8848
Tsangpo
Brahmaputra
Himalaya
Ganga
Yamuna
Sutlej
Indus
Suleiman Ra.
Thar
Narmada
Godavari
Krishna
Western Ghats
Eastern Ghats
C. Comorin
Gulf of Kutch
Plateau of Iran
Great Salt Desert
Elbruz Mts.
Dasht-e Kavir
Hamun
Helmand
Tien Shan
Turfan Basin
Tarim Basin
Tarim
Takla Makan
Lop Nor
Altai
Bogdula 4506
Sayan Mts.
Selenga
Angara
Lena
Aldan
Stanovoy Ra.
Yablonovy Ra.
Plateau of Mongolia
Gobi
Great Khingan Mts.
Manchurian Plain
Amur
Ussuri
Sungari
Great Plain of China
Hwang-ho
Yangtze
Si-kiang
Hong (Red)
China
Koko Nor
Kinabalu 4101

Central Siberian Plateau
West Siberian Plain
Ob
Irtysh
Tobol
Narodnaya 1894
Yenisei
Lower Tunguska
Ob
Verkhoyansk Range
Gydan Ra. (Kolyma)
Srednny Ra.
Indigirka
Kolyma
New Siberian Is.
Wrangel I.
C. Dezhnev
Bering Str.
Chelyuskin
Taimyr Peninsula
Severnaya Zemlya
Laptev Sea
Kara Sea
Novaya Zemlya
Barents Sea
White Sea
Kola Pen.
Kolguyev
North Cape
N. Dvina
Olenek
Ojenek

Projection: Bonne

m ft

1:50 000 000

250 0 250 500 750 1000 miles
250 0 500 1000 1500 km

1:1 000 000

10 ... 10 ... 20 miles
10 ... 0 ... 10 ... 20 ... 30 km

1949–1967 Armistice lines between Israel and the Arab States.

MEDITERRANEAN SEA

LEBANON

SYRIA

Under Israeli Occupation

Cease Fire Line 1967

HAIFA

Hag̱alil (Galilee)

TEL HAZOR

KEFAR NAHUM (CAPERNAUM)

Yam Kinneret (Sea of Galilee) −209

Tiberias

Nazareth

TEL MEGIDDO

'Emeq Yizre'el

Afula

Jenin

Shōmrōn (Samaria)

Nābulus

SHECHEM
JACOB'S WELL

SAMARIA

Netanya

Tūlkarm

Under Israeli Occupation

J O R D A N

TEL ARSHAF
Herzliyya
Ramat HaSharon

TEL AVIV–YAFO (Jaffa)
Ramat Gan
Petah Tiqwa
Bat Yam
Holon

Rishon Le Zion
Nes Ziyyona
Ramla
Rehovot
Lod (Lydda)

Râm Allâh

El Arîha (Jericho)

Hussein (Allenby) Bridge

As Salt

AMMÂN

Az-Zarqâ'

JERUSALEM
(Yerūshalayim, Al Quds)

Ashdod

Qiryat Gat

BET GUVRIN
TEL LAKHISH

Bayt Lahm (Bethlehem)

BURAK SULAYMAN (SOLOMON'S POOLS)

QUMRAN

Ashqelon

Hebron

Gaza

Gaza Strip

Khân Yunis

B A H R E L M I Y E T (DEAD SEA)

MESADA

EGYPT

Be'er Sheva

M i d b a r Y e h u d a

Projection: Conical with two standard parallels

East from Greenwich

Continuation Southwards
1:2 500 000

Gaza
Gaza Strip
Khân Yunis

ISRAEL

Be'er Sheva
Dimona

H a n e g e v

SHIVTA

Mizpe Ramon
1035
Har Ramon

EGYPT

Under Jordan Occupation

Hebron

'Arad

PETRA
1727

Elat
Al 'Aqaba

0 ... 10 ... 20 30 miles
0 ... 10 ... 20 ... 30 km

COPYRIGHT. GEORGE PHILIP & SON. LTD.

1:15 000 000

100   0   100   200   300   400 miles
100   0   100   200   300   400   500   600 km

LEBANON
Bayrût
Jouniet
SYRIA
Dimashq
(Damascus)
Haifa
ISRAEL
Tel Aviv
Yafo
Jerusalem
Amman
JORDAN
Gaza
El 'Arîsh
Bîr el Miyer
Bûr Sa'îd
Ismâ'îliya
El Qantara
El Suweis
(Suez)
el Tîh
Israeli
Occupation
Es Sîna
Khalîg es Suweis
Khalîg el 'Aqaba
2637
2578
El Aqaba
Ma'ân
Tabûk
Dûmat al Jandal
(Al Jawf)
1128

IRAQ
Baghdâd
Rutba
Hît
Al Hillah
Karbalâ'
Al Jazîrah
Kut Dûr
Al 'Amârah
An Nâsiriyah
An Najaf
Al Qurna
Al Basrah
Abadân
Umm Qasr
Al Fao
Bubiyan
Failaka
KUWAIT
Al Kuwayt
(Kuwait)

IRAN
(PERSIA)
Borujerd
Kâshân
Khvor
Ardestân
Dezfûl
4648
Karûn
Masjed Soleymân
Shahrizâ
Yazd
Ahvâz
Khorramshahr
Bandar Shahpur
Bandar-e Bûshehr
Deyyer
Tâheri
Kâzerun
Shîrâz
Jahrom
Neyrîz
Bâft
4419
Kermân
Bam
Zâbol
Dasht-e Lût

AFGHANISTAN

An Nafûd
Hafar al Bâtin
Al Wari'ah
Abu Hadrîya
Ha'il
1814
Al Madînah
Buraidah
Az Zilfî
'Unaizah
Al Majma'ah
Ar Riyâd
(Riyadh)
Duwadami
Sulaimiya
Hilla
1143

SAUDI-ARABIA

PERSIAN GULF
Safaniya
Manifah
Khursaniya
QatÎf
Ad Dammam
Dhahran
BAHRAIN
Al Hufuf
Al Uqayr
QATAR
Doha
Musay'id
UNITED ARAB EMIRATES
(TRUCIAL STATES)
Abu Dhabi
Dubayy
Sharjah
Bandâr 'Abbâs
Minab
Khâmir
2057
Oman
Gâbrik
Jâsk
Gulf of Oman
Suhâr
Al Khâburah
Miskin
3019
Wudham
Masqat
(Muscat)
2151
Sûr
Al Masîrah
Al Khalaf

EGYPT
Aswân
Qena
Qûs
El Uqsur
(Luxor)
Isna
Idfu
Kôm Ombo
Sadd el 'Alî
1st Cataract
El Shallal
Buheiret en Naser
(Lake Naser)
Bîr Shalatein
Es Sahrâ en Nûbîya
(Nubian Desert)
2nd Cataract
Wadi Halfa
3rd Cataract
El Kab
Abu Hamed
Delgo
Argo
El Debba
Kareima
Merowe
Korti
Dongola

RED SEA
Bûr Safâga
Quseir
Ras Banâs
Halaib
2216
Ras Hadarba
Muhammad Qol
Gebel Mîye
Jiddah
Makkah (Mecca)
2565
At Ta'if
Al Lith
Al Qunfidha
Ras Abu Shagara
2635
Bûr Sûdân (Port Sudan)
Suakin
Sinkat
Tokar
Trinkitat
Aqiq
Ras Kasar
Derudub
Karora
2786

Tropic of Cancer

JIBAL ARABIA
Dafina
Mastura
Rabigh Qasr
Usfan
Turaba
Dhurm
Khurm
Laila
Ghail
Qasr Hamam
Ad Dam
Tamra
Na'ifah
Al Ubailah
Umm az Zamul
Yibal
Al Ayn al Muqshin

AR RAB'AL KHÂLÎ
OMAN
ZUFÂR
Shisur
1678
Marbat
Salâlah
Ghubbat al Qamar
Jazâ'ir Khûryân Mûryân
Al Juwara
Al Jazir

SUDAN
Omdurmân
El Khartûm-Bahrî
El Khartûm (Khartoum)
Kassala
El Geteina
Wâd Medanî
Khashm el Girba
Gedaref
Sennar
Singa
Er Roseires
Ed Damer
Atbara
Berber
Adarama
Musmar
Shendi
Wad Hamid
4th Cataract
Kôsti
Ed Dueim

ERITREA
Keren
Akordat
Barentu
Asmera (Asmara)
Mitsiwa
Zula
Mersa Fatma
Dahlak Kebir
Kamaran
Hodeida
Hanish
Zabid
Loheia
3600
Sana
Dhamar
Ibb
3200

YEMEN
Sa'dah
3200
Al Matamma
Marib
Al Khamir
Al Hauta
Shibâm
W. Masila
HADHRAMAWT
5143
Saihut
Ghubbat

SOUTH YEMEN
Al Hawra
Mukalla
Ras al Kalb
Shuqra
Zinjibâr
Al 'Adan (Aden)
Madinat al Shaab
Perim
Bâb el Mandeb
Ahwar
Haura

'Abd al Kûrî
Socotra (South Yemen)
Hadibu
1503
Ras Asir (C. Guardafui)

ETHIOPIA
Aksum
Adwa
Mekele
4620
Dabât
Gonder
Debre Tabor
L. Tana
4154
Mota
Talo
Dembecha
Debre Markos
Alibo
Gebre Tâbor
Gimbi
Nekemte
Sire
Gedo
Addis Abeba (Addis Ababa)
Awash
3381
Hareri
Dire Dawa
Hargeisa
Jima
L. Zway
Asela
L. Shala
Goba
4307
Ginir
L. Abaya
Hula
Arba Minch
L. Shamo
Gidole
L. Burji
Yabelo
Negele
Arero
El Niybo
Chew Bahir (L. Stefanie)
Mega
Moyale
Dolo

Gulf of Aden
Tadjoura
DJIBOUTI
Djibouti
Zeila
Bulhar
Berbera
Karin
Las Khoreh
Erigavo
Bosaso (Bender Cassim)
Candala
El Gal
Alula
Bereda
Bargal
Darror
Ras Hafun
Scusciuban
Handa
Ras Hafun

SOMALI REP.
2406
Borama
Burao
Alnabo
Las Anod
Garoe
Bohotleh
Degeh-Bur
Sasabeneh
Warandab
Domo
Badweina
Welwel
Werder
Geladi
Gerlogubi
Scillave
Imi
Kebri Dehar
Kelafo
Dusa Mareb
Ghelinsor
Iddan
5824
Obbia
Galcaia
El Bur
Bender Beila
Eil
Gardo

INDIAN OCEAN

ZÂIRE
UGANDA
KENYA
Gulu
Lira
Soroti
Mbale
L. Kyoga
4321
Kitale
Lodwar
L. Turkana
North Horr
Marsabit
Wajir
Habaswein
Dif
El Wak
Bardera
Bur Acaba
Baidoa
Lugh Ganana
Bulo Burti
El Dere
Afgoi
Giohar
Uarsciek
Mogadiscio (Mogadishu)
Merca
Brava

Projection: Sanson-Flamsteed's Sinusoidal

East from Greenwich

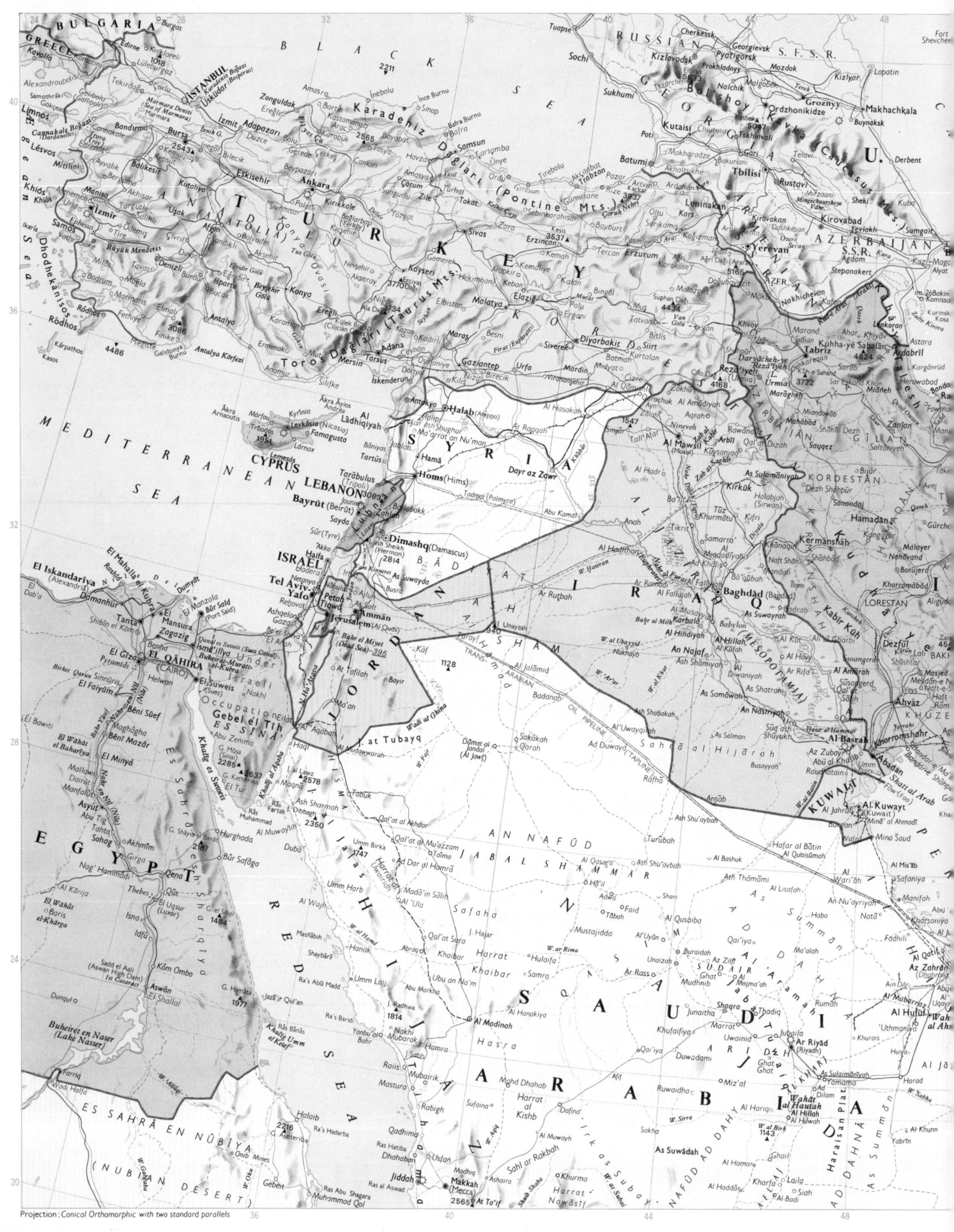

Projection: Conical Orthomorphic with two standard parallels

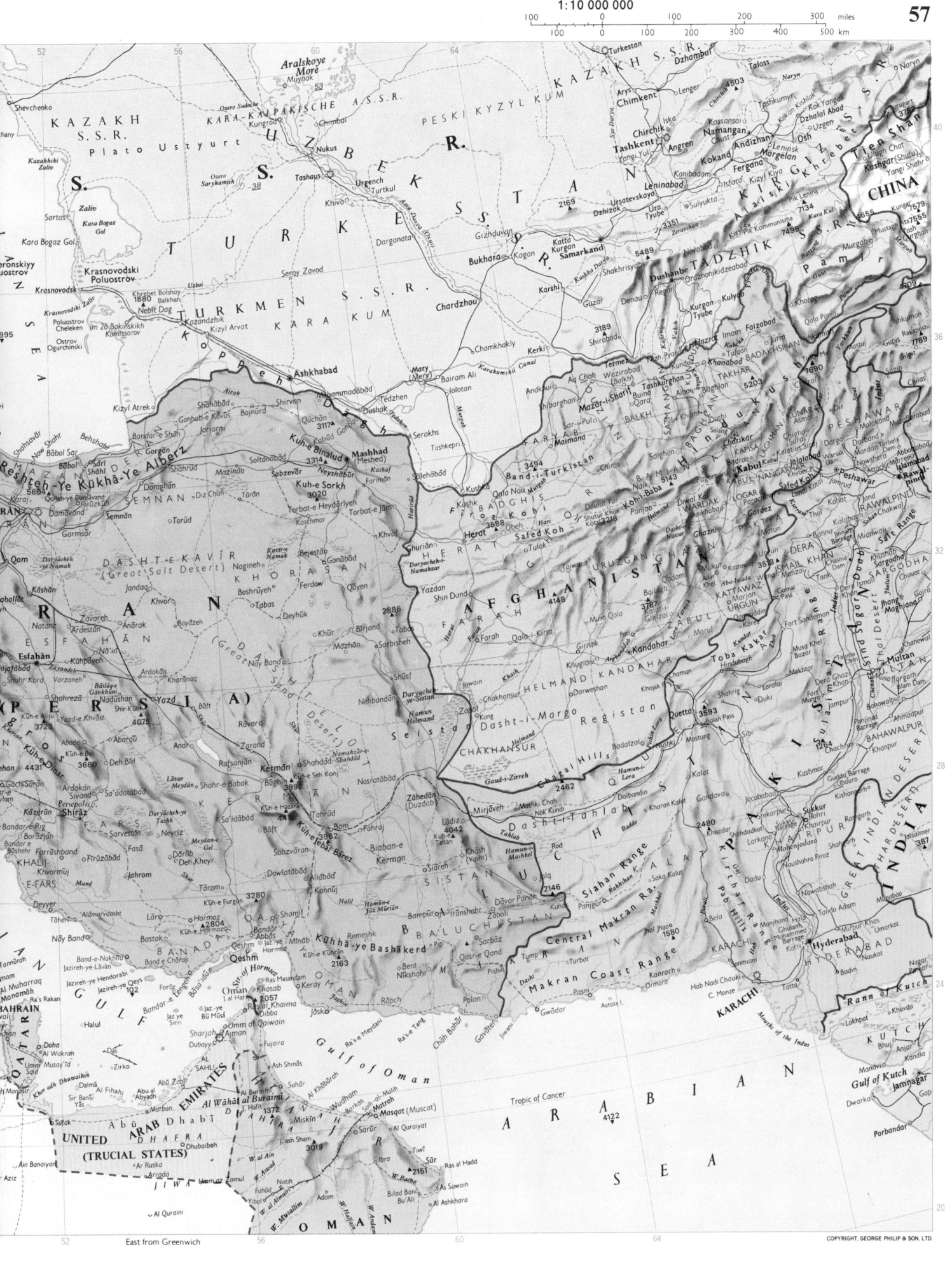

U.S.S.R.

AFGHANISTAN

HERAT · BADGHIS · GHOR · FARAH · URUZGAN · GHAZNI · ZABUL · KANDAHAR · HELMAND · CHAKHANSUR

Kabul · Herat · Kandahar · Quetta

PAKISTAN

BALUCHISTAN · Karachi · KARACHI · Hyderabad · HYDERABAD · Sukkur · KHAIRPUR · Quetta · PESHAWAR · Peshawar · Rawalpindi · RAWALPINDI · Islamabad · Lahore · LAHORE · MULTAN · Multan · BAHAWALPUR

JAMMU AND KASHMIR · Srinagar

Makran Coast Range · Central Makran Range · Siahan Range · Kirthar Range · Pab Hills · Chagai Hills · Toba Kakar

Mouths of the Indus

ARABIAN SEA

Tropic of Cancer

INDIA BHARAT

PUNJAB · Amritsar · Ludhiana · Chandigarh · Ambala · HIMACHAL PRADESH · Simla · Dehra Dun · HARYANA · DELHI · Meerut · Moradabad · Bareilly · Aligarh · Mathura · Agra · Gwalior · Jaipur · Jodhpur · Ajmer · Bikaner · RAJASTHAN · Great Indian Desert (Thar Desert) · Ahmadabad · Jamnagar · Rajkot · Vadodara (Baroda) · Surat · GUJARAT · Kathiawar · Indore · Bhopal · MADHYA PRADESH · Jabalpur · Nagpur · Bombay · MAHARASHTRA · Pune (Poona) · Nasik · Aurangabad · Sholapur · Hyderabad · ANDHRA PRADESH · Secunderabad · Gulbarga

Rann of Kutch · Gulf of Kutch · Gulf of Cambay · DADRA & NAGAR HAVELI · DIU · DAMAN

Satpura Range · Ajanta Range · Balaghat Range

Continuation Southwards on same scale

GOA · Dharwar · Gadag · Hubli · Bellary · Kurnool · Karwar · KARNATAKA · Bangalore · Mysore · Mangalore · Shimoga · Davangere · Coimbatore · Salem · Erode · TAMIL NADU · Madurai · Madras · Vellore · Pondicherry · Cuddalore · Tiruchirappalli · Thanjavur · Trivandrum · Quilon · Calicut (Kozhikode) · Cochin · Trichur · Cape Comorin · Nagercoil · Tirunelveli

Western Ghats · Eastern Ghats · Malabar Coast · Coromandel Coast · Nilgiri Hills · Cardamom Hills · Palni Hills

Palk Strait · Palk Bay · Gulf of Mannar · Adam's Bridge · Jaffna

SRI LANKA (CEYLON) · Colombo · Kandy · Moratuwa · Negombo · Galle · Trincomalee · Batticaloa · Anuradhapura · Adam's Peak 2243 · Mt. Lavinia

Dondra Head

Projection: Conical with two standard parallels

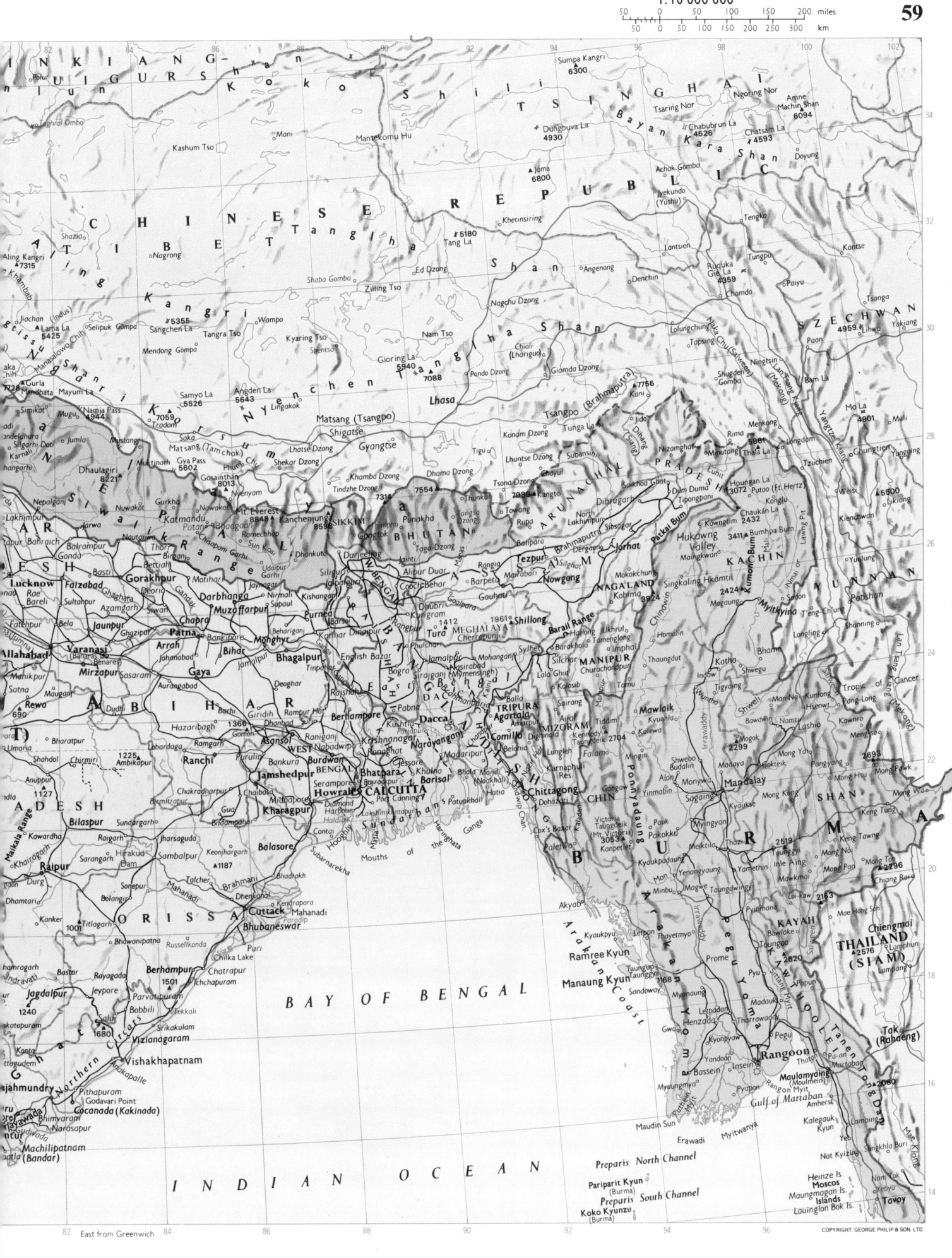

1:10 000 000

50   0   50   100   150   200 miles
100 50 0 50 100 150 200 250 300 km

INKIANG—
niuigurskhan

CHINESE   REPUBLIC

A   TIBET   Tang   tha   Shan   TSINGHAI

SZECHWAN

Lhasa

Tsangpo (Brahmaputra)

ARUNACHAL   PRADESH

YUNNAN

NEPAL

Mt. Everest
8848

SIKKIM

BHUTAN

ASSAM

KACHIN

Katmandu

Lucknow   Faizabad   Gorakhpur   Darbhanga

NAGALAND

MEGHALAYA

MANIPUR

Patna   Arrah   Gaya

BIHAR

Bhagalpur

East   Bengal

Dacca

TRIPURA

MIZORAM   CHIN

Allahabad   Varanasi   Mirzapur

West   Bengal

Agartala

BURMA

MADHYA   PRADESH

Ranchi   Jamshedpur   Kharagpur

ORISSA

Raipur   Cuttack   Bhubaneswar

CALCUTTA   Howrah

Chittagong

SHAN

Mandalay

Irrawaddy

KAYAH

THAILAND
(SIAM)

Vishakhapatnam

BAY   OF   BENGAL

Ramree Kyun

Manaung Kyun

Arakan Coast

PEGU   YOMA

Rangoon

Maulamyaing
Moulmein

Gulf of Martaban

INDIAN   OCEAN

Preparis   North   Channel

Pariparit Kyun
(Burma)

Preparis   South   Channel

Koko Kyunzu
(Burma)

Heinze Is.
Moscos
Islands
Lauinglon Bok Is.

Tavoy

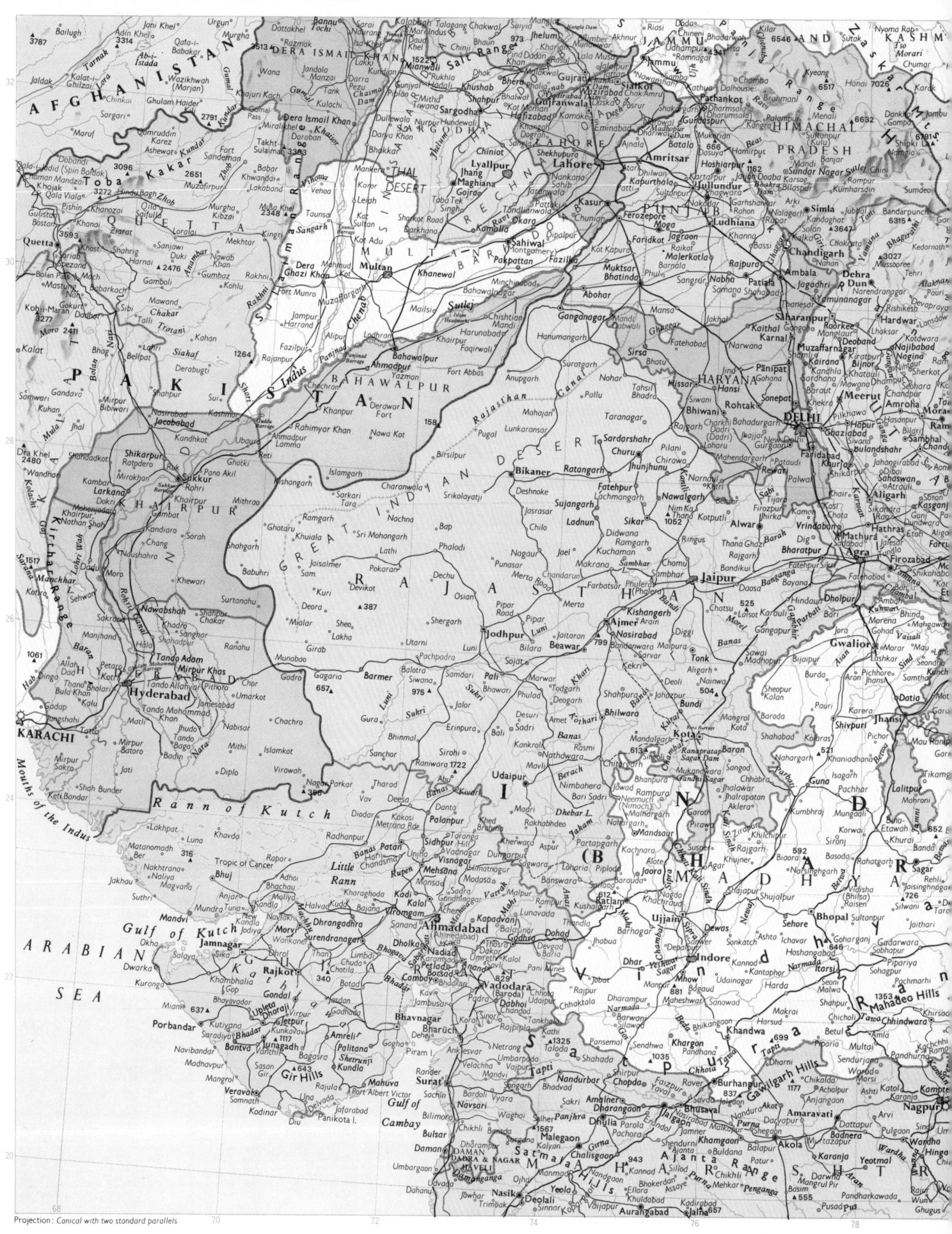

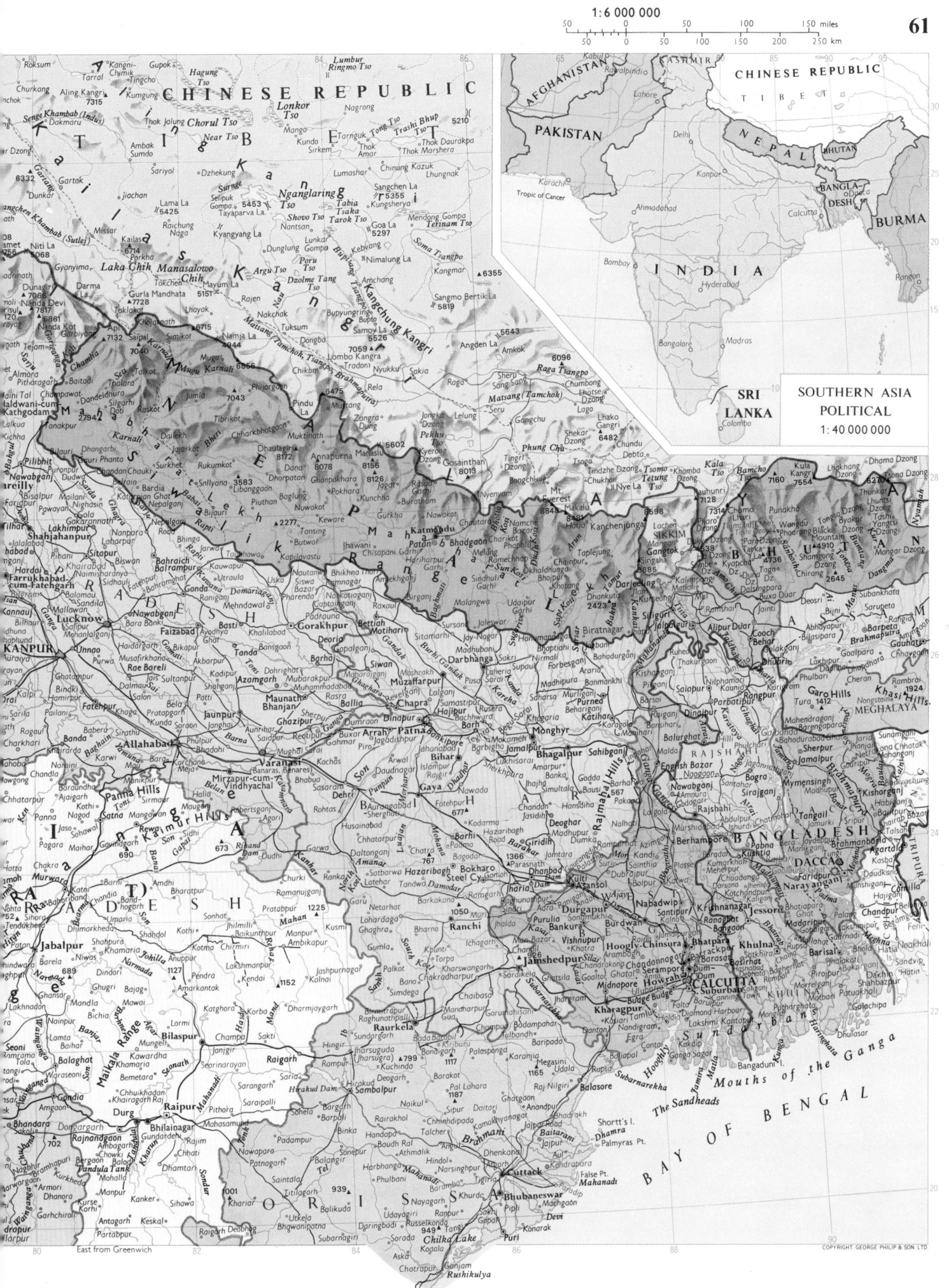

62 SOUTHERN INDIA AND SRI LANKA

1:6 000 000

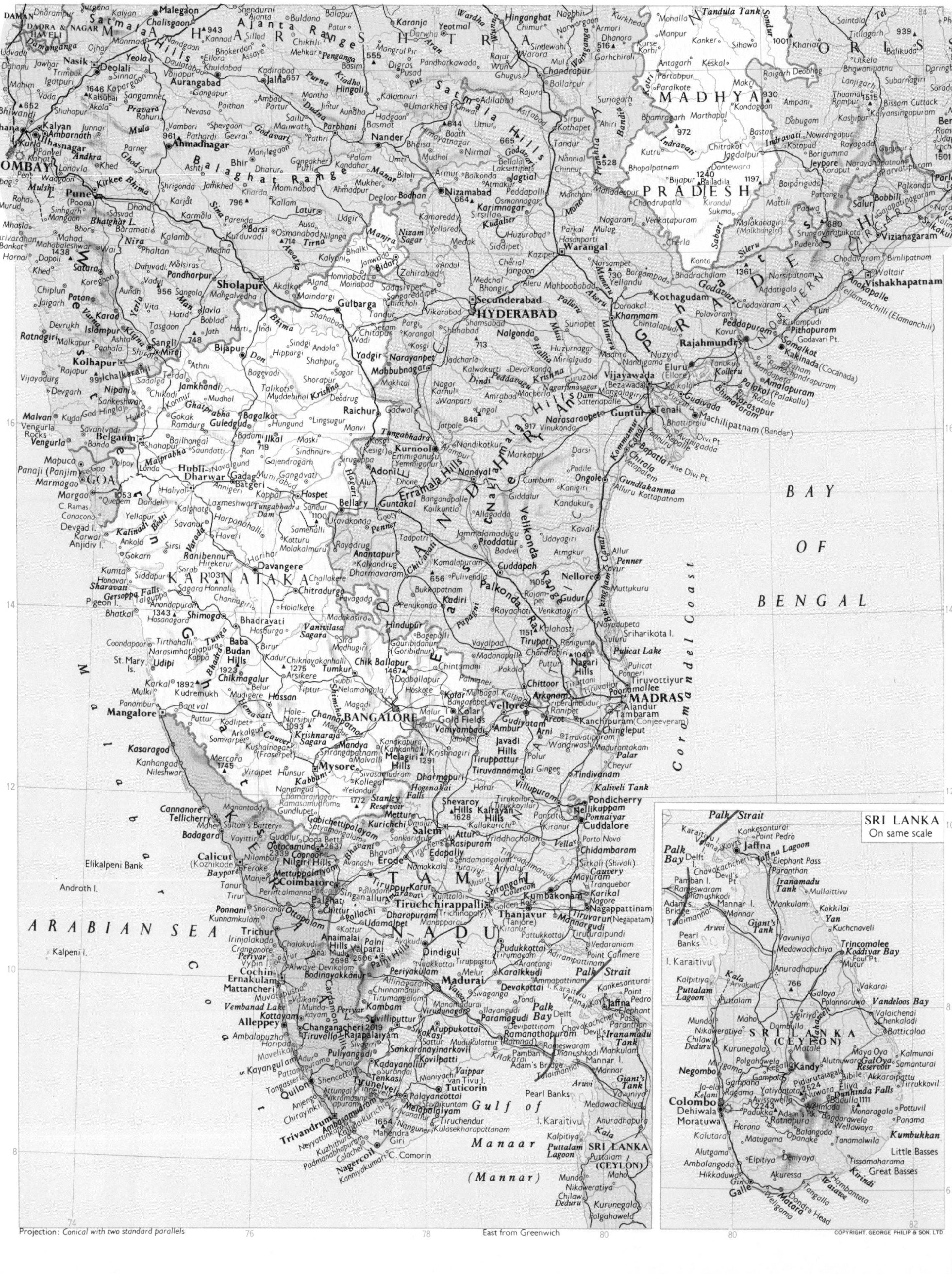

50   0   50   100   150 miles
50   0   50   100   150   200   250 km

MAHARASHTRA

MADHYA PRADESH

BOMBAY

GOA

KARNATAKA

HYDERABAD

Secunderabad

ANDHRA PRADESH

BAY OF BENGAL

ARABIAN SEA

BANGALORE

MADRAS

TAMIL NADU

Coromandel Coast

Gulf of Mannar

(Mannar)

SRI LANKA (CEYLON)

SRI LANKA
On same scale

Palk Strait

Jaffna

SRI LANKA (CEYLON)

Colombo

Kandy

Galle

Projection: Conical with two standard parallels

East from Greenwich

COPYRIGHT. GEORGE PHILIP & SON, LTD

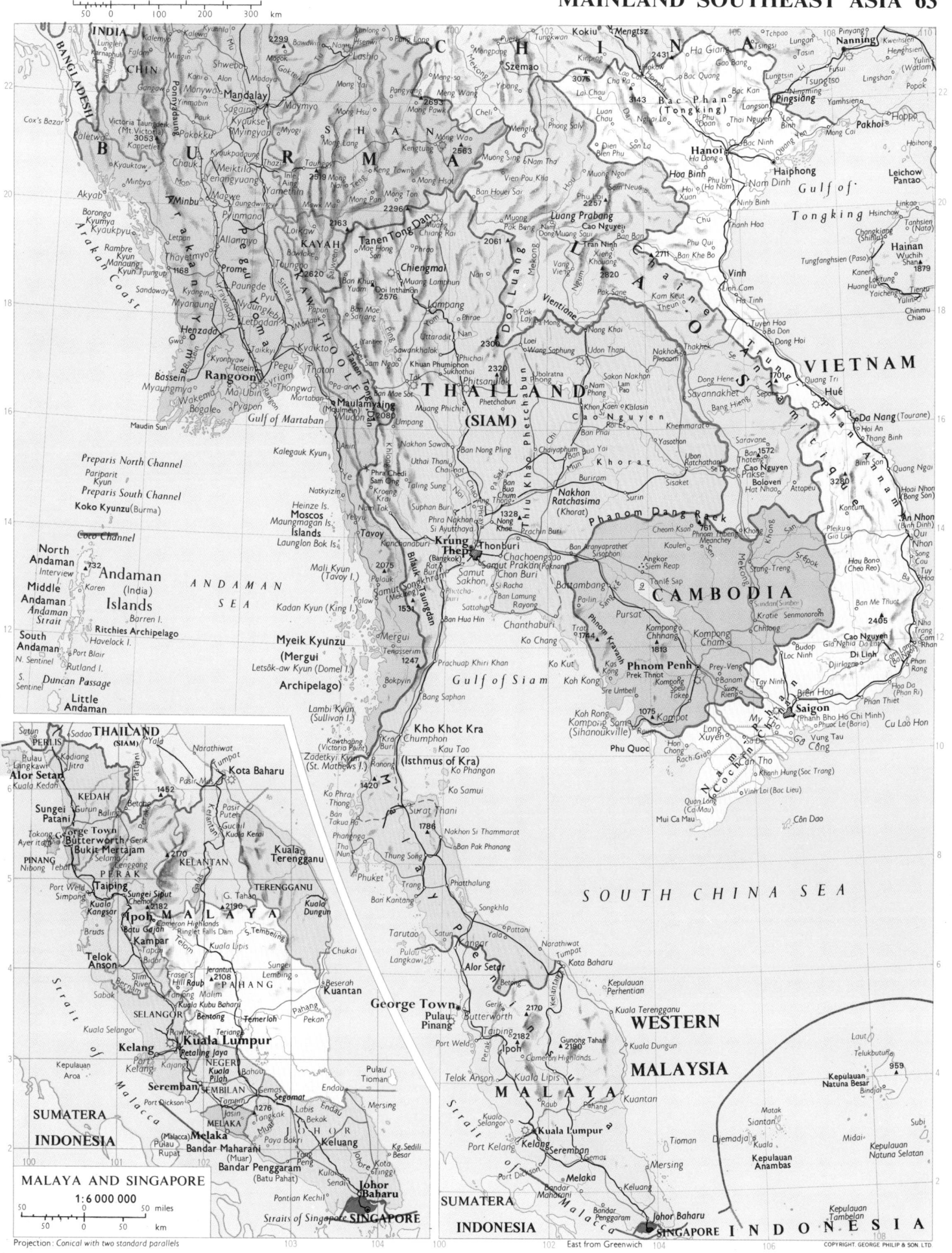

1 : 10 000 000

MALAYA AND SINGAPORE

1 : 6 000 000

Projection : Conical with two standard parallels

East from Greenwich

COPYRIGHT. GEORGE PHILIP & SON. LTD

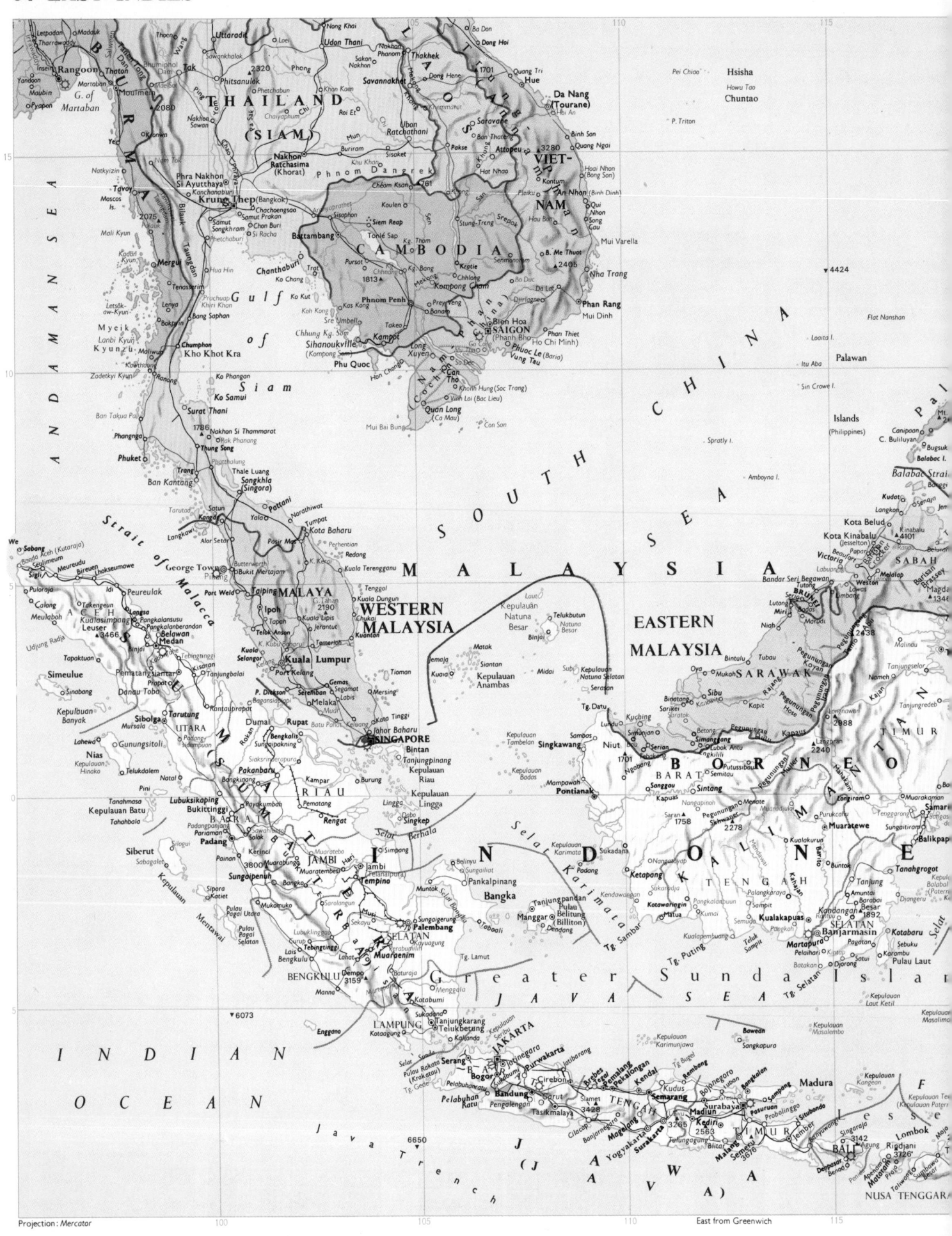

SEA OF JAPAN

PACIFIC OCEAN

SEA OF JAPAN

Sea of Okhotsk

PACIFIC OCEAN

SOUTH KOREA

1:5 000 000

Projection : Conical with two standard parallels

East from Greenwich

| 25 | 0 | 25 | 50 | 75 | 100 miles |
| 25 | 0 | 50 | 100 | 150 | km |

1:10 000 000

East from Greenwich

| 100 | 50 | 0 | 100 | 150 | 200 miles |
| 100 | 0 | 100 | 200 | 300 | km |

Projection : Bonne

Continuation Southwards on same scale

REFERENCE TO PREFECTURES

HOKKAIDŌ DISTRICT		KINKI DISTRICT	
1	Hokkaidō	24	Hyogo
TŌHOKU DISTRICT		25	Kyōto
2	Aomori	26	Shiga
3	Akita	27	Ōsaka
4	Iwate	28	Nara
5	Yamagata	29	Mie
6	Miyagi	30	Wakayama
7	Fukushima	**CHŪGOKU DISTRICT**	
CHŪBU DISTRICT		31	Tottori
8	Niigata	32	Okayama
9	Ishikawa	33	Shimane
10	Toyama	34	Hiroshima
11	Fukui	35	Yamaguchi
12	Gifu	**SHIKOKU DISTRICT**	
13	Nagano	36	Kagawa
14	Yamanashi	37	Tokushima
15	Aichi	38	Ehime
16	Shizuoka	39	Kōchi
KANTŌ DISTRICT		**KYŪSHŪ DISTRICT**	
17	Gumma	40	Fukuoka
18	Tochigi	41	Saga
19	Saitama	42	Nagasaki
20	Ibaraki	43	Kumamoto
21	Tōkyō	44	Ōita
22	Chiba	45	Miyazaki
23	Kanagawa	46	Kagoshima

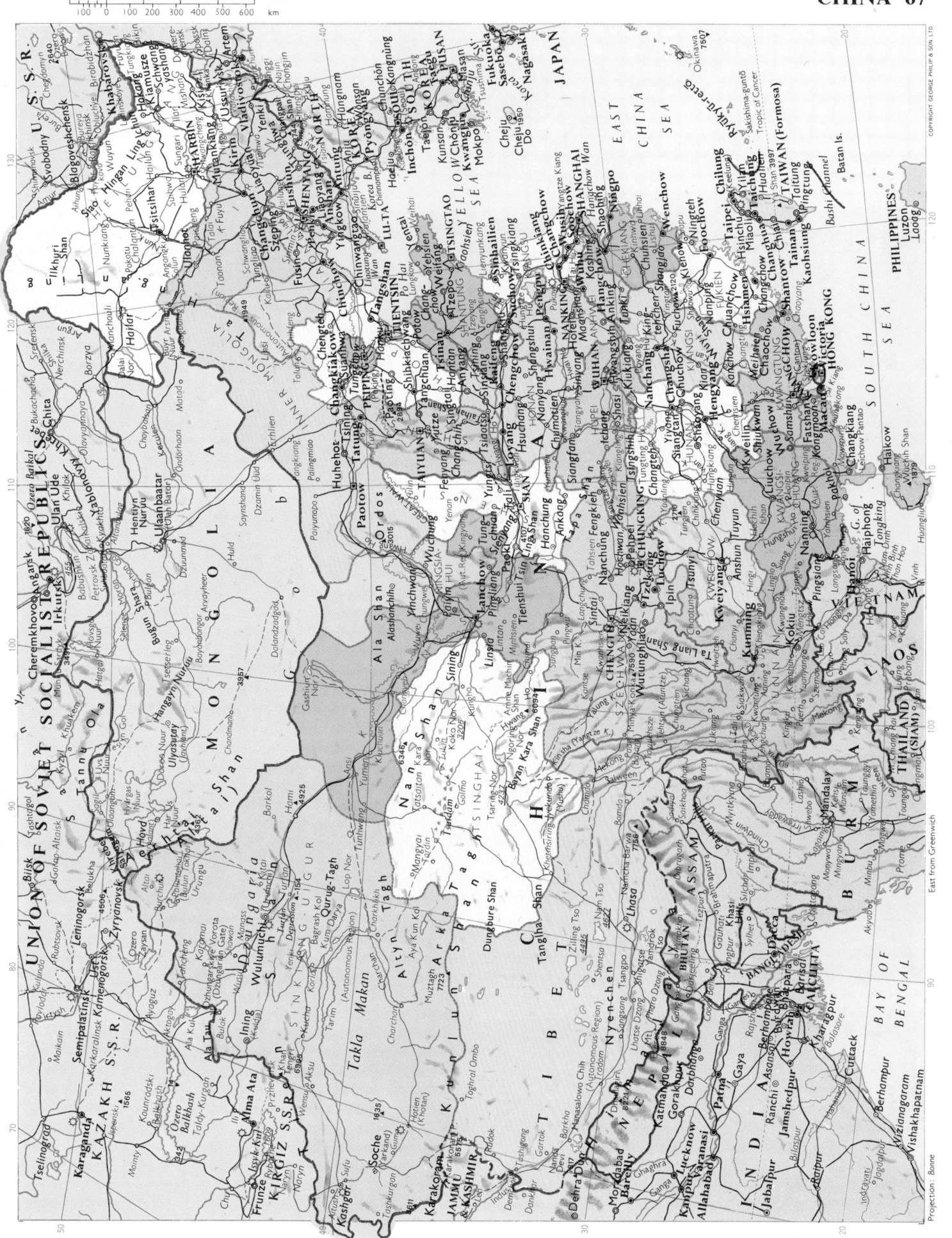

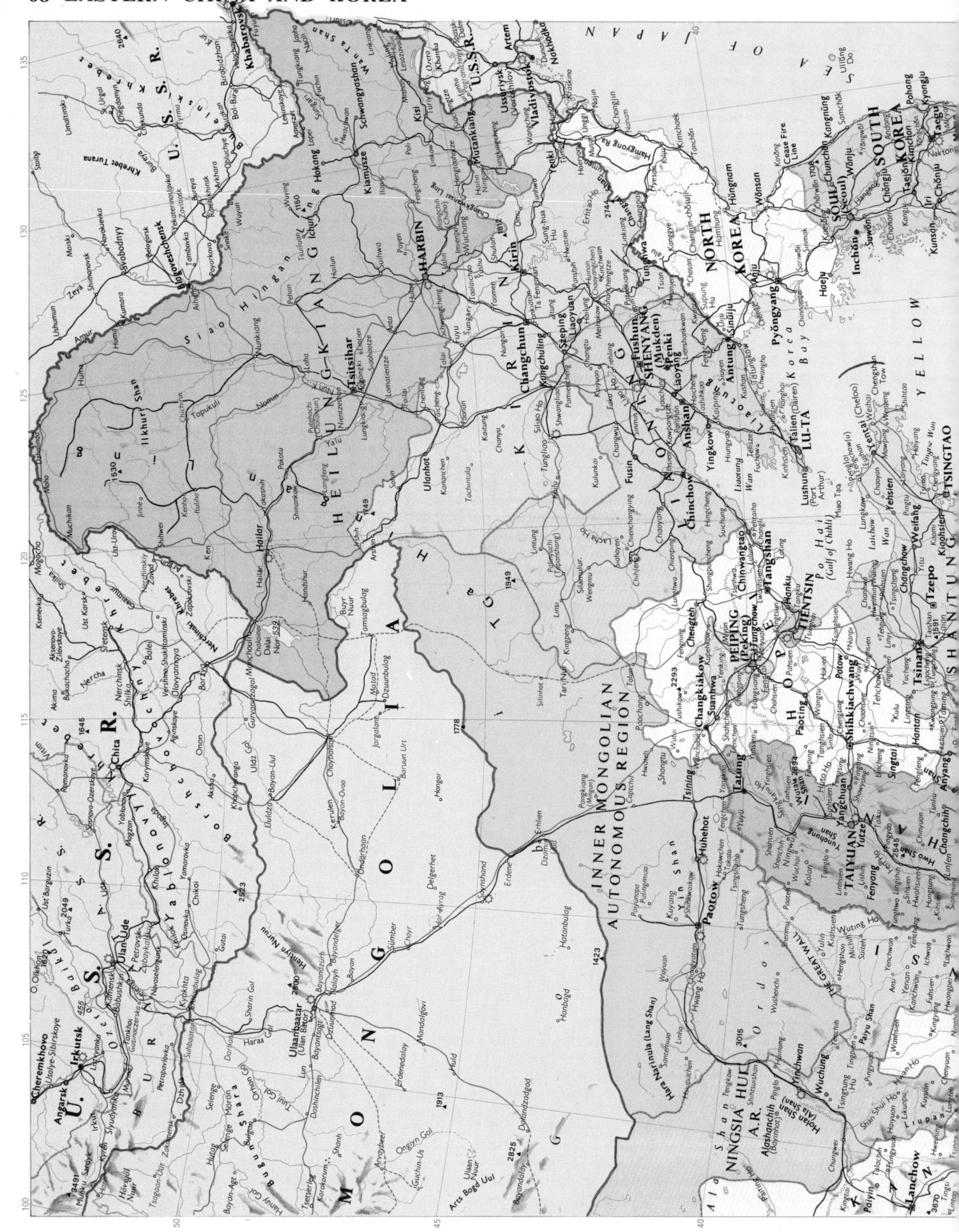

1:10 000 000

50   0   50   100   150   200   250 miles
50 0 50 100 150 200 250 300 350 400 km

PACIFIC OCEAN

RYUKYU

JAPAN

KITAKYUSHU
Fukuoka
Kurume
Sasebo   Omuta   Sendai
Nagasaki   Minamata   Kagoshima
Amakusa   Mokurazaki

Tsushima

Goto-retto

Koshiki-shima
Uji-guntō
Kusagaki-jima

Cheju Do
(Quelpart)

Nansei-shotō

Tokara-guntō

Amami-guntō
Amami-ō-shima
Tokuno-shima
Oki-no-erabu-shima

Okinawa
Naha
Okinawa-guntō
Kume
Miyako-rettō
Yaeyama-rettō
Ishigaki
Iriomote
Sakishima-guntō
Sekibi-shō

Tropic of Cancer

EAST CHINA SEA

SHANGHAI
Nantung
Changshu
Wusih
Soochow
Hangchow
Ningpo
Weichow

CHEKIANG

NANKING
KIANGSU
ANHWEI

HONAN
WUHAN
Hankow
Wuchang
Hanyang

SHENSI
HUPEH

SZECHWAN
CHUNGKING
KWEICHOW
Kweiyang

HUNAN
Changsha
Hengyang

KIANGSI
Nanchang

FUKIEN
Foochow (Minhow)

Chuanchow
Kinmen (Quemoy)
Hsiamen (Amoy)
Changchow
Shantow (Swatow)

TAIWAN (FORMOSA)
Chilung
Keelung
Taipei
Taoyuan
Hsinchu
Taichung
Hualien
Yilan
Changhua
Yunlin
Chiayi
Tainan
Taitung
Kaohsiung
Pingtung

Batan Is.
Babuyan Is.

LUZON
Laoag
Aparri
Vigan

PHILIPPINES

HONGKONG (Br.)
Kowloon
Victoria
Macau (Port.)

KWANGTUNG
KWANGCHOW (Canton)

KWANGSI-CHUANG
NANNING (AD.)

SOUTH CHINA SEA

Tungsha Tao
(Pratas)

Hainan
Haikow

VIETNAM
HANOI
Haiphong

Gulf of Tongking

East from Greenwich

Projection: Lambert's Equivalent Azimuthal

1:40 000 000

200   0   200   400   600   800   1000 miles
200   0   200 400 600 800 1000 1200 1400 1600 km

ATLANTIC OCEAN

British Isles

Bay of Biscay

Alps
Mt. Blanc 4807
Pyrenees
Iberian Peninsula
Corsica
Apennines
Dinaric Alps
Adriatic Sea
Carpathians

Black Sea
Caucasus
Elburus 5633
Caspian Sea
Aral Sea

Anatolia

6578
Madeira
Str. of Gibraltar
Middle Atlas
High Plateaus
Saharan Atlas
High Atlas
Toubkal 4165
Anti Atlas
Dra
Canary Is. 3718
Tenerife
C. Blanc

Mediterranean Sea
C. Bon   Sicily
Malta
G. of Gabes
Chott Djerid
5121   Crete
Cyprus
Levant
Mesopotamia
Tigris
Euphrates
Syrian Desert

Barbary
Tripolitania
Cyrenaica
G. of Sidra
Siwa
Libyan Desert
Egypt
Kufra
El Kharga
1st Cat.
Nile
Arabian Desert
Sinai 2285
Hejaz
Red Sea
Arabia
Persian G.
Bahrain I.
Tropic of Cancer

Igidi
Sahara
S. el Juf
Tuat
Tasili Plateau
Hoggar
Fezzan
Adrar
Air
Bilma
Tibesti 3415
Nubia
Nubian Desert
3rd Cat.
4th Cat.
5th Cat.
6th Cat.
Atbara
Rub' al Khali
Perim I.
Gulf of Aden
Bab el Mandeb
Str. of Bab el Mandeb
Ras Asir
Socotra

C. Vert
Senegambia
Gambia
Senegal
Fouta Djalon
Sudan
Guinea
Niger (Joliba)
Volta
Niger
L. Chad
Wadai
Darfur
Kordofan
White Nile
Blue Nile
Ras Dashan 4620
L. Tana
Ethiopian Highlands
Somali Peninsula
Shabelle

Grain Coast
Gold Coast
Slave Coast
Ivory Coast
C. Palmas
Adamawa Highlands
Cameroon Peak 4070
Macias Nguema Biyoga
Chari
Benue
Bahr el Ghazal
Dar Banda
Bahr el Ghazal
Bahr el Jebel
Uele
L. Mobutu Sese Seko
Chutes Boyoma
Ubangi
Zaire
Congo Basin
Kenya 5199
L. Turkana
Equator

6363
Bight of Benin
Bight of Bonny
Principe
São Tomé
Pagalu
C. Lopez
Gulf of Guinea
Ogoue
Congo
Kasai
Sankuru
Lualaba
Ldi
Amin Dada
L. Kivu
Ituri
Ruwenzori 5109
Elgon 4321
L. Victoria
Kilimanjaro 5895
INDIAN OCEAN
Pemba
Zanzibar

Ascension
Cuango
Kasai
Cuanza
Kwilu
Pool Malebo
Basin
Katanga
L. Tanganyika
Luvua
Mweru
Rungwe 2961
L. Bangweulu
L. Nyasa
Malawi
Ruvuma
C. Delgado
Comoro Is.
Aldabra Is.

St. Helena

ATLANTIC OCEAN

Bié Plateau
C. Frio
Cunene
Cubango
Cuando
Zambezi
Luapula
Mlanje 3000
Shire

Namib Desert
Walvis Bay
Kalahari
Victoria Falls
Matopo
Limpopo
Delagoa Bay
Tropic of Capricorn
Mozambique Channel
Madagascar 2643
Maur
Réunion

Orange
High Veld
3482
Drakensberg
Compass B. 2505
Nieuwveldberge
Gt. Karoo
Swartberg
C. of Good Hope
C. Agulhas
Agulhas Bank
Algoa Bay

Projection: Zenithal Equidistant.   10   West from Greenwich   0   East from Greenwich   10

m   4000 3000 2000 1500 1000 400 200   0   200
ft 12 000 9000 6000 4500 3000 1200 600

1000 2000 4000 6000 m
0 600 3000 6000 12 000 18 000 ft

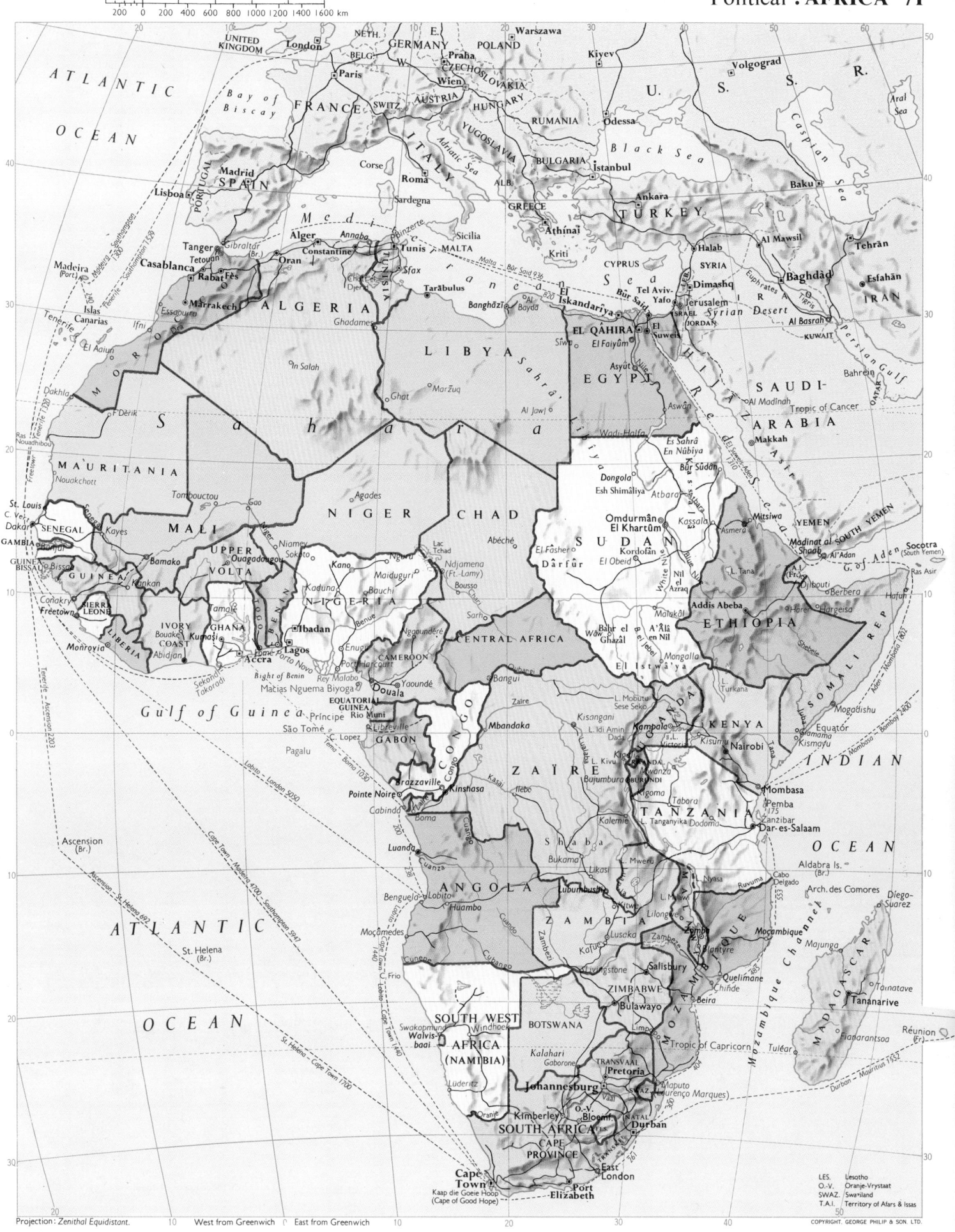

1:40 000 000

Projection: *Zenithal Equidistant.*

West from Greenwich   East from Greenwich

LES.   Lesotho
O.-V.   Oranje-Vrystaat
SWAZ.   Swaziland
T.A.I.   Territory of Afars & Issas

NORTH ATLANTIC

OCEAN

SPAIN

Málaga · Almería

Cádiz · Gibraltar (Br.) · Ceuta (Sp.) · Melilla · Oran · Alger (Algiers) · Constantine · Annaba · Skikda

Tanger · Tetouan · Al-Hoceima · Tlemcen · Sétif

Larache · Kenitra (Port-Lyautey) · Salé · Rabat · Meknès · Fès · Oujda

Casablanca · El Jadida · Berrechid · Khouribga · Saïda · Biskra

Safi · Marrakech · Ksar es Souk · Béchar · Touggourt · El Oued · Gabès

6578 · Madeira (Port.) · Pto. Santo · Funchal

Islas Canarias (Sp.) · Lanzarote · Fuerteventura · Arrecife · Puerto del Rosario

La Palma · Tenerife · Gomera · Sta. Cruz · Las Palmas · Gran Canaria · Hierro

A N T I - A T L A S

M O R O C C O

Dakhla · Pta. Durnford

C. Barbas

Nouadhibou (Port Étienne) · Cite de Cansado

M A U R I T A N I A

El Djouf

Nouakchott · Boutilimit · Aleg

St. Louis · Dagana · Podor · Kaédi

S E N E G A L · Dakar · Kaolack

GAMBIA · Banjul (Bathurst)

GUINEA-BISSAU · Bissau

Conakry

SIERRA LEONE · Freetown

LIBERIA · Monrovia

A L G E R I A

Plateau du Tademaït

Chech · Tanezrouft

A h a g g a r · Tahat · Tamanrasset

Adrar des Iforas

M A L I

Tombouctou · Gao · Bamba

Bamako · Ségou · Mopti

UPPER VOLTA · Ouagadougou · Bobo-Dioulasso

Niamey

N I G E R

Agadez

Aïr (Azbine)

IVORY COAST · Abidjan

GHANA · Accra · Kumasi

TOGO · Lomé

BENIN · Porto-Novo · Cotonou

N I G E R I A · Lagos · Ibadan · Kaduna · Kano · Katsina · Zaria

Benin City · Onitsha · Enugu · Port Harcourt

Bight of Benin

CAMEROON · Mont Cameroun 4070 · Douala

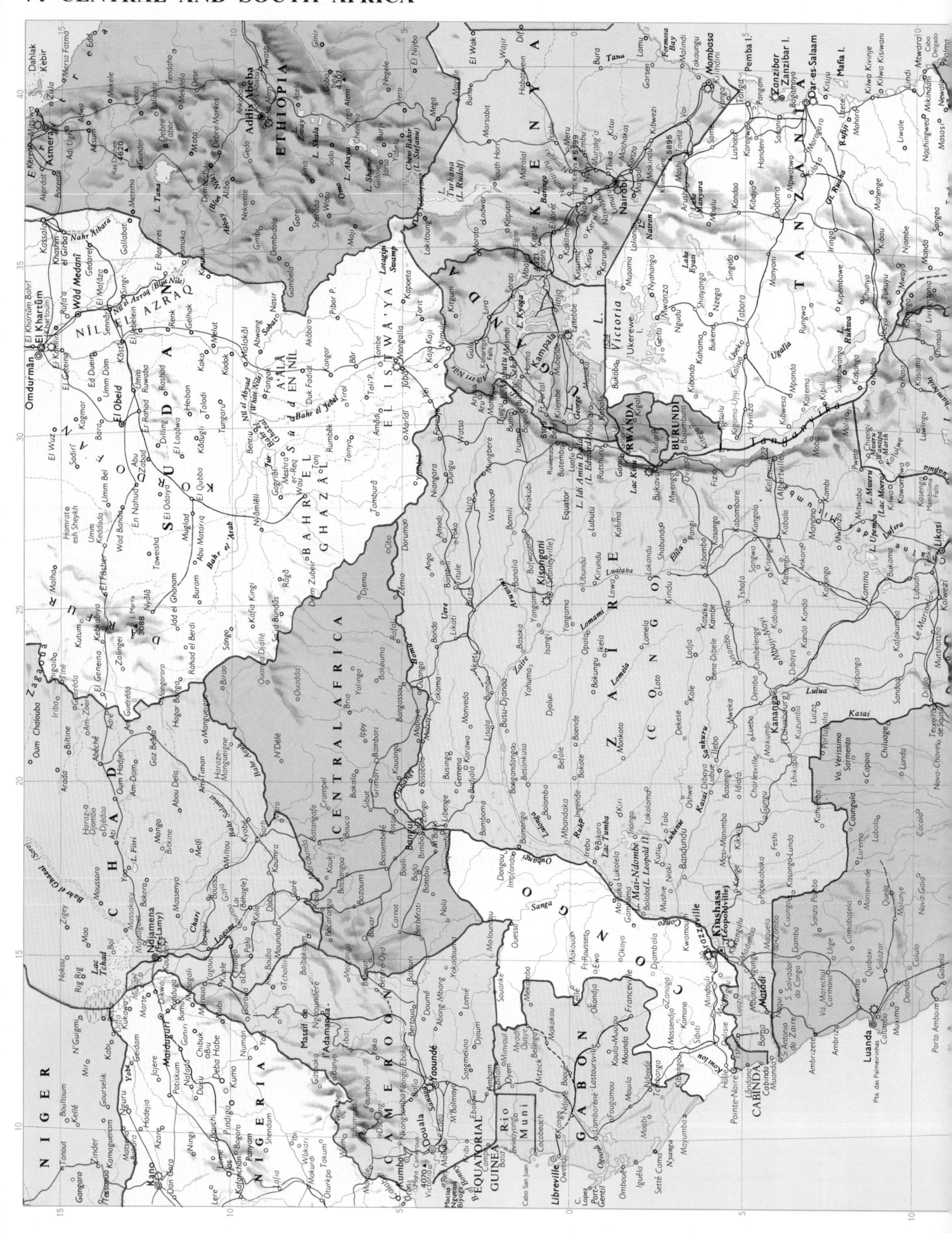

INDIAN OCEAN

MOÇAMBIQUE

MALAWI

ZAMBIA

ZIMBABWE

Salisbury

Bulawayo

BOTSWANA

Kalahari

SOUTH WEST AFRICA (NAMIBIA)

Namib Desert

Windhoek

Okavango Swamps

Caprivi Strip

WESTERN

Nyasa (L. Malawi)

Blantyre

Beira

Maputo

SWAZILAND

TRANSVAAL

Pretoria

Johannesburg

NATAL

Durban

Pietermaritzburg

LESOTHO

ORANJE-VRYSTAAT (O.F.S.)

Bloemfontein

Kimberley

TRANSKEI

CAPE PROVINCE

East London

Port Elizabeth

Cape Town

SOUTH AFRICA

Kaap die Goeie Hoop (C. of Good Hope)

ATLANTIC OCEAN

Tropic of Capricorn

Benguela

Lobito

East from Greenwich

MADAGASCAR
On same scale as General Map
COPYRIGHT GEORGE PHILIP & SON LTD.

INDIAN OCEAN

Antananarivo (Tananarive)

Diégo-Suarez

Majunga

Tuléar

Tamatave

Fianarantsoa

Fort-Dauphin

Tropic of Capricorn

1:15 000 000

100   0   100   200   300   400 miles
100   0   100   200   300   400   500   600 km

Projection: Sanson Flamsteed's Sinusoidal

EUROPE

•Leningrad

Moskva•

Volga

U.   S.   S.   R.

Sverdlovsk•
Omsk•
Novosibirsk•
•Tomsk
Barnaul•

Semipalatinsk•
Karaganda•
L. Balkhash
Alma Ata•
Tashkent•
Samarkand•

AFGHANISTAN
Srinagar•
Lahore•
PAKISTAN
Delhi•
Agra•
Kanpur•
Varanasi•
Ganges
INDIA
Calcutta•
Cuttack•
Hyderabad•
Madras•

Irkutsk•
Ozero
Baykal
•Chita
Ulan
Ude•
Ulaanbaatar•
MONGOLIA
Hovd•
Ulyasutay•

Lena

Blagoveshchensk• Amur

Khabarovsk•

Sea of Okhotsk

Kamchatka
Komandorskie Is.
(U.S.S.R.)
Petropavlovsk•

Sakhalin

A   S   I   A

SINKIANG
UIGUR
Lop Nor•
Wulumuchi•

Kunlun
TIBET
Lhasa•
Mt. Everest
8848

Hoang Ho
Lanchow•
Sian•
Changsha•

CHINA

Peiping•
Tientsin•
Lu-ta•
Tsinan•
Tsingtao•
Nanking•
SHANGHAI
Hangchow•
Wenchow•

Manchuria
Harbin•
Changchun•
Shenyang•
•Antung
KOREA
Sŏul S.•
Pusan•

Vladivostok•

Sea of
Japan
JAPAN
Kyōto•
TOKYO
Yokohama
Osaka Nagoya
Fuji-san 3776

Kuril Is.
10,542
Kuril Trench
Oyashiwo
La Perouse Strait
Hakodate•
•Sendai

Emperor Seamount Chain

3389

KURO
SIWO

7168

Chungking•
Wuhan•

Kweichi Kiang
Foochow•
Hsiamen•
Kunming•
Kwangchow•

Yellow Sea
Kitakyūshū•
Nagasaki•
Kyūshū
Shikoku
South
Honshu
Ridge

8412
Japan Trench
10,554

Bonin Is.

Volcano Is.

Midway Is.
(U.S.)

6603
Lisianski
(U.S.)

P   A

Marcus I.
Necker Ridge
Wake I. (U.S.)

EQUATOR

Taipei•
Taiwan
(Formosa)
HONG KONG•
Hainan

East
China
Sea
Ryūkyū Is.

RANGE

C. Engano

Mariana Is.
U.S. Trust Terr.
Mariana Trench
11,022
Guam (U.S.)
Micronesia

NORTH

Bikini
Atoll

Marshall Is.
U.S. Trust Terr.

BURMA
Rangoon•
THAILAND
(SIAM)
Bangkok•
CAMBODIA

Mergui
Arch.
Isthmus
of
Kra
Andaman Is.

Chengmai

South
China
Sea
Saigon•
Phnom
Penh•

Mindoro
Palawan
PHILIPPINES
Samar
10,497
Mindanao
Mindanao Trench

Yap

Palau Is.

Truk

Eniwetok
Atoll

Caroline Islands
U.S. Trust Territory of the Pacific Islands

Ponape

EQUATORIAL

Ialuit

Makin

Gilbert Is.
(U.K.)

International Date Line

Baker I.
(U.S.)

O

Canton I.

SRI LANKA
Colombo•
Nicobar Is.
1567

George Town•
Kuala Lumpur•
Melaka•
MALAYA
SINGAPORE•
MALAYSIA

Sulu
Sea
Labuan
BRUNEI
SABAH
Kinabalu
4101
SARAWAK

Celebes
Sea

Halmahera

Melanesia

Nauru Is.
Nauru
Ocean I.
(U.K.)

Gulf
of
Siam
C. Camau

Natuna

Nias
Palembang•
Bangka

Borneo

Celebes

Ceram
Buru
Amboina

Dampier Strait

Irian
Jaya
5029
New
Guinea

Admiralty Is.
Bismarck
Arch.
New Ireland

Rabaul•
9103
New Britain

Solomon
Islands
(U.K.)

Tuvalu
(Ellice Is.)

Sta. Cruz I.
(U.K.)

Rotuma

Funafuti

Tokelau

SAM

Wallis
Arch.
Futuna (Fr.)

INDONESIA
Jakarta•
Semarang•
Surabaya•
Java
Sumatra
Sunda
Strait
Christmas I.
(Austral.)
Cocos (Keeling) Is.
(Austral.)

Java Sea
Flores
Sea
Bali
Lombok
Sumbawa
Flores
Banda
Sea
Sumba
Timor
Java
Trench
7450
7440
Tanimbar Is.

Aru Is.

PAPUA
Lae•
•Madang
NEW
GUINEA
Port Moresby•
Louisiade Arch.
(Austral.)

9165

Honiara
Guadalcanal

7570

New
Hebrides
(U.K. & Fr.)

Vanua Levu
Viti Levu
Suva•
FIJI

Niue (Savage)
(N.Z.)

SOUTH

Tonga
Trench

TONGA

INDIAN

OCEAN

Al' Adan - Melbourne 6448

Fremantle 3120

Colombo - Fremantle

1840

1772

Ashmore Is.
Darwin•
Larrimah•
Wyndham•

N.W.
Cape
Onslow•

Arafura Sea
C. Arnhem
Thursday I.
Torres Strait
C. York

Newcastle
Waters•

NORTHERN
TERRITORY

G. of
Carpentaria

Cairns•

Townsville•

Mt. Isa•
Longreach•
QUEENSLAND

Coral Sea

Chesterfield Is.
(Fr.)

Rockhampton•

New
Caledonia
(Fr.)
Noumea•

Loyalty Is.
(Fr.)

Friendly Is.
(N.Z.)
10,822

Shark Bay

Geraldton•

WESTERN AUSTRALIA

Alice Springs•

AUSTRALIA

SOUTH AUSTRALIA

Oodnadatta•
L. Eyre

Maryborough•
Brisbane•
Ipswich•

Norfolk I. (Aust.)

Kermadec Is.
(N.Z.)

Kermadec
Trench
10,047

Perth•
Fremantle•
Albany•
Geographe Bay
K. George Sd.
F. - A. 1353
Cape Town - Fremantle 5615

Kalgoorlie•

Great
Australian Bight

Great
Divide

NEW SOUTH WALES
Sydney•
Newcastle
Wollongong•
Katoomba•
Canberra
Mt. Kosciusko 2230

Lord Howe I. (Aust.)

S - A 1274

Tasman
Sea

Auckland•
Hamilton•
NEW ZEALAND
Palmerston N.
Wellington•

Amsterdam I.
(Fr.)
St. Paul I. (Fr.)

Mid

Oceanic

VICTORIA
Ballarat•
Geelong•
Melbourne•
Adelaide•
Murray
Encounter
Bay

Bass Strait
TASMANIA
Launceston•
Hobart•

W. 1293

Nelson•
Mt. Cook
3764
Christchurch•
Oamaru•
Dunedin•

Cook Strait

Paci

Chatham Is.
(N.Z.)

Crozet Is.
(Fr.)

East

Indian

Cape Town - Melbourne 5814
Cape Town - Hobart 5838

Indian - Antarctic Ridge

Kerguelen
(Fr.)
Heard I. (Aust.)

Rise
Ridge

Invercargill•
Stewart
I.

Auckland Is. (N.Z.)

Macquarie Is.
(Austral.)

Campbell I.
(N.Z.)

Bounty Is. (N.Z.)

Antipodes Is.
(N.Z.)

_ _ _5615_ _ _   Principal Shipping Routes
(Distances in Nautical Miles)

Projection: Bonne

Boundaries of the artesian basins

East from Greenwich

1:12 000 000

AUSTRALASIA
PHYSICAL
1:80 000 000

TASMANIA

on same scale

COPYRIGHT. GEORGE PHILIP & SON. LTD.

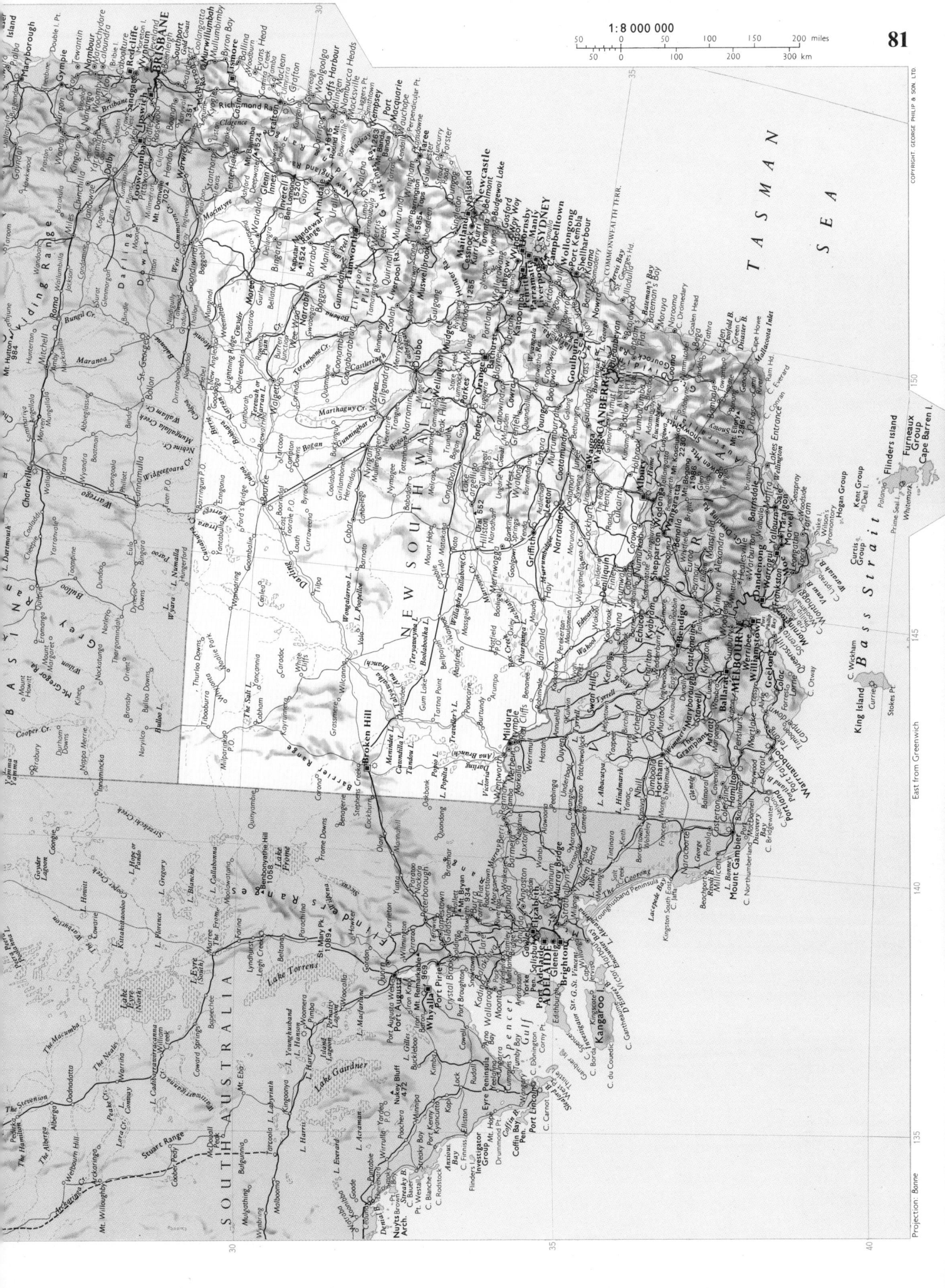

1: 4 500 000

20 0 20 40 60 80 100 miles

20 0 40 80 120 160 km

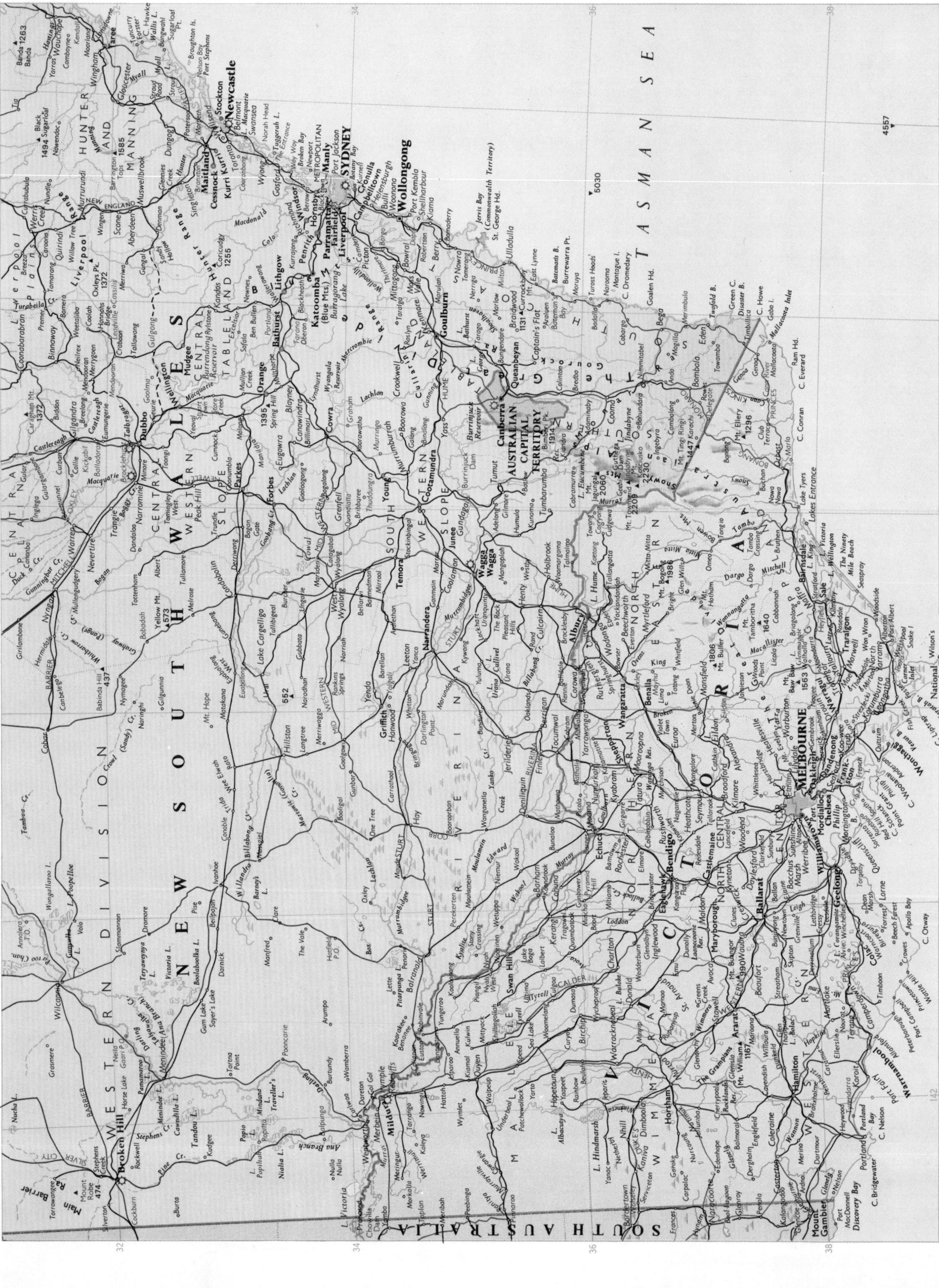

East from Greenwich

Projection: Albers' Equal Area with two standard parallels

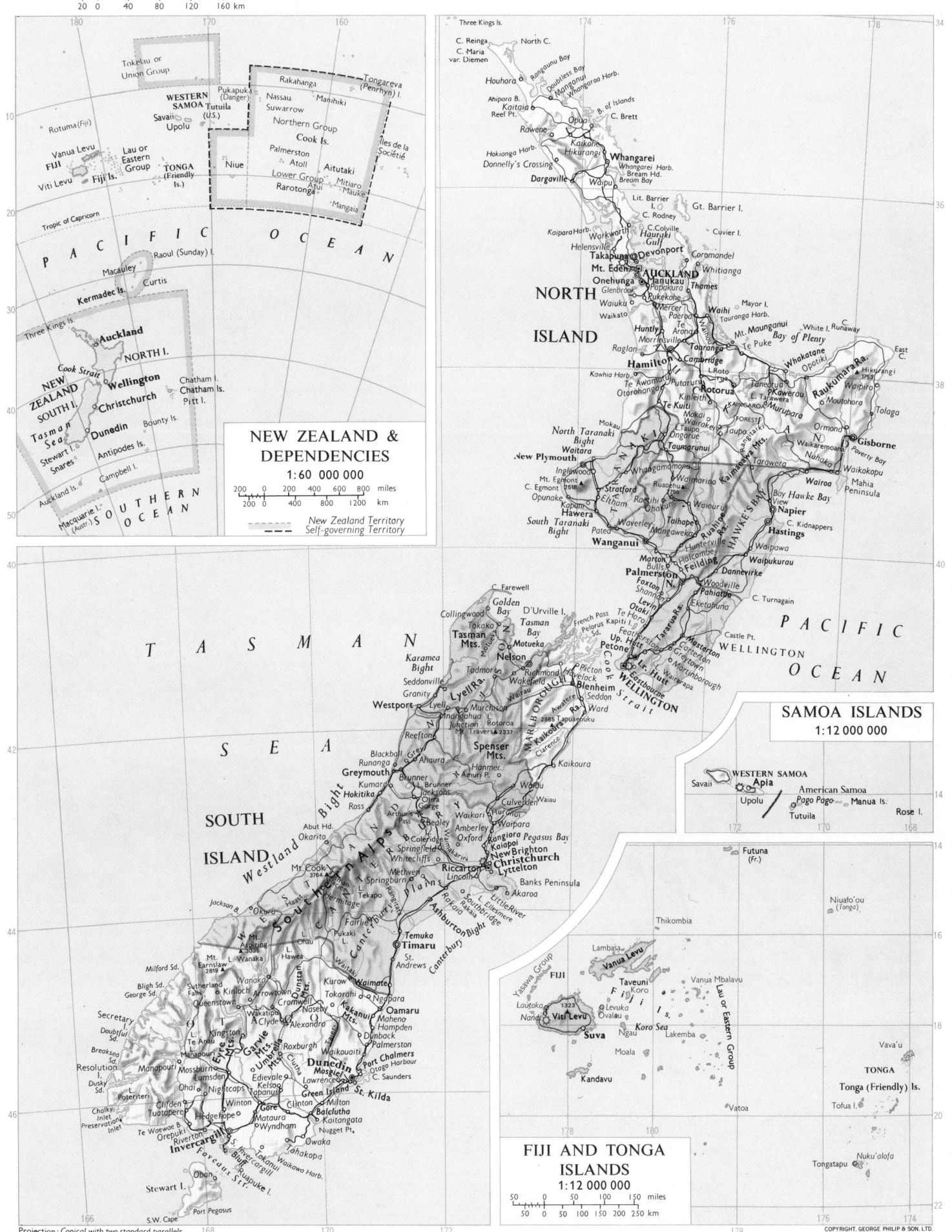

1:6 000 000

miles
20   0   20   40   60   80   100 miles
20   0   40   80   120   160 km

NEW ZEALAND & DEPENDENCIES

1:60 000 000

miles
200   0   200   400   600   800 miles
200   0   400   600   800 km

New Zealand Territory
Self-governing Territory

NORTH ISLAND

SOUTH ISLAND

TASMAN SEA

PACIFIC OCEAN

SOUTHERN OCEAN

SAMOA ISLANDS
1:12 000 000

WESTERN SAMOA
Apia
Savaii
Upolu
American Samoa
Pago Pago
Tutuila
Manua Is.
Rose I.

FIJI AND TONGA ISLANDS
1:12 000 000

miles
50   0   50   100   150 miles
50   0   50   100   150   250 km

FIJI
Vanua Levu
Taveuni
Viti Levu
Suva
Koro Sea
Lau or Eastern Group

TONGA
Tonga (Friendly) Is.
Nuku'alofa
Tongatapu

Projection : Conical with two standard parallels

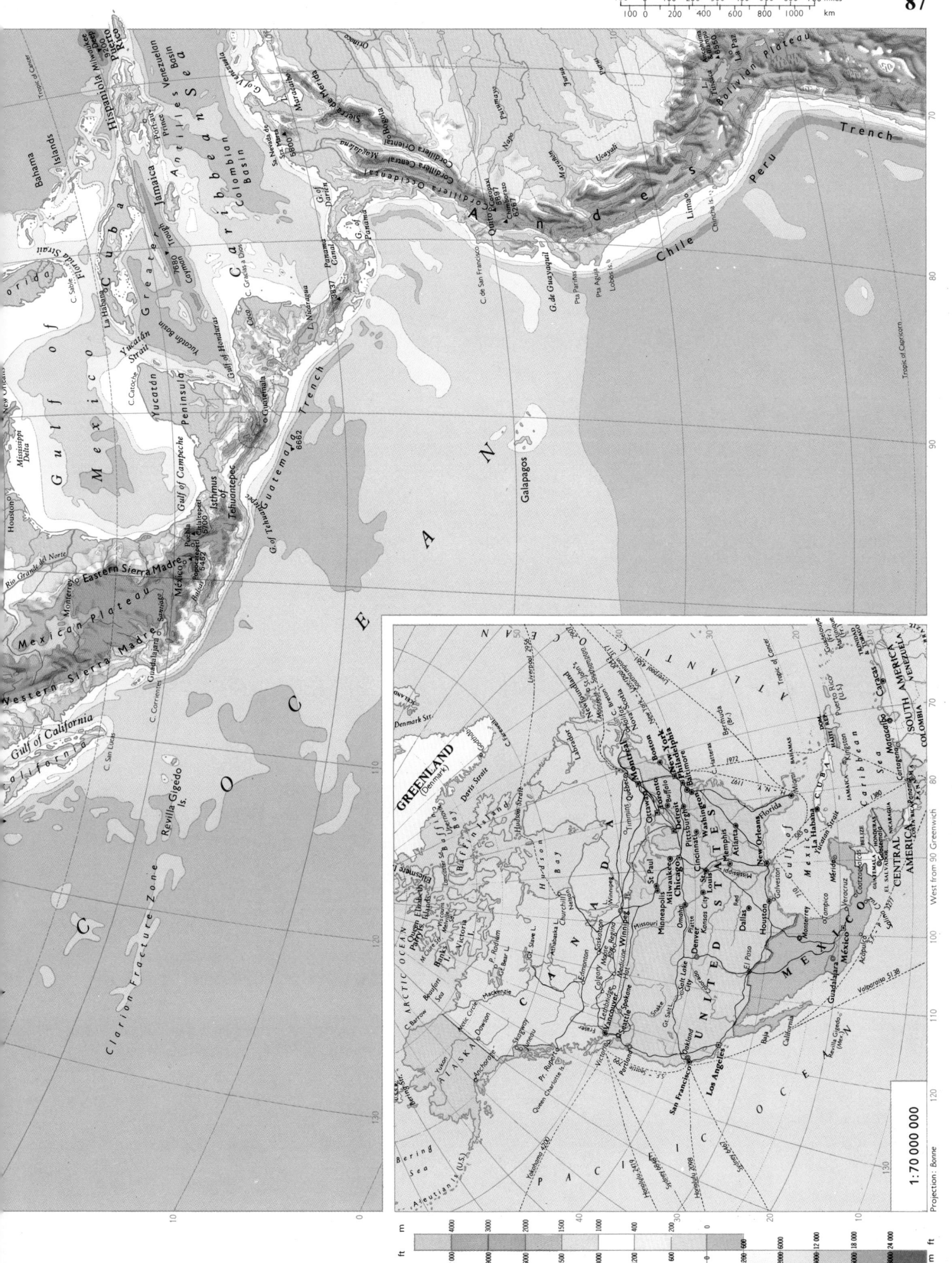

1 : 30 000 000

100   0   100   200   300   400   500   600   700 miles
100 0   200   400   600   800   1000 km

Bahama
Islands
Tropic of Cancer

Puerto Rico
Milwaukee Deep
9200
Hispaniola

Florida Strait
La Habana
Cuba
Greater
Antilles

Venezuelan
Basin

G. of Venezuela
Maracaibo
Sierra de Mérida

Orinoco

Antilles Sea

Jamaica
Caribbean Sea
Trough
7680
Cayman
Caymans

Colombian
Basin

Gulf of Honduras
C. Gracias a Dios
Coco

Cordillera Oriental
Bogotá
Magdalena

Cordillera Central
Quito Cotopaxi 8897
6267 Chimborazo

Cordillera Occidental

Napo

Putumayo

Purús

Juruá

Ucayali

Bolivian Plateau
La Paz
Titicaca
6550
8550
70

A   N   D   E   S

Chile

Peru

Trench

80

Yucatán
Strait
C. Catoche
Yucatán Peninsula

C. S. Antón

Mississippi
Delta
Houston

Gulf of
Mexico

Gulf of Campeche

Guatemala
L. Nicaragua

Panama Canal
Panama
G. of
Darién

G. of
Panamá

C. de San Francisco

G. de Guayaquil
Pta Paríñas

Pta Aguja
Lobos Is.

Chincha Is.

Limão

Tropic of Capricorn

90

Galápagos

New Orleans

Isthmus of Tehuantepec
Guatemala Trench
6662

G. of Tehuantepec

O   C   E   A   N

Rio Grande del Norte
Eastern Sierra Madre
Monterrey
México Puebla
Orizaba Chaltepetl
5700
Bufa Popocatépetl
5452
Santiago
Guadalajara
C. Corrientes

Mexican Plateau

Western Sierra Madre

Gulf of California

California
C. San Lucas

Revilla Gigedo
Is.

Clarion Fracture Zone

C

O

C

E

A

N

10

0

110

120

130

1 : 70 000 000

ARCTIC   OCEAN

GREENLAND
(Denmark)

Denmark Str.

ICELAND

Liverpool 2956
Newfoundland 3517
C. Farewell

St John's
Nova Scotia

Montreal
Québec
Ottawa
Toronto
Buffalo
Detroit
Pittsburgh
Cincinnati
Memphis
Atlanta

Boston
New York
Philadelphia
Washington
Baltimore
C. Hatteras

ATLANTIC

N 50

40

30

Bermuda
(Br.)

1972

Tropic of Cancer

20

Guadeloupe
Martinique
TRINIDAD
Caracas
VENEZUELA
SOUTH AMERICA
COLOMBIA

Puerto Rico
(U.S.)
DOM.
HAITI REP.

Baffin Island

Hudson Strait

Labrador

Ungava

Baffin
Bay

Ellesmere I.

Queen
Elizabeth Is.

Parry Is.

M°Clintock
Melville I.
Banks I.

Victoria
I.

Lancaster Sd.
Devon I.

Hudson

Bay

Churchill

St. Lawrence

C A N A D A

Winnipeg
Regina
Medicine Hat
Calgary

Edmonton

Great Slave L.

Mackenzie

Athabasca
L.

Gt. Bear L.

Beaufort
Sea

Barrow
Arctic Circle

A L A S K A
(U.S.)

Yukon

Dawson

Anchorage
Juneau

Pr. Rupert

Queen Charlotte Is.

Skagway

Vancouver I.
Victoria
Seattle
Spokane
Vancouver
Portland

Fraser

Snake
Columbia

Gt. Salt Lake

Salt Lake
City

San Francisco
Oakland

Los Angeles

Baja
California

Revilla Gigedo Is. (Mex.)

St Paul
Minneapolis
Milwaukee
Chicago
St Louis
Kansas City
Omaha
Denver
Platte

Missouri

Mississippi

Red

Dallas

El Paso

Houston
Galveston

Monterrey
Tampico

Veracruz
México
Guadalajara
Acapulco

M E X I C O

U N I T E D   S T A T E S

Gulf of
Mexico
New Orleans
Florida

Miami

Yucatán Strait
CUBA
La Habana

BAHAMAS

Caribbean
Sea
JAMAICA Kingston

1380

1197

Mérida

BELIZE

GUATEMALA
EL SALVADOR
Coatzacoalcos

HONDURAS
NICARAGUA

COSTA RICA
PANAMA
Panama
Cartagena
Maracaibo

CENTRAL
AMERICA

Valparaiso 5138

P A C I F I C

O C E A N

Bering
Sea
Aleutians (U.S.)

U.S.S.R.
Bering Str.

West from 90 Greenwich

70

80

90

100

110

120

130

Projection : Bonne

m   4000 3000 2000 1500 1000   400   200   0
ft 12 000 9000 6000 4500 3000 1200   600   0   -200 -600 2000 6000 4000 12 000 6000 18 000 8000 24 000 m
                                                                                                                    ft

Projection: Bonne

ALASKA
1:30 000 000

| 100 | 0 | 100 | 200 | 300 miles |
| 100 | 0 | 200 | 400 km |

West from Greenwich

West from Greenwich

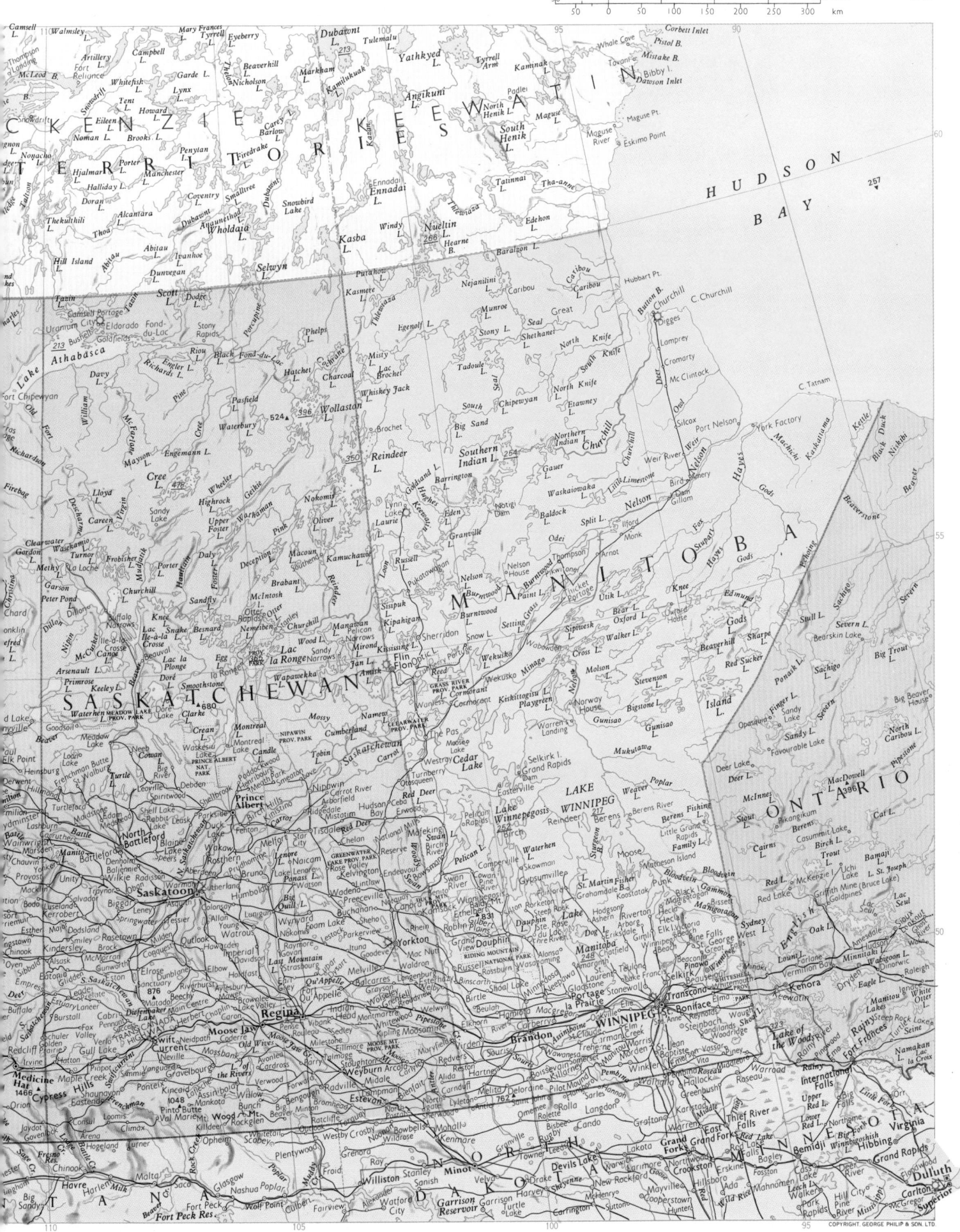

1:7 000 000

50   0   50   100   150   200 miles
50 0 50 100 150 200 250 300 km

HUDSON

BAY

MACKENZIE

TERRITORIES   KEEWATIN

SASKATCHEWAN

MANITOBA

ONTARIO

Lake
Athabasca

Lake
WINNIPEG

Prince
Albert

Saskatoon

Regina

Moose Jaw

Swift
Current

Medicine
Hat

WINNIPEG

Brandon

Portage
la Prairie

NORTH   DAKOTA

MONTANA

MINNESOTA

Duluth

Superior

COPYRIGHT. GEORGE PHILIP & SON. LTD.

HAWAII
1:10 000 000

20 0 20 40 60 80 miles

20 0 40 80 120 km

Projection : Albers' Equal Area with two standard parallels

1:12 000 000

COPYRIGHT. GEORGE PHILIP & SON. LTD.

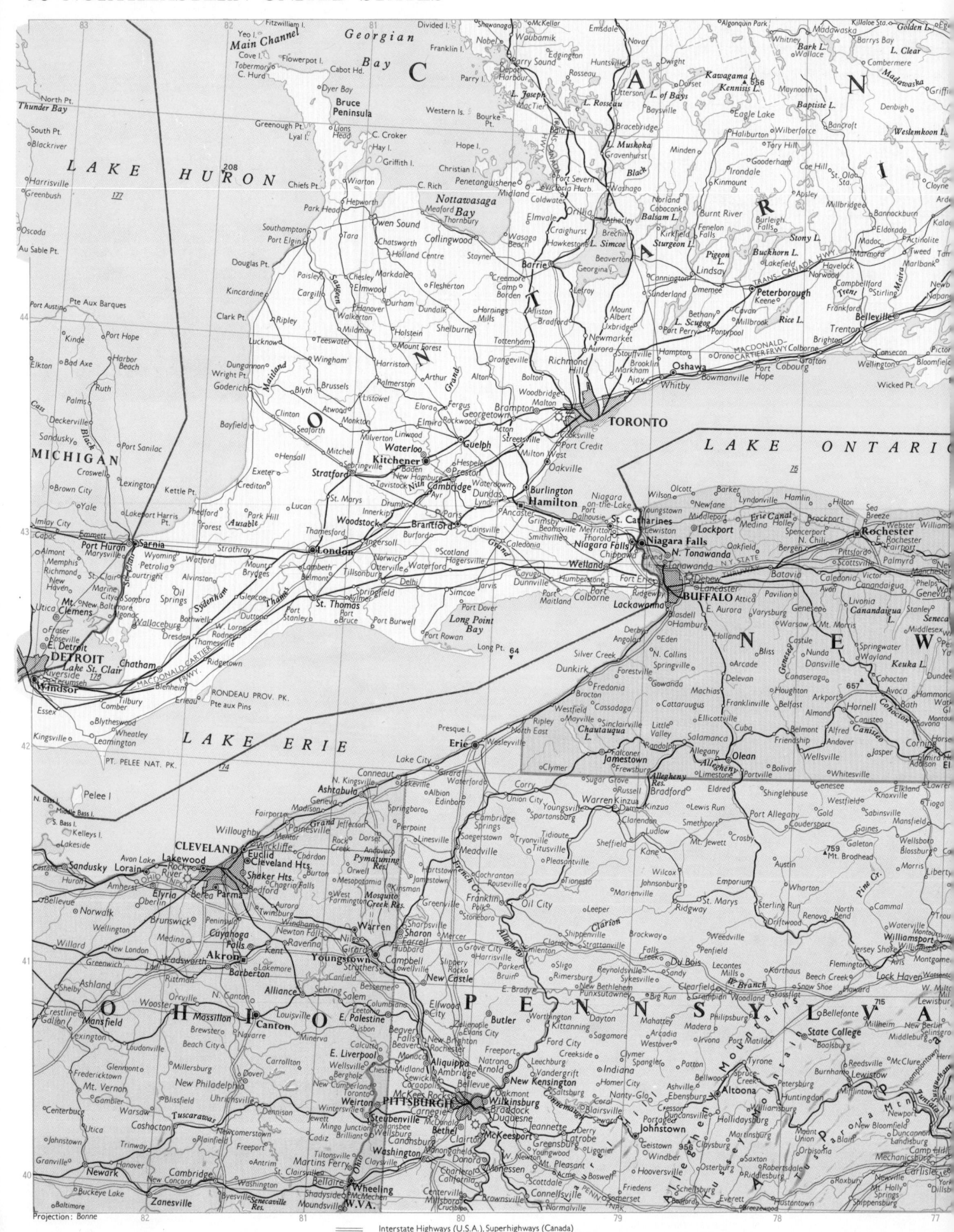

═══ Interstate Highways (U.S.A.), Superhighways (Canada)

═══ Interstate Highways and Superhighways under Construction

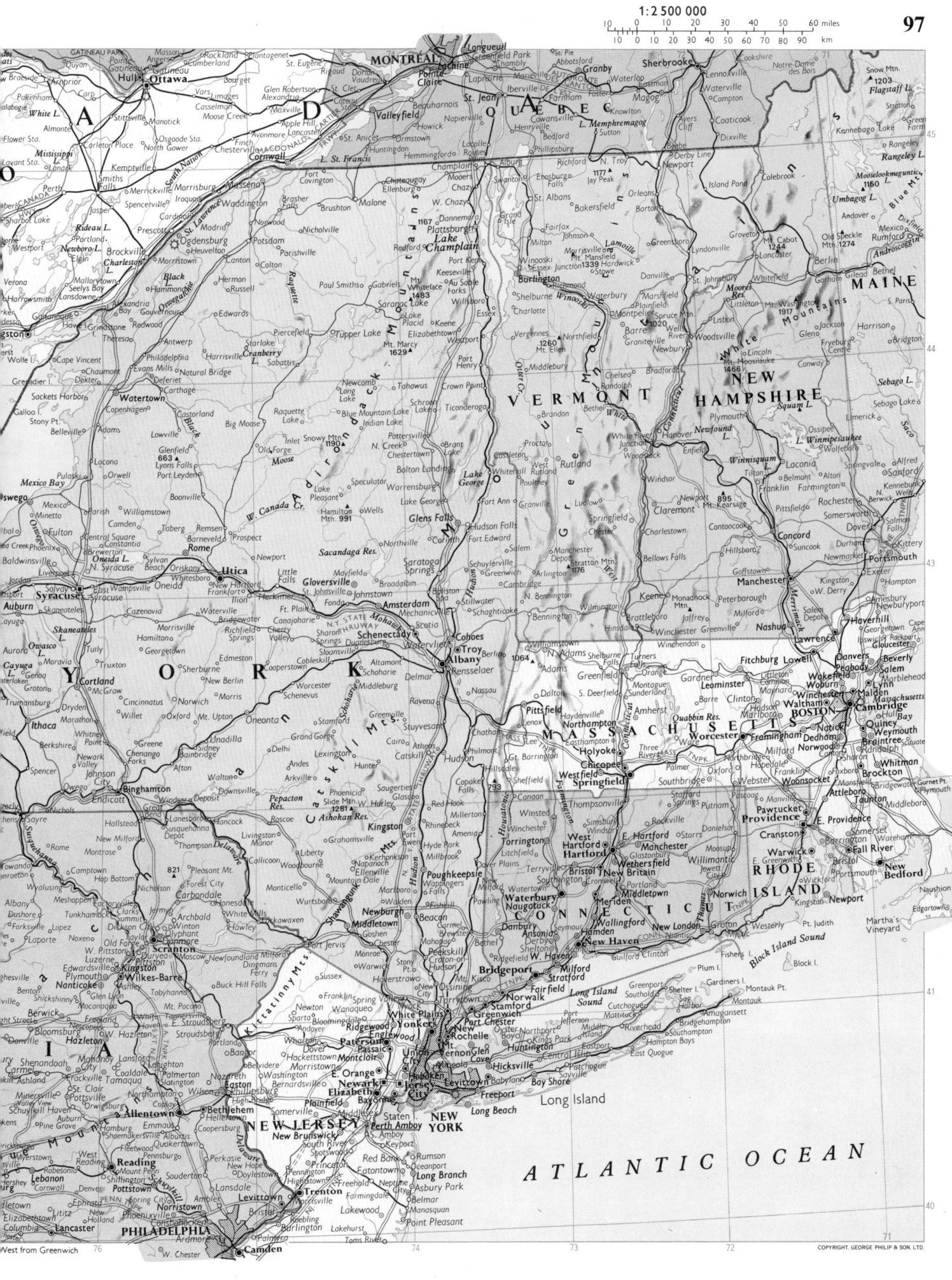

1 : 2 500 000

ATLANTIC OCEAN

West from Greenwich
COPYRIGHT. GEORGE PHILIP & SON. LTD.

LAKE SUPERIOR
LAKE HURON
LAKE ONTARIO
LAKE ERIE
Georgian Bay
ONTARIO
QUEBEC
MICHIGAN
WISCONSIN
ILLINOIS
INDIANA
OHIO
KENTUCKY
WEST VIRGINIA
VIRGINIA
PENNSYLVANIA
NEW YORK
NEW JERSEY
MARYLAND
DELAWARE
CHICAGO
MILWAUKEE
DETROIT
TORONTO
BUFFALO
CLEVELAND
PITTSBURGH
CINCINNATI
PHILADELPHIA
BALTIMORE
WASHINGTON
MONTREAL
BOSTON
Chesapeake Bay

1 : 6 000 000

50 0 50 100 miles

50 0 50 100 150 km

Continuation
Eastwards
On same scale

MAINE

NEW HAMPSHIRE

CANADA

Portland
Portsmouth
Newburyport

NORTH CAROLINA

Raleigh
Wilmington
Cape Fear
Myrtle Beach

SOUTH CAROLINA

Columbia
Charleston
Georgetown
Beaufort

TENNESSEE

Knoxville
Chattanooga
Nashville

GEORGIA

Atlanta
Macon
Columbus
Savannah

ALABAMA

Birmingham
Montgomery
Mobile

MISSISSIPPI

FLORIDA

Jacksonville
St. Augustine
Daytona Beach
Orlando
Tampa
St. Petersburg
Sarasota
Ft. Pierce
West Palm Beach
Ft. Lauderdale
Hollywood
Miami
Miami Beach
EVERGLADES NAT. PARK

Tallahassee
Panama Cy.
Pensacola

GULF OF MEXICO

ATLANTIC OCEAN

BAHAMAS

Grand Bahama I.
Freeport
Great Abaco I.
Little Abaco I.

Projection. Alber's Equal Area with two standard parallels   West from Greenwich

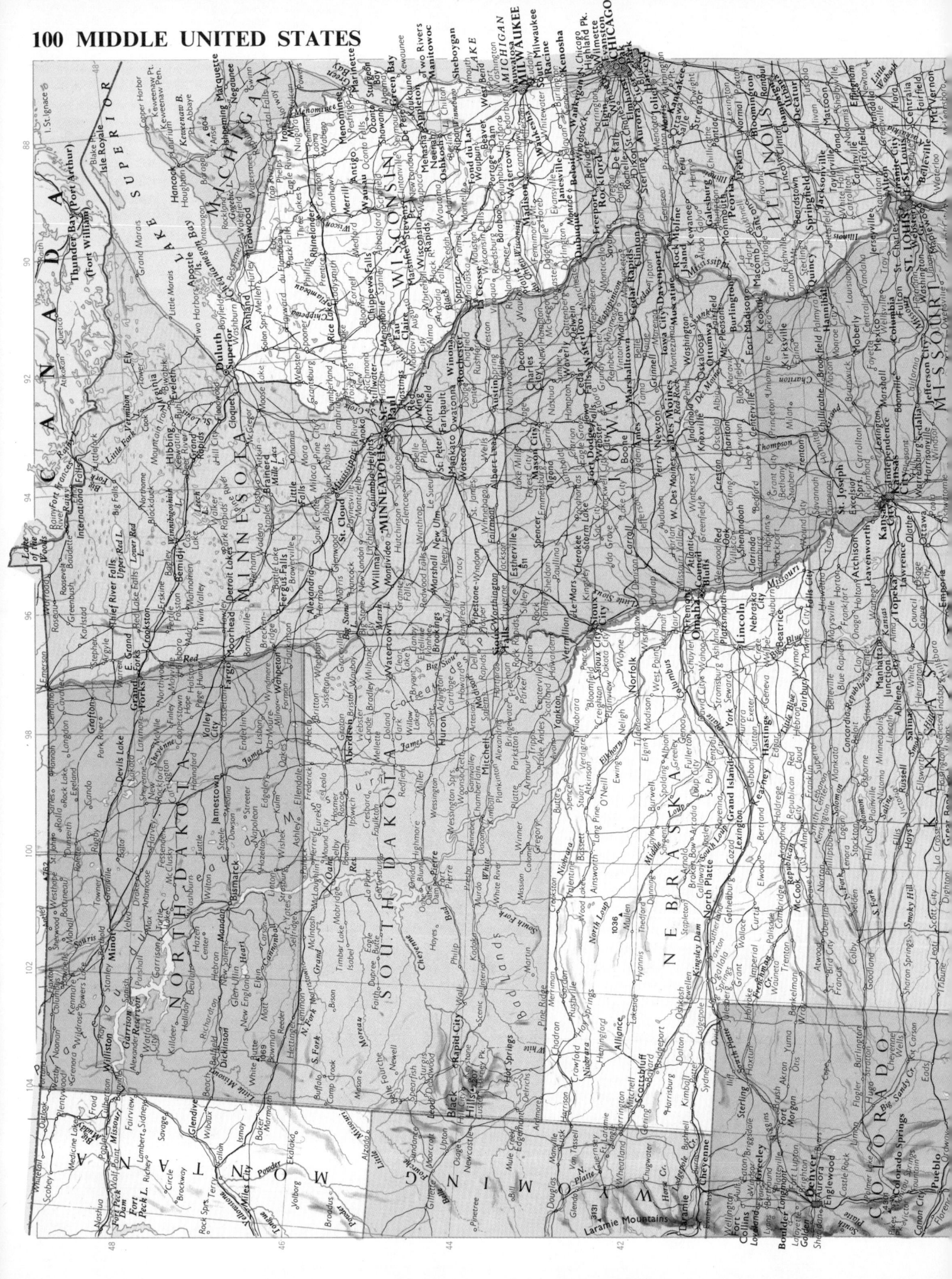

1 : 6 000 000

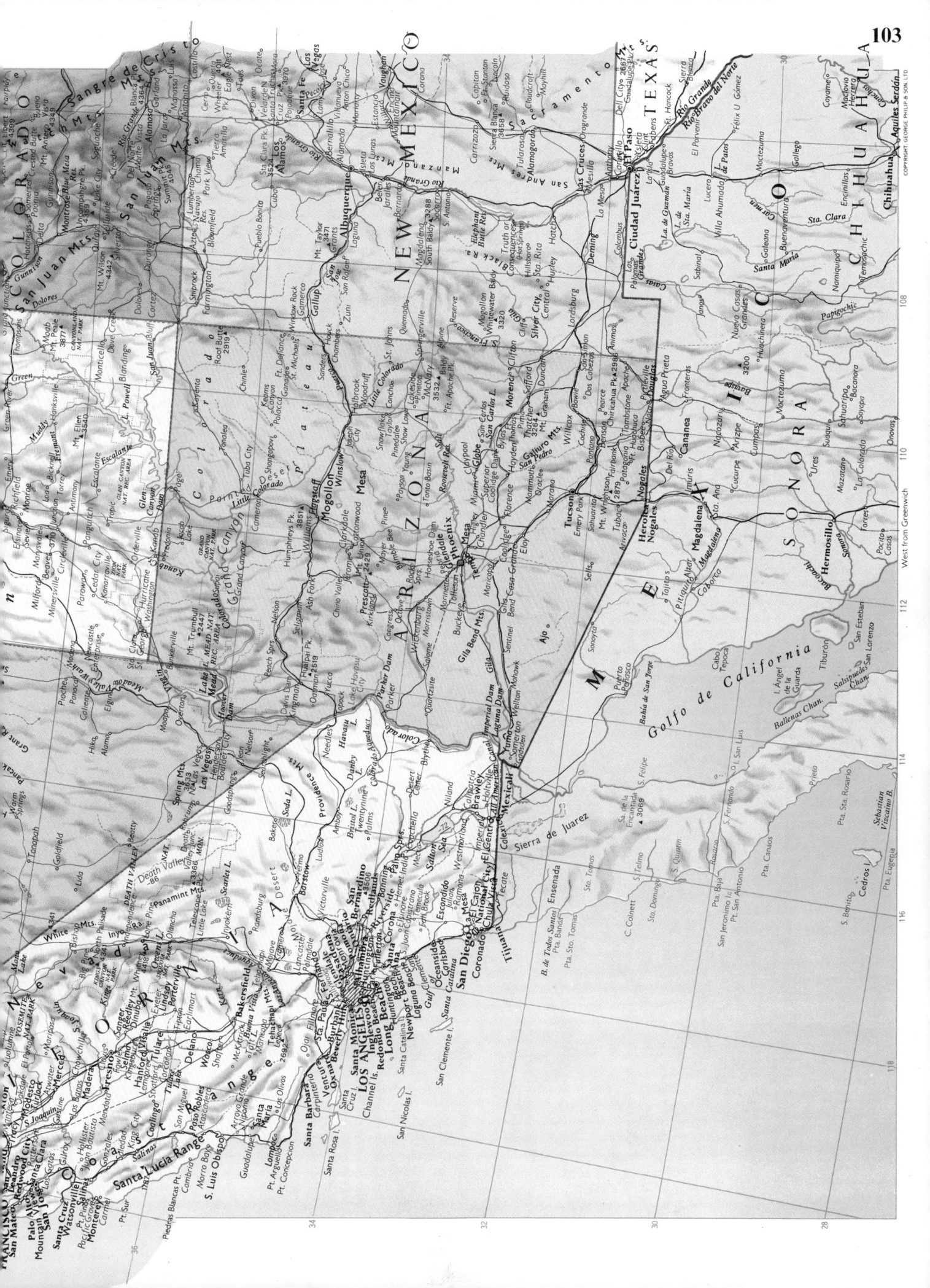

West from Greenwich

1:12 000 000

100 0 100 200 miles
100 0 100 200 300 km

REFERENCE TO NUMBERS

1 Distrito Federal		5 México	
2 Aguascalientes		6 Morelos	
3 Guanajuato		7 Querétaro	
4 Hidalgo		8 Tlaxcala	

G U L F   O F   M E X I C O

P A C I F I C   O C E A N

U N I T E D   S T A T E S

GUATEMALA

BELIZE

HONDURAS

EL SALVADOR

Tropic of Cancer

West from Greenwich

Projection: Bi-polar oblique Conical Orthomorphic

PANAMA CANAL
1:1 000 000

ATLANTIC OCEAN

PACIFIC OC.

CANAL ZONE

REPUBLIC OF PANAMA

Colón

PANAMA

Balboa Heights

Canal Zone 0 5 10 15 miles
0 5 10 15 20 25 km

New Orleans · Houston · Dallas · Fort Worth · San Antonio · Austin · Monterrey · Mexico · Guadalajara · Veracruz · Mérida · Tampico · Chihuahua · Culiacán · Mazatlán · Acapulco · Oaxaca · El Paso · Ciudad Juárez

1:12 000 000.

100 100 200 miles

100 0 100 200 300 km

WINDWARD ISLANDS
1:8 000 000

TRINIDAD & TOBAGO
1:8 000 000

JAMAICA
1:8 000 000

LEEWARD ISLANDS
1:8 000 000

BERMUDA
1:1 000 000

COPYRIGHT GEORGE PHILIP & SON, LTD.

West from Greenwich

Projection: Bi-polar oblique Conical Orthomorphic

Major labels

ATLANTIC OCEAN

CARIBBEAN SEA

PACIFIC OCEAN

GULF OF MEXICO

GREAT ANTILLES

LESSER ANTILLES

GREATER ANTILLES

WINDWARD ISLANDS

LEEWARD ISLANDS

BAHAMAS

GREAT BAHAMA BANK

CUBA

HISPANIOLA

HAITI

DOMINICAN REP.

JAMAICA

PUERTO RICO (U.S.A.)

MEXICO

HONDURAS

NICARAGUA

COSTA RICA

PANAMA

CANAL ZONE

COLOMBIA

VENEZUELA

GUIANA

FLORIDA

MIAMI

La Habana

Santiago de Cuba

Kingston

Port-au-Prince

Santo Domingo

Port of Spain

San Juan

Barranquilla

Cartagena

CARACAS

Maracaibo

Managua

Tegucigalpa

San José

BARBADOS

TRINIDAD & TOBAGO

MARTINIQUE

GUADELOUPE

DOMINICA

ST. LUCIA

GRENADA

ST. VINCENT

Tropic of Cancer

1:30 000 000

100 0 100 200 300 400 500 miles
100 0 200 400 600 800 km

5994

Map labels:

Sa. Nevada de Santa Marta
Barranquilla
5800
Maracaibo
L. Maracaibo
Margarita
Tobago I.
Caracas
Trinidad

G. of
Darien
Panama
Canal
Medellín
Cali
Bogotá
Cord. de Mérida
Llanos
Orinoco
Georgetown
Guiana Highlands
Sierra Pacaraima
2810 Roraima
Serra de Tumucumaque
C. Orange

ATLANTIC
OCEAN

Cordillera Occidental
Cordillera Central
Cordillera Oriental
Guaviare
Meta
Casiquiari
Branco
Essequibo
Courantyne

Equator
Quito
Cotopaxi 5897
Chimborazo 6267
C. de San Francisco
Caquetá
Japurá
Negro
Amazon
Manaus
Marajó I.
Pará
Belém
Fortaleza
São Roque
C. Branco

G. of Guayaquil
Guayaquil
Napo
Putumayo
Marañón
Juruá
Purus
Madeira
Tapajós
Xingu
Tocantins
Parnaíba

Pta. Pariñas
Pta. Aguja
Lobos Is.
Ucayali
Andes
Selvas
Juruá
Aripuana
Roosevelt
Teles Pires
Araguaia
São Francisco
Plateau of Borborema
Recife

Huascarán 6768
Madre de Dios
Guaporé
Arinos
Plateau of Mato Grosso
Brazilian Highlands
Salvador

Chile
Peru
Lima
Chincha Is.
Titicaca
Ancohuma & Illampu 6550
La Paz
Bolivian Plateau
L. Poopó
Brasília
Abrolhos Bank

PACIFIC
Trench
Belo Horizonte
Serra da Mantiqueira
2890 Pico da Bandeira

Tropic of Capricorn
8050
Atacama Desert
Ojos del Salado 6863
Tucumán
Gran Chaco
Pilcomayo
Asunción
Paraná
São Paulo
C. Frio
Rio de Janeiro
Serra do Mar

S. Félix
S. Ambrosio
Salado
Salinas Grandes
Sierra de Córdoba
Bermejo
Uruguay
Iguaçu Falls

Córdoba
L. Mar Chiquita
Entre Rios
Aconcagua 6960
Uspallata Pass
Rosario
Paraná
Pampas
Pôrto Alegre
Lagoa dos Patos

Valparaíso
Santiago
Buenos Aires
Montevideo
La Plata
Rio de la Plata

OCEAN
Arch. de Juan Fernández
Colorado
Negro
Bahía Blanca
Pta. Mogotes

Chiloé I.
Andes
Chubut
Patagonia
G. of San Matias
Valdés Peninsula

Chile Rise
Chonos Archipelago
Taitao Peninsula
G. of Peñas
4058 S. Valentin
G. of San Jorge
Argentine Basin

SOUTH

ATLANTIC

6212

Wellington
Madre de Dios
Magellan's Strait
Santa Inés
Cockburn Chan.
Beagle Chan.
C. Horn
Tierra del Fuego
Staten I.

Falkland Islands
West Falkland
Magellan's Strait
East Falkland

OCEAN

West from Greenwich

Projection: Lambert's Equivalent Azimuthal

COPYRIGHT. GEORGE PHILIP & SON. LTD

m   6000   4000   3000   2000   1000   400   200   0
ft   18 000   12 000   9000   6000   3000   1200   600

200   2000   4000   6000   8000   m
600   6000   12 000   18 000   24 000   ft

1 : 30 000 000

100   0   100   200   300   400   500 miles

100   0   200   400   600   800 km

Projection: Lambert's Equivalent Azimuthal

West from Greenwich

COPYRIGHT. GEORGE PHILIP & SON. LTD.

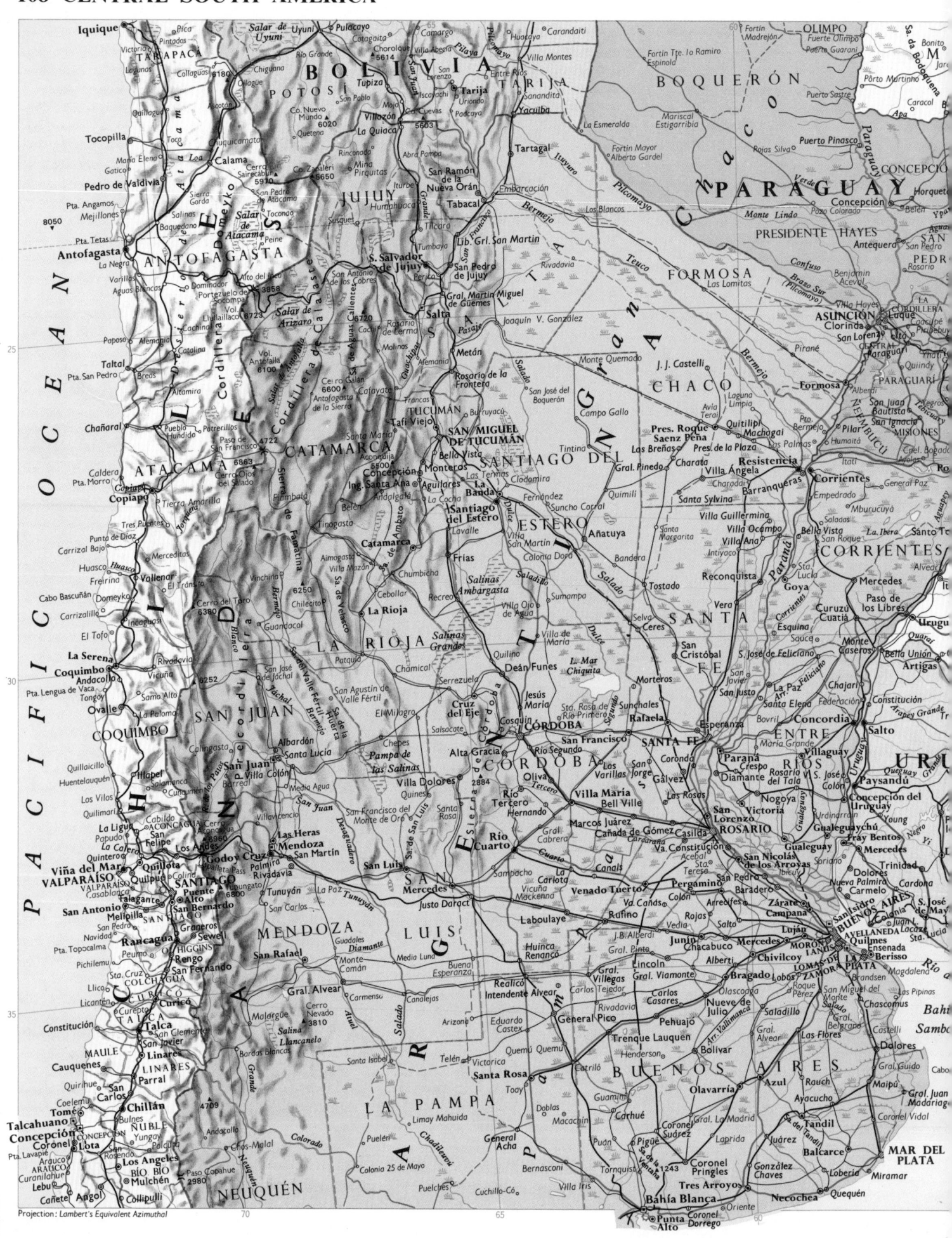

Projection: Lambert's Equivalent Azimuthal

1:16 000 000

100   200   300   400   500 miles
100   0   100   200   300   400   500   600   700   800 km

A T L A N T I C   O C E A N

Equator

RINAM
FR. GUIANA
Paramaribo
Cayenne

AMAPÁ
Macapá
C. do Norte

Estuario do
Rio Amazonas
Ilha Caviana
Ilha de Marajó

AMAZONAS
Santarém
Belém (Pará)

P A R Á

MARANHÃO
São Luís (Maranhão)
Bacabal
Teresina
Parnaíba

CEARÁ
Fortaleza (Ceará)
Sobral

RIO GRANDE
DO NORTE
Natal

PIAUÍ

PARAÍBA
João Pessoa (Paraíba)
Campina Grande

PERNAMBUCO
Caruaru
RECIFE (Pernambuco)

Fernando de Noronha
(Braz.)

Rocas

ALAGOAS
Maceió

SERGIPE
Aracajú

B R A Z I L

G O I A S

B A H I A
Feira de Santana
Salvador (Bahia)

Ilhéus
Vitória da Conquista

MATO GROSSO
Planalto do

Planalto do
Mato Grosso

DIST.
FED.
Brasília
Goiânia

Montes Claros
Diamantina

Nanuque

Campo Grande

M I N A S   G E R A I S
Belo Horizonte
Gov. Valadares

ESPIRITO
SANTO
Vitória

Ribeirão Preto

SÃO
PAULO
Campinas

Juiz de Fora

RIO DE JANEIRO
Niterói
Petrópolis
GUANABARA

Trindade
(Braz.)

6059

1678

1340

1850

COPYRIGHT. GEORGE PHILIP & SON, LTD.

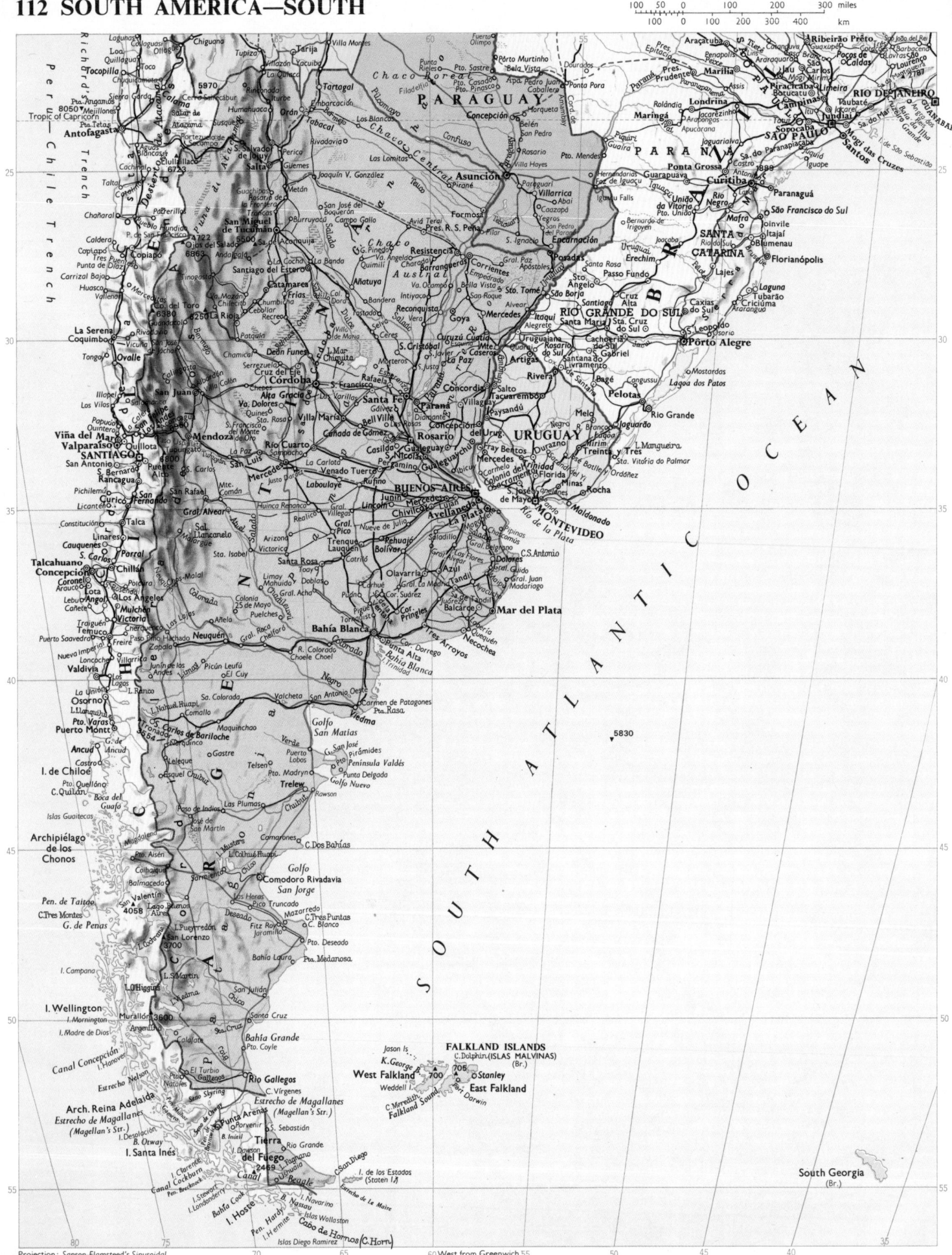

1:16 000 000

100 50 0   100   200   300 miles

100 0 100 200 300 400 km

Projection : Sanson-Flamsteed's Sinusoidal   70   60 West from Greenwich 55   50   45   40

The number in bold type which precedes each name in the index refers to the number of the page where that feature or place will be found.

The geographical co-ordinates which follow the place name are sometimes only approximate but are close enough for the place name to be located.

An open square □ signifies that the name refers to an administrative division of a country while a solid square ■ follows the name of a country.

Rivers have been indexed to their mouth or to their confluence.

The alphabetical order of names composed of two or more words is governed primarily by the first word and then by the second. This is an example of the rule:

> *West Wyalong*
> *West Yorkshire*
> *Westbrook*
> *Westbury*
> *Westerland*
> *Western Australia*

Names composed of a proper name (Gibraltar) and a description (Strait of) are positioned alphabetically by the proper name. All river names are followed by R. If the same word occurs in the name of a town and a geographical feature, the town name is listed first followed by the name or names of the geographical features.

Names beginning with M', Mc are all indexed as if they were spelled Mac.

If the same place name occurs two or more times in the index and all are in the same country, each is followed by the name of the administrative subdivision in which it is located. The names are placed in the alphabetical order of the subdivisions. For example:

> *Stour, R., Dorset*
> *Stour, R., Hereford and Worcester*
> *Stour, R., Kent*
> *Stour, R., Suffolk*

If the same place name occurs twice or more in the index and the places are in different countries they will be followed by the country names and the latter in alphabetical order.

> *Sheffield, U.K.*
> *Sheffield, U.S.A.*

If there is a mixture of these situations, the primary order is fixed by the alphabetical sequence of the countries and the secondary order by that of the country subdivisions. In the latter case the country names are omitted.

> *Rochester, U.K.*
> *Rochester, Minn.* (U.S.A.) are omitted from
> *Rochester, N.H.* (U.S.A.) the index
> *Rochester, N.Y.* (U.S.A.)
> *Rochester, Pa.* (U.S.A.)

The following is a list of abbreviations used in the index

A.S.S.R. – *Autonomous Soviet Socialist Republic*
Ala. – *Alabama*
Alas. – *Alaska*
Ang. – *Angola*
Arch. – *Archipelago*
Arg. – *Argentina*
Ariz. – *Arizona*
Ark. – *Arkansas*
B. – *Baie, Bahía, Bay, Boca, Bucht, Bugt*
B.C. – *British Columbia*
Br. – *British*
C. – *Cabo, Cap, Cape*
C.A.R. – *Central African Republic*
C. Prov. – *Cape Province*
Calif. – *California*
Chan. – *Channel*
Col. – *Colombia*
Colo. – *Colorado*
Conn. – *Connecticut*
Cord. – *Cordillera*
D.C. – *District of Columbia*
Del. – *Delaware*
Dep. – *Dependency*
Des. – *Desert*
Dist. – *District*
Dom. Rep. – *Dominican Republic*
E. – *East*
Eng. – *England*

Fd. – *Fjord*
Fed. – *Federal, Federation*
Fla. – *Florida*
Fr. – *France, French*
G. – *Golfe, Golfo, Gulf, Guba*
Ga. – *Georgia*
Gt. – *Great*
Hants. – *Hampshire*
Hd. – *Head*
Hts. – *Heights*
I.(s) – *Ile, Ilha, Insel, Isla, Island (s)*
Id. – *Idaho*
Ill. – *Illinois*
Ind. – *Indiana*
J. – *Jezero (L.)*
K. – *Kap, Kapp*
Kans. – *Kansas*
Kep. – *Kepulauan (I.)*
Kól. – *Kólpos (B.)*
Ky. – *Kentucky*
L. – *Lac, Lacul, Lago, Lagoa, Lake, Limni, Loch, Lough*
La. – *Louisana*
Ld. – *Land*
Mad. P. – *Madhya Pradesh*
Man. – *Manitoba*
Mass. – *Massachusetts*
Md. – *Maryland*
Me. – *Maine*
Mich. – *Michigan*
Minn. – *Minnesota*

Miss. – *Mississippi*
Mo. – *Missouri*
Mont. – *Montana*
Mt.(s) – *Mont, Monte, Monti, Muntii, Montaña, Mountain (s)*
Mys. – *Mysore*
N. – *North, Northern*
N.B. – *New Brunswick*
N.C. – *North Carolina*
N.D. – *North Dakota*
N.H. – *New Hampshire*
N. Ire. – *Northern Ireland*
N.J. – *New Jersey*
N. Mex. – *New Mexico*
N.S.W. – *New South Wales*
N.Y. – *New York*
N.Z. – *New Zealand*
Nat. Park – *National Park*
Nebr. – *Nebraska*
Neth. – *Netherlands*
Nev. – *Nevada*
Newf. – *Newfoundland*
Nic. – *Nicaragua*
Nig. – *Nigeria*
O.F.S. – *Orange Free State*
Okla. – *Oklahoma*
Ont. – *Ontario*
Oreg. – *Oregon*
Os. – *Ostrov (I.)*
Oz – *Ozero (L.)*
P. – *Pass, Passo, Pasul*

P.N.G. – *Papua New Guinea*
Pa. – *Pennsylvania*
Pak. – *Pakistan*
Pass. – *Passage*
Pen. – *Peninsula*
Pk. – *Peak*
Plat. – *Plateau*
Pol. – *Poluostrov*
Port. – *Portugal, Portuguese*
Prov. – *Province, Provincial*
Pt. – *Point*
Pta. – *Ponta, Punta*
Pte. – *Pointe*
Que. – *Quebec*
Queens. – *Queensland*
R. – *Rio, River*
R.S.F.S.R. – *Russian Soviet Federal Socialist Republic*
Ra.(s) – *Range(s)*
Reg. – *Region*
Rep. – *Republic*
Res. – *Reserve, Reservoir*
S. – *South*
S. Africa – *South Africa*
S.C. – *S. Carolina*
S.D. – *South Dakota*
S. Leone – *Sierra Leone*
S.S.R. – *Soviet Socialist Republic*
Sa. – *Serra, Sierra*
Sask. – *Saskatchewan*
Scot. – *Scotland*

Sd. – *Sound*
Sp. – *Spain, Spanish*
St. – *Saint*
Str. – *Strait, Stretto*
Switz. – *Switzerland*
Tanz. – *Tanzania*
Tas. – *Tasmania*
Tenn. – *Tennessee*
Terr. – *Territory*
Tex. – *Texas*
U.K. – *United Kingdom*
U.S.A. – *United States of America*
U.S.S.R. – *Union of Soviet Socialist Republics*
Ut. P. – *Uttar Pradesh*
Va. – *Virginia*
Vdkhr. – *Vodokhranilishche (Res.)*
Ven. – *Venezuela*
Vic. – *Victoria*
Vt. – *Vermont*
W. – *West*
W. Va. – *West Virginia*
Wis. – *Wisconsin*
Wyo. – *Wyoming*
Yorks. – *Yorkshire*
Yug. – *Yugoslavia*

A

Albardón Amindaion

108 Albardón 31 20s 68 30w
32 Albarracín 40 25n 1 26w
32 Albarracín, Sa. de 40 30n 1 30w
99 Albemarle 35 27n 80 15w
36 Albenga 44 3n 8 12e
30 Alberche, R. 39 58n 4 46w
33 Alberique 39 7n 0 31w
32 Alberes, Mts. 42 28n 2 56w
92 Alberni 49 20n 124 50w
24 Albersdorf 54 8n 9 19e
91 Albert, Canada 45 51n 64 38w
19 Albert, Fr. 50 0n 2 38e
74 Albert, L.= Mobutu Sese Seko, L. 1 30n 31 0e
100 Albert Lea 43 32n 93 20w
74 Albert Nile, R. 3 36n 32 2e
105 Albert Town 18 17n 77 33w
92 Alberta □ 54 40n 115 0w
84 Alberton 38 35s 146 40e
21 Albertville 45 40n 6 22e
74 Albertville= Kalemie 5 55s 29 9e
57 Alberz, Reshteh-Ye-Kūkhā-Ye, Mts. 36 0n 52 0e
20 Albi 43 56n 2 9e
111 Albina, 5 37n 54 15w
36 Albino 45 46n 9 17e
98 Albion 42 15n 84 45w
33 Alboran, I. 35 57n 3 0w
33 Alborea 39 17n 1 24w
45 Ålbôrg 57 2n 9 54e
33 Albox 37 23n 2 8w
31 Albufeira 37 5n 8 15w
33 Albuñol 36 48n 3 11w
103 Albuquerque 35 5n 106 47w
39 Alburno, Mt. 40 32n 15 20e
31 Alburquerque 39 15n 6 59w
84 Albury 36 3s 146 56e
31 Alcácer do Sol 38 22n 8 33w
31 Alcáçovas 38 23n 8 9w
32 Alcalá de Chisvert 40 19n 0 13e
31 Alcalá de Guadaira 37 20n 5 50w
31 Alcalá de los Gazules 36 29n 5 43w
30 Alcalá de Henares 40 28n 3 22w
31 Alcalá la Real 32 27n 3 57w
38 Alcamo 37 59n 12 55e
32 Alcanadre 42 24n 2 7w
32 Alcanadre, R. 41 37n 0 12w
32 Alcanar 40 33n 0 28e
31 Alcanede 39 25n 8 49w
31 Alcanena 39 27n 8 40w
32 Alcaníz 41 2n 0 8w
111 Alcántara, Brazil 2 20s 44 30w
31 Alcântara, Sp. 39 41n 6 57w
33 Alcantarilla 37 59n 1 12w
33 Alcaracejos 38 24n 4 58w
33 Alcaraz 38 40n 2 29w
33 Alcaraz, Sa. de 38 40n 2 20w
33 Alcaudete 37 35n 4 5w
31 Alcazar de San Juan 39 24n 3 12w
33 Alcira 39 9n 0 30w
30 Alcobaça 39 32n 9 0w
30 Alcobendas 40 32n 3 38w
32 Alcolea del Pinar 41 2n 2 28w
31 Alcora 40 5n 0 14w
31 Alcoutim 37 25n 7 28w
33 Alcoy 38 43n 0 30w
32 Alcubierre, Sa. de 41 45n 0 22w
32 Alcublas 39 48n 0 43w
32 Alcudia 39 51n 3 9e
32 Alcudia, B. de 39 45n 3 14e
31 Alcudia, Sa. de la 38 34n 4 30w
71 Aldabra Is. 9 22s 46 28e
51 Aldan, R. 63 28n 129 35e
13 Aldeburgh 52 9n 1 35e
31 Aldeia Nova 37 55n 7 24w
18 Alderney, I. 49 42n 2 12w
13 Aldershot 51 15n 0 43w
72 Aleg 17 3n 13 55w
109 Alegre 20 50s 41 40w
109 Alegrete 29 40s 56 0w
50 Aleisk 52 40n 83 0e
77 Alejandro Selkirk, I. 33 50s 80 15w
49 Aleksandrov Gai 50 15n 48 35e
51 Aleksandrovsk-Sakhalinskiy 50 50n 142 20e
51 Aleksandrovskiy Zavod 50 40n 117 50e
50 Aleksandrovskoye 60 35n 77 50e
28 Aleksandrów Kujawski 52 53n 18 43e
28 Aleksandrów Łódzki 51 49n 19 17e
40 Aleksinac 43 31n 21 12e
109 Além Paraíba 21 52s 42 41w
45 Ålen 62 49n 11 17e
18 Alençon 48 27n 0 4e
94 Alenuihaha Chan. 20 25n 156 0w
56 Aleppo=Ḥalab 36 10n 37 15e
21 Aléria 42 5n 9 30e
92 Alert Bay 50 30n 127 35w
21 Alès 44 9n 4 5e
36 Alessandria 44 54n 8 37e
76 Aleutian Is. 52 0n 175 0w
92 Alexander Arch. 57 0n 135 0w
75 Alexander Bay 28 36s 16 33e
99 Alexander City 32 56n 85 57w
5 Alexander I. 69 0s 70 0w
85 Alexandra 45 14s 169 25e
73 Alexandria=El Iskandarîya 31 0n 30 0e
90 Alexandria, Canada 45 19n 74 38w
41 Alexandria, Rumania 43 57n 25 24e
75 Alexandria, S. Africa 33 38s 26 28e
101 Alexandria, La. 31 20n 92 30w
100 Alexandria, Minn. 45 50n 95 20w
98 Alexandria, Va. 38 47n 77 1w
97 Alexandria Bay 44 20n 75 52w
42 Alexandroúpolis 40 50n 25 24e
32 Alfambra 40 33n 1 5w
32 Alfaro 42 10n 1 50w
41 Alfatar 43 59n 27 13e
24 Alfeld 52 0n 9 49e
109 Alfenas 21 25s 45 57w
37 Alfonsine 44 30n 12 1e
14 Alford 53 16n 0 10e
12 Alfreton 53 6n 1 22w
50 Alga 49 46n 57 20e
31 Algar 36 40n 5 39w
29 Algarve, Reg. 37 15n 8 10w
31 Algeciras 36 9n 5 28w
33 Algemesí 39 11n 0 27w
72 Alger 36 42n 3 8e
72 Algeria ■ 35 10n 3 0e
38 Alghero 40 34n 8 20e
72 Algiers=Alger 36 42n 3 8e
75 Algoabaai 33 50s 25 45e
31 Algodanales 36 54n 3 48w
90 Algonquin Prov. Park 45 35n 78 35w
33 Alhama de Almería 36 57n 2 34w
32 Alhama de Aragón 41 18n 1 54w
33 Alhama de Murcia 37 51n 1 25w
33 Alhambra, Sp. 38 54n 3 4w
103 Alhambra, U.S.A. 34 0n 118 10w
31 Alhaurín el Grande 36 39n 4 41w
32 Aliaga 40 40n 0 42w
42 Aliákmon, R. 40 30n 22 36e
40 Alibunar 45 5n 20 57e
33 Alicante 38 23n 0 30w
33 Alicante □ 38 30n 0 37w
101 Alice 27 47n 98 1w
92 Alice Arm 55 29n 129 23w
82 Alice Downs 17 45s 127 56e
80 Alice Springs 23 40s 135 50e
75 Alicedale 33 15s 26 4e
60 Aligarh 27 55n 78 10e
56 Aligudarz 33 25n 49 45e
30 Alijó 41 16n 7 27w
45 Alingsås 57 56n 12 31e
61 Alipore 22 32n 88 24e
61 Alipur Duar 26 30n 89 35e
96 Aliquippa 40 38n 80 18w
75 Aliwal Nord 30 45s 26 45e
30 Aljezur 37 18n 8 49w
31 Aljustrel 37 55n 8 10w
16 Alkmaar 52 37n 4 45e
103 All American Canal 32 45n 115 0w
61 Allahabad 25 25n 81 58e
93 Allan 51 53n 106 4w
91 Allard Lake 50 40n 63 10w
30 Allariz 42 11n 7 50w
20 Allassac 45 15n 1 29e
86 Allegheny Mts. 38 0n 80 0w
96 Allegheny, R. 40 27n 80 0w
20 Allègre 45 12n 3 41e
104 Allende 28 20n 100 50w
97 Allentown 40 36n 75 30w
26 Allentsteig 48 31n 15 20e
62 Alleppey 9 30n 76 28e
24 Aller, R. 52 57n 9 11e
21 Allevard 45 24n 6 5e
100 Alliance, Nebr. 42 10n 102 50w
96 Alliance, Ohio 40 53n 81 7w
20 Allier, R. 46 58n 3 4e
20 Allier □ 46 25n 3 0e
80 Alligator Creek 19 23s 146 58e
90 Alliston 44 15n 79 55w
14 Alloa 56 7n 3 49w
21 Allos 44 15n 6 38e
62 Alluru Kottapatnam 15 30n 80 10e
90 Alma, Canada 48 35n 71 40w
91 Alma, U.S.A. 43 25n 84 40w
50 Alma Ata 43 15n 76 57e
31 Almada 38 40n 9 9w
80 Almaden 17 22s 144 40e
31 Almadén 38 49n 4 52w
31 Almagro 38 50n 3 45w
33 Almansa 38 51n 1 5w
30 Almanza 42 39n 5 3w
30 Almanzor, P. de 40 15n 5 18w
33 Almanzora, R. 37 14n 1 46w
40 Almaş, Mt. 44 49n 22 12e
32 Almazán 41 30n 2 30w
32 Almazora 39 57n 0 3w
111 Almeirim, Brazil 1 30s 52 0w
31 Almeirim, Port. 39 12n 8 37w
32 Almenara 39 46n 0 14w
16 Almelo 52 22n 6 42e
32 Almenar 41 43n 2 12w
33 Almenara, Sa. de 37 34n 1 32w
31 Almendralejo 38 41n 6 26w
33 Almería 36 52n 2 32w
33 Almería, G. de 36 40n 2 30w
33 Almería □ 37 20n 2 20w
45 Älmhult 56 32n 14 10e
105 Almirante 9 10n 82 30w
43 Almirós 39 11n 22 45e
31 Almodóvar 37 11n 8 2w
31 Almodóvar del Campo 38 43n 4 10w
31 Almogia 36 50n 4 32w
61 Almora 29 38n 79 4e
33 Almoradi 38 7n 0 46w
30 Almorox 40 14n 4 24w
31 Almuñécar 36 43n 3 41w
45 Almvik 57 49n 16 30e
12 Alnwick 55 25n 1 42w
59 Alon 22 12n 95 5e
93 Alonsa 50 50n 99 0w
65 Alor, I. 8 15s 124 30e
63 Alor Setar 6 7n 100 22e
31 Alora 36 49n 4 46w
31 Alosno 37 33n 7 7w
83 Aloysius, Mt. 26 0s 128 38e
30 Alpedrinha 40 6n 7 27w
98 Alpena 45 6n 83 24w
21 Alpes-Maritimes □ 43 55n 7 10e
21 Alpes-de-Haute-Provence □ 44 8n 6 10e
80 Alpha 24 8s 146 39e
36 Alpi Apuane, Mts. 44 7n 10 14e
36 Alpi Atesine, Mts. 46 55n 11 30e
25 Alpi Lepontine, Mts. 46 22n 8 27e
36 Alpi Orobie, Mts. 46 7n 10 0e
25 Alpi Pennine, Mts. 46 0n 7 30e
25 Alpi Retiche, Mts. 46 45n 10 0e
31 Alpiarça 39 15n 8 35w
101 Alpine 30 35n 103 35w
8 Alps, Mts. 47 0n 8 0e
80 Alroy Downs 19 20s 136 5e
45 Als, I. 54 59n 9 55e
19 Alsace, Reg. 48 15n 7 25e
32 Alsasua 42 54n 2 10w
24 Alsfeld 50 44n 9 19e
12 Alston 54 48n 2 26w
46 Alta 69 55n 23 12e
108 Alta Gracia 31 40s 64 30w
92 Alta Lake 50 10n 123 0w
46 Altaelv, R. 69 57n 23 17e
110 Altagracia 10 45n 71 30w
52 Altai, Mts. 48 0n 90 0e
67 Altai, Mts.= Aerhtai Shan, Mts. 48 0n 90 0e
111 Altamira 3 0s 52 10w
39 Altamura 40 50n 16 33e
68 Altanbulag 50 19n 106 30e
25 Altdorf 46 52n 8 36e
33 Altea 38 38n 0 2w
24 Altenberg 50 46n 13 47e
24 Altenburg 50 59n 12 28e
26 Altenmarkt 47 43n 14 39e
31 Alter do Chão 39 12n 7 40w
19 Altkirch 47 37n 7 15e
25 Altmühl, R. 48 55n 11 52e
29 Alto-Alentejo, Reg. 38 50n 7 40w
111 Alto Araguaia 17 15s 53 20w
109 Alto Paraná □ 25 0s 54 50w
13 Alton, U.K. 51 8n 0 59w
100 Alton, U.S.A. 38 55n 90 5w
24 Altona 53 32n 9 56e
96 Altoona 40 32n 78 24w
25 Altstätten 47 22n 9 33e
101 Altus 34 30n 99 25w
67 Altyn Tagh, Mts. 39 0n 89 0e
55 Alula 11 50n 50 45e
65 Alusi 7 35s 131 40e
32 Alustante 40 36n 1 40w
101 Alva 36 50n 98 50w
30 Alvaiázere 39 49n 8 23w
104 Alvarado 18 40n 95 50w
44 Alvdalen, R. 59 23n 13 30e
31 Alverca 38 56n 9 1w
45 Alvesta 56 54n 14 35e
84 Alvie 38 15s 143 30e
31 Alvito 38 15n 8 0w
45 Alvsborgs □ 58 30n 12 30e
46 Älvsbyn 65 39n 20 59e
60 Alwar 27 38n 76 34e
62 Alwaye 10 8n 76 24e
49 Alyat Pristan 39 59n 49 28e
14 Alyth 56 38n 3 15w
73 Am-Timan 11 0n 20 10e
89 Amadjuak 64 0n 72 50w
89 Amadjuak L. 65 0n 71 0w
31 Amadora 38 45n 9 13w
97 Amagansett 40 58n 72 8w
66 Amagasaki 34 42n 135 20e
45 Amager, I. 55 37n 12 37e
66 Amakusa-Shotō, Is. 32 15n 130 10e
44 Åmål 59 2n 12 40e
62 Amalapuram 16 35n 81 55e
43 Amaliás 37 47n 21 22e
60 Amalner 21 5n 75 5e
109 Amambaí 20 30s 56 0w
109 Amambay □ 23 0s 56 0w
50 Amangeldy 50 10n 65 10e
39 Amantea 39 8n 16 3e
111 Amapá 2 5n 50 50w
111 Amapá □ 1 40n 52 0w
111 Amarante, Brazil 6 14s 42 50w
30 Amarante, Port. 41 16n 8 5w
60 Amaravati= Amraoti 20 55n 77 45e
62 Amaravati, R. 10 58n 78 12e
31 Amaraleja 38 12n 7 13w
111 Amargosa 13 2s 39 36w
101 Amarillo 35 14n 101 46w
37 Amaro, Mt. 42 5n 14 6e
56 Amasya 40 40n 35 50e
104 Amatitlán 14 29n 90 38w
111 Amazon= Amazonas, R. 2 0s 53 30w
111 Amazonas, R. 2 0s 53 30w
110 Amazonas □ 4 20s 64 0w
60 Ambala 30 23n 76 56e
62 Ambalangoda 6 15n 80 5e
62 Ambalapuzha 9 25n 76 25e
75 Ambanja 13 40s 48 27e
51 Ambarchik 69 40n 162 20e
108 Ambargasta, Salinas, Reg. 29 0s 64 30w
62 Ambarnath 19 12n 73 22e
62 Ambasamudram 8 43n 77 25e
110 Ambato 1 5s 78 42w
75 Ambatolampy 19 20s 47 35e
25 Amberg 49 25n 11 52e
104 Ambergris Cay 18 0n 88 0w
21 Ambérieu 45 57n 5 20e
85 Amberley 43 9s 172 44e
20 Ambert 45 33n 3 44e
12 Ambleside 54 26n 2 58w
65 Ambon 3 35s 128 20e
75 Ambositra 20 31s 47 25e
103 Amboy 34 33n 115 51w
75 Ambre, C. d' 12 40s 49 10e
96 Ambridge 40 36n 80 15w
62 Ambur 12 47n 78 43e
81 Amby 26 30s 148 11e
50 Amderma 69 45n 61 30e
104 Ameca 20 30n 104 0w
16 Ameland, I. 53 27n 5 45e
37 Amélia 42 34n 12 25e
20 Amèlie-les-Bains-Palalda 42 29n 2 41e
51 Amen 68 45n 180 0e
102 American Falls 42 46n 112 56e
5 American Highland 73 0s 75 0e
85 American Samoa, I. 14 20s 170 0w
109 Americana 22 45s 47 20w
99 Americus 32 0n 84 10w
16 Amersfoort 52 9n 5 23e
83 Amery, Australia 31 9s 117 5e
93 Amery, Canada 56 45n 94 0w
100 Ames 42 0n 93 40w
97 Amesbury 42 50n 70 52w
43 Amfiklia 38 38n 22 35e
42 Amfípolis 40 48n 23 52e
43 Amfissa 38 32n 22 22e
43 Amflokhía 38 52n 21 9e
51 Amga, R. 62 38n 134 32e
51 Amgu 45 45n 137 15e
59 Amherst, Burma 16 0n 97 40e
91 Amherst, Canada 45 48n 64 8w
97 Amherst, Mass. 42 21n 72 30w
96 Amherst, Ohio 41 23n 82 15w
90 Amherstburg 42 6n 83 6w
37 Amiata, Mte. 42 54n 11 40e
19 Amiens 49 54n 2 16e
42 Amindaion 40 42n 21 42e

Amirantes, Is. — Argonne, Mts.

53 Amirantes, Is. 6 0S 53 0E
12 Amlwch 53 24N 4 21W
54 'Ammân 32 0N 35 52E
25 Ammersee, L. 48 0N 11 7E
54 Ammi'ad 32 55N 35 32E
19 Amnéville 49 16N 6 9E
30 Amorebieta 43 13N 2 44W
43 Amorgós, I. 36 50N 25 59E
90 Amos 48 35N 78 5W
69 Amoy=Hsiamen 24 25N 118 4E
32 Amposta 40 43N 0 34E
91 Amqui 48 28N 67 27W
60 Amroati 20 55N 77 45E
60 Amreli 21 35N 71 17E
60 Amritsar 31 35N 74 57E
60 Amroha 28 53N 78 30E
24 Amrum, I. 54 37N 8 21E
16 Amsterdam, Neth. 52 23N 4 54E
97 Amsterdam, U.S.A. 42 58N 74 10W
3 Amsterdam, I. 37 30S 77 30E
26 Amstetten 48 7N 14 51E
50 Amu Darya, R. 43 40N 59 1E
88 Amukta Pass. 52 25N 172 0W
88 Amundsen G. 70 30N 123 0W
5 Amundsen Sea 72 0S 115 0W
51 Amur, R. 52 56N 141 10E
30 Amurrio 43 3N 3 0W
30 Amusco 42 10N 4 28W
43 Amvrakíkós Kól. 39 0N 20 55E
56 An Najaf 32 3N 44 15E
56 An Nasiriyah 31 0N 46 15E
63 An Nhon 13 53N 109 6E
56 An Nu'ayriyah 27 30N 48 30E
15 An Uaimh 53 39N 6 40W
54 Anabta 32 19N 35 7E
102 Anaconda 46 7N 113 0W
102 Anacortes 48 30N 122 40W
101 Anadarko 35 4N 98 15W
30 Anadia 40 26N 8 27W
56 Anadolu, Reg. 38 0W 39 0E
51 Anadyr 64 35N 177 20E
51 Anadyr, R. 64 55N 176 5E
38 Anagni 41 44N 13 8E
92 Anahim Lake 52 28N 125 18W
62 Anai Mudi, Mt. 10 12N 77 20E
62 Anaimalai Hills 10 20N 76 40E
62 Anakapalle 17 42N 83 6E
80 Anakie 23 32S 147 45E
64 Anambas, Kep. 3 20N 106 30E
66 Anan 33 54N 134 40E
60 Anand 22 32N 72 59E
62 Anantapur 14 39N 77 42E
58 Anantnag 33 45N 75 10E
111 Anápolis 16 15S 48 50W
57 Anar 30 55N 55 13E
56 Anatolia, Reg.= Anadolu, Reg. 38 0N 39 0E
108 Añatuya 28 20S 62 50W
18 Ancenis 47 21N 1 10W
88 Anchorage 61 10N 149 50W
30 Ancião 39 56N 8 27W
110 Ancohuma, Mt. 16 0S 68 50W
37 Ancona 43 37N 13 30E
112 Ancud 42 0S 73 50W
112 Ancud, G. de 42 0S 73 0W
108 Andacollo 13 14S 71 6W
44 Andalsnes 62 35N 7 43E
31 Andalucía, Reg. 37 35N 5 0W
99 Andalusia 31 51N 86 30W
63 Andaman Is. 12 30N 92 30E
63 Andaman Sea 13 0N 96 0E
16 Andenne 50 30N 5 5E
25 Andermatt 46 38N 8 35E
24 Andernach 50 24N 7 25E
20 Andernos 44 44N 1 6W
102 Anderson, Calif. 40 30N 122 19W
98 Anderson, Ind. 40 5N 85 40W
99 Anderson, S.C. 34 32N 82 40W
88 Anderson, R. 69 43N 128 58W
106 Andes, Mts. 20 0S 68 0W
62 Andhra Pradesh □ 15 0N 80 0E
43 Andikíthira, I. 35 52N 23 15E
43 Andíparos, I. 37 0N 25 3E
50 Andizhan 41 10N 72 0E
57 Andkhui 36 52N 65 8E
32 Andorra ■ 42 30N 1 30E
13 Andover 51 13N 1 29W
32 Andraitx 39 35N 2 25E
88 Andreanof Is. 51 0N 178 0W
28 Andrespol 51 45N 19 34E
39 Ándria 41 13N 16 17E
40 Andrijevica 42 45N 19 48E
105 Andros, I. 24 30N 78 04
43 Ándros I. 37 50N 24 50E
105 Andros Town 24 43N 77 47W
27 Andrychów 49 51N 19 18E
31 Andújar 38 3N 4 5W
72 Anécho 6 12N 1 34E
105 Anegada I. 18 45N 64 20W
105 Anegada Pass. 18 15N 63 45W
32 Aneto, Pico de 42 37N 0 40E
68 Anganki 47 9N 123 48E
51 Angara, R. 58 6N 93 0E
51 Angarsk 52 30N 104 0E
81 Angaston 34 30S 139 8E
44 Ånge 62 31N 15 35E
104 Angel de la Guarda, I. 29 30N 113 30W
65 Angeles 15 9N 120 35E
45 Ängelholm 56 15N 12 58E
103 Angels Camp 38 8N 120 30W
46 Ångermanälven, R. 62 48N 17 56E
21 Angermünde 53 1N 14 0E
18 Angers 47 30N 0 35E
19 Angerville 48 19N 2 0E
32 Anglés 41 57N 2 38E
12 Anglesey, I. 53 17N 4 20W
20 Anglet 43 29N 1 21W
19 Anglure 48 35N 3 50E
4 Angmagssalik 65 40N 37 20W
74 Ango 4 10N 26 5E
75 Angoche 16 8S 40 0E
108 Angol 37 48S 72 43W
75 Angola ■ 12 0S 18 0E
96 Angola 42 38N 79 2W
20 Angoulême 45 39N 0 10E
20 Angoumois, Reg. 45 30N 0 25E
109 Angra dos Reis 23 0S 44 10W
50 Angren 41 1N 69 45E
105 Anguilla, I. 18 14N 63 5W
80 Angurugu 14 0S 136 25E
14 Angus, Braes of 56 51N 3 0W
45 Anholt, I. 56 42N 11 33E
69 Anhsien 31 30N 104 35E
69 Anhwei □ 33 15N 116 50E
40 Anina 45 5N 21 51E
60 Anjangaon 21 10N 77 20E
60 Anjar 23 6⅛ 70 10E
18 Anjou, Reg. 47 20N 0 15W
68 Anju 39 36N 125 40E
69 Ankang 32 38N 109 5E
56 Ankara 40 0N 32 54E
69 Anking 30 31N 117 2E
24 Anklam 53 51N 13 41E
60 Anklesvar 21 38N 73 3E
98 Ann Arbor 42 17N 83 45W
82 Anna Plains 19 17S 121 37E
72 Annaba 36 50N 7 46E
24 Annaberg-Buchholz 50 34N 12 58E
63 Annam, Reg.= Trung-Phan, Reg. 16 30N 107 30E
63 Annamitique, Chaîne, Mts. 17 0N 106 0E
14 Annan 54 59N 3 16W
14 Annan, R. 54 59N 3 16W
98 Annapolis 38 59N 76 30W
91 Annapolis Royal 44 44N 65 32W
61 Annapurna, Mt. 28 34N 84 50E
21 Annecy 45 55N 6 8E
21 Annecy, L. d' 45 52N 6 10E
21 Annemasse 46 12N 6 16E
67 Anning 24 58N 102 30E
99 Anniston 33 45N 85 50W
21 Annonay 45 15N 4 40E
21 Annot 43 58N 6 38E
43 Ano Viánnos 35 2N 25 21E
100 Anoka 45 10N 93 26W
69 Anping 23 0N 120 6E
25 Ansbach 49 17N 10 34E
68 Anshan 41 3N 122 58E
69 Anshun 26 2N 105 57E
67 Ansi 40 21N 96 10E
32 Ansó 42 51N 0 48W
82 Anson, B. 13 20S 130 6E
97 Ansonia 41 21N 73 6W
90 Ansonville 48 46N 80 43W
14 Anstruther 56 14N 2 40W
65 Ansuda 2 11S 139 22E
68 Anta 46 18N 125 34E
56 Antakya 36 14N 36 10E
75 Antalaha 14 57S 50 20E
56 Antalya 36 52N 30 45E
56 Antalya Körfezi 36 15N 31 30E
75 Antananarivo 18 55S 47 35E
5 Antarctica 90 0S 0 0
5 Antarctic Pen. 67 0S 60 0W
30 Antela, L. de 42 7N 7 40W
108 Antequera, Paraguay 24 8S 57 7W
31 Antequera, Sp. 37 5N 4 33W
103 Anthony 32 1N 106 37W
80 Anthony Lagoon 18 0S 135 30E
21 Antibes 43 34N 7 6E
21 Antibes, C. d' 43 31N 7 7E
91 Anticosti I. 49 20N 62 40W
18 Antifer, C. d' 49 41N 0 10E
100 Antigo 45 8N 89 5W
91 Antigonish 45 38N 61 58W
104 Antigua 14 34N 90 41W
105 Antigua, I. 17 0N 61 50W
105 Antilla 20 40N 75 50W
103 Antimony 38 7N 112 0W
20 Antioche, Pertuis d' 46 5N 1 30W
110 Antioquia 6 40N 75 55W
76 Antipodes Is. 49 45S 178 40E
108 Antofagasta 23 50S 70 30W
108 Antofagasta □ 23 30S 69 0W
108 Antofalla, Mt. 25 33S 67 56W
75 Antongil, B. d' 15 30S 49 50E
109 Antonina 25 26S 48 42W
75 António Enes= Angoche 16 8S 40 0E
18 Antrain 48 28N 1 30W
15 Antrim 54 43N 6 13W
15 Antrim □ 54 55N 6 10W
75 Antsirabe 19 55S 47 2E
68 Antung 40 10N 124 18E
16 Antwerp= Antwerpen 51 13N 4 25E
16 Antwerpen 51 13N 4 25E
16 Antwerpen □ 51 15N 4 40E
62 Anuradhapura 8 22N 80 28E
16 Anvers= Antwerpen 51 13N 4 25E
88 Anvik 62 40N 160 12W
68 Anyang 36 7N 114 26E
65 Anyer-Lor 6 6S 105 56E
69 Anyi 28 50N 115 31E
50 Anzhero Sudzhensk 56 10N 83 40E
38 Ánzio 41 28N 12 37E
32 Aoiz 42 46N 1 22W
66 Aomori 40 45N 140 45E
66 Aomori □ 40 45N 140 40E
60 Aonla 28 16N 79 11E
36 Aosta 45 43N 7 20E
73 Aozou 21 49N 17 25E
65 Aparri 18 22N 121 38E
40 Apatin 45 40N 19 0E
104 Apatzingán 19 0N 102 20W
16 Apeldoorn 52 13N 5 57E
24 Apen 53 12N 7 47E
64 Apenam 8 35S 116 13E
9 Apennines, Mts.= Appennini, Mts. 41 0N 15 0E
104 Apizaco 19 26N 98 9W
24 Apolda 51 1N 11 30E
73 Apollonia= Marsa Susa 32 52N 21 59E
100 Apostle Is. 47 0N 90 30W
109 Apóstoles 27 55S 55 45W
110 Apoteri 4 2N 58 32W
86 Appalachian Mts. 38 0N 80 0W
37 Appennini, Mts. 41 0N 15 0E
36 Appenino Ligure, Mts. 44 30N 9 0E
25 Appenzell □ 47 23N 9 23E
37 Appiano 46 27N 11 27E
12 Appleby 54 35N 2 29W
98 Appleton 44 17N 88 25W
111 Approuagne 4 20N 52 0W
39 Apricena 41 47N 15 25E
21 Apt 43 53N 5 24E
109 Apucarana 23 55S 51 33W
40 Apuseni, Mts. 46 30N 22 45E
57 Aq Chah 37 0N 66 5E
56 'Aqaba 29 31N 35 0E
56 'Aqaba, Khalîj al 28 15N 33 20E
73 Aqiq 18 14N 38 12E
54 Aqraba 32 9N 35 20E
111 Aquidauana 20 30S 55 50W
55 Ar Rab' al Khālī 21 0N 51 0E
54 Ar Ramthā 32 34N 36 0E
56 Ar Raqqah 35 56N 39 1E
56 Ar Riyād 24 41N 46 42E
57 Ar Ruska 23 35N 53 30E
56 Ar Rutbah 33 0N 40 15E
73 Arab, Bahr el, R. 9 2N 29 28E
52 Arabia, Reg. 25 0N 45 0E
70 Arabian Des. 28 0N 32 30E
111 Aracajú 10 55S 37 4W
110 Aracataca 10 38N 74 9W
111 Aracati 4 30S 37 44W
109 Araçatuba 21 10S 50 30W
31 Aracena 37 53N 6 58W
31 Aracena, Sa. de 37 48N 6 40W
111 Araçuai 16 52S 42 4W
54 'Arad 31 17N 35 12E
27 Arad 46 10N 21 20E
27 Arad □ 46 20N 21 45E
32 Aragón, R. 42 13N 1 44W
32 Aragon, Reg. 41 0N 1 0W
38 Aragona 37 24N 13 36E
111 Araguacema 8 50S 49 20W
111 Araguaia, R. 5 21S 48 41W
111 Araguari 18 38S 48 11W
56 Arãk 34 0N 49 40E
59 Arakan Coast 19 0N 94 0E
59 Arakan Yoma, Mts. 20 0N 94 30E
49 Araks, R. 40 1N 48 28E
50 Aral Sea= Aralskoye More 44 30N 66 0E
50 Aralsk 46 50N 61 20E
50 Aralskoye More 44 30N 60 0E
61 Arambagh 22 53N 87 48E
15 Aran, I. 55 0N 8 30W
15 Aran Is. 53 5N 9 42W
32 Arán, Valle de 42 45N 1 0E
30 Aranda de Duero 41 39N 3 42W
30 Aranjuez 40 1N 3 40W
101 Aransas P. 28 0N 97 9W
109 Arapongas 23 29S 51 28W
109 Araranguá 29 0S 49 30W
109 Araraquara 21 50S 48 0W
109 Araras 22 22S 47 23W
84 Ararat 37 16S 143 0E
109 Araruama, L. de 23 0S 42 20W
110 Arauca 7 0N 70 40W
108 Arauco □ 37 50S 73 15W
111 Araxá 19 35S 46 55W
110 Araya, Pen. de 10 40N 64 0W
38 Arbatax 39 57N 9 42E
56 Arbīl 36 15N 44 5E
44 Arboga 59 24N 15 52E
21 Arbois 46 55N 5 46E
14 Arbroath 56 34N 2 35W
38 Arborea 39 46N 8 34E
19 Arc 47 28N 5 34E
20 Arcachon 44 40N 1 10W
20 Arcachon, Bassin d' 44 42N 1 10W
100 Arcadia 44 13N 91 29W
102 Arcata 40 55N 124 4W
37 Arcévia 43 29N 12 58E
48 Archangel= Arkhangelsk 64 40N 41 0E
97 Archbald 41 30N 75 31W
33 Archena 38 9N 1 16W
38 Arci, Mte. 39 47N 8 44E
19 Arcis-sur-Aube 48 32N 4 10E
36 Arco 45 55N 10 54E
93 Arcola 49 40N 102 30W
32 Arcos 41 12N 2 16W
31 Arcos de los Frontera 36 45N 5 49W
62 Arcot 12 53N 79 20E
111 Arcoverde 8 25S 37 4W
89 Arctic Bay 73 2N 85 11W
4 Arctic Ocean 78 0N 160 0W
88 Arctic Red River 67 15N 134 0W
56 Ardabrīl 38 15N 48 18E
31 Ardales 36 53N 4 51W
44 Årdalstangen 61 15N 7 45E
21 Ardeche, R. 44 16N 4 39E
21 Ardèche □ 44 42N 4 16E
15 Ardee 53 51N 6 32W
16 Ardennes, Reg. 49 30N 5 10E
19 Ardennes □ 49 35N 4 40E
19 Ardentes 46 45N 1 50E
57 Ardestan 33 20N 52 25E
14 Ardgour, Reg. 56 45N 5 25W
41 Ardino 41 34N 25 9E
84 Ardlethan 34 22S 146 53E
101 Ardmore, Australia 21 39S 139 11E
101 Ardmore, U.S.A. 34 10N 97 5W
15 Ardnacrusha 52 43N 8 38W
14 Ardnamurchan Pt. 56 44N 6 14W
19 Ardres 50 50N 2 0E
14 Ardrossan 55 39N 4 50W
15 Ards □ 54 35N 5 30W
15 Ards Pen. 54 30N 5 25W
105 Arecibo 18 29N 66 42W
111 Areia Branca 5 0S 37 0W
30 Arenas 40 17N 5 6W
45 Arendal 58 28N 8 46E
32 Arenys de Mar 41 35N 2 33E
36 Arenzano 44 24N 8 40E
110 Arequipa 16 20S 71 30W
74 Arero 4 41N 38 50E
20 Arès 44 47N 1 8E
30 Arévalo 41 3N 4 43W
37 Arezzo 43 28N 11 50E
32 Arga, R. 42 18N 1 47W
31 Argamasilla de Alba 39 8N 3 5W
30 Arganda 40 19N 3 26W
20 Argelès-Gazost 43 0N 0 6W
20 Argelès-sur-Mer 42 34N 3 1E
19 Argent 47 33N 2 25E
37 Argenta 44 37N 11 50E
18 Argentan 48 45N 0 1W
37 Argentário, Mte. 42 23N 11 11E
21 Argentera, Mt. de l' 44 10N 7 18E
36 Argentera, P. 44 11N 7 17E
19 Argenteuil 48 57N 2 14E
91 Argentia 47 18N 53 58W
38 Argentiera, C. dell' 40 44N 8 8E
106 Argentine Basin, Reg. 44 0S 51 0E
112 Argentina ■ 35 0S 66 0W
112 Argentino, L. 50 10S 73 0W
20 Argenton Château 46 59N 0 27W
20 Argenton-sur-Creuse 46 36N 1 30E
18 Argentré 48 5N 0 40W
41 Arges, R. 44 10N 26 45E
73 Argo 19 28N 30 30E
43 Argolikós Kól. 37 20N 22 52E
43 Argolis □ 37 38N 22 50E
19 Argonne, Mts. 49 0N 5 20E

Argos Ayre, Pt. of

43 Árgos 37 40N 22 43 E
43 Argostólion 38 12N 20 33 E
103 Arguello, Pt. 34 34N 120 40W
51 Argun, R. 43 22N 45 55 E
82 Argyle, L. 16 20S 128 40 E
45 Århus 56 8N 10 11 E
39 Ariano Irpino 41 10N 15 4 E
110 Arica, Chile 18 32S 70 20W
110 Arica, Col. 1 30S 75 30W
83 Arid, C. 34 1S 123 10 E
66 Arida 33 29N 135 44 E
20 Ariège, R. 43 31N 1 32 E
20 Ariège □ 42 56N 1 30 E
105 Arima 10 38N 61 17W
14 Arisaig 56 50N 5 40W
62 Ariyalur 11 8N 79 8 E
32 Ariza 41 19N 2 3W
103 Arizona □ 34 20N 111 30W
110 Arjona 10 14N 75 22W
51 Arka 60 15N 142 0 E
67 Arka Tagh, Mts. 36 30N 90 0 E
101 Arkadelphia 34 5N 93 0W
43 Arkadhía □ 38 48N 21 3 E
14 Arkaig, L. 56 58N 5 10W
101 Arkansas, R. 33 48N 91 4W
101 Arkansas □ 35 0N 92 30W
101 Arkansas City 37 4N 97 3W
48 Arkhangelsk 64 40N 41 0 E
15 Arklow 52 48N 6 10W
24 Arkona, C. 54 41N 13 26 E
62 Arkonam 13 7N 79 43 E
20 Arlanc 45 25N 3 42 E
30 Arlanza, R. 42 6N 4 9W
30 Arlanzón, R. 42 3N 4 17W
26 Arlberg P. 49 9N 10 12 E
21 Arles 43 41N 4 40 E
101 Arlington 44 25N 97 4W
16 Arlon 49 42N 5 49 E
45 Arlöy 55 38N 13 5 E
83 Armadale 32 12S 116 0 E
15 Armagh 54 22N 6 40W
15 Armagh □ 54 16N 6 35W
20 Armagnac, Reg. 43 44N 0 10 E
19 Armançon, R. 47 57N 3 30 E
49 Armavir 45 2N 41 7 E
110 Armenia 4 35N 75 45W
49 Armenian S.S.R. □ 40 0N 41 10 E
40 Armeniş 45 13N 22 17 E
19 Armentières 50 40N 2 50 E
81 Armidale 30 30S 151 40 E
92 Armstrong, B.C. 50 25N 119 10W
90 Armstrong, Ont. 50 20N 89 0W
62 Armur 18 48N 78 16 E
19 Arnay-le-Duc 47 10N 4 27 E
32 Arnedo 42 12N 2 5W
16 Arnhem 51 58N 5 55 E
80 Arnhem, B. 12 20S 136 10 E
62 Arni 12 43N 79 19 E
36 Arno, R. 43 31N 10 17 E
96 Arnold 40 36N 79 44W
26 Arnoldstein 46 33N 13 43 E
90 Arnprior 45 23N 76 25W
24 Arnsberg 51 25N 8 10 E
24 Arnstadt 50 50N 10 56 E
31 Aroche 37 56N 6 57 E
30 Arosa, Ria de 42 28N 8 57W
41 Arpaşu de Jos 45 45N 24 38 E
38 Arpino 41 40N 13 35 E
81 Arrabury 26 45S 141 0 E
61 Arrah 25 35N 84 32 E
31 Arraiolos 38 44N 7 59W
14 Arran, I. 55 34N 5 12W
19 Arras 50 17N 2 46 E
20 Arreau 42 54N 0 22 E
20 Arrats, R. 44 6N 0 52 E
72 Arrecife 28 59N 13 40W
108 Arrecifes 34 5S 60 5N
18 Arrée, Mts. d' 48 26N 3 55W
83 Arrino 29 30S 115 40 E
18 Arromanches 49 20N 0 38W
31 Arronches 39 8N 7 16W
20 Arros, R. 43 30N 0 2W
18 Arrou 48 6N 1 8 E
92 Arrowhead 50 40N 117 55W
85 Arrowtown 44 57S 168 50 E
31 Arroyo de la Luz 39 30N 6 38W
20 Ars 46 13N 1 30W
41 Arsache 43 47N 25 45 E
68 Arshan 46 59N 120 0 E
37 Arsiero 45 49N 11 22 E
62 Arsikere 13 15N 76 15 E
19 Ars-sur-Moselle 49 5N 6 4 E
32 Artá 39 40N 3 20 E
43 Árta 39 8N 21 2 E
89 Artemovsk 48 35N 37 55 E
19 Artenay 48 5N 1 50 E
32 Artesa de Segre 41 54N 1 3 E
101 Artesia 32 55N 104 25W
80 Arthur, Pt. 22 7S 150 3 E
108 Artigas 30 20S 56 30W
19 Artois, Reg. 50 20N 2 30 E
56 Artvin 41 14N 41 44 E
65 Aru, Kep. 6 0S 134 30 E
74 Arua 3 1N 30 58 E
111 Aruanã 15 0S 51 10W
105 Aruba, I. 12 30N 70 0W
59 Arunachal Pradesh □ 28 0N 95 0 E
62 Aruppukottai 9 31N 78 8 E
74 Arusha 3 20S 36 40 E
102 Arvada 44 43N 106 6W
68 Arvayheer 46 15N 102 48 E
21 Arve, R. 46 12N 6 8 E
60 Arvi 20 59N 78 16 E
91 Arvida 48 16N 71 14W
46 Arvidsjaur 65 35N 19 10 E
44 Arvika 59 40N 12 36 E
50 Arys 42 26N 68 48 E
48 Arzamas 55 27N 43 55 E
72 Arzew 35 50N 0 23W
37 Arzignano 45 30N 11 20 E
26 Aš 50 13N 12 12 E
54 As Salt 32 2N 35 43 E
56 As Samāwah 31 15N 45 15 E
56 As Sulaimānīyah 24 8N 47 10 E
56 As Sulamāniyah 35 35N 45 29 E
57 As Suwaih 22 10N 59 33 E
56 As Suwayda 32 40N 36 30 E
56 As Suwayrah 32 55N 45 0 E
66 Asahikawa 43 45N 142 30 E
61 Asansol 23 40N 87 1 E
91 Asbestos 45 47N 71 58W
97 Asbury Park 40 15N 74 1W
104 Ascensión, B. de la 19 50N 87 20W
71 Ascension, I. 8 0S 14 15W
26 Aschach 48 23N 14 0 E
25 Aschaffenburg 49 58N 9 8 E
24 Aschersleben 51 45N 11 28 E
37 Ascoli Piceno 42 51N 13 34 E
39 Áscoli Satriano 41 11N 15 32 E
55 Aseb 13 0N 42 40 E
45 Aseda 57 10N 15 20 E
41 Asenovgrad 42 1N 24 51 E
103 Ash Fork 35 14N 112 32W
56 Ash Shāmiyah 31 55N 44 35 E
56 Ash Sharma 28 1N 35 18 E
54 Ash Shuna 32 32N 35 34 E
48 Asha 35 10N 33 38 E
85 Ashburton 43 53S 171 48 E
82 Ashburton, R. 37 52S 145 5 E
82 Ashburton Downs 23 25S 117 4 E
12 Ashby-de-la-Zouch 52 45N 1 29W
54 Ashdod 31 39N 34 35 E
54 Ashdot Yaaqov 32 39N 35 35 E
99 Asheboro 35 43N 79 46W
99 Asheville 35 39N 82 30W
13 Ashford 51 8N 0 53 E
66 Ashikaga 36 28N 139 29 E
12 Ashington 55 12N 1 35W
50 Ashkhabad 38 0N 57 50 E
98 Ashland, Ky. 38 25N 82 40W
96 Ashland, Ohio 40 52N 82 20W
102 Ashland, Oreg. 42 10N 122 38W
97 Ashland, Pa. 40 45N 76 22W
100 Ashland, Wis. 46 40N 90 52W
97 Ashley 41 12N 75 55W
54 Ashquelon 31 42N 34 55 E
96 Ashtabula 41 52N 80 50W
102 Ashton 44 6N 111 30W
12 Ashton-under-Lyne 53 30N 2 8W
1 Asia 45 0N 75 0 E
72 Asilah 35 29N 6 0W
38 Asinara, G. dell' 41 0N 8 30 E
38 Asinara, I. 41 5N 8 15 E
50 Asino 57 0N 86 0 E
55 Asir, Ras 11 55N 51 0 E
55 Asir, Reg. 18 40N 42 30 E
54 Asira esh Shamaliya 32 16N 35 16 E
44 Askim 59 35N 11 10 E
57 Asmar 35 10N 71 27 E
73 Asmera 15 19N 38 55 E
45 Asnen, L. 56 35N 15 45 E
36 Ásola 45 12N 10 25 E
33 Aspe 38 20N 0 40W
85 Aspiring, Mt. 44 23S 168 46W
21 Aspres 44 32N 5 44 E
59 Assam □ 25 45N 92 30 E
16 Asse 50 54N 4 6 E
16 Assen 53 0N 6 35 E
93 Assiniboia 49 40N 106 0W
92 Assiniboine, Mt. 50 52N 115 39W
93 Assiniboine, R. 49 53N 97 8W
109 Assis 22 40S 50 20W
37 Assisi 43 4N 12 36 E
14 Assynt, L. 58 25N 5 10W
49 Astara 38 30N 48 50 E
36 Asti 44 54N 8 11 E
43 Astipálaia, I. 36 32N 26 22 E
30 Astorga 42 29N 6 8W
102 Astoria 46 16N 123 50W
45 Astorp 56 6N 12 55 E
49 Astrakhan 46 25N 48 5 E
30 Asturias, Reg. 43 15N 6 0W
108 Asunción 25 21S 57 30W
73 Aswân 24 4N 32 57 E
73 Aswân High Dam 24 5N 32 54 E
73 Asyût 27 11N 31 4 E
56 At Ta'if 21 5N 40 27 E
106 Atacama Des. 24 0S 69 20W
108 Atacama, Salar de 24 0S 68 20W
108 Atacama □ 27 30S 70 0W
72 Atakpamé 7 31N 1 13 E
43 Atalándi 38 39N 22 58 E
66 Atami 35 0N 139 55 E
72 Atar 20 30N 13 5W
51 Atara 63 10N 129 10 E
31 Atarfe 37 13N 3 40W
50 Atasu 48 30N 71 0 E
73 Atbara 17 42N 33 59 E
73 'Atbara, Nahr, R. 17 40N 33 56 E
50 Atbasar 51 48N 68 20 E
100 Atchison 39 40N 95 0W
32 Ateca 41 20N 1 49W
37 Atessa 42 5N 14 27 E
16 Ath 50 38N 3 47 E
92 Athabasca 54 45N 113 20W
93 Athabasca, L. 59 10N 109 30W
93 Athabasca, R. 58 40N 110 50W
15 Athboy 53 37N 6 55W
15 Athenry 53 18N 8 45W
99 Athens, Ala. 34 49N 86 58W
99 Athens, Ga. 33 56N 83 24W
98 Athens, Ohio 39 52N 82 64W
101 Athens, Tex. 32 11N 95 48W
43 Athens=Athínai 37 58N 23 46 E
80 Atherton 17 17S 145 30 E
43 Athínai 37 58N 23 46 E
15 Athlone 53 26N 7 57W
62 Athni 16 44N 75 6 E
14 Atholl, Forest of 56 51N 3 50W
91 Atholville 48 5N 67 5W
42 Athos, Mt. 40 9N 24 22 E
15 Athy 53 0N 7 0W
51 Atka 60 50N 151 48 E
88 Atka I. 52 15N 174 30W
99 Atlanta 33 50N 84 24W
100 Atlantic 41 25N 95 0W
98 Atlantic City 39 25N 74 25W
1 Atlantic Ocean 0 0 30 0W
72 Atlas, Anti, Mts. 30 0N 8 0W
72 Atlas, Moyen, Mts. 37 0N 5 0W
72 Atlas Saharien, Mts. 34 10N 3 30 E
92 Atlin 59 31N 133 41W
54 Atlit 32 42N 34 56 E
62 Atmakur 14 37N 79 40 E
99 Atmore 31 2N 87 30W
104 Atotonilco 20 20N 98 40W
31 Atouguia 39 20N 9 20W
37 Atri 42 35N 14 0 E
90 Attawapiskat 53 0N 82 30W
90 Attawapiskat L. 52 20N 88 0W
90 Attawapiskat, R. 52 57N 82 18W
26 Attersee 47 55N 13 31 E
26 Attersee, L. 47 52N 13 33 E
19 Attigny 49 28N 4 35 E
43 Attikí □ 38 10N 23 40 E
54 Attil 32 23N 35 4 E
97 Attleboro 41 56N 71 18W
58 Attock 33 52N 72 20 E
88 Attu I. 52 55N 173 0 E
62 Attur 11 35N 78 30 E
45 Atvidaberg 58 12N 16 0 E
100 Atwood 39 52N 101 3W
21 Aubagne 43 17N 5 37 E
19 Aube, R. 48 34N 3 43 E
19 Aube □ 48 15N 4 0 E
21 Aubenas 44 37N 4 24 E
19 Aubigny-sur-Nère 47 30N 2 24 E
20 Aubrac, Mts. d' 44 38N 2 58 E
99 Auburn, Ala. 32 57N 85 30W
102 Auburn, Calif. 38 50N 121 10W
99 Auburn, Me. 44 6N 70 14W
97 Auburn, N.Y. 42 57N 76 39W
20 Aubusson 45 57N 2 11 E
20 Auch 43 39N 0 36 E
19 Auchel 50 30N 2 39 E
85 Auckland 36 52S 174 46 E
76 Auckland Is. 51 0S 166 0 E
20 Aude □ 44 13N 3 15 E
90 Auden 50 17N 87 54W
18 Auderville 49 43N 1 57W
18 Audierne 48 1N 4 34W
19 Audincourt 47 30N 6 50 E
24 Aue 50 34N 12 43 E
24 Auerbach 50 30N 12 25 E
18 Auffay 49 43N 1 7 E
82 Augathella 25 48S 146 35 E
25 Augsburg 48 22N 10 54 E
83 Augusta, Australia 34 22S 115 10 E
39 Augusta, Italy 37 14N 15 12 E
99 Augusta, U.S.A. 33 29N 81 59W
99 Augusta 44 20N 69 46W
75 Augusto Cardoso 12 44S 34 50 E
28 Augustów 53 51N 23 0 E
83 Augustus, Mt. 24 20S 116 50 E
80 Augustus Downs 18 35S 139 55 E
18 Aulne, R. 48 17N 4 16W
19 Aulnoye 46 2N 0 22W
20 Aunis, Reg. 46 0N 0 50W
61 Aurangabad, Bihar 24 25N 84 18 E
60 Aurangabad, Maharashtra 19 50N 75 23 E
18 Auray 47 40N 3 0W
24 Aurich 53 28N 7 30 E
20 Aurillac 44 55N 2 26 E
100 Aurora, Colo. 39 44N 104 55W
98 Aurora, Ill. 41 42N 88 20W
96 Aurora, Ohio 41 21N 81 20W
47 Aust-Agde □ 58 55N 7 40 E
100 Austin, Minn. 43 37N 92 59W
102 Austin, Nev. 39 30N 117 1W
101 Austin, Tex. 30 20N 97 45W
78 Australia ■ 23 0S 135 0 E
84 Australian Alps, Mts. 36 30S 148 8 E
84 Australian Capital Terr. □ 35 15S 149 8 E
5 Australian Dependency □ 73 0S 90 0 E
26 Austria ■ 47 0N 14 0 E
19 Authie, R. 50 21N 1 38 E
104 Autlán 19 40N 104 30W
21 Autun 46 58N 4 17 E
82 Auvergne 15 39S 130 1 E
20 Auvergne, Mts. 45 20N 2 45 E
20 Auvergne, Reg. 45 30N 3 20 E
20 Auvézère, R. 45 12N 0 51 E
19 Auxerre 47 48N 3 32 E
21 Auxonne 47 10N 5 20 E
20 Auzances 46 2N 2 30 E
20 Auzat 45 27N 3 19 E
19 Avallon 47 30N 3 53 E
91 Avalon Pen. 47 0N 53 20W
62 Avanigadda 16 0N 80 56 E
109 Avaré 23 5S 48 55W
42 Ávas 40 57N 25 56 E
111 Aveiro, Brazil 3 10S 55 5W
30 Aveiro, Port. 40 37N 8 38W
30 Aveiro □ 40 40N 8 35W
108 Avellaneda 34 50S 58 10W
39 Avellino 40 54N 14 46 E
44 Averøya, I. 63 0N 7 35 E
39 Aversa 40 58N 14 11 E
110 Aves, Is. de 12 0N 67 40W
19 Avesnes 50 8N 3 55 E
44 Avesta 60 9N 16 10 E
20 Aveyron, R. 44 5N 1 16 E
20 Aveyron □ 44 22N 2 45 E
37 Avezzano 42 2N 13 24 E
14 Aviemore 57 11N 3 50W
39 Avigliano 40 44N 15 41 E
21 Avignon 43 57N 4 50 E
30 Ávila 40 39N 4 43W
30 Ávila, Sa. de 40 40N 5 0W
30 Ávila □ 40 30N 5 0W
30 Avilés 43 35N 5 57W
84 Avoca 37 5S 143 28 E
15 Avoca, R. 52 48N 6 10W
92 Avola, Canada 51 45N 119 30W
39 Avola, Italy 36 56N 15 7 E
39 Avola 36 56N 15 7 E
83 Avon, R., Australia 31 40S 116 7 E
13 Avon, R., Avon 51 30N 2 43W
13 Avon, R., Dorset 50 43N 1 46W
13 Avon, R., Gloucester 51 59N 2 10W
13 Avon □ 51 30N 2 40W
97 Avonmore 45 11N 74 57W
13 Avonmouth 51 30N 2 42W
18 Avranches 48 40N 1 20W
41 Avrig 45 43N 24 21 E
66 Awaji-Shima, I. 34 30N 134 50 E
57 Awali 26 0N 50 30 E
74 Awash 9 1N 40 10 E
85 Awatere, R. 41 37S 174 10 E
14 Awe, L. 56 15N 5 15W
73 Awjilah 29 8N 21 7 E
86 Axel Heiberg Ld. 80 0N 90 0W
20 Ax-les-Thermes 42 44N 1 50 E
13 Axminster 50 47N 3 1W
19 Ay 49 3N 4 0 E
66 Ayabe 35 20N 135 20 E
110 Ayacucho, Arg. 37 5S 58 20W
108 Ayacucho, Peru 13 0S 74 0W
50 Ayaguz 48 10N 80 0 E
31 Ayamonte 37 12N 7 24W
51 Ayan 56 30N 138 16 E
63 Ayer Itam 1 55N 103 11 E
42 Ayía Paraskevi 39 14N 26 16 E
42 Ayíos Evstrátios 39 34N 24 58 E
48 Aykin 62 20N 49 56 E
93 Aylesbury, Canada 50 55N 105 53W
13 Aylesbury, U.K. 51 48N 0 49W
88 Aylmer, L. 64 0N 109 0W
80 Ayr, Australia 19 35S 147 25 E
14 Ayr, U.K. 55 28N 4 37W
14 Ayr, R. 55 29N 4 28W
12 Ayre, Pt. of 54 27N 4 21W

Aytos
Barat □, Java

41 Aytos 42 47N 27 16 E
56 Ayvalik 39 20N 26 46 E
54 Az Zahiriya 31 25N 34 58 E
56 Az Zahrān 26 10N 50 7 E
54 Az-Zarqā' 32 5N 36 4 E
56 Az Zilfi 26 12N 44 52 E
56 Az Zubayr 30 20N 47 50 E
31 Azambuja 39 4N 8 51W
61 Azamgarh 26 35N 83 13 E
56 Āzārbāijān □ 37 0N 44 30 E
72 Azare 11 55N 10 10 E
72 Azbine=Aïr 18 0N 8 0 E
49 Azerbaijan S.S.R. □ 40 20N 48 0 E
31 Aznalcóllar 37 32N 6 17W
54 Azor 32 2N 34 40 E
8 Azores, Is. 38 44N 29 0W
49 Azov 47 3N 39 25 E
49 Azov Sea= Azovskoye More 46 0N 36 30 E
49 Azovskoye More 46 0N 36 30 E
50 Azovy 64 55N 64 35 E
103 Aztec 36 54N 108 0W
105 Azua 18 25N 70 44W
31 Azuaga 38 16N 5 39W
31 Azuer, R. 39 8N 3 36W
105 Azuero, Pen. de 7 40N 80 30W
108 Azul 36 42S 59 43W

B

63 Ba Don 17 45N 106 26 E
30 Baamonde 43 7N 7 44W
57 Baba, Koh-i-, Mts. 34 40N 67 20 E
62 Baba Budan Hills 13 30N 75 40 E
41 Babadag 44 53N 28 48 E
110 Babahoyo 1 40S 79 30W
83 Babakin 32 11S 117 52 E
65 Babelthuap, I. 7 30N 134 36 E
80 Babinda 17 27S 146 0 E
65 Babo 2 30S 133 30 E
57 Bābol 36 40N 52 50 E
57 Babol Sar 36 45N 52 45 E
65 Babuyan Chan. 18 58N 122 0 E
69 Babuyan Is. 19 0N 122 0 E
56 Babylon, Iraq 32 40N 44 30 E
97 Babylon, U.S.A. 40 42N 73 20W
63 Bac Ninh 21 13N 106 4 E
63 Bac-Phan, Reg. 22 0N 105 0 E
63 Bac Quang 22 30N 104 48 E
111 Bacabal 5 20S 56 45W
65 Bacan, I. 1 0S 127 30 E
41 Bacău 46 35N 26 55 E
19 Baccarat 48 28N 6 42 E
25 Bacharach 50 3N 7 46 E
50 Bachelina 57 45N 67 20 E
88 Back, R. 67 15N 95 15W
40 Bačka Palanka 45 17N 19 27 E
40 Bačka Topola 45 48N 19 37 E
25 Backnang 48 57N 9 26 E
65 Bacolod 10 50N 123 0 E
27 Bacs-Kiskun □ 46 43N 19 30 E
27 Bácsalmás 46 8N 19 17 E
26 Bad Aussee 47 43N 13 45 E
24 Bad Driburg 51 44N 9 0 E
25 Bad Ems 51 22N 7 44 E
25 Bad Frankenhausen 51 21N 11 3 E
24 Bad Freienwalde 52 46N 14 2 E
24 Bad Godesberg 50 41N 7 4 E
24 Bad Hersfeld 50 52N 9 42 E
26 Bad Hofgastein 47 17N 13 6 E
25 Bad Homburg 50 17N 8 33 E
24 Bad Honnef 50 39N 7 13 E
26 Bad Ischl 47 44 13 38 E
25 Bad Kissingen 50 11N 10 5 E
25 Bad Kreuznach 49 47N 7 47 E
24 Bad Lauterberg 51 38N 10 29 E
26 Bad Leonfelden 48 31N 14 18 E
25 Bad Mergentheim 49 29N 9 47 E
25 Bad Nauheim 50 24N 8 45 E
24 Bad Oldesloe 53 56N 10 17 E
24 Bad Pyrmont 51 59N 9 5 E
24 Bad Salzuflen 52 8N 8 44 E
24 Bad Segeberg 53 58N 10 16 E
25 Bad Tölz 47 43N 11 34 E
24 Bad Wildungen 51 7N 9 10 E
62 Badagara 11 35N 75 40 E
31 Badajoz 38 50N 6 59W
31 Badajoz □ 38 40N 6 30W
57 Badakhshan □ 36 30N 71 0 E
32 Badalona 41 26N 2 15 E
57 Badalzal 29 50N 65 35 E
56 Badanah 30 58N 41 30 E
64 Badas 4 20N 114 37 E
27 Baden, Austria 48 1N 16 13 E
25 Baden, Switz. 47 28N 8 18 E
25 Baden-Baden 48 45N 8 14 E
25 Baden Württemberg □ 48 40N 9 0 E
14 Badenoch, Reg. 57 0N 4 0W
26 Badgastein 47 7N 13 9 E
57 Badghis □ 35 0N 63 0 E
37 Badia Polèsine 45 6N 11 30 E
60 Badnera 20 48N 77 44 E
62 Badulla 7 1N 81 7 E
31 Baena 37 37N 4 20W
31 Baeza 37 57N 3 25W
89 Baffin B. 72 0N 65 0W
89 Baffin I. 68 0N 77 0W
56 Bafra 41 34N 35 54W
57 Bāft 29 15N 56 38W
62 Bagalkot 16 10N 75 40W
74 Bagamoyo 6 28S 38 55 E
60 Bagasra 21 2N 70 57 E
51 Bagdarin 54 26N 113 36 E
109 Bagé 31 20S 54 15W
56 Baghdād 32 20N 44 30 E
61 Bagherhat 22 40N 89 47 E
38 Bagheira 38 5N 13 30 E
57 Baghīn 30 12N 56 45 E
57 Baghlan 36 12N 69 0 E
57 Baghlan □ 36 0N 68 30 E
37 Bagnacavallo 44 25N 11 58 E
39 Bagnara Cálabria 38 16N 15 49 E
20 Bagnères-de-Bigorre 43 5N 0 9 E
20 Bagnères-de-Luchon 42 47N 0 38 E
36 Bagni di Lucca 41 1N 10 37 E
37 Bagno di Romagna 43 50N 11 59 E
21 Bagnols-sur-Cèze 44 10N 4 36 E
91 Bagotville 48 22N 70 54W
67 Bagrash Kol, L. 42 0N 87 0 E
40 Bagrdan 44 5N 21 11 E
65 Baguio 16 26N 120 34 E
30 Bahabòn de Esgueva 41 52N 3 43W
60 Bahadurgarh 28 40N 76 57 E
105 Bahamas ■ 24 0N 74 0W
63 Bahau 2 48N 102 26 E
60 Bahawalnagar 30 0N 73 15 E
60 Bahawalpur 29 37N 71 40 E
60 Bahawalpur □ 29 5N 71 3 E
61 Baheri 28 45N 79 34 E
111 Bahia= Salvador 13 0S 38 30W
105 Bahia, Is. de la 16 45N 86 15W
111 Bahia □ 12 0N 42 0 E
108 Bahia Blanca 38 35S 62 13W
110 Bahia de Caráquez 0 40S 80 27W
112 Bahia Laura 48 10S 66 30W
110 Bahia Negra 20 5S 58 5W
73 Bahr el Ghazâl □ 7 0N 28 0 E
61 Bahraich 27 38N 81 50 E
57 Bahrain ■ 26 0N 50 35 E
111 Baião 2 50S 49 15W
41 Baicoi 45 3N 25 52 E
91 Baie Comeau 49 12N 68 10W
91 Baie T. Paul 47 28N 70 32W
56 Ba 'iji 35 0N 43 30 E
15 Baile Atha Cliath=Dublin 53 20N 6 18W
31 Bailén 38 8N 3 48W
41 Băileşti 44 1N 23 20 E
62 Bailhongal 15 55N 74 53 E
99 Bainbridge, Ga. 30 53N 84 34W
97 Bainbridge, N.Y. 42 17N 75 29W
88 Baird Mts. 67 10N 160 15W
84 Bairnsdale 37 48S 147 36 E
29 Baixo-Alentejo, Reg. 38 0N 8 40W
27 Baja 46 12N 18 59 E
104 Baja California Norte □ 30 0N 116 0W
104 Baja California Sur □ 26 0N 112 0W
81 Bajimba, Mt. 29 17S 152 6 E
61 Bajitpur 24 13N 91 0 E
80 Bajool 24 30S 150 35 E
50 Bakchar 57 0N 82 5 E
102 Baker, Calif. 36 16N 116 2W
100 Baker, Mont. 46 22N 104 12W
76 Baker I. 0 10N 176 35 E
88 Baker L. 64 0N 97 0W
102 Baker, Mt. 48 50N 121 49W
88 Baker Lake 64 20N 96 10W
90 Baker's Dozen Is. 57 30N 79 0W
103 Bakersfield 35 25N 119 0W
56 Bakhtiari □ 32 0N 49 0 E
49 Bakinskikh Komissarov 39 20N 49 15 E
27 Bakony Forest= Bakony Hegyseg, Reg. 47 10N 17 30 E
27 Bakony Hegyseg, Reg. 47 10N 17 30 E
49 Baku 40 25N 49 45 E
96 Bala 45 2N 79 38 E
54 Bal'a 32 20N 35 6 E
12 Bala, L. 52 53N 3 38W
64 Balabac I. 8 0N 117 0 E
64 Balabac Str. 7 53N 117 5 E
61 Balaghat 21 49N 80 12 E
62 Balaghat Ra. 18 50N 76 30 E
32 Balaguer 41 50N 0 50 E
81 Balaklava, Australia 34 7S 138 22 E
49 Balaklava, U.S.S.R. 44 30N 33 30 E
48 Balakovo 52 4N 47 55 E
61 Balangir 20 43N 83 35 E
60 Balapur 21 22N 76 45 E
48 Balashov 51 30N 43 10 E
61 Balasore 21 35N 87 3 E
27 Balassaguarmat 48 4N 19 15 E
27 Balaton, L. 46 50N 17 40 E
33 Balazote 38 54N 2 9W
104 Balboa 9 0N 79 30W
15 Balbriggan 53 35N 6 10W
108 Balcarce 38 0S 58 10W
41 Balchik 43 28N 28 11 E
85 Balclutha 46 15S 169 45 E
83 Bald, Hd. 35 6S 118 1 E
97 Baldwinsville 43 10N 76 19W
103 Baldy Pk. 33 55N 109 35W
32 Baleares, Is. 39 30N 3 0 E
80 Balfe's Creek 20 12S 145 55 E
64 Bali, I. 8 20S 115 0 E
56 Balikesir 39 35S 27 58 E
64 Balikpapan 1 10S 116 55 E
63 Baling 5 41N 100 55 E
69 Balintang Chan. 19 50N 122 0 E
59 Balipara 26 50N 92 45 E
111 Baliza 16 0S 52 20W
41 Balkan, Mts.= Stara Planina 43 15N 23 0 E
9 Balkan Pen. 42 0N 22 0 E
57 Balkh □ 36 30N 67 0 E
50 Balkhash 46 50N 74 50 E
50 Balkhash, Oz. 46 0N 74 50 E
14 Ballachulish 56 40N 5 10W
83 Balladonia 32 27S 123 51 E
84 Ballarat 37 33S 143 50 E
83 Ballard, L. 29 20S 120 10 E
61 Ballarpur 19 50N 79 23 E
14 Ballater 57 2N 3 2W
61 Ballia 25 46N 84 12 E
83 Ballidu 30 35S 116 45 E
81 Ballina, Australia 28 50S 153 31 E
15 Ballina, Mayo 54 7N 9 10W
15 Ballina, Tipperary 52 49N 8 27W
15 Ballinasloe 53 20N 8 12W
101 Ballinger 31 45N 99 58W
15 Ballinrobe 53 36N 9 13W
15 Ballycastle 55 12N 6 15W
15 Ballymena 54 53N 6 18W
15 Ballymena □ 54 53N 6 18W
15 Ballymoney 55 5N 6 30W
15 Ballymoney □ 55 5N 6 30W
15 Ballyshannon 54 30N 8 10W
112 Balmaceda 46 0S 71 50W
27 Balmazújváros 47 37N 21 21 E
14 Balmoral 57 3N 3 13W
75 Balovale 13 30S 23 15 E
61 Balrampur 27 30N 82 20 E
84 Balranald 34 38S 143 33 E
41 Bals 44 22N 24 5 E
104 Balsas, R. 17 55N 102 10W
49 Balta 48 2N 29 45 E
9 Baltic Sea 56 0N 20 0 E
28 Baltiisk 54 38N 19 55 E
15 Baltimore, Eire 51 29N 9 22W
98 Baltimore, U.S.A. 39 18N 76 37W
58 Baluchistan, Reg. 27 30N 65 0 E
57 Bam 29 7N 58 14 E
72 Bamako 12 34N 7 55W
74 Bambari 5 40N 20 35 E
80 Bambaroo 18 50S 146 10 E
25 Bamberg 49 54N 10 53 E
72 Bamenda 5 57N 10 11 E
57 Bamian □ 35 0N 67 0 E
57 Bampur 27 15N 60 21 E
63 Ban Aranyaprathet 13 41N 102 30 E
63 Ban Bua Yai 15 33N 102 26 E
63 Ban Houei Sai 20 22N 100 32 E
63 Ban Mae Sot 16 40N 98 30 E
63 Ban Nong Pling 15 40N 100 10 E
63 Ban Phai 16 4N 102 44 E
63 Ban Takua Pa 8 55N 98 25 E
57 Banadar Daryay Oman □ 25 30N 56 0 E
74 Banalia 1 32N 25 5 E
72 Banamba 13 29N 7 22W
80 Banana 24 32S 150 12 E
111 Bananal, I. de 11 30S 50 30W
73 Bânâs, Ras 23 57N 35 50 E
60 Banas, R. 25 55N 76 45 E
15 Banbridge 54 26N 6 16W
15 Banbridge □ 54 21N 6 16W
13 Banbury 52 4N 1 21W
14 Banchory 57 3N 2 30W
90 Bancroft 45 3N 77 51W
57 Band-e Charak 26 45N 54 20 E
57 Band-e Nakhīlu 26 58N 53 30 E
61 Banda 25 30N 80 26 E
64 Banda Aceh 5 35N 95 20 E
81 Banda Banda, Mt. 31 10S 152 28 E
65 Banda Sea 6 0S 130 0 E
57 Bandar Abbas 27 15N 56 15 E
63 Bandar Maharani 2 2N 102 34 E
63 Bandar Penggaram 1 50N 102 56 E
64 Bandar Seri Begawan 4 52N 115 0 E
57 Bandar-e Bushetir 28 55N 50 55 E
57 Bandar-e Lengeh 26 35N 54 58 E
57 Bandar-e Ma'shur 30 35N 49 10 E
56 Bandar-e-Pahlavi 37 30N 49 30 E
57 Bandar-e Rig 29 30N 50 45 E
57 Bandar-e Shāh 37 0N 54 10 E
56 Bandar-e Shahpur 30 30N 49 5 E
75 Bandawe 11 58S 34 5 E
109 Bandeira, Pico da 20 26S 41 47W
56 Bandirma 40 20N 28 0 E
15 Bandon 51 44N 8 45W
15 Bandon, R. 51 40N 8 35W
74 Bandundu 3 15S 17 22 E
65 Bandung 6 36S 107 48 E
33 Bañeres 38 44N 0 38W
105 Banes 20 58N 75 43W
92 Banff, Canada 51 20N 115 40W
14 Banff, U.K. 57 40N 2 32W
92 Banff Nat. Park 51 38N 116 22W
63 Bang Saphan 11 14N 99 28 E
75 Bangala Dam 21 7S 31 25 E
62 Bangalore 12 59N 77 40 E
61 Bangaon 23 0N 88 47 E
74 Bangassou 4 55N 23 55 E
73 Banghazı 32 11N 20 3 E
65 Bangil 7 36S 112 50 E
64 Bangka, I., Selatan 3 30S 105 30 E
65 Bangka, I., Utara 7 2S 112 46 E
65 Bangkalan 7 2S 112 46 E
63 Bangkok=Krung Thep 13 45N 100 31 E
59 Bangladesh ■ 24 0N 90 0 E
12 Bangor, Gwynedd 53 13N 4 9W
15 Bangor, N. Down 54 40N 5 40W
97 Bangor, Pa. 40 51N 75 13W
99 Bangor, Me. 44 48N 68 42W
65 Bangued 17 40N 120 37 E
74 Bangui 4 23N 18 35 E
74 Bangweulu, L. 11 0S 30 0 E
105 Bani 18 16N 70 22W
54 Bani Na'im 31 31N 35 10 E
73 Banınah 32 0N 20 12 E
40 Banja Luka 44 49N 17 26 E
65 Banjar 7 24S 108 30 E
64 Banjarmasin 3 20S 114 35 E
65 Banjarnegara 7 24S 109 42 E
72 Banjul 13 28N 16 40W
80 Banka Banka 18 50S 134 0 E
61 Bankipore 25 35N 85 10 E
86 Banks I. 73 30N 120 0W
85 Banks, Pen. 43 45S 173 15 E
61 Bankura 23 11N 87 18 E
15 Bann, R. 55 2N 6 35W
18 Bannalec 47 57N 3 42W
103 Banning 48 44N 91 56W
60 Bannu 33 0N 70 18S
14 Bannockburn 56 5N 3 55W
60 Bañolas 42 16N 2 44 E
30 Baños de Molgas 42 15N 7 40W
27 Banská Bystrica 48 46N 19 14 E
27 Banská Stiavnica 48 25N 18 55 E
60 Banswara 23 32N 74 24 E
65 Banten 6 5S 106 8 E
15 Bantry 51 40N 9 28W
15 Bantry, B. 51 35N 9 50W
65 Bantul 7 55S 110 19 E
60 Bantva 21 29N 70 12 E
62 Bantval 12 55N 75 0 E
41 Banya 42 33N 24 50 E
20 Banyuls 42 29N 3 8 E
62 Bapatla 15 55N 80 30 E
54 Baqa el Gharbiya 32 25N 35 2 E
40 Bar 42 8N 19 8 E
64 Barabai 2 32S 115 34 E
50 Barabinsk 55 20N 78 20 E
100 Baraboo 43 28N 89 46W
105 Baracoa 20 20N 74 30W
108 Baradero 33 52S 59 29S
105 Barahona, Dom. Rep. 18 13N 71 7W
30 Barahona, Sp. 41 17N 2 39W
59 Barail Ra. 25 15N 93 20 E
66 Barak □ 38 20N 140 0 E
59 Barakhola 25 0N 92 45 E
62 Baramati 18 11N 74 33 E
58 Baramula 34 15N 74 20 E
60 Baran 25 9N 76 40 E
92 Baranof 57 0N 135 10W
92 Baranof I. 57 0N 135 10W
48 Baranovichi 53 10N 26 0 E
27 Baranya □ 46 0N 18 15 E
65 Barat □, Java 7 0S 107 0 E

Belmopan Bischofshofen

104 Belmopan 17 18N 88 30W
15 Belmullet 54 13N 9 58W
109 Belo Horizonte 19 55S 43 56W
51 Belogorsk 51 0N 128 20E
40 Belogradchik 43 37N 22 40E
100 Beloit 42 35N 89 0W
48 Belomorsk 64 35N 34 30E
48 Beloretsk 53 58N 58 24E
50 Belovo 54 30N 86 0E
48 Beloye, Oz. 60 10N 37 35E
48 Beloye More 66 0N 38 0E
48 Belozersk 60 0N 37 30E
39 Belpasso 37 37N 15 0E
38 Belsito 37 50N 13 47E
49 Belsty 47 48N 28 0E
81 Beltana 30 48S 138 25E
111 Belterra 2 45S 55 0W
101 Belton 31 4N 97 30W
15 Belturbet 54 6N 7 28W
39 Belvedere Marittimo 39 37N 15 52E
100 Belvidere 42 15N 88 55W
50 Belyy Os. 73 30N 71 0E
50 Belyy Yar 58 26N 84 30E
24 Belzig 52 8N 12 36E
31 Bembézar, R. 38 0N 5 20W
100 Bemidji 47 30N 94 50W
14 Ben Cruachan, Mt. 56 26N 5 8W
73 Ben Gardane 33 11N 11 11E
14 Ben Hope, Mt. 58 24N 4 36W
14 Ben Lawers, Mt. 56 33N 4 13W
81 Ben Lomond, Mt., Australia 30 1S 151 43E
14 Ben Lomond, Mt., U.K. 56 12N 4 39W
14 Ben Macdhui, Mt. 57 4N 3 40W
14 Ben More, Mt. 56 26N 6 2W
14 Ben More Assynt, Mt. 58 7N 4 51W
14 Ben Nevis, Mt. 56 48N 5 0W
14 Ben Wyvis, Mt. 57 40N 4 35W
74 Bena Dibele 4 4S 22 50E
31 Benagalbón 36 45N 4 15W
84 Benalla 36 30S 146 0E
61 Benares=Varanasi 25 22N 83 8E
30 Benavente 38 59N 8 49W
30 Benavides 42 30N 5 54W
14 Benbecula, I. 57 26N 7 20W
81 Benbonyathe Hill 30 25S 139 11E
83 Bencubbin 30 48S 117 52E
102 Bend 44 2N 121 15W
55 Bender Beila 9 30N 50 48E
83 Bendering 32 23S 118 18E
49 Bendery 46 50N 29 50E
84 Bendigo 36 40S 144 15E
54 Bene Beraq 32 5N 34 50E
26 Benešöv 49 46N 14 41E
19 Bénestroff 48 54N 6 45E
39 Benevento 41 7N 14 45E
19 Benfeld 48 22N 7 34E
73 Benghazi=Banghazī 32 11N 20 3E
64 Bengkalis 1 30N 102 10E
64 Bengkulu 3 50S 102 12E
64 Bengkulu □ 3 50S 102 10E
93 Bengough 49 25N 105 10W
75 Benguela 12 37S 13 25E
74 Beni 32 11S 148 43E
73 Beni Mazar 28 32N 30 44E
72 Beni Mellal 32 21N 6 21W
73 Benî Suêf 29 5N 31 6E
32 Benicarló 40 23N 0 23E
33 Benidorm 38 33N 0 9W
72 Benin, B. of 5 0N 3 0E
72 Benin City 6 20N 5 31E
33 Benisa 38 43N 0 3E
108 Benjamin Aceval 24 58S 57 34W
110 Benjamin Constant 4 40S 70 15W
80 Benlidi 24 35S 144 50E
99 Bennettsville 34 38N 79 39W
97 Bennington 42 52N 73 12W
18 Bénodet 47 53N 4 7W
75 Benoni 26 11S 28 18E
25 Bensheim 49 40N 8 38E
103 Benson 31 59N 110 19W
65 Benteng 6 10S 120 30E
101 Benton, Ark. 34 30N 92 35W
100 Benton, Ill. 38 0N 88 55W
98 Benton Harbor 42 10N 86 28W
63 Bentong 3 31N 101 55S
72 Benue, R. 7 47N 6 45E
40 Beograd 44 50N 20 37E
66 Beppu 33 15N 131 30E
54 Ber Dagan 32 1N 34 49E
42 Berati 40 43N 19 59E
73 Berber 18 0N 34 0E
55 Berbera 10 30N 45 2E
74 Berbérati 4 15N 15 40E
33 Berberia, C. 38 39N 1 24E
36 Berceto 44 30N 10 0E
25 Berchtesgaden 47 37N 13 1E
19 Berck 50 25N 1 36E
49 Berdicher 49 57N 28 30E
50 Berdsk 54 47N 83 2E
49 Berdyansk 46 45N 36 50E
55 Bereda 11 45N 51 0E
72 Berekum 7 29N 2 34W
93 Berens River 52 25N 97 0W
27 Berettyóújfalu 47 13N 21 33E
48 Berezniki 59 24N 56 46E
50 Berezovo 64 0N 65 0E
32 Berga 42 6N 1 48E
36 Bergamo 45 42N 9 40E
30 Bergantiños 43 20N 8 40W
24 Bergedorf 53 28N 10 12E
24 Bergen, E. Germany 50 24N 13 26E
16 Bergen, Neth. 52 40N 4 42E
47 Bergen, Norway 60 23N 5 27E
16 Bergen-op-Zoom 51 30N 4 18E
20 Bergerac 44 51N 0 30E
24 Bergheim 50 57N 6 38E
24 Bergisch-Gladbach 50 59N 7 9E
19 Bergues 50 58N 2 24E
16 Bergum 53 13N 5 59E
61 Berhampore 24 2N 88 27E
62 Berhampur 19 15N 84 54E
88 Bering Sea 66 0N 170 0W
4 Bering Str. 65 0N 168 0W
16 Beringen 51 3N 5 14E
51 Beringovskiy 63 3N 179 19E
108 Berisso 34 40S 58 0W
33 Berja 36 50N 2 56W
102 Berkeley 38 0N 122 20W
5 Berkner I. 79 30S 50 0W
41 Berkovitsa 43 16N 23 8E
13 Berkshire □ 51 30N 1 20W
31 Berlanga 38 17N 5 50W
24 Berleburg 51 3N 8 22E
31 Berlenga, I. 39 25N 9 30W
24 Berlin, Germany 52 32N 13 24W
97 Berlin, U.S.A. 44 29N 71 10W
31 Bermeja, Sa. 36 45N 5 11W
32 Bermeo 43 25N 2 47W
105 Bermuda, I. 32 45N 65 0W
25 Bern 46 57N 7 28E
25 Bern □ 46 45N 7 40E
39 Bernalda 40 24N 16 44E
103 Bernalilo 35 17N 106 37W
109 Bernardo de Irigoyen 26 15S 53 40W
24 Bernau 47 53N 12 20E
18 Bernay 49 5N 0 35E
26 Berndorf 47 59N 16 1E
25 Berne=Bern 46 57N 7 28E
25 Berner Alpen, Mts. 46 27N 7 35E
83 Bernier, I. 24 50S 113 12E
25 Bernina, Piz 46 20N 9 54E
26 Beroun 49 57N 14 5E
26 Berounka, R. 50 0N 13 47E
84 Berowra 33 35S 151 12E
21 Berre 43 28N 5 11E
21 Berre, Étang de 43 27N 5 5E
72 Berrechid 33 18N 7 36W
81 Berri 34 14S 140 35E
84 Berrigan 35 38S 145 49E
19 Berry, Reg. 47 0N 2 0E
24 Bersenbrück 52 33N 7 56E
19 Bertincourt 50 5N 2 58E
74 Bertoua 4 30N 13 45E
97 Berwick 41 4N 76 17W
12 Berwick-upon-Tweed 55 47N 2 0W
12 Berwyn Mts. 52 54N 3 26W
27 Berzence 46 12N 17 11E
19 Besançon 47 9N 6 0E
21 Bessèges 44 18N 4 8E
99 Bessemer 46 27N 90 0W
18 Bessin, Reg. 49 21N 1 0W
18 Bessines-sur-Gartempe 46 6N 1 22E
54 Bet Ha 'Emeq 32 58N 35 8E
54 Bet Ha Shitta 32 31N 35 27E
54 Bet Ha'tmeq 32 58N 35 8E
54 Bet Oren 32 43N 34 59E
54 Bet Qeshet 32 41N 35 21E
54 Be't She'an 32 30N 35 30E
54 Bet Shemesh 31 45N 35 0E
54 Bet Yosef 32 34N 35 33E
30 Betanzos 43 15N 8 12W
74 Bétaré-Oya 5 40N 14 5E
32 Betera 39 35N 0 28W
75 Bethanien 26 31S 17 8E
54 Bethany=Eizariya 31 47N 35 15E
97 Bethel, Conn. 41 22N 73 25W
96 Bethel, Pa. 40 20N 80 2W
97 Bethel, Vt. 43 50N 72 37W
54 Bethlehem, Jordan=Bayt Lahm 31 43N 35 12E
75 Bethlehem, S. Africa 28 14S 28 18E
97 Bethlehem, U.S.A. 40 39N 75 24W
75 Bethulie 30 30S 25 29E
19 Béthune 50 30N 2 38E
18 Béthune, R. 49 56N 1 5E
19 Betan Bazoches 48 42N 3 15E
80 Betoota 25 40S 140 42E
61 Bettiah 26 48N 84 33E
36 Béttola 44 46N 9 35E
66 Betung 2 0S 103 10E
41 Beuca 44 14N 24 56E
21 Beuil 44 6N 7 0E
84 Beulah, Australia 35 58S 142 29E
93 Beulah, Canada 50 16N 101 2W
24 Bevensen 53 5N 10 34E
83 Beverley, Australia 32 9S 116 56E
12 Beverley, U.K. 53 52N 0 26W
92 Beverly, Canada 53 36N 113 21W
97 Beverly, U.S.A. 42 32N 70 50W
103 Beverly Hills 34 4N 118 29W
16 Beverwijk 52 28N 4 38E
25 Bex 46 15N 7 0E
72 Beyla 8 30N 8 38W
13 Bexhill 50 51N 0 29E
50 Beyneu 45 10N 55 3E
56 Beypazari 40 10N 31 48E
56 Beyşehir Gölü, L. 37 40N 31 45E
62 Bezawada=Vijayawada 16 31N 80 39E
40 Bezdan 45 28N 18 57E
54 Bezet 33 4N 35 8E
48 Bezhitsa 53 19N 34 17E
20 Béziers 43 20N 3 12E
61 Bhadrakh 21 10N 86 30E
62 Bhadravati 13 49N 76 15E
61 Bhagalpur 25 10N 87 0E
62 Bhaisa 19 10N 77 58E
60 Bhakkar 31 40N 71 5E
61 Bhakra Dam 31 30N 76 45E
59 Bhamo 24 15N 97 15E
62 Bhamragarh 19 30N 80 40E
61 Bhandara 21 5N 79 42E
61 Bhanrer Ra. 23 40N 79 45E
58 Bharūch 21 47N 73 0E
60 Bharatpur 27 15N 77 30E
60 Bhatinda 30 15N 74 57E
62 Bhatkal 13 58N 74 35E
61 Bhatpara 22 50N 88 25E
62 Bhattiprolu 16 7N 80 45E
60 Bhaun 32 55N 72 40E
62 Bhavani 11 27N 77 43E
60 Bhavnagar 21 45N 72 10E
60 Bhera 32 29N 72 57E
60 Bhilwara 25 25N 74 38E
62 Bhima, R. 17 20N 76 30E
62 Bhimavaram 16 30N 81 30E
60 Bhind 26 30N 78 46E
62 Bhiwandi 19 15N 73 0E
60 Bhiwani 28 50N 76 9E
62 Bhiwndi 19 15N 73 0E
62 Bhongir 17 30N 78 56E
60 Bhopal 23 20N 77 53E
62 Bhor 18 12N 73 53E
61 Bhubaneswar 20 15N 85 50E
60 Bhuj 23 15N 69 49E
60 Bhusaval 21 15N 69 49E
61 Bhutan ■ 27 25N 89 50E
27 Biała, R 49 46N 17 40E
28 Biała Piska 53 37N 22 5E
28 Biała Podlaska 52 4N 23 6E
28 Biela Podlaska □ 52 0N 23 0S
28 Białogard 54 2N 15 58E
28 Białystok 53 10N 23 10E
28 Białystok □ 52 50N 23 10E
39 Biancaville 37 39N 14 50E
20 Biarritz 43 29N 1 33W
25 Biasca 46 22N 18 58E
25 Biberach 48 5N 9 49E
30 Bibey, R. 42 24N 7 13W
72 Bibiani 6 30N 2 8W
91 Bic 48 20N 68 41W
39 Bîccari 41 23N 15 12E
72 Bida 9 3N 5 58E
13 Bicester 51 53N 1 9W
62 Bidar 17 55N 77 35E
99 Biddeford 43 30N 70 28E
13 Bideford 51 1N 4 13W
63 Bidor 4 6N 101 15E
75 Bié 12 22S 16 55E
75 Bié Plat. 12 0S 16 0E
102 Bieber 41 4N 121 6W
25 Biel 47 8N 7 14E
28 Bielawa 50 43N 16 37E
27 Bielé Karpaty, Mts. 49 5N 18 0E
24 Bielefeld 52 2N 8 31E
36 Biella 45 33N 8 3E
28 Bielsk Podlaski 52 47N 23 12E
27 Bielsko-Biała 49 50N 19 8E
27 Bielsko Biała 49 45N 19 10E
63 Biên Hoa 10 57N 106 49E
25 Bienne=Biel 47 8N 7 14E
31 Bienvenida 38 18N 6 12W
32 Biescas 42 37N 0 20W
39 Biferno, R. 41 40N 14 38E
90 Big Beaver House 52 59N 89 50W
101 Big Bend Nat. Park 29 15N 103 15W
88 Big Delta 64 15N 145 0W
97 Big Moose 43 49N 74 58W
98 Big Rapids 43 42N 85 27W
93 Big River 53 50N 107 0W
88 Big Salmon 61 50N 136 0W
101 Big Spring 32 10N 101 25W
99 Big Stone Gap 36 52N 82 45W
90 Big Trout L. 53 40N 90 0W
20 Biganos 44 39N 0 59W
93 Biggar, Canada 52 10N 108 0W
14 Biggar, U.K. 55 38N 3 31W
82 Bigge, I. 14 35S 125 10E
81 Biggenden 25 31S 152 4E
102 Bighorn Mts. 44 30N 107 20W
20 Bigorre, Reg. 43 5N 0 2E
102 Bigtimber 45 33N 110 0W
37 Bihać 44 49N 15 57E
61 Bihar 25 5N 85 40E
61 Bihar □ 25 0N 86 0E
27 Bihor □ 47 0N 22 10E
72 Bijagos, Arquipélago dos 11 15N 16 10W
62 Bijapur 26 2N 77 36E
40 Bijeljina 44 46N 19 17E
60 Bijnor 29 27N 78 11E
60 Bikaner 28 2N 73 18E
51 Bikin 46 50N 134 20E
76 Bikini Atoll, I. 12 0N 167 30E
60 Bilara 26 14N 73 53E
61 Bilaspur, Mad. P. 22 2N 82 15E
60 Bilaspur, Punjab 31 19N 76 50E
63 Bilauk Taungdan, Ra. 13 0N 99 0E
30 Bilbao 43 16N 2 56W
40 Bileća 42 53N 18 27E
56 Bilecik 40 5N 30 5E
51 Bilibino 68 3N 166 20E
51 Bilir 65 40N 131 20E
42 Bilishti 40 37N 20 59E
83 Billabalong 27 25S 115 49E
82 Billiluna 19 37S 127 41E
12 Billingham 54 36N 1 18W
102 Billings 45 43N 108 29W
44 Billingsfors 58 59N 12 15E
20 Billom 45 43N 3 20E
73 Bilma 18 50N 13 30E
40 Bilo Gora 45 53N 17 15E
80 Biloela 24 34S 150 31E
101 Biloxi 30 30N 89 0W
73 Biltine 14 40N 20 50E
80 Bilyana 18 5S 145 50E
65 Bima 8 22S 118 49E
60 Bina-Etawah 24 13N 78 14E
65 Binalbagan 10 12N 122 50E
64 Binatang 2 10N 111 40E
80 Binbee 20 19S 147 56E
16 Binche 50 26N 4 10E
83 Bindi Bindi 30 37S 116 22E
75 Bindura 17 18S 31 18E
81 Bingara, N.S.W. 29 40S 150 40E
81 Bingara, Queens. 28 10S 144 37E
25 Bingen 49 57N 7 53E
102 Bingham Canyon 40 31N 112 10W
97 Binghamton 42 9N 75 54W
63 Binh Dinh=An Nhon 13 55N 109 7E
63 Binh Son 15 20N 104 40E
64 Binjai 3 50N 98 30E
54 Binyamina 32 32N 34 56E
73 Binzerte 37 15N 9 50E
108 Bío Bío □ 37 35S 72 0W
37 Biograd 43 56N 15 29E
40 Biokovo 43 23N 17 0E
62 Bir 19 0N 75 54E
73 Bir Atrun 18 15N 26 40E
54 Bir Nabala 31 52N 35 12E
73 Bîr Shalatein 23 5N 35 25E
54 Bir Zeit 31 59N 35 11E
61 Biratnagar 26 18N 87 17E
93 Birch Hills 53 10N 105 10W
84 Birchip 35 52S 143 0E
79 Bird, I. 22 20S 155 20E
80 Birdsville 25 51S 139 20E
82 Birdum 15 50S 133 0E
64 Bireuen 5 14N 96 39E
109 Birigui 21 18S 50 16W
57 Bırjand 32 57N 59 10E
12 Birkenhead 53 24N 3 1W
26 Birkfeld 47 21N 15 45E
41 Bîrlad 46 15N 27 38E
13 Birmingham, U.K. 52 30N 1 55W
99 Birmingham, U.S.A. 33 31N 86 50W
72 Birnin-Kebbi 12 32N 4 12E
51 Birobidzhan 48 50N 132 50E
15 Birr 53 7N 7 55W
93 Birtle 50 30N 101 5W
61 Bisalpur 28 14N 79 48E
103 Bisbee 31 30N 110 0W
20 Biscarrosse, Étang de 44 22N 1 10W
29 Biscay, B. of 45 0N 2 0W
39 Biscéglie 41 14N 16 30E
26 Bischofshofen 47 26N 13 14E

Bischofswerda Brasilia Legal

24 Bischofswerda 51 8N 14 11E
19 Bischwiller 48 47N 7 50E
103 Bishop 37 20N 118 26W
12 Bishop Auckland 54 40N 1 40W
91 Bishop's Falls 49 2N 55 24W
13 Bishop's Stortford 51 52 0 11E
72 Biskra 34 50N 5 52E
28 Biskupiec 53 53N 20 58E
100 Bismarck 46 49N 100 49W
76 Bismark Arch. 3 30S 148 30E
72 Bissau 11 45N 15 45W
93 Bissett 46 14N 78 4W
61 Biswan 27 29N 81 2E
40 Bitola 41 5N 21 21E
39 Bitonto 41 7N 16 40E
24 Bitterfeld 51 36N 12 20E
75 Bitterfontein 31 0S 18 32E
102 Bitterroot Ra. 46 0N 114 20W
38 Bitti 40 29N 9 20E
66 Biwa-Ko, L. 35 15N 135 45E
50 Biysk 52 40N 85 0E
66 Bizen 34 44N 134 9E
72 Bizerte=Binzerte 37 15N 9 50E
45 Bjärka 58 16N 15 44E
40 Bjelašnica, Mt. 43 11N 18 21E
37 Bjelovar 45 56N 16 49E
4 Bjørnøya, I. 74 25N 19 0E
45 Bjuv 56 7N 12 56E
40 Blace 43 18N 21 17E
97 Black, R. 43 59N 76 4W
100 Black Hills, Mts 44 0N 103 50W
13 Black Mts. 51 52N 3 50W
9 Black Sea 43 30N 35 0E
72 Black Volta, R. 8 41N 1 33W
80 Blackall 24 26S 145 27E
80 Blackbull 18 0S 141 7E
12 Blackburn 53 44N 2 30W
102 Blackfoot 43 13N 112 12W
84 Blackheath 33 39S 150 17E
12 Blackpool 53 48N 3 3W
91 Blacks Harbour 45 3N 66 49W
91 Blackville 47 5N 65 58W
80 Blackwater 23 35S 149 0E
15 Blackwater, R., Cork 51 51N 7 50W
15 Blackwater, R., Dungannon 54 31N 6 34W
15 Blackwater, R., Meath 53 39N 6 43W
101 Blackwell 36 55N 97 20W
12 Blaenau Ffestiniog 53 0N 3 57W
20 Blagnac 43 38N 1 24E
49 Blagodarnoye 45 7N 43 37E
40 Blagoevgrad 42 2N 23 5E
51 Blagoveshchensk 50 20N 127 30E
93 Blaine Lake 52 51N 106 52W
80 Blair Atholl, Australia 22 42S 147 31E
14 Blair Atholl, U.K. 56 46N 3 50W
14 Blairgowrie 56 36N 3 20W
92 Blairmore 49 40N 114 25W
41 Blaj 46 10N 23 57E
19 Blamont 48 35N 6 50E
72 Blanc, C.= Ras Nouadhibou 37 15N 9 56E
21 Blanc, Mt. 45 50N 6 52E
112 Blanca, B. 39 10S 61 30W
103 Blanca Pk. 37 35N 105 29W
33 Blanco, C. 39 21N 2 51E
13 Blandford 50 52N 2 10W
103 Blanding 37 35N 109 30W
32 Blanes 41 40N 2 48E
19 Blangy 49 14N 0 17E
26 Blanice 49 10N 14 5E
109 Blanquillo 32 53S 55 37W
27 Blansko 49 22N 16 40E
75 Blantyre 15 45S 35 0E
15 Blarney 51 57N 8 35W
12 Blaydon 54 56N 1 47W
20 Blaye 45 8N 0 40W
84 Blayney 33 32S 149 14E
24 Bleckede 53 18N 10 43E
37 Bled 46 27N 14 7E
26 Bleiburg 46 35N 14 49E
45 Blekinge □ 56 15N 15 15E
85 Blenheim 41 38S 174 5E
13 Bletchley 51 59N 0 54W
72 Blida 36 30N 2 49E
90 Blind River 46 15N 83 0W
65 Blitar 8 5S 112 11E
97 Block I. 41 13N 71 35W
97 Block Island Sd. 41 10N 71 45W
75 Bloemfontein 29 6S 26 14E
18 Blois 47 35N 1 20E
28 Błonie 52 12N 20 37E
97 Bloomingdale 41 0N 74 20W
100 Bloomington, Ill. 40 25N 89 0W
98 Bloomington, Ind. 39 10N 86 30W
97 Bloomsburg 41 0N 76 30W
26 Bludenz 47 10N 9 50E
98 Blue Island 41 40N 87 41W
80 Blue Mud, B. 13 30S 136 0E
97 Blue Mts. 45 15N 119 0W
73 Blue Nile, R.= Nîl el Azraq, R. 10 30N 35 0E
86 Blue Ridge, Mts 36 30N 80 15W
98 Bluefield 37 18N 81 14W
105 Bluefields 12 0N 83 50W
80 Bluff, Australia 23 40S 149 0E
85 Bluff, N.Z. 46 36S 168 21E
83 Bluff Knoll, Mt. 34 23S 118 20E
98 Bluffton 40 43N 85 9W
109 Blumenau 27 0S 49 0W
12 Blyth 55 8N 1 32W
103 Blythe 33 40N 114 33W
101 Blytheville 35 56N 89 55W
72 Bo 7 55N 11 50W
110 Boa Vista 2 48N 60 30W
105 Boaco 12 29N 85 35W
74 Boali 4 48N 18 7E
31 Boatman 27 16S 146 55E
62 Bobbili 18 35N 83 30E
90 Bobcaygeon 44 33N 78 35W
72 Bobo-Dioulasso 11 8N 4 13W
41 Boboc 45 13N 26 59E
28 Bobr R. 52 4N 15 4E
48 Bobruysk 53 10N 29 15E
111 Bocaiuva 17 7S 43 49W
105 Bocas del Toro 9 15N 82 20W
30 Boceguillas 41 20N 3 39W
27 Bochnia 49 58N 29 27E
24 Bocholt 51 50N 6 35E
24 Bochum 51 28N 7 12E
21 Bocognano 42 5N 9 3E
40 Boçsa 45 21N 21 47E
74 Boda 4 19N 17 26E
51 Bodaybo 57 50N 114 0E
83 Boddington 32 50S 116 30E
46 Boden 65 50N 21 42E
25 Bodensee, L. 47 35N 9 25N
62 Bodhan 18 40N 77 55E
62 Bodinayakkanur 10 2N 77 10E
13 Bodmin 50 28N 4 44W
13 Bodmin Moor, Reg. 50 33N 4 36W
46 Bodø 67 17N 14 27E
27 Bodrog, R. 48 15N 21 35E
27 Bodva, R. 48 19N 20 45E
101 Bogalusa 30 50N 89 55W
84 Bogan Gate 33 6S 147 44E
80 Bogantungan 23 41S 147 17E
75 Bogenfels 27 25S 15 25E
81 Boggabri 30 45S 150 0E
13 Bognor Regis 50 47N 0 40W
65 Bogor 6 36S 106 48E
51 Bogorodskoye 52 22N 140 30E
110 Bogota 4 34N 74 0W
50 Bogotal 56 15N 89 50E
61 Bogra 24 26N 89 22E
51 Boguchany 58 40N 97 30E
19 Bohain 49 59N 3 28E
25 Böhmerwald, Mts. 49 30N 12 40E
65 Bohol, I. 9 58N 124 20E
55 Bohotleh 8 20N 46 25E
109 Boi, Pta. do 23 55S 45 15W
91 Boiestown 46 27N 66 26W
102 Boise 43 43N 116 9W
93 Boissevain 49 15N 100 0W
24 Boizenburg 55 16N 13 36E
65 Bojonegoro 7 9S 111 52E
72 Boké 10 56N 14 17W
47 Bokna, Fd. 59 12N 5 30E
74 Bokote 0 12S 21 8E
57 Bol, Kuh-e 30 40N 52 45E
72 Bolama 11 30N 15 30W
18 Bolbec 49 30N 0 30E
41 Boldeşti 45 3N 26 2E
28 Bolesławiec 51 17N 15 37E
110 Bolívar, Arg. 36 2S 60 53W
102 Bolívar, Col. 2 0N 77 0W
110 Bolivia ■ 17 6S 64 0W
106 Bolivian Plat. 19 0S 69 0W
40 Boljevac 45 31N 21 58E
21 Bollène 44 18N 4 45E
44 Bollnäs 61 22N 16 28E
31 Bollullos 37 19N 6 32W
45 Bolmen, L. 56 57N 13 45E
37 Bologna 44 30N 11 20E
19 Bologne 48 10N 5 8E
48 Bologoye 57 55N 34 0E
63 Boloven, Cao Nguyen, Mts. 15 10N 106 30E
61 Bolpur 23 40N 87 45E
37 Bolsena, L. di 42 35N 11 55E
51 Bolshevik, Os. 78 30N 102 0E
49 Bolshoi Kavkaz 42 50N 44 0E
50 Bolshoy Atlym 62 25N 66 50E
51 Bolshoy Shantar, Os. 55 0N 137 42E
12 Bolton 53 35N 2 26W
37 Bolzana 46 30N 11 20E
111 Bom Despacho 19 46S 45 15W
111 Bom Jesus da Lapa 13 10S 43 30W
74 Boma 5 50S 13 4E
84 Bomaderry 34 52S 150 37E
84 Bombala 36 56S 149 15E
62 Bombay 18 55N 72 50E
74 Bomboma 2 25N 18 55E
67 Bomda 29 59N 96 25E
73 Bon, C. 37 1N 11 2E
105 Bonaire, I. 12 10N 68 15W
82 Bonaparte Arch. 15 0S 124 30E
91 Bonaventure 48 5N 63 32W
91 Bonavista 48 40N 53 5W
91 Bonavista B. 48 58N 53 25W
37 Bondeno 44 53N 11 22E
72 Bondoukoro 9 51N 4 25W
72 Bondoukou 8 2N 2 47W
65 Bondowoso 7 56S 113 49E
65 Bone, Teluk, G. 4 10S 120 50E
14 Bo'ness 56 0N 3 38W
73 Bongor 10 35N 15 20E
101 Bonham 33 30N 96 10W
21 Bonifacio 41 24N 9 10E
38 Bonifacio, Bouches de 41 23N 9 10E
76 Bonin Is. 27 0N 142 0E
108 Bonito 21 8S 56 28W
24 Bonn 50 43N 7 6E
102 Bonners Ferry 48 38N 116 21W
18 Bonneval 48 11N 1 24E
21 Bonneville 46 5N 6 24E
83 Bonnie Rock 30 29S 118 22E
70 Bonny, B. of 4 0N 8 0E
93 Bonnyville 54 20N 110 45W
38 Bonorva 40 25N 8 47E
64 Bontang 0 10N 117 30E
65 Bonthain 5 34S 119 56E
16 Boom 51 6N 4 20E
81 Boonah 28 0S 152 35E
100 Boone 42 5N 93 46W
98 Boonville, Ind 38 3N 87 13W
100 Boonville, Mo. 38 57N 92 45W
97 Boonville, N.Y. 43 31N 75 20W
89 Boothia, G. of 70 0N 90 0W
88 Boothia Pen. 70 30N 95 0W
12 Bootle 53 28N 3 1W
74 Booué 0 5S 11 55E
81 Bopeechee 29 35S 137 30E
108 Boquerón 21 30S 60 0W
40 Bor 44 5N 22 7E
45 Borås 57 42N 13 1E
110 Borba 4 12S 59 34W
20 Bordeaux 44 50N 0 36W
83 Borden, Australia 34 3S 118 12E
91 Borden, Canada 46 18N 63 47W
14 Borders □ 55 30N 3 0W
84 Bordertown 36 14S 140 58E
36 Bordighera 43 47N 7 40E
16 Borger, Neth. 52 54N 7 33E
101 Borger, U.S.A. 35 40N 101 20W
36 Borgo 46 3N 11 27E
36 Borgomanera 45 41N 8 28E
36 Borgosésia 45 43N 8 9E
49 Borisoglebsk 51 27N 42 5E
48 Borisov 54 17N 28 28E
110 Borja 4 20S 77 40W
32 Borjas Blancas 41 31N 0 52E
24 Borken 51 3N 9 21E
73 Borkou 18 15N 18 50E
24 Borkum, I. 53 35N 6 41E
44 Borlänge 60 28N 14 33E
5 Borley, C. 66 15S 52 30E
25 Borna 51 8N 12 31E
64 Borneo, I. 1 0N 115 0E
45 Bornholm, I. 55 8N 14 55E
31 Bornos 36 48N 5 42W
51 Borogontsy 62 42N 131 8E
48 Borovichi 58 25N 35 55E
45 Borrby 55 27N 14 10E
32 Borriol 40 4N 0 4W
80 Borroloola 16 4S 136 17E
60 Borsad 22 24N 72 56E
48 Borsod-Abaüj-Zemplén □ 48 20N 21 0E
20 Bort-les-Orgues 45 24N 2 29E
56 Borujerd 33 55N 48 50E
51 Borzya 50 24N 116 31E
40 Bosanska Gradiška 45 9N 17 15E
37 Bosanska Kostajnica 45 11N 16 33E
37 Bosanska Krupa 44 53N 16 10E
37 Bosanski Novi 45 2N 16 22E
55 Bosaso 11 13N 49 8E
13 Boscasble 50 42N 4 42W
39 Boscotrecase 40 46N 14 28E
40 Bosna, R. 45 4N 18 29E
37 Bosna i Hercegovina □ 44 0N 18 0E
41 Bosporus, Str.= Karadeniz Boğazi, Str. 41 10N 29 10E
74 Bossangoa 6 35N 17 30E
101 Bossier City 32 28N 93 38W
12 Boston, U.K. 52 59N 0 2W
97 Boston, U.S.A. 42 20N 71 0W
60 Botad 22 15N 71 40E
84 Botany B. 34 2S 151 6E
41 Botevgrad 42 55N 23 47E
46 Bothnia, G. 63 0N 21 0E
80 Bothwell 42 37N 81 54W
75 Botletle, R. 20 10S 24 10E
41 Botoroaga 44 8N 25 32E
75 Botswana ■ 23 0S 24 0E
109 Botucatu 22 55S 48 30W
91 Botwood 49 6N 55 23W
72 Bou Saâda 35 11N 4 9E
72 Bouaké 7 40N 5 2W
74 Bouar 6 0N 15 40E
72 Bouârfa 32 32N 1 58E
21 Bouches-du-Rhône 43 37N 5 2E
82 Bougainville, C. 13 57S 126 4E
72 Bougouni 11 30N 7 20W
100 Boulder 40 3N 105 10W
103 Boulder City 36 0N 114 58W
80 Boulia 22 52S 139 51E
19 Bouligny 49 17N 5 45E
19 Boulogne-sur-Mer 50 42N 1 36E
102 Bountiful 40 57N 111 58W
20 Bourbon-Lancy 46 37N 3 45E
20 Bourbonnais, Reg. 46 28N 3 0E
45 Bourg 45 3N 0 34W
21 Bourg en Bresse 46 13N 5 12E
20 Bourg Madame 42 29N 1 58E
21 Bourg-de-Péage 45 2N 5 3E
20 Bourges 47 5N 2 22E
45 Bourget, L. du 45 44N 5 52E
18 Bourgneuf 47 2N 1 58W
18 Bourgneuf, B. de 47 3N 2 10W
19 Bourgogne, Reg. 47 0N 4 30E
21 Bourgoin-Jallieu 45 36N 5 17E
81 Bourke 30 8S 145 55E
90 Bourlamaque 48 5N 77 56W
13 Bournemouth 50 43N 1 53W
20 Boussac 46 22N 2 13E
20 Boussens 43 12N 1 2E
7 Bouvet, I. 55 0S 3 30E
92 Bow Island 49 50N 111 23W
83 Bowelling 33 25S 116 30E
80 Bowen 20 0S 148 16E
103 Bowie 32 15N 109 30W
12 Bowland Forest 54 0N 2 30W
98 Bowling Green, Ky. 37 0N 86 25W
98 Bowling Green, Ohio 41 22N 83 40W
80 Bowling Green, C. 19 19S 147 25E
100 Bowman 46 12N 103 21W
90 Bowmanville 43 55N 78 40W
14 Bowmore 55 45N 6 18W
92 Bowness 50 55N 114 25W
84 Bowser 36 19S 146 23E
93 Bowsman 52 15N 101 12W
16 Boxtel 51 36N 5 9E
15 Boyle 53 58N 8 19W
15 Boyne, R. 53 40N 6 34W
70 Boyoma, Chutes 0 12N 25 25E
83 Boyup Brook 33 47S 116 40E
102 Bozeman 45 40N 111 0W
74 Bozoum 6 25N 16 35E
36 Bra 44 41N 7 50E
16 Brabant □ 49 15N 5 20E
37 Brac, I. 43 20N 16 40E
37 Bracciano, L. di 42 6N 12 10E
90 Bracebridge 45 5N 79 20W
44 Bräcke 62 42N 15 32E
40 Brad 46 10N 22 50E
39 Brádano, R. 40 41N 16 20E
96 Braddock 40 24N 79 51W
99 Bradenton 27 25N 82 35W
12 Bradford, U.K. 53 47N 1 45W
96 Bradford, U.S.A. 41 58N 78 41W
91 Bradore Bay 51 27N 57 18W
101 Brady 31 8N 99 25W
14 Braemar 57 2N 3 20W
30 Braga 41 35N 8 32W
30 Braga □ 41 30N 8 30W
108 Bragado 35 2S 60 27W
111 Bragança 1 0S 47 2W
30 Bragança □ 41 30N 6 45W
109 Bragança Paulista 22 55S 46 52W
61 Brahmanbaria 23 50N 91 15E
61 Brahmani, R. 21 0N 85 15E
61 Brahmaputra, R. 26 30N 93 30E
12 Braich-y-Pwll, Pt. 52 47N 4 46W
41 Brăila 45 19N 27 59E
100 Brainerd 46 20N 94 10W
13 Braintree, U.K. 51 53N 0 34E
97 Braintree, U.S.A. 42 11N 71 0W
24 Brake 53 19N 8 30E
24 Brakel 51 43N 9 10E
92 Bralorne 50 50N 123 15W
90 Brampton, Canada 43 42N 79 46W
96 Brampton, U.S.A. 46 0N 97 46W
110 Branco, R. 1 30N 61 15W
45 Brande 55 47N 9 7E
24 Brandenburg 52 24N 12 33E
93 Brandon 49 50N 100 0W
26 Brandýs 50 10N 14 40E
28 Braniewo 54 25N 19 50E
96 Brantford 43 15N 80 15W
20 Brantôme 45 22N 0 39E
84 Branxholme 37 52S 141 49E
111 Brasília 15 55S 47 40W
111 Brasilia Legal 3 45S 55 40W

Braşov Bzenec

Map	Place	Lat.	Long.
41	Braşov	45 7N	25 39E
16	Brasschaat	51 19N	4 27E
27	Bratislava	48 10N	17 7E
51	Bratsk	56 10N	101 3E
97	Brattleboro	42 53N	72 37W
41	Braţul Chilia, R.	45 25N	29 20E
41	Braţul Sfîntu Gheorghe	45 0N	29 20E
41	Braţul Sulina, R.	45 10N	29 20E
26	Braunau	48 15N	13 3E
24	Braunschweig	52 17N	10 28E
13	Braunton	51 6N	4 9W
55	Brava	1 20N	44 8E
103	Brawley	32 58N	115 30W
15	Bray	53 12N	6 6W
19	Bray, Reg.	49 40N	1 40E
19	Bray-sur-Seine	48 25N	3 14E
107	Brazil ■	10 0S	50 0W
98	Brazil	39 30N	87 8W
106	Brazilian Highlands, Mts.	18 0S	46 30W
101	Brazol, R.	30 30N	96 20W
74	Brazzaville	4 9S	15 12E
40	Brčko	44 54N	18 46E
80	Breadalbane	23 48S	139 33E
14	Breadalbane, Reg.	56 30N	4 15W
85	Bream, B.	35 56S	174 35E
85	Bream Head	35 51S	174 36E
65	Brebes	6 52S	109 3E
14	Brechin	56 44N	2 40W
101	Breckenridge	32 48N	98 55W
13	Breckland, Reg.	52 30N	0 40E
27	Breclav	48 46N	16 53E
13	Brecon	51 57N	3 23W
13	Brecon Beacons, Mts.	51 53N	3 27W
16	Breda	51 35N	4 45E
75	Bredasdorp	34 33S	20 2E
84	Bredbo	35 38S	149 10E
26	Bregenz	47 30N	9 45E
46	Breidafjördur	65 20N	23 0W
21	Breil	43 56N	7 31E
111	Brejo	3 41S	42 50W
24	Bremen	53 4N	8 47E
24	Bremerhaven	53 34N	8 35E
102	Bremerton	47 30N	122 48W
31	Brenes	37 32N	5 54W
101	Brenham	30 5N	96 27W
26	Brenner P.	47 0N	11 30E
90	Brent, Canada	46 0N	78 30W
13	Brent, U.K.	51 33N	0 18W
13	Brentwood	51 37N	0 19W
36	Bréscia	45 33N	10 13E
28	Breslau=Wrocław	51 5N	17 5E
19	Bresles	49 25N	2 13E
37	Bressanone	46 43N	11 40E
14	Bressay, I.	60 10N	1 5W
21	Bresse, Plaine de	46 20N	5 10E
20	Bressuire	46 51N	0 30W
18	Brest, Fr.	48 24N	4 31W
48	Brest, U.S.S.R.	52 10N	23 40E
18	Bretagne, Reg.	48 0N	3 0W
41	Bretçu	46 7N	26 18E
19	Breteuil	49 38N	2 18E
20	Breton, Pertuis	46 16N	1 22W
85	Brett, C.	35 10S	174 20E
111	Breves	1 38S	50 25W
81	Brewarrina	30 0S	146 51E
99	Brewer	44 43N	68 50W
97	Brewster	41 23N	73 37W
99	Brewton	31 9N	87 2W
27	Brezno	48 50N	19 40E
74	Bria	6 30N	21 58E
21	Briançon	44 54N	6 39E
19	Briare	47 38N	2 45E
19	Bricon	48 5N	5 0E
18	Bricquebec	49 29N	1 39W
13	Bridgend	51 30N	3 35W
97	Bridgeport	41 12N	73 12W
98	Bridgeton	39 29N	75 10W
83	Bridgetown, Australia	33 58S	116 7E
105	Bridgetown, Barbados	13 0N	59 30W
91	Bridgetown, Canada	44 55N	65 12W
84	Bridgewater, Australia	36 36S	143 59E
91	Bridgewater, Canada	44 25N	64 31W
13	Bridgnorth	52 33N	2 25W
13	Bridgwater	51 7N	3 0W
12	Bridlington	54 4N	0 10W
13	Bridport	50 43N	2 45W
19	Brie, Plaine de la	48 35N	3 10E
19	Brie-Comte Robert	48 40N	2 35E
19	Brienon	48 0N	3 35E
25	Brienzersee, L.	46 44N	7 53E
25	Brig	46 18N	7 59E
12	Brigg	53 33N	0 30W
102	Brigham City	41 30N	112 1W
81	Brighton, Australia	35 1S	138 30E
90	Brighton, Canada	44 3N	77 44W
13	Brighton, U.K.	50 50N	0 9W
18	Brignogan-Plages	48 40N	4 20W
21	Brignoles	43 25N	6 5E
39	Bríndisi	40 39N	17 55E
20	Brioude	45 18N	3 23E
81	Brisbane	27 25S	152 54E
37	Brisighella	44 13N	11 46E
13	Bristol, U.K.	51 26N	2 35W
97	Bristol, Conn.	41 44N	72 37W
97	Bristol, Mass.	41 40N	71 15W
97	Bristol, Pa.	40 7N	74 52W
88	Bristol B.	58 0N	159 0W
13	Bristol Chan.	51 18N	3 30W
101	Bristow	35 5N	96 28W
5	British Antarctic Terr.	66 0S	45 0W
92	British Columbia □	55 0N	125 15W
11	British Is.	55 0N	4 0W
75	Britstown	30 37S	23 30E
90	Britt	45 46N	80 35W
100	Britton	45 50N	97 47W
20	Brive-la-Gaillarde	45 10N	1 32E
30	Briviesca	42 32N	3 19W
80	Brixton	23 32S	144 52E
27	Brno	49 10N	16 35E
60	Broach	21 47N	73 0E
83	Broad Arrow	30 23S	121 15E
14	Broad Law, Mt.	55 30N	3 22W
84	Broadford	37 14S	145 4E
12	Broads, The	52 30N	1 15E
93	Brock	51 27N	108 42W
96	Brockport	43 12N	77 56W
97	Brockton	42 8N	71 2W
90	Brockville	44 37N	75 38W
89	Brodeur Pen.	72 0N	88 0W
14	Brodick	55 34N	5 9W
28	Brodnica	53 15N	19 25E
100	Broken Bow	41 25N	99 35W
84	Broken Hill	31 58S	141 29E
13	Bromley	51 20N	0 5E
45	Bromölla	56 5N	14 25E
45	Brönderslev	57 17N	9 55E
39	Bronte	37 48N	14 49E
80	Bronte Pk.	42 8S	146 30E
100	Brookfield	39 50N	92 50W
101	Brookhaven	31 40N	90 25W
100	Brookings	44 19N	96 48W
88	Brooks Ra.	68 40N	147 0W
83	Brookton	32 22N	116 57E
14	Broom, L.	57 55N	5 15W
82	Broome	18 0S	122 15W
83	Broomehill	33 40S	117 36E
14	Brora	58 0N	3 50W
45	Brösarp	55 44N	14 8E
15	Brosna, R.	53 8N	8 0W
40	Broşteni	47 14N	25 43E
89	Broughton I.	67 35N	63 50W
14	Broughty Ferry	56 29N	2 50W
13	Brown Willy, Mt.	50 35N	4 34W
101	Brownfield	33 10N	102 15W
102	Browning	48 35N	113 10W
93	Brownlee	50 43N	105 59N
100	Brownsville	25 54N	97 30W
101	Brownwood	31 45N	99 0W
19	Bruay	50 29N	2 33E
82	Bruce, Mt.	22 31S	118 6E
90	Bruce Mines	46 20N	83 45W
96	Bruce Pen.	45 0N	81 15W
83	Bruce Rock	31 51S	118 2E
25	Bruchsal	49 9N	8 39E
26	Bruck	47 24N	15 16E
13	Brue, R.	51 10N	2 50W
25	Brugg	47 29N	8 11E
16	Brugge	51 13N	3 13E
92	Brule	53 15N	117 38W
111	Brumado	14 13S	41 40W
19	Brumath	48 43N	7 40E
67	Brunei ■	4 52N	115 0E
80	Brunette Downs	18 38S	135 57E
44	Brunflo	63 4N	14 50E
37	Brunico	46 48N	11 56E
44	Brunkeberg	59 25N	8 30E
85	Brunner	42 27S	171 20E
93	Bruno	52 20N	105 30W
24	Brunsbüttelkoog	53 52N	9 13E
16	Brunssum	50 57N	5 59E
24	Brunswick, W. Germany= Braunschweig	52 17N	10 28E
99	Brunswick, Ga.	31 10N	81 30W
99	Brunswick, Me.	43 53N	69 50W
96	Brunswick, Ohio	41 15N	81 50W
112	Brunswick, Pen.	53 30S	71 30W
83	Brunswick Junction	33 15S	115 50E
40	Brusartsi	43 40N	23 5E
109	Brusque	27 5S	49 0W
16	Brussel	50 51N	4 21E
84	Bruthen	37 43S	147 48E
16	Bruxelles= Brussel	50 51N	4 21E
19	Bruyères	48 10N	6 40E
28	Brwinow	52 9N	20 40E
98	Bryan, Ohio	41 30N	84 30W
101	Bryan, Tex.	30 40N	96 27W
48	Bryansk	53 13N	34 25E
47	Bryne	58 45N	5 36E
40	Brzava, R.	45 21N	20 45E
27	Brzeg	50 52N	17 30E
28	Brzeg Din	51 16N	16 41E
56	Bucak	37 28N	30 36E
110	Bucaramanga	7 0N	73 0W
14	Buchan, Reg.	57 32N	2 8W
14	Buchan Ness, Pt.	57 29N	1 48W
93	Buchanan, Canada	51 40N	102 45W
72	Buchanan, Liberia	5 57N	10 2W
91	Buchans	49 0N	57 2W
24	Buchholz	53 19N	9 51E
24	Bückeburg	52 16N	9 2E
103	Buckeye	33 28N	112 40W
98	Buckhannon	39 2N	80 10W
14	Buckie	57 40N	2 58W
13	Buckingham, U.K.	52 0N	0 59W
90	Buckingham, U.S.A.	45 37N	75 24W
62	Buckingham Canal	14 0N	80 5E
13	Buckinghamshire □	51 50N	0 55W
91	Buctouche	46 30N	64 45W
41	Bucureşti	44 27N	26 10E
98	Bucyrus	40 48N	83 0W
27	Budafok	47 26N	19 2E
59	Budalin	22 20N	95 10E
27	Budapest	47 29N	19 5E
60	Budaun	28 5N	79 10E
13	Bude	50 49N	4 33W
41	Budeşti	44 13N	26 30E
61	Budge Budge	22 30N	88 25E
37	Búdrio	44 31N	11 31E
40	Budva	42 17N	18 50E
110	Buenaventura	29 15S	69 40W
32	Buendia, Pantano de	40 25N	2 43W
108	Buenos Aires	34 30S	58 20W
112	Buenos Aires, L.	46 35S	72 30W
108	Buenos Aires □	34 30	58 20W
93	Buffalo, Canada	50 49N	110 42W
96	Buffalo, U.S.A.	42 55N	78 50W
93	Buffalo Narrows	55 52N	108 28W
28	Bug, R.	51 20N	23 40E
110	Buga	4 0N	77 0W
40	Bugojno	44 2N	17 25E
48	Bugulma	54 38N	52 40E
68	Bugun Shara, Mts.	48 30N	102 0E
48	Buturuslan	53 39N	52 26E
48	Bui	58 23N	41 27E
13	Builth Wells	52 10N	3 26W
30	Buitrago	41 0N	3 38W
31	Bujalance	37 54N	4 23W
40	Bujanovac	42 27N	21 46E
32	Bujaraloz	41 29N	0 10W
74	Bujumbura	3 16S	29 18E
51	Bukachacha	52 55N	116 50E
74	Bukavu	2 20S	28 52E
74	Bukene	4 15S	32 48E
50	Bukhara	39 50N	64 10E
63	Bukit Mertajam	5 22N	100 28E
64	Bukittinggi	0 20S	100 20E
62	Bukkapatnam	14 14N	77 46E
74	Bukoba	1 20S	31 49E
67	Bulak	45 2N	82 5E
60	Bulandshahr	28 28N	77 58E
75	Bulawayo	20 7S	28 32E
41	Bulgaria ■	42 35N	25 30E
55	Bulhar	10 25N	44 30E
83	Bullabulling	31 0S	120 55E
31	Bullaque, R.	39 20N	4 13W
82	Bullara	22 30S	114 2E
83	Bullaring	32 28S	117 40E
33	Bullas	38 2N	1 40W
80	Bullock Creek	17 40S	144 30E
85	Bulls	40 10S	175 24E
19	Bully-les-Mines	50 27N	2 44E
55	Bulo Burti	3 50N	45 33E
60	Bulsar	20 40N	72 58E
51	Bulun	70 37N	127 30E
74	Bumba	2 13N	22 30E
41	Bumbeşti Jiu	45 10N	23 22E
59	Bumhpa Bum, Mt.	26 40N	97 20E
83	Bunbury	33 20S	115 35E
15	Buncrana	55 8N	7 28W
81	Bundaberg	24 54S	152 22E
60	Bundi	25 30N	75 35E
80	Bundooma	24 54S	134 16E
12	Bure, R.	52 38N	1 38E
24	Burg	54 25N	11 10E
41	Burgas	42 33N	27 29E
41	Burgaski Zaliv, B.	42 30N	27 39E
25	Burgdorf, Switz.	47 3N	7 37E
24	Burgdorf, W. Germany	52 27N	10 0E
27	Burgenland □	47 20N	16 20E
91	Burgeo	47 36N	57 34W
75	Burgersdorp	31 0S	26 20E
30	Burgo de Osma	41 35N	3 4W
30	Burgos	42 21N	3 41W
30	Burgos □	42 21N	3 41W
24	Burgstädt	50 55N	12 49E
24	Burgsteinfurt	52 9N	7 23E
31	Burguillos del Cerro	38 23N	6 35W
60	Burhanpur	21 18N	76 20E
65	Burias, I.	13 5N	122 55E
105	Burica, Pta	8 3N	82 51W
54	Burin	32 11N	35 15E
63	Buriram	15 0N	103 0E
80	Burketown	17 45S	139 33E
90	Burks Falls	45 37N	79 10W
102	Burley	42 37N	113 55W
96	Burlington, Canada	43 25N	79 45W
100	Burlington, Colo.	39 21N	102 18W
100	Burlington, Iowa	40 50N	91 5W
100	Burlington, Kans.	38 15N	95 47W
99	Burlington, N.C.	36 7N	79 27W
97	Burlington, N.J.	40 5N	74 50W
102	Burlington, Wash.	48 29N	122 19W
50	Burlyu-Tyube	46 30N	79 10E
59	Burma ■	21 0N	96 30E
83	Burngup	33 0S	118 35E
80	Burnie	41 4S	145 56E
12	Burnley	53 47N	2 15W
102	Burns	43 40N	119 4W
92	Burns Lake	54 20N	125 45W
96	Burnt River	44 40N	78 42E
92	Burntwood, L.	55 35N	99 40W
54	Burqa	32 18N	35 11E
81	Burra	33 40S	138 55E
84	Burrendong Res.	32 45S	149 10E
32	Burriana	39 50N	0 4W
13	Burry Port	51 41N	4 17W
56	Bursa	40 15N	29 5E
12	Burton-on-Trent	52 48N	1 39W
65	Buru, I.	3 30S	126 30E
74	Burundi ■	3 15S	30 0E
64	Burung	0 21N	108 25E
72	Burutu	5 20N	5 29E
12	Bury	53 36N	2 19W
13	Bury St. Edmunds	52 15N	0 42E
51	Buryat A.S.S.R. □	53 0N	110 0E
44	Buskerud □	60 20N	9 0E
40	Busovača	44 6N	17 53E
19	Bussang	47 50N	6 50E
83	Busselton	33 42S	115 15E
16	Bussum	52 16N	5 10E
30	Busto, C.	43 34N	6 28W
36	Busto Arsizio	45 38N	8 50E
74	Busu-Djanoa	1 50N	21 5E
65	Busuanga, I.	12 10N	120 0E
24	Büsum	54 7N	8 50E
74	Buta	2 50N	24 53E
74	Butare	2 31S	29 52E
14	Bute, I.	55 48N	5 2W
74	Butembo	0 9N	29 18E
39	Butera	37 10N	14 10E
74	Butiaba	1 50N	31 20E
96	Butler	40 52N	79 52W
14	Butt of Lewis, Pt.	58 30N	6 20W
102	Butte, Mont.	46 0N	112 31W
100	Butte, Neb.	42 56N	98 54W
63	Butterworth	5 24N	100 23E
65	Butuan	8 52N	125 36E
65	Butung, I.	5 0S	122 45E
49	Buturlinovka	50 50N	40 35E
24	Butzbach	50 24N	8 40E
61	Buxar	25 34N	83 58E
12	Buxton	53 16N	1 54W
51	Buyaga	59 50N	127 0E
68	Buyr Nuur, L.	47 50N	117 35E
41	Buzău	45 10N	26 50E
41	Buzău, R.	45 10N	27 20E
66	Buzen	33 35N	131 5E
37	Buzet	45 24N	13 58E
48	Buzuluk	52 48N	52 12E
97	Buzzards Bay	41 45N	70 38W
41	Byala, Bulgaria	42 53N	27 55E
41	Byala, Bulgaria	43 28N	25 44E
41	Byala Slatina	43 26N	23 55E
28	Bydgoszcz	53 10N	18 0E
28	Bydgoszcz □	53 16N	18 0E
48	Byelorussian S.S.R. □	53 30N	27 0E
103	Bylas	33 11N	110 9W
45	Bylderup	54 58N	9 8E
89	Bylot I.	73 0N	78 0W
75	Byrd Ld.	79 30S	125 0W
5	Byrd Sub-Glacial Basin	82 0S	120 0W
81	Byrock	30 40S	146 27E
81	Byron Bay	28 30S	153 30E
46	Byske	64 59N	21 17E
51	Byrranga, Gory	75 0N	100 0E
27	Bystrzyca Kłodzka	50 19N	16 39E
27	Bytom	50 25N	19 0E
28	Bytów	54 10N	17 30E
27	Bzenec	48 58N	17 18E

C

Carmen de Patagones Chanyi

112 Carmen de Patagones 40 50S 63 0W
80 Carmila 21 53S 149 5E
31 Carmona 37 28N 5 42W
83 Carnarvon, Australia 24 51S 113 42E
75 Carnarvon, S. Africa 30 56S 22 8E
62 Carnatic, Reg. 12 0N 79 0E
31 Carnaxide 38 43N 9 14W
15 Carndonagh 55 15N 7 16W
96 Carnegie 40 24N 80 4W
83 Carnegie, L. 26 5S 122 30E
15 Carnsore Pt. 52 10N 6 20W
111 Carolina 7 10S 47 30W
77 Caroline I. 9 15S 150 3W
65 Caroline Is. 8 0N 150 0E
93 Caron 50 30N 105 50W
39 Carovigno 40 42N 17 40W
27 Carpathians, Mts. . 46 20N 26 0E
41 Carpatii Meridionali, Mts. 45 30N 25 0E
80 Carpentaria, G. of . 14 0S 139 0E
80 Carpentaria Downs 18 44S 144 20E
21 Carpentras 44 3N 5 2E
36 Carpi 44 47N 10 52E
30 Carpio 41 13N 5 7W
36 Carrara 44 5N 10 7E
32 Carrascosa del Campo 40 2N 2 45W
15 Carrick-on-Shannon 53 57N 8 7W
15 Carrick-on-Suir ... 52 22N 7 30W
15 Carrickfergus 54 43N 5 50W
15 Carrickfergus □ ... 54 43N 5 50W
15 Carrickmacross 54 0N 6 43W
81 Carrieton 32 27S 138 27E
30 Carrión, R. 41 53N 4 32W
103 Carrizozo 33 40N 105 57W
100 Carroll 42 2N 94 55W
99 Carrollton 33 36N 85 5W
93 Carrot River 53 50N 101 17W
102 Carson City 39 12N 119 52W
102 Carson Sink 39 50N 118 40W
14 Carstairs 55 42N 3 41W
110 Cartagena, Col. ... 10 25N 75 33W
33 Cartagena, Sp. 37 38N 0 59W
110 Cartago, Col. 4 45N 75 55W
105 Cartago, Costa Rica 9 50N 84 0W
31 Cartaxo 39 10N 8 47W
31 Cartaya 37 16N 7 9W
18 Carteret 49 23N 1 47W
99 Cartersville 34 11N 84 48W
85 Carterton 41 2S 175 31E
101 Carthage, Mo. 37 10N 94 20W
97 Carthage, N.Y. 43 59N 75 37W
91 Cartwright 53 41N 56 58W
111 Caruaru 8 15S 35 55W
110 Carúpano 10 45N 63 15W
101 Caruthersville 36 10N 89 40W
19 Carvin 50 30N 2 57E
31 Carvoeira, C. 39 21N 9 24W
109 Casa Branca, Chile 33 20S 71 25W
31 Casa Branca, Port. 38 29N 8 12W
103 Casa Grande 32 53N 111 51W
111 Casa Nova 9 10S 41 5W
72 Casablanca 33 43N 7 24W
36 Casale Monferrato 45 8N 8 28E
36 Casalmaggiore 44 59N 10 25E
36 Casalpusterlengo .. 45 10N 9 40E
39 Casamássima 40 58N 16 55E
39 Casarano 40 0N 18 10E
104 Casas Grandes 30 22N 108 0W
30 Casatejada 39 54N 5 40W
102 Cascade Ra. 44 0N 122 10W
31 Cascais 38 41N 9 25W
36 Cáscina 43 40N 10 32E
39 Caserta 41 5N 14 20E
15 Cashel 52 31N 7 53W
108 Casilda 33 10S 61 10W
81 Casino 28 52S 153 3E
110 Casiquiare, R. 2 1N 67 7W
26 Cáslav 49 54N 15 22E
32 Caspe 41 14N 0 1W
112 Casper 42 52N 106 27W
9 Caspian Sea 43 0N 50 0E
32 Cassá de la Selva .. 41 53N 2 52E
39 Cassano Iónio 39 47N 16 20E
92 Cassiar Mts. 39 30N 130 30W
75 Cassinga 15 5S 16 23E
38 Cassino 41 30N 13 50E
21 Cassis 43 14N 5 32E
36 Castéggio 45 1N 9 8E
36 Castel San Giovanni 43 4N 9 25E
37 Castel San Pietro .. 44 23N 11 30E
39 Castelbuono 37 56N 14 4E
36 Castelfranco Emilia 44 37N 11 2E
37 Castelfranco Véneto 45 40N 11 56E
38 Castellammare, G. di 35 5N 12 55E
38 Castellammare del Golfo 38 2N 12 53E
39 Castellammare di Stábia 40 47N 14 29E
39 Castellana Grotte . 40 53N 17 10E
21 Castellane 43 50N 6 31E
39 Castellaneta 40 40N 16 57E
32 Castello de Ampurias 42 15N 3 4E
32 Castellón □ 40 15N 0 5W
32 Castellón de la Plana 39 58N 0 3W
32 Castellote 40 48N 0 15W
109 Castelo 20 36S 41 12W
30 Castelo Branco 39 50N 7 31W
30 Castelo Branco □ . 39 52N 7 54W
20 Castelnaudary 43 20N 1 58E
20 Castelsarrasin 44 2N 1 3E
32 Castelltersol 41 45N 2 8E
38 Casteltérmini 37 32N 13 38E
38 Castelvetrano 37 40N 12 46E
84 Casterton 37 30S 141 30E
20 Castets 43 52N 1 6W
37 Castiglione del Lago 43 7N 12 3E
36 Castiglione della Pescáia 42 46N 10 53E
37 Castiglione Fiorentina 43 20N 11 55E
31 Castilblanco 39 17N 5 5W
31 Castilla la Nueva, Reg. 39 45N 3 20W
31 Castilla, Playa de .. 37 0N 6 33W
30 Castilla la Vieja, Reg. 41 55N 4 0W
14 Castle Douglas 54 57N 3 57W
105 Castle Harbour ... 32 17N 64 44W
102 Castle Rock 46 20N 122 58W
15 Castlebar 53 52N 9 17W
15 Castleblayney 54 7N 6 44W
12 Castleford 53 43N 1 21W
92 Castlegar 49 20N 117 40W
84 Castlemaine 37 2S 144 12E
15 Castlereagh 53 47N 8 30W
15 Castlereagh □ 53 47N 8 30W
12 Castletown 54 4N 4 40W
15 Castletown Bearhaven 51 40N 9 54W
80 Castlevale 24 30S 146 48E
92 Castor 52 15N 111 50W
20 Castres 43 37N 2 13E
105 Castries 14 0N 60 50W
109 Castro, Brazil 24 45S 50 0W
112 Castro, Chile 42 30S 73 50W
111 Castro Alves 12 46S 39 33W
31 Castro del Rio 37 41N 4 29W
30 Castro Urdiales ... 43 23N 3 19W
31 Castro Verde 37 41N 8 4W
30 Castropol 43 32N 7 0W
39 Castrovillari 39 49N 16 11E
31 Castuera 38 43N 5 37W
105 Cat I. 24 30N 75 30W
109 Cataguases 21 23S 42 39W
111 Catalão 18 5S 47 52W
32 Cataluña, Reg. 41 40N 1 15E
108 Catamarca 28 30S 65 50W
108 Catamarca □ 28 30S 65 50W
109 Catanduva 21 5S 48 58W
39 Catánia 37 31N 15 4E
39 Catanzaro 38 54N 16 38E
65 Catarman 12 28N 124 1E
20 Catine, Reg. 46 30N 0 15W
79 Cato, I. 23 15S 155 32E
104 Catoche, C. 21 40N 87 0W
33 Catral 38 10N 0 47W
110 Catrimani 0 27N 61 41W
97 Catskill 42 14N 73 52W
97 Catskill Mts. 42 15N 74 15W
96 Cattaraugus 42 22N 78 52W
37 Cattólica 43 58N 12 43E
38 Cattólica Eraclea .. 37 27N 13 24E
49 Caucasus Mts.= Bolshoi Kavkaz . 42 50N 44 0E
111 Caucia 3 40S 38 55W
18 Caudebec 49 30N 0 42E
33 Caudete 38 42N 1 2W
19 Caudry 50 7N 3 22E
18 Caulnes 48 18N 2 10W
39 Caulónia 38 23N 16 25E
108 Cauquenes 36 0S 72 30W
91 Causapscal 48 19N 67 12W
62 Cauvery, R. 11 10N 79 51E
39 Cava dei Tirreni 40 42N 14 42E
30 Cávado, R. 41 32N 8 48W
21 Cavaillon 43 50N 5 2E
21 Cavalaire 43 10N 6 33E
15 Cavan □ 53 58N 7 10W
15 Cavan 54 0N 7 22W
84 Cavendish 37 31S 142 2E
111 Caviana, I. 0 15N 50 0W
65 Cavite 14 20N 120 55E
40 Cavtat 42 35N 18 13E
111 Caxias 5 0S 43 27W
109 Caxias do Sul 29 10S 51 10W
74 Caxito 8 30S 13 30E
110 Cayambe 0 3N 78 22W
111 Cayenne 5 0N 52 18W
19 Cayeux-sur-Mer ... 50 10N 1 30E
105 Cayman Is. 19 40N 79 50W
104 Cayo 17 10N 89 0W
97 Cayuga L. 42 45N 76 45W
33 Cazorla, Sa. de 38 5N 2 55W
41 Căzăneşti 44 36N 27 3E
20 Cazaux, Étang de . 44 30N 1 10E
20 Cazères 43 13N 1 5E
37 Čazma 45 45N 16 39E
75 Cazombo 12 0S 22 48E
33 Cazorla 37 55N 3 2W
30 Cea, R. 42 0N 5 36W
15 Ceanannas Mor ... 53 42N 6 53W
111 Ceara □ 5 0S 40 0W
111 Ceará=Fortaleza .. 3 35S 38 35W
30 Cebollera, Sa. de .. 42 0N 2 30W
30 Cebreros 40 27N 4 28W
65 Cebu 10 30N 124 0E
65 Cebu, I. 10 23N 123 58E
38 Ceccano 41 34N 13 18E
36 Cécina 43 19N 10 33E
30 Ceclavin 39 50N 6 45W
103 Cedar City 37 41N 113 3W
101 Cedar Creek Res. . 32 15N 96 0W
100 Cedar Falls 42 39N 92 29W
93 Cedar L. 53 30N 100 30W
100 Cedar Rapids 42 0N 91 38W
99 Cedartown 34 1N 85 15W
92 Cedarvale 55 1N 128 22W
102 Cedarville 41 37N 120 13W
30 Cedeira 43 39N 8 2W
111 Cedro 6 34S 39 3W
104 Cedros, I. de 28 10N 115 20W
81 Ceduna 32 7S 133 46E
39 Cefalù 38 3N 14 1E
30 Cega, R. 41 33N 4 46W
27 Cegléd 47 11N 19 47E
39 Céglie Messápico .. 40 39N 17 31E
104 Celaya 20 31N 100 37W
15 Celbridge 53 20N 6 33W
65 Celebes, I.= Sulawesi, I. 2 0S 120 0E
65 Celebes Sea 3 0N 123 0E
37 Celje 46 16N 15 18E
24 Celle 52 37N 10 4E
30 Celorico da Beira . 40 38N 7 24W
20 Cenon 44 50N 0 33W
109 Centenario do Sul . 22 48S 51 37W
96 Centerville 40 3N 79 59W
100 Centerville 31 15N 95 56W
37 Cento 44 43N 11 16E
103 Central 32 46N 108 9W
14 Central □ 56 12N 4 25W
20 Central, Massif 45 0N 3 10E
74 Central Africa ■ .. 7 0N 20 0E
97 Central Islip 40 49N 73 13W
58 Central Makan Ra. 26 30N 64 15E
100 Centralia, Ill. 38 32N 89 5W
102 Centralia, Wash. .. 46 46N 122 59W
39 Centúripe 37 37N 14 41E
40 Čepin 45 32N 18 34E
38 Ceprano 41 33N 13 30E
41 Ceptura 45 1N 26 21E
65 Ceram, I.= Seram, I. 3 10S 129 0E
20 Cerbère 42 26N 3 10E
41 Cerbu 44 46N 24 46E
31 Cercal 37 48N 08 40W
32 Cerdaña 42 22N 1 35E
20 Cère, R. 44 55N 1 53E
108 Ceres, Arg. 29 55S 61 55W
75 Ceres, S. Africa ... 33 21S 19 18E
20 Céret 42 30N 2 42E
39 Cerignola 41 17N 15 53E
56 Çerkeş 40 40N 32 58E
37 Cerknico 45 48N 14 21E
41 Cernavodă 44 22N 28 3E
19 Cernay 47 48N 7 10E
104 Cerralvo, I. 24 20N 109 45E
104 Cerritos 22 20N 100 20W
32 Cervera 41 40N 1 16E
30 Cervera de Pisuerga 42 51N 4 30W
37 Cérvia 44 15N 12 20E
39 Cervinara 41 2N 14 36E
21 Cervione 42 20N 9 29E
30 Cervo 43 40N 7 24W
37 Cesena 44 9N 12 14E
37 Cesenático 44 12N 12 22E
26 Česká Lípa 50 43N 14 35E
26 Česká Socialistická □ .. 49 30N 15 0E
27 Česká Třebová 49 54N 16 27E
26 České Budějovice . 48 55N 14 25E
26 České Velenice ... 48 45N 15 1E
26 Český Brod 50 4N 14 52E
26 Český Krumlov ... 48 43N 14 21E
27 Český Těšín 49 45N 18 39E
84 Cessnock 33 0S 151 15E
37 Cetina, R. 43 26N 16 42E
40 Cetinje 42 23N 18 59E
72 Ceuta 35 52N 5 26W
20 Cevennes, Mts. 44 10N 3 50E
56 Ceyhan 37 4N 35 47E
62 Ceylon= Sri Lanka ■ 7 30N 80 50E
21 Chablais, Reg. 46 20N 6 45E
19 Chablis 47 47N 3 48E
108 Chacabuco 34 40S 60 27W
63 Chachoengsao 13 45N 101 12E
108 Chaco □ 25 0S 61 0W
73 Chad ■ 12 30N 17 15E
73 Chad, L. 13 30N 14 30W
100 Chadron 42 50N 103 0W
57 Chagai Hills 29 30N 63 0E
21 Chagny 46 57N 4 45E
3 Chagos Arch. 6 0S 72 0E
57 Chāh Bahār 25 20N 60 40E
61 Chaibasa 22 33N 85 49E
60 Chaj Doab, Reg. .. 32 0N 73 0E
108 Chajari 30 42N 58 0W
57 Chakhansur 31 10N 62 0E
57 Chakhansur □ 30 25N 62 0E
60 Chaklashi 22 40N 72 52E
61 Chakradharpur 22 45N 85 40E
60 Chakwal 32 50N 72 45E
20 Chalais 45 16N 0 3E
62 Chalakudi 10 18N 76 20E
19 Chalindrey 47 48N 5 26E
69 Chaling 26 55N 113 30E
60 Chalisgaon 20 30N 75 10E
20 Challans 46 50N 2 0W
110 Challapata 19 0S 66 50W
19 Challerange 49 18N 4 46E
21 Chalon-sur-Saône . 46 48N 4 50E
19 Châlons-sur-Marne 48 58N 4 20E
30 Chamartín de la Rosa 40 28N 3 40W
60 Chamba 32 35N 76 10E
60 Chambal, R. 26 30N 79 15E
98 Chambersburg 39 53N 77 41W
21 Chambéry 45 34N 5 55E
75 Chambeshi 10 58S 31 5E
97 Chambly 45 27N 73 17W
91 Chambord 48 25N 72 6W
67 Chamdo 31 21N 97 2E
21 Chamonix 45 55N 6 51E
61 Champa 22 2N 82 43E
19 Champagne, Reg. . 49 0N 4 40E
19 Champagne, Plaine de 49 0N 4 0E
21 Champagnole 46 45N 5 55E
100 Champaign 40 8N 88 14W
19 Champaubert 48 50N 3 45E
97 Champlain 46 27N 72 24W
97 Champlain, L. 44 30N 73 20W
104 Champotón 19 20N 90 50W
108 Chañaral 26 15S 70 50W
60 Chanasma 23 44N 72 5E
61 Chanda 19 57N 79 25E
88 Chandalar 67 30N 148 30W
60 Chandausi 28 27N 78 49E
101 Chandeleur Sd. ... 29 58N 88 40W
61 Chandernagore 22 52N 88 24E
91 Chandler, Canada . 48 18N 64 46W
103 Chandler, U.S.A. .. 33 20N 111 56W
61 Chandpur, India. .. 23 8N 90 42E
60 Chandpur, Pak. ... 29 8N 78 19E
62 Changanacheri 9 25N 76 31E
68 Changchih 36 7N 113 0E
69 Changchow, Fukien 24 32N 117 44E
69 Changchow, Kiangsu 31 45N 120 0E
68 Changchow, Shantung 36 55N 118 3E
68 Changchun 43 58N 125 9E
69 Changhua 24 2N 120 30E
68 Changkiakow 40 52N 114 45E
69 Changkiang 21 7N 110 21E
68 Changli 39 40N 119 19E
68 Changpai 41 26N 128 0E
68 Changpai Shan, Mts. 42 0N 128 0E
69 Changping, Fukien 25 30N 117 33E
68 Changping, Peiping 40 15N 116 15E
69 Changpu 24 2N 117 31E
69 Changsha 28 5N 113 1E
69 Changshu 31 33N 120 45E
69 Changtai 24 34N 117 50E
69 Changteh 29 12N 111 43E
69 Changting 25 46N 116 30E
68 Changwu 42 21N 122 45E
67 Changyeh 39 0N 100 59E
62 Channaptna 12 40N 77 15E
13 Channel Is. 49 30N 2 40W
63 Chanthaburi 12 38N 102 12E
19 Chantilly 49 12N 2 38E
20 Chantonnay 46 40N 1 3W
101 Chanute 37 45N 95 25W
67 Chanyi 25 56N 104 1E

Chao Phraya, R. Circle

63 Chao Phraya, R. 13 32N 100 36 E
69 Chaoan 23 45N 117 11 E
69 Chaochow 23 45N 116 32 E
69 Chaohwa 32 16N 105 41 E
67 Chaotung 27 30N 103 40 E
68 Chaoyang 41 46N 120 16 E
104 Chapata, L. 20 10N 103 20w
50 Chapayevo 50 25N 51 10 E
48 Chapayevsk 53 0N 49 40 E
109 Chapecó 27 14s 52 41w
99 Chapel Hill 35 53N 79 3w
90 Chapleau 47 45N 83 30w
61 Chapra 25 48N 84 50 E
110 Charagua 19 45s 63 10w
110 Charambira, Pta. 4 20N 77 30w
110 Charaña 17 30s 69 35w
108 Charata 27 13s 61 14w
67 Charchan 38 4N 85 16 E
67 Charchan, R. 39 0N 86 0 E
13 Chard, U.K. 50 52N 2 59w
93 Chard, U.S.A. 55 55N 111 10w
50 Chardara 41 16N 67 59 E
50 Chardzhou 39 0N 63 20 E
20 Charente □ 45 50N 0 36w
20 Charente, R. 45 57N 1 5w
20 Charente-Maritime □ 45 50N 0 35w
73 Chari, R. 12 58N 14 31 E
57 Charikar 35 0N 69 10 E
67 Charkhlikh 39 16N 88 17 E
16 Charleroi 50 24N 4 27 E
98 Charles, C. 37 10N 75 52w
100 Charles City 43 2N 92 41w
101 Charleston, Mass. 34 2N 90 3w
99 Charleston, S.C. 32 47N 79 56w
98 Charleston, W. Va. 38 24N 81 36w
105 Charlestown, Nevis 17 8N 62 37w
97 Charlestown, U.S.A. 38 29N 85 40w
81 Charleville, Australia 26 24s 146 15 E
15 Charleville, Eire=Rath Luire 52 21N 8 40w
19 Charleville-Mézières 49 44N 4 40 E
99 Charlotte 35 16N 80 46w
105 Charlotte Amalie 18 22N 64 56w
98 Charlottesville 38 1N 78 30w
91 Charlottetown 46 19N 63 3w
84 Charlton 36 16s 143 24 E
100 Charlton 40 59N 93 20w
90 Charlton I. 52 0N 79 20w
91 Charny 46 43N 71 15w
21 Charolles 46 27N 4 16 E
20 Charroux 46 9N 0 25 E
80 Charters Towers 20 5s 146 13 E
18 Chartres 48 29N 1 30 E
108 Chascomús 35 30s 58 0w
41 Chatal Balkan=Udvoy, Mts. 42 50N 26 50 E
88 Chatanika 65 7N 147 31w
20 Château Chinon 47 4N 3 56 E
18 Château-du-Loir 47 40N 0 25 E
18 Château Gontier 47 50N 0 42w
19 Château Porcien 49 31N 4 13 E
18 Château Renault 47 36N 0 56 E
19 Château Thierry 49 3N 3 20 E
18 Château-la-Vallière 47 30N 0 20 E
18 Châteaubourg 48 7N 1 25w
18 Châteaubriant 47 43N 1 23w
18 Châteaudun 48 3N 1 20 E
18 Châteaulin 48 11N 4 8w
20 Châteaumeillant 46 35N 2 12 E
20 Châteauneuf-sur-Charente 45 36N 0 3w
19 Châteauneuf-sur-Loire 47 52N 2 13 E
20 Châteauroux 46 50N 1 40 E
20 Châtelaillon Plage 46 5N 1 5w
20 Châtelguyon 45 55N 3 4 E
20 Châtellerault 46 50N 0 30 E
13 Chatham, U.K. 51 22N 0 32 E
91 Chatham, N.B. 47 2N 65 28w
96 Chatham, Ont. 42 23N 82 15w
98 Chatham, Alas. 57 30N 135 0w
97 Chatham, N.Y. 42 21N 73 32w
76 Chatham Is. 44 0s 176 40w
92 Chatham Str. 57 0N 134 40w
20 Châtillon-en-Bazois 47 3N 3 39 E
21 Châtillon-en-Diois 44 41N 5 29 E
20 Châtillon-sur-Indre 46 48N 1 10 E
19 Châtillon-sur-Seine 47 50N 4 33 E
20 Châtillon-sur-Sèvre 46 56N 0 45w
99 Chattahoochee 30 43N 84 51w
99 Chattanooga 35 2N 85 17w
19 Chaulnes 49 48N 2 47 E
19 Chaumont 48 7N 5 8 E
19 Chauny 49 37N 3 12 E
21 Chaussin 46 59N 5 22 E
20 Chauvigny 46 34N 0 39 E
111 Chaves, Brazil 0 15s 49 55w
30 Chaves, Port. 41 45N 7 32w
26 Cheb 50 9N 12 20 E
48 Cheboksary 56 8N 47 30 E
98 Cheboygan 45 38N 84 29w
68 Chefoo=Yentai 37 30N 121 21 E
51 Chegdomyn 51 7N 132 52 E
102 Chehallis 46 44N 122 59w
69 Cheju 33 28N 126 30 E
69 Cheju Do, I. 33 29N 126 34 E
69 Chekiang □ 29 30N 120 0 E
112 Chelforó 39 0s 66 40w
50 Chelkar 47 40N 59 32 E
50 Chelkar Tengiz Solonchak 48 0N 62 30 E
19 Chelles 48 52N 2 33 E
28 Chełm 51 8N 23 30 E
28 Chełm □ 51 20N 23 20 E
28 Chełmno 53 20N 18 30 E
13 Chelmsford 51 44N 0 29 E
28 Chełmno 53 20N 18 30 E
84 Chelsea 38 5s 145 8 E
13 Cheltenham 51 55N 2 5w
50 Chelyabinsk 55 10N 61 35 E
92 Chemainus 48 54N 123 41w
75 Chemba 17 11s 34 53 E
48 Chemikovsk 54 58N 56 0w
18 Chemillé 47 14N 0 45w
63 Chemor 4 44N 101 6 E
102 Chemult 43 14N 121 54w
60 Chenab, R. 29 23N 71 2 E
69 Chengchow 34 47N 113 46 E
67 Chengkiang 24 58N 102 59 E
68 Chengteh 41 0N 117 55 E
68 Chengting 38 8N 114 37 E
67 Chengtu 30 45N 104 0 E
68 Chengyang 36 20N 120 16 E
69 Chenhsien 25 45N 112 37 E
69 Chenning 25 57N 105 51 E
68 Chentung 46 2N 123 1 E
69 Chenyuan 27 0N 108 20 E
41 Chepelare 41 44N 24 40 E
105 Chepo 9 10N 79 6w
13 Chepstow 51 39N 2 41w
100 Chequamegon B. 46 40N 90 30w
19 Cher □ 47 10N 2 30 E
18 Cherbourg 49 39N 1 40w
72 Cherchell 36 35N 21 63 E
48 Cherdyn 60 20N 56 20 E
51 Cheremkhovo 53 32N 102 40 E
50 Cherepanovo 54 15N 83 30 E
49 Cherkassy 49 30N 32 0 E
41 Cherni, Mt. 42 35N 23 28 E
48 Chernigov 51 28N 31 20 E
49 Chernovtsy 48 0N 26 0 E
51 Chernoye 70 30N 89 10 E
100 Cherokee 42 40N 95 30w
48 Cheropovets 59 5N 37 55 E
112 Cherquenco 38 35s 72 0w
51 Cherskogo Khrebet 65 0N 143 0 E
41 Cherven-Bryag 43 17N 24 7 E
13 Cherwell, R. 51 44N 1 15w
98 Chesapeake B. 38 0N 76 12w
12 Cheshire □ 53 14N 2 30w
33 Cheste 39 30N 0 41w
12 Chester, U.K. 53 12N 2 53w
98 Chester, Pa. 39 54N 75 20w
99 Chester, S.C. 34 44N 81 13w
12 Chesterfield 53 14N 1 26w
88 Chesterfield Inlet 63 30N 91 0w
76 Chesterfield Is. 19 52s 158 15 E
104 Chetumal 18 30N 88 20w
104 Chetumal, B. de 18 40N 88 10w
20 Chevanceaux 45 18N 0 14w
12 Cheviot, The, Mt. 55 28N 2 8w
12 Cheviot Hills 55 20N 2 30w
74 Chew Bahir, L. 4 40N 30 50 E
102 Chewelah 48 25N 117 56w
100 Cheyenne 41 9N 104 49w
100 Cheyenne, R. 44 40N 101 15w
60 Chhindwara 22 2N 78 59 E
63 Chi, R. 15 13N 104 45 E
69 Chiai 23 29N 120 25 E
75 Chianje 15 35s 13 40 E
104 Chiapas □ 17 0N 92 45w
39 Chiaramonte Gulfi 37 1N 14 41 E
36 Chiari 45 31N 9 55 E
36 Chiávari 44 20N 9 20 E
36 Chiavenna 46 18N 9 23 E
66 Chiba 35 30N 140 7 E
66 Chiba □ 35 30N 140 20 E
75 Chibemba 15 48s 14 8 E
90 Chibougamau 49 56N 74 24w
98 Chicago 41 45N 87 40w
98 Chicago Heights 41 29N 87 37w
92 Chichagof I. 58 0N 136 0w
13 Chichester 50 50N 0 47w
104 Chichén Itzá 20 40N 88 34w
66 Chichibu 36 5N 139 10 E
68 Chichirin 50 35N 123 45 E
101 Chickasha 35 0N 98 0w
31 Chiclana de la Frontera 36 26N 6 9w
110 Chiclayo 6 42s 79 50w
102 Chico 39 45N 121 54w
112 Chico, R. 43 50s 66 25w
97 Chicopee 42 6N 72 37w
91 Chicoutimi 48 28N 71 5w
62 Chidambaram 11 20N 79 45 E
89 Chidley, C. 60 30N 64 15w
25 Chiemsee, L. 47 53N 12 27 E
74 Chiengi 8 38s 29 10 E
63 Chiengmai 18 55N 98 55 E
37 Chienti, R. 43 18N 13 45 E
36 Chieri 45 0N 7 50 E
19 Chiers, R. 49 39N 5 0 E
37 Chieti 42 22N 14 10 E
68 Chihfeng 42 10N 118 56 E
69 Chihing 25 2N 113 45 E
69 Chihkiang 27 21N 109 45 E
68 Chihli, G. of=Po Hai, G. 38 30N 119 0 E
69 Chihsien 35 29N 114 1 E
104 Chihuahua 28 40N 106 3w
104 Chihuahua □ 28 40N 106 3w
50 Chiilí 44 10N 66 55 E
62 Chik Ballapur 13 25N 77 45 E
62 Chikmagalur 13 15N 75 45 E
62 Chikodi 16 26N 74 38 E
58 Chilas 35 25N 74 5 E
81 Childers 25 15s 152 17 E
101 Childress 34 30N 100 50w
107 Chile ■ 35 0s 71 15w
110 Chilete 7 10s 78 50w
75 Chililabombwe 12 18s 27 43 E
61 Chilka L. 19 40N 85 25 E
108 Chillán 36 40s 72 10w
100 Chillicothe, Mo. 39 45N 93 30w
98 Chillicothe, Ohio. 39 53N 82 58w
92 Chilliwack 49 10N 122 0w
112 Chiloé, I. de 42 50s 73 45w
104 Chilpancingo 17 30N 99 40w
84 Chiltern 36 10s 146 36 E
13 Chiltern Hills 51 44N 0 42w
69 Chilung 25 3N 121 45 E
75 Chilwa, L. 15 15s 35 40 E
67 Chimai 34 0N 101 39 E
110 Chimborazo, Mt. 1 20s 78 55w
110 Chimbote 9 0s 78 35w
50 Chimkent 42 40N 69 25 E
59 Chin □ 22 0N 93 0 E
67 China ■ 35 0N 100 0 E
105 Chinandega 12 30N 87 0w
110 Chincha Alta 13 20s 76 0w
81 Chinchilla 26 45s 150 38 E
33 Chinchilla de Monte Aragón 38 53N 1 40w
68 Chinchow 41 10N 121 2 E
75 Chinde 18 45s 36 30 E
59 Chindwin, R. 21 26N 95 15 E
69 Ching Ho, R. 34 20N 109 0 E
62 Chingleput 12 42N 79 58 E
75 Chingola 12 31s 27 53 E
75 Chingole 13 4s 34 17 E
68 Chinhae 35 9N 128 58 E
60 Chiniot 31 45N 73 0 E
68 Chinju 35 12N 128 2 E
69 Chinkiang 32 2N 119 29 E
103 Chino Valley 34 54N 112 28w
18 Chinon 47 10N 0 15 E
93 Chinook, Canada 51 28N 110 59w
102 Chinook, U.S.A. 48 35N 109 19w
61 Chinsura 22 53N 88 27 E
62 Chintamani 13 26N 78 3 E
68 Chinwangtao 40 0N 119 31 E
37 Chióggia 45 13N 12 15 E
92 Chip Lake 53 35N 115 35w
75 Chipata 13 38s 32 28 E
31 Chipiona 36 44N 6 26w
62 Chiplun 17 31N 73 34 E
96 Chippawa 43 5N 79 10w
13 Chippenham 51 27N 2 7w
100 Chippewa, R. 44 25N 92 10w
100 Chippewa Falls 44 56N 91 24w
104 Chiquimula 14 51N 89 37w
110 Chiquinquira 5 37N 73 50w
62 Chirala 15 50N 80 20 E
60 Chirawa 28 14N 75 42 E
62 Chirayinkil 8 41N 76 49 E
50 Chirchik 81 58N 69 15 E
88 Chirikof I. 55 50N 155 35w
105 Chiriquí, G. de 8 0N 82 10w
105 Chiriquí, L. de 9 10N 82 0w
105 Chiriqui, Mt. 8 55N 82 35w
75 Chiromo 16 30s 35 7 E
41 Chirpan 42 10N 25 19 E
75 Chisamba 14 55s 28 20 E
60 Christian Mandi 29 50N 72 55 E
51 Chita 52 0N 113 25 E
62 Chitapur 17 10N 76 50 E
75 Chitembo 13 30s 16 50 E
60 Chitorgarh 24 52N 74 43 E
62 Chitradurga 14 15N 76 28 E
105 Chitré 7 59N 80 27w
59 Chittagong 22 19N 91 55 E
61 Chittagong □ 24 5N 91 25 E
62 Chittoor 13 15N 79 5 E
62 Chittur 10 40N 76 45 E
33 Chiva 39 27N 0 41w
36 Chivasso 45 10N 7 52 E
108 Chivilcoy 35 0s 60 0w
26 Chlumec 50 9N 15 29 E
28 Chodziez 52 58N 17 0 E
62 Chodavaram 17 40N 82 50 E
112 Choele Choel 39 11s 65 40w
19 Choisy 48 45N 2 24 E
28 Choinice 53 42N 17 40 E
20 Cholet 47 4N 0 52w
105 Choluteca 13 20N 87 14w
75 Choma 16 48s 26 59 E
60 Chomu 27 15N 75 40 E
26 Chomutov 50 28N 13 23 E
63 Chon Buri 13 21N 101 1 E
68 Chonan 36 56N 127 3 E
110 Chone 0 40s 80 0w
68 Chongjin 41 51N 129 58 E
68 Chŏngju, N. Korea 39 41N 125 13 E
68 Chŏngju, S. Korea 36 39N 127 27 E
68 Chŏnju 35 50N 127 4 E
112 Chonos, Arch. de los 45 0s 75 0w
60 Chopda 21 20N 75 15 E
12 Chorley 53 39N 2 39w
27 Chorzow 50 18N 19 0 E
66 Chóshi 35 45N 140 45 E
28 Choszczno 53 7N 15 25 E
102 Choteau 47 50N 112 10w
68 Choybalsan 48 3N 114 28 E
85 Christchurch, N.Z. 43 33s 172 47w
13 Christchurch, U.K. 50 44N 1 47w
75 Christiana 27 52s 25 8 E
82 Christmas Creek 18 29s 125 23 E
77 Christmas I. 1 58N 157 27w
26 Chrudim 49 58N 15 43 E
27 Chrzanów 50 10N 19 21 E
50 Chu 43 36N 73 42 E
69 Chu Kiang, R. 24 50N 113 37 E
69 Chuanchow 24 57N 118 31 E
69 Chuanhsien 25 50N 111 12 E
66 Chūbu □ 36 45N 137 0 E
112 Chubut, R. 43 20s 65 5w
68 Chucheng 36 0N 119 16 E
69 Chuchow 27 56N 113 3 E
48 Chudskoye, Oz. 58 13N 27 30 E
88 Chugiak 61 25N 149 30w
66 Chūgoku □ 35 0N 133 0 E
66 Chūgoku-Sanchi, Mts. 35 0N 133 0 E
69 Chuhsien 30 51N 107 1 E
63 Chukai 4 13N 103 25 E
51 Chukotskiy Khrebet 68 0N 175 0 E
51 Chukotskoye More 68 0N 175 0w
103 Chula Vista 33 44N 117 8w
69 Chumatien 33 0N 114 4 E
51 Chumikan 54 40N 135 10 E
63 Chumphon 10 35N 99 14 E
68 Chuncho E9n 37 58N 127 44 E
69 Chunghsien 30 17N 108 4 E
69 Chungking 29 30N 106 30 E
67 Chungtien 28 0N 99 30 E
68 Chungwei 37 35N 105 10 E
60 Chunian 31 10N 74 0 E
74 Chunya 8 30s 33 27 E
25 Chur 46 52N 9 32 E
93 Churchill 58 45N 94 5w
93 Churchill, R., Man. 58 47N 94 12w
91 Churchill, R., Newf. 53 30N 60 10w
92 Churchill Pk. 58 10N 125 10w
60 Churu 28 20N 75 0 E
69 Chusan, I. 30 0N 122 20 E
48 Chuvash A.S.S.R. □ 53 30N 48 0 E
48 Chuvovoy 58 15N 57 40 E
65 Cianjur 6 81s 107 7 E
109 Cianorte 23 37s 52 37w
65 Cibatu 7 8s 107 59 E
98 Cicero 41 48N 87 48w
28 Ciechanów 52 52N 20 38 E
28 Ciechanow □ 53 0N 20 0 E
105 Ciego de Avila 21 50N 78 50w
110 Ciénaga 11 0N 74 10w
105 Cienfuegos 22 10N 80 30w
26 Cieplice Slaskie Zdrój 50 50N 15 40 E
20 Cierp 42 55N 0 40 E
27 Cieszyn 49 45N 18 35 E
33 Cieza 38 17N 1 23w
32 Cifuentes 40 47N 2 37w
31 Cijara, Pantano, Res. 39 18N 4 52w
65 Cilacap 7 43s 109 0 E
101 Cimarron, R. 36 10N 96 17w
65 Cimahi 6 53s 107 33 E
36 Cimone, Mte. 44 12N 10 42 E
41 Cîmpina 45 10N 25 45 E
41 Cîmpulung 45 17N 25 3 E
32 Cinca, R. 41 26N 0 21 E
98 Cincinnati 39 10N 84 26w
37 Cíngoli 43 23N 13 10 E
21 Cinto, Mt. 42 24N 8 54 E
38 Circéo, Mte. 41 14N 13 3 E
88 Circle 47 26N 105 35w

Coonana Dalkeith

83 Coonana 31 0S 123 0E
62 Coondapoor 13 42N 74 40E
81 Coongoola 27 43S 145 47E
62 Coonoor 11 10N 76 45E
99 Cooper 39 57N 75 7W
81 Cooper Creek, R., L. 28 0S 139 0E
81 Coorong, The 35 50S 139 20E
83 Coorow 29 50S 115 59E
81 Cooroy 26 22S 152 54E
102 Coos Bay 43 26N 124 7W
84 Cootamundra 34 36S 148 1E
15 Cootehill 54 5N 7 5W
33 Cope, C. 37 26N 1 28W
45 Copenhagen=København 55 41N 12 34E
39 Copertino 40 17N 18 2W
108 Copiapó 27 15S 70 20E
37 Copparo 44 52N 11 49E
88 Copper Center 62 10N 145 25W
90 Copper Cliff 46 30N 81 4W
92 Copper Mountain 49 20N 120 30W
88 Coppermine 68 0N 116 0W
41 Copşa Mică 46 6N 24 15E
12 Coquet, R. 55 22N 1 37W
74 Coquilhatville=Mbandaka 0 1N 18 18E
108 Coquimbo 30 0S 71 20W
108 Coquimbo □ 30 0S 71 0W
41 Corabia 43 48N 24 30E
110 Coracora 15 5S 73 45W
89 Coral Harbour 64 0N 83 0W
90 Coral Rapids 50 20N 81 40W
76 Coral Sea 15 0S 150 0E
96 Coraopolis 40 30N 80 10W
39 Corato 41 12N 16 22E
19 Corbeil-Essonnes 48 36N 2 25E
20 Corbières, Mts. 42 55N 2 35E
98 Corbin 37 0N 84 3W
31 Corbones, R. 37 36N 5 39W
13 Corby 52 29N 0 41W
33 Corcoles, R. 39 12N 2 40W
103 Corcoran 36 6N 119 35W
30 Corcubión 42 56N 9 12W
99 Cordele 31 55N 83 49W
108 Córdoba, Arg. 31 20S 64 10W
108 Córdoba, Arg. □ 31 22S 64 15W
104 Córdoba, Mexico 26 20N 103 20W
31 Córdoba, Sp. 37 50N 4 50W
108 Córdoba □, Arg. 31 22S 64 15W
31 Córdoba □, Sp. 38 5N 5 0W
65 Cordon 16 42N 121 32E
88 Cordova 60 36N 145 45W
80 Corfield 21 40S 143 21E
42 Corfu, I.=Kérkira, I. 39 38N 19 50E
30 Corgo 42 56N 7 25W
30 Coria 40 0N 6 33W
39 Corigliano Cálabro 39 36N 16 31E
43 Corinth, Greece=Kórinthos 37 56N 22 55E
99 Corinth, U.S.A. 34 54N 88 30W
43 Corinth Canal 37 48N 23 0E
111 Corinto, Brazil 18 20S 44 30W
105 Corinto, Nic. 12 30N 87 10W
15 Cork 51 54N 8 30W
15 Cork □ 51 54N 8 30W
38 Corleone 37 48N 13 16E
56 Çorlu 41 11N 27 49E
93 Cormorant 54 5N 100 45W
105 Corn Is. 12 0N 83 0W
109 Cornélio Procópio 23 7S 50 40W
91 Corner Brook 49 0N 58 0W
102 Corning, Calif. 39 56N 122 9W
96 Corning, N.Y. 42 10N 77 3W
90 Cornwall 45 5N 74 45W
13 Cornwall □ 50 26N 4 40W
110 Coro 11 30N 69 45W
111 Coroatá 4 20S 44 0W
110 Corocoro 17 15S 69 19W
85 Coromandel 36 45S 175 31E
62 Coromandel Coast Reg. 12 30N 81 0E
103 Corona 33 49N 117 36W
103 Coronado 32 45N 117 9W
105 Coronado, B. de 9 0N 83 40W
88 Coronation G. 68 0N 114 0W
108 Coronda 31 58S 60 56W
108 Coronel 37 0S 73 10W
108 Coronel Bogado 27 11S 56 18W
108 Coronel Dorrego 38 40S 61 10W
108 Coronel Oviedo 25 24S 56 30W
108 Coronel Pringles 38 0S 61 30W
108 Coronel Suárez 37 30S 62 0W
109 Corpus 27 10S 55 30W
101 Corpus Christi 27 50N 97 28W
30 Corral de Almaguer 39 45N 3 10W
36 Corréggio 44 46N 10 47E
20 Corrèze □ 45 20N 1 50E
15 Corrib, L. 53 25N 9 10W
108 Corrientes 27 30S 58 45W
108 Corrientes □ 28 0S 57 0W
105 Corrientes, C., Cuba 21 43N 84 30W
110 Corrientes, C., Col. 5 30N 77 34W
83 Corrigin 32 18S 117 45E
96 Corry 41 55N 79 39W
21 Corse, C. 43 1N 9 25E
21 Corse, I. 42 0N 9 0E
21 Corsica, I.=Corse, I. 42 0N 9 0E
101 Corsicana 32 5N 96 30W
21 Corte 42 19N 9 11E
31 Cortegana 37 52N 6 49W
103 Cortez 37 24N 108 35W
37 Cortina d'Ampezzo 46 32N 12 9E
97 Cortland 42 35N 76 11W
37 Cortona 43 16N 12 0E
31 Coruche 38 57N 8 30W
56 Çorum 40 30N 35 5E
110 Corumbá 19 0S 57 30W
102 Corvallis 44 36N 123 15W
104 Cosamalopan 18 23N 95 50W
39 Cosenza 39 17N 16 14E
41 Coşereni 44 38N 26 35E
96 Coshocton 40 17N 81 51W
19 Cosne-sur-Loire 47 24N 2 54E
108 Cosquín 31 15S 64 30W
36 Cossato 45 34N 8 10E
33 Costa Blanca, Reg. 38 25N 0 10W
32 Costa Brava, Reg. 41 30N 3 0E
31 Costa del Sol, Reg. 36 30N 4 30W
32 Costa Dorada, Reg. 40 45N 1 15E
105 Costa Rica ■ 10 0N 84 0W
41 Costeşti 44 40N 24 53E
38 Cost Smeralda 41 5N 9 35E
25 Coswig 51 52N 12 31E
65 Cotabato 7 8N 124 13E
21 Côte d'Azur, Reg. 43 25N 6 50E
19 Côte d'Or □ 47 30N 4 50E
21 Côte d'Or, Reg. 47 10N 4 50E
18 Cotentin, Reg. 49 30N 1 30W
19 Côtes de Meuse, Reg. 49 15N 5 22E
18 Côtes-du-Nord □ 48 28N 2 50W
72 Cotonou 6 20N 2 25E
110 Cotopaxi, Mt. 0 30S 78 30W
13 Cotswold Hills 51 42N 2 10W
102 Cottage Grove 43 48N 123 2W
24 Cottbus 51 44N 14 20E
24 Cottbus □ 51 43N 13 30E
103 Cottonwood 34 48N 112 1W
31 Couço 38 59N 8 17W
102 Coulee City 47 44N 119 12W
19 Coulommiers 48 50N 3 3E
21 Coulon, R. 43 51N 5 0E
88 Council, Alas. 64 55N 163 45W
102 Council, Id. 44 45N 116 30W
100 Council Bluffs 41 20N 95 50W
21 Couronne, C. 43 19N 5 3E
18 Courseulles 49 20N 0 29W
21 Cours 46 7N 4 19E
92 Courtenay 49 45N 125 0W
18 Courville 48 28N 1 15E
18 Coutances 49 3N 1 28W
20 Coutras 45 3N 0 8W
30 Covilhã 40 17N 7 31W
99 Covington, Ga. 33 36N 83 50W
98 Covington, Ky. 39 5N 84 30W
93 Cowan 52 5N 100 45W
83 Cowan, L. 31 45S 121 45E
84 Cowangie 35 12S 141 26E
90 Cowansville 45 14N 72 46W
14 Cowdenbeath 56 7N 3 20W
81 Cowell 33 38S 136 40E
13 Cowes 50 45N 1 18W
84 Cowra 33 49S 148 42E
111 Coxim 18 30S 54 55W
59 Cox's Bazar 21 25N 92 3E
104 Cozumel, I. de 20 30N 86 40W
75 Cradock 32 8S 25 36E
102 Craig 40 32N 107 44W
15 Craigavon □ 54 27N 6 26W
41 Craiova 44 21N 23 48E
74 Crampel 7 8N 19 8E
93 Cranberry Portage 54 36N 101 22W
80 Cranbrook, Tas. 42 0S 148 5E
83 Cranbrook, W. Australia 34 20S 117 35E
92 Cranbrook Canada 49 30N 115 55W
97 Cranston 41 47N 71 27W
41 Crasna 46 32N 27 51E
111 Crateús 5 10S 40 50W
111 Crato, Brazil 7 10S 39 25W
31 Crato, Port. 39 16N 7 39W
21 Crau, Reg. 43 32N 4 40E
98 Crawfordsville 40 2N 86 51W
13 Crawley 51 7N 0 10W
19 Crécy 48 50N 2 53E
93 Cree L. 57 30N 107 0W
19 Creil 49 15N 2 34E
36 Crema 45 21N 9 40E
36 Cremona 45 8N 10 2E
19 Crépy 49 37N 3 32E
19 Crépy-en-Valois 49 14N 2 54E
37 Cres, I. 44 58N 14 25E
102 Crescent City 41 45N 124 12W
108 Crespo 32 2S 60 20W
90 Cressman 47 40N 72 55W
21 Crest 44 44N 5 2E
92 Creston, Canada 49 10N 116 40W
100 Creston, U.S.A. 41 0N 94 20W
99 Crestview 30 45N 86 35W
43 Crete=Kriti, I. 35 10N 25 0E
43 Crete, Sea of 26 0N 25 0E
32 Creus, C. 42 20N 3 19E
20 Creuse □ 46 0N 2 0E
20 Creuse, R. 47 0N 0 34E
37 Crevalcore 44 41N 11 10E
33 Crevillente 38 12N 0 48W
12 Crewe 53 6N 2 28W
109 Criciúma 28 40S 49 23W
14 Crieff 56 22N 3 50W
37 Crikvenica 45 11N 14 40E
49 Crimea=Krymskaya, Reg. 45 0N 34 0E
24 Crimmitschau 50 48N 12 23E
14 Crinan 56 4N 5 30W
104 Cristóbal 9 10N 80 0W
101 Crockett 31 20N 95 30W
21 Croisette, C. 43 13N 5 20E
82 Croker, I. 11 12S 132 32E
14 Cromarty 57 40N 4 2W
12 Cromer 52 56N 1 18E
85 Cromwell 45 3S 169 14E
84 Cronulla 34 3S 151 8E
105 Crooked I. 22 50N 74 10W
100 Crookston 47 50N 96 40W
12 Cross Fell, Mt. 54 44N 2 29W
15 Crosshaven 51 48N 8 19W
97 Croton-on-Hudson 41 19N 73 55W
39 Crotone 39 5N 17 6E
102 Crow Agency 45 40N 107 30W
15 Crow Hd. 51 34N 10 9W
101 Crowley 30 15N 92 20W
97 Crown Point 41 24N 87 23W
92 Crowsnest P. 49 40N 114 40W
80 Croydon, Australia 18 15S 142 14E
13 Croydon, U.K. 51 18N 0 5W
18 Crozon 48 15N 4 30W
109 Cruz Alta 28 40S 53 32W
108 Cruz del Eje 30 45S 64 50W
109 Cruzeiro 22 50S 45 0W
109 Cruzeiro do Oeste 23 46S 53 4W
110 Cruzeiro do Sul 7 35S 72 35W
81 Crystal Brook 33 21S 138 13E
101 Crystal City 38 15N 90 23W
27 Csongrád 46 43N 20 12E
27 Csongrád □ 46 32N 20 15E
27 Csurgo 46 16N 17 9E
75 Cuamba 14 45S 36 22E
75 Cuando, R. 14 0S 19 30E
31 Cuba 38 10N 7 54W
105 Cuba ■ 22 0N 79 0W
83 Cuballing 32 50S 117 15E
110 Cucui 1 10N 66 50W
110 Cúcuta 7 54N 72 31W
62 Cuddalore 11 46N 79 45E
62 Cuddapah 14 30N 78 47E
30 Cudillero 43 33N 6 9W
83 Cue 27 20S 117 55E
30 Cuéllar 41 23N 4 21E
32 Cuenca, Sp. 40 5N 2 10W
110 Cuenca, Ecuador 2 50S 79 9W
32 Cuenca, Sp. □ 40 0N 2 0W
32 Cuenca, Sa. de 39 55N 1 50W
104 Cuernavaca 18 50N 99 20W
101 Cuero 29 5N 97 17W
111 Cuiabá 15 30S 56 0W
14 Cuillin Hills 57 14N 6 15W
21 Cuiseaux 46 30N 5 22E
104 Cuitzeo, L. 19 55N 101 5W
20 Culan 46 34N 2 20E
84 Culcairn 35 41S 147 3E
30 Culebra, Sa. de la 41 55N 6 20W
104 Culiacán 24 50N 107 40W
33 Cúllar de Baza 37 35N 2 34W
14 Cullen 57 45N 2 50W
82 Cullen, Pt. 11 50S 141 47E
33 Cullera 39 9N 0 17W
14 Culloden Moor 57 29N 4 7W
21 Culoz 45 47N 5 46E
85 Culverden 42 47S 172 49E
110 Cumaná 10 30N 64 5W
92 Cumberland, Canada 49 40N 125 0W
98 Cumberland, U.S.A. 39 40N 78 43W
89 Cumberland Pen. 67 0N 65 0W
86 Cumberland Plat. 36 0N 84 30W
89 Cumberland Sd. 65 30N 66 0W
31 Cumbres Mayores 38 4N 6 39W
12 Cumbria □ 54 44N 2 55W
12 Cumbrian, Mts. 54 30N 3 0W
31 Cummins 34 16S 135 44E
83 Cunderdin 31 39S 117 15E
75 Cunene, R. 17 20S 11 50E
36 Cúneo 44 23N 7 32E
81 Cunnamulla 28 4S 145 41E
93 Cupar, Canada 51 0N 104 10W
14 Cupar, U.K. 56 20N 3 0W
110 Cupica, G. de 6 25N 77 30W
40 Ćuprija 34 57N 21 26E
105 Curaçao 12 10N 69 0W
19 Cure, R. 47 40N 3 41E
110 Curiapo 8 33N 61 5W
108 Curicó 34 55S 71 20W
108 Curicó □ 34 50S 71 15W
109 Curitiba 25 20S 49 10W
111 Currais Novos 6 13S 36 30W
111 Curralinho 1 35S 49 30W
80 Currawilla 25 10S 141 20E
102 Currie 40 16N 114 45W
80 Curtis, I. 23 40S 151 15E
111 Curuçá 0 35S 47 50W
111 Cururupu 1 50S 44 50W
108 Curuzú Cuatiá 29 50S 58 5W
111 Curvelo 18 45S 44 27W
84 Curya 35 53S 142 54E
101 Cushing 31 43N 94 50W
36 Cusna, Mte. 44 17N 10 23E
20 Cusset 46 8N 3 28E
100 Custer 43 45N 103 38W
102 Cut Bank 48 40N 112 15W
39 Cutro 39 1N 16 58E
61 Cuttack 20 25N 85 57E
83 Cuvier, C. 23 14S 113 22E
24 Cuxhaven 53 51N 8 41E
96 Cuyahoga Falls 41 8N 81 30W
110 Cuzco, Mt. 20 0S 66 50W
110 Cuzco 13 32S 72 0W
80 Cygnet 43 8S 147 1E
56 Cyprus ■ 35 0N 33 0E
73 Cyrenaica=Barqa Reg. 27 0N 20 0E
73 Cyrene=Shahhat 32 39N 21 18E
27 Czechoslovakia ■ 49 0N 17 0E
27 Czechowice Dziedzice 49 54N 18 59E
27 Czeladz 50 16N 19 2E
28 Czempiń 52 9N 16 33E
27 Czerwionka 50 7N 18 37E
27 Częstochowa 50 49N 19 7E
28 Czestichowa □ 50 50N 19 0E
28 Człuchów 53 41N 17 22E

D

63 Da, R. 16 0N 107 0E
63 Da Lat 12 3N 108 32E
63 Da Nang 16 10N 108 7E
72 Dabakala 8 15N 4 20W
60 Dabhoi 22 10N 73 20E
28 Dąbie 53 27N 14 45E
72 Dabola 10 50N 11 5W
27 Dabrowa Gornieza 50 15N 19 10E
27 Dabrowa Tarnówska 50 10N 21 0E
61 Dacca 23 43N 90 26E
61 Dacca □ 24 0N 90 0E
25 Dachau 48 16N 11 27E
110 Dadanawa 3 0N 59 30W
60 Dadau 26 45N 67 45E
49 Dagesta A.S.S.R. □ 42 30N 47 0E
65 Dagupan 16 3N 120 33E
72 Dahomey ■=Benin ■ 8 0N 2 0E
31 Daimiel 39 5N 3 35W
15 Daingean 53 18N 7 15W
68 Dairen=Talien 39 0N 121 31E
73 Dairût 27 34N 30 43E
83 Dairy Creek 25 12S 115 48E
66 Daisetsu-Zan, Mt. 43 30N 142 57E
80 Dajarra 21 42S 139 30E
72 Dakar 14 34N 17 29W
72 Dakhla 23 50N 15 53W
49 Dakhovskaya 44 13N 40 13E
60 Dakor 22 45N 73 11E
40 Dakovica 42 22N 20 26E
40 Dakovo 45 19N 18 24E
68 Dalai Nor, L. 49 0N 117 50E
44 Dalälven, R. 60 38N 17 27E
68 Dalandzadgad 43 35N 104 30E
58 Dalbandin 28 53N 64 25E
14 Dalbeattie 54 56N 3 49W
81 Dalby 27 11S 151 16E
101 Dalhart 36 4N 102 31W
91 Dalhousie 48 0N 66 26W
54 Daliyat el Karmel 32 41N 35 3E
40 Dalj 45 29N 18 59E
14 Dalkeith 55 54N 3 4W

E

Fiñana Fukuyama

33 Fiñana 37 10N 2 50W
14 Findhorn 57 30N 3 45W
98 Findlay 41 0N 83 41W
18 Finistère □ 48 20N 4 20W
30 Finisterre 42 54N 9 16W
30 Finisterre, C. 42 50N 9 19W
80 Finke 25 34S 134 35E
46 Finland ■ 70 0N 27 0E
48 Finland, G. of 60 0N 26 0E
84 Finley 35 38S 145 35E
92 Finnegan 51 7N 112 5W
80 Finnigan, Mt. 15 49S 145 17E
81 Finniss, C. 33 38S 134 51E
46 Finnmark □ 69 30N 25 0E
45 Finspång 58 45N 15 43E
25 Finsteraarhorn, Mt. 46 31N 8 10E
24 Finsterwalde 51 37N 13 42E
36 Fiorenzuola 44 56N 9 54E
37 Firenze 43 47N 11 15E
21 Firminy 45 23N 4 18E
60 Firozabad 27 10N 78 25E
41 Fîrţaneşti 45 48N 27 59E
57 Fīrūzābād 28 52N 52 35E
57 Fīrūzkūh 35 50N 52 40E
83 Fisher 30 30S 131 0E
97 Fishers I. 41 16N 72 2W
13 Fishguard 51 59N 4 59W
97 Fitchburg 42 35N 71 47W
32 Fitero 42 4N 1 52W
112 Fitz Roy 47 10S 67 0W
99 Fitzgerald 31 45N 83 10W
80 Fitzroy, R., Queens. 23 32S 150 52E
82 Fitzroy, R., W. Australia 17 31S 138 35E
82 Fitzroy Crossing 18 9S 125 38E
36 Fivizzana 44 14N 10 8E
74 Fizi 4 17S 28 55E
45 Fjellerup 56 29N 10 34E
44 Fla 60 25N 9 26E
103 Flagstaff 35 10N 111 40W
47 Flåm 60 52N 7 14E
12 Flamborough Hd. 54 8N 0 4W
102 Flaming Gorge L. 41 15N 109 30W
16 Flandre Occidentale □ 51 0N 3 0E
16 Flandre Orientale □ 51 0N 4 0E
16 Flandres, Plaines des 51 10N 3 15E
14 Flannan Is. 58 9N 7 52W
102 Flathead L. 47 50N 114 0W
80 Flattery, C., Australia 14 58S 145 21E
102 Flattery, C., U.S.A. 48 21N 124 31W
12 Fleetwood 53 55N 3 1W
47 Flekkefjord 58 18N 6 39E
44 Flen 59 4N 16 35E
24 Flensburg 54 46N 9 28E
18 Flers 48 47N 0 33W
13 Fletton 52 34N 0 13W
93 Flin Flon 54 46N 101 53W
83 Flinders, B. 34 19S 114 9E
80 Flinders, I. 40 0S 148 0E
81 Flinders, Ras. 31 30S 138 30E
12 Flint, U.K. 53 15N 3 7W
98 Flint, U.S.A. 43 0N 83 40W
77 Flint I. 11 26S 151 48W
32 Flix 41 14N 0 32E
19 Flixecourt 50 0N 2 5E
12 Flodden 55 37N 2 8W
100 Flora 38 40N 88 30W
37 Florence, Italy= Firenze 43 47N 11 15E
99 Florence, Ala. 34 50N 87 50W
103 Florence, Ariz. 33 0N 111 25W
102 Florence, Oreg. 44 0N 124 3W
99 Florence, S.C. 34 5N 79 50W
110 Florencia 1 36N 75 36W
104 Flores 16 50N 89 40W
65 Flores, I. 8 35S 121 0E
65 Flores Sea 6 30S 124 0E
111 Floriano 6 50S 43 0W
109 Florianópolis 27 30S 48 30W
100 Florida 34 7S 56 10W
99 Florida □ 28 30N 82 0W
87 Florida Str. 25 0N 80 0W
27 Floridsdorf 48 15N 16 25E
42 Flórina 40 48N 21 26E
42 Flórina □ 40 45N 21 20E
47 Florø 61 35N 5 1E
32 Flumen, R. 41 50N 0 25W
38 Flumendosa, R. 39 30N 9 25E
16 Flushing= Vlissingen 51 26N 3 34E
5 Flying Fish, C. 72 30S 103 0W
93 Foam Lake 51 40N 103 15W
40 Foča 43 31N 18 47E
41 Focşani 45 41N 27 15E
39 Fóggia 41 28N 15 31E
91 Fogo 49 43N 54 17W
26 Fohnsdorf 47 12N 14 40E
24 Föhr, I. 54 40N 8 30E
20 Foix 42 58N 1 38E
20 Foix, Reg. 43 0N 1 30E
43 Fokís □ 38 30N 22 15E
43 Folégandros, I. 36 37N 24 55E
90 Foleyet 48 15N 82 25W
37 Foligno 42 58N 12 40E
13 Folkestone 51 5N 1 11E
36 Follónica, G. di 42 54N 10 53E
93 Fond du Lac, Canada 59 20N 107 10W
100 Fond-du-Lac, U.S.A. 43 46N 88 26W
38 Fondi 41 21N 13 25E
30 Fonfría 41 37N 6 9W
104 Fonseca, G. de 13 10N 87 40W
19 Fontainebleau 48 24N 2 40E
110 Fonte Boa 2 25S 66 0W
20 Fontenay-le-Comte 46 28N 0 48W
69 Foochow 26 5N 119 18E
19 Forbach 49 10N 6 52E
84 Forbes 33 22S 148 0E
61 Forbesganj 26 17N 87 18E
32 Forcall, R. 40 40N 0 12W
25 Forchheim 49 42N 11 4E
96 Ford City 40 47N 79 11W
4 Forel, Mt. 66 52N 36 55W
92 Forest Lawn 51 4N 114 0W
92 Forestburg 52 35N 112 1W
91 Forestville 48 48N 69 20W
20 Forez, Mts. du 45 40N 3 50E
14 Forfar 56 40N 2 53W
19 Forges-les-Eaux 49 37N 1 30E
37 Forlí 44 14N 12 2E
12 Formby Pt. 53 33N 3 7W
33 Formentera, I. 38 40N 1 30E
32 Formentor, C. 39 58N 3 13E
38 Fórmia 41 15N 13 34E
111 Formiga 20 27S 45 25W
36 Formigine 44 37N 10 51E
108 Formosa, Arg. 26 15S 58 10W
111 Formosa, Brazil 15 32S 47 20W
108 Formosa □ 25 0S 60 0W
69 Formosa= Taiwan ■ 24 0N 121 0E
111 Formosa, Sa. 12 0S 55 0W
69 Formosa Str. 24 40N 124 0E
30 Fornos de Algodres 40 48N 7 32W
36 Fornovo di Taro 44 42N 10 7E
14 Forres 57 37N 3 38W
83 Forrest 38 22S 143 40E
101 Forrest City 35 1N 90 47W
44 Fors 60 14N 16 20E
80 Forsayth 18 33S 143 34E
44 Forsmo 63 16N 17 11E
24 Forst 51 43N 15 37E
102 Forsyth 46 14N 106 37W
90 Fort Albany 52 15N 81 35W
73 Fort-Archambault =Sarh 9 5N 18 23E
92 Fort Assinboine 54 20N 114 45W
14 Fort Augustus 57 9N 4 40W
102 Fort Benton 47 50N 110 40W
102 Fort Bragg 39 28N 123 50W
102 Fort Bridger 41 22N 110 20W
89 Fort Chimo 58 9N 68 12W
93 Fort Chipewyan 58 46N 111 9W
100 Fort Collins 40 30N 105 4W
90 Fort Coulonge 45 50N 76 45W
75 Fort-Dauphin 25 2S 47 0E
100 Fort Dodge 42 29N 94 10W
93 Fort Frances 48 35N 93 25W
88 Fort Franklin 65 30N 123 45W
90 Fort George 53 40N 79 0W
90 Fort George, R. 53 50N 77 0W
88 Fort Good Hope 66 14N 128 40W
92 Fort Graham 56 38N 124 35W
103 Fort Hancock 31 19N 105 56W
90 Fort Hope 51 30N 88 10W
91 Fort Kent 47 12N 68 30W
73 Fort-Lamy= Ndjamena 12 4N 15 8E
100 Fort Laramie 42 15W 104 30W
99 Fort Lauderdale 26 10N 80 5W
92 Fort Liard 60 20N 123 30W
92 Fort Mackay 57 12N 111 41W
91 Fort McKenzie 56 50N 69 0W
92 Fort Macleod 49 45N 113 30W
72 Fort MacMahon 29 51N 1 45E
88 Fort McPherson 67 30N 134 55W
100 Fort Madison 40 39N 91 20W
72 Fort Mirabel 29 31N 2 55E
100 Fort Morgan 40 10N 103 50W
99 Fort Myers 26 30N 82 0W
92 Fort Nelson 58 50N 122 30W
88 Fort Norman 64 57N 125 30W
99 Fort Payne 34 25N 85 44W
102 Fort Peck 47 1N 105 30W
102 Fort Peck Res. 47 40N 107 0W
99 Fort Pierce 27 29N 80 19W
74 Fort Portal 0 40N 30 20E
92 Fort Providence 61 20N 117 30W
93 Fort Qu'Appelle 50 45N 103 50W
92 Fort Resolution 61 10N 114 40W
74 Fort-Rousset 0 29S 15 55E
90 Fort Rupert 51 30N 78 40W
92 Fort St. James 54 30N 124 10W
92 Fort St. John 56 15N 120 50W
60 Fort Sandeman 31 20N 69 25E
92 Fort Saskatchewan 53 40N 113 15W
101 Fort Scott 38 0N 94 40W
88 Fort Selkirk 62 43N 137 22W
90 Fort Severn 56 0N 87 40W
92 Fort Simpson 61 45N 121 30W
50 Fort Slevchenko 44 30N 50 10E
101 Fort Smith 35 25N 94 25W
101 Fort Stockton 30 48N 103 2W
101 Fort Sumner 34 24N 104 8W
99 Fort Valley 32 33N 83 52W
92 Fort Vermilion 58 30N 115 57W
75 Fort Victoria 20 8S 30 55E
98 Fort Wayne 41 5N 85 10W
90 Fort William, Canada= Thunder Bay 48 20N 89 10W
14 Fort William, U.K. 56 48N 5 8W
101 Fort Worth 32 45N 97 25W
88 Fort Yukon 66 35N 145 12W
111 Fortaleza 3 35S 38 35W
105 Fort-de-France 14 36N 61 5W
82 Fortescue, R. 21 20S 116 5E
14 Forth, Firth of 56 5N 2 55W
14 Fortrose 57 35N 4 10W
102 Fortuna 48 38N 124 8W
88 Forty Mile 64 20N 140 30W
21 Fos 43 20N 4 57E
37 Fossacesia 42 15N 14 30E
36 Fossano 44 39N 7 40E
5 Fossil Bluff 71 15S 69 0W
37 Fossombrone 43 41N 12 49E
98 Fostoria 41 8N 83 25W
18 Fougères 48 21N 1 14W
14 Foula, I. 60 10N 2 5W
13 Foulness, I. 51 26N 0 55E
72 Foumban 5 45N 10 50E
20 Fourchambault 47 0N 3 3E
82 Fourcroy, C. 11 45S 130 2E
19 Fourmies 50 1N 4 2E
43 Foúrnoi, I. 37 36N 26 32E
72 Fouta Djalon, Mts. 11 20N 12 10W
85 Foveaux, Str. 46 42S 168 10E
13 Fowey 50 20N 4 39W
83 Fowlers, B. 31 59S 132 34E
69 Fowning 33 30N 119 40E
93 Fox Valley 50 30N 109 25W
89 Foxe Basin 68 30N 77 0W
89 Foxe Chan. 66 0N 80 0W
89 Foxe Pen. 65 0N 76 0W
85 Foxton 40 29S 175 18E
15 Foyle, L. 55 6N 7 18W
15 Foynes 52 37N 9 6W
30 Foz 43 33N 7 20W
109 Foz do Iguaçu 25 30S 54 30W
97 Frackville 40 46N 76 15W
32 Fraga 41 32N 0 21E
97 Framingham 42 17N 71 25W
111 Franca 20 25S 47 30W
37 Francavilla al Mare 42 25N 14 16E
39 Francavilla Fontana 40 32N 17 35E
17 France ■ 47 0N 3 0E
74 Franceville 1 38S 13 35E
19 Franche Comté, Reg. 46 30N 5 50E
91 Francis Harbour 52 34N 55 44W
75 Francistown 21 11S 27 32E
39 Francofonte 37 13N 14 50E
91 François 47 34N 56 44W
24 Frankenberg 51 3N 8 47E
25 Frankenwald, Mts. 50 18N 11 36E
98 Frankfort, Ind. 40 20N 86 33W
98 Frankfort, Ky. 38 12N 85 44W
24 Frankfurt □ 52 30N 14 0E
25 Frankfurt am Main 50 7N 8 40E
24 Frankfurt an der Oder 52 50N 14 31E
25 Fränkishe Alb. 49 20N 11 30E
100 Franklin, Nebr. 40 9N 98 55W
97 Franklin, N.H. 43 28N 71 39W
97 Franklin, N.J. 41 9N 74 38W
96 Franklin, Pa. 41 22N 79 45W
99 Franklin, Tenn. 35 54N 86 53W
98 Franklin, W. Va. 38 38N 79 21W
88 Franklin, Reg. 71 0N 99 0W
102 Franklin D. Roosevelt L. 48 30N 118 16W
88 Franklin Mts. 66 0N 125 0W
88 Franklin Str. 72 0N 96 0W
84 Frankston 38 8S 145 8E
50 Frantsa Iosifa, Zemlya, Is. 76 0N 62 0E
90 Franz 48 25N 85 30W
38 Frascati 41 48N 12 41E
96 Fraser 42 32N 82 57W
81 Fraser, I. 25 15S 153 10E
92 Fraser, R. 49 9N 123 12W
92 Fraser Lake 54 0N 124 50W
14 Fraserburgh 47 41N 2 0W
63 Fraser's Hill 3 43N 101 43E
41 Frăteşti 43 59N 25 59E
25 Frauenfeld 47 34N 8 54E
108 Fray Bentos 33 10S 58 15W
82 Frazier Downs 18 48S 121 42E
45 Fredericia 55 34N 9 45E
98 Frederick, Md. 39 25N 77 23W
101 Frederick, Okla. 34 22N 99 0W
98 Fredericksburg 38 16N 77 29W
91 Fredericton 45 57N 66 40W
45 Frederiksborg □ 55 50N 12 10E
4 Frederikshåb 62 0N 49 30W
45 Frederikshavn 57 28N 10 31E
45 Frederikssund 55 50N 12 3E
45 Frederiksvaerk 55 58N 12 2E
96 Fredonia 42 26N 79 20W
44 Fredrikstad 59 13N 10 57E
97 Freehold 40 15N 74 18W
97 Freeland 41 3N 75 48W
105 Freeport, Bahamas 26 30N 78 35W
100 Freeport, Ill. 42 18N 89 40W
97 Freeport, N.Y. 40 39N 73 35W
101 Freeport, Tex. 28 55N 95 22W
72 Freetown 8 30N 13 10W
31 Fregenal de la Sierra 38 10N 6 39W
24 Freiberg 50 55N 13 20E
25 Freiburg 48 0N 7 50E
112 Freire 39 0S 72 50W
25 Freising 48 24N 11 27E
26 Freistadt 48 30N 14 30E
24 Freital 51 0N 13 40E
21 Fréjus 43 25N 6 44E
83 Fremantle 32 1S 115 47E
100 Fremont, Nebr. 41 30N 96 30W
98 Fremont, Ohio 41 20N 83 5W
84 French, I. 38 20S 145 22E
111 French Guiana ■ 4 0N 53 0W
55 French Terr. of the Afars & Issas ■ 11 30N 42 15E
111 Fresco, R. 6 39S 51 59W
104 Fresnillo 23 10N 103 0W
103 Fresno 36 47N 119 50W
30 Fresno Alhandigo 40 42N 5 37W
25 Freudenstadt 48 27N 8 25E
80 Frewena 19 50S 135 50E
108 Frías 28 40S 65 5W
25 Fribourg 46 49N 7 9E
25 Fribourg □ 45 40N 7 0E
25 Friedberg 50 19N 8 45E
25 Friedrichshafen 47 39N 9 29E
26 Friesach 46 57N 14 24E
16 Friesland □ 53 5N 5 50E
75 Frio, C. 18 0S 12 0E
24 Fritzlar 51 8N 9 19E
37 Friuli Venezia Giulia □ 46 0N 13 0E
89 Frobisher B. 63 0N 67 0W
13 Frome 51 16N 2 17W
98 Front Royal 38 55N 78 10W
31 Fronteira 39 3N 7 39W
104 Frontera 18 30N 92 40W
20 Frontignan 43 27N 3 45E
38 Frosinone 41 38N 13 20E
44 Frösö 63 11N 14 35E
98 Frostburg 39 43N 78 57W
44 Frôvi 59 28N 15 24E
41 Frumoasa 46 28N 25 48E
50 Frunze 42 54N 74 36E
111 Frutal 20 0S 49 0W
27 Frýdek Místek 49 40N 18 20E
43 Fthiótis □ 38 50N 22 25E
68 Fuchin 47 10N 132 0E
69 Fuchow 27 50N 116 14E
66 Fuchu 34 34N 133 14E
69 Fuchun Kiang, R. 30 10N 120 9E
31 Fuengirola 36 32N 4 41W
31 Fuente de Cantos 38 15N 6 18W
31 Fuente el Fresno 39 14N 3 46W
31 Fuente Ovejuna 38 15N 5 25W
31 Fuentes de Andalucia 37 28N 5 20W
32 Fuentes de Ebro 31 31N 0 38W
31 Fuentes de León 38 5N 6 32W
30 Fuentes de Oñoro 40 33N 6 52W
108 Fuerte Olimpo 21 0S 58 0W
72 Fuerteventura, I. 28 30N 14 0W
57 Fujaira 25 7N 56 18E
66 Fuji 35 9N 138 39E
66 Fuji-san, Mt. 35 22N 138 44E
66 Fuji-no-miya 35 20N 138 40E
66 Fujisawa 35 22N 139 29E
69 Fukien □ 26 0N 117 30E
66 Fukuchiyama 35 25N 135 9E
66 Fukui 36 0N 136 10E
66 Fukui □ 36 0N 136 12E
66 Fukuoka 33 30N 130 30E
66 Fukuoka □ 33 30N 131 0E
66 Fukushima 37 30N 140 15E
66 Fukushima □ 37 30N 140 15E
66 Fukuyama 34 35N 133 20E

Fulda Giong, Teluk B.

24 Fulda 50 32N 9 41 E
24 Fulda, R. 51 25N 9 39 E
103 Fullerton 33 52N 117 58W
100 Fulton, Mo. 38 50N 91 55W
97 Fulton, N.Y. 43 20N 76 22W
19 Fumay 50 0N 4 40 E
20 Fumel 44 30N 0 58 E
66 Funabashi 35 45N 140 0 E
76 Funafuti, I. 8 30S 179 0 E
72 Funchal 32 45N 16 55W
110 Fundación 10 31N 74 11W
30 Fundão 40 8N 7 30W
91 Fundy, B. of 45 0N 66 0W
72 Funtua 11 31N 7 17 E
56 Furat, Nahr al, R. 33 30N 43 0 E
109 Furnas, Reprêsa de, L. 20 45S 46 0W
12 Furness 54 14N 3 8W
26 Fürstenfeld 47 3N 16 3 E
25 Furstenfeldbruck 48 10N 11 15 E
24 Furstenwalde 52 20N 14 3 E
25 Fürth 49 29N 11 0 E
89 Fury & Hecla Str. 69 40N 81 0W
110 Fusagasugá 4 21N 74 22W
68 Fushan 37 30N 121 5 E
68 Fushun 42 0N 123 59 E
68 Fusin 42 12N 121 33 E
25 Füssen 47 12N 121 33 E
69 Futing 27 15N 120 10 E
69 Futsing 25 46N 119 29 E
76 Futuna, I. 14 25S 178 20 E
69 Fuyang 30 5N 119 56 E
68 Fuyu 45 10N 124 50 E
12 Fylde, R. 53 47N 2 56W
45 Fyn, I. 55 20N 10 30 E
14 Fyne, L. 56 0N 5 20W
45 Fyns □ 55 15N 10 30 E

G

72 Gabès 33 53N 10 2 E
73 Gabès, G. de 34 0N 10 30 E
74 Gabon ■ 0 10S 10 0 E
75 Gaborone 24 37S 25 57 E
97 Gabriels 44 26N 74 12W
41 Gabrovo 42 52N 25 27 E
57 Gach-Sārān 30 15N 50 45 E
40 Gacko 43 10N 18 33 E
62 Gadag 15 30N 75 45 E
60 Gadarwara 22 50N 78 50 E
33 Gádor, Sa. de 36 57N 2 45W
99 Gadsden, Ala. 34 1N 86 0W
103 Gadsden, Ariz. 32 35N 114 47W
62 Gadwal 16 10N 77 50 E
41 Găesti 44 48N 25 14 E
38 Gaeta 41 12N 13 35 E
38 Gaeta, G. di 41 0N 13 25 E
99 Gaffney 35 10N 81 31W
72 Gafsa 34 24N 8 51 E
91 Gagetown 45 46N 66 29W
72 Gagnoa 6 4N 5 55W
91 Gagnon 51 50N 68 5W
20 Gah 43 12N 0 27W
61 Gahmar 25 27N 83 55 E
61 Gaibandha 25 20N 89 36 E
26 Gail, R. 46 36N 13 53 E
20 Gaillac 43 54N 1 54 E
18 Gaillon 49 10N 1 20 E
96 Gaines 41 45N 77 35W
99 Gainesville, Fla. 29 38N 82 20W
99 Gainesville, Ga. 34 17N 83 47W
101 Gainesville, Tex. 33 40N 97 10W
12 Gainsborough 53 23N 0 46W
81 Gairdner, L. 32 0S 136 0 E
14 Gairloch, L. 57 43N 5 45W
75 Galangue 13 48S 16 3 E
77 Galápagos, Is. 0 0N 89 0W
14 Galashiels 55 37N 2 50W
41 Galaţi 45 27N 28 2 E
39 Galatina 40 10N 18 10 E
39 Galátone 40 8N 18 3 E
99 Galax 36 42N 80 57W
43 Galaxídhion 38 22N 22 23 E
83 Galena 27 50S 114 41 E
33 Galera 37 45N 2 33W
100 Galesburg 40 57N 90 23W
48 Galich 58 23N 42 18 E
30 Galicia, Reg. 42 43N 8 0W
54 Galilee= Hagalil, Reg. 32 53N 35 18 E
54 Galilee, Sea of= Kinneret, Yam 32 49N 35 36 E
36 Gallarte 45 40N 8 48 E
99 Gallatin 36 24N 86 27W
62 Galle 6 5N 80 10 E
32 Gállego, R. 41 39N 0 51W
112 Gallegos, R. 51 35S 69 0W
110 Gallinas, Pta. 12 28N 71 40W
39 Gallipoli 40 8N 18 0 E
98 Gallipolis 38 50N 82 10W
46 Gällivare 67 7N 20 32 E
32 Gallocanta, L. de 40 58N 1 30W
14 Galloway, Reg. 55 0N 4 25W
14 Galloway, Mull of 54 38N 4 50W
103 Gallup 35 30N 108 54W
96 Galt= Cambridge 43 21N 80 19W
26 Galtür 46 58N 10 11 E
30 Galve de Sorbe 41 13N 3 10W
101 Galveston 29 15N 94 48W
101 Galveston B. 29 30N 94 50W
108 Gálvez 32 0S 61 20W
15 Galway 53 16N 9 4W
15 Galway, B. 53 10N 9 20W
15 Galway □ 53 16N 9 3W
66 Gamagori 34 50N 137 14 E
72 Gambaga 10 30N 0 28W
72 Gambia ■ 13 20N 15 45W
72 Gambia, R. 13 28N 16 34W
82 Gambier, C. 11 56S 130 57 E
104 Gamboa 9 8N 79 42W
103 Gamerco 35 33N 108 56W
20 Gan 0 10S 71 10 E
54 Gan Shamu'el 32 28N 34 56 E
54 Gan Yavne 31 48N 34 42 E
90 Gananoque 44 20N 76 10W
61 Gandak, R. 25 32N 85 5 E
91 Gander 49 1N 54 33W
32 Gandesa 41 3N 0 26 E
72 Gandi 12 55N 5 49 E
33 Gandía 38 58N 0 9W
61 Ganga, Mouths of the 21 30N 90 0 E
61 Ganga, R. 23 22N 90 32 E
60 Ganganagar 29 56N 73 56 E
60 Gangapur 26 32N 76 37 E
62 Gangavati 15 30N 76 36 E
59 Gangaw 22 5N 94 15 E
61 Ganges, R.= Ganga, R. 23 22N 90 32 E
61 Gangtok 27 20N 88 40 E
60 Ganj 27 45N 78 47 E
20 Gannat 46 7N 3 11 E
27 Ganserdorf 48 20N 16 43 E
72 Gao 18 0N 1 0 E
72 Gaoual 11 45N 13 25W
21 Gap 44 33N 6 5 E
111 Garanhuns 8 50S 36 30W
102 Garberville 40 11N 123 50W
109 Garça 22 14S 49 37W
21 Gard □ 44 2N 4 10 E
36 Garda, L. di 45 40N 10 40 E
24 Gardelegen 52 32N 11 21 E
101 Garden City 38 0N 100 45W
57 Gardez 33 31N 68 59 E
102 Gardiner 45 3N 110 53W
97 Gardner 42 35N 72 0W
55 Gardo 9 18N 49 20 E
102 Garfield 47 3N 117 8W
43 Gargaliánoi 37 4N 21 38 E
39 Gargano, Testa del, Pt. 41 49N 16 12 E
38 Garigliano, R. 41 13N 13 45 E
102 Garland 41 47N 112 10W
50 Garm 39 0N 70 20 E
25 Garmisch-Partenkirchen 47 30N 11 5 E
57 Garmsār 35 20N 52 25 E
61 Garo Hills 25 30N 90 30 E
55 Garoe 8 35N 48 40 E
20 Garonne, R. 45 2N 0 36W
20 Garrigues, Reg. 43 40N 3 30 E
102 Garrison 46 37N 112 56W
100 Garrison Res. 47 30N 102 0W
88 Garry, L. 65 40N 100 0W
90 Garson 50 5N 96 50W
20 Gartempe, R. 46 48N 0 50 E
67 Gartok 31 59N 80 30 E
24 Gartz 54 17N 13 21 E
65 Garut 7 14S 107 53 E
31 Garvão 37 42N 8 21W
85 Garvie, Mts. 45 27S 169 59 E
98 Gary 41 35N 87 20W
110 Garzón 2 10N 75 40W
17 Gascogne, G. de 44 0N 2 0W
20 Gascogne, Reg. 43 45N 0 20 E
83 Gascoyne, R. 24 52S 113 37 E
83 Gascoyne Junction 25 3S 115 12 E
72 Gashaka 7 20N 11 29 E
91 Gaspé 48 52N 64 30W
91 Gaspé, C. 48 48N 64 7W
91 Gaspé Pass. 49 10N 64 0W
91 Gaspé Pen. 48 45N 65 40W
91 Gaspesian Prov. Park 49 0N 66 45W
99 Gastonia 35 17N 81 10W
43 Gastoúni 37 51N 21 15 E
42 Gastoúri 39 34N 19 54 E
112 Gastre 42 10S 69 15W
33 Gata, C. de 36 41N 2 13W
30 Gata, Sa. de 40 20N 6 20W
40 Gătaia 45 26N 21 30 E
14 Gatehouse of Fleet 54 53N 4 10W
12 Gateshead 54 57N 1 37W
19 Gatinais, Reg. 48 5N 2 40 E
20 Gâtine, Hauteurs de 46 40N 0 50W
97 Gatineau 45 28N 75 40W
90 Gatineau Nat. Park 45 30N 75 52W
75 Gatooma 18 21S 29 55 E
104 Gatun 9 16N 79 55W
104 Gatun L. 9 7N 79 56W
31 Gaucín 36 31N 5 19W
61 Gauhati 26 5N 91 55 E
5 Gaussberg, Mt. 66 45S 89 0 E
32 Gavá 41 18N 2 0 E
20 Gavarnie 42 44N 0 3W
57 Gavater 25 10N 61 23 E
43 Gávdhos, I. 34 50N 24 6 E
31 Gavião 39 28N 7 50W
44 Gavle 60 41N 17 13 E
44 Gävleborgs □ 61 20N 16 15 E
36 Gavorrano 42 55N 10 55 E
18 Gavray 49 55N 1 20W
60 Gawilgarh Hills 21 15N 76 45 E
81 Gawler 34 30S 138 42 E
61 Gaya 24 47N 85 4 E
81 Gayndah 25 35S 151 39 E
54 Gaza 31 30N 34 28 E
54 Gaza Strip 31 29N 34 25 E
56 Gaziantep 37 6N 37 23 E
28 Gdańsk 54 22N 18 40 E
28 Gdansk □ 54 10N 18 30 E
28 Gdynia 54 35N 18 33 E
73 Gebeit Mine 21 3N 36 29 E
73 Gedaref 14 2N 35 28 E
54 Gedera 31 49N 34 46 E
20 Gèdre 42 47N 0 2 E
45 Gedser 54 35N 11 55 E
84 Geelong 38 2S 144 20 E
83 Geelvink, Chan. 28 30S 114 10 E
16 Geeraadsbergen 50 45N 3 53 E
24 Geesthacht 53 25N 10 20 E
73 Geili 16 1N 32 37 E
44 Geilo 60 32N 8 14 E
25 Geislingen 47 55N 8 37 E
74 Geita 2 48S 32 12 E
39 Gela 37 3N 14 15 E
39 Gela, G. di 37 0N 14 8 E
16 Gelderland □ 52 5N 6 10 E
16 Geldrop 51 25N 5 32 E
16 Geleen 50 57N 5 49 E
56 Gelibolu 40 28N 26 43 E
25 Gelnhausen 50 12N 9 12 E
24 Gelsenkirchen 51 30N 7 5 E
24 Gelting 54 43N 9 53 E
63 Gemas 2 37N 102 36 E
16 Gembloux 50 34N 4 43 E
74 Gemena 3 20N 19 40 E
37 Gemona del Fruiuli 46 16N 13 7 E
25 Gemünden 50 3N 9 43 E
20 Gençay 46 23N 0 23 E
108 General Acha 37 20S 64 38W
108 General Alvear 36 0S 60 0W
108 General Artigas 26 52S 56 16W
108 General Juan Madariaga 37 0S 57 0W
108 General Martin Miguel de Güemes 24 50S 65 0W
108 General Pico 35 45S 63 50W
108 General Pinedo 27 15S 61 30W
112 General Roca 30 0S 67 40W
41 General Toshevo 43 42N 28 6 E
108 General Viamonte 35 1S 61 3W
108 General Villegas 35 0S 63 0W
96 Genesee, R. 43 16N 77 36W
25 Geneva= Genève, Switz. 46 12N 6 9 E
96 Geneva, U.S.A. 42 53N 77 0W
25 Geneva, L.= Léman, L. 46 26N 6 30 E
25 Genève 46 12N 6 9 E
31 Genil, R. 37 42N 5 19W
21 Génissiat, Barrage de 46 1N 5 48 E
16 Genk 50 58N 5 32 E
38 Gennargentu, Mt. del 39 59N 9 19 E
36 Genova 44 24N 8 56 E
36 Génova, G. di 44 0N 9 0 E
16 Gent 51 2N 3 37 E
24 Genthin 52 24N 12 10 E
83 Geographe, B. 33 30S 115 15 E
83 Geographe, Chan. 24 30S 113 0 E
75 George 33 58S 22 29 E
97 George, L. 43 30N 73 30W
89 George R.=Port Nouveau-Quebec 58 30N 65 50W
80 George Town Australia 41 5S 148 55 E
63 George Town, W. Malaysia 5 25N 100 19 E
80 Georgetown, Australia 18 17S 143 33 E
90 Georgetown, Ont. 43 40N 80 0W
91 Georgetown, P.E.I. 46 13N 62 24W
72 Georgetown, Gambia 13 30N 14 47W
110 Georgetown, Guyana 6 50N 58 12W
99 Georgetown, U.S.A. 33 22N 79 15W
99 Georgia □ 32 0N 82 0W
92 Georgia Str. 49 20N 124 0W
90 Georgian B. 45 15N 81 0W
49 Georgian S.S.R. □ 41 0N 45 0 E
49 Georgiu-Dezh 51 3N 39 20 E
49 Georgiyevsk 44 12N 43 28 E
24 Gera 50 53N 12 5 E
24 Gera □ 50 45N 11 30 E
83 Geraldton, Australia 28 48S 114 32 E
90 Geraldton, Canada 49 44N 86 59W
19 Gérardmer 48 3N 6 50 E
88 Gerdine, Mt. 61 32N 152 50W
56 Gerede 40 45N 32 10 E
33 Gérgal 37 7N 2 31W
25 Gerlafingen 47 10N 7 34 E
55 Gerlogubi 6 53N 45 3 E
92 Germansen Landing 55 43N 124 40W
75 Germiston 26 15S 28 5 E
66 Gero 35 48N 137 14 E
27 Gerlachovka, Mt. 49 11N 20 7 E
32 Gerona 41 58N 2 46 E
32 Gerona □ 42 11N 2 30 E
20 Gers □ 43 35N 0 38 E
20 Gers, R. 44 9N 0 39 E
24 Geseke 51 38N 8 29 E
30 Getafe 40 18N 3 44W
20 Gevaudan, Reg. 44 40N 3 40 E
40 Gevgelija 41 9N 22 30 E
21 Gex 46 21N 6 3 E
102 Geyser 47 17N 110 30W
46 Geysir 64 19N 20 18W
54 Gezer 31 52N 34 55 E
61 Ghaghara, R. 25 45N 84 40 E
72 Ghana ■ 6 0N 1 0W
72 Ghardaîa 32 31N 3 37 E
56 Ghat 24 59N 10 19 E
61 Ghatal 22 40N 87 46 E
62 Ghatprabha, R. 16 21N 75 51 E
73 Ghazal, Bahr el, R. 9 31N 30 25 E
72 Ghazaouet 35 8N 1 50W
60 Ghaziabad 28 42N 77 35 E
61 Ghazipur 25 38N 83 35 E
57 Ghazni 33 30N 68 17 E
57 Ghazni □ 33 0N 68 0 E
36 Ghedi 45 24N 10 16 E
41 Gheorghe Gheorghiu-Dej 46 17N 26 47 E
21 Ghisonaccia 42 1N 9 26 E
57 Ghor □ 34 0N 64 20 E
90 Ghost River 51 25N 83 20W
72 Ghudāmes 30 11N 9 29 E
57 Ghuriān 34 17N 61 25 E
15 Giant's Causeway 55 15N 6 30W
36 Giaveno 45 3N 7 20 E
105 Gibara 21 0N 76 20W
38 Gibellina 37 48N 13 0 E
75 Gibeon 25 7S 17 45 E
31 Gibraléon 37 23N 6 58W
31 Gibraltar ■ 36 7N 5 22W
31 Gibraltar, Str. of 35 55N 5 40W
82 Gibson, Des. 24 0S 126 0 E
19 Gien 47 40N 2 36 E
24 Giessen 50 34N 8 40 E
24 Gifhorn 52 29N 10 32 E
66 Gifu 35 30N 136 45 E
66 Gifu □ 36 0N 137 0 E
104 Giganta, Sa. de la 25 30N 111 30W
14 Gigha, I. 55 42N 5 45W
36 Giglio, I. 42 20N 10 52 E
20 Gignac 43 39N 3 32 E
30 Gijón 43 32N 5 42W
103 Gila, R. 32 43N 114 33W
103 Gila Bend 32 57N 112 43W
56 Gilan □ 37 0N 49 0 E
76 Gilbert Is. 1 0N 176 0 E
93 Gilbert Plains 51 9N 100 28W
80 Gilbert River 18 9S 142 50 E
83 Gilgai 31 15S 119 56 E
84 Gilgandra 31 42S 148 39 E
58 Gilgit 35 50N 74 15 E
93 Gillam 56 20N 94 40W
80 Gilliat 20 40S 141 28 E
13 Gillingham 51 23N 0 34 E
90 Gilmour 44 48N 77 37W
103 Gilroy 37 10N 121 37W
80 Gindie 23 45S 148 10 E
83 Gingin 31 22S 115 37 E
54 Ginnosar 32 51N 35 32 E
39 Ginosa 40 35N 16 45 E
39 Gióia, G. di 38 30N 15 50 E
39 Gióia del Colle 40 49N 16 55 E
39 Gióia Táuro 38 26N 15 53 E
43 Gióna, Mt. 38 38N 22 14 E
65 Giong, Teluk, B. 4 50N 118 20 E

Giovi, P. del Great Victoria Des.

21 Giovi, P. del 44 30N 8 55E
39 Giovinazzo 41 10N 16 40E
60 Gir Hills 21 0N 71 0E
27 Giraltovce 49 7N 21 32E
96 Girard 41 10N 80 42W
110 Girardot 4 18N 74 48W
14 Girdle Ness 57 9N 2 2W
56 Giresun 40 45N 38 30E
73 Girga 26 17N 31 55E
61 Giridih 24 10N 86 21E
57 Girishk 31 47N 64 24E
20 Gironde, R. 45 30N 1 0W
20 Gironde □ 44 45N 0 30W
32 Gironella 42 2N 1 53E
14 Girvan 55 15N 4 50W
85 Gisborne 38 39S 178 5E
45 Gislaved 57 18N 13 32E
19 Gisors 49 15N 1 40E
39 Giugliano in Campania 40 55N 14 12E
37 Giulianova 42 45N 13 58E
41 Giurgiu 43 52N 25 57E
54 Giv'at Olga 32 28N 34 53E
54 Giv'atayim 32 4N 34 49E
19 Givet 50 8N 4 49E
21 Givors 45 35N 4 45E
57 Gizhiga 62 0N 150 27E
51 Gizhiginskaya Guba 61 0N 158 0E
28 Gîzycko 54 2N 21 48E
42 Gjirokastra 40 7N 20 16E
88 Gjoa Haven 68 20N 96 0W
44 Gjøvik 60 47N 10 43E
91 Glace Bay 46 11N 59 58W
92 Glacier B. Nat. Monument 58 45N 136 30W
102 Glacier Nat. Park 48 40N 114 0W
101 Gladewater 32 30N 94 58W
80 Gladstone, Queens. 23 52S 151 16E
81 Gladstone, S. Australia 33 17S 138 22E
93 Gladstone, Canada 50 20N 99 0W
44 Glåma, R. 59 12N 10 57E
25 Glarus 47 3N 9 4E
14 Glasgow, U.K. 55 52N 4 14W
98 Glasgow, U.S.A. 37 2N 85 55W
13 Glastonbury 51 9N 2 42W
24 Glauchau 50 50N 12 33E
48 Glazov 58 0N 52 30E
92 Gleichen 50 50N 113 0W
26 Gleisdorf 47 6N 15 44E
14 Glen Affric 57 15N 5 0W
103 Glen Canyon Dam 37 0N 111 25W
103 Glen Canyon Nat. Recreation Area 37 30N 111 0W
14 Glen Coe 56 40N 5 0W
97 Glen Cove 40 51N 73 37W
14 Glen Garry 57 3N 5 7W
14 Glen More 57 12N 4 30E
84 Glen Thompson 37 38S 142 35E
84 Glenalbyn 36 30S 143 48E
18 Glénans, Is. de 47 42N 4 0W
85 Glenbrook 33 46S 150 37E
103 Glendale, Ariz. 33 40N 112 8W
103 Glendale, Calif. 34 7N 118 18W
102 Glendale, Oreg. 42 44N 123 29W
100 Glendive 47 7N 104 40W
81 Glenelg 34 58S 138 30E
84 Glenelg, R. 38 3S 141 9E
15 Glengariff 51 45N 9 33W
80 Glengyle 24 48S 139 37E
81 Glenn Innes 29 44S 151 44E
84 Glennies Creek 32 30S 151 8E
80 Glenorchy 36 55S 142 41E
80 Glenore 17 50S 141 12E
80 Glenormiston 22 55S 138 50E
102 Glenrock 42 53N 105 55W
14 Glenrothes 56 12N 3 11W
97 Glens Falls 43 20N 73 40W
15 Glenties 54 48N 8 18W
92 Glenwood, Canada 49 21N 113 24W
100 Glenwood, U.S.A. 45 38N 95 21W
102 Glenwood Springs 39 39N 107 15W
27 Gliwice 50 22N 18 41E
103 Globe 33 25N 110 53W
26 Glödnitz 46 53N 14 7E
26 Gloggnitz 47 41N 15 56E
28 Głogów 51 37N 16 5E
75 Glorieuses, Is. 11 30S 47 20E
12 Glossop 53 27N 1 56W
84 Gloucester, Australia 32 0S 151 59E
13 Gloucester, U.K. 51 52N 2 15W
97 Gloucester, U.S.A. 42 38N 70 39W
13 Gloucestershire □ 51 44N 2 10W
97 Gloversville 43 5N 74 18W
28 Głowno 51 59N 19 42E
27 Glubczyce 50 13N 17 52E
24 Glücksburg 54 48N 9 34E
24 Glückstadt 53 46N 9 28E
26 Gmünd, Kärnten, 46 54N 13 31E
26 Gmünd, Niederösterreich 48 45N 15 0E
26 Gmunden 47 55N 13 48E
28 Gniezno 52 30N 17 35E
83 Gnowangerup 33 58S 117 59E
63 Gô Công 10 12N 107 0E
62 Goa 15 33N 73 59E
62 Goa □ 15 33N 73 59E
61 Goalpara 26 10N 90 40E
14 Goat Fell, Mt. 55 37N 5 11W
74 Goba 7 1N 39 59E
75 Gobabis 22 16S 19 0E
68 Gobi, Des. 44 0N 111 0E
62 Gobichettipalayam 11 31N 77 21E
24 Goch 51 40N 6 9E
62 Godavari, R. 16 37N 82 18E
62 Godavari Pt. 17 0N 82 20E
91 Godbout 49 20N 67 38W
90 Goderich 43 45N 81 41W
105 Golfito 8 41N 83 5W
4 Godhavn 69 15N 53 38W
60 Godhra 22 49N 73 40E
27 Gödöllö 47 38N 19 25E
108 Godoy Cruz 32 56S 68 52W
93 Gods L. 54 40N 94 10W
4 Godthåb 64 10N 51 46W
75 Goei Hoop, K.die =Good Hope, C. of 34 24S 18 30E
16 Goeree 51 50N 4 0E
16 Goes 51 30N 3 55E
90 Gogama 47 35N 81 35W
80 Gogango 23 40S 150 2E
28 Gogolin 50 30N 18 0E
73 Gogriâl 8 30N 28 0E
111 Goiânia 16 35S 49 20W
111 Goias □ 12 10S 48 0W
26 Goisern 47 38N 13 38E
66 Gojo 34 21N 135 42E
60 Gojra 31 10N 72 40E
62 Gokak 16 11N 74 52E
62 Gokarn 14 33N 74 17E
59 Gokteik 22 26N 97 0E
44 Göl 57 4N 9 42E
61 Gola Gokarannath 28 4N 80 28E
70 Gold Coast 4 0N 1 40W
28 Goldap 54 19N 22 19E
92 Golden, Canada 51 20N 117 0W
100 Golden, U.S.A. 39 42N 105 30W
85 Golden B. 40 40S 172 50E
62 Golden Rock 10 45N 78 48E
93 Goldfields 37 45N 117 13W
99 Goldsboro 35 24N 77 59W
82 Goldsworthy 20 21S 119 30E
31 Golega 39 24N 8 29W
28 Goleniów 53 35N 14 50E
105 Golfito 8 41N 83 5W
21 Golo, R. 42 31N 9 32E
14 Golspie 57 58N 3 58W
28 Golub Dobrzyń 53 7N 19 2E
74 Goma 1 37S 29 10E
61 Gomati, R. 25 32N 83 11E
48 Gomel 52 28N 31 0E
72 Gomera, I. 28 10N 17 5W
104 Gómez Palacio 25 40N 104 40W
24 Gommern 52 54N 11 47E
57 Gonābād 34 15N 58 45E
105 Gonaïves 19 20N 72 50W
61 Gonda 27 9N 81 58E
60 Gondal 21 58N 70 52E
73 Gonder 12 23N 37 30E
61 Gondia 21 30N 80 10E
30 Gondomar, Port 41 10N 8 35W
30 Gondomar, Sp. 42 7N 8 45W
19 Gondrecourt 48 26N 5 30E
54 Gonen 33 7N 35 39E
101 Gonzales 29 30N 97 30W
108 González Chaves 38 2S 60 5W
75 Good Hope, C. of 34 24S 18 30E
12 Goole 53 42N 0 52W
84 Goolgowi 33 58S 154 39E
83 Goomalling 31 19S 116 49E
81 Goondiwindi 28 30S 150 21E
16 Goor 52 13N 6 33E
91 Goose Bay 53 15N 60 20W
62 Gooty 15 7N 77 41E
61 Gopalganj 23 1N 89 55E
25 Göppingen 48 42N 9 40E
33 Gor 37 23N 2 58W
28 Gora R. 52 7N 17 28E
61 Gorakhpur 26 47N 83 32E
40 Goražde 43 40N 18 56E
30 Gorbea, Peña 43 1N 2 50W
105 Gorda, Pta. 14 10N 83 10W
100 Gordon 42 49N 102 6W
83 Gordon River 34 10S 117 15E
80 Gordonvale 17 5S 145 50E
81 Gore, Australia 28 17S 151 29E
74 Gore, Ethiopia 8 12N 35 32E
85 Gore, N.Z. 46 5S 168 58E
15 Gorey 52 41N 6 18W
110 Gorgona, I. 3 0N 78 10W
49 Goris 39 31N 46 23E
37 Gorizia 45 56N 13 37E
28 Gorka 51 39N 16 58E
48 Gorki=Gorkiy 56 20N 44 0E
48 Gorkiy 56 20N 44 0E
48 Gorkovskoye Vdkhr 57 2N 43 4E
27 Gorlice 49 35N 21 11E
24 Görlitz 51 10N 14 59E
49 Gorlovka 48 25N 37 58E
41 Gorna Oryakhovitsa 43 7N 25 40E
40 Gornja Tuzla 44 35N 18 46E
40 Gornji Milanovac 44 0N 20 29E
40 Gornji Vakuf 43 57N 17 34E
50 Gorno Filinskoye 60 5N 70 0E
48 Gornyatski 67 49N 64 20E
65 Gorontalo 0 35N 123 13E
15 Gort 53 4N 8 50W
48 Goryn, R. 52 8N 27 17E
28 Gorzów Wielkopolski 52 43N 15 15E
28 Gorzów Wielkopolski □ 52 40N 15 20E
84 Gosford 33 23S 151 18E
98 Goshen 41 36N 85 46W
24 Goslar 51 55N 10 23E
37 Gospič 44 35N 15 23E
13 Gosport 50 48N 1 8W
40 Gostiva 41 48N 20 57E
28 Gostyń 51 50N 17 3E
28 Gostynin 52 26N 19 29E
45 Göteborg 57 43N 11 59E
45 Göteborgs och Bohus □ 58 30N 11 30E
45 Götene 58 33N 13 30E
24 Gotha 50 56N 10 42E
47 Gotland, I. 57 30N 18 30E
41 Gotse Delchev 41 43N 23 46E
66 Gōtsu 35 0N 132 14E
24 Göttingen 51 31N 9 55E
27 Gottwaldov 49 14N 17 40E
16 Gouda 52 1N 4 42E
7 Gough, I. 40 10S 9 45W
90 Govin Res. 48 35N 74 40W
84 Goulburn 32 22S 149 31E
73 Gounou-Gaya 9 38N 15 31E
20 Gourdon 44 44N 1 23E
19 Gournay 49 29N 1 44E
97 Gouverneur 44 18N 75 30W
20 Gouzon 46 12N 2 14E
105 Governor's Harbour 25 10N 76 14W
13 Gower, Pen. 51 35N 5 10W
108 Goya 29 10S 59 10W
75 Graaff-Reinet 32 13S 24 32E
24 Grabow 53 17N 11 31E
37 Gračac 44 18N 15 57E
105 Gracias a Dios, C. 15 0N 83 20W
37 Grado, Italy 45 40N 13 20E
30 Grado, Sp. 43 23N 6 4W
41 Graeca, L. 44 5N 26 10E
81 Grafton, Australia 29 35S 152 0E
100 Grafton, U.S.A. 48 30N 97 25W
39 Gragnano 40 42N 14 30E
90 Graham, Canada 49 20N 90 30W
99 Graham, N.C. 36 5N 79 22W
101 Graham, Tex. 33 7N 98 38W
92 Graham I. 53 40N 132 30W
5 Graham Ld. 65 0S 64 0W
93 Grahamdale 51 30N 98 34W
75 Grahamstown 33 19S 26 31E
21 Graie, Alpi, Mts. 45 30N 7 10E
70 Grain Coast, Reg. 4 20N 10 0W
111 Grajaú 5 50S 46 30W
28 Grajewo 53 39N 22 30E
20 Gramat 44 48N 1 43E
14 Grampian □ 57 20N 2 45W
14 Grampian Highlands, Mts. 56 50N 4 0W
42 Gramshi 40 52N 20 12E
72 Gran Canaria, I. 27 55N 15 35W
106 Gran Chaco, Reg. 25 0S 61 0W
36 Gran Paradiso, Mt. 49 33N 7 17E
37 Gran Sasso d'Italia, Mts. 42 25N 13 30E
105 Granada, Nic. 11 58N 86 0W
31 Granada, Sp. 37 10N 3 35W
31 Granada □ 37 5N 4 30W
15 Granard 53 47N 7 30W
90 Granby 45 25N 72 45W
105 Grand Bahama I. 26 40N 78 30W
91 Grand Bank 47 6N 55 48W
72 Grand Bassam 5 10N 3 49W
105 Grand Bourg 15 53N 61 19W
103 Grand Canyon 36 10N 112 45W
103 Grand Canyon Nat. Park 36 15N 112 20W
105 Grand Cayman, I. 19 20N 81 20W
102 Grand Coulee Dam 48 0N 118 50W
91 Grand Falls 47 2N 67 46W
92 Grand Forks, Canada 49 0N 118 30W
100 Grand Forks, U.S.A. 48 0N 97 3W
98 Grand Haven 43 3N 86 13W
100 Grand Island 40 59N 98 25W
103 Grand Junction 39 0N 108 30W
72 Grand Lahou 5 10N 5 0W
18 Grand Lieu, L. de 47 6N 1 40W
100 Grand Marais 47 45N 90 25W
90 Grand' Mère 46 36N 72 40W
93 Grand Rapids, Canada 53 12N 99 19W
98 Grand Rapids, Mich. 42 57N 85 40W
100 Grand Rapids, Minn. 47 19N 93 29W
25 Grand St-Bernard, Col. du 45 53N 7 11E
102 Grand Teton, Mt. 43 45N 110 57W
30 Grandas de Salime 43 13N 6 53W
112 Grande, B. 50 30S 68 20W
109 Grande, I. 23 9S 44 14W
94 Grande, R. 25 57N 97 9W
91 Grand Baie 48 19N 70 52W
91 Grande-Entrée 47 30N 61 40W
92 Grande Prairie 55 15N 118 50W
91 Grande Rivière 48 26N 64 30W
108 Grandes, Salinas, Reg. 29 37S 64 56W
31 Grândola 38 12N 8 35W
19 Grandvillers 49 40N 1 57E
108 Graneros 34 5S 70 45W
14 Grangemouth 56 1N 3 43W
44 Grängesberg 60 6N 15 1E
102 Grangeville 45 57N 116 4W
100 Granite City 38 45N 90 3W
85 Granity 41 39S 171 51E
111 Granja 3 17S 40 50W
30 Granja de Moreruela 41 48N 5 44W
31 Granja de Torrehermosa 38 19N 5 35W
32 Granollers 41 39N 2 18E
24 Gransee 53 0N 13 10E
12 Grantham 52 55N 0 39W
14 Grantown-on-Spey 57 19N 3 36W
103 Grants 35 14N 107 57W
102 Grants Pass 42 30N 123 22W
102 Grantsville 40 35N 112 32W
18 Granville 48 50N 1 35W
33 Grao de Gandía 39 0N 0 27W
102 Grass Valley 39 18N 121 0W
21 Grasse 43 38N 6 56E
25 Graubünden □ 46 45N 9 30E
20 Graulhet 43 45N 1 58E
32 Graus 42 11N 0 20E
20 Grave, Pte. de 45 34N 1 4W
93 Gravelbourg 49 50N 105 35W
19 Gravelines 51 0N 2 10E
90 Gravenhurst 44 52N 79 20W
81 Gravesend, Australia 29 35S 150 20E
13 Gravesend, U.K. 51 25N 0 22E
39 Gravina di Púglia 40 48N 16 25E
19 Gray 47 27N 5 35E
13 Grays 51 28N 0 23E
93 Grayson 50 45N 102 40W
26 Graz 47 4N 15 27E
31 Grazalema 36 46N 5 23W
40 Grdelica 42 55N 22 3E
105 Great Abaco I. 26 15N 77 10W
80 Great Australian Basin 24 30S 143 0E
83 Great Australian Bight 33 30S 130 0E
105 Great Bahama Bank 23 15N 78 0W
85 Great Barrier I. 37 12S 175 25E
80 Great Barrier Reef 19 0S 149 0E
102 Great Basin 40 0N 116 30W
88 Great Bear L. 65 0N 120 0W
100 Great Bend 38 25N 98 55W
73 Great Bitter Lake 30 15N 32 40E
15 Great Blasket, I. 52 5N 10 30W
8 Great Britain, I. 54 0N 2 15W
84 Great Divide, Mts. 23 0S 146 0E
80 Great Dividing Range 25 0S 147 0E
105 Great Exuma I. 23 30N 75 50W
102 Great Falls 47 27N 111 12W
105 Great Inagua I. 21 0N 73 20W
60 Great Indian Des. 28 0N 72 0E
12 Great Orme's Hd. 53 20N 3 52W
12 Great Ouse, R. 52 47N 0 22E
86 Great Plains 42 0N 100 0W
74 Great Ruaha, R. 7 56S 37 52E
102 Great Salt L. 41 0N 112 30W
102 Great Salt Lake Des. 40 20N 113 50W
82 Great Sandy Des. 21 0S 124 0E
92 Great Slave L. 61 30N 114 20W
99 Great Smoky Mt. Nat. Park 35 39N 83 30W
83 Great Victoria Des. 29 30S 126 30E

Hallandsås Mt. Hindukush, Mts.

45 Hallandsås Mt. 56 23N 13 0E
16 Halle, Belgium 50 44N 4 13W
24 Halle, E. Germany 51 29N 12 0E
24 Halle □ 51 28N 11 58E
44 Hällefors 59 46N 14 30E
26 Hallein 47 40N 13 5E
81 Hallett 33 25S 138 55E
5 Halley Bay 76 30S 27 0W
44 Hallingdalselv, R. 60 24N 9 35E
46 Hällnäs 64 18N 19 40E
82 Halls Creek 18 20S 128 0E
44 Hallsberg 59 5N 15 7E
44 Hallstahammar 59 38N 16 15E
26 Hallstatt 47 33N 13 38E
97 Hallstead 41 56N 75 45W
65 Halmahera, I. 0 40N 128 0E
45 Halmstad 56 37N 12 56E
73 Halq el Oued 36 53N 10 10E
24 Haltern 51 44N 7 10E
56 Hamā 35 5N 36 40E
66 Hamada 34 50N 132 10E
56 Hamadān 34 52N 48 32E
56 Hamadān □ 35 0N 48 40E
66 Hamamatsu 34 45N 137 45E
44 Hamar 60 48N 11 7E
24 Hamburg, Germany 53 32N 9 59E
96 Hamburg, U.S.A. 40 37N 95 38W
97 Hamden 41 21N 72 56W
47 Häme □ 61 30N 24 30E
47 Hämeenlinna 61 3N 24 26E
83 Hamelin Pool 26 22S 114 20E
24 Hameln 52 7N 9 24E
82 Hamersley Ra. 22 0S 117 45E
68 Hamhung 40 0N 127 30E
67 Hami 42 54N 93 28E
84 Hamilton, Australia 37 37S 142 0E
105 Hamilton, Bermuda 32 15N 64 45W
96 Hamilton, Canada 43 20N 79 50W
85 Hamilton, N.Z. 37 47S 175 19E
14 Hamilton, U.K. 55 47N 4 2W
102 Hamilton, Mont. 46 20N 114 6W
98 Hamilton, Ohio 39 20N 84 35W
80 Hamilton Hotel 22 45S 140 40E
97 Hamilton Mt. 43 25N 74 22W
93 Hamiota 50 11N 100 38W
99 Hamlet 34 56N 79 40W
24 Hamm 51 40N 7 58E
44 Hammarö, I. 59 20N 13 30E
46 Hammerfest 70 33N 23 50E
98 Hammond, Ind. 41 40N 87 30W
101 Hammond, La. 30 30N 90 28W
85 Hampden 45 18S 170 50E
13 Hampshire □ 51 3N 1 20W
98 Hampton 37 4N 76 8W
56 Hamra 24 2N 38 55E
44 Hamrånge 60 59N 17 5E
69 Han Kiang, R. 30 32N 114 22E
69 Hanchung 33 10N 107 2E
100 Hancock 47 10N 88 35W
55 Handa, Japan 34 53N 137 0E
66 Handa, Somalia 10 37N 51 2E
74 Handeni 5 25S 38 2E
27 Handlová 48 45N 18 35E
54 Hanegev, Reg. 30 50N 35 0E
92 Haney 49 12N 122 40W
103 Hanford 36 25N 119 45W
69 Hangchow 30 12N 120 1E
69 Hangchow Wan, G. 30 30N 121 30E
47 Hangö 59 59N 22 57E
68 Hanh 51 32N 100 35E
54 Hanita 33 5N 35 10E
69 Hankow 30 32N 114 20E
68 Hanku 39 16N 117 50E
85 Hanmer 42 32S 172 50E
92 Hanna 51 40N 112 0W
100 Hannibal 39 42N 91 22W
24 Hannover 52 23N 9 43E
45 Hanö, B. 55 45N 14 60E
45 Hanö, I. 56 0N 14 50E
63 Hanoi 21 5N 150 40E
90 Hanover, Canada 44 9N 81 2W
97 Hanover, N.H. 43 43N 72 17W
98 Hanover, Pa. 39 46N 76 59W
112 Hanover, I. 50 58S 74 40W
60 Hansi 29 10N 75 57E
68 Hantan 36 42N 114 30E
69 Hanyang 30 30N 114 19E
46 Haparanda 65 52N 24 8E
91 Happy Valley 155 53N 60 10W
60 Hapur 28 45N 77 45E
68 Har-Ayrag 45 50N 109 30E
67 Har Us Nuur, L. 48 0N 92 0E
54 Har Yehuda, Reg. 31 40N 35 0E
56 Harad 24 15N 49 0E
55 Haradera 4 33N 47 38E
68 Harbin 45 46N 126 51E
91 Harbour Breton 47 29N 55 50W
91 Harbour Deep 50 25N 56 30W
91 Harbour Grace 47 40N 53 22W
24 Harburg 53 27N 9 58E
60 Harda 22 27N 77 5E
47 Hardanger Fd. 60 15N 6 0E
75 Hardap Dam 24 28S 17 48E
16 Harderwijk 52 21N 5 36E
75 Harding 30 22S 29 55E
60 Hardwar 29 58N 78 16E
112 Hardy, Pen. 55 30S 68 20W
55 Harer 9 20N 42 8E
18 Harfleur 49 30N 0 10E
55 Hargeisa 9 30N 44 2E
62 Harihar 14 32N 75 44E
62 Haripad 9 14N 76 28E
12 Harlech 52 52N 4 7W
102 Harlem 48 29N 108 39W
16 Harlingen, Neth. 53 11N 5 25E
101 Harlingen, U.S.A. 26 30N 97 50W
13 Harlow 51 47N 0 9E
102 Harlowton 46 30N 109 54W
102 Harney L. 43 0N 119 0W
102 Harney Basin 43 30N 119 0W
100 Harney Pk. 43 52N 103 33W
44 Härnösand 62 38N 18 5E
30 Haro 42 35N 2 55W
62 Harpanahalli 14 47N 75 59E
99 Harriman 36 0N 84 35W
91 Harrington Harbour 50 31N 59 30W
14 Harris, I. 57 50N 6 55W
98 Harrisburg, Ill. 37 42N 88 30W
97 Harrison, N.Y. 40 58N 73 43W
101 Harrison, Ohio 36 10N 93 4W
96 Harrisburg, Pa. 40 18N 76 52W
88 Harrison B. 70 25N 151 0W
98 Harrisonburg 38 28N 78 52W
100 Harrisonville 38 45N 93 45W
90 Harriston 43 57N 80 53W
12 Harrogate 53 59N 1 32W
13 Harrow 51 35N 0 15W
97 Hartford 41 47N 72 41W
91 Hartland 46 20N 67 32W
13 Hartland Pt. 51 2N 4 32W
12 Hartlepool 54 42N 1 11W
75 Hartley 18 10S 30 7E
92 Hartley Bay 46 4N 80 45W
93 Hartney 49 30N 100 35W
99 Hartsville 34 23N 80 2W
60 Harunabad 29 35N 73 2E
83 Harvey, Australia 33 4S 115 48E
98 Harvey, U.S.A. 41 40N 87 40W
13 Harwich 51 56N 1 18E
60 Haryana 29 0N 76 10E
24 Harz, Mts. 51 40N 10 40E
13 Haslemere 51 5N 0 41W
20 Hasparren 43 24N 1 18W
62 Hassan 13 0N 76 5E
16 Hasselt 50 56N 5 21E
72 Hassi Messaoud 31 15N 6 35E
72 Hassi R'Mel 32 35N 3 24E
45 Hässleholm 56 9N 13 46E
85 Hastings, N.Z. 39 39S 176 52E
13 Hastings, U.K. 50 51N 0 36E
98 Hastings, Mich. 42 40N 85 20E
100 Hastings, Neb. 40 34N 98 22W
103 Hatch 32 45N 107 8W
40 Hateg 45 36N 22 55E
67 Hatgal 50 40N 100 0E
60 Hathras 27 36N 78 6E
61 Hatia I. 22 50N 91 20E
99 Hatteras, C. 35 10N 75 30W
101 Hattiesburg 31 20N 89 20W
27 Hatvan 47 40N 19 45E
47 Haugesund 59 23N 5 13E
41 Haunţii Sebeşului, Mt. 45 30N 23 30E
55 Haura 13 50N 47 35E
85 Hauraki, G. 36 35S 175 5E
26 Hausruck, Mts. 48 6N 13 30E
19 Haut-Rhin □ 48 0N 7 15E
21 Haute-Corse □ 42 30N 9 20E
20 Haute-Garonne □ 43 28N 1 30E
20 Haute-Loire □ 45 5N 3 50E
19 Haute-Marne □ 48 10N 5 20E
91 Hauterive 49 10N 68 25W
19 Hautmont 50 15N 3 55E
19 Haute-Saône □ 47 45N 6 10E
21 Haute-Savoie □ 46 0N 6 20E
20 Haute-Vienne □ 45 50N 1 10E
21 Hautes-Alpes □ 44 40N 6 30E
20 Hautes-Pyrénées □ 43 0N 0 10E
13 Havant 50 51N 0 59W
90 Havelock 44 26N 77 53W
85 Havelock North 39 42S 176 53E
13 Haverfordwest 51 48N 4 59W
97 Haverhill 42 50N 71 2W
62 Haveri 14 53N 75 24E
13 Havering 51 33N 0 20E
97 Haverstraw 41 12N 73 58W
26 Havlíckuv Brod 49 36N 15 33E
102 Havre 48 40N 109 34W
91 Havre St. Pierre 50 18N 63 33W
56 Havza 41 0N 35 35E
94 Hawaii □ 20 0N 155 0W
94 Hawaii, I. 20 0N 155 0W
85 Hawea, L. 44 28S 169 19E
85 Hawera 39 35S 174 19E
14 Hawick 55 25N 2 48W
90 Hawk Junction 48 5N 84 35W
85 Hawke, B. 39 25S 177 20E
81 Hawker 31 59S 138 22E
85 Hawke's Bay □ 39 45S 176 35E
91 Hawke's Harbour 53 2N 55 50W
91 Hawkesbury, Nova Scotia 45 40N 61 10W
90 Hawkesbury, Ont. 45 35N 74 40W
102 Hawthorne 38 37N 118 47W
84 Hay, Australia 34 30S 144 51E
13 Hay, U.K. 52 4N 3 9W
92 Hay River 60 50N 115 50W
19 Hayange 49 20N 6 2E
103 Hayden 40 30N 107 22W
80 Haydon 18 0S 141 30E
88 Hayes, Mt. 63 37N 146 43W
93 Hayes, R. 57 3N 92 9W
13 Hayling I. 50 40N 1 0W
100 Hays 38 55N 99 25W
13 Haywards Heath 51 0N 0 5W
57 Hazārān, Kūh-e, Mt. 29 35N 57 20E
98 Hazard 37 18N 83 10W
61 Hazaribagh 23 58N 85 26E
19 Hazebrouck 50 42N 2 31E
92 Hazelton 55 20N 127 42W
97 Hazleton 40 58N 76 0W
54 Hazor 33 2N 35 2E
57 Hazrat Imam 37 15N 68 50E
102 Healdsburg 38 33N 122 51W
12 Heanor 53 1N 1 20W
3 Heard I. 53 0S 74 0E
90 Hearst 49 40N 83 41W
91 Heart's Content 47 54N 53 27W
91 Heath Steele 48 30N 66 20W
81 Hebel 28 59S 147 48E
91 Hebertville 47 0N 71 30W
14 Hebrides, Inner, Is. 57 20N 6 40W
14 Hebrides, Outer, Is. 57 50N 7 25W
89 Hebron, Canada 58 10N 62 50W
54 Hebron, Jordan 31 32N 35 6E
92 Hecate Str. 53 10N 130 30W
44 Hedemora 60 18N 15 58E
44 Hedmark □ 61 45N 11 0E
16 Heemstede 52 19N 4 37E
16 Heerde 52 24N 6 2E
16 Heerenveen 52 57N 5 55E
16 Heerlen 50 55N 6 0E
24 Heide 54 10N 9 7E
25 Heidelberg 49 23N 8 41E
25 Heidenheim 48 40N 10 10E
75 Heilbron 27 16S 27 59E
25 Heilbronn 49 8N 9 13E
24 Heiligenstadt 51 22N 10 9E
68 Heilungkiang □ 47 30N 129 0E
47 Heinola 61 13N 26 10E
93 Heinsburg 53 50N 110 30W
59 Heinze Is. 14 25N 97 45E
46 Hekla, Mt. 63 56N 19 35W
101 Helena, Ark. 34 30N 90 35W
102 Helena, Mont. 46 40N 112 0W
14 Helensburgh 56 0N 4 44W
85 Helensville 36 41S 174 29E
54 Helez 31 36N 34 39E
45 Helgasjön, L. 57 0N 14 54E
24 Heligoland, I. 54 10N 7 51E
75 Hell-Ville 13 25S 48 16E
16 Hellendoorn 52 24N 6 27E
33 Hellín 38 31N 1 40W
57 Helmand, Hamun 31 0N 61 0E
57 Helmand □ 31 0N 64 0E
57 Helmand, R. 31 12N 61 34E
16 Helmond 51 29N 5 41E
14 Helmsdale 58 7N 3 40W
24 Helmstedt 52 16N 11 0E
45 Helsingborg 56 3N 12 42E
47 Helsingfors= Helsinki 60 15N 25 3E
45 Helsingør 56 2N 12 35E
47 Helsinki 60 15N 25 3E
13 Helston 50 7N 5 17W
12 Helvellyn, Mt. 54 31N 3 1W
73 Helwân 29 50N 31 20E
13 Hemel Hempstead 51 45N 0 28W
32 Henares, R. 40 24N 3 30W
20 Hendaye 43 23N 1 47W
98 Henderson, Ky. 37 50N 87 38W
99 Henderson, N.C. 36 18N 78 23W
101 Henderson, Tex. 32 5N 94 49W
99 Hendersonville 35 21N 82 28W
81 Hendon 28 5S 151 50E
16 Hengelo 52 15N 6 48E
69 Hengyang 26 57N 112 28E
19 Hénin Beaumont 50 25N 2 58E
18 Hennebont 47 49N 3 19W
24 Henningsdorf 52 38N 13 13E
90 Henrietta Maria, C. 55 10N 82 30W
74 Henrique de Carvalho 9 39S 20 24E
101 Henryetta 35 2N 96 0W
84 Henty 35 30N 147 0E
59 Henzada 17 38N 95 35E
102 Heppner 45 27N 119 34W
57 Herat 34 20N 62 7E
57 Herat □ 34 20N 62 7E
20 Hérault □ 43 34N 3 15E
20 Hérault, R. 43 17N 3 26E
93 Herbert 50 30N 107 10W
80 Herbert Downs 23 0S 139 11E
40 Hercegnavi 42 30N 18 33E
13 Hereford, U.K. 52 4N 2 42W
101 Hereford, U.S.A. 34 50N 102 28W
13 Hereford and Worcester □ 52 14N 1 42W
16 Herentals 51 12N 4 51E
24 Herford 52 7N 8 40E
19 Héricourt 47 32N 6 55E
25 Herisau 47 22N 9 17E
97 Herkimer 43 0N 74 59W
18 Herm, I. 49 30N 2 28W
26 Hermagor-Pressegger See, L. 46 38N 13 23E
84 Hermidale 31 30S 146 42E
102 Hermiston 45 50N 119 16W
85 Hermitage 43 44S 170 5E
112 Hermite, I. 55 50S 68 0W
56 Hermon, Mt.= Sheikh, Jabal ash 33 20N 26 0E
104 Hermosillo 29 10N 111 0W
27 Hernad R. 47 56N 21 8E
109 Hernandarias 25 20S 54 50W
108 Hernando 32 28S 64 50W
24 Herne 51 33N 7 12E
13 Herne Bay 51 22N 1 8E
45 Herning 56 8N 9 0E
90 Heron Bay 48 40N 85 25W
56 Herowabad 37 37N 48 32E
30 Herrera de Pisuerga 42 35N 4 20W
31 Herrera del Duque 39 10N 5 3W
101 Herrin 37 50N 89 0W
45 Herrljunga 58 5N 13 5E
16 Herstal 50 40N 5 38E
13 Hertford 51 47N 0 4W
13 Hertford □ 51 51N 0 5W
30 Hervás 40 16N 5 52W
77 Hervey Is. 19 30S 159 0W
24 Herzberg 51 38N 10 20E
54 Herzliyya 32 10N 34 50E
26 Herzogenburg 48 17N 15 41E
24 Hessen □ 50 57N 9 20E
24 Hettstedt 51 39N 11 30E
18 Heve, C. de la 49 30N 0 5E
27 Heves □ 47 50N 20 0E
89 Hewett, C. 70 30N 68 0W
12 Hexham 54 58N 2 7W
12 Heysham 54 5N 2 53W
84 Heywood 38 8S 141 37E
100 Hibbing 47 30N 93 0W
99 Hickory 35 46N 81 17W
97 Hicksville 40 46N 73 30W
66 Hida Sammyaku, Mts. 36 0N 137 10E
104 Hidalgo □ 20 30N 99 10W
104 Hidalgo del Parral 26 10N 104 50W
26 Hieflau 47 36N 14 46E
72 Hierro, I. 27 57N 17 56W
69 Hifung 22 59N 115 17E
66 Higashiósaka 34 39N 135 35E
83 Higginsville 31 42S 121 38E
99 High Point 35 57N 79 58W
92 High Prairie 55 30N 116 30W
92 High River 50 30N 113 50W
13 High Wycombe 51 37N 0 45W
70 High Veld 26 30S 30 0E
14 Highland □ 57 30N 4 50W
98 Highland Park, Ill. 42 10N 87 50W
98 Highland Park, Mich. 42 25N 83 6W
32 Hijar 41 10N 0 27W
56 Hijāz, Reg. 26 0N 37 30E
66 Hikari 33 58N 131 56E
66 Hikone 35 15N 136 10E
85 Hikurangi 37 54S 178 5E
24 Hildersheim 52 9N 9 55E
16 Hillegom 52 18N 4 35E
45 Hillerød 55 56N 12 19E
13 Hillingdon 51 33N 0 29W
100 Hillsboro, Kan. 38 28N 97 10W
102 Hillsboro, Oreg. 45 31N 123 0W
101 Hillsboro, Tex. 32 0N 97 10W
90 Hillsport 49 27N 85 34W
84 Hillston 33 30S 145 31E
94 Hilo 19 44N 155 5W
16 Hilversum 52 14N 5 10E
60 Himachal Pradesh □ 31 30N 77 0E
52 Himalaya, Mts. 29 0N 84 0E
66 Himeji 34 50N 134 40E
66 Himi 36 50N 137 0E
45 Himmerland, Reg. 56 50N 9 38E
56 Hims=Homs 34 40N 36 45E
80 Hinchinbrook, I. 18 20S 146 15E
13 Hinckley 52 33N 1 21W
60 Hindaun 26 44N 77 5E
84 Hindmarsh, L. 35 50S 141 55E
57 Hindukush, Mts. 36 0N 71 0E

J

K

Knud Rasmussen Ld. Kurya

4 Knud Rasmussen Ld. 80 0N 55 0W
27 Knurów 50 13N 18 38 E
89 Koartac 61 5N 69 36W
65 Koba 6 37S 134 37 E
66 Kobe 34 45N 135 10 E
45 København 55 41N 12 34 E
25 Koblenz 50 21N 7 36 E
28 Kobyłka 52 21N 21 10 E
40 Kočane 41 53N 22 27 E
40 Kočani 41 55N 22 25 E
37 Kočevje 45 39N 14 50 E
66 Kōchi 33 30N 133 35 E
66 Kōchi □ 33 40N 133 30 E
62 Kodaikanal 10 13N 77 32 E
62 Koddiyar B. 8 33N 81 15 E
88 Kodiak 57 48N 152 23W
88 Kodiak I. 57 30N 152 45 E
60 Kodinar 20 46N 70 46 E
73 Kodok 9 53N 32 7 E
26 Köflach 47 4N 15 4 E
72 Koforidua 6 3N 0 17W
66 Kōfu 35 40N 138 30 E
45 Køge 55 27N 12 11 E
45 Køge, B. 55 30N 12 20 E
58 Kohat 33 40N 71 29 E
59 Kohima 25 35N 94 10 E
5 Kohler Ra. 77 0S 110 0W
83 Kojonup 33 48S 117 10W
50 Kokand 40 30N 70 57 E
92 Kokanee Glacier Prov. Park 49 47N 117 10W
50 Kokchetav 53 20N 69 10 E
54 Kokhav Mikha'el 31 37N 34 40 E
67 Kokiu 23 22N 103 6 E
46 Kokkola 63 50N 23 8 E
63 Koko Kyunzu, Is. 14 10N 93 30 E
67 Koko Nor, L. 37 0N 100 0 E
98 Kokomo 40 30N 86 6W
89 Koksoak, R. 58 30N 68 10W
75 Kokstad 30 32S 29 29 E
51 Kokuora 61 30N 145 0 E
48 Kola 68 45N 33 8 E
68 Kolan 38 43N 111 32 E
62 Kolar 13 12N 78 15 E
62 Kolar Gold Fields 12 58N 78 16 E
41 Kolarovgrad 43 27N 26 42 E
40 Kolašin 42 50N 19 31 E
45 Kolding 55 30N 9 29 E
65 Kolepom, I. 8 0S 138 30 E
48 Kolguyev 69 20N 48 30 E
62 Kolhapur 16 43N 74 15 E
26 Kolín 50 2N 15 9 E
62 Kollegal 12 9N 77 9 E
62 Kolleru L. 16 40N 81 10 E
24 Köln 50 56N 9 58 E
28 Koło 52 14N 18 40 E
28 Kołobrzeg 54 10N 15 35 E
48 Kołomna 55 8N 38 45 E
49 Kolomyya 48 31N 25 2 E
59 Kolosib 24 15N 92 45 E
50 Kolpashevo 58 20N 83 5 E
48 Kolskiy Pol. 67 30N 38 0 E
48 Kolskiy Zaliv 69 23N 34 0 E
74 Kolwezi 10 40S 25 25 E
51 Kolyma, R. 64 40N 153 0 E
27 Komárno 47 49N 18 5 E
27 Komarom 47 43N 18 7 E
27 Komarom □ 47 35N 18 20 E
66 Komatsu 36 25N 136 30 E
48 Komi A.S.S.R. 64 0N 55 0 E
27 Komló 46 15N 18 16 E
66 Komoro 36 19N 138 26 E
42 Komotini 41 9N 25 26 E
40 Komovi, Mt. 42 40N 19 40 E
63 Kompong Cham 11 54N 105 30 E
63 Kompong Som 10 38N 103 30 E
51 Komsomolets, Os. 80 30N 95 0 E
51 Komsomolsk 50 30N 137 0 E
51 Kondakovo 69 20N 151 30 E
83 Kondinin 32 34S 118 8 E
72 Koudougou 12 10N 2 20W
51 Kondratyevo 57 30N 98 30 E
5 Kong Haakon VII Hav, Sea 65 0S 20 0 E
68 Kongju 36 30N 127 0 E
59 Konglu 27 13N 97 57 E
69 Kongmoon 22 35N 113 1 E
74 Kongolo 5 22S 27 0 E
44 Kongsberg 59 39N 9 39 E
48 Königsberg= Kaliningrad 54 42N 20 32 E
28 Konin 52 12N 18 15 E
28 Konin □ 52 15N 18 20 E
40 Konjic 43 42N 17 58 E
48 Konosha 61 0N 40 5 E
49 Konotop 51 12N 33 7 E
28 Końskie 51 15N 20 23 E
28 Konstantynów Łódźki 51 45N 19 20 E
25 Konstanz 47 39N 9 10 E
72 Kontagora 10 23N 5 27 E
56 Konya 37 52N 32 35 E
83 Kookynie 29 17S 121 22 E
82 Kooline 22 57S 116 20 E
83 Koolyanobbing 30 48S 119 46 E
81 Koonibba 31 58S 133 27 E
83 Koorda 30 48S 117 35 E
92 Kootenay Nat. Park 51 0N 116 0W
84 Koo-wee-rup 38 13S 145 28 E
40 Kopaonik, Mts. 43 10N 21 0 E
62 Kopargaon 19 51N 74 28 E
47 Kopervik 59 17N 5 17 E
50 Kopeysk 55 7N 61 37 E
44 Köping 59 31N 16 3 E
62 Koppal 15 23N 76 5 E
44 Kopparbergs □ 61 20N 14 15 E
37 Koprivnica 46 12N 16 45 E
40 Korab, Mt. 41 44N 20 40 E
24 Korbach 51 17N 8 50 E
42 Korça 40 37N 20 50 E
42 Korça □ 40 40N 20 50 E
37 Korčula, I. 42 57N 17 0 E
56 Kordestān □ 36 0N 47 0 E
73 Kordofān □ 13 0N 29 0 E
68 Korea B. 39 0N 124 0 E
62 Koregaon 17 40N 74 10 E
72 Korhogo 9 29N 5 28 E
43 Korinthiakós Kól. 38 16N 22 30 E
43 Korinthía □ 37 50N 22 35 E
43 Kórinthos 37 26N 22 55 E
66 Kōriyama 37 24N 140 23 E
67 Korla 41 45N 86 4 E
37 Kornat, I. 43 50N 15 20 E
85 Koro Sea 17 30S 179 45W
84 Koroit 38 18S 142 24 E
43 Koróni 36 48N 21 57 E
28 Koronowo 53 19N 17 55 E
27 Körös, R. 46 30N 142 42 E
51 Korsakov 46 30N 142 42 E
45 Korsør 55 20N 11 9 E
28 Korsze 54 11N 21 9 E
16 Kortrijk 50 50N 3 17 E
84 Korumburra 38 26S 145 50 E
51 Koryakskiy Khrebet, Mts. 61 0N 171 0 E
43 Kos, I. 36 50N 27 15 E
28 Koscierzyna 54 8N 17 59 E
101 Kosciusko 33 3N 89 34W
92 Kosciusko I. 56 0N 133 40W
84 Kosciusko, Mt. 36 27S 148 16 E
62 Kosgi 16 58N 77 43 E
60 Kosi 27 48N 77 29 E
27 Košice 48 42N 21 15 E
40 Kosjerić 44 0N 19 55 E
48 Koslan 63 28N 48 52 E
40 Kosovska-Mitrovica 42 54N 20 52 E
37 Kostajnica 45 17N 16 30 E
41 Kostenets 42 15N 23 52 E
73 Kôstî 13 8N 32 43 E
48 Kostroma 57 50N 41 58 E
28 Kostrzyn 52 24N 17 14 E
28 Koszalin 54 12N 16 8 E
28 Koszalin □ 54 10N 16 10 E
27 Köszeg 47 23N 16 33 E
60 Kot Adu 30 30N 71 0 E
60 Kot Moman 32 13N 73 0 E
60 Kota 25 14N 75 49 E
63 Kota Baharu 6 7N 102 14 E
64 Kota Kinabalu 6 0N 116 12 E
63 Kota Tinggi 1 44N 103 53 E
64 Kotabaru 3 20S 116 20 E
64 Kotabumi 4 49S 104 46 E
64 Kotawaringin 2 28S 111 27 E
48 Kotelnich 58 20N 48 10 E
62 Kothagudam 17 30N 80 40 E
62 Kothapet 19 21N 79 28 E
24 Köthen 51 44N 11 59 E
47 Kotka 60 28N 26 55 E
48 Kotlas 61 15N 47 0 E
88 Kotlik 63 2N 163 33W
40 Kotor 42 25N 18 47 E
40 Kotoriba 46 37N 16 48 E
60 Kotri 25 22N 68 22 E
43 Kótronas 36 38N 22 29 E
26 Kotschach Mauthern 46 40N 13 0 E
62 Kottayam 9 35N 76 33 E
62 Kottur 10 34N 76 56 E
88 Kotzebue 66 53N 162 39W
43 Koufonísi, I. 34 56N 26 8 E
74 Koula-Moutou 1 15S 12 25 E
80 Koumala 21 38S 149 15 E
50 Kounradskiy 47 20N 75 0 E
111 Kourou 5 9N 52 39W
72 Kouroussa 10 45N 9 45W
40 Kovačica 45 5N 20 38 E
48 Kovdor 67 34N 30 22 E
48 Kovel 51 10N 25 0 E
62 Kovilpatti 9 10N 77 50 E
48 Kovrov 56 25N 41 25 E
62 Kovur, Andhra Pradesh 17 3N 81 39 E
62 Kovur, Andhra Pradesh 14 30N 80 1 E
69 Kowloon 22 20N 114 15 E
69 Koyiu 23 2N 112 28 E
88 Koyukuk, R. 64 56N 157 30W
42 Kozáni 40 19N 21 47 E
42 Kozáni □ 40 20N 21 45 E
40 Kozara, Mts. 45 0N 17 0 E
40 Kozarac 44 58N 16 48 E
62 Kozhikode= Calicut 11 15N 75 43 E
48 Kozhva 65 10N 57 0 E
28 Kozmin 51 48N 17 27 E
28 Kozuchów 51 45N 15 35 E
72 Kpandu 7 2N 0 18 E
63 Kra, Isthmus of= Kra, Kho Khot 10 15N 99 30 E
63 Kra, Kho Khot 10 15N 99 30 E
63 Kra Buri 10 22N 98 46 E
40 Kragujevac 44 2N 20 56 E
27 Kracków 50 4N 19 57 E
27 Krakow □ 50 5N 20 0 E
65 Kraksaan 7 43S 113 23 E
40 Kraljevo 43 44N 20 41 E
26 Kralupy 50 13N 14 20 E
49 Kramatorsk 48 50N 37 30 E
44 Kramfors 62 55N 17 48 E
37 Kranj 46 16N 14 22 E
37 Krapina 46 10N 15 52 E
27 Krapkowice 50 29N 17 55 E
48 Krasavino 60 58N 46 26 E
51 Kraskino 42 45N 130 58 E
26 Kraslice 50 19N 12 31 E
27 Krasnik 50 55N 22 5 E
49 Krasnodar 45 5N 38 50 E
48 Krasnokamsk 58 0N 56 0 E
50 Krasnoselkupsk 65 20N 82 10 E
50 Krasnoturinsk 59 39N 60 1 E
48 Krasnoufimsk 56 30N 57 37 E
50 Krasnouralsk 58 0N 60 0 E
50 Krasnovodsk 40 0N 52 52 E
48 Krasnovishersk 60 23N 56 59 E
51 Krasnoyarsk 56 8N 93 0 E
28 Krasnystaw 50 57N 23 5 E
49 Krasnyy Yar 46 43N 48 23 E
24 Krefeld 51 20N 6 22 E
43 Kremaston, L. 38 52N 21 30 E
49 Kremenchug 49 5N 33 25 E
49 Kremenchugskoye, Vdkhr. 49 20N 32 30 E
40 Kremenica 40 55N 21 25 E
26 Krems 48 25N 15 36 E
26 Kremsmünster 48 3N 14 8 E
41 Krichem 46 16N 24 28 E
62 Krishna, R. 15 43N 80 55 E
62 Krishnagiri 12 32N 78 16 E
61 Krishnanagar 23 24N 88 33 E
47 Kristiansand 58 5N 7 50 E
45 Kristianstad 56 5N 14 7 E
45 Kristianstads □ 56 0N 14 0 E
44 Kristiansund 63 10N 7 45 E
44 Kristinehamn 59 18N 14 13 E
46 Kristinestad 62 18N 21 25 E
43 Kriti, I. 35 15N 25 0 E
43 Kritsá 35 10N 25 41 E
40 Kriva Palanka 42 11N 22 19 E
49 Krivoy Rog 47 51N 33 20 E
40 Križevci 46 3N 16 32 E
37 Krk, I. 45 5N 14 56 E
37 Krka, R. 45 50N 15 30 E
26 Krkonoše, Mts. 50 50N 15 30 E
27 Krnov 50 5N 17 40 E
28 Krobia 51 47N 16 59 E
26 Kročehlavy 50 8N 14 9 E
27 Kroměříž 49 18N 17 21 E
45 Kronobergs □ 56 45N 14 30 E
48 Kronshtadt 60 5N 29 35 E
75 Kroonstad 27 43S 27 19 E
51 Kropotkin 58 50N 115 10 E
28 Krośniewice 52 15N 19 11 E
27 Krosno 49 35N 21 56 E
27 Krosno □ 49 30N 21 40 E
28 Krosno Odrz 52 3N 15 7 E
28 Krotoszyn 51 42N 17 23 E
37 Krsko 45 57N 15 30 E
75 Krugersdorp 26 5S 27 46 E
41 Krumovgrad 41 29N 25 38 E
63 Krung Thep 13 45N 100 35 E
27 Krupinica, R. 48 5N 18 53 E
40 Kruševac 43 35N 21 28 E
44 Krylbo 60 7N 16 15 E
49 Krymskaya 44 57N 37 50 E
28 Krzyz 52 52N 16 0 E
72 Ksar El Boukhari 35 5N 2 52 E
72 Ksar-el-Kebir 35 0N 6 0W
64 Kuala 2 46N 105 47 E
64 Kuala Dungun 4 46N 103 25 E
63 Kuala Kangsar 4 49N 100 57 E
63 Kuala Kubu Baharu 3 35N 101 38 E
63 Kuala Lipis 4 22N 102 5 E
63 Kuala Lumpur 3 9N 101 41 E
63 Kuala Pilah 2 45N 102 14 E
63 Kuala Selangor 3 20N 101 15 E
63 Kuala Terengganu 5 20N 103 8 E
64 Kualakapuas 2 55S 114 20 E
64 Kualakurun 1 10S 113 50 E
64 Kualapembuang 3 14S 112 38 E
64 Kualasimpang 4 16N 98 4 E
63 Kuantan 3 49N 103 20 E
49 Kuba 41 21N 48 22 E
58 Kubak 27 10N 63 10 E
49 Kuban, R. 45 20N 37 30 E
66 Kubokawa 33 12N 133 8 E
67 Kucha 41 50N 82 30 E
60 Kuchaman 27 13N 74 47 E
26 Kuchenspitze, Mt. 47 3N 10 14 E
64 Kuching 1 33N 110 25 E
66 Kuchinotsu 32 36N 130 11 E
64 Kudat 7 0N 116 42 E
65 Kudus 6 48N 110 51 E
73 Kufra, El Wâhât et 24 17N 23 15 E
26 Kufstein 47 35N 12 11 E
26 Kuhnsdorf 46 37N 14 38 E
57 Kūhpāyeh 32 44N 52 20 E
83 Kukerin 33 13S 118 0 E
42 Kukësi □ 42 15N 20 15 E
40 Kula, Bulgaria 43 52N 22 36 E
40 Kula, Yug. 45 37N 19 32 E
61 Kula Kangri, Mt. 28 14N 90 47 E
63 Kulai 1 44N 103 35 E
62 Kulasekharapattanam 8 20N 78 0 E
80 Kulgera 25 50S 133 18 E
83 Kulin 32 40S 118 2 E
83 Kulja 30 35S 117 31 E
50 Kulsary 46 59N 54 1 E
61 Kulti 23 43N 86 50 E
50 Kulunda 52 45N 79 15 E
50 Kulyab 37 55N 69 50 E
67 Kum Darya, R. 41 0N 89 0 E
50 Kum Tekei 43 10N 79 30 E
64 Kumai 2 52S 111 45 E
66 Kumamoto 32 45N 130 45 E
66 Kumamoto □ 32 30N 130 40 E
40 Kumanovo 42 9N 21 42 E
85 Kumara 42 37S 171 12 E
83 Kumari 32 45S 121 30 E
72 Kumasi 6 41N 1 38 E
72 Kumba 4 36N 9 24 E
62 Kumbakonam 10 58N 79 25 E
81 Kumbarilla 27 15S 150 55 E
66 Kumagaya 36 9N 139 22 E
48 Kumertau 52 46N 55 47 E
44 Kumla 59 8N 15 10 E
25 Kummerower See 53 49N 12 52 E
72 Kumo 10 1N 11 12 E
59 Kumon Bum, Mts. 26 0N 97 15 E
62 Kumta 14 29N 74 32 E
57 Kunar □ 35 15N 71 0 E
60 Kunch 26 0N 79 10 E
83 Kundip 33 42S 120 10 E
60 Kundla 21 21N 71 25 E
57 Kunduz 36 50N 68 50 E
57 Kunduz □ 36 50N 68 50 E
45 Kungälv 57 54N 12 0 E
68 Kungchuling 43 31N 124 58 E
67 Kungho 36 28N 100 45 E
50 Kungrad 43 6N 58 54 E
45 Kungsbacka 57 30N 12 7 E
44 Kungsör 59 25N 16 5 E
27 Kunhegyes 47 22N 20 36 E
69 Kunhsien 32 30N 111 17 E
65 Kuningan 6 59S 108 29 E
59 Kunlong 23 20N 98 50 E
52 Kunlun Shan, Mts. 36 0N 82 0 E
67 Kunming 25 11N 102 37 E
62 Kunnamkulam 10 38N 76 7 E
68 Kunsan 35 59N 126 35 E
82 Kununurra 15 40S 128 39 E
80 Kunwarara 22 25S 150 7 E
46 Kuopio 62 53N 27 35 E
46 Kuopio □ 63 25N 27 10 E
65 Kupang 10 19S 123 39 E
92 Kupreanof I. 56 50N 133 30W
40 Kupres 44 1N 17 15 E
49 Kura, R. 39 24N 49 24 E
62 Kurandvad 16 45N 74 39 E
66 Kurashiki 34 40N 133 50 E
66 Kurayoshi 35 26N 133 50 E
62 Kurduvadi 18 8N 75 29 E
41 Kŭrdzhali 41 38N 25 21 E
66 Kure 34 14N 132 32 E
50 Kurgaldzhino 50 35N 70 20 E
50 Kurgan 55 30N 65 0 E
62 Kurichchi 11 36N 77 35 E
51 Kurilskiye Os. 45 0N 150 0 E
66 Kurino 31 57N 130 43 E
62 Kurla 19 5N 72 52 E
62 Kurnool 15 45N 78 0 E
85 Kurow 44 4S 170 29 E
84 Kurri Kurri 32 50S 151 28 E
61 Kurseong 26 56N 88 18 E
48 Kursk 51 42N 36 11 E
40 Kuršumlija 43 9N 21 19 E
66 Kurume 33 15N 130 30 E
62 Kurunegala 7 30N 80 18 E
51 Kurya 61 15N 108 10 E

Louis Trichardt Maiduguri

75 Louis Trichardt 23 0S 25 55E
91 Louisbourg 45 55N 60 0W
90 Louiseville 46 20N 73 0W
76 Louisiade Arch. 11 10S 153 0E
101 Louisiana □ 30 50N 92 0W
98 Louisville, Ky. 38 15N 85 45W
101 Louisville, Miss. 33 7N 89 3W
20 Loulay 46 3N 0 30W
31 Loulé 37 9N 8 0W
26 Louny 50 20N 13 48E
100 Loup City 41 19N 98 57E
20 Lourdes 43 6N 0 3W
75 Lourenço Marques= Maputo 25 58S 32 32E
31 Lourinha 39 14N 9 17W
30 Lousã 40 7N 8 14W
81 Louth, Australia 30 30S 145 8E
15 Louth, Eire 53 47N 6 33W
12 Louth, U.K. 53 23N 0 0
15 Louth □ 53 55N 6 30W
43 Loutra-Aidhipsoú 38 54N 23 2E
18 Louviers 49 12N 1 10E
93 Love 53 29N 104 9W
41 Lovech 43 8N 24 43E
100 Loveland 40 27N 105 4W
102 Lovelock 40 17N 118 25W
30 Lovios 41 55E 8 4W
47 Lovisa 60 28N 26 12E
26 Lovosice 50 30N 14 2E
37 Lovran 45 18N 14 15E
40 Lovrin 45 58N 20 48E
97 Lowell 42 38N 71 19W
85 Lower Hutt 41 10S 174 55E
13 Lowestoft 52 29N 1 44E
28 Łowicz 52 6N 19 55E
97 Lowville 43 48N 75 30W
81 Loxton 34 28S 140 31E
76 Loyalty Is 21 0S 167 30E
69 Loyang 34 41N 112 28E
69 Loyung 24 25N 109 25E
20 Lozère □ 44 35N 3 30E
40 Loznica 44 32N 19 14E
68 Lu-ta 39 0N 121 31E
74 Lualaba, R. 0 26N 25 20E
74 Luanda 8 58S 13 9E
63 Luang Prabang 19 45N 102 10E
75 Luangwa, R. 15 40N 30 25E
75 Luanshya 13 3S 28 28E
30 Luarca 43 32N 6 32W
28 Lubań 51 5N 15 15E
65 Lubang Is. 13 50N 120 12E
28 Lubartów 51 28N 22 42E
54 Lubban 32 9N 35 14E
24 Lübben 51 56N 13 54E
101 Lubbock 33 40N 102 0W
24 Lübeck 53 52N 10 41E
74 Lubefu 4 47S 24 27E
28 Lubin 51 24N 16 11E
28 Lublin 51 12N 22 38E
28 Lublin □ 51 5N 22 30E
28 Lubliniec 50 43N 18 45E
56 Lubnān, Mts. 34 0N 36 0E
28 Lubon 52 21N 16 51E
28 Lubsko 51 45N 14 57E
64 Lubuklinggau 3 15S 102 55E
64 Lubuksikaping 0 10N 100 15E
75 Lubumbashi 11 32S 27 28E
74 Lubutu 0 45S 26 30E
88 Lucania, Mt. 60 48N 141 25W
36 Lucca 43 50N 10 30E
14 Luce B. 54 45N 4 48W
65 Lucena, Philippines 13 56N 121 37E
31 Lucena, Sp. 37 27N 4 31W
32 Lucena del Cid 40 9N 0 17W
27 Lučenec 48 18N 19 42E
39 Lucera 41 30N 15 20E
33 Luchena, R. 37 44N 1 50W
24 Lüchow 52 58N 11 8E
69 Luchow 29 2N 105 10E
24 Luckenwalde 52 5N 13 11E
61 Lucknow 26 50N 81 0E
20 Luçon 46 28N 1 10W
37 Ludbreg 46 15N 16 38E
24 Lüdenscheid 51 13N 7 37E
75 Lüderitz 26 41S 15 8E
60 Ludhiana 30 57N 75 56E
98 Ludington 43 58N 86 27W
13 Ludlow 52 23N 2 42W
41 Ludus 46 29N 24 5E
44 Ludvika 60 8N 15 14E
25 Ludwigsburg 48 53N 9 11E
25 Ludwigshafen 49 27N 8 27E
24 Ludwigslust 53 19N 11 28E
101 Lufkin 31 25N 94 40W
48 Luga 58 40N 29 55E
25 Lugano 46 0N 8 57E
25 Lugano, L. di 46 0N 9 0E
49 Lugansk= Voroshilovgrad 48 35N 39 29E
55 Lugh Ganana 3 48N 42 40E
30 Lugo, Sp. 43 2N 7 35W
37 Lugo, It. 44 25N 11 53E
30 Lugo □ 43 0N 7 30W
40 Lugoj 45 42N 21 57E
30 Lugones 43 26N 5 50W
50 Lugovoy 43 0N 72 20E
36 Luino 46 0N 8 24E
111 Luis Correia 3 0S 41 35W
108 Luján 34 45S 59 5W
69 Lukang 24 0N 120 19E
61 Lukhisarai 27 11N 86 5E
41 Lukovit 43 13N 24 11E
28 Łuków 51 56N 22 23E
75 Lukulu 14 35S 23 25E
46 Luleå 65 35N 22 10E
74 Lulonga, R. 0 43N 18 23E
74 Lulua, R. 5 2S 21 7E
74 Luluabourg= Kananga 5 55S 22 18E
99 Lumberton 34 37N 78 59W
85 Lumsden 45 44S 168 27E
68 Lun 47 55N 105 1E
60 Lunavada 23 8N 73 37E
45 Lund 55 41N 13 12E
75 Lundazi 12 20S 33 7E
13 Lundy, I. 51 10N 4 41W
12 Lune, R. 54 2N 2 50W
24 Lüneburg 53 15N 10 23E
24 Lüneburger Heide, Reg. 53 0N 10 0E
21 Lunel 43 39N 7 31E
24 Lunen 51 36N 7 31E
91 Lunenburg 44 22N 64 18W
19 Lunéville 48 36N 6 30E
68 Lunghwa 41 15N 117 51E
68 Lungkiang 47 22N 123 4E
68 Lungkow 37 40N 120 25E
59 Lungleh 22 55N 92 45E
68 Lungsi 35 0N 104 35E
60 Luni, R. 24 40N 71 15E
74 Luofu 0 1S 29 15E
41 Lupeni 45 21N 23 13E
108 Luque 37 35N 4 16W
19 Lure 47 40N 6 30E
15 Lurgan 54 28N 6 20W
75 Lusaka 15 28S 28 16E
42 Lushnja 40 55N 19 41E
74 Lushoto 4 47S 38 20E
68 Lushun 38 48N 121 16E
75 Luso 11 47S 19 52E
20 Lussac-les-Châteaux 46 24N 0 43E
13 Luton 51 53N 0 24W
64 Lutong 4 30N 114 0E
48 Lutsk 50 50N 25 15E
5 Lützow Holnbukta, B. 69 0S 38 0E
16 Luxembourg 49 37N 6 9E
16 Luxembourg ■ 50 0N 6 0E
16 Luxembourg □ 49 58N 5 30E
19 Luxeuil-les-Bains 47 49N 6 24E
73 Luxor=El Uqsur 25 41N 32 38E
20 Luy, R. 43 39N 1 8W
48 Luza 60 39N 47 10E
25 Luzern 47 3N 8 18E
25 Luzern □ 47 2N 7 55E
111 Luziania 16 20S 48 0W
65 Luzon, I. 16 0N 121 0E
20 Luzy 46 47N 3 58E
49 Lvov 49 40N 24 0E
68 Lwanhsien 39 45N 118 45E
28 Lwówek Śl 51 7N 15 38E
51 Lyakhovskiye Os. 73 40N 141 0E
60 Lyallpur 31 30N 73 5E
41 Lyaskovets 43 6N 25 44E
14 Lybster 58 18N 3 16W
45 Lyckeby 56 12N 15 37E
46 Lycksele 64 38N 18 40E
54 Lydda=Lod 31 57N 34 54E
75 Lydenburg 25 10S 30 29E
85 Lyell 41 48S 172 4E
85 Lyell, Ra. 41 38S 172 20E
13 Lyme Regis 50 44N 2 57W
13 Lymington 50 46N 1 32W
98 Lynchburg 37 23N 79 10W
84 Lyndhurst, N.S.W. 33 41N 149 2E
80 Lyndhurst, Queens. 18 56S 144 30E
97 Lyndonville 44 32N 72 1W
97 Lynn 42 28N 70 57W
93 Lynn Lake 56 51N 101 3W
13 Lynton 51 14N 3 50W
21 Lyon 45 46N 4 50E
21 Lyonnais, Reg. 45 45N 4 15E
83 Lyons, R. 25 2N 115 9W
97 Lyons Falls 43 37N 75 22W
26 Lysá 50 11N 14 51E
45 Lysekil 58 17N 11 26E
48 Lysra 57 7N 57 47E
12 Lytham St. Annes 53 45N 2 58W
85 Lyttelton 43 35S 172 44E
41 Lyubimets 41 50N 26 5E

M

54 Ma'ad 32 37N 35 36E
69 Maanshan 31 40N 118 30E
16 Maas, R. 51 49N 5 1E
16 Maastricht 50 50N 5 40E
12 Mablethorpe 53 21N 0 14E
109 Macaé 20 20S 41 55W
101 McAllen 26 12N 98 15W
101 McAlester 34 57N 95 40W
111 Macapá 0 5N 51 10W
80 McArthur, R. 15 54S 136 40E
111 Macau 5 0S 36 40W
69 Macau ■ 22 16N 113 35E
92 McBride 53 20N 120 10W
102 McCammon 42 41N 112 11W
12 Macclesfield 53 16N 2 9W
93 McClintock 57 45N 94 15W
88 M'Clintock Chan. 71 0N 103 0W
101 McComb 31 20N 90 30W
100 McCook 40 15N 100 35W
3 McDonald I. 54 0S 73 0E
82 Macdonnell, Ras. 23 40S 133 0E
81 McDouall Peak 29 51S 134 55E
88 Macdougall, L. 66 20N 98 30W
14 Macduff 57 40N 2 30W
90 Mace 48 55N 80 0W
30 Maceda 42 16N 7 39W
30 Macedo de Cavaleiros 41 31N 6 57W
111 Maceió 9 40S 35 41W
72 Macenta 8 35N 9 20W
37 Macerata 43 19N 13 28E
102 McGill 35 27N 114 50W
15 Macgillycuddy's Reeks, Mts. 52 2N 9 45W
108 Machagai 26 56S 60 2W
74 Machakos 1 30S 37 15E
110 Machala 3 10S 79 50W
51 Machetna 61 20N 172 20E
30 Machichaco, C. 43 28N 2 47W
110 Machiques 10 4N 72 34W
13 Machynlleth 52 36N 3 51W
72 Macias Nguema Biyoga, I. 3 30N 8 40E
81 Macintyre, R. 28 38S 150 47E
30 Macizo Galaico 42 30N 7 30W
80 Mackay, Australia 21 36S 148 39E
102 Mackay, U.S.A. 43 58N 113 37W
82 Mackay, L. 22 40S 128 35E
96 McKees Rocks 40 27N 80 3W
96 McKeesport 40 21N 79 50W
92 Mackenzie 55 20N 123 5W
88 Mackenzie, Reg. 61 30N 144 30W
88 Mackenzie, R. 69 15N 134 8W
110 Mackenzie City 6 0N 58 10W
88 Mackenzie Mts. 64 0N 130 0W
80 McKinlay 21 16S 141 17E
88 McKinley, Mt. 63 10N 151 0W
4 McKinley Sea 84 0N 10 0W
101 McKinney 33 10N 96 40W
93 Macklin 52 20N 109 56W
81 Macksville 30 40S 152 56E
81 Maclean 29 26S 153 16E
75 Maclear 31 2S 28 23E
81 Macleay, R. 30 52S 153 1E
92 McLennan 55 42N 116 50W
83 McLeod, L. 24 9S 113 47E
92 McLure 50 55N 120 20W
86 M'Clure Str. 74 40N 117 30W
102 McMinnville, Oreg. 45 16N 123 11W
99 McMinnville, Tenn. 35 43N 85 45W
93 McMurray 56 45N 111 27W
103 McNary 34 4N 109 53W
100 Macomb 40 25N 90 40W
38 Macomer 40 16N 8 48E
21 Mâcon 46 19N 4 50E
99 Macon 32 50N 83 37W
100 McPherson 38 25N 97 40W
76 Macquarie Is. 54 36S 158 55S
84 Macquarie, R. 30 7S 147 24E
5 Mac Robertson Coast 68 30S 63 0E
15 Macroom 51 54N 8 57W
56 Madā'in Sālih 26 51N 37 58E
75 Madagascar ■ 20 0S 47 0E
73 Madama 22 0N 14 0E
62 Madanapalle 13 33N 78 34E
76 Madane 5 0S 145 46E
61 Madaripur 23 2N 90 15E
59 Madauk 17 56N 96 52E
96 Madawaska 45 30N 77 55W
59 Madaya 22 20N 96 10E
38 Maddalena, I. 41 15N 9 23E
39 Maddaloni 41 4N 14 23E
104 Madden L. 9 20N 79 37W
72 Madeira, I. 32 50N 17 0W
110 Madeira, R. 3 22S 58 45W
103 Madera 37 0N 120 1W
61 Madhupur 24 18N 86 37E
60 Madhya Pradesh □ 21 50N 81 0E
55 Madinat al Shaab 12 50N 45 0E
74 Madingou 4 10S 13 33E
98 Madison, Ind. 38 42N 85 20W
100 Madison, S.D. 44 0N 97 8W
100 Madison, Wis. 43 5N 89 25W
98 Madisonville 37 42N 86 30W
65 Madiun 7 38S 111 32E
62 Madras, India 13 8N 80 19E
102 Madras, U.S.A. 44 40N 121 10W
104 Madre, Laguna 25 0N 97 30W
110 Madre de Dios, R. 10 59S 66 8W
112 Madre de Dios, I. 50 20S 75 10W
104 Madre del Sur, Sa. 17 30N 100 0W
104 Madre Occidental, Sa. 27 0N 107 0W
104 Madre Oriental, Sa. 25 0N 100 0W
30 Madrid 40 25N 3 45W
30 Madrid □ 40 30N 3 45W
31 Madridejos 39 28N 3 33W
31 Madrona, Sa. 38 27N 4 16W
31 Madroñera 39 26N 5 42W
65 Madura, I. 7 0N 113 20E
65 Madura, Selat 7 30S 113 20E
83 Madura Motel 31 55S 127 0E
62 Madurai 9 55N 78 10E
62 Madurantakam 12 30N 79 50E
66 Maebashi 36 23N 139 4E
41 Măeruş 45 53N 25 31E
13 Maesteg 51 36N 3 40W
105 Maestra, Sa. 20 15N 77 0W
32 Maestrazgo, Mts. de 40 30N 0 25W
75 Maevatanana 16 56S 46 49E
93 Mafeking, Canada 52 40N 101 10W
75 Mafeking, S.Africa 25 50S 25 38E
74 Mafia I. 7 45S 39 50E
109 Mafra 36 10N 50 0W
51 Magadan 59 30N 151 0E
74 Magadi 1 54S 36 19E
112 Magallanes, Estrecho de, Str. 52 30S 75 0W
110 Magangue 9 14N 74 45W
91 Magdalen Is. 47 30N 61 40W
104 Magdalena, Mexico 30 50N 112 0W
103 Magdalena, U.S.A. 34 10N 107 20W
112 Magdalena, I., Chile 44 42S 73 10W
104 Magdalena, I., Mexico 24 40N 112 15W
24 Magdeburg 52 8N 11 36E
24 Magdeburg □ 52 20N 11 40E
54 Magdi'el 32 10N 34 54E
15 Magee, I. 54 48N 5 44W
65 Magelang 7 29S 110 13E
36 Maggiorasca, Mt. 44 33N 9 29E
36 Maggiore, L. 46 0N 8 35E
54 Maghar 32 54N 35 24E
15 Magherafelt 54 45N 6 36W
15 Magherafelt □ 54 45N 6 36W
37 Magione 43 10N 12 12E
39 Máglie 40 8N 18 17E
43 Magnisía □ 39 24N 22 46E
50 Magnitogorsk 53 20N 59 0E
101 Magnolia 33 18N 93 12W
91 Magog 45 18N 72 9W
92 Magrath 49 25N 112 50W
33 Magro, R. 39 11N 0 25W
111 Maguarinho, C. 0 15S 48 30W
59 Magwe 20 10N 95 0E
56 Mahābād 36 50N 45 45E
61 Mahabharat Lekh, Mts. 28 30N 82 0E
62 Mahad 18 6N 73 29E
55 Mahaddei Uen 3 0N 45 32E
60 Mahadeo Hills 22 20N 78 30E
75 Mahalapye 23 1S 26 51E
57 Mahallāt 33 55N 50 30E
61 Mahanadi, R. 20 0N 86 25E
61 Mahananda, R. 24 29N 88 18E
97 Mahanoy City 40 48N 76 10W
60 Maharashtra □ 19 30N 75 30E
62 Mahboobabad 17 42N 80 2E
62 Mahbubnagar 16 45N 77 59E
73 Mahdia 35 28N 11 0E
62 Mahé 11 42N 75 34E
85 Maheno 45 10S 170 50E
85 Mahia Pen. 39 9S 177 55E
61 Mahoba 25 15N 79 55E
32 Mahón 39 50N 4 18E
91 Mahone Bay 44 27N 64 23W
60 Mahuva 25 7N 71 46E
74 Mai-Ndombe, L. 2 0S 18 0E
13 Maidenhead 51 31N 0 42W
93 Maidstone, Canada 53 5N 109 20W
13 Maidstone, U.K. 51 16N 0 31E
73 Maiduguri 12 0N 13 20E

Maijdi Martapura, Kalimantan

61 Maijdi 22 48N 91 10E
61 Maikala Ra. 22 0N 81 0E
19 Mailly-le-Camp 48 41N 4 12E
15 Main, R. 54 43N 6 18W
25 Main, R. 50 0N 8 18E
99 Maine □ 45 20N 69 0W
18 Maine, Reg. 48 0N 0 0E
18 Maine-et-Loire □ 47 31N 0 30W
59 Maingkwan 26 15N 96 45E
14 Mainland, I., Orkney 59 0N 3 10W
14 Mainland, I., Shetland 60 15N 1 22W
60 Mainpuri 27 18N 79 4E
25 Mainz 50 0N 8 17E
108 Maipú 37 0S 58 0W
110 Maiquetía 10 36N 66 57W
59 Mairabari 26 30N 92 30E
105 Maisí, C. 20 10N 74 10W
19 Maisse 48 24N 2 21E
84 Maitland 32 44S 151 36E
66 Maizuru 35 25N 135 22E
65 Majalengka 6 55S 108 14E
54 Majd el Kurum 32 56N 35 15E
65 Majene 3 27S 118 57E
40 Majevica, Mts. 44 45N 18 50E
75 Majunga 17 0S 47 0E
61 Makalu, Mt. 27 54N 87 6E
51 Makarovo 57 40N 107 45E
40 Makarska 43 18N 17 2E
65 Makasar, Selat, Str. 1 0S 118 20E
50 Makat 47 39N 53 19E
42 Makedhonia □ 40 39N 53 19E
72 Makeni 8 55N 12 5W
49 Makeyevka 48 0N 38 0E
75 Makgadikgadi Salt Pans 20 40S 25 45E
49 Makhachkala 43 0N 47 15E
74 Makindu 2 17S 37 49E
50 Makinsk 52 37N 70 26E
56 Makkah 21 30N 39 54E
91 Makkovik 55 0N 59 10W
51 Maklakovo 58 16N 92 29E
27 Makó 46 14N 20 33E
74 Makokou 0 40N 12 50E
58 Makran Coast Ra. 25 40N 4 0E
56 Māku 39 15N 44 31E
66 Makurazaki 31 15N 130 20E
72 Makurdi 7 45N 8 32E
49 Mal Usen, R. 48 50N 49 39E
37 Mala Kapela, Mts. 44 45N 15 30E
62 Malabar Coast, Reg. 11 0N 75 0E
63 Malacca, Str. of 3 0N 101 0E
27 Malacky 48 27N 17 0E
102 Malad City 41 10N 112 20W
31 Málaga 36 43N 4 23W
31 Málaga □ 36 38N 4 58W
75 Malagasy Rep.= Madagascar ■ 19 0S 46 0E
31 Malagón 39 11N 3 52W
31 Malagón, R. 37 35N 7 29W
73 Malakâl 9 33N 31 50E
58 Malakand 34 40N 71 55E
51 Malamyzh 50 0N 136 50E
65 Malang 7 59S 112 35E
74 Malanje 9 30S 16 17E
44 Mälaren, L. 59 30N 17 10E
90 Malartic 48 9N 78 9W
56 Malatya 38 25N 38 20E
75 Malawi ■ 13 0S 34 0E
75 Malawi, L. 12 30S 34 30E
63 Malay Pen. 5 0N 102 0E
63 Malaya □ 4 0N 102 0E
56 Malayer 28 22N 56 38E
64 Malaysia ■ 5 0N 110 0E
80 Malbon 21 5S 140 17E
31 Malbooma 30 41S 134 11E
28 Malbork 54 3N 19 10E
24 Malchow 53 29N 12 25E
83 Malcolm 28 51S 121 25E
97 Malden 42 26N 71 5W
77 Malden I. 4 3S 154 59W
53 Maldive Is. 2 0N 73 0W
109 Maldonado 35 0S 55 0W
27 Malé Karpaty, Mts. 48 30N 17 20E
60 Malegaon 20 30N 74 30E
60 Malerkotla 30 32N 75 58E
19 Malesherbes 48 15N 2 24E
32 Malgrat 41 39N 2 46E
73 Malha 15 8N 26 12E
72 Mali ■ 15 0N 10 0W
40 Mali, Kanal 45 36N 19 24E
15 Malin Hd. 55 18N 7 16W
74 Malindi 3 12S 40 5E
65 Malingping 6 45S 106 2E
84 Mallacoota, Inlet 34 40S 149 40E
14 Mallaig 57 0N 5 50W
61 Mallawan 27 4N 80 12E
73 Mallawi 27 44N 30 44E
43 Mállia 35 17N 25 27E
32 Mallorca, I. 39 30N 3 0E
15 Mallow 52 8N 8 39W
46 Malmberget 67 11N 20 40E
45 Malmö 55 36N 12 59E
45 Malmöhus □ 55 45N 13 30E
41 Malnaş 46 2N 25 49E
65 Malolos 14 50N 21 2E
97 Malone 44 50N 74 19W
31 Malpartida 39 26N 6 30W
30 Malpica 43 19N 8 50W
102 Malta 48 20N 107 55W
73 Malta ■ 35 50N 14 30E
12 Malton 54 9N 0 48W
65 Maluku, Is. 3 0S 128 0E
44 Malung 60 42N 13 44E
62 Malvalli 12 28N 77 8E
62 Malvan 16 2N 73 30E
13 Malvern, U.K. 52 7N 2 19W
101 Malvern, U.S.A. 34 22N 92 50W
13 Malvern Hills 52 0N 2 19W
111 Mamanguape 6 50S 35 4W
65 Mamasa 2 55S 119 20E
18 Mamers 48 21N 0 22E
39 Mámmola 38 23N 16 13E
103 Mammoth 32 46N 110 43W
69 Mamoi 26 0N 119 25E
110 Mamoré, R. 10 23S 65 53W
72 Mamou 10 15N 12 0W
64 Mampawah 0 30N 109 5E
28 Mamry, L. 54 8N 21 42E
72 Man 7 30N 7 40W
12 Man, I. of 54 15N 4 30W
59 Man Na 23 27N 97 19E
111 Mana 5 45N 53 55W
62 Manaar, G. of 8 30N 79 0E
110 Manacapuru 3 10S 60 50W
32 Manacor 39 32N 3 12E
65 Manado 1 40N 124 45E
105 Managua 12 0N 86 20W
105 Managua, L. de 12 20N 86 30W
75 Mananjary 21 13S 48 20E
85 Manapouri, L. 45 32S 167 32E
61 Manaslu, Mt. 28 33N 84 33E
67 Manass 44 20N 86 21E
59 Manaung Kyun, I. 18 45N 93 40E
110 Manaus 3 0S 60 0W
31 Mancha Real 37 48N 3 39W
18 Manche □ 49 10N 1 20W
12 Manchester, U.K. 53 30N 2 15W
97 Manchester, Conn. 41 47N 72 30W
97 Manchester, N.H. 42 58N 71 29W
68 Manchouli 49 46N 117 24E
109 Mandaguari 23 32S 51 42W
47 Mandal 58 2N 7 25E
65 Mandala, Puncak, Mt. 4 30S 141 0E
59 Mandalay 22 0N 96 10E
68 Mandalgovi 45 40N 106 22E
56 Mandali 33 52N 45 28E
100 Mandan 46 50N 101 0W
65 Mandar, Teluk, G. 3 35S 119 4E
75 Mandimba 14 22S 35 33E
61 Mandla 22 39N 80 30E
45 Mandø, I. 55 18N 8 33E
75 Mandritsara 15 50S 48 49E
60 Mandsaur 24 3N 75 8E
83 Mandurah 32 32S 115 43E
39 Mandúria 40 25N 17 38E
60 Mandvi 22 51N 69 22E
62 Mandya 12 30N 77 0E
73 Manfalût 27 20N 30 52E
39 Manfredónia 41 40N 15 55E
39 Manfredónia, G. di 41 30N 16 10E
62 Mangalagiri 16 26N 80 36E
41 Mangalia 43 50N 28 35E
62 Mangalore 12 55N 74 47E
30 Manganeses 41 45N 5 43W
85 Mangaweka 39 48S 175 47E
64 Manggar 2 50S 108 10E
58 Mangla Dam 33 32N 73 50E
65 Mangole, I. 1 50S 125 55E
85 Mangonui 35 1S 173 32E
30 Mangualde 40 38N 7 48W
109 Mangueira, L. 33 0S 52 50W
67 Mangyai 38 6N 91 37E
50 Mangyshlak Pol. 43 40N 52 30E
100 Manhattan 39 10N 96 40W
111 Manhuaçu 20 15S 42 2W
37 Maniago 46 11N 12 40E
110 Manicoré 6 0S 61 10W
91 Manicouagan, L. 51 25N 68 15W
77 Manihiki, I. 11 0S 161 0W
65 Manila 14 40N 121 3E
65 Manila B. 14 0N 120 0E
84 Manildra 33 11S 148 41E
81 Manilla 30 45S 150 43E
59 Manipur □ 24 30N 94 0E
56 Manisa 38 38N 27 30E
98 Manistee 44 15N 86 20W
98 Manistique 45 59N 86 18W
93 Manitoba □ 55 30N 97 0W
93 Manitoba, L. 50 40N 98 30W
100 Manitou Springs 38 52N 104 55W
90 Manitoulin I. 45 40N 82 30W
98 Manitowoc 44 8N 87 40W
110 Manizales 5 5N 75 32W
62 Manjeri 11 7N 76 11E
56 Manjil 36 46N 49 30E
83 Manjimup 34 15S 116 6E
62 Manjra, R. 18 49N 77 52E
100 Mankato, Kans. 39 49N 98 11W
100 Mankato, Minn. 44 8N 93 59W
72 Mankono 8 10N 6 10W
32 Manlleu 42 2N 2 17E
84 Manly 33 48S 151 14E
81 Mannahill 32 26S 139 59E
62 Mannargudi 10 45N 79 32E
25 Mannheim 49 28N 8 29E
92 Manning 56 53N 117 39W
38 Mannu, C. 40 2N 8 24E
38 Mannu, R. 40 50N 8 23E
81 Mannum 34 57S 139 12E
65 Manokwari 0 54N 134 0E
74 Manono 7 18S 27 25E
21 Manosque 43 49N 5 47E
32 Manresa 41 48N 1 50E
60 Mansa, India 30 0N 75 27E
74 Mansa, Zambia 11 13S 28 55E
89 Mansel I. 62 0N 80 0W
84 Mansfield, Australia 37 0S 146 0E
12 Mansfield, U.K. 53 8N 1 12W
96 Mansfield, U.S.A. 40 45N 82 30W
97 Mansfield, Mt. 44 33N 72 49W
30 Mansilla de las Mules 42 30N 5 25W
20 Mansle 45 52N 0 9E
110 Manta 1 0S 80 40W
103 Manteca 37 50N 121 12W
19 Mantes-la-Jolie 49 0N 1 41E
102 Manti 39 23N 111 32W
109 Mantiqueira, Sa. da 22 0S 44 0W
36 Mántova 45 10N 10 47E
65 Manukan 8 14N 123 3E
85 Manukau 37 2S 174 54E
62 Manwath 19 19N 76 32E
49 Manych-Gudilo, Oz. 46 24N 42 38E
74 Manyoni 5 45S 34 55E
60 Manzai 32 20N 70 15E
30 Manzaneda, Cabeza de 42 12N 7 15W
105 Manzanillo, Cuba 20 20N 77 10W
104 Manzanillo, Mexico 19 0N 104 20W
105 Manzanillo, Pta. 9 30N 79 40W
73 Mao 14 4N 15 19E
93 Maple Creek 49 55N 109 27W
100 Maplewood 38 33N 90 18W
62 Mapuca 15 36N 73 46E
57 Maputo 25 58S 32 32E
56 Maqnā 28 25N 34 50E
112 Maquinchao 41 15S 68 50W
109 Mar Sa. do 25 30S 49 0W
108 Mar Chiquita, L. 30 40S 62 50W
108 Mar del Plata 38 0S 57 30W
111 Marabá 5 20S 49 5W
110 Maracaibo 10 40N 71 37W
110 Maracaibo, L. de 9 40N 71 30W
109 Maracaju 21 38S 55 9W
110 Maracay 10 15N 67 36W
73 Maradah 29 4N 19 4E
72 Maradi 13 35N 8 10E
56 Maragheh 37 30N 46 12E
111 Marajó, I. de 1 0S 49 30W
56 Marand 38 30N 45 45E
75 Marandellas 18 5S 31 42E
111 Maranguape 3 55S 38 50W
111 Maranhão=São Luís 2 39S 44 15W
111 Maranhão □ 5 0S 46 0W
37 Marano, L. di 45 42N 13 13E
110 Marañón, R. 4 50S 75 35W
56 Maraş 37 37N 36 53E
41 Mărăşeşti 45 52N 27 5E
31 Marateca 38 34N 8 40W
43 Marathókambos 37 43N 26 42E
80 Marathon 20 51S 143 32E
55 Marbat 17 0N 54 45E
31 Marbella 36 30N 4 57W
82 Marble Bar 21 9S 119 44E
97 Marblehead 42 29N 70 51W
24 Marburg 50 49N 8 44E
27 Marcal, R. 47 41N 17 32E
36 Marcaria 45 7N 10 34E
13 March 57 33N 0 5E
37 Marche □ 43 22N 13 10E
20 Marche, Reg. 46 5N 2 10E
16 Marche-en-Famenne 50 14N 5 19E
31 Marchena 37 18N 5 23W
39 Marcianise 41 3N 14 16E
19 Marck 50 57N 1 57E
108 Marcos Juárez 32 42S 62 5W
76 Marcus I. 24 0N 153 45E
97 Marcy, Mt. 44 7N 73 55W
58 Mardan 34 12N 72 2E
56 Mardin 37 20N 40 36E
14 Maree, L. 57 40N 5 30W
80 Mareeba 16 59S 145 28E
37 Maremma, Reg. 42 45N 11 15E
62 Margao 14 12N 73 58E
92 Margaret Bay 51 20N 127 20W
82 Margaret River 18 0S 126 30E
20 Margaride, Mts. de la 44 43N 3 38E
110 Margarita, Is. de 11 0N 64 0W
13 Margate 51 23N 1 24E
39 Margharita d'Savoia 41 25N 16 5E
48 Mari A.S.S.R. □ 56 30N 48 0E
85 Maria van Diemen, C. 34 29S 172 40E
45 Mariager, Fd. 56 42N 10 19E
76 Mariana Is. 17 0N 145 0E
105 Marianao 23 8N 82 24W
99 Marianna 30 45N 85 15W
75 Mariano Machado 13 2S 14 40E
26 Mariánské Lázně 49 57N 12 41E
26 Mariazell 47 47N 15 19E
55 Marib 15 25N 45 20E
45 Maribo 54 48N 11 30E
37 Maribor 46 36N 15 40E
89 Maricourt 61 36N 71 57W
105 Marie-Galante, I. 15 56N 61 16W
47 Mariehamn 60 5N 19 57E
75 Mariental 24 36S 18 0E
96 Marienville 41 27N 79 8W
45 Mariestad 58 43N 13 50E
99 Marietta, Ga. 34 0N 84 30W
98 Marietta, Ohio 39 27N 81 27W
105 Marigot 15 32N 61 18W
50 Marniisk 56 10N 87 20E
109 Marília 22 0S 50 0W
65 Marinduque, I. 13 25N 122 0E
98 Marinette 45 4N 87 40W
109 Maringá 23 35S 51 50W
101 Marion, Ill. 37 45N 88 55W
98 Marion, Ind. 40 35N 85 40W
100 Marion, Iowa 42 2N 91 36W
98 Marion, Ohio 40 38N 83 8W
99 Marion, S.C. 34 11N 79 22W
99 Marion, Va. 36 51N 81 29W
21 Maritimes, Alpes, Mts. 44 10N 7 10E
41 Maritsa 42 1N 25 50E
57 Marjan 32 5N 68 20E
62 Markapur 15 44N 79 19E
45 Markaryd 56 28N 13 35E
12 Market Drayton 52 55N 2 30W
13 Market Harborough 52 29N 0 55W
12 Market Rasen 53 24N 0 20W
5 Markham, Mt. 83 0S 164 0E
28 Marki 52 20N 21 2E
43 Markoupoulon 37 53N 23 57E
40 Markovac 44 14N 21 7E
48 Marks 51 45N 46 50E
25 Marktredwitz 50 1N 12 2E
97 Marlboro 42 19N 71 33W
80 Marlborough 22 46S 149 52E
85 Marlborough □ 41 45S 173 33E
13 Marlborough Downs 51 25N 1 55W
19 Marle 49 43N 3 47E
101 Marlin 31 25N 96 50W
62 Marmagao 15 25N 73 56E
20 Marmande 44 30N 0 10E
56 Marmara Denizi, Sea 40 45N 28 15E
37 Marmolada, Mt. 46 25N 11 55E
90 Marmora 44 28N 77 41W
19 Marne □ 49 0N 4 10E
19 Marne, R. 48 49N 2 24E
75 Maroantsetra 15 26S 49 44E
81 Maroochydore 26 35S 153 10W
27 Maros, R. 46 15N 20 13E
75 Marovoay 16 6S 46 39E
77 Marquesas Is. 9 0S 139 30W
98 Marquette 46 30N 87 21W
73 Marra, J. 7 20N 27 35E
72 Marrakech 31 40N 8 0W
80 Marrawah 40 56S 144 41E
81 Marree 29 39S 138 1E
31 Marroqui, Pta. 36 0N 5 37W
73 Marsa Brega 30 30N 19 20E
73 Marsa Susa 32 52N 21 59E
74 Marsabit 2 18N 38 0E
38 Marsala 37 48N 12 25E
37 Marsciano 42 54N 12 20E
84 Marsden 33 47N 147 32E
21 Marseille 43 18N 5 23E
100 Marshall, Minn. 44 25N 95 45W
100 Marshall, Mo. 39 8N 93 15W
101 Marshall, Tex. 32 29N 94 20W
76 Marshall Is. 9 0N 171 0E
100 Marshalltown 42 0N 93 0W
100 Marshfield 44 42N 90 10W
44 Märsta 59 37N 17 52E
59 Martaban 16 30N 97 35E
59 Martaban, G. of 15 40N 96 30E
64 Martapura, Kalimantan 3 22S 114 56E

Monclava Moyle □

104 Monclava 26 50N 101 30W
91 Moncton 46 7N 64 51W
30 Mondego, C. 40 11N 8 54W
30 Mondego, R. 40 9N 8 52W
37 Mondolfo 43 45N 13 8E
30 Mondoñedo 43 25N 7 23W
36 Mondovì 44 23N 7 56E
38 Mondragone 41 8N 13 52E
96 Monessen 40 9N 79 50W
31 Monesterio 38 6N 6 15W
90 Monet 48 10N 75 40W
37 Monfalcone 45 49N 13 32E
30 Monforte de Lemos 42 31N 7 33W
59 Mong Kung 21 35N 97 35E
59 Mong Pan 20 19N 98 22E
59 Mong Pawk 22 4N 99 16E
59 Mong Ton 20 25N 98 45E
59 Mong Wa 21 26N 100 27E
59 Mong Yai 22 28N 98 3E
83 Monger, L. 29 25S 117 5E
61 Monghyr 25 23N 86 30E
73 Mongo 12 14N 18 43E
67 Mongolia ■ 47 0N 103 0E
75 Mongu 15 16S 23 12E
20 Monistrol 45 17N 14 11E
93 Monk 47 7N 69 59W
80 Monkira 24 46S 140 30E
13 Monmouth, U.K. 51 48N 2 43W
100 Monmouth, U.S.A. 40 50N 90 40W
105 Mono, Pta. del 12 0N 83 30W
39 Monópoli 40 57N 17 18E
27 Monor 47 21N 19 27E
33 Monóvar 38 28N 0 53W
32 Monreal del Campo 40 47N 1 20W
38 Monreale 38 6N 13 16E
101 Monroe, La. 32 32N 92 4W
98 Monroe, Mich. 41 55N 83 26W
99 Monroe, N.C. 35 2N 80 37W
100 Monroe, Wis. 42 38N 89 40W
72 Monrovia, Liberia 6 18N 10 47W
103 Monrovia, U.S.A. 34 7N 118 1W
16 Mons 50 27N 3 58E
37 Monsélice 43 13N 11 45E
45 Monsterås 57 3N 16 33E
21 Mont Cenis, Col du 45 15N 6 54E
92 Mont Joli 48 37N 68 10W
90 Mont Laurier 46 35N 75 30W
18 Mont St. Michel 48 40N 1 30W
90 Mont Tremblant Prov. Park 46 30N 74 30W
37 Montagnana 45 13N 11 29E
91 Montague 46 10N 62 39W
104 Montague, I. 31 40N 144 46W
20 Montaigu 46 59N 1 18W
32 Montalbán 40 50N 0 45W
39 Montalbano Iónica 40 17N 16 33E
32 Montalbo 39 53N 2 42W
37 Montalcino 43 4N 11 30E
30 Montalegre 41 49N 7 47W
39 Montalto Uffugo 39 25N 16 9E
102 Montana □ 6 0S 73 0W
19 Montargis 48 0N 2 43E
20 Montauban 44 0N 1 21E
97 Montauk 41 3N 71 57W
97 Montauk Pt. 41 4N 71 52W
19 Montbard 47 38N 4 20E
19 Montbéliard 47 31N 6 48E
32 Montblanch 41 23N 1 4E
21 Montbrison 45 36N 4 3E
20 Montcalm, Pic de 42 40N 1 25E
21 Montceau-les-Mines 46 40N 4 23E
97 Montclair 40 53N 74 49W
20 Mont-de-Marsan 43 54N 0 31W
19 Montdidier 49 38N 2 35E
111 Monte Alegre 2 0S 54 0W
111 Monte Azul 15 9S 42 53W
21 Monte Carlo 43 46N 7 23E
108 Monte Caseros 30 10S 57 50W
30 Monte Redondo 39 53N 8 50W
36 Monte Rosa, Mt. 45 55N 7 50E
38 Monte San Giovanni 41 38N 13 31E
40 Monte San Guiliano 43 20N 11 42E
39 Monte Sant 'Angelo 41 42N 15 59E
38 Monte Santu, C. di 40 5N 9 42E
90 Montebello 45 40N 74 55W
37 Montebelluna 45 47N 12 3E
18 Montebourg 49 30N 1 20W
36 Montecatini 43 55N 10 48E
110 Montecristi 1 0S 80 40W
36 Montecristo, I. 42 20N 10 20E
37 Montefiascone 42 31N 12 2E
105 Montego Bay 18 30N 78 0W
82 Montejinnie 16 40S 131 45E
21 Montélimar 44 33N 4 45E
31 Montellano 36 59N 5 36W
104 Montemorelos 25 11N 99 42W
31 Montemor-o-Nova 38 40N 8 12W
109 Montenegro □ 42 40N 19 20E
37 Montepulciano 43 5N 11 46E
19 Montereau 48 22N 2 57E
103 Monterey 36 35N 121 57W
110 Montería 8 46N 75 53W
108 Monteros 27 11S 65 30W
37 Monterotondo 42 3N 12 36E
104 Monterrey 25 40N 100 30W
111 Montes Claros 16 30S 43 50W
32 Montes de Toledo 39 35N 4 30W
102 Montesano 47 0N 123 39W
39 Montesarchio 41 5N 14 37E
37 Montesilvano 42 30N 14 8E
37 Montevarchi 43 30N 11 32E
109 Montevideo 34 50S 56 11W
18 Montfort-sur Meuse 48 8N 1 58W
13 Montgomery, U.K. 52 34N 3 9W
99 Montgomery, U.S.A. 32 20N 86 20W
97 Monticello, N.Y. 41 37N 74 42W
103 Monticello, Utah 37 55N 109 27W
36 Montichiari 45 28N 10 29E
19 Montigny-les-Metz 49 7N 6 10E
31 Montijo 38 52N 6 39W
31 Montilla 37 36N 4 40W
100 Montivideo 44 55N 95 40W
20 Montluçon 46 22N 2 36E
91 Montmagny 46 58N 70 43E
19 Montmédy 49 30N 5 20E
21 Montmélian 45 30N 6 4E
19 Montmirail 48 51N 3 30E
20 Montmoreau 45 23N 0 7E
91 Montmorency 46 53N 71 11W
20 Montmorillon 46 26N 0 50E
19 Montmort 48 55N 3 49E
80 Monto 24 52S 151 12E
18 Montoire 47 45N 0 52E
31 Montoro 38 1N 4 27W
102 Montpelier, Id. 42 15N 11 29W
97 Montpelier, Vt. 44 15N 72 38W
20 Montpellier 43 37N 3 52E
20 Montpon-Ménestrol 45 2N 0 11E
90 Montreal 45 31N 73 34W
20 Montrejeau 43 6N 0 35E
19 Montreuil 50 27N 1 45E
18 Montreuil-Bellay 47 8N 0 9W
25 Montreux 46 26N 6 55E
18 Montrichard 47 20N 1 10E
14 Montrose, U.K. 56 43N 2 28W
103 Montrose, U.S.A. 38 30N 107 52W
32 Montsant, Sa. de 41 17N 0 1E
32 Montsech, Sa. del 42 0N 0 45E
32 Montseny 42 49N 1 2E
105 Montserrat, I. 16 40N 62 10W
32 Montserrat, Mt. 41 36N 1 49E
21 Mont-sous-Vaudrey 46 58N 5 36E
30 Montuenga 41 3N 4 38W
32 Montuiri 39 34N 2 59E
59 Monywa 22 7N 95 11E
36 Monza 45 35N 9 15E
16 Monze 16 17S 27 29E
58 Monze, C. 24 47N 66 37E
32 Monzón 41 52N 0 10E
83 Mooliabeenee 31 20S 116 2E
90 Moonbeam 49 20N 82 10W
81 Moonie 27 46S 150 20E
81 Moonta 34 6S 137 32E
83 Moora 30 37S 115 58E
80 Mooraberree 25 13S 140 54E
83 Moorarie 25 56S 117 35E
83 Moore, L. 29 50S 117 35E
83 Moore River 31 6S 115 32E
14 Moorfoot Hills 55 44N 3 8W
100 Moorhead 47 0N 97 0W
25 Moosburg 48 28N 11 57E
90 Moose, R. 43 37N 75 22W
97 Moose Creek 45 15N 74 58W
90 Moose Factory 52 20N 80 40W
93 Moose Jaw 50 30N 105 30W
100 Moose Lake 46 27N 92 48W
93 Moosomin 50 9N 101 40W
90 Moosonee 51 25N 80 51W
75 Mopeia Velha 17 30S 35 40E
72 Mopti 14 30N 4 0W
110 Moquegua 17 15S 70 46W
27 Mór 47 25N 18 12E
31 Móra, Sp. 40 15N 0 45W
44 Mora, Sweden 61 2N 14 38E
32 Mora de Ebro 41 6N 0 38E
32 Mora la Nueva 41 7N 0 39E
60 Moradabad 28 50N 78 50E
28 Morąg 53 55N 19 56E
31 Moral de Calatrava 38 51N 3 33W
30 Moraleja 40 6N 6 43W
105 Morant Pt. 17 55N 76 12W
14 Morar, L. 56 57N 5 40W
33 Moratalla 38 14N 1 49W
62 Moratuwa 6 45N 79 55E
27 Morava, R. 48 10N 16 59E
40 Moravița 45 17N 21 14E
83 Morawa 29 13S 116 0E
110 Morawhanna 8 30N 59 40W
14 Moray Firth 57 50N 3 30W
36 Morbegno 46 8N 9 34E
18 Morbihan □ 47 55N 2 50W
18 Mordelles 48 5N 1 52W
93 Morden 49 15N 98 10W
84 Mordialloc 38 1S 145 6E
48 Mordovian A.S.S.R. □ 54 20N 44 30E
44 Møre og Romsdal □ 63 0N 9 0E
12 Morecambe 54 5N 2 52W
12 Morecambe B. 54 7N 3 0W
81 Moree 29 28S 149 54E
99 Moorhead City 34 46N 76 44W
104 Morelia 19 40N 101 11W
80 Morella 23 0S 143 47E
104 Morelos □ 18 40N 99 10W
60 Morena 26 30N 78 9E
31 Morena, Sa. 38 20N 4 0W
103 Morenci 33 7N 109 20W
19 Moret 48 22N 2 48E
81 Moreton, I. 27 10S 153 25E
19 Moreuil 49 46N 2 30E
21 Morez 46 31N 6 2E
101 Morgan City 29 40N 91 15W
99 Morganton 35 46N 81 48W
98 Morgantown 39 39N 75 58W
18 Morgat 48 15N 4 32E
19 Morhange 48 55N 6 38E
92 Morinville 53 49N 113 41W
66 Morioka 39 45N 141 8E
18 Morlaix 48 36N 3 52W
19 Mormant 48 37N 2 52E
80 Mornington, I., Australia 16 30S 139 30E
112 Mornington, I., Chile 49 50S 75 30W
65 Moro G. 6 30N 123 0E
72 Morocco ■ 32 0N 5 50W
74 Morogoro 6 50S 37 40E
104 Moroleón 20 8N 101 32W
105 Morón 22 0N 78 30W
68 Mörön, R. 47 14N 110 37E
108 Morón 34 40S 58 40W
32 Morón de Almazán 41 29N 2 27W
31 Morón de la Frontera 37 6N 5 28W
75 Morondavo 20 17S 44 27E
65 Morotai, I. 2 10N 128 30E
74 Moroto 2 28N 34 42E
12 Morpeth 55 11N 1 41W
101 Morrilton 35 10N 92 45W
111 Morrinhos 17 45S 49 10W
85 Morrinsville 37 40S 175 32E
93 Morris 49 25N 97 30W
83 Morris, Mt. 26 9S 131 4E
90 Morrisburg 44 55N 75 7W
97 Morristown, N.J. 40 48N 74 30W
99 Morristown, Tenn. 36 18N 83 20W
97 Morrisville 42 54N 75 39W
108 Morro, Pta. 27 6S 71 0W
103 Morro Bay 35 27N 120 54W
110 Morrosquillo, G. de 9 35N 75 40W
48 Morshansk 53 28N 41 50E
44 Mörsil 63 19N 13 40E
18 Mortagne, Orne 48 30N 0 32E
20 Mortagne, Vendée 46 59N 0 57W
19 Mortagne, R. 48 33N 6 27E
18 Mortain 48 40N 0 57W
36 Mortara 45 15N 8 43E
108 Morteros 30 50S 62 0W
111 Mortes, R. 11 45S 50 44W
84 Mortlake 38 5S 142 50E
84 Morundah 34 57S 146 19E
21 Morvan, Mts. du 47 5N 4 0E
81 Morven 26 22S 147 5E
14 Morvern, Reg. 56 38N 5 44W
60 Morvi 22 25N 72 5E
84 Morwell 38 10S 146 22E
25 Mosbach 49 21N 9 9E
59 Moscos Is. 14 0N 97 45E
102 Moscow 46 45N 116 59W
48 Moscow=Moskva 55 45N 37 35E
25 Mosel, R. 50 22N 7 36E
19 Moselle □ 48 59N 6 33E
85 Mosgiel 45 53S 170 21E
74 Moshi 3 22S 37 18E
46 Mosjøen 65 51N 13 12E
48 Moskva 55 45N 27 35E
48 Moskva, R. 55 5N 38 50E
27 Mosonmagyaróvár 47 52N 17 18E
110 Mosquera 2 35N 78 30W
96 Mosquito Cr. Res. 41 22N 80 45W
105 Mosquitos, G. de los 9 15N 81 0W
44 Moss 59 27N 10 40E
84 Moss Vale 34 32S 150 25E
93 Mossbank 50 0N 106 0W
85 Mossburn 45 41S 168 15E
75 Mosselbaai 34 11S 22 8E
74 Mossendjo 2 55S 12 42E
84 Mossgiel 33 15S 144 30E
80 Mossman 16 28S 145 23E
111 Mossoró 5 10S 37 15W
75 Mossuril 14 58S 40 42E
26 Most 50 31N 13 38E
72 Mostaganem 35 54N 0 5E
40 Mostar 43 22N 17 50E
56 Mosul=Al Mawsil 36 20N 43 5E
32 Mota del Cuervo 39 30N 2 52W
45 Motala 58 32N 15 1E
14 Motherwell 55 48N 4 0W
61 Motihari 26 37N 85 1E
32 Motilla del Palancar 39 34N 1 55W
39 Mótlola 40 38N 17 0E
31 Motril 36 44N 3 37W
85 Motueka 41 7S 173 1E
74 Mouila 1 50S 11 0E
20 Moulins 46 35N 3 19¼
59 Moulmein= Maulamyaing 16 30N 97 40E
99 Moultrie 31 11N 83 47W
73 Moundou 8 40N 16 10E
96 Moundsville 39 53N 80 43W
99 Mount Airy 36 31N 80 37W
81 Mount Barker 34 38S 117 40E
98 Mount Carmel, Ill. 38 20N 87 48W
97 Mount Carmel, Pa. 40 46N 76 25W
96 Mount Clemens 42 35N 82 50W
80 Mount Coolon 21 25S 147 25E
75 Mount Darwin 16 47S 31 38E
80 Mount Douglas 21 35S 146 50E
85 Mount Eden 36 53S 174 46E
92 Mount Edgecumbe 57 3N 135 21W
82 Mount Elizabeth 16 0S 125 50E
90 Mount Forest 43 59N 80 43W
84 Mount Gambier 37 50S 140 46E
80 Mount Garnet 17 41S 145 7E
81 Mount Hope 34 7S 135 23E
80 Mount Isa 20 42S 139 26E
83 Mount Keith 27 15S 120 30E
97 Mount Kisco 41 12N 73 44W
80 Mount Larcom 23 48S 150 59E
83 Mount Magnet 28 2S 117 47E
85 Mount Maunganui 37 40S 176 14E
80 Mount Molloy 16 42S 145 20E
80 Mount Morgan 23 40S 150 25E
83 Mount Narryer 26 30S 115 55E
82 Mount Newman 23 18S 119 45E
100 Mount Pleasant, Iowa 41 0N 91 35W
98 Mount Pleasant, Mich. 43 38N 84 46W
101 Mount Pleasant, Texas 33 5N 95 0W
102 Mount Pleasant, Utah 39 40N 111 29W
102 Mount Rainier Nat. Park 46 50N 121 20W
92 Mt. Revelstoke Nat. Park 51 6N 118 0W
92 Mount Robson 52 56N 119 15W
98 Mount Sterling 38 0N 84 0W
80 Mount Surprise 18 10S 144 17E
100 Mount Vernon, Ill. 38 19N 88 55W
97 Mount Vernon, N.Y. 40 57N 73 49W
96 Mount Vernon, Ohio 40 20N 82 30W
102 Mount Vernon, Wash. 48 27N 122 18W
81 Mount Willoughby 27 58S 134 8E
102 Mountain Home 43 3N 115 52W
92 Mountain Park 52 50N 117 15W
103 Mountain View 37 26N 122 5W
103 Mountainair 34 35N 106 15W
15 Mountmellick 53 7N 7 20W
80 Moura, Australia 24 35S 149 58E
110 Moura, Brazil 1 25S 61 45W
31 Moura, Port. 38 7N 7 30W
73 Mourdi, Depression du 18 10N 23 0E
20 Mourenx 43 23N 0 36W
19 Mourmelon-le Grand 49 8N 4 22E
15 Mourne, Mts. 54 10N 6 0W
15 Mourne, R. 54 45N 7 25W
16 Mouscron 50 45N 3 12E
25 Moutier 47 16N 7 21E
21 Moutiers 45 29N 6 31E
85 Moutohora 38 27S 177 32E
69 Mowming 21 50N 110 32E
68 Mowping 37 25N 121 34E
74 Moyale 3 30N 39 0E
15 Moyle □ 55 10N 6 15W

Nipigon, L. Oakville, Man.

90 Nipigon, L. 49 40N 88 30W
111 Niquelandia 14 27S 48 27W
62 Nira, R. 17 58N 7 8E
66 Nirasaki 35 42N 138 27E
62 Nirmal 19 3N 78 20E
40 Niš 43 19N 21 58E
31 Nisa 39 30N 2 41W
55 Nisab 14 25N 46 29E
40 Nišava, R. 43 22N 21 46E
39 Niscemi 37 8N 14 21E
66 Nishinomiya 34 45N 135 20E
43 Nísiros, I. 36 35N 27 12E
45 Nissan, R. 43 22N 21 46E
45 Nissum, Fd. 56 20N 8 11E
109 Niterói 22 52S 43 0W
14 Nith, R. 55 0N 3 35W
27 Nitra 48 19N 18 4E
27 Nitra, R. 47 46N 18 10E
16 Nivelles 50 35N 4 20E
19 Nivernais, Reg. 47 0N 3 40E
62 Nizamabad 18 45N 78 7E
59 Nizamghat 28 20N 95 45E
51 Nizhne Kolymsk 68 40N 160 55E
50 Nizhne-Vartovskoye 60 56N 76 38E
51 Nizhneangarsk 56 0N 109 30E
51 Nizhneudinsk 55 0N 99 20E
50 Nizhniy Tagil 57 45N 60 0E
56 Nizip 37 1N 37 46E
27 Nizké Tatry, Mts. 48 55N 20 0E
54 Nizzanim 31 42N 34 37E
74 Njombe 9 0S 34 35E
72 Nkambe 6 35N 10 40E
72 Nkawkaw 6 36N 0 49W
74 Nkhata Bay 11 33S 34 16E
75 Nkhota Kota 12 55S 34 15E
72 Nkongsamba 4 55N 9 55E
88 Noatak 67 34N 162 59W
66 Nobeoka 32 36N 131 41E
30 Noblejas 39 58N 3 26W
39 Nocera Inferiore 40 45N 14 37E
39 Noci 40 47N 17 7E
66 Noda 47 30N 142 5E
104 Nogales, Mexico 31 36N 94 29W
103 Nogales, U.S.A. 31 33N 110 59W
66 Nōgata 33 48N 130 54E
18 Nogent-le-Rotrou 48 20N 0 50E
19 Nogent-sur-Seine 48 30N 3 30E
83 Noggerup 33 32S 116 5E
51 Noginsk 55 50N 38 25E
108 Nogoya 32 24S 59 50W
27 Nograd □ 48 0N 19 30E
30 Nogueira de Ramuin 42 21N 7 43W
32 Noguera Pallaresa, R. 42 15N 0 54E
32 Noguera Ribagorzana, R. 41 40N 0 43E
60 Nohar 29 11N 74 49E
63 Noi, R. 17 5N 105 2E
18 Noire, Mts., Finistere 48 11N 3 40W
20 Noire, Mts., Tarn 43 26N 2 12W
20 Noirétable 45 48N 3 46E
20 Noirmoutier 47 0N 2 15W
20 Noirmoutier, Î. de 46 58N 2 10W
58 Nok Kundi 28 50N 62 45E
51 Nokhhuysk 60 0N 117 45E
39 Nola 40 54N 14 29E
21 Nolay 46 58N 4 35E
36 Noli, C. di 44 12N 8 26E
88 Nome 64 30N 165 30W
18 Nonancourt 48 47N 1 11E
18 Nonant-le-Pin 48 42N 0 12E
80 Nonda 20 40S 142 28E
63 Nong Khae 14 29N 100 53E
63 Nong Khai 17 50N 102 46E
20 Nontron 45 31N 0 40E
82 Noonamah 12 38S 131 4E
81 Noondoo 28 35S 148 30E
16 Noord Beveland, I. 51 45N 3 50E
16 Noord Brabant □ 51 40N 5 0E
16 Noord Holland □ 52 30N 4 45E
16 Noordoost-Polder 52 45N 5 45E
16 Noordwijk 52 14N 4 26E
92 Nootka I. 49 40N 126 50W
44 Nora 59 32N 15 2E
90 Noranda 48 20N 79 0E
44 Norberg 60 4N 15 56E
37 Nórcia 42 50N 13 5E
19 Nord □ 50 15N 3 30E
24 Nord-Friesische, Is. 54 50N 8 20E
24 Nord-Ostsee Kanal 54 5N 9 15E
24 Nord-Süd Kanal 53 0N 10 32E
4 Nordaustlandet 79 55N 23 0E
45 Nordborg 55 5N 9 50E
24 Norddeich 53 37N 7 10E
92 Nordegg 52 29N 116 5W
24 Norden 53 35N 7 12E
24 Nordenham 53 29N 8 28E
24 Norderney 53 42N 7 9E
24 Norderney, I. 53 42N 7 15E
24 Nordhausen 51 29N 10 47E
24 Nordhorn 52 27N 7 4E
46 Nordkapp, Norway 71 11N 25 48E
4 Nordkapp, Svalbard 80 31N 20 0E
46 Nordland □ 65 40N 13 0E
25 Nördlingen 48 50N 10 30E
24 Nordrhein Westfalen □ 51 45N 7 30E
24 Nordstrand, I. 54 27N 8 50E
51 Nordvik 73 40N 110 57E
45 Nordyllands □ 57 0N 10 0E
15 Nore, R. 52 25N 6 58W
100 Norfolk, Nebr. 42 3N 97 25W
98 Norfolk, Va. 36 52N 76 15W
12 Norfolk □ 52 39N 1 0E
76 Norfolk I. 28 58S 168 3E
51 Norilsk 69 20N 88 0E
100 Normal 40 30N 89 0W
101 Norman 35 12N 97 30W
88 Norman Wells 65 40N 126 45W
18 Normandie, Reg. 48 45N 0 10E
18 Normandie, Collines de 48 55N 0 45W
90 Normandin 48 49N 72 31W
80 Normanton 17 40S 141 10E
83 Nornalup 35 0S 116 49E
112 Norquinco 41 51S 70 55W
45 Norrahammar 57 43N 14 7E
46 Norrbotten □ 66 45N 23 0E
45 Nørresundby 57 5N 9 52E
97 Norristown 40 9N 75 15W
45 Norrköping 58 37N 16 11E
44 Norrtälje 59 46N 18 42E
83 Norseman 32 8S 121 43E
45 Norsholm 58 31N 15 59E
51 Norsk 52 30N 130 0E
111 Norte, C. do 1 40N 49 55W
85 North, C. 34 23S 173 4E
85 North I. 38 0S 176 0E
97 North Adams 42 42N 73 6W
1 North America 45 0N 100 0W
63 North Andaman, I. 13 15N 92 40E
6 North Atlantic Ocean 30 0N 50 0W
93 North Battleford 52 50N 108 10W
90 North Bay 46 20N 79 30W
90 North Belcher Is. 56 30N 79 0W
92 North Bend, Canada 49 50N 121 35W
102 North Bend, Oreg. 43 28N 124 7W
96 North Bend, Pa. 41 20N 77 42W
14 North Berwick 56 4N 2 44W
99 North Carolina □ 35 30N 80 0W
14 North Channel 55 0N 5 30W
98 North Chicago 42 19N 87 50W
100 North Dakota □ 47 30N 100 0W
83 North Dandalup 32 31S 115 58E
15 North Down □ 54 40N 5 45W
13 North Downs 51 17N 0 30W
9 North European Plain 55 0N 25 0E
13 North Foreland, Pt. 51 22N 1 28E
92 North Kamloops 50 40N 120 25W
68 North Korea ■ 40 0N 127 0E
59 North Lakhimpur 27 15N 94 10E
14 North Minch 58 5N 5 55W
100 North Platte 41 10N 100 50W
4 North Pole 90 0N 0 0E
14 North Ronaldsay, I. 59 20N 2 30W
93 North Saskatchewan, R. 53 15N 105 6W
8 North Sea 56 0N 4 0E
91 North Sydney 46 12N 60 21W
97 North Syracuse 43 8N 76 8W
96 North Tonawanda 43 5N 78 50W
101 North Truchas Pk. 36 0N 105 30W
12 North Tyne, R. 54 59N 2 8W
14 North Uist, I. 57 40N 7 15W
92 North Vancouver 49 25N 123 20W
105 North Village 32 15N 64 45W
12 North Walsham 52 49N 1 22E
82 North West, C. 21 45S 114 9E
14 North West Highlands, Mts. 57 35N 5 2W
88 North West Territories □ 65 0N 100 0W
12 North York Moors 54 25N 0 50W
12 North Yorkshire □ 54 10N 1 25W
12 Northallerton 54 20N 1 26W
83 Northam 31 35S 116 42E
83 Northampton, Australia 28 21S 114 33E
13 Northampton, U.K. 52 14N 0 54W
97 Northampton, Mass. 42 22N 72 39W
97 Northampton, Pa. 40 38N 75 24W
13 Northampton □ 52 16N 0 55W
80 Northampton Downs 24 35S 145 48E
83 Northcliffe 34 36S 116 7E
24 Northeim 51 42N 10 0E
15 Northern Ireland ■ 54 45N 7 0W
78 Northern Territory □ 16 0S 133 0E
100 Northfield 44 37N 93 10W
97 Northport 45 8N 85 39W
12 Northumberland □ 55 12N 2 0W
80 Northumberland, Is. 21 45S 150 20E
91 Northumberland Str. 46 20N 64 0W
12 Northwich 53 16N 2 30W
88 Norton Sd. 64 0N 165 0W
24 Nortorf 54 14N 10 47E
97 Norwalk, Conn. 41 7N 73 27W
96 Norwalk, Ohio 41 15N 82 37W
46 Norway ■ 67 0N 11 0E
93 Norway House 53 55N 98 50W
5 Norwegian Dependency 75 0S 15 0E
4 Norwegian Sea 66 0N 1 0E
12 Norwich, U.K. 52 38N 1 17E
97 Norwich, Conn. 41 33N 72 5W
97 Norwich, N.Y. 42 32N 75 30W
97 Norwood 42 10N 71 10W
50 Nosok 70 10N 82 20E
57 Nosratabad 29 55N 60 0E
14 Noss Hd. 58 29N 3 4W
75 Nossob, R. 26 55S 20 37E
28 Noteć R. 52 44N 15 26E
43 Notios Evvoïkos, Kól. 38 20N 24 0E
92 Notikewin 57 15N 117 5W
39 Noto 36 52N 15 4E
44 Notodden, Reg. 59 35N 9 17E
91 Notre Dame B. 49 45N 55 30W
89 Notre Dame de Koartac=Koartac 60 55N 69 40W
89 Notre Dame d'Ivugivik= Ivugivik 62 20N 78 0W
96 Nottawasaga B. 44 40N 80 30W
12 Nottingham 52 57N 1 10W
12 Nottinghamshire □ 53 10N 1 0W
72 Nouadhibou 21 0N 17 0W
72 Nouakchott 18 20N 15 50W
76 Noumea 22 17S 166 30E
75 Nouport 31 10S 24 57E
90 Nouveau Comptoir 53 2N 78 55W
19 Nouzonville 49 48N 4 44E
27 Nová Bana 48 28N 18 39E
26 Nová Bystrice 49 2N 15 8E
111 Nova Cruz 6 28S 35 25W
109 Nova Esperança 23 8S 52 13W
109 Nova Friburgo 22 10S 42 30W
111 Nova Granada 20 29S 49 19W
40 Nova Gradiška 45 17N 17 28E
109 Nova Iguaçu 22 45S 43 28W
75 Nova Lisboa= Huambo 12 42S 15 54E
26 Nova Paka 50 29N 15 30E
91 Nova Scotia □ 45 10N 63 0W
75 Nova Sofola 20 7S 34 48E
111 Nova Venecia 18 45S 40 24E
41 Nova Zagora 42 32N 25 59E
41 Novaci 45 10N 23 42E
36 Novara 45 27N 8 36E
48 Novaya Ladoga 60 7N 32 16E
50 Novaya Lyalya 58 50N 60 35E
51 Novaya Sibir, Os. 75 10N 150 0E
50 Novaya Zemlya, I. 75 0N 56 0E
27 Nové Mesto 49 33N 16 7E
27 Nové Zámky 47 59N 18 11E
33 Novelda 38 24N 0 45W
36 Novellara 44 50N 10 43E
48 Novgorod 58 30N 31 25E
40 Novi Bečej 45 36N 20 10E
40 Novi Kneževac 46 4N 20 8E
41 Novi Krichim 42 22N 24 31E
36 Novi Lígure 44 45N 8 47E
41 Novi Pazar, Bulgaria 43 25N 27 15E
40 Novi Pazar, Yug. 43 12N 20 28E
40 Novi-Sad 45 18N 19 52E
37 Novi Vinodolski 45 10N 14 48E
109 Nôvo Hamburgo 29 37S 51 7W
109 Novo Horizonte 21 28S 49 13W
74 Novo Redondo 11 10S 13 48E
49 Novocherkassk 47 27N 40 5E
50 Novokazalinsk 45 40N 61 40E
48 Novokiybyshevsk 53 7N 49 58E
50 Novo-kuznetsk 54 0N 87 10E
48 Novomoskovsk 54 5N 38 15E
49 Novorossiyk 44 43N 37 52E
49 Novoshakhtinsk 47 39N 39 58E
50 Novosibirsk 55 0N 83 5E
51 Novosibirskiye Os. 75 0N 140 0E
48 Novotroitsk 51 10N 58 15E
49 Novouzensk 50 32N 48 17E
40 Novska 45 19N 17 0E
26 Novy Bydžov 50 14N 15 29E
28 Nõvy Dwór 52 26N 20 44E
27 Nový Jičín 49 15N 18 0E
57 Now Shahr 36 40N 51 40E
84 Nowa Nowa 37 44S 148 3E
28 Nowa Sól 51 48N 15 44E
28 Nowe Warpno 53 42N 14 18E
59 Nowgong 26 20N 92 50E
28 Nowogrod 53 14N 21 53E
84 Nowra 34 53S 150 35E
27 Nowy Sącz 49 40N 20 41E
30 Noya 42 48N 8 53W
18 Noyant 47 30N 0 6E
19 Noyers 47 40N 4 0E
19 Noyon 49 34N 3 0E
18 Nozay 47 34N 1 38W
75 Nsanje 16 55S 35 12E
72 Nsawam 5 50N 0 24W
75 Nuanetsi 21 22S 30 45E
70 Nubian Des. 21 30N 33 30E
73 Nûbîya, Es Sahrâ en 21 30N 33 30E
108 Ñuble □ 37 0S 72 0W
108 Nueva Palmira 33 52S 58 20W
104 Nueva Rosita 28 0N 101 20W
108 Nueve de Julio 35 30S 60 50W
105 Nuevitas 21 30N 77 20W
112 Nuevo, G. 43 0S 64 30W
104 Nuevo Laredo 27 30N 99 40W
104 Nuevo León □ 25 0N 100 0W
85 Nuhaka 39 3S 177 45E
19 Nuits 47 10N 4 56E
21 Nuits St. Georges 47 10N 4 56E
73 Nukheila 19 1N 26 21E
50 Nukus 42 20N 59 40E
88 Nulato 64 43N 158 6W
32 Nules 39 51N 0 9W
82 Nullagine 21 53S 120 6E
83 Nullarbor 31 26S 130 55E
83 Nullarbor Plain 31 20S 128 0E
66 Numata 36 38N 139 3E
66 Numazu 35 7N 138 51E
44 Numedal 60 6N 9 6E
84 Numurkah 36 0S 145 26E
13 Nuneaton 52 32N 1 29W
88 Nunivak I. 60 0N 166 0W
68 Nunkiang 49 11N 125 12E
16 Nunspeet 52 21N 5 45E
38 Núoro 40 20N 9 20E
25 Nürnberg 49 26N 11 5E
64 Nusa Tenggara Barat 8 50S 117 30E
65 Nusa Tenggara Timur □ 9 30S 122 0E
58 Nushki 29 35N 65 59E
89 Nutak 57 30N 61 59W
62 Nuwara Eliya 6 58N 80 55E
75 Nuweveldberge 32 10S 21 45E
62 Nuzvid 16 47N 80 51E
83 Nyabing 33 30S 118 7E
97 Nyack 41 5N 73 57W
74 Nyahanga 2 20S 33 37E
73 Nyâlâ 12 2N 24 58E
75 Nyasa, L. 12 0S 34 30E
45 Nyborg 55 18N 10 47E
45 Nybro 56 44N 15 55E
50 Nyda 66 40N 73 10E
67 Nyenchen, Ra. 30 30N 95 0E
74 Nyeri 0 23S 36 56E
27 Nyirbátor 47 49N 22 9E
27 Nyíregyháza 48 0N 21 47E
46 Nykarleby 63 32N 22 31E
45 Nykøbing 54 56N 11 52E
45 Nykøbing Mors 56 49N 8 51E
45 Nyköping 58 45N 17 0E
75 Nylstroom 24 42S 28 22E
26 Nymburk 50 10N 15 1E
44 Nynäshamn 58 54N 17 57E
84 Nyngan 31 30S 147 8E
25 Nyon 46 23N 6 14E
21 Nyons 44 22N 5 10E
84 Nyora 38 20S 145 41E
27 Nysa 50 40N 17 22E
28 Nysa, R. 52 4N 14 46E
51 Nyurba 63 17N 118 20E
74 Nzega 4 10S 33 12E
72 Nzérékoré 7 49N 8 48W

O

100 Oahe Dam 44 28N 100 25W
100 Oahe Res. 45 30N 100 15W
94 Oahu, I. 21 30N 158 0W
102 Oak Creek 40 15N 106 59W
98 Oak Park 41 55N 87 45W
99 Oak Ridge 36 1N 84 5W
101 Oakdale 30 50N 92 28W
12 Oakengates 52 42N 2 29W
102 Oakesdale 47 11N 117 9W
81 Oakey 27 25S 151 43E
12 Oakham 52 40N 0 43W
103 Oakland 37 50N 122 18W
84 Oakleigh 37 54S 145 6E
96 Oakmont 40 31N 79 50W
82 Oakover, R. 20 43S 120 33E
102 Oakridge 43 47N 122 31W
93 Oakville, Man. 49 56N 97 58W

Osby Paranavaí

45 Osby 56 23N 13 59E
101 Osceola 35 40N 90 0W
25 Oschatz 51 17N 13 8E
24 Oschersleben 52 2N 11 13E
38 Oschiri 40 43N 9 7E
40 Osečina 44 23N 19 34E
96 Oshawa 43 50N 78 45W
100 Oshkosh 44 3N 88 35W
72 Oshogbo 7 48N 4 37E
41 Osica de Jos 44 14N 24 20E
28 Osieczna 51 55N 16 40E
40 Osijek 45 34N 18 41E
37 Osimo 43 40N 13 30E
49 Osipenko= Berdyansk 46 45N 36 49E
100 Oskaloosa 41 18N 92 40W
45 Oskarshamn 57 15N 16 27E
44 Oslo 59 55N 10 45E
44 Oslofjorden 58 30N 10 0E
62 Osmanabad 18 5N 76 10E
56 Osmaniye 37 5N 36 10E
24 Osnabrück 52 16N 8 2E
109 Osorio 29 53S 50 17W
112 Osorno 40 25S 73 0W
16 Oss 51 46N 5 32E
80 Ossa, Mt. 41 80S 146 0E
33 Ossa de Montiel 38 58N 2 45W
97 Ossining 41 9N 73 50W
24 Oste, R. 53 33N 9 10E
16 Ostend=Oostende 51 15N 2 50E
24 Osterburg 52 47N 11 44E
44 Østerdalen 62 0N 10 40E
45 Östergötlands □ 58 24N 15 34E
24 Osterholz-Scharmbeck 53 14N 8 48E
44 Östersund 63 10N 14 38E
44 Østfold □ 59 25N 11 25E
24 Ostfriesische Is. 53 45N 7 15E
25 Ostfriesland, Reg. 53 20N 7 40E
44 Östhammar 60 16N 18 22E
27 Ostrava 49 51N 18 18E
28 Ostrgog 52 37N 16 33E
28 Ostróda 53 42N 19 58E
28 Ostrołeka 53 4N 21 38E
28 Ostrołeka □ 53 0N 21 30E
41 Ostrov 43 40N 24 9E
28 Ostrów Mazowiecka 52 50N 21 51E
28 Ostrów Wielkopolski 51 39N 17 49E
27 Ostrowiec-Swietokrzyski 50 57N 21 23E
40 Ostrozac 43 43N 17 49E
28 Ostrzeszów 51 25N 17 52E
39 Ostuni 40 44N 17 34E
42 Osumi, R. 40 48N 19 52E
66 Ōsumi-Kaikyō, Str. 30 55N 131 0E
66 Ōsumi-Shotō, Is. 30 30N 130 45E
31 Osuna 37 14N 5 8W
97 Oswego 43 29N 76 30W
97 Oswego, R. 43 28N 76 31W
12 Oswestry 52 52N 3 3W
27 Oświęcim 50 2N 19 11E
85 Otago □ 44 45S 169 10E
66 Ōtake 34 27N 132 25E
85 Otaki 40 45S 175 10E
66 Otaru 43 13N 141 0E
26 Otava 61 39N 27 4E
110 Otavalo 0 20N 78 20W
42 Otelec 45 36N 20 50E
30 Otero de Rey 43 6N 7 36W
102 Othello 46 53N 119 8W
85 Otira Gorge 42 53S 171 33E
75 Otjiwarongo 20 30S 16 33E
85 Otorohanga 38 11S 175 12E
39 Otranto 40 9N 18 28E
39 Otranto, C. d' 40 7N 18 30E
66 Ōtsu 42 35N 143 40E
44 Otta 61 46N 9 32E
62 Ottapalam 10 46N 76 23E
90 Ottawa, Canada 45 27N 75 42W
100 Ottawa, Ill. 41 20N 88 55W
100 Ottawa, Kans 38 40N 95 10W
89 Ottawa Is. 59 50N 80 0W
90 Ottawa, R. 45 20N 73 58W
24 Otterndorf 53 47N 8 52E
93 Otter Rapids 55 42N 104 46W
26 Ottersheim 48 21N 14 12E
45 Otterup 55 30N 10 22E
100 Ottumwa 41 0N 92 25W
72 Oturkpo 7 10N 8 15E
112 Otway, B. 53 30S 74 0W
84 Otway, C. 38 52S 143 31E
112 Otway, Seno de 53 5S 71 30W
28 Otwock 52 5N 21 20E
26 Ötz 47 13N 10 53E
26 Ötztaler Alpen, Mts. 46 58N 11 0E
72 Ouagadougou 12 25N 1 30W
72 Ouallene 24 41N 1 11E
72 Ouargla 31 59N 5 25E
72 Ouarzazate 30 55N 6 55W
74 Oubangi, R. 0 30S 17 42E
19 Ouche, R. 47 6N 5 16E
16 Oudenaarde 50 50N 3 37E
18 Oudon 47 22N 1 19W
75 Oudtshoorn 33 35S 22 14E
18 Ouessant, I. d' 48 28N 5 6W
74 Ouesso 1 37N 16 5E
72 Ouezzane 34 51N 5 42W
72 Ouidah 6 25N 2 0E
72 Oujda 34 41N 1 45W
72 Ouled Djellal 34 28N 5 2E
46 Oulu 65 1N 25 29E
46 Oulu □ 64 36N 27 20E
46 Oulujärvi, L. 64 25N 27 0E
16 Our, R. 49 53N 6 18E
111 Ouricuri 7 53S 40 5W
109 Ourinhos 23 0S 49 54W
109 Ouro Fino 22 16S 46 25W
109 Ouro Prêto 20 20S 43 30W
80 Ouse 42 25S 146 42E
13 Ouse, R., E. Sussex 50 47N 0 3E
12 Ouse, R., N. Yorks 53 42N 0 41W
18 Oust, R. 47 39N 2 6W
75 Outjo 20 5S 16 7E
93 Outlook 51 30N 107 0W
19 Outreau 50 40N 1 36E
84 Ouyen 35 1S 142 22E
36 Ovada 44 39N 8 40E
85 Ovalau, I. 17 40S 178 48E
108 Ovalle 30 33S 71 18W
75 Ovamboland, Reg. 17 20S 16 30E
30 Ovar 40 51N 8 40E
16 Over Flakkee, I. 51 45N 4 5E
16 Overijssel □ 52 25N 6 35E
16 Overpelt 51 12N 5 20E
30 Oviedo 43 25N 5 50W
30 Oviedo □ 43 20N 6 0W
44 Oviksfjällen, Mts. 63 0N 13 49E
85 Owaka 46 27S 169 40E
66 Owase 34 7N 136 5E
100 Owatonna 44 3N 93 17W
97 Owego 42 6N 76 17W
90 Owen Sound 44 35N 80 55W
74 Owendo 0 17N 9 30E
98 Owensboro 37 40N 87 5W
72 Owo 7 18N 5 30E
98 Owosso 43 0N 84 10W
45 Oxelösund 58 43N 17 15E
13 Oxford, U.K. 51 45N 1 15W
97 Oxford, Mass. 42 7N 71 52W
99 Oxford, N.C. 36 19N 78 36W
13 Oxford □ 51 45N 1 15W
93 Oxford House 54 46N 95 16W
103 Oxnard 34 10N 119 14W
66 Oyama 36 18N 139 48E
74 Oyem 1 37N 11 35E
51 Oymyakon 63 25N 143 10E
72 Oyo 7 46N 3 56E
21 Oyonnax 46 16N 5 40E
97 Oyster Bay 40 52N 73 32W
65 Ozamiz 8 15N 123 50E
99 Ozark 31 29N 85 39W
86 Ozark Plat. 37 20N 91 40W
100 Ozarks, L. of the 38 10N 93 0W
38 Ozieri 40 35N 9 0E
28 Ozorków 51 57N 19 16E
41 Ozun 45 47N 25 50E

P

63 Pa Sak, R. 14 11 100 40E
67 Paan 30 0N 99 3E
59 Pa-an 16 45N 97 40E
75 Paarl 33 45S 18 46E
28 Pabianice 51 40N 19 20E
61 Pabna 24 1N 89 18E
110 Pacaraima, Sa. 5 0N 63 0W
110 Pacasmayo 7 20S 79 35W
38 Paceco 37 59N 12 32E
60 Pachhar 24 40N 77 42E
39 Pachino 36 43N 15 4E
60 Pachora 20 38N 75 29E
104 Pachuca 20 10N 98 40W
103 Pacific Groves 37 36N 121 58W
77 Pacific Ocean 10 0N 140 0W
18 Pacy 49 2N 1 22E
65 Padalarang 7 50S 107 30E
64 Padang 1 0S 100 20E
93 Paddockwood 53 30N 105 30W
24 Paderborn 51 42N 8 44E
88 Padlei 62 10N 97 5W
89 Padloping Island 67 0N 63 0W
62 Padmanabhapuram 8 16N 77 17E
37 Pádova 45 24N 11 52E
60 Padra 22 15N 73 7E
61 Padrauna 26 54N 83 59E
13 Padstow 50 33N 4 57W
98 Paducah, Ky. 37 0N 88 40W
101 Paducah, Tes. 34 3N 100 16W
85 Paeroa 37 23S 175 41E
37 Pag, I. 44 50N 15 0E
65 Pagadian 7 55N 123 30E
71 Pagalu, I. 1 35S 3 35E
43 Pagastikós Kól. 39 15N 23 12E
103 Page 47 11N 97 37W
57 Paghman 34 36N 68 57E
37 Paglieta 42 10N 14 30E
85 Pago Pago 14 16S 170 43W
103 Pagosa Springs 37 16N 107 1W
90 Pagwa River 50 2N 85 14W
94 Pahala 20 25N 156 0W
63 Pahang, R. 3 32N 102 28E
63 Pahang □ 3 30N 103 9E
85 Pahiatua 40 27S 175 50E
68 Paicheng 45 40N 122 52E
13 Paignton 50 26N 3 33W
18 Paimboeuf 47 17N 2 0W
18 Paimpol 48 48N 3 4W
96 Painesville 41 42N 81 18W
90 Paint Hills= Nouveau Comptoir 53 2N 78 55W
103 Painted Des. 36 40N 112 0W
14 Paisley 55 51N 4 27W
110 Paita 5 5S 81 0W
68 Paiyin 36 45N 104 4E
30 Pajares 43 0N 5 48W
63 Pak Lay 18 15N 101 27E
63 Pak Sane 18 22N 103 39E
62 Pakala 13 29N 79 8E
64 Pakanbaru 0 30N 101 15E
69 Pakhoi 21 30N 109 10E
58 Pakistan ■ 30 0N 70 0E
59 Pakokku 21 30N 95 0E
69 Pakongchow 23 50N 113 0E
60 Pakpattan 30 25N 73 16E
40 Pakrac 45 17N 17 12E
27 Paks 46 38N 18 55E
63 Pakse 15 5N 105 52E
57 Paktya □ 33 0N 69 15E
32 Palafrugell 41 55N 3 10E
39 Palagonía 37 20N 14 43E
43 Palaiokastron 35 12N 26 18E
62 Palakol 16 31N 81 46E
32 Palamós 41 50N 3 10E
51 Palana 59 10N 160 10E
64 Palangkaraya 2 16S 113 56E
60 Palanpur 24 10N 72 25E
75 Palapye 22 30S 27 7E
62 Palar, R. 12 28N 80 9E
99 Palatka 29 40N 81 40W
65 Palau Is. 7 30N 134 30E
63 Palauk 13 10N 98 40E
63 Palaw 13 0N 98 50E
64 Palawan, I. 10 0N 119 0E
64 Palawan Is. 10 0N 115 0E
62 Palayancottai 8 45N 77 45E
40 Pale 43 50N 18 38E
65 Paleleh 1 10N 121 50E
64 Palembang 3 0S 104 50E
30 Palencia 42 1N 4 34W
30 Palencia □ 42 31N 4 33W
38 Palermo 38 8N 13 20E
101 Palestine 31 42N 95 35W
59 Paletwa 21 30N 92 50E
62 Palghat 10 46N 76 42E
60 Pali 25 50N 73 20E
72 Palimé 6 57N 0 37E
100 Palisade 40 35N 101 10W
60 Palitana 21 32N 71 49E
62 Palk B. 9 30N 79 30E
62 Palkonda 18 36N 83 48E
62 Palkonda Ra. 13 50N 79 20N
80 Palm, Is. 18 40S 146 35E
103 Palm Springs 33 51N 116 35W
32 Palma 39 33N 2 39E
33 Palma, B. de 39 30N 2 39E
8 Palma, I. 28 45N 17 50W
31 Palma del Rio 37 43N 5 17W
38 Palma di Montechiaro 37 12N 13 46E
105 Palma Soriano 20 15N 76 0W
111 Palmares 8 41S 35 36W
109 Palmas 26 29S 52 0W
72 Palmas, C. 4 27N 7 46W
109 Palmeira 25 25S 50 0W
111 Palmeira dos Indios 9 25S 36 30W
31 Palmela 38 32N 8 57W
88 Palmer 61 35N 149 10W
5 Palmer Ld. 73 0S 60 0W
85 Palmerston 45 29S 170 43E
85 Palmerston North 40 21S 175 39E
97 Palmerton 40 47N 75 36W
39 Palmi 38 21N 15 51E
108 Palmira, Arg. 32 59S 68 25W
110 Palmira, Col. 3 32N 76 16W
97 Palmyra 34 5N 77 18W
77 Palmyra Is. 5 52N 162 5W
62 Palni 10 30N 77 30E
62 Palni Hills 10 14N 77 33E
103 Palo Alto 37 25N 122 8W
39 Palo del Colle 41 4N 16 43E
65 Palopo 3 0S 120 16E
33 Palos, C. de 37 38N 0 40W
56 Palu 38 45N 40 0E
60 Palwal 28 8N 77 19E
65 Pamekason 7 10S 113 29E
68 Pamiencheng 43 16N 124 4E
20 Pamiers 43 7N 1 39E
99 Pamlico Sd. 35 20N 76 0W
101 Pampa 35 35N 100 58W
65 Pampanua 4 22S 120 14E
106 Pampas, Reg. 34 0S 64 0W
110 Pamplona 7 23N 72 39W
32 Pana 39 25N 89 0W
41 Panagyurishte 42 49N 24 15E
62 Panaji 15 25N 73 50E
104 Panama 9 0N 79 25W
105 Panamá ■ 8 48N 79 55W
104 Panamá, B. de 8 50N 79 20W
105 Panamá, G. de 8 4N 79 20W
104 Panama Canal 9 10N 79 56W
99 Panama City 30 10N 105 41W
65 Panarukan 7 40S 113 52E
65 Panay, I. 11 10N 122 30E
65 Panay G. 11 0N 122 30E
40 Pančevo 44 52N 20 41E
30 Pancorbo, P. 42 32N 3 5W
62 Pandharpur 17 41N 75 20E
60 Pandhurna 21 36N 78 35E
109 Pando 34 30S 56 0W
50 Panfilov 44 30N 80 0E
59 Pang-Long 23 11N 98 45E
42 Pangaíon Óros 40 50N 24 0E
74 Pangani 5 25S 38 58E
64 Pangkalanberandan 4 1N 98 20E
64 Pangkalansusu 4 2N 98 42E
89 Pangnirtung 66 8N 65 44W
103 Panguitch 37 52N 112 30W
59 Pangyang 22 10N 98 45E
60 Panipat 29 25N 77 2E
84 Panitya 35 15S 141 0E
57 Panjao 34 21N 67 0E
58 Panjgur 27 0N 64 5E
62 Panjim=Panaji 15 25N 73 50E
64 Pankalpinang 2 0S 106 0E
61 Panna 24 40N 80 15E
62 Pannuru 16 5N 80 34E
109 Panorama 21 21S 51 51W
62 Panruti 11 46N 79 35E
68 Panshih 42 55N 126 3E
38 Pantellaria, I. 36 52N 12 0E
104 Pánuco 22 0N 98 25W
62 Panvel 18 59N 73 10E
72 Panyam 9 27N 9 8E
68 Paochang 41 46N 115 30E
69 Paoki 34 25N 107 15E
39 Páola 39 21N 16 2E
67 Paoshan 25 7N 99 9E
68 Paoting 38 50N 115 30E
68 Paotow 40 35N 110 3E
69 Paoying 33 10N 119 20E
27 Papá 47 22N 17 30E
105 Papagayo, G. del 10 4N 85 50W
62 Papagni, R. 14 10N 78 30E
85 Papakura 37 45S 174 59E
104 Papantla 20 45N 97 41W
64 Papar 5 45N 116 0E
43 Papas, Ákra 38 13N 21 6E
24 Papenburg 53 7N 7 25E
76 Papua New Guinea ■ 8 0S 145 0E
37 Papuča 44 22N 15 30E
40 Papuk, Mts. 45 30N 17 30E
111 Pará=Belém 1 20S 48 30W
111 Pará □ 3 20S 52 0W
111 Paracatú 17 10S 46 50W
81 Parachilna 31 10S 138 21E
40 Paraćin 43 54N 21 27E
31 Paradas 37 18N 5 29W
61 Paradip 20 15N 86 35E
102 Paradise 47 27N 114 54W
101 Paragould 36 5N 90 30W
109 Paraguaçu Paulista 22 22S 50 35W
110 Paraguaipoa 11 21N 71 57W
110 Paraguaná, Penide. 12 0N 70 0W
108 Paraguari 25 36S 57 0W
108 Paraguarí □ 26 0S 57 10W
107 Paraguay ■ 23 0S 57 0W
108 Paraguay, R. 27 18S 58 38W
111 Paraiba □ 7 0S 36 0W
109 Paraíba do Sul, R. 21 37S 41 3W
47 Parainen 60 18N 22 18E
72 Parakou 9 25N 2 40E
43 Parálion-Astrous 37 25N 22 45E
62 Paramagudi 9 31N 78 39E
111 Paramaribo 5 50N 55 10W
108 Paraná, Arg. 32 0S 60 30W
111 Paraná, Brazil 12 30S 47 40W
108 Paraná, R. 33 43S 59 15W
109 Paraná □ 24 30S 51 0W
109 Paranaguá 25 30S 48 30W
109 Paranapanema, R. 22 40S 53 9W
109 Paranavaí 23 4S 52 28W

Phatthalung Port Cartier

63 Phatthalung 7 39N 100 6E
99 Phenix City 32 30N 85 0W
63 Phetchaburi 16 25N 101 8E
63 Phichai 17 22N 100 10E
98 Philadelphia 40 0N 75 10W
42 Philippi 41 0N 24 19E
8 Philippine Trench= Mindanao Trench 8 0N 128 0E
65 Philippines ■ 12 0N 123 0E
84 Phillip, I. 38 30S 145 12E
97 Phillipsburg 40 43N 75 12W
81 Phillott 27 53S 145 50E
102 Philomath 44 28N 123 21W
63 Phitsanulok 16 50N 100 12E
63 Phnom Penh 11 33N 104 55E
103 Phoenix 33 30N 112 10W
77 Phoenix Is. 3 30S 172 0W
97 Phoenixville 40 12N 75 29W
63 Phra Nakhon Si Ayutthaya 14 25N 100 30E
63 Phu Doan 21 40N 105 10E
63 Phu Loi, Mt. 20 14N 103 14E
63 Phu Ly 20 35N 105 50E
63 Phu Quoc, I. 10 15N 104 0E
63 Phuket 8 0N 98 28E
60 Phul 30 19N 75 14E
36 Piacenza 45 2N 9 42E
81 Pialba 25 20S 152 45E
81 Pian Creek 30 2S 148 12E
21 Piana 42 14N 8 38E
31 Pias 38 1N 7 29W
28 Piaseczno 52 5N 21 2E
28 Piastów 52 12N 20 48E
41 Piatra 43 51N 25 9E
111 Piaui □ 7 0S 43 0W
37 Piave, R. 45 32N 12 44E
39 Piazza Armerina 37 21N 14 20E
19 Picardie, Plaine de 50 0N 2 0E
19 Picardie, Reg. 50 0N 2 15E
101 Picayune 30 40N 89 40W
12 Pickering 54 15N 0 46W
90 Pickle Crow 51 30N 90 0W
8 Pico, I. 38 28N 28 20W
112 Pico Truncado 46 40S 68 10W
30 Picos Anceres, Sa. de 42 51N 6 52W
19 Picquigny 49 56N 2 10E
84 Picton, Australia 34 12S 150 34E
90 Picton, Canada 44 1N 77 9W
85 Picton, N.Z. 41 18S 174 3E
91 Pictou 45 41N 62 42W
92 Picture Butte 49 55N 112 45W
112 Picún Leufú 39 30S 69 5W
62 Pidurutalagala, Mt. 7 10N 80 50E
31 Piedrabuena 39 0N 4 10W
103 Piedras Blancas Pt. 35 45N 121 18W
104 Piedras Negras 28 35N 100 35W
36 Piermonte □ 45 0N 7 30E
97 Piercefield 44 13N 74 35W
42 Piería □ 40 13N 22 25E
100 Pierre 44 23N 100 20W
19 Pierrefonds 49 20N 3 0E
27 Piešťany 48 35N 17 50E
75 Piet Retief 27 1S 30 50E
39 Pietraperzia 37 26N 14 8E
75 Pietermaritzburg 29 35S 30 25E
75 Pietersburg 23 54S 29 25E
36 Pietrasanta 43 57N 10 12E
90 Pigeon River 48 1N 89 42W
108 Pigüé 37 36S 62 25W
75 Piketberg 32 55S 18 40E
98 Pikeville 37 30N 82 30W
28 Piła 53 10N 16 48E
28 Piła □ 53 0N 17 0E
108 Pilar 26 50S 58 10W
111 Pilar 14 30S 49 45W
28 Piława 51 58N 21 31E
108 Pilcomayo, R. 25 21S 57 42W
61 Pilibhit 28 40N 78 50E
28 Pilica, R. 51 52N 21 17E
42 Pilion, Mt. 39 27N 23 7E
60 Pilkhawa 28 43N 77 42E
28 Pillau=Baltiisk 54 38N 19 55E
43 Pilos 36 55N 21 42E
103 Pima 32 54N 109 50W
81 Pimba 31 18S 136 46E
63 Pinang □ 5 25N 100 15E
105 Pinar del Rio 22 26N 83 40W
93 Pinawa 50 15N 95 50W
92 Pincher Creek 49 30N 113 35W
60 Pind Dadan Khan 32 55N 73 47E
83 Pindar 28 30S 115 47E
72 Pindiga 9 58N 10 53E
42 Pindos Óros 40 0N 21 0E
42 Pindus Mts.= Pindos Óros 40 0N 21 0E
91 Pine, C. 46 37N 53 30W
101 Pine Bluff 34 10N 92 0W
82 Pine Creek 13 49S 131 49E
93 Pine Falls 50 51N 96 11W
92 Pine Point 60 50N 114 40W
48 Pinega, R. 64 8N 41 54E
80 Pinehill 23 38S 146 57E
36 Pinerolo 44 47N 7 21E
37 Pineto 42 36N 14 4E
75 Pinetown 29 48S 30 54E
101 Pineville 31 22N 92 30W
19 Piney 48 22N 4 21E
63 Ping, R. 15 42N 100 9E
83 Pingaring 32 40S 118 32E
83 Pingelly 32 29S 116 59E
69 Pingkiang 28 45N 113 30E
68 Pingliang 35 32N 106 50E
69 Pingsiang 22 2N 106 55E
69 Pingtingshan 33 43N 113 28E
69 Pingtung 22 38N 120 30E
68 Pingyao 37 12N 112 10E
109 Pinhal 22 10S 46 46W
30 Pinhel 40 18N 7 0W
68 Pinhsien 35 10N 108 10E
83 Pinjarra 32 37S 115 52E
84 Pinnaroo 35 13S 140 56E
105 Pinos, I. de 21 40N 82 40W
103 Pinos, Pt. 36 50N 121 57W
31 Pinos Puente 37 15N 3 45W
65 Pinrang 3 46S 119 34E
48 Pinsk 52 10N 26 8E
93 Pinto Butte, Mt. 49 22N 107 25W
83 Pintumba 31 50S 132 18E
69 Pinyang 23 12N 108 35E
48 Pinyug 60 5N 48 0E
103 Pioche 38 0N 114 35N
36 Piombino 42 54N 10 30E
28 Pionki 51 29N 21 28E
28 Piotrków Trybunalski 51 23N 19 43E
28 Piotrków Trybunalski □ 51 20N 19 30E
60 Pipar 26 25N 73 31E
60 Pipariya 22 45N 78 23E
100 Pipestone 44 0N 96 20W
91 Pipmuacan Res. 49 40N 70 25W
82 Pippingarra 20 27S 118 42E
98 Piqua 40 10N 84 10W
109 Piracicaba 22 45S 47 30W
111 Piracuruca 3 50S 41 50W
43 Piraeus= Piraiévs 37 57N 23 42E
43 Piraiévs 37 57N 23 42E
43 Piraiévs □ 37 0N 23 30E
109 Pirajui 21 59S 49 29W
37 Piran 45 31N 13 33E
108 Pirané 25 44S 59 7W
41 Pirdop 42 40N 24 10E
43 Pirgos, Ilia 37 40N 21 27E
43 Pírgos, Messinia 36 50N 22 16E
18 Piriac-sur-Mer 47 23N 2 31W
108 Piribebuy 25 29S 57 3W
111 Piripiri 4 15S 41 46W
25 Pirmasens 49 12N 7 30E
24 Pirna 50 57N 13 57E
61 Pirojpur 22 35N 90 1E
40 Pirot 43 9N 22 39E
65 Piru 3 3S 128 12E
36 Pisa 43 43N 10 23E
110 Pisagua 19 40S 70 15W
110 Pisco 13 50S 76 5W
41 Piscu 45 30N 27 43E
26 Pisek 49 19N 14 10E
39 Pisticci 40 24N 16 33E
36 Pistóia 43 57N 10 53E
30 Pisuerga, R. 41 33N 4 52W
28 Pisz 53 38N 21 49E
109 Pitanga 24 46S 51 44W
77 Pitcairn I. 25 5S 130 5W
46 Pitea 65 20N 21 25E
41 Piteşti 44 52N 24 54E
62 Pithapuram 17 10N 82 15E
83 Pithara 30 20E 116 35E
42 Píthion 41 24N 26 40E
19 Pithiviers 48 10N 2 13E
14 Pitlochry 56 43N 3 43W
102 Pittsburg, Calif. 38 1N 121 50W
101 Pittsburg, Kans. 37 21N 94 43W
96 Pittsburgh, Pa. 40 25N 79 55W
101 Pittsburgh, Tex. 32 59N 94 58W
97 Pittsfield 42 28N 73 17W
97 Pittston 41 19N 75 50W
81 Pittsworth 27 41S 151 37E
110 Piura 5 5S 80 45W
91 Placentia 47 20N 54 0W
102 Placerville 38 47N 120 51W
105 Placetas 22 15N 79 44W
97 Plainfield 40 37N 74 28W
101 Plainview 34 10N 101 40W
101 Plaquemine 30 20N 91 15W
30 Plasencia 40 3N 6 8W
37 Plaški 45 4N 15 22E
91 Plaster Rock 46 53N 67 22W
108 Plata, R. de la 34 45S 57 30W
110 Plato 9 47N 74 47W
100 Platte, R. 41 4N 95 53W
100 Platteville 40 18N 104 47W
25 Plattling 48 46N 12 53E
97 Plattsburgh 44 41N 73 30W
100 Plattsmouth 41 0N 96 0W
24 Plauen 50 29N 12 9E
40 Plavnica 42 10N 19 20E
98 Pleasantville 39 25N 74 30W
18 Plélan-le-Grand 48 0N 2 7W
18 Pléneuf-val-André 48 37N 2 32W
85 Plenty, B. of 37 45S 177 0E
48 Plesetsk 62 40N 40 10E
91 Plessisville 46 14N 71 46W
28 Pleszew 51 53N 17 47E
41 Pleven 43 26N 24 37E
40 Ploče 43 4N 17 26E
28 Płock 52 32N 19 40E
18 Ploëmeur 47 44N 3 26W
18 Ploërmel 47 55N 2 26W
41 Ploieşti 44 57N 26 5E
24 Plön 54 8N 10 22E
28 Płonsk 52 37N 20 21E
28 Płoty 53 48N 15 18E
18 Plouaret 48 37N 3 28W
26 Ploucnice 50 47N 14 13E
18 Ploudalmézeau 48 34N 4 41W
41 Plovdiv 42 8N 24 44E
75 Plumtree 20 27S 27 55E
18 Pluvigner 47 46N 3 1W
105 Plymouth, Montserrat 16 42N 62 13W
13 Plymouth, U.K. 50 23N 4 9W
98 Plymouth, Ind. 41 20N 86 19W
97 Plymouth, N.H. 43 44N 71 41W
97 Plymouth, Pa. 41 17N 76 0W
26 Plzeň 49 45N 13 22E
28 Pniewy 52 31N 16 16E
37 Po, Foci del 44 52N 12 30E
36 Po, R. 44 57N 12 4E
68 Po Hai, G. 38 40N 119 0E
51 Pobedino 49 51N 142 49E
30 Pobladura de Valle 42 6N 5 44W
102 Pocatello 42 50N 112 25W
26 Pochlarn 48 12N 15 12E
109 Poços de Caldas 21 50S 46 45W
26 Poděbrady 50 9N 15 8E
51 Podkamenndya Tunguska 61 50N 90 26E
26 Podmokly 50 48N 14 10E
48 Podolsk 55 30N 37 30E
48 Podporozny 60 55N 34 2E
40 Podravska Slatina 45 42N 17 45E
24 Poel, I. 54 0N 11 25E
37 Poggibonsi 43 27N 11 8E
42 Pogradeci 40 57N 20 48E
68 Pohang 36 8N 129 23E
37 Pohorje, Mt. 46 30N 15 7E
40 Poiana Ruscăi Mt. 45 45N 22 25E
90 Point Edward 43 10N 82 30W
97 Point Pleasant 38 50N 82 7W
97 Pointe Claire 45 26N 73 49W
74 Pointe-Noire 4 48S 12 0E
105 Pointe-à-Pitre 16 10N 61 30W
19 Poissy 48 55N 2 0E
20 Poitou, Plaines du 46 30N 0 1W
20 Poitou, Reg. 46 25N 0 15W
19 Poix 49 47N 2 0E
19 Poix Terron 49 38N 4 38E
28 Pojezierze Mazurski, Reg. 53 40N 21 0E
81 Pokataroo 29 30S 148 34E
74 Poko 3 7N 26 52E
68 Pokotu 48 46N 121 54E
51 Pokrovsk 61 29N 129 6E
30 Pola de Lena 43 10N 5 49W
30 Pola de Siero 43 24N 5 39W
103 Polacca 35 52N 110 25W
28 Poland ■ 52 0N 20 0E
5 Polar Sub-Glacial Basin 85 0S 100 0E
13 Polden Hills 51 7N 2 50W
27 Polgar 47 54N 21 6E
68 Poli 8 34N 12 54E
43 Políaigos, I. 36 45N 24 38E
39 Policastro, G. di 39 55N 15 35E
28 Police 53 33N 14 33E
39 Polignano a Mare 41 0N 17 12E
21 Poligny 46 50N 5 42E
43 Polikhnitos 39 4N 26 10E
65 Polillo Is. 14 56N 122 0E
39 Polístena 38 25N 16 4E
62 Pollachi 10 35N 77 0E
32 Pollensa 39 54N 3 2E
50 Polnovat 63 50N 66 5E
48 Polotsk 55 30N 28 50E
41 Polski Trumbosh 43 20N 25 38E
41 Polsko Kosovo 43 23N 25 38E
102 Polson 47 45N 114 12W
49 Poltava 49 35N 34 35E
62 Polur 12 32N 79 11E
48 Polyarny 69 8N 33 20E
111 Pombal, Brazil 6 55S 37 50W
30 Pombal, Port. 39 55N 8 40W
103 Pomona 34 2N 117 49W
41 Pomorie 42 26N 27 41E
99 Pompano 26 12N 80 6W
76 Ponape, I. 6 55N 158 10E
101 Ponca City 36 40N 97 5W
105 Ponce 18 1N 66 37W
89 Pond Inlet 72 30N 75 0W
62 Pondicherry 11 59N 79 50E
30 Ponferrada 42 32N 6 35W
62 Ponnani 10 45N 75 59E
59 Ponnyadaung, Mts. 22 0N 94 10E
48 Ponoi 67 0N 41 0E
92 Ponoka 52 35N 113 40W
65 Ponorogo 7 52S 111 29E
20 Pons 45 35N 0 34W
18 Pont-Audemer 49 21N 0 30E
91 Pont Lafrance 47 40N 64 58W
21 Pont St. Esprit 44 16N 4 40E
18 Pont-l'Abbé 47 52N 4 15W
18 Pont-l'Evêque 49 18N 0 11E
109 Ponta Grossa 25 0S 50 10W
19 Pont-à-Mousson 45 54N 6 1E
109 Ponta Pora 22 20S 55 35W
21 Pontarlier 46 54N 6 20E
18 Pontaubault 48 40N 1 20W
101 Pontchartrain, L. 30 12N 90 0W
18 Pontchâteau 47 26N 2 8W
31 Ponte de Sor 39 17N 7 57W
21 Ponte Leccia 42 28N 9 13E
109 Ponte Nova 20 25S 42 54W
38 Pontecorvo 41 28N 13 40E
36 Pontedera 43 40N 10 37E
12 Pontefract 53 42N 1 19W
93 Ponteix 49 46N 107 29W
30 Pontevedra 42 26N 8 40W
30 Pontevedra, Ria de 42 22N 8 45W
30 Pontevedra □ 42 25N 8 39W
100 Pontiac, Ill. 40 50N 88 40W
98 Pontiac, Mich. 42 40N 83 20W
63 Pontian Kechil 1 29N 103 23E
64 Pontianak 0 3S 109 15E
56 Pontine Mts.= Karadeniz Dağlari, Mts. 41 30N 35 0E
18 Pontivy 48 5N 3 0W
19 Pontoise 49 3N 2 5E
18 Pontorson 48 34N 1 30W
36 Pontrémoli 44 22N 9 52E
13 Pontypool 51 42N 3 1W
13 Pontypridd 51 36N 3 21S
38 Ponziane, Is. 40 55N 13 0E
81 Poochera 32 43S 134 51E
13 Poole 50 42N 2 2W
62 Poona=Pune 18 29N 73 57E
62 Poonamelle 13 3N 80 10E
110 Poopó, L. 18 30S 67 35W
83 Popanyinning 32 40S 117 2E
110 Popayán 2 27N 76 36W
16 Poperinge 50 51N 2 42E
51 Popigay 71 55N 110 47E
101 Poplar Bluff 36 45N 90 22W
104 Popocatepetl, Mt. 19 10N 98 40W
37 Popovača 45 30N 16 41E
41 Popovo 43 21N 26 18E
27 Poprád 49 3N 20 18E
60 Porbandar 21 44N 69 43E
31 Porcuna 37 52N 4 11W
88 Porcupine, R. 66 35N 145 15W
37 Pordenone 45 58N 12 40E
41 Pordim 43 23N 24 51E
37 Poreč 45 14N 13 36E
109 Porecatu 22 43S 51 24W
21 Poretta 42 35N 9 28E
47 Pori 61 29N 21 48E
46 Porjus 66 57N 19 50E
47 Porkkala 59 59N 24 26E
110 Porlamar 10 57N 63 51W
30 Prma, R. 42 29N 5 28W
18 Pornic 47 7N 2 5W
51 Poronaysk 49 20N 143 0E
43 Póros 37 30N 23 30E
21 Porquerolles, Î. de 43 0N 6 13E
36 Porretta, P. 44 9N 10 59E
44 Porsgrunn 59 10N 9 40E
81 Port Adelaide 34 46S 138 30E
92 Port Alberni 49 15N 124 50W
60 Port Albert Victor 21 0N 71 30E
90 Port Alfred 48 18N 70 53W
92 Port Alice 50 25N 127 25W
96 Port Allegany 41 49N 78 17W
102 Port Angeles 48 0N 123 30W
90 Port Arthur, Canada= Thunder Bay 48 25N 89 10W
68 Port Arthur, China= Lushun 38 48N 121 16E
101 Port Arthur, U.S.A. 30 0N 94 0W
Thunder Bay 48 25N 89 10W
81 Port Augusta 32 30S 137 50E
91 Port aux Basques 47 32N 59 8W
32 Port Bou 42 25N 3 9E
81 Port Broughton 33 37S 137 56E
91 Port Cartier 50 10N 66 50W

Port Chalmers Pulaski, N.Y.

85 Port Chalmers 45 49 S 170 30 E
97 Port Chester 41 0 N 73 41 W
90 Port Colborne 42 50 N 79 10 W
92 Port Coquitlam 49 20 N 122 45 W
96 Port Credit 43 34 N 79 35 W
78 Port Darwin 12 18 S 130 55 E
105 Port de Paix 19 50 N 72 50 W
63 Port Dickson 2 30 N 101 49 E
80 Port Douglas 16 30 S 145 30 E
92 Port Edward 54 14 N 130 18 W
90 Port Elgin 44 25 N 81 25 W
75 Port Elizabeth 33 58 S 25 40 E
14 Port Ellen 55 39 N 6 12 W
12 Port Erin 54 5 N 4 45 W
72 Port Étienne= Nouadhibou 21 0 N 17 0 W
84 Port Fairy 38 22 S 142 12 E
74 Port-Gentil 0 47 S 8 40 E
14 Port Glasgow 55 57 N 4 40 W
72 Port Harcourt 4 43 N 7 5 E
92 Port Hardy 50 41 N 127 30 W
89 Port Harrison= Inoucdouac 58 25 N 78 15 W
82 Port Hedland 20 25 S 118 35 E
97 Port Henry 44 0 N 73 30 W
91 Port Hood 46 0 N 61 32 W
90 Port Hope 44 0 N 78 20 W
96 Port Huron 43 0 N 82 28 W
97 Port Jervis 41 22 N 74 42 W
84 Port Kembla 34 29 S 150 56 E
63 Port Klang 3 0 N 101 21 E
20 Port La Nouvelle 43 1 N 3 3 E
15 Port Laoise 53 2 N 7 20 W
101 Port Lavaca 28 38 N 96 38 W
81 Port Lincoln 34 42 S 135 52 E
72 Port-Lyautey= Kenitra 34 15 N 6 40 W
81 Port Macquarie 31 25 S 152 54 E
91 Port Maitland 44 0 N 66 2 W
92 Port Mellon 49 32 N 123 31 W
91 Port Menier 49 51 N 64 15 W
76 Port Moresby 9 24 S 147 8 E
93 Port Nelson 57 5 N 92 56 W
75 Port Nolloth 29 17 S 16 52 E
89 Port Nouveau-Quebec 58 30 N 65 50 W
105 Port of Spain 10 40 N 61 20 W
102 Port Orchard 47 31 N 122 47 W
90 Port Perry 44 6 N 78 56 W
81 Port Pirie 33 10 S 137 58 E
88 Port Radium 66 10 N 117 40 W
73 Port Said= Bûr Sa'îd 31 16 N 32 18 E
75 Port St. Johns= Umzimvubu 31 38 S 29 33 E
21 Port-St.-Louis 43 23 N 4 50 E
91 Port St. Servain 51 21 N 58 0 W
75 Port Shepstone 30 44 S 30 28 E
92 Port Simpson 54 30 N 130 20 W
90 Port Stanley 42 40 N 81 10 W
73 Port Sudan= Bûr Sûdân 19 32 N 37 9 E
13 Port Talbot 51 35 N 3 48 W
102 Port Townsend 48 0 N 122 50 W
20 Port-Vendres 42 32 N 3 8 E
48 Port Vladimir 69 25 N 33 6 E
81 Port Wakefield 34 12 S 138 10 E
63 Port Weld 4 50 N 100 38 E
15 Portadown 54 27 N 6 26 W
100 Portage 43 31 N 89 25 W
93 Portage la Prairie 49 58 N 98 18 W
31 Portalegre 39 19 N 7 25 W
31 Portalégre □ 39 15 N 7 40 W
101 Portales 34 12 N 103 25 W
15 Portarlington 53 10 N 7 10 W
105 Port-au-Prince 18 40 N 72 20 W
21 Port-de-Bouc 43 24 N 4 59 E
18 Port-en-Bessin 49 20 N 0 45 W
103 Porterville 36 5 N 119 0 W
20 Portet 43 31 N 1 25 E
13 Porthcawl 51 28 N 3 42 W
31 Portimão 37 8 N 8 32 W
84 Portland, Australia 33 13 S 149 59 E
97 Portland, Conn. 41 34 N 72 39 W
99 Portland, Me. 43 40 N 70 15 W
102 Portland, Oreg. 45 35 N 122 30 W
13 Portland Bill 50 31 N 2 27 W
13 Portland I. 50 32 N 2 25 W
89 Portland Promontory 59 0 N 78 0 W
12 Portmadoc 52 51 N 4 8 W
91 Portneuf 46 43 N 71 55 W
21 Porto, Fr. 42 16 N 8 38 E
30 Porto, Port. 41 8 N 8 40 W
30 Porto □ 41 8 N 8 20 W
21 Porto, G. de 42 17 N 8 34 E
109 Pôrto Alegre 30 5 S 51 3 W
75 Porto Amélia= Pemba 12 58 S 40 30 E
111 Pôrto de Móz 1 41 S 52 22 W
38 Porto Empédocle 37 18 N 13 30 E
111 Porto Franco 9 45 S 47 0 W
111 Porto Grande 0 42 N 51 24 W
108 Pôrto Murtinho 21 45 S 57 55 W
111 Porto Nacional 10 40 S 48 30 W
72 Porto-Novo 6 23 N 2 42 E
37 Porto Recanati 43 26 N 13 40 E
37 Porto San Giórgio 43 11 N 13 49 E
111 Porto Seguro 16 20 S 39 0 W
37 Porto Tolle 44 57 N 12 20 E
38 Porto Torres 40 50 N 8 23 E
109 Porto União 26 10 S 51 0 W
21 Porto-Vecchio 41 35 N 9 16 E
110 Porto Velho 8 46 S 63 54 W
36 Portoferráio 42 50 N 10 20 E
37 Portogruaro 45 57 N 12 50 E
102 Portola 39 49 N 120 28 W
37 Portomaggiore 44 41 N 11 47 E
36 Portovénere 44 2 N 9 50 E
110 Portoviejo 1 0 S 80 20 W
14 Portpatrick 54 50 N 5 7 W
14 Portree 57 25 N 6 11 W
15 Portrush 55 13 N 6 40 W
13 Portsmouth, U.K. 50 48 N 1 6 W
97 Portsmouth, N.H. 43 5 N 70 45 W
98 Portsmouth, Ohio 38 45 N 83 0 W
97 Portsmouth, R.I. 41 35 N 71 44 W
98 Portsmouth, Va. 36 50 N 76 50 W
14 Portsoy 57 41 N 2 41 W
46 Porttipahta, I. 68 5 N 26 40 E
30 Portugalete 43 19 N 3 4 W
29 Portugal ■ 40 0 N 7 0 W
72 Portuguese Guinea ■= Guinea Bissau ■ 12 0 N 15 0 W
15 Portumna 53 5 N 8 12 W
112 Porvenir 53 10 S 70 30 W
47 Provoo 60 27 N 25 50 E
109 Posadas, Arg. 27 30 S 56 0 W
31 Posadas, Sp. 37 47 N 5 11 W
69 Poseh 23 50 N 106 0 E
65 Poso 1 20 S 120 55 E
111 Posse 14 4 S 46 18 W
24 Pössneck 50 42 N 11 34 E
90 Poste de la Baleine 55 20 N 77 40 W
72 Poste Maurice Cortier 22 14 N 1 2 E
37 Postojna 45 46 N 14 12 E
75 Potchefstroom 26 41 S 27 7 E
39 Potenza 40 40 N 15 50 E
37 Potenza, R. 43 25 N 13 40 E
37 Potenza Picena 43 22 N 13 37 E
30 Potes 43 15 N 4 42 W
75 Potgietersrus 24 10 S 29 3 E
49 Poti 42 10 N 41 38 E
72 Potiskum 11 39 N 11 2 E
98 Potomac, R. 38 0 N 76 20 W
110 Potosí 19 38 S 65 50 W
108 Potosí □ 20 30 S 67 0 W
65 Potatan 10 56 N 122 38 E
68 Potow 38 8 N 116 31 E
24 Potsdam, E. Germany 52 23 N 13 4 E
97 Potsdam, U.S.A. 44 40 N 74 59 W
24 Potsdam □ 52 40 N 13 30 E
97 Pottersville 42 38 N 84 45 W
97 Pottsdown 40 17 N 75 40 W
97 Pottsville 40 39 N 76 12 W
92 Pouce Coupe 55 40 N 120 10 W
97 Poughkeepsie 41 40 N 73 57 W
19 Pouilly 47 18 N 2 57 E
109 Pouso Alegre 11 55 S 57 0 W
85 Poverty B. 38 43 S 178 0 E
30 Póvoa de Varzim 41 25 N 8 46 W
48 Povenets 62 48 N 35 0 E
90 Powassan 46 5 N 79 25 W
100 Powder, R. 46 44 N 105 26 W
102 Powder River 43 5 N 107 0 W
102 Powell 44 45 N 108 45 W
103 Powell, L. 37 25 N 110 45 W
92 Powell River 49 48 N 125 20 W
13 Powys □ 52 20 N 3 30 W
69 Poyang 28 59 N 116 40 E
69 Poyang Hu, L. 29 10 N 116 10 E
51 Poyarkovo 49 38 N 128 45 E
30 Poza de la Sal 42 35 N 3 31 W
40 Požarevac 44 35 N 21 18 E
40 Požega 45 21 N 17 41 E
28 Poznań 52 25 N 17 0 E
28 Poznań □ 52 30 N 18 0 E
33 Pozo Alcón 37 42 N 2 56 W
110 Pozo Almonte 20 10 S 69 50 W
31 Pozoblanco 38 23 N 4 51 W
39 Pozzallo 36 44 N 15 40 E
39 Pozzuoli 40 49 N 14 7 E
40 Praca 43 47 N 18 43 E
63 Prachin Buri 14 0 N 101 25 E
20 Prades 42 38 N 2 23 E
111 Prado 17 20 S 39 20 W
37 Pragersko 46 27 N 15 42 E
26 Prague=Praha 50 5 N 14 22 E
26 Praha 50 5 N 14 22 E
20 Prahecq 46 19 N 0 26 W
41 Prahova, R. 44 43 N 26 27 E
40 Prahovo 44 18 N 22 39 E
41 Praid 46 32 N 25 10 E
111 Prainha 1 45 S 53 30 W
80 Prairie 20 50 S 144 35 E
102 Prairie City 45 27 N 118 44 W
100 Prairie du Chien 43 1 N 91 9 W
100 Prairies, Coteau des 44 0 N 97 0 W
64 Praja 8 39 S 116 37 E
111 Prata 19 25 S 49 0 W
37 Prato 43 53 N 11 5 E
37 Prátola Peligna 42 7 N 13 51 E
101 Pratt 37 40 N 98 45 W
30 Pravia 43 30 N 6 12 W
108 Precordillera 30 0 S 69 1 W
37 Predáppio 44 7 N 11 58 E
40 Predejane 42 51 N 22 9 E
93 Preeceville 52 0 N 102 50 W
92 Premier 56 4 N 130 1 W
40 Prenj, Mt. 43 33 N 17 53 E
24 Prenzlau 53 19 N 13 51 E
40 Prepansko, J. 40 45 N 21 0 E
63 Preparis North Chan. 15 12 N 93 40 E
63 Preparis South Chan. 14 36 N 93 40 E
27 Prerov 49 28 N 17 27 E
90 Prescott, Canada 44 45 N 75 30 W
103 Prescott, U.S.A. 34 35 N 112 30 W
40 Preševo 42 19 N 21 39 E
108 Presidencia Roque Saenz Peña 26 50 S 60 30 W
108 Presidente de la Plaza 27 0 S 60 0 W
109 Presidente Epitácio 21 46 S 52 6 W
108 Presidente Hayes □ 24 0 S 59 0 W
109 Presidente Prudente 15 45 S 54 0 W
41 Preslav 43 10 N 26 52 E
27 Prešov 49 0 N 21 15 E
99 Presque Isle 46 40 N 68 0 W
72 Prestea 5 22 N 2 7 W
13 Presteign 52 17 N 3 0 W
96 Preston, Canada 43 25 N 80 20 W
12 Preston, U.K. 53 46 N 2 42 W
14 Prestonpans 55 58 N 3 0 W
14 Prestwick 55 30 N 4 38 W
75 Pretoria 25 44 S 28 12 E
43 Préveza 38 57 N 20 47 E
88 Pribilov Is. 56 0 N 170 0 W
26 Příbram 49 41 N 14 2 E
102 Price 39 40 N 110 48 W
32 Priego 40 38 N 2 21 W
31 Priego de Córdoba 37 27 N 4 12 W
75 Prieska 29 40 S 22 42 E
27 Prievidza 48 46 N 18 36 E
40 Prijedor 44 58 N 16 41 E
49 Prikaspiyskaya Nizmennost 47 30 N 50 0 E
49 Prikumsk 44 30 N 44 10 E
40 Prilep 41 21 N 21 37 E
49 Priluki 50 30 N 32 15 E
93 Prince Albert 53 15 N 105 50 W
93 Prince Albert Nat. Park 54 0 N 106 25 W
88 Prince Albert Pen. 72 0 N 116 0 W
88 Prince Albert Sd. 70 25 N 115 0 W
89 Prince Charles I. 68 0 N 76 0 W
3 Prince Edward Is. 45 15 S 39 0 E
91 Prince Edward I. □ 44 2 N 77 20 W
92 Prince George 53 50 N 122 50 W
86 Prince of Wales, C. 53 50 N 131 30 W
80 Prince of Wales, I., Australia 10 35 S 142 0 E
88 Prince of Wales I., Canada 73 0 N 99 0 W
92 Prince of Wales I., U.S.A. 53 30 N 131 30 W
92 Prince Rupert 54 20 N 130 20 W
80 Princess Charlotte, B. 14 15 S 144 0 E
5 Princesse Astrid Kyst 71 0 S 10 0 E
5 Princesse Ragnhild Kyst 71 0 S 30 0 E
92 Princeton, Canada 49 27 N 120 30 W
98 Princeton, Ind. 38 20 N 87 35 W
98 Princeton, Ky. 37 6 N 87 55 W
97 Princeton, N.J. 40 18 N 74 40 W
98 Princeton, W.Va. 37 21 N 81 8 W
71 Principé, I. 1 37 N 7 25 E
30 Prior, C. 43 34 N 8 17 W
48 Priozersk 61 2 N 30 4 E
48 Pripyat, R. 51 20 N 30 20 E
40 Priština 42 40 N 21 13 E
99 Pritchard 30 47 N 88 5 W
24 Pritzwalk 53 10 N 12 11 E
38 Priverno 41 29 N 13 10 E
40 Prizren 42 13 N 20 45 E
38 Prizzi 37 44 N 13 24 E
65 Probolinggo 7 46 S 113 13 E
62 Proddatur 14 45 N 78 30 E
104 Progreso 21 20 N 89 40 W
42 Prokletije, Mt. 42 30 N 19 45 E
50 Prokopyevsk 54 0 N 87 3 E
40 Prokuplje 43 16 N 21 36 E
59 Prome 18 45 N 95 30 E
111 Propriá 10 13 S 36 51 W
21 Propriano 41 41 N 8 52 E
80 Proserpine 20 21 S 148 36 E
102 Prosser 46 11 N 119 52 W
27 Prostějov 49 30 N 17 9 E
41 Provadiya 43 12 N 27 30 E
21 Provence, Reg. 43 40 N 5 45 E
97 Providence 41 41 N 71 15 W
90 Providence Bay 45 41 N 82 15 W
105 Providencia, I. de 13 25 N 81 26 W
51 Provideniya 64 23 N 173 18 W
92 Provincial Cannery 51 33 N 127 36 W
19 Provins 48 33 N 3 15 E
102 Provo 40 16 N 111 37 W
93 Provost 52 25 N 110 20 W
40 Prozor 43 50 N 17 34 E
109 Prudentópolis 25 12 S 50 57 W
80 Prudhoe, I. 21 23 S 149 45 E
88 Prudhoe Bay 70 10 N 148 0 W
93 Prudhomme 52 22 N 105 47 W
27 Prudnik 50 20 N 17 38 E
28 Pruszcz Gdańska 54 17 N 19 40 E
28 Pruszków 52 9 N 20 49 E
49 Prut, R. 45 28 N 28 12 E
5 Prydz B. 69 0 S 74 0 E
28 Przasnysz 53 2 N 20 45 E
27 Przemysl 49 50 N 22 45 E
27 Przemysl □ 50 0 N 22 0 E
50 Przhevalsk 42 30 N 78 20 E
43 Psará, I. 38 37 N 25 38 E
48 Pskov 57 50 N 28 25 E
27 Pszczyna 49 59 N 18 58 E
42 Ptolemaís 40 30 N 21 43 E
110 Pucallpa 8 25 S 74 30 W
69 Puchi 29 42 N 113 54 E
41 Pucioasia 45 4 N 25 26 E
62 Pudukkottai 10 28 N 78 47 E
104 Puebla 19 0 N 98 10 W
104 Puebla □ 18 30 N 98 0 W
31 Puebla de Guzman 37 33 N 7 15 W
30 Puebla de Sanabria 42 4 N 6 38 W
100 Pueblo 38 20 N 104 40 W
108 Puente Alto 33 32 S 70 35 W
31 Puente Genil 37 22 N 4 47 W
32 Puente la Reina 42 40 N 1 49 W
30 Puenteareas 42 10 N 8 28 W
30 Puentedeume 43 24 N 8 10 W
67 Puerh 23 11 N 100 56 E
105 Puerto Armuelles 8 20 N 83 10 W
110 Puerto Asís 0 30 N 76 30 W
110 Puerto Ayacucho 5 40 N 67 35 W
104 Puerto Barrios 15 40 N 88 40 W
110 Puerto Berrío 6 30 N 74 30 W
110 Puerto Bolívar 3 10 S 79 55 W
110 Puerto Cabello 10 28 N 68 1 W
105 Puerto Cabezas 14 0 N 83 30 W
110 Puerto Carreño 6 12 N 67 22 W
105 Puerto Cortes 15 51 N 88 0 W
104 Puerto Cortés 8 20 N 82 20 W
112 Puerto Coyle 50 54 S 69 15 W
110 Puerto Cumarebo 11 29 N 69 21 W
31 Puerto de Santa María 36 35 N 6 15 W
72 Puerto del Rosario 28 30 N 13 52 W
112 Puerto Deseado 47 45 S 66 0 W
110 Puerto Páez 6 13 N 67 28 W
110 Puerto Leguizamo 0 12 S 74 46 W
112 Puerto Lobos 42 0 S 65 3 W
33 Puerto Lumbreras 37 34 N 1 48 W
112 Puerto Madryn 42 48 S 65 4 W
33 Puerto Mazarrón 37 34 N 1 15 W
112 Puerto Montt 41 28 S 72 57 W
112 Puerto Natales 51 45 S 72 25 W
105 Puerto Padre 21 13 N 76 35 W
108 Puerto Pinasco 22 30 S 57 50 W
112 Puerto Pirámides 42 35 S 64 20 W
110 Puerto Piritu 10 5 N 65 0 W
105 Puerto Plata 19 40 N 70 45 W
65 Puerto Princesa 9 55 N 118 50 E
112 Puerto Quellón 43 7 S 73 37 W
31 Puerto Real 36 33 N 6 12 W
105 Puerto Rico, I. 18 15 N 66 45 W
112 Puerto Saavedra 38 47 S 73 24 W
110 Puerto Suárez 18 58 S 57 52 W
112 Puerto Varas 41 19 S 72 59 W
31 Puertollano 38 43 N 4 7 W
112 Pueyrredón, L. 47 20 S 72 0 W
48 Pugachev 52 0 N 48 55 E
102 Puget Sd. 47 15 N 123 30 W
39 Puglia □ 41 0 N 16 30 E
40 Pui 45 30 N 23 4 E
32 Puig Mayor, Mt. 39 49 N 2 47 E
32 Puigcerda 42 24 N 1 50 E
19 Puisaye, Collines de la 47 35 N 3 30 E
85 Pukaki, L. 44 5 S 170 1 E
93 Pukatawagan 55 45 N 101 20 W
85 Pukekohe 37 12 S 174 55 E
37 Pula 39 0 N 9 0 E
108 Pulacayo 20 25 S 66 41 W
68 Pulantien 39 25 N 122 0 E
97 Pulaski, N.Y. 43 32 N 76 9 W

Reading, U.S.A. Ronsard, C.

97 Reading, U.S.A. 40 20N 75 53W
108 Realicó 35 0S 64 15W
20 Réalmont 43 48N 2 10E
65 Rebi 5 30S 134 7E
37 Recanati 43 24N 13 32E
40 Recas 45 46N 21 30E
60 Rechna Doab, Reg. 31 35N 73 30E
111 Recife 8 0S 35 0W
24 Recklinghausen 51 36N 7 10E
108 Reconquista 29 10S 59 45W
101 Red, R. 48 10N 97 0W
97 Red Bank 40 21N 74 4W
102 Red Bluff 40 11N 122 11W
92 Red Deer 52 20N 113 50W
93 Red Lake 51 1N 94 1W
100 Red Oak 41 0N 95 10W
100 Red Wing 44 32N 92 35W
28 Reda 54 40N 18 19E
13 Redbridge 51 35N 0 7E
12 Redcar 54 37N 1 4W
93 Redcliff 50 10N 110 50W
81 Redcliffe 27 12S 153 0E
84 Redcliffs 34 16S 142 10E
102 Redding 40 30N 122 25W
13 Redditch 52 18N 1 57W
103 Redlands 34 0N 117 0W
83 Redmond, Australia 34 55S 117 40E
102 Redmond, U.S.A. 44 19N 121 11W
18 Redon 47 40N 2 6W
105 Redonda, I. 16 58N 62 19W
30 Redondela 42 15N 8 38W
31 Redondo 38 39N 7 37W
103 Redondo Beach 33 52N 118 26W
13 Redruth 50 14N 5 14W
92 Redstone 52 8N 123 42W
93 Redvers 49 35N 101 40W
92 Redwater 53 55N 113 0W
103 Redwood City 37 30N 122 15W
15 Ree, L. 53 35N 8 0W
103 Reedley 34 40N 119 27W
102 Reedsport 43 45N 124 4W
85 Reefton 42 6S 171 51E
28 Rega, R. 53 52N 15 16E
39 Regalbuto 37 40N 14 38E
54 Regavim 32 32N 35 2E
25 Regen 48 58N 13 9E
25 Regen, R. 49 1N 12 6E
25 Regensburg 49 1N 12 7E
36 Reggio nell'Emilia 44 42N 10 38E
39 Réggio di Calábria 38 7N 15 38E
93 Regina 50 30N 104 35W
57 Registan, Reg. 30 15N 65 0E
109 Registro 24 30S 47 50W
31 Reguengos de Monsaraz 38 25N 7 32W
75 Rehoboth 17 55S 15 5E
54 Rehovot 31 54N 34 48E
24 Reichenbach 50 36N 12 19E
83 Reid 35 17S 149 8E
80 Reid River 19 40S 146 48E
99 Reidsville 36 21N 79 40W
13 Reigate 51 14N 0 11W
32 Reillo 39 54N 1 53W
19 Reims 49 15N 4 0E
54 Reina 32 43N 35 18E
112 Reina Adelaida, Arch. 52 20S 74 0W
93 Reindeer L. 57 20N 102 20W
85 Reinga, C. 34 25S 172 43E
30 Reinosa 43 2N 4 15W
30 Reinosa, P. 42 56N 4 10W
51 Rekinniki 60 38N 163 50E
111 Remanso 9 41S 42 4W
65 Rembang 6 42S 111 21E
57 Remeshk 26 55N 58 50E
19 Remiremont 48 0N 6 36E
24 Remscheid 51 11N 7 12E
97 Remsen 43 19N 75 11W
24 Rendsburg 54 18N 9 41E
51 Rene 66 2N 179 25W
90 Renfrew, Canada 45 30N 76 40W
14 Renfrew, U.K. 55 52N 4 24W
64 Rengat 0 30S 102 45E
108 Rengo 34 25S 70 52W
62 Renigunta 13 38N 79 30E
73 Renk 11 47N 32 49E
16 Renkum 51 58N 5 43E
81 Renmark 34 11S 140 43E
18 Rennes 48 7N 1 41W
18 Rennes, Bassin de 48 0N 2 0W
102 Reno 39 30N 119 0W
32 Renteria 43 19N 1 54W
102 Renton 47 30N 122 9W
61 Reotipur 25 33N 83 45E
62 Repalle 16 2N 80 45E
100 Republican, R. 39 3N 96 48W
89 Repulse Bay 66 30N 86 30W
32 Requena 39 30N 1 4W
40 Resen 41 5N 21 0E
93 Reserve 33 50N 108 54W
108 Resistencia 27 30S 59 0W
40 Reşiţa 45 18N 21 53E
89 Resolution I., Canada 61 30N 65 0W
85 Resolution, I., N.Z. 45 40S 166 40E
104 Retalhulen 14 33N 91 46W
19 Rethel 49 30N 4 20E
43 Réthímnon 35 15N 24 40E
43 Réthímnon □ 35 23N 24 28E
18 Rétiers 47 55N 1 25W
71 Réunion, Í. 22 0S 56 0E
32 Reus 41 10N 1 5E
25 Reutlingen 48 28N 9 13E
26 Reutte 47 29N 10 42E
20 Revel 43 28N 2 0E
61 Revelganj 25 50N 84 40E
92 Revelstoke 51 0N 118 0W
19 Revigny 48 50N 5 0E
77 Revilla Gigedo Is. 18 40N 112 0W
19 Revin 49 55N 4 39E
61 Rewa 24 33N 81 25E
60 Rewari 28 15N 76 40E
102 Rexburg 43 45N 111 50W
72 Rey Malabo 3 45N 8 50E
46 Reykanes, Pen. 63 48N 22 40W
46 Reykjavik 64 10N 21 57E
104 Reynosa 26 5N 98 18W
56 Reza'iyeh 37 40N 45 0E
13 Rhayader 52 19N 3 30W
16 Rheden 52 0N 6 3E
24 Rheine 52 17N 7 25E
25 Rheinland-Pfalz □ 50 50N 7 0E
24 Rheydt 51 10N 6 24E
19 Rhinau 48 19N 7 43E
100 Rhinelander 45 38N 89 29W
72 Rhir, C. 30 38N 9 54W
36 Rho 45 31N 9 2E
97 Rhode Island □ 41 38N 71 37W
75 Rhodesia=Zimbabwe 20 0S 28 30E
41 Rhodope, Mts. = Rhodopi Planina 41 40N 24 20E
41 Rhodopi Planina 41 40N 24 20E
13 Rhondda 51 39N 3 30W
21 Rhône □ 45 54N 4 35E
21 Rhône, R. 43 28N 4 42E
14 Rhum, I. 57 0N 6 20W
12 Rhyl 53 19N 3 29W
111 Riachão 7 20S 46 37W
30 Riansares, R. 39 32N 3 18W
64 Riau □ 1 0N 102 35E
64 Riau, Kep. 0 30N 104 20E
30 Riaza, R. 41 16N 3 29W
30 Ribadavia 42 17N 8 8W
30 Ribadeo 43 35N 7 5W
30 Ribadesella 43 30N 5 7W
32 Ribas 42 19N 2 15E
111 Ribas do Rio Pardo 20 27S 53 46W
29 Ribatejo, Reg. 39 15N 8 30W
12 Ribble, R. 54 13N 2 20W
45 Ribe □ 55 34N 8 30E
45 Ribe 55 19N 8 44E
19 Ribeauville 48 10N 7 20E
19 Ribécourt 49 30N 2 55E
30 Ribeira 42 36N 8 58W
109 Ribeirão Prêto 21 10S 47 50W
38 Ribera 37 30N 13 13E
24 Ribnitz-Damgarten 54 14N 12 24E
26 Řičany 50 0N 14 40E
85 Riccarton 43 32S 172 37E
37 Riccione 44 0N 12 39E
100 Rice Lake 44 10N 78 10W
75 Richards B. 28 48S 32 6E
97 Richford 45 0N 72 40W
91 Richibucto 46 42N 64 54W
102 Richland 44 49N 117 9W
80 Richmond, Australia 20 43S 143 8E
85 Richmond, N.Z. 41 4S 173 12E
75 Richmond, S. Africa 29 54S 30 8E
13 Richmond, Surrey 51 28N 0 18W
12 Richmond, Yorks. 54 24N 1 43W
102 Richmond, Calif. 38 0N 122 30W
98 Richmond, Ind. 39 50N 84 50W
98 Richmond, Ky. 37 40N 84 20W
102 Richmobd, Utah 41 55N 111 48W
98 Richmond, Va. 37 33N 77 27W
90 Richmond Gulf, L. 56 20N 75 50W
96 Richmond Hill 43 52N 79 27W
98 Richwood 38 17N 80 32W
32 Ricla 41 31N 1 24W
93 Ridgedale 53 0N 104 10W
90 Ridgetown 42 26N 81 52W
97 Ridgewood 40 59N 74 7W
96 Ridgway 41 25N 78 43W
93 Riding Mountain Nat. Park 50 55N 100 25W
26 Ried 48 14N 13 30E
37 Rienza, R. 46 49N 11 47E
24 Riesa 51 19N 13 19E
39 Riesi 37 16N 14 4E
37 Rieti 42 23N 12 50E
102 Rifle 39 40N 107 50W
48 Riga 56 53N 24 8E
91 Rigolet 54 10N 58 23W
37 Rijeka 45 20N 14 21E
40 Rijeka Crnojevica 42 24N 19 1E
16 Rijssen 52 19N 6 30E
16 Rijswijk 52 4N 4 22E
102 Riley 39 18N 96 50W
19 Rilly 49 11N 4 3E
27 Rimavaská Sobota 48 22N 20 2E
44 Rimbo 59 44N 18 21E
37 Rimini 44 3N 12 33E
41 Rîmnicu Sărat 45 26N 27 3E
41 Rîmnicu Vîlcea 45 9N 24 21E
91 Rimouski 48 27N 68 30W
15 Rineanna 52 42N 85 7W
45 Ringe 55 13N 10 28E
44 Ringerike 60 7N 10 16E
45 Ringkøbing 56 5N 8 15E
45 Ringkøbing □ 56 15N 8 30E
45 Ringsjön, L. 55 55N 13 30E
45 Ringsted 55 25N 11 46E
24 Rinteln 52 11N 9 3E
33 Rio, Pta. del 36 49N 2 24W
111 Rio Amazonas, Estuario do 1 0N 49 0W
110 Rio Branco, Brazil 9 58S 67 49W
109 Rio Branco, Uruguay 32 34S 53 25W
109 Rio Brilhante 21 48S 54 33W
105 Rio Claro 10 20N 61 25W
109 Rio Claro 22 19S 47 35W
108 Rio Cuarto 33 10S 64 25W
109 Rio de Janeiro 23 0S 43 12W
109 Rio de Janeiro □ 22 50S 43 0W
109 Rio do Sul 27 95S 49 37W
112 Rio Gallegos 51 35S 69 15W
109 Rio Grande, Arg. 53 50S 67 45W
112 Rio Grande, Brazil 32 0S 52 20W
94 Rio Grande, R. 37 47N 106 15W
111 Rio Grande do Norte □ 5 45S 36 0W
109 Rio Grande do Sul □ 30 0S 54 0W
111 Rio Largo 9 28S 35 50W
110 Rio Mulatos 19 40S 66 50W
74 Rio Muni □ 1 30N 10 0E
109 Rio Negro 26 0S 50 0W
109 Rio Pardo 15 55S 42 30W
108 Río Segundo 31 40S 63 58W
108 Río Tercero 32 10S 64 5W
30 Rio Tinto 41 11N 8 34W
111 Rio Verde, Brazil 17 43S 50 56W
104 Río Verde, Mexico 21 56N 99 59W
102 Rio Vista 38 11N 121 44W
110 Riobamba 1 50S 78 45W
20 Riom 45 54N 3 7E
110 Ríohacha 11 33N 72 55W
39 Rionero in Vulture 40 55N 15 40E
110 Ríosucio 5 30N 75 40W
110 Rioscio 7 27N 77 7W
96 Ripley 44 4N 81 32W
32 Ripoll 42 15N 2 13E
12 Ripon, U.K. 54 8N 1 31W
100 Ripon, U.S.A. 43 51N 88 50W
39 Riposto 37 44N 15 12E
40 Risan 42 32N 18 42E
20 Riscle 43 39N 0 5W
54 Rishon Le Zion 31 58N 34 48E
54 Rishpon 32 12N 34 49E
18 Risle, R. 49 26N 0 23E
41 Rîsnov 45 35N 25 27E
45 Risør 58 43N 9 13E
63 Ritchies Arch. 12 10N 93 5E
96 Rittman 40 57N 81 48W
102 Ritzville 47 10N 118 21W
36 Riva 45 53N 10 50E
18 Riva Bella-Ouistreham 49 17N 0 18W
108 Rivadavia 29 50S 70 35W
105 Rivas 11 30N 85 50W
21 Rive-de-Gier 45 32N 4 37E
109 Rivera 31 0S 55 50W
97 Riverhead 40 53N 72 40W
93 Riverhurst 50 55N 106 50W
75 Riversale 34 7S 21 15E
103 Riverside, Calif. 34 0N 117 15W
102 Riverside, Wyo. 41 12N 106 57W
81 Riverton, Australia 34 10S 138 46E
93 Riverton, Canada 51 5N 97 0W
85 Riverton, N.Z. 46 21S 168 0E
102 Riverton, U.S.A. 43 1N 108 27W
20 Rivesaltes 42 47N 2 50E
36 Riviera 44 0N 8 30E
91 Rivière Bleue 47 26N 69 2W
91 Rivière du Loup 47 50N 69 30W
91 Rivière Pentecôte 49 57N 67 1W
36 Rivoli 45 3N 7 31E
56 Riyadh = Ar Riyád 24 41N 46 42E
56 Rize 41 0N 40 30E
44 Rjukan 59 54N 8 33E
30 Roa 41 41N 3 56W
21 Roanne 46 3N 4 4E
99 Roanoke, Ala. 33 9N 85 23W
98 Roanoke, Va. 37 19N 79 55W
99 Roanoke Rapids 36 36N 77 42W
105 Roatán, I. de 16 23N 86 26W
75 Robertson 33 46S 19 50E
90 Roberval 48 32N 72 15W
77 Robinson Crusoe, I. 33 50S 78 30W
93 Roblin 51 21N 101 25W
92 Robson, Mt. 53 10N 119 10W
101 Robstown 27 47N 97 40W
31 Roca, C. da 38 40N 9 31W
111 Rocas, Is. 4 0S 34 1W
37 Roccastrada 43 0N 11 10E
109 Rocha 34 30S 54 25W
12 Rochdale 53 36N 2 10W
20 Rochefort 45 56N 0 57W
100 Rochelle 41 55N 89 5W
92 Rocher River 61 12N 114 0W
84 Rochester, Australia 36 22S 144 41E
13 Rochester, U.K. 51 22N 0 30E
100 Rochester, Minn. 44 1N 92 28W
97 Rochester, N.H. 43 19N 70 57W
96 Rochester, N.Y. 43 10N 77 40W
96 Rochester, Pa. 40 41N 80 17W
99 Rock Hill 34 55N 81 2W
100 Rock Island 41 30N 90 35W
105 Rock Sound 24 54N 76 12W
102 Rock Springs 46 55N 106 11W
8 Rockall, I. 57 37N 13 42W
5 Rockefeller Plat. 84 0S 130 0W
100 Rockford, Ill. 42 20N 89 0W
100 Rockford, Mich. 43 7N 85 33W
80 Rockhampton 23 22S 150 32E
83 Rockingham 32 15S 115 38E
97 Rockville, Conn. 41 51N 72 27W
99 Rockland, Ma. 44 6N 69 8W
98 Rockville, Md. 39 7N 77 10W
83 Rocky Gully 34 30S 117 0E
99 Rocky Mount 35 55N 77 48W
92 Rocky Mountain House 52 22N 114 55W
86 Rocky Mts. 48 0N 113 0W
96 Rocky River 41 30N 81 40W
92 Rockyford 51 13N 113 8W
44 Rødberg 60 17N 8 56E
45 Rødby 54 41N 11 23E
45 Rødbyhavn 54 39N 11 22E
91 Roddickton 50 51N 56 8W
20 Rodez 44 21N 2 33E
42 Rodhópi □ 41 10N 25 30E
43 Ródhos 36 15N 28 10E
43 Ródhos, I. 36 15N 28 10E
85 Rodney, C. 36 17S 174 50E
3 Rodriguez, I. 20 0S 65 0E
82 Roebourne 20 44S 117 9E
82 Roebuck, B. 18 5S 122 20E
82 Roebuck Plains P.O. 17 56S 122 28E
16 Roermond 51 12N 6 0E
89 Roes Welcome Sd. 65 0N 87 0W
16 Roeselare 50 57N 3 7E
47 Rogaland □ 59 12N 6 20E
37 Rogaska Slatina 46 15N 15 42E
101 Rogers 36 20N 94 0W
90 Roggan River 54 24N 78 5W
21 Rogliano 42 57N 9 30E
60 Rohtak 28 55N 76 43E
19 Roisel 49 58N 3 6E
108 Rojas 34 10S 60 45W
26 Rokycany 49 43N 13 35E
109 Rolândia 23 5S 52 0W
101 Rolla 38 0N 91 42W
80 Rollingstone 19 2S 146 24E
80 Rolleston 43 35S 172 24E
105 Rolleville 23 41N 76 0W
37 Roma, Italy 41 54N 12 30E
81 Roma, Australia 26 32S 148 49E
51 Roman 43 8N 23 54E
21 Romans 45 3N 5 3E
88 Romanzof, C. 61 49N 165 56W
37 Rome, Italy= Roma 41 54N 12 30E
99 Rome, Ga. 34 20N 85 0W
97 Rome, N.Y. 43 14N 75 29W
45 Romeleåsen, Reg. 55 34N 13 33E
19 Romilly 48 31N 3 44E
13 Romney Marsh 51 0N 1 0E
45 Rømø, I. 55 10N 8 30E
19 Romorantin-Lanthenay 47 21N 1 45E
44 Romsdal 62 25N 7 50E
14 Ronaldsay, North I. 59 23N 2 26W
14 Ronaldsay, South I. 58 47N 2 56W
111 Roncador, Sa. do 12 30S 52 30W
31 Ronda 36 46N 5 12W
31 Ronda, Sa. de 36 44N 5 3W
44 Rondane, Reg. 61 57N 9 50E
96 Rondeau Prov. Park 42 16N 81 51W
110 Rondônia □ 11 0S 63 0W
111 Rondonópolis 16 28S 54 38W
45 Rønne 55 6N 14 44E
5 Ronne Ld. 83 0S 70 0W
45 Ronneby 56 12N 15 17E
83 Ronsard, C. 24 46S 113 10E

St. George's I. San Francisco del Oro

105 St. George's I. 32 22N 64 40W
19 St. Germain 48 53N 2 5E
20 St. Germain de Calberte 44 13N 3 48E
20 St. Germain-des-Fossés 46 12N 3 26E
21 St. Gervais, Haute Savoie 45 53N 6 42E
20 St. Gervais, Puy de Dôme 46 4N 2 50E
20 St. Gilles-Croix-de-Vie 46 41N 1 55W
21 St. Gilles-du-Gard 43 40N 4 26E
20 St. Girons 42 59N 1 8E
25 St. Goar 50 31N 7 43E
71 St. Helena, I. 15 55S 5 44W
75 St. Helenabaai 32 40S 18 10E
80 St. Helens, Australia 41 20S 148 15E
12 St. Helens, U.K. 53 28N 2 44W
102 St. Helens, U.S.A. 45 55N 122 50W
18 St. Helier 49 11N 2 6W
90 St. Hyacinthe 45 40N 72 58W
13 St. Ives, Cambridge 52 20N 0 5W
13 St. Ives, Cornwall 50 13N 5 29W
90 St. Jean 45 20N 73 50W
93 St. Jean Baptiste 49 15N 97 20W
20 St. Jean-d'Angély 45 57N 0 31W
20 St. Jean-de-Luz 43 23N 1 39W
21 St.-Jean-de-Maurienne 45 16N 6 28E
20 St. Jean-de-Monts 46 47N 2 4W
20 St. Jean-du-Gard 47 7N 3 52E
90 St. Jérôme 45 55N 74 0W
26 St. Johann 47 22N 13 12E
91 St. John 45 20N 66 8W
91 St. John, L. 48 40N 72 0W
105 St. John's, Antigua 17 6N 61 51W
91 St. John's, Canada 47 45N 52 40W
97 St. Johnsbury 44 25N 72 1W
97 St. Johnsville 43 0N 74 43W
98 St. Joseph, Mich. 42 6N 86 29W
100 St. Joseph, Mo. 39 46N 94 51W
90 St. Jovite 46 8N 74 38W
19 St. Julien-du-Sault 48 2N 3 18E
20 St. Junien 45 53N 0 55E
19 St. Just-en-Chaussée 49 30N 2 25E
85 St. Kilda 45 53S 170 31E
105 St. Kitts, I. 17 20N 62 40W
93 St. Laurent 50 25N 97 58W
21 St. Laurent-du-Pont 45 23N 5 45E
91 St. Lawrence 46 54N 55 23W
91 St. Lawrence, G. of 48 25N 62 0W
88 St. Lawrence, I. 63 0N 170 0W
91 St. Lawrence, R. 49 15N 67 0W
91 St. Leonard 47 12N 67 58W
20 St. Léonard-de-Noblat 45 49N 1 29E
90 St. Lin 45 44N 73 46W
18 St. Lô 49 7N 1 5W
72 St. Louis, Senegal 16 8N 16 27W
100 St. Louis, U.S.A. 38 40N 90 20W
105 St. Lucia, I. 14 0N 60 50W
75 St. Lucia, L. 28 5S 32 30E
105 St. Lucia Chan. 14 15N 61 0W
105 St. Maarten, I. 18 0N 63 5W
20 St. Maixent 46 24N 0 12W
18 St. Malo 48 39N 2 1W
18 St. Malo, G. de 48 50N 2 30W
21 St. Mandrier 43 4N 5 56E
105 St. Marc 19 10N 72 5W
21 St. Marcellin 45 9N 5 20E
102 St. Maries 47 17N 116 34W
19 St. Martin 50 42N 1 38E
105 St. Martin, I. 18 0N 63 0W
91 St. Martins 45 22N 65 38W
20 St. Martory 43 9N 0 56E
80 St. Marys, Australia 41 32S 148 11E
96 St. Marys, U.S.A. 41 30N 78 33W
13 St. Marys, I. 49 55N 6 17W
18 St. Mathieu, Pte. de. 48 20N 4 45W
88 St. Matthew I. 60 30N 172 45W
19 St. Maur 48 48N 2 30E
20 St. Médard-de-Guizières 45 1N 0 4W
13 St. Michael's Mt. 50 7N 5 30W
25 St. Moritz 46 30N 9 50E
18 St. Nazaire 47 17N 2 12W
13 St. Neots 52 14N 0 16W
19 St. Nicolas 48 38N 6 18E
16 St. Niklaas 51 10N 4 8E
19 St. Omer 50 45N 2 15E
91 St. Pacôme 47 24N 69 58W
20 St. Palais 45 40N 1 8W
91 St. Pamphile 46 58N 69 48W
91 St. Pascal 47 32N 69 48W
92 St. Paul, Canada 51 34N 57 47W
20 St. Paul, Fr. 43 44N 1 3W
100 St. Paul, U.S.A. 44 54N 93 5W
3 St. Paul, I. 30 40S 77 34E
20 St. Paul-de-Fenouillet 42 50N 2 28E
100 St. Peter 44 15N 93 57W
13 St. Peter Port 49 27N 2 31W
99 St. Petersburg 27 45N 82 40W
91 St. Pierre, Canada 46 40N 56 0W
20 St. Pierre, Fr. 45 57N 1 19W
90 St. Pierre, L. 46 10N 72 50W
18 St. Pierre-Église 49 40N 1 24W
18 St. Pierre-en-Port 49 48N 0 30E
91 St. Pierre et Miquelon □ 46 49N 56 15W
20 St. Pierre-le-Moutier 46 48N 3 7E
18 St. Pierre-sur-Dives 49 2N 0 1W
19 St. Pol 50 21N 2 20E
19 St. Pol-sur-Mer 51 1N 2 20E
26 St. Polten 48 12N 15 37E
20 St. Pons 43 30N 2 45E
20 St. Pourcain-sur-Sioule 46 18N 3 18E
19 St. Quentin 49 50N 3 16E
21 St. Rambert d'Alban 45 17N 1 35E
21 St. Raphaël 43 25N 6 46E
18 St. Servan 48 38N 2 0E
18 St. Sever Calvados 48 50N 1 3W
91 St. Siméon 47 51N 69 54W
91 St. Stephen 45 16N 67 17W
20 St. Sulpice la Pointe 43 46N 1 41E
20 St. Sulpice-Laurière 46 3N 1 29E
90 St. Thomas, Canada 42 47N 81 12W
96 St. Thomas, U.S.A. 38 23N 92 13W
105 St. Thomas, Virgin Is. 18 21N 64 56W
90 St. Tite 46 45N 72 40W
21 St. Tropez 43 17N 6 38E
16 St. Troud 50 48N 5 10E
18 St. Vaast-la-Hougue 49 35N 1 17W
26 St. Valentin 48 10N 14 32E
19 St. Valéry 50 10N 1 38E
18 St. Valéry-en-Caux 49 52N 0 43E
21 St. Vallier 43 42N 6 51E
20 St. Varent 46 53N 0 13W
26 St. Veit 46 46N 14 21E
105 St. Vincent, I. 13 10N 61 10W
20 St. Vincent-de-Tyrosse 43 39N 1 18W
105 St. Vincent Pass. 13 30N 61 0W
93 St. Walburg 53 39N 109 12W
25 St. Wendel 49 28N 7 10E
26 St. Wolfgang 47 44N 13 27E
20 St. Yrieux 45 31N 1 12E
18 Ste. Adresse 49 31N 0 5E
91 Ste. Anne de Beaupré 47 2N 70 58W
19 Ste. Benoîte 49 47N 3 30E
91 Ste. Cecile 47 56N 64 34W
20 Ste. Hermine 46 32N 1 4W
105 Ste. Marie 14 48N 61 1W
75 Ste. Marie, C. 25 36S 45 8E
19 Ste. Marie-aux-Mines 48 10N 7 12E
91 Ste. Marie de la Madeleine 46 26N 71 0W
18 Ste. Maur 47 7N 0 37E
21 Ste. Maxime 43 19N 6 39E
19 Ste. Menehould 49 5N 4 54E
18 Ste. Mère Église 49 24N 1 19W
105 Ste. Rose 16 20N 61 45W
93 Ste. Rose du lac 51 10N 99 30W
20 Saintes 45 45N 0 37W
20 Saintonge, Reg. 45 40N 0 50W
59 Sairang 23 50N 92 45E
66 Saitama □ 36 25N 137 0E
110 Sajama, Mt. 18 6S 68 54W
66 Sakai 34 30N 135 30E
66 Sakaide 34 32N 133 50E
66 Sakaiminato 35 33N 133 15E
66 Sakata 38 55N 139 56E
51 Sakhalin 51 0N 143 0E
54 Sakhnin 32 52N 35 12E
69 Sakishima-guntō, Is. 24 30N 124 0E
75 Sakrivier 30 54S 20 28E
44 Sala 59 58N 16 35E
39 Sala Consilina 40 23N 15 35E
77 Sala-y-Gomez, I. 26 28S 105 28W
108 Saladillo 35 40S 59 55W
72 Salaga 8 31N 0 31W
30 Salamanca, Sp. 40 58N 5 39W
96 Salamanca, U.S.A. 42 10N 78 42W
30 Salamanca □ 40 57N 5 40W
43 Salamis 37 56N 23 30E
30 Salas 43 25N 6 15W
30 Salas de los Infantes 42 2N 3 17W
65 Salatiga 7 19S 110 30E
48 Salavat 53 21N 55 55E
110 Salaverry 8 15S 79 0W
65 Salawati, I. 1 7S 130 54E
74 Salazar 9 18S 14 54E
19 Salbris 47 25N 2 3E
75 Saldanha 33 0S 17 58E
84 Sale, Australia 38 7S 147 0E
12 Sale, U.K. 53 26N 2 19W
72 Salé 34 3N 6 48W
50 Salekhard 66 30N 66 25E
62 Salem, India 11 40N 78 11E
97 Salem, Mass. 42 29N 70 53W
96 Salem, Ohio 40 52N 80 50W
102 Salem, Oreg. 45 0N 123 0W
98 Salem, Va. 37 19N 80 8W
97 Salem Depot 42 47N 71 12W
38 Salemi 37 49N 12 47E
21 Salernes 43 34N 6 15E
39 Salerno 40 40N 14 44E
39 Salerno, G. di 40 35N 14 45E
12 Salford 53 30N 2 17W
27 Salgótarján 48 5N 19 47E
56 Salihli 38 29N 28 9E
75 Salima 13 47S 34 26E
100 Salina 38 50N 97 40W
104 Salina Cruz 16 10N 95 10W
111 Salinas, Brazil 16 20S 42 10W
103 Salinas, U.S.A. 36 40N 121 38W
105 Salinas, B. de 11 4N 85 45W
33 Salinas, C. de 39 16N 3 4E
111 Salinópolis 0 40S 47 20W
31 Salir 47 14N 8 2W
81 Salisbury, Australia 34 46S 138 38E
75 Salisbury, Rhodesia 17 50S 31 2E
13 Salisbury, U.K. 51 4N 1 48W
98 Salisbury, Md. 38 20N 75 38W
99 Salisbury, N.C. 35 42N 80 29W
13 Salisbury Plain 51 13N 2 0W
41 Săliște 45 45N 23 56E
102 Salmon 45 12N 113 56W
102 Salmon, R. 45 51N 116 46W
92 Salmon Arm 50 40N 119 15W
97 Salmon Falls 42 55N 114 59W
83 Salmon Gums 32 59S 121 38E
102 Salmon River Mts. 45 0N 114 30W
47 Salo 60 22N 23 3E
31 Salobreña 36 44N 3 35W
21 Salon 43 39N 5 6E
13 Salop □ 52 36N 2 45W
32 Salou, C. 41 3N 1 10E
20 Salses 42 50N 2 55E
62 Salsette I. 19 5N 72 50E
49 Salsk 46 28N 41 30E
36 Salsomaggiore 44 48N 9 59E
102 Salt Lake City 40 45N 111 58W
60 Salt Ra. 32 30N 72 25E
108 Salta 24 47S 65 25W
108 Salta □ 24 48S 65 30W
14 Saltcoats 55 38N 4 47W
45 Saltholm, I. 55 38N 12 43E
104 Saltillo 25 30N 100 57W
108 Salto, Arg. 34 20S 60 15W
108 Salto, Uruguay 31 20S 58 10W
103 Salton Sea 33 20N 116 0W
72 Saltpond 5 15N 1 3W
44 Saltsjöbaden 59 15N 18 20E
92 Saltspring 48 54N 123 37W
73 Salum 31 31N 25 7E
62 Salur 18 27N 83 18E
36 Saluzzo 44 39N 7 29E
111 Salvador, Brazil 13 0S 38 30W
93 Salvador, Canada 52 20N 109 25W
104 Salvador ■ 13 50N 89 0W
31 Salveterra de Magos 39 1N 8 47W
30 Salvora, I. 42 30N 8 58W
59 Salween, R. 16 31N 97 37E
26 Salza, R. 47 40N 14 43E
26 Salzach, R. 48 12N 12 56E
26 Salzburg 47 48N 13 2E
26 Salzburg □ 47 25N 13 15E
24 Salzgitter 52 2N 10 22E
24 Salzwedel 52 50N 11 11E
63 Sam Neua 20 29N 104 0E
63 Sam Ngao 17 18N 99 0E
101 Sam Rayburn Res. 31 15N 94 20W
50 Sama 60 10N 60 15E
30 Sama de Langreo 43 18N 5 40W
51 Samagaltai 50 36N 95 3E
62 Samalkot 17 3N 82 13E
57 Samangan □ 36 15N 67 40E
65 Samar, I. 12 0N 125 0E
54 Samaria, Reg.= Shomron, Reg. 32 15N 35 13E
64 Samarinda 0 30S 117 9E
50 Samarkand 39 40N 67 0E
61 Sambalpur 21 28N 83 58E
60 Sambhar 26 52N 11 16E
108 Samborombón, B. 36 5S 57 20W
16 Sambre, R. 50 28N 4 52E
68 Samchŏk 37 27N 129 10E
19 Samer 50 38N 1 44E
85 Samoa Is. 14 0S 171 0W
21 Samoëns 46 5N 6 45E
41 Samokov 42 20N 23 33E
30 Samos 42 44N 7 20W
43 Sámos, I. 37 45N 26 50E
42 Samothráki, I. 40 28N 25 38E
65 Sampang 7 11S 113 13E
32 Samper de Calanda 41 11N 4 2W
64 Sampit 2 20S 113 0E
69 Samshui 23 7N 112 58E
45 Samsø, I. 55 52N 10 37E
56 Samsun 41 15N 36 15E
63 Samut Prakan 13 32N 100 40E
63 Samut Sakhon 13 31N 100 20E
63 Samut Songkhram 13 24N 100 1E
72 San 13 15N 4 45W
30 San Adrián, C. de 43 21N 8 50W
77 San Ambrosio, I. 26 21S 79 52W
105 San Andrés, I. de 12 42N 81 46W
104 San Andrés Tuxtla 18 30N 95 20W
101 San Angelo 31 30N 100 30W
108 San Antonio, Chile 33 40S 71 40W
101 San Antonio, U.S.A. 29 30N 98 30W
105 San Antonio, C. 21 50N 84 57W
33 San Antonio, C. de 38 48N 0 12E
33 San Antonio Abad 38 59N 1 19E
105 San Antonio de los Banos 22 54N 82 31W
112 San Antonio Oeste 40 40S 65 0W
39 San Bartolomeo 41 24N 15 1E
36 San Benedetto 45 2N 10 57E
101 San Benito 26 5N 97 32W
103 San Bernardino 34 7N 117 18W
65 San Bernardino Str. 12 37N 124 12E
108 San Bernardo 33 40S 70 50W
110 San Bernardo, I. de 9 45N 75 50W
105 San Blas, Cord. de 9 15N 78 30W
108 San Carlos, Arg. 33 50S 69 0W
65 San Carlos, Philippines 10 29N 123 25E
109 San Carlos, Uruguay 34 46S 54 58W
110 San Carlos, Ven. 1 55N 67 4W
110 San Carlos, Ven. 9 40N 68 36W
112 San Carlos de Bariloche 41 10S 71 25W
32 San Carlos de la Rápita 40 37N 0 35E
110 San Carlos del Zulia 9 1N 71 55W
103 San Carlos L. 33 13N 110 24W
38 San Cataldo 37 30N 13 58E
32 San Celoni 41 42N 2 30E
33 San Clemente, Sp. 39 24N 2 25W
103 San Clemente, U.S.A. 33 29N 117 45W
103 San Clemente I. 33 0N 118 30W
105 San Cristóbal, Dom. Rep. 18 25N 70 6W
110 San Cristóbal, Ven. 7 46N 72 14W
104 San Cristóbal de las Casas 16 50N 92 33W
39 San Demétrio Corone 39 34N 16 22E
103 San Diego 32 50N 117 10W
112 San Diego, C. 54 40S 65 10W
37 San Dona di Piave 45 38N 12 34E
108 San Estanislao 24 39S 56 26W
30 San Esteban de Gormaz 41 34N 3 13W
36 San Felice sul Panaro 44 51N 11 9E
108 San Felipe, Chile 32 43S 70 50W
110 San Felipe, Ven. 10 20N 68 44W
32 San Felíu de Guíxals 41 45N 3 1E
107 San Felix, I. 26 30S 80 0W
108 San Fernando, Chile 34 30S 71 0W
65 San Fernando, Philippines 15 5N 120 37E
65 San Fernando, Philippines 16 40N 120 23E
31 San Fernando, Sp. 36 22N 6 17W
105 San Fernando, Trinidad 10 20N 61 30W
103 San Fernando, U.S.A. 34 15N 118 29W
110 San Fernando de Apure 7 54N 67 28W
110 San Fernando de Atabapo 4 3N 67 42W
39 San Fernando di Puglia 41 18N 16 5E
108 San Francisco, Arg. 31 30S 62 5W
103 San Francisco, U.S.A. 37 35N 122 30W
103 San Francisco, R. 32 59N 109 22W
105 San Francisco de Macoris 19 19N 70 15W
104 San Francisco del Oro 26 52N 105 50W

Seymour, Australia — Siverek

84 Seymour, Australia 36 58 S 145 10 E
98 Seymour, U.S.A. 39 0 N 85 50 W
21 Seyssel 45 57 N 5 49 E
19 Sézanne 48 40 N 3 40 E
38 Sezze 41 30 N 13 3 E
73 Sfax 34 49 N 10 48 E
41 Sfintu-Gheorghe 45 52 N 25 48 E
16 's-Gravenhage 52 7 N 4 17 E
75 Shabani 20 17 S 30 2 E
41 Shabla 43 31 N 28 32 E
74 Shabunda 2 40 S 27 16 E
50 Shadrinsk 56 5 N 63 38 E
13 Shaftesbury 51 0 N 2 12 W
62 Shahabad, Andhra Pradesh 17 10 N 78 11 E
60 Shahabad, Punjab 30 10 N 76 55 E
61 Shahabad, Ut.P. 27 36 N 79 56 E
57 Sháhábád, Iran 37 40 N 56 50 E
60 Shahada 21 33 N 74 30 E
62 Shahapur 15 50 N 74 34 E
56 Shāhbād 34 10 N 46 30 E
68 Shahcheng 40 18 N 115 27 E
57 Shahdād 30 30 N 57 40 E
73 Shahhat 32 40 N 21 35 E
57 Shāhī 36 30 N 52 55 E
61 Shahjahanpur 27 54 N 79 57 E
62 Shahpur, Karnataka 16 40 N 76 48 E
60 Shahpur, Mad.P. 22 12 N 77 58 E
56 Shāhpūr, Iran 38 12 N 44 45 E
57 Shahrezā 32 0 N 51 55 E
57 Shāhrūd 36 30 N 55 0 E
57 Shahsavār 36 45 N 51 12 E
57 Shaikhabad 34 0 N 68 45 E
60 Shajapur 23 20 N 76 15 E
96 Shaker Heights 41 29 N 81 36 W
49 Shakhty 47 40 N 40 10 E
48 Shakhunya 57 40 N 47 0 E
72 Shaki 8 41 N 3 21 E
69 Shalu 24 24 N 120 26 E
57 Sham, Jabal ash 23 10 N 57 5 E
57 Shamil 29 32 N 77 18 E
74 Shamo, L. 5 45 N 37 30 E
97 Shamokin 40 47 N 76 33 W
75 Shamva 17 18 S 31 34 E
59 Shan □ 21 30 N 98 30 E
68 Schanchengtze 42 2 N 123 47 E
72 Shanga 9 1 N 5 2 E
75 Shangani, R. 18 41 S 27 10 E
68 Shangchih 45 10 N 127 59 E
69 Schangchwan Shan, I. 21 35 N 112 45 E
69 Shanghai 31 10 N 121 25 E
69 Shangjao 28 25 N 117 25 E
69 Shangkiu 34 28 N 115 42 E
69 Shangshui 33 42 N 115 4 E
68 Shanh 47 5 N 103 5 E
85 Shannon 40 33 S 175 25 E
15 Shannon, R. 52 30 N 9 53 W
68 Shansi □ 37 0 N 113 0 E
69 Shantow 23 25 N 116 40 E
68 Shantung □ 37 0 N 118 0 E
69 Shanyang 33 39 N 110 2 E
69 Shaohing 30 0 N 120 32 E
69 Shaowu 27 25 N 117 30 E
69 Shaoyang 27 10 N 111 30 E
14 Shapinsay, I. 59 2 N 2 50 W
56 Shaqra 25 15 N 45 16 E
68 Sharin Gol 49 12 N 106 27 E
57 Sharjah 25 23 N 55 26 E
83 Shark, B. 25 15 S 133 20 E
96 Sharon, Pa. 41 14 N 80 31 W
97 Sharon, Mass. 42 5 N 71 11 W
48 Sharya 58 12 N 45 40 E
75 Shashi 21 40 S 28 40 E
69 Shasi 30 16 N 112 20 E
102 Shasta, Mt. 41 45 N 122 0 W
102 Shasta Res. 40 50 N 122 15 W
93 Shaunavon 49 35 N 108 40 W
97 Shawangunk Mts. 41 35 N 74 30 W
100 Shawano 44 45 N 88 38 W
90 Shawinigan 46 35 N 72 50 W
101 Shawnee 35 15 N 97 0 W
55 Shebele, Wabi 2 0 N 44 0 E
98 Sheboygan 43 46 N 87 45 W
91 Shediac 46 14 N 64 32 W
13 Sheerness 51 26 N 0 47 E
54 Shefar'am 32 48 N 35 10 E
12 Sheffield, U.K. 53 23 N 1 28 W
97 Sheffield, U.S.A. 42 6 N 73 23 W
60 Shegaon 20 48 N 76 59 E
61 Sheikhpura 25 9 N 85 53 E
60 Shekhupura 31 42 N 73 58 E
69 Shekki 22 30 N 113 15 E
69 Sheklung 23 5 N 113 55 E
91 Shelburne, Nova Scotia 43 47 N 65 20 W
90 Shelburne, Ont. 44 4 N 80 15 W
102 Shelby, Mont. 48 30 N 111 59 W
99 Shelby, N.C. 35 18 N 81 34 W
98 Shelbyville, Ind. 39 30 N 85 42 W
99 Shelbyville, Tenn. 35 30 N 86 25 W
91 Sheldrake 50 20 N 64 51 W
51 Shelikhova Zaliv 59 30 N 157 0 E
93 Shell Lake 53 19 N 107 6 W
93 Shellbrook 53 13 N 106 24 W
91 Shelter Bay 50 30 N 67 20 W
88 Shelton, Alaska 55 20 N 105 0 W
97 Shelton, Conn. 41 18 N 73 7 W
102 Shelton, Wash. 47 15 N 123 6 W
49 Shemakha 40 50 N 48 28 E
100 Shenandoah, Iowa 40 50 N 95 25 W
97 Shenandoah, Pa. 40 49 N 76 13 W
98 Shenandoah, R. 39 19 N 77 44 W
62 Shencottah 8 59 N 77 18 E
72 Shendam 9 10 N 9 30 E
73 Shendî 16 46 N 33 33 E
60 Shendurni 20 39 N 75 36 E
42 Shëngjeni 41 50 N 19 35 E
68 Shensi □ 35 0 N 109 0 E
68 Shenyang 41 35 N 123 30 E
84 Shepparton 36 18 S 145 25 E
13 Sherborne 50 56 N 2 31 W
72 Sherbro I. 7 30 N 12 40 W
91 Sherbrooke 45 24 N 71 57 W
102 Sheridan 44 50 N 107 0 W
101 Sherman 33 40 N 96 35 W
61 Sherpur 25 1 N 90 3 E
93 Sherridon 55 10 N 101 5 W
16 s'Hertogenbosch 51 41 N 5 19 E
12 Sherwood Forest 53 5 N 1 5 W
75 Shesheke 17 50 S 24 0 E
14 Shetland □ 60 30 N 1 30 W
62 Shevaroy Hills 11 58 N 78 12 E
50 Shevchenko 44 25 N 51 20 E
54 Shevut'Am 32 19 N 34 55 E
55 Shibam 16 0 N 48 36 E
57 Shibarghan 36 40 N 65 48 E
66 Shibushi 31 25 N 131 0 E
91 Shickshock Mts. 48 40 N 66 30 W
14 Shiel, L. 56 48 N 5 32 W
66 Shiga □ 35 20 N 136 0 E
67 Shigatse 29 10 N 89 0 E
68 Shihkiachwang 38 0 N 114 32 E
69 Shihpu 29 12 N 121 58 E
68 Shihwei 51 28 N 119 59 E
42 Shijaku 41 21 N 19 33 E
60 Shikarpur, India 28 17 N 78 7 E
60 Shikarpur, Pak. 27 57 N 68 39 E
60 Shikohabad 27 6 N 78 38 E
66 Shikoku, I. 33 45 N 133 30 E
66 Shikoku □ 33 30 N 133 30 E
15 Shillelagh 52 46 N 6 32 W
51 Shilka 52 0 N 115 55 E
97 Shillington 40 18 N 75 58 W
59 Shillong 25 30 N 92 0 E
66 Shimada 34 49 N 138 19 E
66 Shimane □ 35 0 N 132 30 E
51 Shimanovsk 52 15 N 127 30 E
66 Shimizu 35 0 N 138 30 E
66 Shimodate 36 20 N 139 55 E
62 Shimoga 13 57 N 75 32 E
66 Shimonoseki 33 58 N 131 0 E
50 Shimpek 44 50 N 74 10 E
14 Shin, L. 58 7 N 4 30 W
57 Shin Dand 33 12 N 62 8 E
66 Shingú 33 40 N 135 33 E
74 Shinyanga 3 45 S 33 27 E
91 Shippegan 47 45 N 64 45 W
66 Shirane-San, Mt. 35 40 N 138 15 E
57 Shiráz 29 42 N 52 30 E
75 Shire, R. 17 42 S 35 19 E
62 Shirol 16 47 N 74 41 E
60 Shirpur 21 21 N 74 57 E
69 Shiukwan 24 58 N 113 3 E
60 Shivpuri 25 18 N 77 42 E
66 Shizuoka 35 0 N 138 30 E
66 Shizuoka □ 35 15 N 138 40 E
42 Shkodra 42 6 N 19 20 E
42 Shkodra □ 42 5 N 19 20 E
42 Shkumbini, R. 41 1 N 19 26 E
93 Shoal Lake 50 30 N 100 35 W
13 Shoeburyness 51 13 N 0 49 E
68 Shohsien 39 30 N 112 25 E
62 Sholapur 17 43 N 75 56 E
51 Shologontsy 66 13 N 114 14 E
54 Shomera 33 4 N 35 17 E
54 Shómrón, Reg. 32 15 N 35 13 E
62 Shoranur 10 46 N 76 19 E
62 Shorapur 16 31 N 76 48 E
102 Shoshone 43 0 N 114 27 W
75 Shoshong 22 0 S 26 30 E
103 Show Low 34 16 N 110 0 W
101 Shreveport 32 30 N 93 50 W
12 Shrewsbury 52 42 N 2 45 W
62 Shrivardhan 18 10 N 73 3 E
69 Shucheng 31 25 N 117 2 E
69 Shuikiahu 32 14 N 117 4 E
88 Shumagin Is. 55 0 N 159 0 W
50 Shumikha 55 15 N 63 30 E
54 Shunat Nimran 31 54 N 35 37 E
69 Shunchang 26 52 N 117 48 E
88 Shungnak 66 53 N 157 2 W
55 Shuqra 13 22 N 45 34 E
57 Shúsf 31 50 N 60 5 E
56 Shushtar 32 0 N 48 50 E
54 Shuweika 32 20 N 35 1 E
68 Shwangliano 43 39 N 123 40 E
59 Shwebo 22 30 N 95 45 E
59 Shwegu 24 15 N 96 50 E
58 Shyok 34 15 N 78 5 E
58 Shyok, R. 35 13 N 75 53 E
63 Si Racha 13 20 N 101 10 E
58 Siahan Ra. 27 30 N 64 40 E
67 Siakwan 25 45 N 100 10 E
60 Sialkot 32 32 N 74 30 E
63 Siam=Thailand ■ 15 0 N 100 0 E
69 Sian 34 2 N 109 0 E
69 Sian Kiang, R. 22 30 N 110 10 E
69 Siangfan 32 15 N 112 2 E
69 Siangtan 28 0 N 112 55 E
69 Siangyang 32 18 N 111 0 E
68 Siao Hingan Ling, Mts. 49 0 N 127 0 E
65 Siargao, I. 9 52 N 126 3 E
42 Siátista 40 15 N 21 33 E
48 Siauhai 55 56 N 23 15 E
93 Sibbald 51 24 N 110 10 W
37 Sibenik 43 48 N 15 54 E
64 Siberut, I. 1 30 S 99 0 E
60 Sibi 29 30 N 67 48 E
74 Sibiti 3 38 S 13 19 E
41 Sibiu 45 45 N 24 9 E
41 Sibiu □ 45 50 N 24 15 E
64 Sibolga 1 50 N 98 45 E
59 Sibsagar 27 0 N 94 36 E
64 Sibu 2 19 N 111 51 E
65 Sibutu Pass. 4 50 N 120 0 E
65 Sibuyan, I. 12 25 N 122 40 E
65 Sibuyan Sea 12 50 N 122 20 E
67 Sichang 28 0 N 102 10 E
39 Sicilia □ 37 30 N 14 30 E
39 Sicilia, I. 37 30 N 14 30 E
38 Sicilian Chan. 37 20 N 12 20 E
110 Sicuani 14 10 S 71 10 W
40 Šid 45 6 N 19 16 E
62 Siddipet 18 0 N 79 0 E
39 Siderno Marina 38 16 N 16 17 E
42 Sidhirókastron 37 20 N 21 46 E
60 Sidhpur 23 56 N 71 25 E
73 Sîdi Barrâni 31 32 N 25 58 E
72 Sidi bel Abbès 35 13 N 0 10 W
72 Sidi Ifni 29 29 N 10 3 W
14 Sidlaw Hills 56 32 N 3 10 W
13 Sidmouth 50 40 N 3 13 W
92 Sidney, Canada 48 39 N 123 24 W
98 Sidney, U.S.A. 40 18 N 84 6 W
65 Sidoardjo 7 30 S 112 46 E
24 Sieburg 50 48 N 7 12 E
28 Siedlce 52 10 N 22 20 E
28 Siedlce □ 52 0 N 22 0 E
24 Sieg, R. 50 45 N 7 5 E
24 Siegen 50 52 N 8 2 E
63 Siem Reap 13 20 N 103 52 E
37 Siena 43 20 N 11 20 E
69 Sieyang 34 20 N 108 48 E
28 Sieradź 51 37 N 18 41 E
28 Sieradź □ 51 30 N 18 40 E
28 Sierpc 52 55 N 19 43 E
72 Sierra Leone ■ 9 0 N 12 0 W
102 Sierra Nevada, Mts. 40 0 N 121 0 W
25 Sierre 46 17 N 7 31 E
43 Sífnos, I. 37 0 N 24 45 E
20 Sigean 43 2 N 2 58 E
41 Sighisoara 46 12 N 24 50 E
64 Sigli 5 25 N 96 0 E
46 Siglufjördur 66 12 N 18 55 W
110 Sigsig 3 0 S 78 50 W
30 Sigüenza 41 3 N 2 40 W
72 Siguiri 11 31 N 9 10 W
103 Sigurd 38 57 N 112 0 W
63 Sihanoukville = Kompong Som 10 40 N 103 30 E
69 Sihsien 29 55 N 118 23 E
56 Siirt 37 57 N 41 55 E
69 Si Kiang, R. 22 0 N 114 0 E
69 Sikandarabad 28 30 N 77 39 E
60 Sikandra Rao 27 43 N 78 24 E
60 Sikar 27 39 N 75 10 E
72 Sikasso 11 7 N 5 35 W
101 Sikeston 36 52 N 89 35 W
51 Sikhote Alin Khrebet 46 0 N 136 0 E
43 Síkinos, I. 36 40 N 25 8 E
61 Sikkim □ 27 50 N 88 50 E
30 Sil, R. 42 27 N 7 43 W
64 Silamulun, R. 43 20 N 121 0 E
54 Sīlat adh Dhahr 32 19 N 35 11 E
37 Silba 44 24 N 14 41 E
59 Silghat 26 35 N 93 0 E
61 Siliguri 26 45 N 88 25 E
41 Silistra 44 6 N 27 19 E
44 Siljan, L. 60 55 N 14 45 E
45 Silkeborg 56 10 N 9 32 E
75 Silva Porto=Bié 12 22 S 16 55 E
103 Silver City, Panama Canal Zone 9 21 N 79 53 W
103 Silver City, U.S.A. 32 50 N 108 18 W
31 Silves 37 11 N 8 26 W
54 Silwan 31 59 N 35 15 E
26 Silz 47 16 N 10 56 E
64 Simanggang 1 15 N 111 25 E
90 Simcoe, Canada 42 50 N 80 20 W
90 Simcoe, L. 44 20 N 79 20 W
51 Simenga 62 50 N 107 55 E
40 Simeria 45 51 N 23 1 E
64 Simeulue, I. 2 45 N 95 45 E
49 Simferopol 44 55 N 34 3 E
43 Sími, I. 36 35 N 27 50 E
60 Simla 31 2 N 77 15
93 Simmie 49 56 N 108 6 W
63 Simpang 4 50 N 100 40 E
25 Simplonpass 46 15 N 8 0 E
80 Simpson, Des. 25 0 S 137 0 E
45 Simrishamn 55 33 N 14 22 E
62 Sina, R. 17 23 N 75 54 E
73 Sinâ', Gebel el Tîh Es 29 0 N 33 30 E
73 Sinai = Es Sinâ' 29 0 N 34 0 E
41 Sinaia 45 21 N 25 38 E
104 Sinaloa □ 25 50 N 108 20 W
37 Sinalunga 43 12 N 11 43 E
40 Sînandrei 45 52 N 21 13 E
110 Sincelejo 9 18 N 75 24 W
69 Sincheng 34 25 N 113 56 W
111 Sincorá, Sa. do 13 30 S 41 0 W
60 Sind, R. 26 26 N 79 14 E
65 Sindangbarang 7 27 S 107 9 E
60 Sindsagar Doab, Reg. 32 0 N 71 30 E
31 Sines 37 56 N 8 51 E
31 Sines, C. de 37 58 N 8 53 W
32 Sineu 39 39 N 3 0 E
69 Sinfeng 26 59 N 106 55 E
73 Singa 13 10 N 33 57 E
65 Singaparna 7 23 S 108 4 E
63 Singapore ■ 1 17 N 103 51 E
63 Singapore, Str. of 1 10 N 103 40 E
25 Singen 47 45 N 8 50 E
74 Singida 4 49 S 34 48 E
42 Singitikós Kól. 40 6 N 24 0 E
59 Singkling Hkamti 26 0 N 95 45 E
64 Singkawang 1 0 N 109 5 E
64 Singkep 0 30 S 140 20 E
68 Singtai 37 2 N 114 30 E
69 Singtze 29 30 N 116 4 E
69 Sinhailien 34 31 N 119 0 E
68 Sinhsien 38 25 N 112 45 E
69 Sinhwa 27 36 N 111 6 E
67 Sining 36 35 N 101 50 E
56 Sinjār 36 19 N 41 52 E
54 Sinjil 32 3 N 35 15 E
73 Sinkat 18 55 N 36 49 E
68 Sinkiang 35 35 N 111 25 E
67 Sinkiang-Uigur □ 42 0 N 85 0 E
68 Sinkin 39 30 N 122 29 E
38 Sînnai 39 18 N 9 13 E
111 Sinnamary 5 23 N 52 57 W
73 Sinnûris 29 26 N 30 31 E
41 Sinoe, L. 44 35 N 28 50 E
56 Sinop 42 1 N 35 11 E
69 Sinsiang 35 15 N 113 55 E
64 Sintang 0 5 N 111 35 E
31 Sintra 38 47 N 9 25 W
68 Sinuiju 40 5 N 124 24 E
69 Sinyang 32 6 N 114 2 E
25 Sion 46 14 N 7 20 E
100 Sioux City 42 32 N 96 25 W
100 Sioux Falls 43 35 N 96 40 W
90 Sioux Lookout 50 10 N 91 50 W
105 Siparia 10 15 N 61 30 W
69 Siping 33 25 N 114 10 E
105 Siquia, R. 12 30 N 84 30 W
57 Sir Bani Yas, I. 24 20 N 54 0 E
80 Sir Edward Pellew Group, Is. 15 40 S 137 10 E
88 Sir James McBrien, Mt. 62 7 N 127 41 W
62 Sira 13 41 N 76 49 E
39 Siracusa 37 4 N 15 17 E
61 Sirajganj 24 25 N 89 47 E
41 Siret, R. 47 55 N 26 5 E
60 Sironj 24 5 N 77 45 E
43 Síros, I. 37 28 N 24 57 E
60 Sirsa 29 33 N 75 4 E
62 Sirsi 14 40 N 74 49 E
62 Sirsilla 18 23 N 78 49 E
37 Sisak 45 30 N 16 21 E
63 Sisaket 15 8 N 104 23 E
63 Sisante 39 25 N 2 12 W
63 Sisophon 13 31 N 102 59 E
57 Sistan Baluchistan □ 27 0 N 62 0 E
30 Sistema Central 40 40 N 5 55 W
61 Sitamarhi 26 37 N 85 30 E
61 Sitapur 27 38 N 80 45 E
32 Sitges 41 17 N 1 47 E
42 Sithonia, Pen. 40 0 N 23 45 E
92 Sitka 57 9 N 134 58 W
59 Sittang Myit, R. 18 20 N 96 45 E
16 Sittard 51 0 N 5 52 E
65 Situbondo 7 45 S 114 0 E
62 Sivakasi 9 24 N 77 47 E
57 Sivand 30 5 N 52 55 E
56 Sivas 39 43 N 36 58 E
56 Siverek 37 50 N 39 25 E

Teano Tocopilla

39 Teano 41 15N 14 1E
31 Teba 36 59N 4 55W
72 Tébessa 35 28N 8 9E
64 Tebingtinggi 3 38S 102 1E
20 Tech, R. 42 36N 3 3E
104 Tecuala 22 24N 105 30W
41 Tecuci 45 51N 27 27E
50 Tedzhen 37 23N 60 31E
12 Tees, R. 54 34N 1 16W
12 Teesside 54 37N 1 13W
110 Tefé 3 25S 64 50W
65 Tegal 6 52S 109 8E
16 Tegelen 51 20N 6 9E
61 Teghra 25 30N 85 34E
105 Tegucigalpa 14 10N 87 0W
68 Tehchow 37 28N 116 18E
57 Tehrān 35 44N 51 30E
57 Tehrān □ 35 30N 51 0E
67 Tehtsin 28 45N 98 58E
104 Tehuacán 18 20N 97 30W
104 Tehuantepec 16 10N 95 19W
104 Tehuntepec, Istmo de 17 0N 94 30W
13 Teifi, R. 52 7N 4 42W
13 Teign, R. 50 33N 3 29W
13 Teignmouth 50 33N 3 30W
41 Teiuş 46 12N 23 40E
75 Teixeira da Silva 12 12S 15 52E
74 Teixeira de Sousa 10 42S 22 12E
31 Tejo, R. 38 40N 9 24W
85 Tekapo, L. 43 48S 170 32E
104 Tekax 20 20N 89 30W
50 Tekeli 44 50N 79 0E
56 Tekirdag 40 58N 27 30E
62 Tekkali 18 43N 84 24E
54 Tel Aviv-Yafo 32 4N 34 48E
54 Tel Mond 32 15N 34 56E
104 Tela 15 40N 87 28W
64 Telanaipura = Jambi 1 38S 103 30E
49 Telavi 42 0N 45 30E
92 Telegraph Creek 58 0N 131 10W
44 Telemark □ 59 30N 8 30E
30 Teleno 42 23N 6 22W
12 Telford 52 42N 2 29W
26 Telfs 47 19N 11 4E
68 Telisze 39 50N 112 0E
92 Telkwa 54 41N 126 56W
98 Tell City 38 0N 86 44W
62 Tellicherry 11 45N 75 30E
63 Telok Anson 4 0N 101 10E
112 Telsen 42 30S 66 50W
24 Teltow 52 24N 13 15E
64 Telukbetung 5 29S 105 17E
64 Telukbutun 4 5N 108 7E
64 Telukdalem 0 45N 97 50E
72 Tema 5 41N 0 0E
65 Temanggung 7 18S 110 10E
63 Tembeling, R. 4 4N 102 20E
31 Tembleque 39 41N 3 30W
13 Teme, R. 52 9N 2 18W
63 Temerloh 3 27N 102 25E
50 Temir 49 8N 57 6E
50 Temirtou 53 10N 87 20E
90 Temiskaming 46 44N 79 5W
84 Temora 34 30S 147 30E
103 Tempe 33 26N 111 59W
64 Tempino 1 55S 103 23E
38 Témpio Pausania 40 53N 9 6E
101 Temple 31 5N 97 28W
15 Templemore 52 48N 7 50W
24 Templin 53 8N 13 31E
112 Temuco 38 50S 72 50W
85 Temuka 44 14S 171 17E
62 Tenali 16 15N 80 35E
104 Tenancingo 18 98N 99 33W
104 Tenango 19 0N 99 40W
63 Tenasserim 12 6N 99 3E
21 Tenay 45 55N 5 30E
13 Tenby 51 40N 4 42W
21 Tenda 44 5N 7 34E
72 Tenerife, I. 28 20N 16 40W
65 Tengah□, Java 7 0S 110 0E
64 Tengah□, Kalimantan 2 20S 113 0E
67 Tengchung 24 58N 98 30E
69 Tenghsien 35 10N 117 10E
50 Tengiz, Oz. 50 30N 69 0E
62 Tenkasi 8 55N 77 20E
80 Tennant Creek 19 30S 134 0E
99 Tennessee, R. 37 0N 88 20W
99 Tennessee □ 36 0N 86 30W
66 Tenryū-Gawa, R. 34 39N 137 47E
81 Tenterfield 29 0S 152 0E
111 Teófilo Otoni 17 15S 41 30W
104 Teotihuacan 19 44N 98 50W
104 Tepic 21 30N 104 54W
26 Teplice 50 39N 13 48E
32 Ter, R. 42 1N 3 12E
30 Tera, R. 38 56N 8 3W
37 Téramo 42 40N 13 40E
84 Terang 38 3S 142 59E
8 Terceira, I. 38 43N 24 13W
62 Terdal 16 33N 75 9E
40 Teregova 45 10N 22 16E
49 Terek, R. 43 44N 46 33E
63 Terengganu □ 4 53N 103 0E
111 Teresina 5 2S 42 45W
28 Terespol 52 5N 23 36E
19 Tergnier 49 40N 3 17E
63 Teriang 3 15N 102 26E
39 Terlizzi 41 8N 16 32E
50 Termez 37 0N 67 15E
38 Términi Imerese 37 59N 13 51E
104 Términos, L. de 18 35N 91 30W
65 Ternate 0 45N 127 25E
16 Terneuzen 51 20N 3 50E
37 Terni 42 34N 12 38E
26 Ternitz 47 43N 16 2E
81 Terowie 38 10S 138 50E
92 Terrace 54 30N 128 35W
38 Terracina 41 17N 13 12E
37 Terranuova 43 38N 11 35E
20 Terrasson 45 7N 1 19E
5 Terre Adélie 67 0S 140 0E
98 Terre Haute 46 30N 75 13W
101 Terrell 32 44N 96 19W
97 Terryville 41 41N 73 1W
16 Terschelling, I. 53 25N 5 20E
32 Teruel 40 48N 1 8W
32 Teruel □ 40 48N 1 0E
41 Tervel 43 45N 27 28E
46 Tervola 66 6N 24 59E
40 Tešica 43 27N 21 45E
72 Tessalit 20 12N 1 0E
13 Test, R. 51 7N 1 30W
20 Tet, R. 42 44N 3 2E
75 Tete 16 13S 33 33E
41 Teteven 42 58N 24 17E
72 Tetouan 35 30N 5 25W
40 Tetovo 42 1N 21 2E
51 Tetyukhe = Dalnergorsk 44 40N 135 50E
93 Teulon 50 30N 97 20W
14 Teviot, R. 55 36N 2 26W
81 Tewantin 26 27S 153 3E
13 Tewkesbury 51 59N 2 8W
101 Texarkana, Ark. 33 25N 94 0W
101 Texarkana, Tex. 33 25N 94 0W
81 Texas 28 49S 151 15E
101 Texas □ 31 30N 98 30W
101 Texas City 27 20N 95 20W
16 Texel, I. 53 5N 4 50E
104 Teziutlán 19 50N 97 30W
59 Tezpur 26 40N 92 45E
75 Thabana Ntlenyana 29 30S 29 9E
75 Thabazimbi 24 40S 26 4E
63 Thailand ■ 16 0N 101 0E
63 Thakhek 17 25 104 45E
58 Thal 33 28N 70 33E
60 Thal Desert 31 0N 71 30E
81 Thallon 28 30S 148 57E
25 Thalwil 47 17N 8 35E
13 Thame, R. 51 52N 0 47W
85 Thames 37 7S 175 34E
90 Thames, R., Canada 42 19N 82 28W
13 Thames, R., U.K. 51 28N 0 43E
62 Thana 19 12N 72 59E
60 Thanesar 30 1N 76 52E
13 Thanet, I. 51 21N 1 20E
63 Thang Binh 15 50N 108 20E
82 Thangoo P.O. 18 10S 122 22E
80 Thangool 24 29S 150 35E
63 Thanh Hoa 19 35N 105 40E
62 Thanjavur 10 48N 79 12E
19 Thann 47 48N 7 5E
19 Thaon 48 15N 6 25E
81 Thargomindah 27 58S 143 46E
59 Tharrawaddy 17 30N 96 0E
42 Thásos, I. 40 40N 24 40E
103 Thatcher 32 54N 109 46W
59 Thaton 17 0N 97 39E
20 Thau, Étang de 43 23N 3 36E
59 Thaungdut 24 30N 94 30E
59 Thayetmyo 19 19N 95 11E
59 Thazi 21 0N 96 5E
105 The Bight 24 19N 75 24W
102 The Dalles 45 40N 121 11W
105 The Flatts 32 19N 64 45W
68 The Great Wall of China 37 30N 109 0E
105 The Grenadines 12 40N 61 15W
16 The Hague = s'Gravenhage 52 7N 7 14E
83 The Johnston Lakes 32 25S 120 30E
93 The Pas 53 45N 101 15W
81 Theebine 26 0S 152 30E
20 Thenon 45 9N 1 4E
80 Theodore 24 55S 150 3E
42 Thermaikós Kól. 40 15N 22 45E
102 Thermopolis 43 14N 108 10E
43 Thermopylae 38 48N 22 45E
42 Thesprotia □ 39 27N 20 22E
42 Thessalía □ 39 30N 22 0E
90 Thessalon 46 20N 83 30W
42 Thessaloníki 40 38N 23 0E
42 Thessaloníki □ 40 45N 23 0E
13 Thetford 52 25N 0 44E
91 Thetford Mines 46 8N 71 18W
81 Thevenard 32 9S 133 38E
101 Thibodaux 29 48N 90 49W
93 Thicket Portage 55 25N 97 45W
100 Thief River Falls 48 15N 96 10W
37 Thiene 45 42N 11 29E
19 Thierache, Reg. 49 51N 3 45E
20 Thiers 45 52N 3 33E
72 Thiès 14 50N 16 51W
74 Thika 1 1S 37 5E
19 Thionville 49 20N 6 10E
43 Thíra, I. 36 23N 25 27E
12 Thirsk 54 15N 1 20W
45 Thisted 56 57N 8 42E
43 Thíval 38 19N 23 19E
20 Thiviers 45 25N 0 54E
99 Thomasville, Ala. 31 55N 87 42W
99 Thomasville, Fla. 30 50N 84 0W
99 Thomasville, N.C. 35 5N 80 4W
93 Thompson 55 50N 97 34W
97 Thompsonville 42 0N 72 37W
63 Thonburi 13 50N 100 36W
21 Thonon 46 22N 6 29E
12 Thornaby on Tees 54 36N 1 19W
96 Thorold 43 8N 79 13W
20 Thouars 46 59N 0 13W
42 Thráki □ 41 9N 25 30E
42 Thrakikón Pélagos 40 30N 25 0E
102 Three Forks 45 5N 111 40W
92 Three Hills 51 43N 113 15W
97 Three Rivers 28 30N 98 10W
4 Thule 76 0N 68 0W
25 Thun 46 45N 7 38E
90 Thunder Bay 48 25N 89 10E
92 Thunder River 52 13N 119 20W
25 Thunersee 46 42N 7 42E
63 Thung Song 8 10N 99 40E
25 Thurgau □ 47 34N 9 10E
24 Thüringer Wald 50 35N 11 0E
15 Thurles 52 40N 7 53W
26 Thurn P. 47 19N 12 24E
90 Thurso, Canada 45 36N 75 15W
14 Thurso, U.K. 58 34N 3 31W
5 Thurston I. 72 0S 100 0W
45 Thy, Reg. 57 0N 8 30E
72 Tiaret 35 28N 1 21E
72 Tiassalé 5 58N 4 57W
109 Tibaji 24 19S 50 19W
37 Tiber, R. 41 44N 12 14E
54 Tiberias 32 47N 35 32E
73 Tibesti 21 0N 17 30E
67 Tibet □ 32 30N 86 0E
52 Tibet, Plateau of 35 0N 90 0E
81 Tibooburra 29 26S 142 1E
45 Tibro 58 28N 14 10E
104 Tiburón, I. 29 0N 112 30W
36 Ticino, R. 45 9N 9 14E
25 Ticino □ 46 20N 8 45E
97 Ticonderoga 43 40N 73 28E
104 Ticul 20 20N 89 50W
45 Tidaholm 58 12N 13 55E
72 Tidjikdja 18 4N 11 35W
68 Tiehling 42 25N 123 51E
16 Tiel 51 54N 5 5E
16 Tielt 51 0N 3 20E
52 Tien Shan, Mts. 42 0N 80 0E
16 Tienen 50 48N 4 57E
69 Tienshui 34 30N 105 34E
68 Tientsin 39 10N 117 0E
69 Tientung 23 47N 107 2E
31 Tierra de Barros 38 40N 6 30W
30 Tierra de Campos 42 5N 4 45W
112 Tierra del Fuego, I. 54 0S 69 0W
30 Tiétar, R. 39 55N 5 50W
109 Tietê, R. 20 40S 51 35W
98 Tiffin 41 8N 83 10W
54 Tifrah 31 19N 34 42E
99 Tifton 31 28N 83 32W
65 Tifu 3 39S 126 18E
41 Tigăneşti 44 44N 26 8E
83 Tignish 46 58N 63 57W
56 Tigris, R. = Dijlah, Nahr 31 0N 47 25E
51 Tigu 29 48N 91 38E
59 Tigyaing 23 45N 96 10E
104 Tijuana 32 30N 117 10W
104 Tikal 17 2N 89 35W
49 Tikhoretsk 45 56N 40 5E
51 Tiksi 71 50N 129 0E
16 Tilburg 51 31N 5 6E
90 Tilbury, Canada 42 17N 84 23E
13 Tilbury, U.K. 51 27N 0 24E
51 Tilhat 28 0N 79 45E
51 Tilichiki 61 0N 166 5E
90 Tillsonburg 42 53N 80 55W
43 Tílos, I. 36 27N 27 27E
81 Tilpa 30 58S 144 30E
48 Timanskiy Kryazh 65 58N 50 5E
85 Timaru 44 23S 171 14E
43 Timbákion 35 4N 24 45E
72 Timbuktu= Tombouctou 16 50N 3 0W
42 Timfi Oros, Mt. 39 59N 20 45E
43 Timfristós, Mt. 38 57N 21 50E
40 Timiş, R. 44 51N 20 39E
40 Timişoara 4543 1 21 15E
90 Timmins 48 28N 81 25W
40 Timok, R. 44 13N 22 40E
111 Timon 5 8S 42 52W
65 Timor, I. 9 0S 125 0E
82 Timor, Sea 10 0S 127 0E
72 Timris, C. 19 15N 16 30W
65 Timur□, Java 7 20S 112 0E
64 Timur□, Kalimantan 1 15N 117 0E
62 Tindivanam 12 15N 79 35E
72 Tindouf 27 50N 8 4W
45 Tinglev 54 57N 9 13E
83 Tinkurrin 33 0S 117 38E
43 Tínos, I. 37 33N 25 8E
33 Tiñoso, C. 37 32N 1 6W
69 Tinpak 21 40N 111 15E
81 Tintinara 35 48S 140 2E
31 Tinto, R. 37 12N 6 55W
63 Tioman, Pulau 2 50N 104 10E
59 Tipongpani 27 20N 95 55E
15 Tipperary 52 28N 8 10W
15 Tipperary □ 52 37N 7 55W
13 Tipton 52 32N 2 4W
62 Tiptur 13 15N 76 26E
54 Tīra 32 14N 34 56E
57 Tirān 32 45N 51 0E
42 Tirana 41 18N 19 49E
42 Tirana-Durresi □ 41 35N 20 0E
36 Tirano 46 13N 10 11E
49 Tiraspol 46 55N 29 35E
54 Tirat Karmel 32 46N 34 58E
54 Tirat Tsevi 32 26N 35 51E
54 Tirat Yehuda 32 1N 34 56E
56 Tire 38 5N 27 50E
56 Tirebolu 40 58N 38 45E
14 Tiree, I. 56 31N 6 49W
41 Tîrgovişte 44 55N 25 27E
41 Tîrgu-Cârbuneşti 44 58N 23 31E
41 Tîrgu-Jiu 45 5N 23 19E
41 Tîrgu-Mureş 46 31N 24 38E
41 Tîrgu Ocna 46 15N 26 37E
41 Tîrgu Sacuesc 46 0N 26 8E
58 Tirich Mir, Mt. 36 15N 71 35E
41 Tîrnaveni 46 19N 24 13E
42 Tírnavos 39 45N 22 18E
26 Tirol □ 47 3N 10 43E
38 Tirso, L. del 40 8N 8 56E
38 Tirso, R. 39 52N 8 33E
62 Tiruchchirappalli 10 45N 78 45E
62 Tiruchendur 8 29N 78 7E
62 Tirunelveli 8 45N 77 45E
62 Tirupati 13 45N 79 30E
62 Tiruppur 11 6N 77 21E
62 Tiruppattur 12 30N 78 30E
62 Tiruturaipundi 10 32N 79 41E
62 Tiruvalla 9 23N 76 33E
62 Tiruvallur 13 9N 79 57E
62 Tiruvannamalai 12 10N 79 12E
62 Tiruvarur 10 46N 79 38E
62 Tiruvatipuram 12 39N 79 33E
62 Tiruvottiyur 13 10N 80 22E
40 Tisa, R. 45 15N 20 17E
93 Tisdale 52 50N 104 0W
27 Tisza, R. 45 15N 20 17E
27 Tiszaföldvár 76 59N 20 15E
27 Tiszafured 47 38N 20 50E
51 Tit-Ary 71 58N 127 1E
110 Titicaca, L. 15 30S 69 30W
40 Titigrad 42 30N 19 19E
40 Titov Veles 41 46N 21 47E
40 Titovo Uzice 43 55N 19 50E
74 Titule 3 15N 25 31E
96 Titusville 41 35N 79 39W
40 Tivat 42 28N 18 43E
13 Tiverton 50 54N 3 30W
37 Tívoli 41 58N 12 45E
57 Tiwī 22 45N 59 12E
72 Tizi-Ouzou 36 48N 4 2E
104 Tizimín 21 0N 88 1W
45 Tjörn, I. 58 0N 11 35E
104 Tlaxcala □ 19 30N 98 20W
104 Tlaxiaco 17 10N 97 40W
72 Tlemcen 34 52N 1 15W
28 Tłuszcz 52 25N 21 25E
60 Toba Tek Singh 31 30N 69 0E
105 Tobago, I. 11 10N 60 30W
33 Tobarra 38 35N 1 41W
65 Tobelo 1 25N 127 56E
80 Tobermorey, Australia 22 12S 138 0E
90 Tobermory, Canada 45 12N 81 40W
14 Tobermory, U.K. 56 37N 6 4W
50 Tobolsk 58 0N 68 10E
73 Tobruk = Tubruq 32 7N 23 55E
111 Tocantinopolis 6 20S 47 25W
111 Tocantins, R. 1 45S 49 10W
99 Toccoa 34 35N 83 19W
66 Tochigi 36 25N 139 45E
66 Tochigi □ 36 45N 139 45E
31 Tocina 37 37N 5 44W
44 Töckfors 59 30N 11 50E
108 Tocopilla 22 5S 70 10W

Utrecht, Neth. Vila Nova de Gaia

16 Utrecht, Neth. 52 3N 5 8E
75 Utrecht, S. Africa 27 38S 30 20E
16 Utrecht, Netherlands □ 52 6N 5 7E
31 Utrera 37 12N 5 48W
66 Utsunomiya 36 30N 139 50E
61 Uttar Pradesh □ 27 0N 80 0E
63 Uttaradit 17 36N 100 5E
12 Uttoxeter 52 53N 1 50W
47 Uudenmaa □ 60 25N 23 0E
68 Uuldza 49 8N 112 10E
47 Uusikaupunki 60 47N 21 28E
101 Uvalde 29 15N 99 48W
50 Uvat 59 5N 68 50E
74 Uvinza 5 5S 30 24E
74 Uvira 3 22S 29 3E
67 Uvs Nuur, L. 50 20N 92 30E
66 Uwajima 33 10N 132 35E
104 Uxmal 20 22N 89 46W
108 Uyuni 20 35S 66 55W
108 Uyuni, Salar de 20 10S 68 0W
50 Uzbek S.S.R. 40 5N 65 0E
20 Uzerche 45 25N 1 35E
21 Uzès 44 1N 4 26E

V

75 Vaal, R. 29 4S 23 38E
46 Vaasa 63 10N 21 35E
46 Vaasa □ 63 6N 23 0E
27 Vác 47 49N 19 10E
109 Vacaria 28 31S 50 52W
21 Vaccares, Étang de 43 32N 4 34E
60 Vadnagar 23 47N 72 40E
46 Vadsø 70 3N 29 50E
26 Vaduz 47 8N 9 31E
45 Vaggeryd 57 30N 14 10E
30 Vagos 40 33N 8 42W
27 Váh, R. 47 55N 18 0E
5 Vahsel B. 75 0S 35 0W
50 Vaigach 70 10N 59 0E
62 Vaigai, R. 9 20N 79 0E
18 Vaiges 48 2N 0 30W
60 Vaijapur 19 58N 74 45E
62 Vaikam 9 45N 76 25E
41 Vakarel 42 35N 23 40E
90 Val d'Or 48 7N 77 47W
93 Val Marie 49 15N 107 45W
30 Valadares 41 5N 8 38W
41 Valahia □ 44 35N 25 0E
25 Valais □ 46 12N 7 45E
27 Valasské Meziříčí 49 29N 17 59E
44 Valbo 60 40N 17 4E
112 Valchete 40 40S 66 20W
19 Val-d'Oise □ 49 5N 2 0E
37 Valdagno 45 38N 11 18E
48 Valdayskaya Vozvyshennost 57 0N 33 40E
31 Valdeazogues, R. 38 45N 4 55W
45 Valdemarsvik 58 14N 16 40E
31 Valdepeñas, Ciudad Real 38 43N 3 25W
31 Valdepeñas, Jaen 31 33N 3 47W
30 Valderaduey, R. 41 31N 5 42W
32 Valderrobres 40 53N 0 9E
112 Valdés, Pen. 42 30S 63 45W
88 Valdez 61 14N 146 10W
112 Valdivia 39 50S 73 14W
37 Valdobbiádene 45 53N 12 0E
99 Valdosta 30 50N 83 48W
44 Valdres 61 0N 9 3E
111 Valença, Brazil 13 20S 39 5W
30 Valença, Port. 42 1N 8 34W
111 Valença da Piaui 6 20S 41 45W
21 Valence 44 57N 4 54E
20 Valence-d'Agen 44 8N 0 54E
33 Valencia, Sp. 39 27N 0 23W
110 Valencia, Ven. 10 11N 68 0W
33 Valencia, G. de 39 30N 0 20E
33 Valencia, Reg. 39 25N 0 45W
33 Valencia □ 39 20N 0 40W
31 Valencia de Alcantara 39 25N 7 14W
30 Valencia de Don Juan 42 17N 5 31W
31 Valencia del Ventoso 38 15N 6 29W
19 Valenciennes 50 20N 3 34E
41 Vălenii-de-Munte 45 12N 26 3E
15 Valentia, I. 51 54N 10 22W
100 Valentine 42 50N 100 35W
36 Valenza 45 2N 8 39E
110 Valera 9 19N 70 37W
39 Valguarnera Caropepe 37 30N 14 22E
21 Valinco, G. de 41 40N 8 52E
40 Valjevo 44 18N 19 53E
16 Valkenswaard 51 21N 5 29E
32 Vall de Uxó 40 49N 0 15W
104 Valladolid, Mexico 20 30N 88 20W
30 Valladolid, Sp. 41 38N 4 43W
30 Valladolid □ 41 38N 4 43W
36 Valle d'Aosta □ 45 45N 7 22E
110 Valle de la Pascua 9 13N 66 0W
104 Valle de Santiago 20 25N 101 15W
30 Vallecas 40 23N 3 41W
102 Vallejo 38 12N 122 15W
108 Vallenar 28 30S 70 50W
100 Valley City 46 57N 98 0W
90 Valleyfield 45 15N 74 8W
92 Valleyview 55 5N 117 25W
32 Valls 41 18N 1 15E
30 Valmaseda 43 11N 3 12W
19 Valmy 49 5N 4 45E
18 Valognes 49 30N 1 28W
108 Valparaíso 33 2S 71 40W
108 Valparaíso □ 33 2S 71 40W
75 Valsbaai 34 15S 18 40E
36 Valtellino 46 9N 10 2E
31 Valverde del Camino 37 35N 6 47W
30 Valverde del Fresno 40 15N 6 51W
43 Vamos 35 24N 24 13E
62 Vamsadhara, R. 18 21N 84 8E
101 Van Buren, Ark. 35 28N 94 18W
91 Van Buren, Me. 47 10N 68 1W
82 Van Diemen, C. 16 30S 139 46E
82 Van Diemen, G. 12 0S 132 0E
56 Van Gölü 38 30N 43 0E
98 Van Wert 40 52N 84 31W
92 Vancouver, Canada 49 20N 123 10W
102 Vancouver, U.S.A. 45 44N 122 41W
92 Vancouver I. 49 50N 126 30W
100 Vandalia 38 57N 89 4W
45 Vandborg 56 32N 8 10E
92 Vanderhoof 54 0N 124 0W
80 Vandyke 24 8S 142 45E
45 Vänern, L. 58 47N 13 50E
45 Vänersborg 58 26N 12 27E
63 Vang Vieng 18 58N 102 32E
74 Vanga 4 35S 39 12E
62 Vaniyambadi 12 46N 78 44E
51 Vankarem 67 51N 175 50W
90 Vankleek Hill 45 32N 74 40W
46 Vännäs 63 58N 19 48E
18 Vannes 47 40N 2 47W
44 Vansbro 60 32N 14 15E
85 Vanua Levu, I. 15 45S 179 10E
21 Var, R. 43 39N 7 12E
21 Var □ 43 27N 6 18E
62 Varada, R. 14 56N 75 41E
18 Varades 47 25N 1 1W
61 Varanasi 25 22N 83 8E
37 Varaždin 46 20N 16 20E
36 Varazze 44 21N 8 36E
45 Varberg 57 17N 12 20E
40 Vardar, R. 40 35N 22 50E
45 Varde 55 38N 8 29E
24 Varel 53 23N 8 9E
20 Varennes-sur-Allier 49 12N 5 0E
40 Vareš 44 12N 18 23E
36 Varese 45 49N 8 50E
109 Varginha 21 33S 45 25W
44 Värmdö, I. 59 18N 18 45E
44 Värmlands □ 59 45N 13 0E
41 Varna 43 13N 27 56E
45 Värnamo 57 10N 14 3E
26 Varnsdorf 49 56N 14 38E
40 Varvarin 43 43N 21 20E
19 Varzy 47 22N 3 20E
27 Vas □ 47 10N 16 55E
31 Vascão, R. 37 31N 7 31W
32 Vascongadas, Reg. 42 50N 2 45W
43 Vasilikón 38 25N 23 40E
44 Västerås 59 37N 16 38E
46 Västerbotten □ 64 58N 18 0E
46 Västerdalälven, R. 60 33N 15 8E
44 Västernorrlands □ 63 30N 17 40E
45 Västervik 57 43N 16 43E
44 Västmanlands □ 89 5N 16 20E
37 Vasto 42 8N 14 40E
20 Vatan 47 4N 1 50E
37 Vatican City 41 54N 12 27E
39 Vaticano, C. 38 38N 15 50E
46 Vatnajökull 64 30N 16 30W
45 Vättern, L. 58 25N 14 30E
21 Vaucluse □ 44 3N 5 10E
19 Vaucouleurs 48 37N 5 40E
25 Vaud □ 46 35N 6 30E
103 Vaughan 34 37N 105 12W
21 Vauvert 43 42N 4 17E
92 Vauxhall 50 5N 112 9W
45 Växjö 56 52N 14 50E
50 Vaygach, Os. 70 0N 60 0E
24 Vechta 52 47N 8 18E
16 Vechte, R. 52 35N 6 5E
27 Vecsés 47 26N 19 19E
62 Vedaraniam 10 25N 79 50E
16 Veendam 53 5N 6 25E
16 Veenendaal 52 2N 5 34E
46 Vefsna, R. 65 50N 13 12E
30 Vegadeo 45 27N 7 4W
46 Vegafjord 65 37N 12 0E
92 Vegreville 53 30N 112 5W
31 Vejer de la Frontera 36 15N 5 59W
45 Vejle □ 55 2N 11 22E
37 Vela Luka 42 59N 16 44E
20 Velay, Mts. du 45 0N 3 40E
37 Velebit Planina, Mts. 44 50N 15 20E
37 Velebitski Kanal 44 45N 14 55E
42 Velestínon 39 23N 22 45E
110 Vélez 6 2N 73 43W
33 Velez Blanco 37 41N 2 5W
31 Vélez Málaga 36 48N 4 5W
33 Vélez Rubio 37 41N 2 5W
37 Velika Kapela, Mts. 45 10N 15 5E
40 Velika Morava, R. 44 43N 21 3E
40 Velika Plana 44 20N 21 1E
40 Veliki Backu, Kanal 45 45N 19 15E
48 Velikiy Ustyug 60 47N 46 20E
48 Velikiye Luki 56 25N 30 32E
62 Velikonda Ra. 14 45N 79 10E
41 Velingrad 42 4N 23 58E
37 Velino, Mt. 42 10N 13 20E
26 Velke Meziřici 49 21N 16 1E
38 Velletri 41 43N 12 43E
45 Vellinge 55 29N 13 0E
62 Vellore 12 57N 79 10E
16 Velsen 52 27N 4 40E
48 Velsk 61 10N 42 5E
24 Velten 52 40N 13 11E
62 Vembanad L. 9 36N 76 15E
21 Venaco 42 14N 9 10E
108 Venado Tuerto 33 50S 62 0W
21 Vence 43 43N 7 6E
31 Vendas Novas 38 39N 8 27W
20 Vendée □ 46 40N 1 20W
19 Vendeuvre 48 14N 4 27E
18 Vendôme 47 47N 1 3E
32 Vendrell 41 10N 1 30E
45 Vendsyssel, Reg. 57 22N 10 15E
37 Véneta, L. 45 19N 12 13E
37 Veneto □ 45 30N 12 0E
37 Venézia 45 27N 12 20E
110 Venezuela ■ 8 0N 65 0W
110 Venezuela, G. de 11 30N 71 0W
62 Vengurla 15 53N 73 45E
37 Venice=Venézia 45 27N 12 20E
21 Vénissieux 45 43N 4 53E
62 Venkatagiri 14 0N 79 35E
62 Venkatapuram 18 20N 80 30E
16 Venlo 51 22N 6 11E
16 Venraij 51 31N 6 0E
30 Venta de S. Rafael 40 42N 4 12W
36 Ventimiglia 43 50N 7 39E
13 Ventnor 50 35N 1 12W
21 Ventoux, Mt. 44 10N 5 17E
48 Ventspils 57 25N 21 32E
103 Ventura 34 16N 119 25W
108 Vera, Arg. 29 30S 60 20W
33 Vera, Sp. 37 15N 1 15W
104 Veracruz 19 10N 96 10W
104 Veracruz □ 19 0N 96 15W
60 Veraval 20 53N 70 27E
36 Vercelli 45 19N 8 25E
112 Verde, R. 41 56S 65 5W
24 Verden 52 56N 9 15E
21 Verdon, R. 43 43N 5 46E
19 Verdun 49 12N 5 24E
21 Verdun-sur-le-Doubs 46 54N 5 0E
75 Vereeniging 26 38S 27 57E
32 Vergara 43 9N 2 28W
42 Vergoritis, L. 40 45N 21 45E
30 Verín 41 57N 7 27W
49 Verkhniy Baskunchak 48 5N 46 50E
51 Verkhoyansk 67 50N 133 50E
51 Verkhoyanskiy Khrebet 66 0N 129 0E
19 Vermenton 47 40N 3 42E
93 Vermilion 53 20N 110 50W
93 Vermilion, R. 53 44N 110 18W
93 Vermilion Bay 49 50N 93 20W
100 Vermillion 42 50N 96 56W
97 Vermont □ 43 40N 72 50W
102 Vernal 40 28N 109 35W
90 Verner 46 25N 80 8W
18 Verneuil 48 45N 0 56E
92 Vernon, Canada 50 20N 119 15W
18 Vernon, Fr. 49 5N 1 30E
101 Vernon, U.S.A. 34 0N 99 15W
42 Véroia 40 34N 22 18E
38 Véroli 41 43N 13 24E
36 Verona 45 27N 11 0E
19 Versailles 48 48N 2 8E
72 Verte, C. 14 45N 17 30W
18 Vertou 47 10N 1 28W
19 Vertus 48 54N 4 0E
16 Verviers 50 37N 5 52E
19 Vervins 49 50N 3 53E
21 Vescovato 42 30N 9 26E
26 Veselí n Luž 49 12N 14 43E
49 Veselovskoye, Vdkhr. 47 0N 41 0E
19 Vesle, R. 49 23N 3 38E
19 Vesoul 60 40N 6 11E
47 Vest-Agde □ 58 30N 7 0E
44 Vestfold □ 59 15N 10 0E
45 Vestjællands □ 55 30N 11 20E
46 Vestmannaejar, Is. 63 27N 20 15W
4 Vestspitsbergen, I. 78 40N 17 0E
39 Vesuvio, Mt. 40 50N 14 22E
27 Veszprém 47 8N 17 57E
27 Veszprém □ 47 5N 17 55E
27 Vésztö 46 55N 21 16E
62 Vetapalem 15 47N 80 18E
45 Vetlanda 57 24N 15 3E
41 Vetovo 43 42N 26 16E
37 Vettore, Mt. 44 38N 7 5E
25 Vevey 46 28N 6 51E
20 Vézère, R. 44 53N 0 53E
110 Viacha 16 30S 68 5W
36 Viadana 44 55N 10 30E
111 Viana 3 0S 44 40W
30 Viana del Bollo 42 10N 7 10W
31 Viana do Alentejo 38 20N 8 0W
30 Viana do Castelo 41 42N 8 50W
30 Vianna do Castelo □ 41 50N 8 30W
111 Vianopolis 16 40S 48 35W
31 Viar, R. 37 36N 5 50W
36 Viaréggio 43 52N 10 13E
39 Vibo Valéntia 38 40N 16 5E
45 Viborg 56 27N 9 23E
45 Viborg □ 56 30N 9 20E
20 Vic-Fézensac 43 47N 0 19E
37 Vicenza 45 32N 11 31E
32 Vich 41 58N 2 19E
20 Vichy 46 9N 3 26E
101 Vicksburg 32 22N 90 56W
39 Vico del Gargano 41 54N 15 57E
111 Vicosa 9 28S 36 25W
20 Vic-sur-Cère 44 59N 2 38E
96 Victor 42 58N 77 24W
81 Victor Harbour 35 30S 138 37E
108 Victoria, Arg. 32 40S 60 10W
79 Victoria, Australia 21 16S 149 3E
72 Victoria, Cameroon 4 1N 9 10E
92 Victoria, Canada 48 30N 123 25W
112 Victoria, Chile 38 22S 72 29W
69 Victoria, Hong Kong 22 25N 114 15E
64 Victoria, Malaysia 5 20N 115 20E
101 Victoria, U.S.A. 28 50N 97 0W
74 Victoria, L. 1 0S 33 0E
82 Victoria, R. 15 12S 129 43E
93 Victoria Beach 50 45N 96 32W
105 Victoria de las Tunas 20 58N 76 59W
75 Victoria Falls 17 58S 25 45E
88 Victoria I. 71 0N 11 0W
15 Victoria Ld. 75 0S 160 0E
59 Victoria Taungdeik, Mt. 21 15N 93 55E
75 Victoria West 31 25S 23 4E
91 Victoriaville 46 4N 71 56W
103 Victorville 34 32N 117 18W
99 Vidalia 32 13N 82 25W
21 Vidauban 43 25N 6 27E
40 Vidin 43 59N 22 52E
30 Vidio, C. 43 35N 6 14W
112 Viedma 40 50S 63 0W
112 Viedma, L. 49 30S 72 30W
30 Vieira 41 38N 8 8W
32 Viella 42 43N 0 44E
24 Vienenburg 51 57N 10 35E
27 Vienna = Wien 48 12N 16 22E
21 Vienne 45 31N 4 53E
18 Vienne, R. 47 13N 0 5E
20 Vienne □ 45 53N 0 42E
63 Vientiane 18 7N 102 35E
24 Viersen 51 15N 6 23E
25 Vierwaldstättersee, L. 47 0N 8 30E
19 Vierzon 47 13N 2 5E
39 Vieste 41 53N 16 10E
63 Vietnam ■ 16 0N 108 0E
21 Vif 45 5N 5 41E
65 Vigan 17 35N 120 28E
36 Vigévano 45 18N 8 50E
111 Vigia 0 50S 48 5W
20 Vignemale, Pic de 42 47N 0 10W
36 Vignola 44 29N 11 0E
30 Vigo 42 12N 8 41W
30 Vigo, Ria de 42 15N 8 45W
62 Vijayadurg 16 30N 73 25E
62 Vijayawada 16 31N 80 39E
62 Vikramasingapuram 8 40N 76 47E
50 Vikulovo 56 50N 70 40E
75 Vila Cabral = Lichinga 13 13S 35 11E
31 Vila de Rei 39 41N 8 9W
30 Vila do Conde 41 21N 8 45W
31 Vila Franca de Xira 38 57N 8 59W
75 Vila Machado 19 15S 34 14E
30 Vila Nova de Foscôa 41 5N 7 9W
30 Vila Nova de Gaia 41 4N 8 40W

Wallal Willimantic

81 Wallal 26 32s 146 7e
82 Wallal Downs 19 47s 120 40e
81 Wallaroo 33 56s 137 39e
12 Wallasey 3 26s 3 2w
84 Wallerawang 33 25s 150 4e
80 Wallahallow 17 50s 135 50e
97 Wallingford 43 27n 72 58w
76 Wallis Arch. 13 20s 176 20e
102 Wallowa 45 40n 117 35w
12 Wallsend 54 59n 1 30w
81 Wallumbilla 26 33s 149 9e
12 Walney, I 54 5n 3 15w
84 Walpeup 35 10s 142 2e
13 Walsall 52 36n 1 59w
101 Walsenburg 37 42n 104 45w
24 Walsrode 52 51n 9 37e
62 Waltair 17 44n 83 23e
24 Waltershausen 50 53n 10 33e
90 Waltham, Canada 45 57n 76 57w
97 Waltham, U.S.A. 42 22n 71 12w
75 Walvisbaai 23 0s 14 28e
75 Walvis Bay = Walvisbaai 23 0s 14 28e
74 Wamba 2 10n 27 57e
31 Wanaaring 29 38s 144 0e
85 Wanaka, L. 44 33s 169 7e
65 Wanapiri 4 30s 135 50e
97 Wanaque 41 3n 74 17w
81 Wanbi 34 46s 140 17e
62 Wandiwash 12 30n 79 30e
81 Wandoan 26 5s 149 55e
85 Wanganui 39 35s 175 3e
84 Wangaratta 36 21s 146 19e
81 Wangary 34 33s 135 29e
68 Wangtu 38 42n 115 4e
69 Wanhsien 30 45n 108 20e
75 Wankie 18 18s 26 30e
93 Wanless 54 11n 101 21w
69 Wanning 18 45n 110 28e
69 Wantsai 28 1n 114 5e
69 Wanyang Shan, Mts. 26 30n 113 30e
69 Wanyuan 32 3n 108 16e
102 Wapato 46 30n 120 25w
55 Warandab 7 20n 44 2e
62 Warangal 17 58n 79 45e
85 Ward 41 49s 174 11e
57 Wardak □ 34 15n 68 0e
60 Wardha 20 45n 78 39e
97 Ware 42 16n 72 15w
24 Waren 53 30n 12 41e
24 Warendorf 51 57n 8 0e
81 Warialda 29 29s 150 33e
65 Warkopi 1 12s 134 9e
85 Warkworth 36 24s 174 41e
13 Warley 52 30n 2 0w
93 Warman 52 25n 106 30w
75 Warmbad, S.W. Africa 28 25s 18 42e
75 Warmbad, S.W. Africa 19 14s 13 51e
84 Warncoort 38 30s 143 45e
102 Warner Ra. 41 30s 120 20w
99 Warner Robins 32 41n 83 36w
24 Warnemünde 54 9n 12 5e
83 Waroona 32 50s 115 55e
60 Warora 20 14n 79 1e
84 Warracknabeal 36 9s 142 26e
84 Warragul 38 10s 145 58e
81 Warrego, R. 30 24s 145 21e
84 Warren, Australia 31 42s 147 51e
96 Warren, Ohio 41 18n 80 52w
96 Warren, Pa. 41 52n 79 10w
101 Warren 33 35n 92 3w
15 Warrenpoint 54 7n 6 15w
100 Warrensburg 38 45n 93 45w
75 Warrenton, S. Africa 28 9s 24 47e
102 Warrenton, U.S.A. 46 11n 123 59w
72 Warri 5 30n 5 41e
12 Warrington, U.K. 53 25n 2 38w
99 Warrington, U.S.A. 30 22n 87 16w
84 Warrnambool 38 25s 142 30e
58 Warsak Dam 34 10n 71 25e
98 Warsaw 41 14n 85 50w
28 Warszawa 52 13n 21 0e
28 Warszawa □ 52 35n 21 0e
28 Warta, R. 52 35n 14 39e
13 Warwick □ 52 20n 1 30w
81 Warwick, Australia 28 10s 152 1e
13 Warwick, U.K. 52 17n 1 36w
97 Warwick, U.S.A. 41 43n 71 25w
92 Wasa 49 45n 115 50w
86 Wasatch Mts. 40 30n 111 15w
103 Wasco, Calif. 35 37n 119 16w
102 Wasco, Oreg. 45 45n 120 46w
100 Waseca 44 3n 93 31w
12 Wash, The 52 58n 0 20w
96 Washago 44 46n 79 21w
102 Washington □ 47 45n 120 30w
98 Washington, D.C. 38 52n 77 0w
98 Washington, Ind. 38 40n 87 8w
100 Washington, Iowa 41 20n 91 45w
100 Washington, Mo. 38 33n 91 1w
97 Washington, N.J. 40 45n 74 59w
99 Washington, N.C. 35 35n 77 1w
98 Washington, Ohio 39 34n 83 26w
96 Washington, Pa. 40 10n 80 20w
77 Washington I. 4 43n 160 24w
97 Washington, Mt. 44 15n 71 18w
16 Wassenaar 52 8n 4 24e
24 Wasserkuppe, Mt. 50 30n 9 56e
90 Waswanipi 49 30n 77 0w
65 Watangpone 4 29s 120 25e
97 Waterbury 41 32n 73 0w
15 Waterford 52 16n 7 8w
15 Waterford □ 51 10n 7 40w
16 Waterloo, Belgium 50 43n 4 25e
100 Waterloo, Iowa 42 27n 92 20w
96 Waterloo, N.Y. 42 54n 76 53w
97 Watertown, N.Y. 43 58n 75 57w
100 Watertown, S.D. 44 57n 97 5w
100 Watertown, Wis. 43 15n 88 45w
99 Waterville 44 35n 69 40w
97 Watervliet 42 46n 73 43w
65 Wates 7 53s 110 6e
13 Watford 51 38n 0 23w
83 Watheroo 30 15s 116 0w
105 Watling, I. 24 0n 74 30w
93 Watrous 51 40n 105 25w
74 Watsa 3 4n 29 30e
83 Watson 30 19s 131 41e
92 Watson Lake 60 12n 129 0w
103 Watsonville 37 58n 121 49w
25 Wattwil 47 18n 9 6e
84 Waubra 37 21s 143 39e
84 Wauchope 31 28s 152 45e
93 Waugh 49 40n 95 20w
98 Waukegan 42 22n 87 54w
100 Waukesha 43 0n 88 15w
100 Waupun 43 38n 88 44w
100 Wausau 44 57n 89 40w
98 Wauwatosa 43 6n 87 59w
82 Wave Hill 17 32n 131 0e
13 Waveney, R. 52 28n 1 45e
85 Waverley 39 46s 174 37e
100 Waverly 42 40n 92 30w
16 Wavre 50 43n 4 38e
73 Wâw 7 45n 28 1e
101 Waxahachie 32 22n 96 53w
80 Wayatinah 42 19s 146 27e
99 Waycross 31 12n 82 25w
98 Waynesboro, Pa. 39 46n 77 32w
98 Waynesboro, Va. 38 4n 78 57w
99 Waynesville 35 31n 83 0w
57 Wazirabad, Afghanistan 36 44n 66 47e
60 Wazirabad, Pak. 32 30n 74 8e
13 Weald, The 51 7n 0 9e
12 Wear, R. 54 55n 1 22w
101 Weatherford 32 45n 97 48w
97 Webster 42 4n 71 54w
100 Webster City 42 30n 93 50w
100 Webster Green 38 38n 90 20w
65 Weda 0 30n 127 50e
112 Weddell I. 51 50s 61 0w
5 Weddell Sea 72 30s 40 0w
84 Wedderburn 36 20s 143 33e
91 Wedgeport 43 44n 65 59w
81 Wee Waa 30 11s 149 26e
102 Weed 41 29n 122 22w
16 Weert 51 15n 5 43e
28 Wegliniec 51 18n 15 10e
69 Wei Ho, R. 35 45n 114 30e
24 Weida 50 47n 12 3e
68 Weifang 36 47n 119 10e
68 Weihai 37 30n 122 10e
25 Weilheim 47 50n 11 9e
24 Weimar 51 0n 11 20e
69 Weinan 34 30n 109 35e
25 Weingarten 47 49n 9 39e
25 Weinheim 47 50n 11 9e
80 Weipa 12 24s 141 50e
93 Weir River 57 0n 94 10w
96 Weirton 40 22n 80 35w
102 Weiser 44 10n 117 0w
25 Weissenburg 49 2n 10 58e
24 Weissenfels 51 11n 11 58e
24 Weisswasser 51 30n 14 36e
26 Wêitra 48 41n 14 54e
26 Weiz 47 13n 15 39e
28 Wejherow 54 35n 18 12e
93 Wekusko 54 45n 99 45w
31 Welbourn Hill 27 21s 134 6e
98 Welch 37 29n 81 36w
25 Welden 48 27n 10 40e
75 Welkom 28 0s 26 50e
96 Welland 43 0n 79 10w
12 Welland, R. 52 53n 0 2e
80 Wellesley, Is. 17 20s 139 30e
13 Wellingborough 52 18n 0 41w
84 Wellington, Australia 32 30s 149 0e
90 Wellington, Canada 43 57n 77 20w
85 Wellington, N.Z. 41 19s 174 46e
12 Wellington, U.K. 52 42n 2 31w
101 Wellington, U.S.A. 37 15n 97 25w
85 Wellington □ 40 8s 175 36e
112 Wellington, I. 49 30s 75 0w
12 Wells, Norfolk 52 57n 0 51e
13 Wells, Somerset 51 12n 2 39w
102 Wells, U.S.A. 41 8n 115 0w
83 Wells, L. 26 44s 123 15w
97 Wells River 44 9n 72 4w
96 Wellsburg 40 15n 80 36w
28 Welna, R. 42 9n 77 53w
26 Wels 48 9n 14 1e
84 Welshpool, Australia 38 42s 146 26e
13 Welshpool, U.K. 52 40n 3 9w
12 Wem 52 52n 2 45w
102 Wenatchee 47 30n 120 17w
69 Wenchang 19 38n 110 42e
72 Wenchi 7 46n 2 8w
69 Wenchow 28 0n 120 35e
102 Wendell 42 50n 114 51w
69 Wensiang 34 35n 110 40e
12 Wensleydale 54 20n 2 0w
67 Wensu 41 15n 80 14e
68 Wenteng 25 15s 23 16e
84 Wentworth 34 2s 141 54e
75 Wepener 29 42s 27 3e
75 Werda 25 15s 23 16e
24 Werdau 50 45n 12 20e
24 Werder 52 23n 12 56e
24 Werdohl 51 15n 7 47e
25 Werne 51 38n 7 38e
24 Wernigerode 51 49n 0 45e
84 Werribee 37 54s 144 40e
84 Werris Creek 31 8s 150 38e
25 Wertheim 49 44n 9 32e
24 Wesel 51 39n 6 34e
24 Weser, R. 53 32n 8 34e
91 Wesleyville 49 8n 53 36w
80 Wessel, Is. 11 10s 136 45e
98 West Bend 43 25n 88 10w
61 West Bengal □ 25 0n 90 0e
13 West Bromwich 52 32n 2 1w
100 West Des Moines 41 30n 93 45w
112 West Falkland, I. 51 30s 60 0w
100 West Frankfort 37 56n 89 0w
24 West Germany ■ 51 0n 9 0e
13 West Glamorgan □ 51 40n 3 55w
97 West Hartford 41 45n 72 45w
97 West Haven 41 18n 72 57w
101 West Helena 34 30n 90 40w
101 West Memphis 35 5n 90 3w
13 West Midlands □ 52 30n 2 0w
101 West Monroe 32 32n 92 7w
99 West Palm Beach 26 44n 80 3w
97 West Pittston 41 19n 75 49w
105 West Pt. 18 14n 78 30w
101 West Point, Miss. 33 36n 88 38w
98 West Point, Va. 37 35n 76 47w
13 West Sussex □ 50 55n 0 30w
98 West Virginia □ 39 0n 18 0w
84 West Wyalong 33 56s 147 10e
12 West Yorkshire □ 53 45n 1 40w
99 Westbrook 43 41n 70 21w
80 Westbury 41 30s 146 51e
24 Westerland 54 51n 8 20e
78 Western Australia □ 25 0s 118 0e
62 Western Ghats, Mts. 15 30n 74 30e
14 Western Isles □ 57 30n 7 10w
63 Western Malaysia □ 4 0n 10 2e
85 Western Samoa ■ 14 0s 172 0w
16 Westerschelde, R. 51 25n 4 0e
24 Westerstede 51 15n 7 55e
24 Westerwald, Mts. 50 39n 8 0e
97 Westfield 42 9n 72 49w
85 Westland □ 43 33s 169 59e
92 Westlock 54 20n 113 55w
15 Westmeath □ 53 30n 7 30w
98 Westminster 39 34s 77 1w
103 Westmorland 33 2n 115 42w
64 Weston, Malaysia 5 10n 115 35e
98 Weston, U.S.A. 39 3n 80 29w
13 Weston-super-Mare 51 20n 2 59w
15 Westport, Eire 53 44n 9 31w
85 Westport, N.Z. 41 46s 171 37e
14 Westray, I. 59 18n 3 0w
92 Westview 49 50n 124 31w
102 Westwood 40 26n 121 0w
65 Wetar, I. 7 30s 126 30e
92 Wetaskiwin 52 55n 113 24w
97 Wethersfield 41 43n 72 40w
16 Wetteren 51 0n 3 53e
24 Wetzlar 50 33n 8 30e
101 Wewaka 35 10n 96 35w
15 Wexford 52 20n 6 28w
15 Wexford □ 52 20n 6 40w
93 Weyburn 49 40n 103 50w
26 Weyer 47 51n 14 40e
13 Weymouth, U.K. 50 36n 2 28w
97 Weymouth, U.S.A. 42 13n 70 53w
85 Whakatane 37 57s 177 1e
89 Whale, R. 57 40n 67 0w
93 Whale Cove 62 10n 93 0w
14 Whalsay, I. 60 22n 1 0w
85 Whangamomona 39 8s 174 44e
85 Whangarei 35 43s 174 21e
85 Whangaroa, Harbour 35 4s 173 46e
12 Wharfe, R. 53 51n 1 7w
100 Wheatland 42 4n 105 58w
103 Wheeler Pk. 38 57n 114 15w
96 Wheeling 40 2n 80 41w
12 Whernside, Mt. 54 14n 2 24w
96 Whitby, Canada 43 50n 78 50w
12 Whitby, U.K. 54 29n 0 37w
98 White, R., Ind. 38 25n 87 44w
101 White, R., Ark. 33 53n 91 3w
81 White Cliffs 30 50s 143 10e
13 White Horse, Vale of 51 37n 1 30w
97 White Mts. 44 15n 71 15w
73 White Nile, R. = Nîl el Abyad 9 30n 31 40e
97 White Plains 41 2n 73 44e
90 White River 48 35n 85 20w
97 White River Junc. 43 28n 72 20w
48 White Sea= Beloye More 66 30n 38 0e
102 White Sulphur Springs 46 35n 111 0w
85 Whitecliffs 43 26s 171 55e
97 Whitefield 44 23n 71 37w
102 Whitefish 48 25n 114 22w
97 Whitehall, N.Y. 43 32n 73 28w
102 Whitehall, Wis. 44 20n 91 19w
12 Whitehaven 54 33n 3 35w
92 Whitehorse 60 45n 135 10w
93 Whiteshell Prov. Park 50 0n 95 25w
80 Whitewood 21 28s 143 30e
93 Whitewood 50 20n 102 20w
14 Whithorn 54 55n 4 25w
85 Whitianga 36 47s 175 41e
97 Whitman 42 4n 70 55w
103 Whitney, Mt. 36 35n 118 14w
97 Whitney Point 42 19n 75 59w
13 Whitstable 51 21n 1 2e
80 Whitsunday, I. 20 15s 149 4e
88 Whittier 60 46n 148 48w
91 Whittle, C. 50 11n 60 8w
81 Whyalla 33 2s 137 30e
90 Wiarton 44 50n 81 10w
101 Wichita 37 40n 97 29w
101 Wichita Falls 33 57n 98 30w
14 Wick 58 26n 3 5w
103 Wickenburg 33 58n 112 45w
83 Wickepin 32 50s 117 30e
96 Wickliffe 41 46n 81 29w
15 Wicklow 53 0n 6 2w
15 Wicklow □ 52 59n 6 25w
15 Wicklow Mts. 53 0n 6 30w
83 Widgiemooltha 31 30s 121 34e
12 Widnes 53 22n 2 44w
28 Wiecbork 53 22n 17 30e
25 Wiedenbrück 51 50n 8 18e
28 Wielbark 53 24n 20 55e
28 Wieluń 51 15n 18 40e
27 Wien 48 12n 16 22e
27 Wiener Neustadt 47 49n 16 16e
28 Wieprz, R. 51 34n 21 49e
16 Wierden 52 22n 6 35e
25 Wiesbaden 50 7n 8 17e
12 Wigan 53 33n 2 38w
14 Wigtown 54 52n 4 27w
14 Wigtown B. 54 46n 4 15w
84 Wilcannia 31 30s 143 26e
24 Wildeshausen 52 54n 8 25e
26 Wildon 46 52n 15 31e
98 Wildwood 39 5n 74 46w
26 Wilhelmsburg, Austria 48 6n 15 36e
24 Wilhelmsburg, W. Germany 53 28n 10 1e
24 Wilhelshaven 53 30n 8 9e
97 Wilkes-Barre 41 15n 75 52w
15 Wilkes Ld. 69 0s 120 0e
5 Wilkes Sub-Glacial Basin 68 0s 140 0e
93 Wilkie 52 27n 108 42w
96 Wilkinsburg 40 26n 79 50w
96 Willard 41 3n 82 44w
103 Willcox 32 13n 109 53w
105 Willemstad 12 5n 69 0w
82 Willeroo 15 14s 131 37e
81 William Creek 28 58s 136 22e
83 Williams, Australia 33 0s 117 0e
103 Williams, U.S.A. 35 16n 112 11w
92 Williams Lake 52 20n 122 10w
98 Williamsburg 37 17n 76 44w
98 Williamson 37 46n 82 17w
96 Williamsport 41 18n 77 1w
84 Williamstown, Australia 37 46s 144 58e
97 Williamstown, U.S.A. 42 41n 73 12w
97 Willimantic 41 45n 72 12w

Williston Yoweragabbie

100 Williston 48 10N 103 35W
102 Willits 39 28N 123 17W
100 Willmar 45 5N 95 0W
96 Willoughby 41 38N 81 26W
84 Willow Tree 31 40S 150 45E
75 Willowmore 33 15S 23 30E
80 Willows, Australia 23 45S 147 25E
102 Willows, U.S.A. 39 30N 122 10W
98 Wilmette 42 6N 87 44W
98 Wilmington, Del. 39 45N 75 32W
99 Wilmington, N.C. 34 14N 77 54W
98 Wilmington, Ohio 39 29N 83 46W
99 Wilson 35 44N 77 54W
103 Wilson, Mt. 37 55N 105 3W
84 Wilson's Promontory 39 5S 146 28E
13 Wilton 51 5N 1 52W
13 Wiltshire □ 51 20N 2 0W
83 Wiluna 26 40S 120 25E
19 Wimereux 50 45N 1 37E
13 Winchester, U.K. 51 4N 1 19W
97 Winchester, Conn. 41 53N 73 9W
98 Winchester, Ind. 40 10N 84 56W
98 Winchester, Ky. 38 0N 84 8W
98 Winchester, Va. 39 14N 78 8W
12 Windermere, L. 54 20N 2 57W
75 Windhoek 22 35S 17 4E
26 Windischgarsten 47 42N 14 21E
80 Windorah 25 24S 142 36E
13 Windrush, R. 51 42N 1 25W
84 Windsor, Australia 33 34S 150 44E
91 Windsor, Nova Scotia 44 59N 64 5W
90 Windsor, Ont. 42 25N 83 0W
13 Windsor, U.K. 51 28N 0 36W
105 Windward Is. 13 0N 63 0W
92 Winfield, Canada 52 58N 114 26W
101 Winfield, U.S.A. 37 15N 97 0W
84 Wingen 31 50S 150 58E
90 Wingham 43 55N 81 25W
90 Winisk, R. 55 17N 85 5W
93 Winkler 49 15N 98 0W
26 Winklern 46 52N 12 53E
72 Winneba 5 25N 0 36W
102 Winnemucca 41 0N 117 45W
93 Winnepegosis, L. 52 40N 100 0W
98 Winnetka 42 8N 87 46W
101 Winnfield 31 57N 92 38W
82 Winning 23 9S 114 32E
93 Winnipeg 49 50N 97 15W
93 Winnipeg, L. 52 30N 98 0W
93 Winnipegosis 52 40N 100 0W
97 Winnipesaukee, L. 43 35N 71 20W
100 Winona 44 2N 91 45W
97 Winooski 44 31N 73 11W
97 Winooski, R. 44 30N 73 15W
16 Winschoten 53 9N 7 3E
103 Winslow 35 2N 110 41W
97 Winsted 41 55N 73 4W
99 Winston-Salem 36 7N 80 15W
99 Winter Haven 28 0N 81 42W
99 Winter Park 28 34N 81 19W
25 Winterthur 47 30N 8 44E
80 Winton 22 21S 143 0E
85 Winton 46 8S 168 20E
19 Wintzenheim 48 4N 7 17E
81 Wirrulla 32 24S 134 31E
12 Wisbech 52 39N 0 10E
100 Wisconsin □ 44 30N 90 0W
100 Wisconsin Rapids 44 25N 89 50W
14 Wishaw 55 46N 3 55W
28 Wisła, R. 54 22N 18 55E
27 Wisłoka, R. 50 27N 21 23E
24 Wismar 53 53N 11 23E
19 Wissant 50 52N 1 40E
19 Wissembourg 49 2N 7 57E
75 Witbank 25 51S 29 14E
12 Witham, R. 52 56N 0 4E
12 Withernsea 53 43N 0 2W
13 Witney 51 47N 1 29W
75 Witsand 34 24S 20 50E
24 Witten 51 26N 7 19E
24 Wittenberg 51 51N 12 39E
24 Wittenberge 53 0N 11 44E
24 Wittenburg 53 30N 11 4E
82 Wittenoom 22 15S 118 20E
24 Wittengen 52 43N 10 43E
24 Wittow, I. 54 37N 13 21E
24 Wittstock 53 10N 12 30E
25 Witzenhausen 51 20N 9 50E
28 Wkra R. 52 27N 20 44E
65 Wlingi 8 5S 112 25E
28 Włocławek 52 39 19 2E
28 Wrocław 51 10N 17 0E
97 Woburn 42 31N 71 7W
84 Wodonga 36 5S 146 50E
27 Wodzisław Śl. 50 1N 18 26E
65 Wokam, I. 5 45S 134 28E
90 Wolfe I. 44 7N 76 27E
24 Wolfenbüttel 52 10N 10 33E
26 Wolfsberg 46 50N 14 52E
24 Wolfsburg 52 27N 10 49E
24 Wolgast 54 3N 13 46E
112 Wollaston, Is. 55 40S 67 30W
93 Wollaston L. 58 20N 103 30W
88 Wollaston Pen. 69 30N 113 0W
84 Wollongong 34 25S 150 54E
28 Wołomin 51 21N 16 39E
93 Wolseley 50 25N 103 15W
86 Wolstenholme, C. 62 50N 78 0W
13 Wolverhampton 52 35N 2 6W
80 Wonarah P.O. 19 55S 136 20E
81 Wondai 26 20S 151 49E
83 Wongan Hills 30 53S 116 42E
68 Wŏnju 37 30N 127 59E
68 Wŏnsan 39 20N 127 25E
84 Wonthaggi 38 29S 145 31E
92 Wood Buffalo Nat. Park 59 30N 113 0W
83 Woodanilling 33 31S 117 24E
84 Woodend 37 20N 144 33E
102 Woodland 38 40N 121 50W
93 Woodridge 49 20N 96 20W
83 Woodroffe, Mt. 26 20S 131 45E
93 Woods, L. of the 49 30N 94 30W
80 Woodstock, Australia 19 22S 142 45E
91 Woodstock, N.B. 46 11N 67 37W
90 Woodstock, Ont 43 10N 80 45W
13 Woodstock, U.K. 51 51N 1 20W
96 Woodstock, Vt. 43 37N 72 31W
100 Woodstock, Ill. 42 17N 88 30W
97 Woodsville 44 10N 72 0W
85 Woodville 40 20S 175 53E
101 Woodward 36 24N 99 28W
83 Woolgangie 31 12S 120 35E
81 Woolgoolga 30 7S 153 12E
81 Woombye 26 40S 152 55E
84 Woomelang 35 37S 142 40E
83 Woomera 31 9S 136 56E
84 Woonona 34 32S 150 49E
97 Woonsocket 42 0N 71 30W
100 Woonsockett 44 5N 98 15W
83 Wooramel 25 45S 114 40E
83 Wooramel, R. 25 47S 114 10E
83 Wooroloo 31 45S 116 25E
96 Wooster 40 38N 81 55W
75 Worcester, S. Africa 33 39S 19 27E
13 Worcester, U.K. 52 12N 2 12W
97 Worcester, U.S.A. 42 14N 71 49W
26 Wörgl 47 29N 12 3E
12 Workington 54 39N 3 34W
12 Worksop 53 19N 1 9W
102 Worland 44 0N 107 59W
25 Worms 49 37N 8 21E
83 Worsley 33 15S 116 2E
26 Wörther See, L. 46 37N 14 19E
13 Worthing 50 49N 0 21W
100 Worthington 43 35N 95 30W
65 Wosi 0 15S 128 0E
92 Wrangell 56 30N 132 25W
88 Wrangell Mts. 61 40N 143 30W
14 Wrath, C. 58 38N 5 0W
12 Wrekin, The, Mt. 52 41N 2 35W
12 Wrexham 53 5N 3 0W
92 Wright, Canada 51 45N 121 30W
65 Wright, Philippines 11 42N 125 2E
88 Wrigley 63 0N 123 30W
28 Wrocław 51 5N 17 5E
28 Wrocław □ 51 0N 17 0E
28 Września 52 21N 17 36E
83 Wubin 30 8S 116 30E
68 Wuchang, Heilungkiang 44 51N 127 10E
69 Wuchang, Hupei 30 34N 114 25E
69 Wuchow 23 26N 111 19E
69 Wuchung 38 4N 106 12E
69 Wuhan 30 32N 114 22E
69 Wuhu 31 21N 118 30E
72 Wukari 7 57N 9 42E
59 Wuntho 23 55N 95 45E
24 Wuppertal 51 15N 7 8E
83 Wurarga 28 15S 116 12E
25 Würzburg 49 46N 9 55E
24 Wurzen 51 21N 12 45E
69 Wusih 31 30N 120 30E
67 Wusu 44 10N 84 55E
68 Wutai Shan 39 4N 113 35E
67 Wutunghliao 29 25N 104 0E
67 Wuwei 38 0N 102 30E
69 Wuyi Shan, Mts. 26 40N 116 30E
68 Wuying 48 10N 129 20E
68 Wuyuan 41 45N 108 30E
83 Wyalkatchem 31 8S 117 22E
98 Wyandotte 42 14N 83 13W
81 Wyandra 27 12S 145 56E
84 Wycheproot 36 0N 143 17E
13 Wye, R. 51 37N 2 39W
13 Wymondham 52 34N 1 7E
82 Wyndham 15 33S 128 3E
81 Wynnum 27 29S 152 58E
81 Wynyard, Australia 40 59S 145 45E
93 Wynyard, Canada 51 45N 104 10W
Canada 51 45N 104 10W
102 Wyoming □ 42 48N 109 0W
84 Wyong 33 14S 151 24E
28 Wyrzysk 53 10N 17 17E
28 Wyszków 52 36N 21 25E
98 Wytheville 37 0N 81 3W

X

42 Xánthi 41 10N 24 58E
42 Xánthi □ 41 10N 24 58E
98 Xenia 39 42N 83 57W
63 Xieng Khouang 19 17N 103 25E
43 Xilókastron 38 4N 22 43E
75 Xinavane 25 2S 32 47E
111 Xingu, R. 1 30S 51 53W
43 Xiniás, L. 39 2N 22 12E
111 Xique-Xique 10 40S 42 40W

Y

80 Yaamba 23 8S 150 22E
67 Yaan 30 0N 102 59E
41 Yablanitsa 43 2N 24 5E
51 Yablonovy Khrebet 53 0N 114 0E
54 Ya'Bud 32 27N 35 10E
108 Yacuiba 22 0S 63 25W
62 Yadgir 16 45N 77 5E
54 Yagur 32 45N 35 4E
69 Yaicheng 18 14N 109 7E
102 Yakima 46 42N 120 30W
68 Yakoshih 49 13N 120 35E
66 Yaku-Shima, I. 30 20N 130 30E
51 Yakut A.S.S.R. □ 66 0N 125 0E
88 Yakutat 59 50N 139 44W
51 Yakutsk 62 5N 129 40E
80 Yalboroo 20 50S 148 30E
83 Yalgoo 23 16S 116 39E
104 Yalkubul, Pta. 21 32N 88 37W
84 Yallourn 38 10S 146 18E
49 Yalta 44 30N 34 10E
68 Yalu, R. 47 30N 123 30E
67 Yalung Kiang, R. 32 0N 100 0E
50 Yalutorovsk 56 30N 65 40E
66 Yamagata 37 55N 140 20E
66 Yamagata □ 38 30N 140 0E
66 Yamaguchi 34 10N 131 32E
66 Yamaguchi □ 34 20N 131 40E
50 Yamal Pol. 71 0N 70 0E
56 Yamama 24 5N 47 30E
66 Yamanashi □ 35 40N 138 40E
84 Yamba 29 30S 153 22E
41 Yambol 42 30N 26 36E
65 Yamdena, I. 7 45S 131 20E
59 Yamethin 20 26N 96 9E
82 Yampi, Sd. 15 15S 123 30E
69 Yamhsien 21 45N 108 31E
41 Yamrukohal, Mt. 42 44N 24 52E
54 Yamun 32 29N 35 14E
61 Yamuna, R. 27 0N 78 30E
66 Yanai 33 58N 132 7E
62 Yanam 16 47N 82 15E
48 Yanaul 56 25N 55 0E
83 Yandanooka 29 18S 115 29E
59 Yandoon 17 2N 95 39E
74 Yangambi 0 47N 24 20E
69 Yangchow 32 25N 119 25E
68 Yangchuan 38 0N 113 29E
50 Yangi-Yer 40 17N 68 48E
69 Yangtze Kiang, R. 31 40N 122 0E
100 Yankton 42 55N 97 25W
81 Yanna 26 58S 146 0E
69 Yanping 22 25N 112 0E
41 Yantra, R. 43 35N 25 37E
69 Yao Shan, Mts. 24 0N 110 0E
74 Yaoundé 3 50N 1 35E
65 Yap Is. 9 30N 138 10E
65 Yapen, I. 1 50S 136 0E
65 Yapen, Teluk, G. 1 30S 136 0E
80 Yaraka 24 53S 144 3E
48 Yaransk 57 13N 47 56E
13 Yare, R. 52 40N 1 45E
48 Yarensk 61 10N 49 8E
67 Yarkand= Soche 38 24N 77 20E
58 Yarkhun, R. 36 30N 72 45E
91 Yarmouth 43 53N 65 45W
48 Yaroslavl 57 35N 39 55E
83 Yarra Yarra Lakes 29 12S 115 45E
82 Yarraloola 21 34S 115 52E
81 Yarraman 26 46S 152 1E
50 Yar-Sale 66 50N 70 50E
51 Yartsevo 60 20N 90 0E
110 Yarumal 6 58N 75 24W
85 Yasawa Is. 17 0S 177 23E
63 Yasothon 15 50N 104 10E
84 Yass 34 50S 149 0E
54 Yas'ur 32 54N 35 10E
88 Yathkyed, L. 63 0N 98 0W
66 Yatsushiro 32 30N 130 40E
54 Yattah 31 27N 35 6E
60 Yaval 21 10N 75 42E
54 Yavne 31 52N 34 45E
66 Yawatehama 33 27N 132 24E
57 Yazd 31 55N 54 27E
57 Yazdan 33 30N 60 50E
101 Yazoo City 32 48N 90 28W
26 Ybbs 48 12N 15 4E
59 Ye 15 15N 97 51E
83 Yealering 32 35S 117 30E
59 Yebyu 14 15N 98 13E
33 Yecla 38 35N 1 5W
68 Yehsien 37 12N 119 58E
51 Yelanskoye 61 25N 128 0E
81 Yelarbon 28 33S 150 49E
48 Yelets 52 40N 38 30E
14 Yell, I. 46 42N 2 20W
62 Yellamanchilli 38 0N 117 20E
62 Yellandu 17 36N 80 20E
83 Yellowdine 31 18S 119 39E
92 Yellowhead P. 53 0N 118 30W
92 Yellowknife 62 30N 114 10W
88 Yellowknife, R. 63 30N 113 30W
102 Yellowstone Nat. Park 44 35N 110 0W
102 Yellowtail Res. 45 6N 108 8W
80 Yelvertoft 20 13S 138 53E
55 Yemen ■ 15 0N 44 0E
59 Yenangyaung 20 30N 95 0E
69 Yencheng 36 44N 110 2E
51 Yeniseysk 58 39N 92 4E
50 Yenisey, R. 68 0N 86 30E
50 Yeniseyskiy Zaliv 72 20N 81 0E
68 Yenki 43 12N 129 30E
68 Yentai 37 30N 121 22E
51 Yenyuka 58 20N 121 30E
13 Yeo, R. 51 1N 2 46W
60 Yeola 20 0N 74 30E
60 Yeotmal 20 20N 78 15E
13 Yeovil 50 57N 2 38W
80 Yeppoon 23 5S 150 47E
49 Yerevan 40 10N 44 20E
51 Yermakovo 52 35N 126 20E
51 Yerofey Pavlovich 54 0N 122 0E
54 Yeroham 30 59N 34 55E
49 Yershov 51 15N 48 27E
13 Yes Tor 50 41N 3 59E
20 Yeu, Î.d' 46 42N 2 20W
69 Yeungchun 22 15N 111 40E
69 Yeungkong 21 55N 112 0E
49 Yeysk Stavo 46 40N 38 12E
108 Yhatí 25 45S 56 35W
109 Yhú 25 0S 56 0W
42 Yiannitsa 40 46N 22 24E
57 Yibal 22 10N 56 8E
69 Yilan 24 47N 121 44E
68 Yin Shan, Mts. 41 0N 111 0E
68 Yinchwan 38 30N 106 20E
69 Yingcheng 31 0N 113 44E
68 Yingkow 40 38N 122 30E
69 Yingtan 28 12N 117 0E
42 Yioura, I. 39 23N 24 10E
74 Yirga Alem 6 34N 38 29E
43 Yíthion 36 46N 22 34E
68 Yitu 36 40N 118 24E
69 Yiyang 28 45N 112 16E
54 Yizre'el 32 34N 35 19E
46 Ylivieska 64 4N 24 28E
101 Yoakum 29 20N 97 10W
65 Yogyakarta 7 49S 110 22E
66 Yokkaichi 35 0N 136 30E
66 Yokohama 35 30N 139 32E
66 Yokosuka 35 20N 139 40E
66 Yonago 35 25N 133 19E
68 Yŏngchŏn 35 55N 138 55E
97 Yonkers 40 57N 73 51W
19 Yonne □ 47 50N 3 40E
19 Yonne, R. 48 23N 2 58E
54 Yoqne'am 32 39N 35 7E
83 York, Australia 31 52S 116 47E
12 York, U.K. 53 38N 1 7W
100 York, Nebr. 40 55N 97 35W
98 York, Pa. 39 57N 76 43W
80 York, C. 75 55N 66 25W
82 York, Sd. 14 30S 125 0E
93 York Factory 57 0N 92 30W
12 York Wolds 54 0N 0 30W
81 Yorke, Pen. 34 40S 137 35E
93 Yorkton 51 11N 102 28W
83 Yornup 34 2S 116 10E
103 Yosemite Nat. Park 31 50N 119 30W
48 Yoshkar Ola 56 49N 47 10E
69 Yŏsu 34 47N 127 45E
54 Yotvata 29 53N 35 2E
15 Youghal 51 58N 7 51W
84 Young 34 19S 148 18E
108 Young 32 44S 57 36W
81 Younghusband, Pen. 34 45S 139 15E
96 Youngstown 43 16N 79 2W
83 Yoweragabbie 28 10S 117 30E